eGIRLS, eCITIZENS

eGIRLS, eCITIZENS

EDITED BY

Jane Bailey and Valerie Steeves

University of Ottawa Press
2015

uOttawa

The University of Ottawa Press gratefully acknowledges the support extended to its publishing list by Canadian Heritage through the Canada Book Fund, by the Canada Council for the Arts, by the Federation for the Humanities and Social Sciences through the Awards to Scholarly Publications Program and by the University of Ottawa.
Copy editing: Susan James, Joanne Muzak
Proofreading: Barbara Ibronyi, Michael Waldin
Typesetting: Counterpunch Inc.
Cover design: Aline Corrêa de Souza, eGirls logo designed by Miriam Martin

Library and Archives Canada Cataloguing in Publication

eGirls, eCitizens / edited by Jane Bailey and Valerie Steeves.

(Law, technology and media)
Includes bibliographical references and index.
Issued in print and electronic formats.
ISBN 978-0-7766-2257-6 (paperback). – ISBN 978-0-7766-2259-0 (pdf). – ISBN 978-0-7766-2258-3 (epub)

1. Teenage girls. 2. Young women. 3. Social media. 4. Internet – Social aspects. 5. Cyberfeminism. I. Bailey, Jane, 1965– , author, editor II. Steeves, Valerie M., 1959– , author, editor III. Series: Law, technology and society

HQ1178.E45 2015   305.23082   C2015-902889-2
                                            C2015-902890-6

Printed and bound in Great Britain by
Marston Book Services Ltd, Oxfordshire

Table of Contents

Acknowledgements

We are grateful to the girls and young women who gave up their time to meet with eGirls Project researchers to talk about their seamlessly integrated online/offline lives and to offer their first person insights on how their equal right to eCitizenship can be enhanced. Thanks also to all of the contributors to the book and to the workshop and conference that preceded it — especially to the fabulous team of students who have supported us throughout the life of The eGirls Project, including: Sarah Heath, Trevor Milford, Virginia Lomax, Jess Warwick, Miriam Martin, Roya Baryole, Ashley Butts, Hayley Crooks, Sarah Deveau, Hannah Draper, Suzie Dunn, Claire Feltrin, Valerie Fernandes, Mouna Hanna, Jill Lewis, Stela Murrizi, Tony Verbora, Julia Williams, Nerissa Yan, Kaitlin Waechter, Anne-Dahlie Cledanor, and Emily Assaf.

We have also benefited from the remarkable collaboration with our friends and eGirls Project co-researchers Jacquelyn Burkell, Priscilla Regan, Madelaine Saginur and Jane Tallim, as well as our organizational partners MediaSmarts, The Centre for Law, Technology and Society and the Office of the Privacy Commissioner of Canada.

We gratefully acknowledge the financial support we received from the Social Sciences and Humanities Research Council's Partnership Development Program and Connections Program, the Shirley Greenberg Chair for Women and the Legal Profession, the University of Ottawa, the Centre for Law Technology and Society, the Canadian Women's Foundation, and the Law Foundation of Ontario.

Thanks also to our dear friend and colleague Ian Kerr, for bringing us together in the On the Identity Trail Project and encouraging us to dream big.

Thanks most of all to our families, friends and loved ones without whose patience and support none of this would be possible. The experiences, passions and critiques of our own lifelong focus groups — Val's Sarah, Melissa, Ben, Aly and Bethany and Jane's Helen and Grace — are at the heart of this book.

Introduction: Cyber-Utopia? Getting beyond the Binary Notion of Technology as Good or Bad for Girls

Jane Bailey and Valerie Steeves

This volume is the culmination of a labour of love more formally known as The eGirls Project, a three-year research initiative funded by a Social Sciences and Humanities Research Council (SSHRC) partnership development grant that began in 2011. We hope, however, that this ending is also a beginning; an invitation to future research, education and policy initiatives, and grassroots activism aimed at ensuring substantively equal opportunities for girls and young women to participate in our digitally networked society.

Together we co-led an interdisciplinary, intersectoral, international eGirls Project team investigation of the relationship between gender, privacy, and equality in online social networking. We conducted qualitative interviews and focus groups with girls (aged 15 to 17) and young women (aged 18 to 22) to explore their firsthand experiences of and perspectives on these issues. Our team of academic investigators included Dr. Jacquelyn Burkell (University of Western Ontario, Faculty of Information and Media Studies), Dr. Priscilla M. Regan (George Mason University, Department of Public and International Affairs), Jane Tallim (Executive Director, MediaSmarts), and Madelaine Saginur (Executive Director, Centre for Law, Technology and Society; CLTS). Our institutional partners included MediaSmarts (Canada's leading digital literacy education organization), the CLTS (a University of Ottawa–based research centre committed to fostering interdisciplinary knowledge exchange and mobilization about law, technology, and society), and the Office of the Privacy Commissioner of Canada (OPC; mandated by Parliament to act as an ombudsman and guardian of privacy in Canada).

The project was born of our researchers' shared interests in and concerns around the future of privacy, identity, and equality in our increasingly digitally networked world. Our mutual interests were in part fostered by several of our team members' prior involvement in the multi-year SSHRC-funded On the Identity Trail Project led by our colleague and friend Dr. Ian Kerr. Within the crucible of the On the Identity Trail Project, and through the connections between Professor Bailey's research on the equality implications of technology for socially vulnerable community members (particularly women and girls) and the rich insights gained from students in her cyberfeminism class, Dr. Steeves's research on youth privacy and its gendered dimensions, and her collaborative efforts with Drs. Burkell and Regan, as well as MediaSmarts and the OPC, these and other pressing issues relating to young Canadians online were initially recognized and forged.

The origin of the eGirls Project was also grounded in our sense of dissatisfaction with the scholarly and policy dialogues around technology, especially as they related to girls and young women. The 1990s were punctuated by utopian forecasts of what digital technologies would mean, not only for the economy (including promises about the riches that lay along the information superhighway[1]), but also for the expressive freedoms and liberties of all citizens (such as John Perry Barlow's "Declaration of the Independence of Cyberspace"[2]). While some feminist scholars worried that digital communications technologies might represent the latest examples of patriarchal technological control,[3] others predicted that girls and young women were particularly well situated to reap the benefits of digitized communications networks.[4] Some feminist cyber-optimists metaphorically imagined the possibility of using the network to subvert patriarchy entirely.[5] Others spoke of the ways in which individual actions might achieve revolutionary collective goals, including taking back the pen from the concentrated control of mainstream media. It was imagined that girls' and young women's firsthand accounts of the richness and diversity of their lives would proliferate in cyberspace, thereby undermining (and perhaps even destroying) stereotypical mainstream scripts that had previously constrained them.[6]

By the early 2000s, however, academic and policy dialogues had become increasingly interlaced with dystopian accounts of digital communications technology focused on danger and risk,[7] particularly in relation to girls and young women. In Canada, the fears aroused by these dystopian accounts were (and continue to be) used as justifications for expanded state and law enforcement powers, especially powers of surveillance.[8] Too often, little to no effort has been made to specifically tie these expanded surveillance powers to the dangers claimed, or to address the underlying systemic factors that disproportionately expose girls and young women to sexualized attacks. At the same time, an impressive burgeoning body of surveillance scholarship has remained largely inattentive to the constraining forces confronted by girls and women,[9] while policymakers have focused on individualistic approaches, many of which responsibilize girls for exposing themselves to harm and blame parents for failing to sufficiently monitor and control their daughters.[10]

We suspected that girls' and young women's lived experiences with digitized communications were far more complicated than the dichotomous utopian and dystopian poles of debate. Perhaps more pressingly, we were concerned that neither theory nor policy was sufficiently informed by the lived experiences of girls and young women themselves. We envisioned the eGirls Project as a vehicle for examining these suspected gaps and imagining how they might be bridged. We were also deeply interested in knowing how girls and young women would feel about the ways they and their experiences were characterized in both scholarly and policy dialogues.

The eGirls Project proceeded in five stages. In the first and second stages, we analyzed the critical scholarship and Canadian federal parliamentary debates focused on the topic of girls, young women, and technology, to examine how critical scholars and policymakers have talked about girls and young women in general and their online experiences in particular, and the predictions that were made about the implications of technology for girls' and young women's lived equality.[11] In the third stage, we conducted interviews and focus groups with girls and young women aged 15 to 17 and 18 to 22 to ask them about their experiences of privacy, gender, identity, and equality in online social networks, as well as for their reactions to the characterizations and predictions drawn from our review of critical scholarship and policy. In the fourth stage, we compared the results of our critical scholarship and policy analyses with the findings from the focus groups and interviews, in order to reflect on the gaps between our participants' actual experiences and the scholarly and policy predictions about and descriptions of those experiences. Finally, in the fifth stage, we mobilized the insights gained in the earlier phases at a public conference held in March 2014, where many of the authors in this volume made presentations.[12]

Our findings from the eGirls Project interviews and focus groups, together with our reflections on their implications for scholarship and policy, are reported on in the chapters in this collection authored by Jane Bailey, Valerie Steeves, Jacquelyn Burkell and Madelaine Saginur, Priscilla M. Regan and Diana L. Sweet, and Sarah Heath.[13] At the time of writing, eGirls Project partner MediaSmarts is intensively engaged in developing a multimedia educational unit designed to address the issues and concerns voiced by our participants. When completed, that unit will be made freely available on the MediaSmarts website.

As we proceeded through the various phases of the eGirls Project, we were struck by how often decontextualized, individualistic accounts of technology and of girls surfaced. These narrow accounts seemed predestined to breed the kinds of unidimensional utopian/dystopian descriptions of and predictions about the impact of digital communications technologies on lived equality for girls and young women that had inspired the eGirls Project in the first place. Like many feminists who had confronted other types of social issues before us, we craved a contextualized analysis, one that moved beyond any individual or any one technology or platform, one that moved away from isolationist, victim-blaming judgment focused on risk avoidance. We imagined developing an approach grounded in the voices and experiences of girls and young women that sought neither to infantilize them nor to responsibilize them, but rather to respond to their own perceptions of their seamlessly integrated online/offline existences in a supportive, empathetic way. We hoped this approach could help to break policy free from abstract, objectified narratives and instead ground new reforms premised on girls' and young women's situated knowledge and experiences.

Along the way, it occurred to us that too much of the theoretical and policy dialogue suffered from what Lessig years ago termed

the fallacy of "is-ism" — the mistake of confusing how something is with how it must be. There is certainly a way that cyberspace *is*. But how cyberspace *is* is not how it has to be …. The possible architectures of something we would call "the Net" are many, and the character of life within those different architectures is diverse.[14]

Lessig's approach challenged utopian accounts of the anarchic, unregulable, freedom-producing "nature" of the internet, positing both that how the internet "is" depended on how the network was coded, and that the underlying code was subject to change.[15] A change in code could alter the architecture or "'built environment' of social life in cyberspace."[16] Since code and thus the architecture of cyberspace could be shaped by and interact with other kinds of regulators of human behaviour — markets, social norms, and laws — Lessig suggested that there was no reason to presume that the internet architecture would be designed in ways that promoted freedom.[17] In fact, he predicted that markets, social norms, and laws might coalesce in ways that encouraged changes in code that would fundamentally shift cyberspace from a once-presumed space of freedom to a space of unprecedented control.[18] Lessig's claims, however, were not advanced fatalistically. That architecture, markets, social norms, and laws *could* coalesce in the direction of de-liberation did not mean that they necessarily *would*, nor that citizens had to passively accept whatever the powers-that-be handed them. Instead, he suggested that "technology is plastic," and so susceptible to being "made to reflect any set of values we think important."[19]

In terms of the eGirls Project, Lessig's identification of the multiplicity of interactive forces at work in shaping what online communications *are, will be,* or *can be* offers a framework for unearthing the oversimplifications involved in the dichotomous utopian/dystopian accounts of technology's meaning for and impact on girls and young women found in the scholarly and policy discourses. Perhaps more important, it offers hope for imagining that genuinely egalitarian online spaces, though not inevitable, are nevertheless possible. Whether digitized communication networks ultimately enhance girls' and young women's freedom and lived social equality depends not just upon the existence of an expressive platform, but also on how that platform is constructed within a capitalist marketplace, the social norms and practices of those who inhabit it and those who design its architecture, and any laws that regulate those spaces and those within them, as well as the interactions between all of these forces.

We envisioned this volume as a vehicle for pushing forward scholarly and policy dialogue that shifts away from dichotomous good/bad, dystopian/utopian, on-one-hand/on-the-other-hand accounts of girls, young women, and technology toward a more empathetic, intersectional, and contextual account. We also sought to deepen our understanding of the ways social markers such as immigration status, ethnicity, rural/urban living, class, race, sexuality, gender identity, (dis)ability, and age intersect in the lives of girls and young women. Such an account must be both grounded in the voices of girls and young women and open to responses that move beyond neo-liberal discourses of risk and responsibility to acknowledge how the market, architecture, social norms, and laws (or the absence of laws) coalesce and interact to complicate substantively equal navigation of online social spaces by girls and young women. Each of the chapters in this volume grapples with one or more of these aspects of the online environment, and what their interactions may imply about the prospect of a lived social equality for girls and young women.

PART I: It's Not That Simple:
Complicating Girls' Experiences on Social Media

> Hi Barbie.
> Hi Ken!
> Do you want to go for a ride?
> Sure Ken!
> Jump in ...[20]

Part I of the book consists of three chapters that explore the complexities of online life. Like Barbie in the Aqua song, girls have been invited to travel the information superhighway by policymakers and feminist cyber-optimists alike. However, as utopian forecasts have given way to dystopian predictions, the sociotechnical spaces that girls inhabit no longer look quite so simple.

Bailey's chapter sets the stage by making the case for putting girls' own lived experiences at the centre of policy debates to ensure that their needs as a marginalized group will deeply inform the policy options that shape their online environment. Drawing on the eGirls data, she highlights the gap between the problems that Canadian federal policymakers have focused on and the problems that our participants would like to see addressed. She then gives voice to the messages that our participants expressly wished to pass on to policymakers. First and foremost, our participants wanted policymakers to know that the online environment can be particularly difficult for girls to navigate (as compared to boys) because the publicity it enables — which is a large part of the benefit — also creates a "powder keg" where one misstep can permanently damage their reputations. They accordingly called upon policymakers to address the ways that online architectures open them up to judgment and shaming if they fail to perform a narrow, highly stereotyped way of being a "girl." To get the policy response right, policymakers must stop focusing solely on criminal responses that typically make girls responsible for their own safety. Instead, they should limit the ways in which corporations invade girls' online privacy for profit, and regulate media representations that reinforce stereotypes and set girls up for conflict.

Milford builds on these themes in his essay on cyberfeminism. He suggests that we can move beyond responsibilization and better protect girls' online privacy by troubling the dichotomies that too often structure debates about girls and technology. He revisits feminist engagement with technology issues and suggests that binary thinking — offline vs. online, risks vs. benefits, vulnerability vs. agency — has limited our theoretical capacity to challenge policies that constrain girls' agency in the name of protecting them from harm. By maintaining the tension between poles in a fully integrated online/offline social environment that is *both* liberating *and* constraining, we can better understand how girls experience online representations as instances of both agency and vulnerability. Milford concludes that, in this environment, agency can best be promoted by providing girls with control over the disclosure and sharing of their own images. And, since agency can only be fully experienced once we address the constraining impact of the stereotypical media representations that increasingly colonize online spaces, this approach will also help focus policy attention on ongoing, systemic patterns of discrimination and bias across a range of intersections including gender, sexuality, and race.

Kanai's chapter explores notions of online agency in greater detail. She argues that feminist scholars should be careful to distance themselves from neo-liberal, postfeminist discourses that position girlhood as an ongoing project of self-improvement. The constant self-surveillance and discipline required in such a project are consistent with the commercial agenda behind social media, but they also work to collapse agency into a highly disciplined performance of self as a "brand." Instead, Kanai applies a Foucauldian understanding of discipline to reinvigorate the interrogation of online spaces as complex, mediated sites of power, in which heightened conditions of surveillance and intimacy invite particular gendered practices of (self-)control. By complicating our understanding of social media in this way, we will be able to map the tensions that exist in girls' online self-presentations and more empathetically appreciate how they "do identity" in the highly fraught and complex mediatized social environment in which they live.

The chapters by Bailey, Milford, and Kanai all call for a deeper examination of the market forces and social norms that combine to constrain girls' agency on social media. The next section of the book seeks to complicate our understanding, not of the environment per se, but of the rich diversity of experiences of the girls who live there.

PART II: Living in a Gendered Gaze

I'm a Barbie girl, in the Barbie world.
Life in plastic, it's fantastic![21]

Part II consists of five chapters that use the results of qualitative research to explore the lived experience of girls more fully by examining intersections between gender and other identity markers, including immigrant status, race, and rural/urban living, and the impacts of stereotypical mainstream representations of femininity on peer surveillance, online conflict, and gender and sexual culture among youth.

Ndengeyingoma provides a fascinating overview of the ways that recently immigrated girls use social media to deepen their friendship connections and to bridge the social dislocation that is part of the immigration experience. In doing so, she highlights the benefits that attract many girls to networked media – the real value of easy and ongoing contact with friends and family, and the freedom to explore new relationships and social roles in relative anonymity. She also reminds us that every girl is situated within a wide range of socio-economic, cultural, and linguistic experiences, and that these factors intersect and play out in diverse ways. Ndengeyingoma's participants spoke of how difficult it can be to bridge gaps between the expectations of the members of their community of origin and the relationships and opportunities they experience in their host country. Although they, like non-immigrant girls, worried about the possibility of being monitored online by others, recently immigrated girls faced a more onerous burden because they were open to being judged for failing to satisfy the norms of either the community of origin or the community of the host country.

Burkell and Saginur explore intersecting differences between girls who live in cities and girls who live in rural areas. Using the eGirls data, they compare and contrast urban and rural girls' experiences on social media. Again, the commonalities are striking. Although rural girls were very aware of their "rural-ness" (unlike urban girls, who never defined themselves as city girls) and felt that city girls were much more successful at "amping up" their virtual appearance through the use of makeup and Photoshop, the experiences of both groups of girls were very similar. Both used social media to reinforce their real-world connections to people who lived in their communities and to keep in touch with family and friends who lived far away; and both reported a similar level of pressure to conform to the expectations of peers. However, rural girls were more likely to take online conflict offline, and attempt to resolve issues face to face. Burkell and Saginur suggest that this may be linked to the fact that their real-world social circles were more limited in size and space, and also more interconnected ("everyone knows everyone"); this amplified the potentially destructive impact of ongoing conflict and increased the need to intervene face to face to repair breaches in relationships. Again, this illustrates the complexities of online life and the importance of accounting for the diverse constraints that girls experience because they are situated differently.

Early discussions of girls and technology suggested that girls retreated to the privacy of the bedroom to create a liminal space in which to experiment with media representations of femininity and to pursue their cultural goals of "becoming" young women. This retreat was a conflicted victory; although it underscored the transgressive potential of access to communications technologies and the ways in which girls exercised agency as cultural producers, it also suggested that public spaces continued to be closed to girls. As new technologies emerged, however, some scholars argued that the line between the privacy of the bedroom and the publicity of online performativity was blurring. These scholars celebrated the networked bedroom as a hybrid public/private space that enhanced the emancipatory potential of resistive identities.

Steeves uses the eGirls Project data to test this claim, and to explore the relationship between privacy, publicity, and resistance on social media. Her analysis reveals a complex and contradictory set of affordances and constraints. Although the publicity enjoyed on social media made it easier for eGirls participants to cultivate professional relationships with potential clients and employers, the easy slide between private experimentation and public perfor-mance opened them up to harsh judgment, especially from peers, if they stepped outside the narrow confines of a highly stylized and stereotypical performance of femininity. Steeves concludes that resistive and potentially emancipatory identity experimenta-tion is more likely to occur if the privacy of the virtual bedroom is protected from commercial interests that seek to replicate the kinds of stereotypes that constrain girls' enjoyment of the public sphere, and if girls are given more control over the virtual traces they leave in the public sphere.

Regan and Sweet explore the nature of online stereotypes in greater detail by examining the ways that eGirls participants mobilized the term "drama" to describe the kinds of conflicts they experience on social media. They suggest that discussions of drama are closely linked to "mean girl" discourses that pathologize femi-nine social aggression and implicitly treat male aggression as neutral. Policy interventions using this lens accordingly overregulate girls. However, eGirls participants also talked about drama as a form of highly gendered peer surveillance; whereas boys' behaviours were generally overlooked or accepted as neutral, girls were closely moni-tored to ensure that their behaviour conformed to gendered norms. In addition, eGirls participants talked about drama as an enjoyable form of entertainment, where stereotypical performances of gender were attended to for pleasure. Regan and Sweet conclude that policy interventions must attend to these alternative understandings of drama and, rather than punishing girls for social aggression, regulate the companies that own social media. By requiring online companies to provide users with more tools to control the flow of their infor-mation online, and by restricting the use of media stereotypes in online advertising, policymakers could constrain the environmental elements that encourage this kind of conflict.

Ringrose and Harvey examine the digital affordances that mediate gender through four case studies that explore networked teens' gender and sexual culture among economically and racially marginalized young people in London, England. They suggest that, although old binaries between boy and girl continue to play out in a hierarchy of gender power that privileges maleness, networked technologies add a layer of temporal, spatial, and performative complexity. Because networked devices enable a high level of visibility, there is an increased demand for photos of girls' bodies. Creating these images can be pleasurable for girls, but it is also risky because they have little control over the use of the images once they are given to a boy. Boys, for their part, perform masculinity by collecting photos and selectively displaying them online in order to assert territorial claims against other boys. This translates into offline behaviours, including increased male judgment of girls' bodies and increased sexual touching of girls as a form of "joking."

PART III: Dealing with Sexualized Violence

You can brush my hair,
Undress me anywhere.[22]

The kinds of affordances that Ringrose and Harvey highlight make it more difficult to deal with sexual violence online, because these affordances continue to play out in ways that dismiss violence against women and simultaneously blame them for their victimization. Part III addresses these difficulties and suggests that we need new theoretical, legal, and policy responses to address the harms associated with sexual violence in digital spaces.

Fairbairn opens this part of the book by arguing that the prevalent understanding of sexual violence as physical assault limits our ability to address the harms of online behaviours such as trolling, revenge porn, rape threats, and cyber-harassment. Given the blurring boundary between online and offline spaces, it is imperative that we define, document, and prevent violence against girls and women in all its manifestations. New definitions and new forms of data gathering are required because the interplay between power and control in digital spaces is complex and multifaceted. Moreover, the types of violence girls and women experience online are often discounted because they are perceived as "not real" or as the result of girls' and women's naiveté. Fairbairn concludes that, if we assume online violence can be ignored, we will continue to blame victims for the harms they experience. If, on the other hand, we acknowledge the real psychological and emotional harms that women experience when they are threatened, humiliated, and abused online, we will be able to create supportive responses that place online sexual violence within a spectrum of harmful behaviours.

Slane examines the nature of online sexual violence by analyzing the arguments made in the *NJ v. Ravi* case. In 2010, Dharun Ravi, a student at Rutgers University, used a webcam to film his roommate, Tyler Clementi, engaged in intimate activity with another man. Clementi subsequently committed suicide and Ravi was charged with a series of offences, including bias intimidation. Slane focuses on the meaning ascribed by both the prosecution and the defence to Ravi's and Clementi's online conversations in the context of the bias intimidation charges. She argues that online communications must be understood in context, especially when criminal charges have been laid against a young person, particularly with respect to the degree of privacy/publicity expected in relation to communication on particular online platforms and to memes like "lol" and "hehehe" that superficially suggest levity, but can also be used as "covers" for deeper concerns. Her discussion of the relationship between homophobic expressions and heteronormative performances of masculinity underlines the importance of addressing the complexities that equality-seeking groups face in online communications. In addition, understanding masculine and feminine stereotypes is a critical component of understanding girls' and young women's experiences online because these same stereotypes shape and constrain the gender and sexual performances available to them.

Shariff and DeMartini explore the meaning of sexualized violence in cases where sexts are distributed without consent in order to attack a girl's reputation. They place the issues within three broader trends: the misogynist backlash against girls and women who use networked technologies to challenge online sexual violence; the gendered meanings attributed to the harms associated with the non-consensual distribution of intimate images, as well as notions of responsibility and culpability; and the reactive response of legislators and educators. Their analysis reinforces Fairbairn's claims that online sexualized violence typically implicates misogynist discourses about victim blaming and male privilege. Empirical data from the Define the Line projects at McGill University illustrates how easily young people can internalize these discourses, especially given the punitive approach that policymakers and educators are using to address the issues. They argue that policymakers should instead proactively address systemic factors such as rape culture and misogyny, and use education to help young people decode the discriminatory messages around them and interact in ways that are respectful of and empathetic to others.

Angrove extends the discussion about sexual violence by looking at sexualized cyberbullying as an education, and education law, issue. She reviews cyberbullying initiatives in three Canadian provinces – Ontario, Nova Scotia, and British Columbia – to assess how well current initiatives actively promote a school culture that celebrates equality. All three jurisdictions have amended their education laws to respond to bullying, but only Ontario and Nova Scotia have gone beyond gender-neutral terminology to address gendered violence directly. More recently, Ontario has amended its curricular guidelines to incorporate issues such as diversity, consent, and the impact of media on body image and gender identity. Since teachers are mandated to teach young people about good citizenship, she suggests that there is untapped potential within the school system to devise more creative educational responses grounded in human rights and equality education.

PART IV: eGirls, eCitizens

Imagination, life is your creation.[23]

The final part of the book builds on the insights of the previous chapters, and outlines various interventions that can, and do, provide girls with the tools and knowledge they need to actively take up the role of engaged citizen.

Johnson's chapter argues that, to date, most interventions that focused on safety issues have had negative impacts on girls, who may be deprived of opportunities online due to exaggerated fears about unknown sexual predators. Johnson suggests that media literacy education is a corrective, because it encourages young people to develop the skills they need to use, understand, and create with digital technologies. Placing digital literacy within a broader context of digital citizenship also steers us away from punitive responses based on fears about safety from unknown predators, and moves us toward interventions that will encourage young people to develop the empathy, ethical perspective, and activist stance that are at the heart of acting responsibly online. He outlines a number of educational initiatives created by MediaSmarts, Canada's largest digital literacy organization, that promote digital literacy, and urges educators to take gender into account in digital literacy education. In particular, since girls rely on social norms to negotiate a comfortable degree of online privacy, educators who teach online privacy issues should take as a starting point the need to have respect for the privacy expectations of others. Similarly, he suggests that educational initiatives that address cyberbullying, sexting, and media stereotypes should take into account the gendered nature of these harms, and call upon everyone – boys and girls – to act as responsible digital citizens.

Heath uses the eGirls data to examine how girls use privacy settings and other technical tools to protect their online security. From the eGirls participants' perspective, the technical design of the sites they inhabit creates particular security risks because the design makes it difficult for them to control the flow of the information they post there. They were especially concerned by design features that identify them when they wish to be anonymous, or make it hard to maintain a boundary between their various audiences. They were also uncomfortable with the commercial collection and use of their information. However, they actively engaged with their own security, and used a number of strategies to protect it. When faced with interactions that were deemed inappropriate, "creepy," strange, or unfamiliar, they would block or delete users, carefully manage the types of information they revealed, or disengage from particular conversations. In doing so, they demonstrated a strong resilience with respect to managing their own security.

Rosenblatt and Tushnet's chapter illustrates how digitally literate young women can use network tools for their own purposes, to express themselves and to push back against constraining stereotypes. They analyze the experiences of young women who create fanworks (fictional works that remix characters from popular culture to create new narratives) and conclude that remix culture provides a unique opportunity for girls and young women to develop selfhood, emotional maturity, and professional skills, and to explore the intersections between gender, sexuality, and ability/disability. Unlike commercial works, where female producers are underrepresented, fandom works are dominated by girls and young women who are otherwise marginalized in mainstream storylines. Existing copyright laws, which permit the creation of new, non-commercial works that incorporate elements of copyrighted materials, provide a space for girls to insert their own stories and create and consume works about people who look, act, and feel like they do.

Shade's chapter examines the Stop the Meter campaign, in which young women used YouTube to speak out against user-based billing and encourage others to sign the Stop the Meter petition. The chapter illustrates how young women can engage with policies and practices that shape the online environment in thoughtful and creative ways. This provides an important counterpoint to the type of self-branding discussed by Kanai, and confirms concerns raised by many of the authors in this book about the commercialization of the digital spaces girls inhabit. Shade notes optimistically that despite the ways in which media culture encourages commodification of feminine sexuality, the fact that some young women are engaging in political debate and civic action online is encouraging.

Bringing It All Together

eGirls, eCitizens challenges binary utopian/dystopian discourses and calls for the creation of more nuanced understandings that are both grounded in girls' situated knowledges and mindful of the ways that the sociotechnical environment shapes their experiences. Not only should policymakers take girls' own experiences into account, they must think more critically about how intersecting identity markers and stereotypes create constraints and affordances particular to girls and young women in networked environments. Sexual violence is one of those constraints, requiring policy responses that meaningfully address the barriers to equality that girls face through both reactive and proactive initiatives. As we move to address constraints, it is essential that we continue to promote the creation of online spaces that provide opportunities for girls and young women to articulate their own perspectives, challenge stereotypes, and fully participate as networked citizens.

Notes

1   Daniel Brassard, *Information Superhighway* (Ottawa: Library of Parliament, Parliamentary Research Branch, 1994), <http://publications.gc.ca/Collection-R/LopBdP/BP/bp385-e.htm>.

2   John Perry Barlow, "Declaration of the Independence of Cyberspace" (1996), <https://projects.eff.org/~barlow/Declaration-Final.html>.

3   Renate Klein, "The Politics of Cyberfeminism: If I'm a Cyborg Rather than a Goddess Will Patriarchy Go Away?" in *Cyberfeminism: Connectivity, Critique, Creativity*, eds. Susan Hawthorne & Renate Klein (Australia: Spinifex, 1999), 186.

4   Michele White, "Too Close to See: Men, Women, and Webcams" *New Media & Society* 5:1 (2003): 7; Hille Koskela, "Webcams, TV Shows and Mobile Phones: Empowering Exhibitionism," *Surveillance and Society* 2:3 (2004): 199; Sadie Plant, "On the Matrix: Cyberfeminist Simulations," in *Cultures of Internet: Virtual Spaces, Real Histories, Living Bodies*, ed. Rob Shields (London: SAGE, 1996), 170; Donna Haraway, "A Cyborg Manifesto: Science, Technology and Socialist-Feminism in the Late Twentieth Century," in *Simians, Cyborgs and Women: The Reinvention of Nature*, ed. Donna Haraway (New York: Routledge, 1991), 149.

5   Plant, *supra* note 4.

6   White, *supra* note 4; Koskela, *supra* note 4; Terri M. Senft, *Camgirls: Celebrity and Community in the Age of Social Networks* (New York: Peter Lang, 2008).

7   Jane Bailey & Valerie Steeves, "Will the Real Digital Girl Please Stand Up?", in *New Visualities, New Technologies: The New Ecstasy of Communication*, ed. J. Macgregor Wise & Hille Koskela (Burlington, VT: Ashgate, 2013).

8   West Coast LEAF, *#Cybermisogyny: Using and Strengthening Canadian Legal Responses to Gendered Hate and Harassment* (British Columbia: 2014): 13, <http://www.westcoastleaf.org/wp-content/uploads/2014/10/2014-REPORT-CyberMisogyny.pdf>.

9   Valerie Steeves & Jane Bailey, "Living in the Mirror: Understanding Young Women's Experiences with Online Social Networking," in *Expanding the Gaze: Gender, Public Space and Surveillance*, eds. Emily Van De Meulen, Amanda Glasbeek & Rob Heynen (Toronto: University of Toronto Press: forthcoming).

10   Bailey & Steeves, *supra* note 7.

11   Jane Bailey, "Time to Unpack the Juggernaut?: Reflections on the Canadian Federal Parliamentary Debates on 'Cyberbullying,'" *Dalhousie Law Journal* 35 [forthcoming], archived at *Social Sciences Research Network*, <http://papers.ssrn.com/sol3/papers.cfm?abstract_id=2448480>.; Hannah Draper, "Canadian Policy Process Review 1994–2011", <http://

egirlsproject.files.wordpress.com/2013/10/canada-federal-policy-review-2012.pdf>; Trevor Milford, "Assessing Girls' Online Experience through a Cyberfeminist Lens: A Review of Relevant Literature", <http://egirlsproject.files.wordpress.com/2012/10/milford_critical-lit-review-memo-sep-19-2011.pdf>.

12 Our conference "eGirls, eCitizens: Putting Theory, Policy and Education into Dialogue with the Voices of Girls and Young Women" was made possible through generous funding from a SSHRC Connections grant, the Shirley E. Greenberg Chair in Women and the Legal Profession, the Canadian Women's Foundation, the University of Ottawa, and the Centre for Law, Technology and Society.

13 Within these chapters we often refer to both teen and adult participants as girls, rather than using the lengthier expression, girls and young women, because that is the language that our participants used to refer to themselves. Similarly, when referring to males, we use the term boys rather than the lengthier expression, boys and young men, again because this is the language our participants used.

14 Lawrence Lessig, *Code Version 2.0* (New York: Basic Books, 2006), 32, <http://codev2.cc/download+remix/Lessig-Codev2.pdf>.

15 *Ibid.*, at 6.

16 *Ibid.*, at 121.

17 *Ibid.*, at 6 and 123.

18 *Ibid.*, at 38.

19 *Ibid.*, at 32.

20 Claus Norreen & Lene Nystrom."Barbie Girl." Aquarium. Universal Music 1997, <http://www.azlyrics.com/lyrics/aqua/barbiegirl.html>.

21 *Ibid.*

22 *Ibid.*

23 *Ibid.*

PART I

IT'S NOT THAT SIMPLE: COMPLICATING GIRLS' EXPERIENCES ON SOCIAL MEDIA

A Perfect Storm: How the Online Environment, Social Norms, and Law Shape Girls' Lives

Jane Bailey

Constructed as commodities and markets, trained to be nurturers and caregivers, and having their wants and voices trivialized and dismissed, Canadian girls need to have their realities recognized, and require support, resources, and programs which address their specific concerns.[1]

Introduction

It is all too easy for members of dominant social groups to assume that their way of knowing the world reflects both the way the world *is* and the way others see and experience it. Factors like economic status, sex, race, ability, religion, sexual orientation, and gender identity centre the experiences of the privileged as objective reality, while marginalizing the experiences of non-dominant groups as if they were subjective exceptions. As Grillo and Wildman put it:

> Members of dominant groups assume that their perceptions are the pertinent perceptions, that their problems are the problems that need to be addressed, and that in discourse they should be the speaker rather than the listener.[2]

Despite these perceptions, people's understandings of the world are heavily influenced by their own experiences, which are dramatically affected by intersecting aspects of situation and identity.[3] In a jurisdiction such as Canada (as well as in other jurisdictions subject to international human rights conventions discussed in this chapter), where those in charge of the policy agenda disproportionately represent privileged communities,[4] there is a significant risk that policies and programs will be developed in ways that have little to do with the lived experiences of marginalized community members. At best, such policies may have little import for marginalized community members, and at worst may harm them. Recognizing and addressing knowledge gaps between policymakers and marginalized community members is therefore critical to developing meaningful policy processes and responses for all community members. This chapter focuses on the gap between Canadian federal policymakers (who are largely white, male adults with an average age of about 50) and Canadian girls, particularly when it comes to technology-related policy. I argue that demographic differences relating to age and gender, among other factors, and international instruments asserting the rights of the child, and in particular the girl child, necessitate consultation with and the participation of girls in the development of technology-related policies affecting them.

Recognition of knowledge gaps between adults and children, between women and men, between boys and girls, and between girls and women has made its way onto the international policymaking stage over the last two decades. Policy scholarship and international law recognize that policies and programs affecting children do not adequately reflect and incorporate children's knowledge.[5] Children[6] bear internationally recognized human rights that entitle them both to participate on issues that affect them (according to their level of maturity),[7] and to have their best interests and rights protected.[8] Adults are dutybound to facilitate realization of children's rights and to ensure that children's best interests are protected.[9] Scholars and those involved in community programming assert, "Children have unique bodies of knowledge about their lives, needs and concerns – together with ideas and views that derive from their direct experiences."[10] As a result, they ought to be considered experts in their everyday lives,[11] be understood as educators of adults about their lives,[12] and be afforded *meaningful*[13] opportunities to participate in decisions, policies, and programming that affect them. At the same time, limitations in their autonomy and life experience will often mean that their participation and decision-making requires respectful adult support.[14]

Similarly, recognition that gender can intersect with other axes of discrimination in ways that materially impact on women's experiences of the world has produced national and international calls for mainstreaming gender analysis at every stage of the policy process.[15] Responses to gaps based on age and gender (and the intersections of each with other axes of discrimination) cannot, however, be presumed to address the needs of *girls*, who are marginalized by their gender among children and by their age among women.[16] Among children, girls' needs are likely to differ from boys' needs (particularly in a sexist society),[17] while in terms of age, girls' needs may well differ from those of women (particularly in a society that prioritizes adults).[18] In light of this, the United Nations Committee on the Rights of the Child urges that States parties:

> pay special attention to the right of the girl child to be heard, to receive support, if needed, to voice her view and her view be given due weight, as gender stereotypes and patriarchal values undermine and place severe limitations on girls in the enjoyment of the right [of children to be heard under Article 12 of the Convention on the Rights of Children].[19]

Girls, then, must be consulted and engaged in developing policies and programming that affect them.[20] Responding to issues that impact children and youth in ways that are meaningful to girls will often require addressing systemic factors of sexism, racism, poverty, and other intersecting axes of discrimination that can structure girls' experiences.[21] It is essential to understand the different impacts of policy on males and females of different backgrounds, not only because generic programs are often not universally effective,[22] but also because, as Jiwani notes:

> gender-neutral descriptions obscure root causes of violence, and leave underlying gender-related dynamics unnamed and invisible. Instead, structured and systemic social problems appear as random, un-patterned, and individualized.[23]

Meaningful inclusion of the varied realities of children, women, and girls in the policy process enhances the likelihood that policies and programming will produce positive outcomes. Equally important, incorporating their voices in the policy process creates opportunities for women and children to develop enhanced citizenship and participation skills that are central to democracy.[24] It can also unearth issues and responses that might otherwise be invisible to those whose life experiences are not marked by vulnerabilities based on, among other things, gender, age, race, and their complex intersections.[25] I suggest that fulfilling our international obligations to girls not only requires listening to them to better understand their firsthand perspectives on their everyday lives, but also requires addressing environmental factors that impede the exercise of their rights and their ability to flourish.

The interviews and focus groups with girls (aged 15 to 17) and young women (aged 18 to 22) reported in this chapter derive from concerns about a particular kind of policy: Canadian federal technology-related policy developments as they affect children (and particularly girls). Specifically, eGirls Project researchers were concerned about whether federal policy – particularly policy that is focused on amendments to criminal law as a way to address such issues as online child pornography, luring, and (more recently) "cyberbullying"[26] – was addressing issues and adopting approaches that reflected girls' and young women's experiences in their daily lives. As a result, we decided to ask girls and young women for their firsthand perspectives. We asked both about their experiences with online social media, and about the issues and responses identified as significant by policymakers during debates in the Canadian federal parliament and related committees from 1994 forward, on topics relating to children, youth, girls (where mentioned), and technology.

As reported previously,[27] our analysis of these debates revealed a focus on online sexual predation, online child pornography, and the age of consent, typically using gender-neutral language that effectively caused girls to disappear from the policy agenda (even in relation to sexualized violence statistically far more likely to affect girls) except when girls were used to exemplify victimhood, risky sexualized behaviour, and general irrationality. The debates we reviewed centred attention on individuals, in many ways paralleling earlier policy around violence prevention and girls previously analyzed by the Alliance of Five Research Centres on Violence (FREDA).[28] Areas of focus included unknown "sexual predators and naïve, negligent and irresponsible parents" and "extreme sexual abuse of babies and very young children that currently fall outside of the acceptable scope of the mainstream [corporate] agenda."[29] Left largely unconsidered were underlying systemic issues such as the mainstream corporate trade in stereotypical representations of girls' sexuality,[30] although these issues were occasionally raised in policy submissions on "cyberbullying."[31] The relatively rare instances where participants in the policy process broke from gender neutrality included specific examples of girls who had committed suicide following incidents described as "cyberbullying,"[32] and more generic comments about "girls" that cast them in the "roles of criminals, naïve victims, know-it-alls in need of education and sometimes as sexual provocateurs placing men in danger of criminalization."[33]

Given the way policymakers defined the issues, reactions were, by and large, punitive, reactive, and individuated. Others have noted that related public educational responses have also responsibilized girls targeted by online harassment as authors of their own misfortune, in need of training about the dangers of unknown sexual predators.[34] The qualitative research reported upon here was designed, in part, to better understand the relevance of the policy agenda formulated by adults from girls' and young women's own perspectives, based on their experiences of their everyday digitally networked lives.

Methodology

In January and February of 2013, researchers with the eGirls Project held a series of interviews and focus groups with girls (ages 15 to 17) and young women (ages 18 to 22). All participants used interactive online media (such as social networking, blogging, and/or user-generated video sites) as a regular part of their social lives. Half of our sample resided in an urban Ontario setting and half resided in a rural Ontario setting.[35]

We interviewed six girls aged 15 to 17 and six young women aged 18 to 22. An additional twenty-two participated in four focus group discussions, as follows: (1) seven girls aged 15 to 17 living in the urban setting; (2) five girls aged 15 to 17 living in the rural setting; (3) six young women aged 18 to 22 living in the urban setting and (4) four young women aged 18 to 22 living in the rural setting. A professional research house recruited our participants on the basis of sex, age (either 15 to 17 or 18 to 22), and location of residence (urban or rural). While participants were not recruited on the basis of self-identification with regard to other aspects of their identities, such as race, ethnicity, gender identity, or sexual orientation, our participant group included members of racialized, linguistic, and various religious groups.

In the interviews and the focus groups, we explored, among other things, the types of visual and textual representations the participants used online to express their identities as girls and young women, and the benefits and pitfalls they experienced on social media. We also asked for their views on the issues and policy responses focused on by policymakers (as identified in the review of federal parliamentary debates previously reported on and summarized above).

With participant permission, the interviews and focus group were audiotaped and transcribed by our research assistants for analysis. All identifying information was removed from the transcripts, and pseudonyms were used to identify participants.[36]

Our Findings

In this chapter, we focus on our participants' responses to questions about what policymakers should know about being a girl online, as well as their recommendations as to what policymakers should do to address the issues of concern to them.

What Policymakers Should Know about Being a Girl Online

Some of our participants worked to distance themselves from the *other* girls who spent too much time seeking attention online or posted "bad" or "inappropriate" photos of themselves, perhaps implicitly assuming that they were expected to do so in light of the negative attention focused on girls judged to have behaved in these ways.[37] Many also, however, identified themselves as engaging or having engaged (at an earlier stage in their lives) in those kinds of online practices. Perhaps because many of them were able to see themselves in the *other* girl they sometimes described, most of our participants offered empathetic explanations that went beyond simplistically *blaming* individual girls. Instead, they contextualized these practices within a broader framing of the benefits of online interaction and self-exploration, the impacts of mediatized stereotypes of white, heteronormative female beauty, and technological architectures that simultaneously enabled and limited control over their fully integrated online/offline lives.

It Isn't all Bad

Many of our participants stressed that policymakers should not focus solely on the negative side of online life. Most emphasized the social and entertainment aspects of keeping in touch with others online. As one would expect in a fully integrated online/offline existence, this also included maintaining intimate relationships, sometimes employing strategies that allowed them to sexually express themselves without being exposed to an undue risk of negative judgment. As Andrea (age 22) put it:

> I do send pictures to my boyfriend. But I always make sure my face is not in there ... Because even though I don't think he'd spread them around, if he lost his phone and it wasn't password protected there, that would not be good.

While also appreciating the social and relational aspects of online interaction, one of our participants emphasized its value as a tool of social and political change for women:

> One in six people around the world are using internet. So, I think this could help foster equality, principles of equality, principles of social justice, all that, I think it has the potential ... Whereas in real life there's ... systemic reasons why [women] can't achieve equality to men ... online, I think if we use it right, it's possible. (Alessandra, age 21)

Adults Are Sending Mixed Messages

Our participants told us that, while many adults had initially discouraged girls from being online because of the risks of sexual predation, girls were now actively encouraged to participate. For example, Eve (age 16) observed:

> Three years ago, people were saying, like a lot of news channels, are like Facebook is bad, yeah a lot of sexual offenders are using this ... young girls, don't use Facebook ... and now they're like, please come to us and like us on Facebook, and then maybe you get a chance to win ... you know, it's ironic.

Give Girls a Break as They Navigate This Complex Environment

Notwithstanding that it appeared that adults now *wanted* girls to be online, our participants felt that adults had no idea how hard it was to *be* a girl online. As Beth (age 16) said, policymakers needed to understand that "it's hard" to be a girl online because:

> No matter what you do, you're doing something wrong. Like, if you don't have social media, your friends can't reach you. If you do have social media, creeps are everywhere. And it's just, like, no matter if you say yes to something, you say no to something, they're going to judge you for whatever you choose.

Similarly, Amelia (age 18) focused on the fact that communication on online social media had become the "norm" for girls, such that "you don't talk to people in person so much anymore." In light of this transition, she called for policymakers to

> Have a bit of understanding as to … where we're coming from, 'cause if you're going to change the way that we're going to be socializing and, like, living day to day … we have to cope with that in some way and it's going to change the way we're acting and it's going to change a lot of things, so try not to be so … negative upon the ways that people use it because … it's all changing, it's all new, so we have to learn as we go.

Nicole (age 16) summarized:

> I think they have to kinda give girls a break [laughter], 'cause it's difficult online, 'cause there's so many sites that you can do, and they're so distracting, and you could be cyberbullied, and it can kinda drive people crazy.

Nicole's comments about "cyberbullying" hint at a gap between our participants' perspectives toward online "dangers" and those of policymakers. While federal policymakers tended toward a focus on stranger danger, many of our participants revealed a much more complex conception of "danger" and its sources in their online lives.

Life on a Powder Keg: Fear of the "Big Fuse" and Reputational Ruin
When our participants discussed issues of online fears or dangers, they tended to focus on the danger of making that one mistake that could expose them to permanent reputational harm and social ruin, a danger they often associated with "bad" or "inappropriate" images, which frequently revolved around sexualized self-representations. Josée (age 15) evoked powder keg imagery when she explained that although she marked most pictures she posted of herself "private," she wouldn't be concerned if they got out because "it's not stuff which would be, like, a big fuse if it would get … public."

Unlike Canadian policymakers, however, our participants' conceptions of "danger" focused far less on unknown sexual predators and far more on attacks by peers, which they understood to be rooted in unfair social standards and expectations of particular concern. In this vein, a number of participants referred to the situation of Amanda Todd, the British Columbia teen who committed suicide after being blackmailed and taunted after she flashed her breasts in an online forum and someone uploaded a screenshot of the image to an online porn site.[38] For example, Monique (age 16) lamented the unfairness of the situation:

> We like all know … if you're going to send a picture of that, like you know what can happen, but it's still not fair about how bad your reputation can get affected … one bad decision that she made doesn't change who she is, like posting one slutty picture doesn't make you a slut, it doesn't change who you are, like it's not fair how easily like your whole entire image can get changed on one image, like one picture.

Others evoked powder keg imagery through different examples. For example, Keira (age 21) posited:

> It makes you worry about to which extent they can use information … [What if someone] had no clue at 17 years old that they wanted to be Prime Minister one day. And let's say in one picture they're smoking a joint, and there's a photo of them on Facebook, and it ruins them.

Becky (age 19) noted, "If you understand the internet, you know you can't go back. It's always there … absolutely everything is out there."

Alessandra (age 21) opined, "Everything you put up there can be traced back to you forever." The potentially permanent outcomes of each and every posting decision led Laura (age 18) to emphasize that by the age of twelve girls should be told

> There's danger outside there, in the social media. That it's really dangerous, and, like, if you post something it's never going to be deleted, so think twice about what you're going to post or what picture you're going to take, or which video you're going to do … in the short term, it can make you feel good for, like, two or three days. But if you look at it in five, six years when you're trying to get a job and your boss is going to look up … you're going to get in trouble.

Many of our participants felt that girls' reputations were particularly vulnerable to attack, creating a gendered risk of developing a permanent negative record. They offered various reasons for and explanations of that vulnerability, many of which related to exposure to "cyberbullying," discussions that again focused on attacks by peers rather than on the unknown sexual predators policymakers had tended to focus on.

"Cyberbullying" Is Rooted in Homophobia and (possibly) Sexism

There was strong agreement among our participants that "cyberbullying" is often based in homophobia. Josie (age 16) recounted the following:

> Like, my friend X is bi[sexual], so he does get a lot of comments, like, "Oh, you're so gross," or it's just really annoying. 'Cause that kind of stuff annoys me. He'll get ragged on because he's bi. So that stuff bothers me, too.

However, Jill (age 20) felt that, in relation to "cyberbullying" among girls, "it's not sexist or homophobic" because she believed girls were more accepting of the LGBTQ community than boys. Eve (age 16) emphasized that other kinds of factors, such as racism, were also often at play in "cyberbullying."

Even though all of our participants recognized the application of different standards to girls, particularly around appearance and sexuality, only a handful of them (Brianne, age 20, Lynda, age

17, Allessandra, age 21, and Andrea, age 22) explicitly agreed that "cyberbullying" was often informed not only by homophobia, but also by sexism. As Brianne (age 20) put it,

> Bullying is mostly based on, like, weight and what you look like, and obviously your sexual orientation. So yeah, bullying is based on that. And it's probably our society.

According to Beth (age 16),

> Homophobia is a big thing, but also, like, some people refuse to post, like, topless pictures, and they'll get hate for that. Or if you do post topless pictures, you'll get hate for that. Or if, pretty much anything you do is something wrong in someone's eyes.

Andrea (age 22) recalled the following online posting linking sexism and homophobia:

> I read something on Facebook; it was a picture and it was just black and it said, "Homophobia: the fear that gay men will treat you the same way you treat straight women." [laughter] It seems so true.

A few of our participants identified specific examples of "cyberbullying" they considered to be sexist. Alessandra (age 21) noted:

> Let's take for example victim blaming Amanda Todd ... let's look at the core issue here – misogyny, sexism, exploitation, and abuse of young girls, no no no! People are too busy victim-blaming Amanda Todd [mimics in high-pitched voice], "Well, she shouldn't have sent those pictures, what was she thinking, like, this girl's a slut!" and it reinforces that, and so, those ideologies contribute to rape victims being, "Well, what were you doing walking alone at 12 o'clock anyways?"

Lynda (age 17) recalled a less notorious incident as one she understood to exemplify sexism:

> It all started off with a small comment and it could escalate to everybody getting involved, [such as] calling out [a girl for]

trying to get in between [another girl and her boyfriend, but the "cyberbullying" was] only towards the girl and no one assumes that the guy has anything to do with it … no one said anything to him, just her.

Likewise, Alessandra (age 21) now understood what she called "beefs" between girls over boyfriends during her high school years through the lens of learned sexism:

> Ninety-nine percent of the time, the starting of the beef had to do with cheating, you know what I mean, boyfriends cheating or not being faithful or being attracted to other girls … The media has taught us to be in competition with one another and that's why there's not a lot of women's solidarity, they're quick to fight with another girl in defence of a guy, well that guy's the cheater, that guy's the guy that should be eliminated from the circle, so that's why guys are at a privilege in high school.

While some of our participants did not explicitly agree that sexism informed "cyberbullying," many perceived clear gendered differences in the frequency and nature of "cyberbullying."

Girls Are Targeted More Often than Boys and in Different Ways

A number of our participants felt that girls were more likely than boys to be targets of "cyberbullying": (Nicole (age 16), Clare (age 16), and Amelia (age 18). As Nicole put it, "Girls are still considered the weaker gender, they get bullied more." Clare and Amelia speculated that girls were attacked more because they participated and disclosed more online than boys. Clare noted that girls would sometimes blog something, intending it for strangers, but

> if somebody from school found it, then they'd laugh about it or share it around and everyone would laugh about it [or if a girl posted a picture that wasn't] necessary they'll call them out on it.

Interestingly, Clare also felt boys might get attacked for posting photos of themselves because doing so "looks gay," on the basis of her view that posting pictures of yourself is "seen as more of a female thing."

A number of our participants felt that girls were targeted for "cyberbullying" for reasons quite different than those for which boys were targeted. As Brianne (age 20) put it,

> I think girls, it's more that they pick on, like, weight and, like, looks and stuff. Guys, it's more, like, well, "You haven't tapped that many girls yet," kind of thing. Like, "You're not a man," or "You haven't been with, like, twenty girls yet, so you're not a man." And girls, it's like, "Oh, well she's slept with, like, twenty guys, so, you know, like, she's dirty," and stuff like that. So it's different.

Nicole (age 16) and Amelia (age 18) both felt that girls were more likely to be targeted about their looks than boys. As Nicole put it, "taking a blow at someone's appearance, weight, size, height, those are all things that offend girls a lot more than guys, I think." She connected this to unrealistic media images of girls:

> You gotta learn to accept yourself before others will … With all the magazines out, the right appearance is size two … But realistically, that's not going to happen for everyone.

Amelia also felt that boys were likely to "cyberbully" girls by trying to "pressure you into … send[ing] them a picture or, you know, like, pressure you into doing something." She recalled a female Facebook friend having posted a status line that said,

> You know you're a real man when you tell me that if I don't send you a picture of myself like naked that you're going to post a picture of someone's breasts and put them on Facebook and tag me and say that they're mine."

Amelia noted that girls often confront a dilemma, that is,

> 'Cause what would he do with that actual picture of you if you sent it? And if you don't, he's going to try and target you anyways to the public eye and make you look trashy.

And yet, Amelia felt that the consequences of complying with a request for a naked photo were much more negative for girls than they would be for boys, which she felt wasn't "really fair":

> I don't think it would bother [guys] at all 'cause guys, you know, they have ... they can have the mindset where, you know, like, oh yeah, well, I'm getting lucky and you're not, and I think guys are different in that sense than girls.

Given her view that girls were more likely than boys to suffer negative targeting for engaging in sex (or being alleged to have engaged in sex), Amelia felt that one of the most effective ways to attack a girl was by

> posting something saying, you know, they slept with somebody or hooked up with somebody ... and, you know, accusing them of being trashy or slutty ... If you posted something like that, that would obviously be more damaging, I think, to a girl's image.

Interestingly, however, Amelia felt it was "hard to say" if sexism informed "cyberbullying,", noting with respect to online equality, "For me at least I don't really view [it as] any different, where, like, guys are more than girls, or girls are more than guys, type thing online."

A Perfect Storm

A number of our participants felt that girls were more exposed to "cyberbullying" (and to online sexual predation) than boys because girls posted more, sought more attention, and therefore opened themselves up to a greater risk of judgment. However, when asked to explain their thinking as to why that might be, our participants contextualized girls' choices within a complex set of interactions—involving personal preferences, social norms, gendered marketing practices, and technical architectures—that might be described as a "perfect storm."

Architectures That Incent Disclosure

Catlin (age 19) indicated that (at least in high school), success tended to be measured by one's friend and follower counts, suggesting that the *way* that social media sites are designed can create incentives to expand networks to include unknown people. As Monica (age 16) put it:

> Yeah, lots of people would just accept people and just so they have another friend … Like, the more friends you have, the more popular [you are], kind of thing.

In this way, online environments structured to elicit disclosure of information may inadvertently set girls up for surveillance and judgment, particularly when understood in the context of social norms pressuring the very kinds of stereotypical performances connected with online attacks by peers.

Social Norms That Invite Stereotypical Performances of Femininity and Sexuality

For many of our participants, visibility was understood to be a critical component of success online. However, some highlighted gendered, heteronormative expectations around how to achieve visibility. Lynda (age 17) wanted policymakers to understand the "pressure that's put on girls" to be like the images they see in magazines and on television:

> You feel like you need to be perfect, or live up to everyone's expectations of you. And the media's expectations of what girls are supposed to be like.

In her view, the internet worsened the situation "because you see other girls' profiles and they're, like, portrayed as like super pretty and all that, and you try to be like that. I guess, girls feel pressured to be like that."

Alicia (age 17) indicated that emulating these stereotypes allows girls to compete for attention and amass followers, which can simultaneously both enhance self-determination and create a sense of vulnerability. As Clare (age 16) put it:

> Girls are, they kind of feel pressured to be on, like, a lot of social media sites and posting pictures of themselves, and then if they're getting a lot of guy followers, they'll feel pressures to like cater their pictures or the style of their picture more towards

the guy followers, 'cause they're getting a lot of them, and that they don't necessarily post the pictures because … they don't want to be respected by people, but they want attention, I guess. And they want, like, they want to gain a following, so they feel more powerful, so that's why they do it.

Some participants, such as Alessandra (age 21) and Cindy (age 20), felt that the competition set up between heterosexual girls for male attention increased girls' exposure to predators. Others also felt that the publicness of online social media tended to "make more drama," which "makes [it] more difficult for everyone."

Technical Architectures Can Facilitate Conflict

A number of our participants felt that certain kinds of online platforms created conditions ripe for conflict and harassment. Our rural minor focus group participants agreed that the social media site Ask. fm[39] was particularly problematic. As Paula (age 17) put it:

> It's so bad. It's just, people asking people these questions, but a lot of them are negative.

Beth (age 16) agreed, noting, "Like, Ask.fm, I've had friends that, like, people said, 'Go kill yourself; you're no good in the world,' – things like that." Similarly, interviewee Nicole (age 16) called Ask.fm "a big one" for "cyberbullying," saying "it's like asking people, 'Come bully me please'."

However, Josie (age 16) also suggested that Ask.fm users could opt not to publish negative comments. This suggests that users aren't aware of that option or, as Monica (age 16) suggested, it might reflect a "trend" toward garnering attention, even if it is negative attention:

> Monica (age 16): I don't know if you've heard of the Amanda Todd thing, but her thing spread around the internet like crazy, and she ended her life because of it and she was only like 14, 15 years old … it's turning that kind of stuff into a trend, which is the worst thing that could happen, right?
> Researcher: What do you mean by turning into a trend? Do you mean it's a trend on Twitter?

Monica (age 16): No, no, like people are doing it almost for attention, like, it's the worst attention you could get, but almost turning into that.

Simple default settings can also add to online "drama." For example, Catlin (age 19) noted that certain platforms automatically disclose to the sender of a message whether the recipient has read it, creating tension when the recipient doesn't respond immediately.

Technical Architectures Can Complicate Self-Help Privacy Strategies

Keira (age 21) and Andrea (age 22) — both participants in our urban adult focus group — felt that platform architecture and complex user agreements complicated their use of self-help strategies. For example, they felt that some platforms were structured to create a sense that disclosure of a considerable amount of information was necessary, when it actually wasn't. Keira indicated that this could lead to a feeling of uncomfortable "exposure," especially to unknown "friends." For that reason, some participants preferred platforms that made it easier to post only what you wanted to, with interviewee Clare (age 16) noting,

> I think Instagram, you really don't have to give any information about yourself, it's all shown in the pictures pretty much, it depends what you wanna show them, and then on like, I know, on Facebook you have to include a lot of information, your school, hometown, everything, so that's a lot more personal. And on, like, Tumblr, it's basically completely anonymous, you can leave anonymous messages, so like they don't know like anything about you, so you need no information for something like that.

More than one participant said they didn't know how online service providers used their data. Some weren't certain how privacy settings worked, either. For example, Monica (age 16) said,

> I think I do [use the privacy settings]. I'm not 100 percent sure, but I think I have, it's like only my friends can see my stuff, I think that's the setting that way.

Others, including Nicole (age 16), noted that privacy-setting defaults on some platforms changed frequently, making it more difficult to maintain a consistent level of privacy. Inconsistencies between platforms with respect to privacy also created confusion. As Nicole described it, whereas a fight on Facebook would be accessible only to friends of friends,

> [On Twitter] you're fighting in front of literally everyone ... if you don't have your password protected.

Andrea (age 22) noted a bait-and-switch scheme under which she was lured with a free app, only to find out later that in order to keep it, she had to disclose personal information:

> Yeah, 'cause you can, like, add an app or something – like, the 8Tracks you said, and sometimes it does it at first, or a month down the road it will ask if it can access your friends or your information, and you don't really know what it wants to really access now. And you press cancel and you can't use it, and you're like, "Fuck." So I have to accept it.

Trish (age 18) also noted that using some platforms can lead to enormous growth in your number of followers just by adding a single person:

> So you don't even know who you're talking to ... That's kind of creepy.

Catlin (age 19) expressed concern about the mandated tie between her phone plan and having to open a Google account, because

> every time I take a picture on my phone, it automatically uploads to my Google account. Automatically. It doesn't matter how many times I try to delete it, because I can't even delete it off my phone ... 'Cause when you first get an Android, you have to get a Google account. So now everything gets uploaded to my Google account.

Similarly, some participants, such as Kathleen (age 20), expressed concern about the ways that platforms automatically integrated postings from other platforms, "so that everyone knows what you're up to."

In the Face of This Perfect Storm, What Should Policymakers Do?

While our participants did not dismiss the use of criminal and other individual sanctions to address certain kinds of online behaviours (such as non-consensual distribution of intimate images), a number of their suggestions emphasized policy approaches that broadened the policymaking lens beyond reactions to individuals. Some of their suggestions would bring online platform providers under greater scrutiny and directly target underlying systemically discriminatory social and marketing norms and practices that they understood to heavily influence girls' ability to freely navigate their seamlessly integrated online/offline world.

Surveillance Is a Problem, Not a Solution

Many of our participants expressed as much or more concern about online surveillance by family members, employers, and peers as about surveillance by unknown adults. As Courtney (age 17) put it, "I was getting stalked by my family." As discussed above, for many of our participants, peer surveillance and monitoring were integral components of "cyberbullying."

Sometimes different forms of surveillance intersected. Amelia (age 18) blocked certain members of her church community from following her on Twitter and refrained from posting drinking photos on Facebook out of respect for her parents. She explained,

> My mom doesn't want pictures of me drinking on Facebook just because I'm friends with people who are from, just, like, the church community, and she said, "I just don't want people seeing that and making judgments," and I said, "Why are you so worried about what people will think, when it's not what they think of you, it's what they think of me?" But she explained it to me … you are my child, I've raised you a way, and I don't want people to make judgments about me from your actions.

Similarly, 20-year-old Kathleen's parents worried about

> just random strangers. Employers. Anything that could give a
> negative image or be misinterpreted in any way. Not that there's
> really bad pictures of me, but just, like, a picture doesn't explain
> the story, so it could be misinterpreted in many different ways.

As a result, Monica (age 16) identified a need for solutions that don't involve "parents standing looking over your shoulder. You can't really have that … Like you don't have any privacy." Alessandra (age 21) also rejected surveillance-based policy interventions at a more general level:

> I feel like [online child pornography is] exploited in the media
> to implement policies that permit spying, which inflict on our
> rights, you know, as Canadians.

Regulate Platform Providers to Improve Our Privacy

While recognizing that privacy settings were available and useful, some of our participants noted that they could be unduly complicated and time-consuming to use. As a result, as Nicole (age 16) put it:

> You have to, like, name off every single person that you want to
> see, and some people just don't have the time.

Others noted that, even after going to the trouble of taking down material, the fact that it could be maintained in storage with service providers in perpetuity created a lasting sense of unease. Brianne (age 20) suggested:

> That if you wanted something deleted, that it should be com-
> pletely gone. Like, it should not be traceable ever again. Because
> there's, like, people think that one picture's funny of you; if
> you're hanging out with friends and they take a picture that
> they think is funny and you think is horrible, you know … and
> even though it takes a while, they might actually delete it, but it's
> not actually gone … It would be better if, like, I'd feel better if I
> knew that when I deleted an account or something, everything's
> gone, instead of them having my information.

Alessandra (age 20) went farther, emphasizing that users should have greater control over sales of their photos to third party users, an approach she felt could be particularly significant for young women, noting the sexual double standard applied to girls:

> [If] they're selling your information, like your pictures, that's putting you at risk, *that* is a violation of privacy … because if a girl's father … [sees] their daughter on this advertisement on a porno site, I think it is more … you can have a lot more negative backlash than if … a father sees his son on the advertisement of a porno site … just because of social constructions of male and female sexuality she'd be faced [with] harsher consequences socially.

Other participants expressed similar concerns, with Amelia (age 18) noting, "You should have the right to authorize whether or not they use your information … or your photos."

Platform Providers Should Make It Easier to Remove "Cyberbullying"

Some of our participants felt service providers should make it easier to stop "cyberbullying." Jill (age 20) suggested clearer language on social networking sites about "what 'cyberbullying' is," so that both "a direct, bad comment" and "several comments that are slightly negative" could be removed quickly. Kathleen (age 20) emphasized the importance of quick responses to "deal with the situation right away." Josée (age 15) urged greater security measures to protect against hackers, as well as increased staff at service providers to deal with these "kinds of problems because [in her view] there [are] a lot of cases."

Provide Support for Targets of "Cyberbullying"

Our participants emphasized the need for improved support for targets of "cyberbullying." Keira (age 21) highlighted the carry-over between online harassment and the school environment and suggested the appointment of

> a counsellor at school that is aware of what's going on [on] Facebook. I mean, like, you get home and your interaction with the people at school continues until ten o'clock at night. You know? And so much is going on, not just happening in

the hallways—it's happening on the internet. And I think that schools, I think that schools should be a lot more involved in that.

Mackenzie (age 20) also stressed that targets should know they have adults to talk to who will really listen to what they are saying.

Both Josée (age 15) and Alessandra (age 21) suggested that there was a real risk of declining online participation unless "cyberbullying" is addressed. Alessandra felt this was particularly true for members of marginalized communities, noting that Aboriginal persons who posted their support for social justice movements such as Idle No More[40] were at "risk of racialized attacks" not faced by non-Aboriginals.

Address Problematic Underlying Social Norms, Not Just the Symptoms

Alessandra adamantly advocated that effectively addressing the problem of online sexualized harassment and stigma for girls required proactive educational responses aimed at systemic prejudices:

> If I was talking to a policymaker, then I would say, "You want to eradicate the issue, or you wanna help limit the online bullying, and the sexual harassment of girls online … and even just the idea of girls sending out these pictures of them[selves] with bikinis, or bras, or lingerie, and … that coming back to haunt them for the rest of their lives? You want to eradicate that, you have to implement women's studies and both men and women need to take these courses … That's the kind of activities that are going to challenge … sexism and oppression of women."

She contrasted these kinds of initiatives with more individually oriented responses typically aimed exclusively at girls, stressing it was important for high school curricula to incorporate teaching *all* youth

> to start deconstructing and unlearning … the ideologies that if a woman gets raped then she should take self-defence or she shouldn't have done this, or what she should've done differently as opposed to tackling the core issue: no, there's a guy that's a rapist. We gotta teach people not to rape, not how not to get raped.

Moreover, she concluded that

> [Girls need to learn by high school that] we're supposed to be allies … we're not supposed to be fighting each other, we're supposed to be working together. We're supposed to keep an eye out on these issues for each other.

Discussion

Our qualitative results – while not generalizable, nor representative of the full diversity of girls' and young women's experiences – nevertheless illustrate two issues highlighted in the literature on the importance of incorporating girls and young women as participants in policy processes that affect them. First, our results suggest that there are gaps in knowledge between policymakers and our participants. Second, they suggest that other kinds of policy approaches may be important to facilitating realization of girls' and young women's rights, including their right to full participation in the e-society that policymakers have identified as essential to Canada's economic well-being.[41]

Gaps in Knowledge
Canadian federal policy debates related to children and technology have tended to focus on sexualized dangers posed by unknown adults. In contrast, many of our participants were clear that being online wasn't "all bad." When they did discuss online fears and dangers, their concerns tended to relate more to harassment and surveillance by known others (apart from stranger-related concerns they sometimes expressed about their younger sisters and girl cousins). This kind of gap seems to reflect a well-documented trend of policymaker focus on sexual threats from unknown predators despite clear evidence that girls and women are most at risk of violence from people known to them.[42]

Notwithstanding Canadian policymakers' tendency to speak about online risks in gender-neutral terms (even with respect to forms of violence statistically far more likely to affect girls),[43] our participants clearly perceived differences based on gender, race, and membership in the LGBTQ community. Most understood girls to be more exposed to online attacks than boys, in no small part because they felt girls were subject to greater negative scrutiny in relation to their appearance and sexuality than boys. However, they also noted that gay and gender-non-conforming boys were also exposed, particularly for engaging in stereotypically "female behaviours," such as posting selfies. While most of our participants were reluctant to say that "sexism" informed online attacks, their descriptions of their everyday experiences with the different standards applied to boys and girls readily parallels the double standard applied to girls' expressions of sexuality identified in the literature.[44] They also suggest the influence of social norms around gender conformity that construct and constrain performances of "proper" masculinity and femininity,[45] often in ways that render "acting like a girl" a debilitating insult to boys.

When Canadian policy debate relating to technology and children broke from gender neutrality, it was typically to discuss specific examples of girls who had committed suicide in connection with "cyberbullying," or to discuss girls generically. Generic discussions tended toward caricatures, such as the sexual temptress or the naïve know-it-all,[46] focusing on behaviours by imaginary girls isolated from the social context and constructions that give them meaning.[47]

Our participants also sometimes discussed individual girls who had committed suicide, particularly Amanda Todd. However, their concerns did not end with addressing the individual perpetrators involved or the individual girls themselves. Instead, they emphasized what they saw as the unfair consequences of sexualized exposure for girls, as opposed to boys, essentially highlighting a systemic sexual double standard, usually without explicitly using the language of sexism or inequality. Some of our participants also relied on caricatures of *other* girls, often in ways that seemed to allow them to distance themselves from sexualized self-representations[48] and images that might be thought of as too attention seeking. In contrast with the policy debates, however, our participants simultaneously provided empathetic, contextualized understandings of stereotypically sexualized self-representations as part of negotiating a complex environment influenced by desires, norms, markets, and technological architectures, which our participants, again, understood to produce quite different consequences for girls than for boys.

Our participants described living a seamlessly integrated offline/online existence,[49] which unsurprisingly incorporated all aspects of life, including expression of and experimentation with sexuality, self-image, and desire. Many said that online visibility was integral to social success. They also identified the ways that social norms around visibility interacted with other kinds of norms, including market pressures to emulate mediatized heteronormative stereotypes of beauty and sexuality as a recognizable way of achieving visibility.[50] Unrealistic mediatized norms acted both as an enabler of recognition, and a constraint on diverse expressions of sexuality and desire.[51] In addition, our participants understood themselves, as girls, to be scrutinized particularly intensely online (as compared to boys), leading to an exaggerated risk of lasting reputational effects for crossing over the fine line between expressions of socially acceptable sexualized beauty and being a "slut."[52]

Our participants also described a world in which online architectures made experimentation with different kinds of self-representations particularly risky for girls. The perceived gendered risk of losing control over one's online image appeared to make privacy exceptionally important to them (at least until sexual double standards are systematically dismantled). However, they noted that online spaces were often architected in such a way as to undermine both their privacy *per se* and privacy strategies. Many noted the ways that online social media sites were structured to incent and reward disclosure (such as through friend counts), and to make it difficult to exercise privacy strategies that allow for particular performances to be accessible only to particular audiences. Many were unclear as to what service providers were able to do with information posted by and about them.[53] Moreover, some expressed discomfort with the permanence of the record, noting that even when they deleted their accounts or photos, the files still resided on a hard drive controlled by the service provider. Our participants went further to say that online social media sites could be set up in ways that invited "cyberbullying" by, for example, specifically facilitating attention seeking through inviting questions to be asked anonymously. In terms of redress, they noted that service provider policies on when information would be taken down were often less than clear.

Unexplored Approaches

As Jiwani noted in her research on violence prevention and girls, the process of identifying knowledge gaps between policymakers and girls and young women can bring into relief other kinds of approaches that could better facilitate realization of girls' and young women's rights.[54] Our participants highlighted possibilities for two different sorts of responses: (1) policy targeted at a variety of other actors beyond girls themselves and unknown sexual predators; and (2) programs aimed at underlying systems of discrimination that inform the everyday kinds of problems they understood to be most salient to girls and young women. I discuss some concrete examples of policies that could respond to the issues raised in the conclusion below.

Conclusion

The composite of online life that our participants drew for us revealed a complicated interaction between personal preferences and desires, social norms, gendered marketing practices, and online architectures that shape girls' online lives,[55] which invites analysis of how and whether the law should or would intervene. To date, legal interventions have tended toward reactive criminal law responses that mask the underlying systemic issues and the corporate practices that inform them, and offer limited redress. Our participants described a world in which architectures structured to maximize disclosure (and minimize privacy) lead to perceiving high counts of "friends" and "likes" as "popularity." These architectural constraints combine with social norms and marketing practices that encourage emulation of mediatized representations of female beauty and sexuality as ways of competing for recognition (often, for heterosexual girls, from males). Together, these produce a perfect storm, incenting self-disclosure that simultaneously promises on the one hand celebrity and recognition, but on the other hand a gendered risk of shame and harassment that is complicated by the enduring consequences of unnecessarily permanent digital records.

These interactions invite policy responses that take into account the difficulty of navigating this complex environment, without compromising girls' capacity to thrive in their digitally networked existences. Moreover, they invite consideration of proactive policy alternatives that are not aimed primarily at further responsibilizing girls themselves by counselling them to further limit their online participation.[56] Alternative responses aimed at promotion of a more egalitarian society[57] could involve:

- curricular reform in our education system to enhance the critical media and digital literacy skills of *all* youth, as well as their understanding of human rights, in order to assist them to unpack and challenge discriminatory social norms and widely marketed white, heteronormative stereotypes of femininity and sexuality that, among other things, set girls up for gendered shaming, and for competition for male attention;[58]

- enhanced corporate accountability for unrealistically narrow media representations of girls and women that work to constrain their choices, and ignore other non-mainstream representations and diverse realities;[59]
- and intervening on corporate practices that structure online environments in ways that make it difficult for girls to exercise privacy strategies and set them up to surveil one another.

Policymakers are internationally obligated to facilitate the voices of girl children and to protect their best interests. Our results illustrate how policymakers' understanding of the "dangers" to girls and young women online can vary in important ways from those of girls and young women themselves. Meaningfully facilitating girls' and young women's voices will require specific initiatives to engage girls and young women from a rich diversity of backgrounds and experiences in the project of understanding and improving the conditions of our e-society. It is also likely to mean public intervention on the habits and practices of other actors who profit from the perfect storm that currently mediates girls' and young women's e-quality.

Acknowledgements

Thanks to the Social Sciences and Humanities Research Council for their generous support of the eGirls Project.

Notes

1   Yasmin Jiwani, *Violence Prevention and the Girl Child* (Vancouver: The Alliance of Five Research Centres on Violence, FREDA Centre, 1999), 5, last modified February 1999, <http://fredacentre.com/wp-content/uploads/2010/09/Jiwani-et-al-1999-Violence-Prevention-and-the-Girl-Child-.pdf>.

2   Trina Grillo & Stephanie M. Wildman, "Obscuring the Importance of Race: The Implication of Making Comparisons between Racism and Sexism (Or Other-Isms)," *Duke Law Journal* 40:2 (1991): 397.

3   Kimberley Crenshaw, "Mapping the Margins: Intersectionality, Identity Politics, and Violence against Women of Color," *Stanford Law Review* 43:6 (1991): 1279.

4   For example, in the 2011 federal election, elected MPs were 74 percent male, 90 percent were not members of a visible minority group (over 60 percent of elected women were not members of minority groups), 74 percent had completed some post-secondary education, and their average age was 49.79 years, notwithstanding that women comprised the majority of the Canadian population, and ethnic minorities comprised almost 20 percent of the population. See: Mary-Rose Brown, *Edging towards Diversity: A Statistical Breakdown of Canada's 41st Parliament, with Comparisons to the 40th Parliament* (Ottawa: Public Policy Forum, June 2011), 10, <http://www.ppforum.ca/sites/default/files/edging_towards_diversity_final.pdf>; Jerome H. Black, "Racial Diversity in the 2011 Federal Election: Visible Minority Candidates and MPs," *Canadian Parliamentary Review* 36:3 (2013): 22; "Women in Federal Politics," Equal Voice, last modified March 2013, <http://www.equalvoice.ca/pdf/women_in_federal_politics_fact_sheet_march_2013.pdf>; and Jerome H. Black, "Minority Women in the 35th Parliament: A New Dimension of Social Diversity," *Canadian Parliamentary Review* 20:1 (1997): 19.

5   Gerison Lansdown, Shane Jimerson & Reza Shahroozi, "Children's Rights and School Psychology: Children's Right to Participation," *Journal of School Psychology* 52:3 (2014): 4–7; Terry Barber, "Young People and Civic Participation: A Conceptual Overview," *Youth & Policy* 96 (2007): 32; Barry Percy-Smith, "'You Think You Know? ... You have no Idea': Youth Participation in Health Policy Development," *Health Education Research* 22:6 (2007): 880.

6   Defined for purposes of this discussion as persons under 18 years of age.

7   United Nations Committee on the Rights of the Child, *Convention on the Rights of the Child*, GA Res 40/25, UN GAOR, 44th Sess., U.N. Doc A/RES/44/25 (New York: United Nations Office of the High Commissioner for Human Rights, 1990), Article 3, accessed 23 September 2014, <http://www.ohchr.org/en/professionalinterest/pages/crc.aspx>; Natasha Blanchet-Cohen & Christophe Bedeaux, "Towards a Rights-Based Approach to Youth Programs: Duty-Bearers' Perspectives," *Children and Youth Services Review* 38 (2014): 76, subsequently called "Duty-Bearers' Perspectives"; United Nations Committee on the Rights of the Child, *The Right of the Child to be Heard*, CRC, 55 Sess., General Comment No 12 UN Doc CRC/C/GC/12 (New York: United Nations Convention on the Rights

of the Child, 2009), para 72–73, <http://www2.ohchr.org/english/bodies/ crc/docs/AdvanceVersions/CRC-C-GC-12.pdf>.

8   Susan Bennett, Stuart Hart & Kimberly Ann Svevo-Cianci, "The Need for a General Comment for Article 19 of the UN Convention on the Rights of the Child: Toward Enlightenment and Progress for Child Protection," *Child Abuse & Neglect* 33:11 (2009): 786.

9   Blanchet-Cohen & Bedeaux, *supra* note 7 at 76; Roger Hart & Michael Schwab, "Children's Rights and the Building of Democracy: A Dialogue on the International Movement for Children's Participation," *Children and the Environment* 24:3 (1997): 179; Percy-Smith, *supra* note 5 at 889.

10   Lansdown et al, *supra* note 5 at 6.

11   Roger Hart, Collette Daiute, Semil Iltus, David Kritt, Michaela Rome & Kim Sabo, "Developmental Theory and Children's Participation in Community Organizations," *Children and the Environment* 24:3 (1997): 33; Percy-Smith, *supra* note 5 at 889; Ariadne Vroman & Philippa Collin, "Everyday Youth Participation? Contrasting Views from Australian Policymakers and Young People," *Young: Nordic Journal of Youth Research* 18:1 (2010): 109.

12   Ben Kirshner, "Youth Activism as a Context for Learning and Development," *American Behavioral Scientist* 51:3 (2007): 371.

13   Barry Percy-Smith & Danny Burns, "Exploring the Role of Children and Young People as Agents of Change in Sustainable Community Development," *Local Environment* 18:3 (2013): 324.

14   Lansdown et al, *supra* note 5 at 4.

15   Status of Women Canada, *Gender-Based Analysis: A Guide for Policy-Making* (Ottawa: Status of Women Canada, 1996), 4, 7, last updated September 1998, <http://www.pacificwater.org/userfiles/file/IWRM/Toolboxes/ gender/gender_based_analysis.pdf>; United Nations Commission on the Status of Women, *Progress in Mainstreaming a Gender Perspective into the Development, Implementation and Evaluation of National Policies and Programmes, With a Particular Focus on Challenges and Achievements in the Implementation of the Millennium Development Goals for Women and Girls*, ESC, 58 Sess., Annex, Agenda Item 3(a), E/CN.6/2014/4 (New York: United Nations Commission on the Status of Women, 2014), 7/20, 17/20, 14/20.

16   Nura Taefi, "The Synthesis of Age and Gender: Intersectionality, International Human Rights Law and the Marginalisation of the Girl-Child," *The International Journal of Children's Rights*, 17:3 (2009): 345; Calhoun Research and Development, C. Lang Consulting & Irene Savoie, *Girls in Canada 2005* (Toronto and Shediac, NB: Canadian Women's Foundation, 2005), ii–iv, <http://www.canadianwomen.org/sites/canadianwomen. org/files/PDF%20-%20Girls%20in%20Canada%20Report%202005.pdf>; Girls Action Foundation, *Amplify: Designing Spaces and Programs for Girls, A Toolkit* (Montreal: Girls Action Foundation, 2010), 16, <http://

girlsactionfoundation.ca/en/download/file/fid/1549>; Yasmin Jiwani, Helene Berman & Catherine Ann Cameron, "Violence Prevention and the Canadian Girl Child," *International Journal of Child, Youth and Family Studies* 1:2 (2010): 143.

17 Jiwani et al, *supra* note 16 at 135; Jennifer Tipper, *The Canadian Girl-Child: Determinants of the Health and Well-being of Girls and Young Women*, (Ottawa: Canadian Institute of Child Health, 1997), 6, accessed 23 September 2014, <http://www.cich.ca/PDFFiles/cndgirlchildeng.pdf>.

18 Girls Action Foundation, *supra* note 16 at 1; Taefi, *supra* note 16 at 345; Jiwani et al, *supra* note 16 at 135; United Nations Entity for Gender Equality and the Empowerment of Women, *Platform for Action: The Girl-Child Diagnosis* (Beijing: United Nations Fourth World Conference on Women, 1995), para 263–264, <http://www.un.org/womenwatch/daw/beijing/platform/girl.htm#object1>; Tipper, *supra* note 17 at 6.

19 United Nations Committee, *The Right of the Child to Be Heard, supra* note 7 at para 77.

20 Girls Action Foundation, *supra* note 16 at 13, 38, 42; United Nations Commission on the Status of Women, *Agreed Conclusions on Access and Participation of Women and Girls in Education, Training and Science and Technology, Including for the Promotion of Women's Equal Access to Full Employment and Decent Work* (New York: United Nations Commission on the Status of Women, 2014), Art. 21, <http://www.un.org/womenwatch/daw/csw/csw55/agreed_conclusions/AC_CSW55_E.pdf>; United Nations Commission on the Status of Women, *International Day of the Girl Child*, GA Res. 66/170. UN GAOR 66th Sess., U.N. Doc A/RES/66/170 (New York: United Nations Commission on the Status of Women, 2012), 1; Tipper, *supra* note 17 at 6.

21 United Nations Commission on the Status of Women, *Agreed Conclusions, supra* note 20 at Art. 21; Jiwani et al, *supra* note 16 at 137.

22 Jiwani et al, *supra* note 16 at 135; Debra J. Pepler, Dirsten C. Madsen, Christopher D. Webster & Kathryn S. Levene, *The Development and Treatment of Girlhood Aggression* (London: Lawrence Erlbaum, 2005), 180; Terrie E Moffitt, Avshalom Caspi, Michael Rutter & Phil A. Silva, *Sex Differences in Antisocial Behaviour: Conduct Disorder, Delinquency, and Violence in the Dunedin Longitudinal Study* (New York: Cambridge University Press, 2001), 182.

23 Jiwani et al, *supra* note 16 at 137.

24 Blanchet-Cohen & Bedeaux, *supra* note 7 at 76; Shareefa Fulat & Raza Jaffrey, "Muslim Youth Helpline: A Model of Youth Engagement in Service Delivery," *Youth & Policy* 92 (2006): 168–169, <http://www.youthandpolicy.org/wp-content/uploads/2013/07/youthandpolicy92.pdf>; Hart & Schwab, *supra* note 9 at 178. See also the discussion of girls' and young women's civic participation in Shade, Chapter XVI.

25   Girls Action Foundation, *supra* note 16 at 17; Jiwani, *supra* note 1 at 14; United Nations Commission on the Status of Women, *Agreed Conclusions, supra* note 20 at Art. 6, 9, 17; UN Web Services Section, Department of Public Information, *UN's International Day of the Girl Child* (New York: United Nations, 2013), <http://www.un.org/en/events/girlchild>; Jiwani et al, *supra* note 16 at 134.

26   I have placed the term "cyberbullying" in quotation marks in this chapter to reiterate my concern expressed in earlier writing that the widespread use of the term itself to describe a remarkable variety of situations and behaviours risks obscuring fundamental differences between those situations and behaviours. In particular, its application to situations of sexual, racial, and other forms of identity-based online harassment can too easily eclipse underlying systemic structures of discrimination that disproportionately expose members of particular groups to attack and violence: Jane Bailey, "Time to Unpack the Juggernaut?: Reflections on the Canadian Federal Parliamentary Debates on Cyberbullying," (2014), 48, unpublished, archived at Social Sciences Research Network, <http://papers.ssrn.com/sol3/papers.cfm?abstract_id=2448480>.

27   The results of our review of these debates are reported in Jane Bailey & Valerie Steeves, "Will the Real Digital Girl Please Stand Up? Examining the Gap Between Policy Dialogue and Girls' Accounts of their Digital Experiences," in *New Visualities, New Technologies: The New Ecstasy of Communication*, eds. Greg Wise & Hille Koskela (Farnham: Ashgate Publishing, 2013), 41–66.

28   Jiwani et al, *supra* note 16 at 137; Jiwani, *supra* note 1.

29   Bailey & Steeves, *supra* note 27 at 56.

30   These were also the sorts of issues focused upon by media in this general timeframe: Steven Roberts & Aziz Douai, "Moral Panics and Cybercrime: How Canadian Media Cover Internet Child Luring," *Journal of Canadian Media Studies* 10:1 (2012): 12–13.

31   Bailey, *supra* note 26.

32   *Ibid.*, at 22.

33   Bailey & Steeves, *supra* note 27 at 56.

34   Lara Karaian, "Policing 'Sexting': Responsibilization, Respectability and Sexual Subjectivity in Child Protection/Crime Prevention Responses to Teenagers' Digital Sexual Expression," *Theoretical Criminology* 18:3 (2013): 2–3.

35   For a rural/urban comparative analysis, see Burkell & Saginur, Chapter V.

36   Our rural adult focus group included Catlin (19), Laura (18), Trish (18), and Brianne (20). Our rural minor focus group included Courtney (17), Chelsea (17), Paula (17), Beth (16), and Josie (16). Our urban adult focus

group included Keira (21), Donna (19), Jill (20), Andrea (22), Ashley (18), and Kathleen (20). Our urban minor focus group included Vicky (17), Eve (16), Abby (17), Jacquelyn (17), Lauryn (17), Monique (16), and Jane (16). Our rural adult interviewees were Cassandra (19), Becky (19), and Amelia (18). Our rural minor interviewees were Monica (16), Lynda (17), and Nicole (16). Our urban adult interviewees were Alessandra (21), Mackenzie (20), and Cindy (20). Our urban minor interviewees were Alicia (17), Clare (16), and Josée (15).

37   For further details, see Steeves, Chapter VI.

38   Andree Lau, "Amanda Todd: Bullied Teen Commits Suicide," *The Huffington Post*, 11 October 2012, <http://www.huffingtonpost.ca/2012/10/11/amanda-todd-teen-bullying-suicide-youtube_n_1959668.html>.

39   *"Ask and Answer,"* Ask.fm, <http://www.ask.fm>.

40   For further information on this important social justice movement see: "CStreet Campaign," *Idle No More*, <http://www.idlenomore.ca>.

41   "Minister Clement Updates Canadians on Canada's Digital Economy Strategy," *Government of Canada: Industry Canada News Releases*, last modified 22 November 2010, <http://www.ic.gc.ca/eic/site/064.nsf/eng/06096.html>.

42   Jiwani, *supra* note 1 at 14.

43   Mirroring the tendency documented by FREDA in connection with violence prevention and the girl child. As noted above, however, exceptions were made in situations where specific girls or caricatures of girls were used as examples of victimhood, risky sexualized behaviour, and general irrationality: Bailey & Steeves, *supra* note 27.

44   Jessica Ringrose, Laura Harvey, Rosalind Gill & Sonia Livingstone, "Teen Girls, Sexual Double Standards and 'Sexting': Gendered Value in Digital Image Exchange," *Feminist Theory* 14:3 (2013): 305.

45   Elizabeth J. Meyer, *Gender, Bullying and Harassment: Strategies to End Sexism and Homophobia in Schools* (New York: Teachers College Press, 2009), 6–9, 21–22, <https://tesl-ej.org/~teslejor/pdf/ej61/r1.pdf>.

46   Bailey & Steeves, *supra* note 27 at 56.

47   In much the same way that FREDA documented a media tendency to isolate delinquent girls and girl-on-girl violence from the social context of physical and sexual abuse that often informs it.

48   Caroline Caron, "Sexy Girls as the 'Other': The Discursive Processes of Stigmatizing Girls," (paper presented at the Canadian Communication Association Conference, University of British Columbia, Vancouver, BC., 4–6 June 2008), 6, <http://archivesic.ccsd.cnrs.fr/docs/00/35/28/31/PDF/Girls_as_the_Other.doc.pdf>.

49   Valerie Steeves, *Young Canadians in a Wired World: Phase II: Trends and Recommendations* (Ottawa: Media Awareness Network, 2005), 21, <http://

mediasmarts.ca/sites/default/files/pdfs/publication-report/full/YCWWII-trends-recomm.pdf>.

50   Valerie Steeves & Jane Bailey, "Living in the Mirror: Understanding Young Women's Experiences with Online Social Networking," in *Expanding the Gaze: Gender, Public Space and Surveillance*, eds. Amanda Glasbeek, Rob Haynen & Emily Van der Muelen (Toronto: University of Toronto Press, forthcoming 2015).

51   Ringrose et al, *supra* note 44 at 312.

52   *Ibid.*, at 317; Jane Bailey, Valerie Steeves, Jacquelyn Burkell & Priscilla Regan, "Negotiating with Gender Stereotypes on Social Networking Sites: From 'Bicycle Face' to Facebook," *Journal of Communication Inquiry* 37 (2013): 11.

53   It has been clear for some time that privacy policies are not always written in understandable ways, especially in terms of facilitating youth understanding: Anca Micheti, Jacquelyn Burkell & Valerie Steeves, "Fixing Broken Doors: Strategies for Drafting Privacy Policies Young People Can Understand," *Bulletin of Science, Technology & Society* 30:2 (2010): 130; Office of the Privacy Commissioner of Canada, *Privacy for Everyone: Report on the* Personal Information Protection and Electronic Documents Act (Ottawa: Office of the Privacy Commissioner of Canada, 2011), 21, <https://www.priv.gc.ca/information/ar/201112/2011_pipeda_e.pdf>.

54   Jiwani et al, *supra* note 16 at 134.

55   Lawrence Lessig, *Code Version 2.0* (New York: Basic Books, 2006), 123.

56   For further discussion of responsibilization, see Karaian, *supra* note 34.

57   Elizabeth Meyer, "New Solutions for Bullying and Harassment: A Post-Structural, Feminist Approach," in *School Bullying: New Theories in Context*, eds. Robin May Schott & Dorte Marie Sondergaard (Cambridge: Cambridge University Press, 2014), 209.

58   See Steeves, Chapter VI; "Resisting Stereotypes and Working for Change," MediaSmarts, <http://mediasmarts.ca/gender-representation/women-and-girls/resisting-stereotypes-and-working-change>.

59   Eileen L. Zurbriggen, Rebecca L. Collins, Sharon Lamb, Tomi-Ann Roberts, Deborah L. Tolman, L. Monique Ward & Jeanne Blake, *Report of the APA Task Force on the Sexualization of Girls* (Washington, DC: American Psychological Association), 38, <http://www.apa.org/pi/women/programs/girls/report-full.pdf>.

CHAPTER II

Revisiting Cyberfeminism: Theory as a Tool for Understanding Young Women's Experiences

Trevor Scott Milford

Introduction: Troubling Binary Thinking

Early cyberfeminists conceptualized cyberspaces as fundamentally liberating, theorizing their capacity to move beyond the traditional binaries and limitations of popular gender and feminist politics. Human-machine mergers made possible by technology were imagined as facilitators of "post-gender worlds":[1] and virtual spaces were initially envisioned as utopian sites of unrestricted, transcendent emancipation from gender-related constraints.[2] Cyberspaces showed promise to disrupt conventional patriarchal hierarchies, colonial power interests, and militarized, commercialized technologies of advanced capitalism,[3] representing a "brave new world." In this brave new world, the hierarchical and subjugating logic underscoring social binaries and privileging male over female, hetero- over homosexual, Caucasian over non-Caucasian, and even human over animal could be restructured on a socio-political scale to address deep-seated disparity and ultimately move toward social equality.[4]

However, despite this utopian outlook, it quickly became apparent that online spaces are locales in which feminist issues manifest.[5] As Gajjala notes, early cyberfeminist frameworks "reduce[d] the problem of inequality ... to just a problem of material access to equipment, wiring and technical training."[6] Issues of online inequality instead extend to broader socio-political contexts that impact the construction of cyberspatial environments themselves on a cultural level, where narrative discourses of linear patriarchal, colonial, and capitalist progress routinely are furthered within these constructions.[7] These discourses have the potential to restrict women's agency online, potentially undermining their equal participation in digital society. Policy and political discourses that address issues of online inequality – in addition to many contemporary cyberfeminist discourses – also show tendencies to adopt these linear progress narratives. In the process of adopting these narratives, simplistic binary notions relating to gender and virtual space are regularly accepted instead of critiqued, including notions of online vs. offline, virtual spaces as liberating vs. constraining, virtual experience as vulnerable vs. empowering, and regulatory approaches to virtual issues that focus on policy responses vs. self-regulation. In many cases this acceptance perpetuates the very binary notions that early cyberfeminists theorized cyberspaces could overcome.

Instead of complicating the intersection of gender and cyberspatial environments, cyberfeminist critiques and legal responses to gendered online issues have too often stagnated, typically investing in yet another artificial dichotomy: virtual spaces as utopian or dystopian, with nothing in between. The "brave new world" foreseen by early cyberfeminists has become an anti-utopia fraught with gendered risk, which can then be used to justify current trends in legal responses that include responsibilization, criminalization, and surveillance of women online. Yet the same critique that can be levelled at early cyberfeminist views of cyberspaces as inherently utopian can also be levelled at the framing of virtual spaces as inherently dystopian: it's just not that simple.

This chapter strives to move beyond this dichotomous vision of cyberspace by building on major areas of cyberfeminist debate to disturb commonly accepted binary notions surrounding gender and online spaces, and considering how cyberfeminists can work together to achieve common goals. In doing so, it maps the trajectory of major contemporary cyberfeminist discourses to consider how cyberfeminist critique could ultimately be mobilized to move beyond these artificial binaries, critiquing current policy initiatives that attempt to govern gender and virtual spaces and contemplating new directions for future regulatory strategies. Finally, this chapter looks at how future cyberfeminist research initiatives could work to fill these gaps and engage in discussions that are ultimately more productive, inclusive, intersectional, and empowering.

Online vs. Offline:
Complicating Feminist Critique and the Virtual Divide

Cyberfeminisms are not a unified feminist movement with a cohesive political or theoretical agenda. Although many self-identified cyberfeminists refuse to define cyberfeminism altogether, according to Flanagan and Booth, the term "cyberfeminism" refers to "a sporadic, tactical, contradictory set of theories, debates, and practices"[8] relating to gender and digital culture. Daniels suggests that because the contexts of cyberfeminist discourses are not unified, rather than referring to a monolithic singular cyberfeminism, it is more useful to refer to plural cyberfeminisms.[9] "Cyberfeminisms" is inclusive of the diverse theoretical and political stances that cyberfeminists occupy when engaging in discussions on gender and digital culture or technology, reflecting that the common ground between theoretical cyberfeminist variants is a "sustained focus on gender and digital technologies and on [feminist] practices."[10] More important than semantic theoretical divisions between "camps" of cyberfeminists is that cyberfeminists share a belief that women should attempt to empower themselves via the appropriation and control of virtual technology in ways that continue to express their identities as females.[11] Depending on the theoretical position, this can entail restructuring virtual technology itself to promote gender equality, increasing women's access to existing virtual technology, or a combination of both.

Conceptualizing cyberfeminisms as a plurality is an attempt to reconcile differences between various feminist frameworks that could fall under a digital purview. Through this theoretical lens, questions of difference between schools of cyberfeminist thought become less important, and cyberfeminists, regardless of their differences, can begin to integrate a variety of theoretical backgrounds and intersectional viewpoints into emergent feminist discourses. Such integration is a reparative[12] move away from divisive interfeminist disputes, recognizing that diverse cyberfeminist perspectives can simultaneously yield fruitful theoretical discussions while working toward a common goal of greater online equality. This chapter will embrace this operationalization of cyberfeminist theoretical thought, in the spirit of acknowledging the diverse perspectives that cyberfeminisms encompass.

If cyberfeminisms refer to a combined focus on gender, digital technologies, and feminist practices, it is helpful next to consider whether cyberfeminisms can be separated from other feminisms. Is a sustained focus on digital technology enough for a feminist framework to be considered cyberfeminist? In order to answer this question, it is necessary to first deconstruct the dichotomy between online and offline spaces so as to examine whether it is accurate to say that any feminist framework does *not* have a vested interest in – or at the very least, does not apply to – digital technology. I begin by outlining the theoretical concept of the cyborg. I then draw upon this theoretical construct and its feminist implications to consider the relationships between ubiquitous technologization, gender, techno-spatial processes of identity formation, and the replication of offline inequalities within online spaces. In doing so, I attempt to illustrate the confluence between online and offline realms and better situate how all feminisms can, in fact, be considered cyberfeminisms.

Donna Haraway[13] notes that technologized and non-technologized spheres, or online and offline spheres, intersect in complex ways, concluding that "virtual" and "real" life is an inaccurate binary construct. To transcend absolutist, dichotomized thinking, she puts forth the concept of the "cyborg" to suggest that human and machine have become one. Haraway offers that, "The [theoretical] cyborg is a creature in a post-gender world"[14] where human and machine have become fused figuratively in terms of conflated identity and often literally in terms of shared physical space, whether via technological interaction or corporeally shared space such as implantation with medical technology. Cyborgs contest the underlying ideologies of broader political structures which assume that power binaries are natural as opposed to socially constructed, questioning the fundamental nature of what it means to be human. Paasonen agrees with Haraway that, "The cyborg stands as a metaphor of feminist subject, a boundary figure that moves across the hierarchical categories of the natural and the artificial ... without positioning technology as a masculine other of women and nature."[15] Sadie Plant shares that considering virtual worlds through the theoretical lens of the cyborg is important because it creates space for women within already existing cultures and also because of its potential to undermine material offline realities of patriarchal control, which are often replicated online.[16] As Sandoval likewise asserts, "'Cyborg consciousness' has a long lineage sited in forms of opposition to domination."[17] This lineage, she offers, complements the cyborg metaphor particularly well, because both advocate new or reconceptualized techniques of social interaction, including how we collectively think, act, and live.

The idea that cyborg consciousness is rooted in forms of opposition to domination implies a need to reflect on how offline inequalities can be replicated within technospaces. Social inequalities from the offline realm — in particular, offline violence against women and other gender-related disparities — are also reflected in virtual contexts.[18] Much like offline spaces, online spaces deeply entrench sexism, racism, and homophobia;[19] technological architectures, as Gajjala has pointed out, structurally entrench hegemonic colonialism, capitalism, and patriarchy.[20] Feminist tools of critique traditionally used offline can be mobilized to combat and theorize inequality that is replicated in online spaces, ultimately granting women greater online agency and reducing gendered online violence.[21] Virtual contexts are further inseparable from "real life" in terms of the pivotal role they play in identity formation and identity performance.

The need to challenge constraining gender stereotypes in virtual spaces is particularly acute for girls and young women. Although girls are confident about their ability to use networked technologies as economic actors (e.g., employee, entrepreneur), the public nature of online performances amplifies the impact of online stereotypes and opens them up to harsh judgment from peers, particularly as they seek to express themselves as *girls becoming women*.[22] Extending cyberfeminist literature — which focuses largely on women — to help us theorize the relationship between technology and gender for girls is especially important, as it may help us better understand the ways that networked spaces create affordances and constraints for girls seeking to inhabit feminine identities.

Game scholars, such as Lehdonvirta, have looked at the role of online spaces within identity formation, criticizing the virtual/non-virtual divide more explicitly and arguing that such a dichotomy is a "treacherous fantasy."[23] Taylor writes that, "To imagine that we can segregate these things — … virtual and real — not only misunderstands our relationship with technology, but our relationship with culture"[24] and ultimately builds academic research upon false assumptions. Virtual spaces often flow into other mediums and forums that can be either online or offline. Non-virtual social worlds, social economies, and social institutions similarly permeate virtuality and are complexly intertwined with virtual worlds, virtual economies, and virtual institutions that each shape individuals' lives and identities, which are reflected both on line and off line.[25] Virtual spaces, then, are fused together with "real" life into one social space that encompasses both online and offline realities. Virtual citizens perform identity similarly to offline citizens, despite potentially feeling freer to experiment with identity on line;[26] online spheres are also subject to similar feminist critiques as offline spheres, rather than providing transcendent spaces for gender-neutral self-expression as early cyberfeminists envisioned.

With the ubiquitous technologization that characterizes life in the new millennium,[27] many contemporary Western subjects are unable to escape the fusion of offline and online life that stems from pervasive reliance on technology. Corporeality is linked to identity and subjectivity, as Haraway's cyborg metaphor suggests, blurring the lines between the virtual and the non-virtual. For example, in Canada, the internet penetration rate in 2011 was 81.6 per cent,[28] meaning that only 18.4 per cent of Canadians did not use some form of virtual technology. Smartphone use is widespread; debit and credit cards are relied upon for financial transactions; closed-circuit surveillance is extensive. It is nearly impossible to avoid interaction with digital technology in the course of living contemporary life; the daily life of most Canadians is saturated with the use of virtual technology. As Haraway has argued, this reliance on technology means that contemporary subjects can potentially be theorized as embodying cyborg subjectivity and can therefore be subjected to cyberfeminist critiques relating to technologization. Since most members of the Canadian public can conceivably be interpellated as feminist subjects by virtue of living technologized lives, it stands to reason that most Canadians also have a vested interest in the various feminist critiques that can be made of technologized spaces. While additional research is required to more deeply conceptualize the relationship between cyborg subjectivity and corporeality, both in generally Western and in specifically Canadian contexts, future work could build upon these themes by considering the argument that most Canadians stand as Harawayan metaphors of feminist subject. Such potential research has wide-reaching implications for the spread of cyberfeminist initiatives to wider Western populations, Canada included.

As this section has sketched, *online* and *offline* are absolutist terms that do not adequately capture the complex intersections between virtual technology, gender inequality, and "real" life: focusing on one to the exclusion of the other does a disservice to [cyber] feminist goals of combatting gendered inequality, since the inequalities entrenched in both "real" and virtual realms are inseparable. In addition, as several scholars point out,[29] cyberfeminisms are inherently inclusive, plural, non-monolithic, and integrative of diverse feminist perspectives. It stands to reason, then, that traditional offline feminisms can be mobilized within cyberfeminist frameworks, and that traditional cyberfeminisms can be mobilized within offline feminist frameworks. After all, the central difference between cyberfeminisms and non-cyberfeminisms is simply a focus on digital technology—and since digital technology cannot be separated from offline life, this is, in effect, not a difference at all.[30] While online spaces do have unique nuances with feminist implications, feminist tools of critique are, by nature of this close relationship, in fact cyberfeminist tools of critique. It is time for this false dichotomy to be acknowledged, so that all those concerned with gendered inequalities may come together in a ubiquitously technologized world.

Agency vs. Vulnerability: Liberation, Constraint, Risk, and Self-Disclosure

Discourses on gender and virtual spaces have traditionally either painted virtual spaces as inherently liberating or inherently constraining for girls and women (as well as those from other gender-related minorities, including those who identify as transgendered, non-gender normative, and/or non-heterosexual). It has been established that although early cyberfeminists viewed virtual spaces in a utopian way that stressed their liberating potential, later discourses on gender and virtual spaces—which have been echoed by policymakers and popular media—stress the potential risk, although cyberfeminist scholars are beginning to question whether there are ways to interpret these risks as liberating. These discourses that construct a risk/benefit binary appear alongside discourses dichotomizing girls' online experiences as either empowering (agential) or vulnerable.

This section adopts the perspective that constraints or risks can indeed be liberating and that vulnerability is not necessarily disempowering, suggesting that it is a false dichotomy to see online spaces as either liberating or constraining, or to see girls' virtual experiences as either empowering or vulnerable. In this section I begin to examine nuances of risk-centred media, policy, and theoretical debate, considering the implications of these nuances for online identity and self-expression. After establishing a working definition for online agency and using it to begin considering issues related to surveillance, privacy, and self-disclosure, I then view issues related to media stereotypes, authenticity, and body image through this lens. I advocate moving away from cyberfeminist discussions that focus on false risk/benefit binaries like liberation vs. constraint and empowerment vs. vulnerability, looking at how girls' experiences might be reoperationalized as simultaneously empowering and vulnerable as opposed to exclusively one or the other. My goal is to embrace more critical discussions that aim to maximize agency while minimizing constraint for all girls within virtual environments.

Contemporary media, theoretical, and policy discourses have established diverse potential constraints upon girls' and women's free and empowering virtual experiences. These discourses have been approached from both cyberfeminist and non-cyberfeminist theoretical perspectives, and by self-identified cyberfeminists as well as non-cyberfeminists. While some question conceptualizing online spaces solely as risk-based, all contribute to the current prevalence of risk in discourses surrounding girls and virtual technology. This is not to say that discussions of risk should cease altogether. Rather, these discussions should be reframed to focus on the potential for liberation and increased agency in girls' use of virtual technology, the reduction of potential constraints upon them, and an ultimate goal of increasing virtual gender equality rather than bolstering patriarchal protectionism.

Risks identified in media, policy, and theoretical debates on girls and young women and digital technology include (among others): surveillance by other online users,[31] privacy risks,[32] concerns related to self-disclosure (particularly in terms of future employment, sexual harassment, reputational damage, or constraints on higher education),[33] potential sexualization and resulting miscellaneous threats to personal safety in response to self-images that are posted online,[34] other reputational risks,[35] body image risks related to internalization of gendered media representations,[36] and cyberbullying and cyber gender harassment.[37] Upon looking at each of these issues more deeply, however, it becomes clear that not all of these areas are exclusively sites of risk and constraint for girls in virtual spaces. Without discounting that for some they may indeed represent constraints upon agency or unrestricted use of virtual technology, for many girls and young women these areas can also facilitate liberation. Even when these areas do present certain constraints, research has shown that girls are aware of these constraints and are cognizant of potential online risk, proactively enacting strategies to independently manage them.[38]

Policy, media, and many theoretical discourses have linked online gendered risk to online publicity, invoking publicity as a thread that underscores a multitude of gendered risk-based discourses about femininity online. Various scholars have identified that such discourses often condemn – or at the very least problematize – girls' and women's online self-disclosure.[39] These discourses suggest that girls and women who publicly self-present online can subject themselves to many of the aforementioned risks, including increased surveillance,[40] privacy intrusions,[41] unwanted sexual intrusions by males,[42] reputational concerns,[43] employment-related concerns,[44] and cyberbullying or cyber gender harassment.[45]

Too often, popular discourses neoliberally and patriarchically responsibilize girls and young women to self-protect against potential online risk, or recommend that they be protected through legislative initiatives,[46] accepting online risks and gendered constraints as inevitable and focusing on identifying and managing gendered characteristics that could precipitate negative behaviours. In doing so, these discourses latently blame girls for attracting online risk, situating those who experience gender-related victimization as less or more blameworthy, depending on how well they self-protect against it. Cyberfeminisms acknowledge that such discourses entrench gender inequality. First, these discourses neglect to consider that "risks" are not simply constraining and could simultaneously be a source of agency or liberation. Second, in neglecting to consider the root causes of systemically entrenched constraints upon empowerment and free expression for girls online, they do nothing to actually address issues of inequality. Instead, they merely provide individualistic band-aid solutions that function on a micro-level, as opposed to a macro-level, to responsibilize individual girls and young women.

Before dissecting specific constraints to illustrate how they can simultaneously be liberating, it is important to consider the role of agency in women's virtual citizenship. While there is some disagreement within cyberfeminisms regarding how and by whom "agency" should be defined,[47] Koskela offers a helpful conceptualization, arguing that agency is found in the act of presenting, as opposed to the act of being seen. It cannot be simply a matter of who is looking at content that is posted online, since in presenting their private lives on the internet, posters are aware that anyone may see content that is posted. A partial answer, she suggests, is that agency refers to "what, how and when [online content] is controlled by the person(s) whose images are circulated."[48]

Although girls and young women usually have *some* control over which images of themselves are circulated online, Koskela cautions that *exactly how* these pictures will be used and disseminated is beyond their control. She warns that self-disclosed content "obviously can be used for repressive purposes as easily as for empowering purposes."[49] The mere fact that online photos can be used for undesirable purposes such as control, surveillance, sexualization, slander, or other forms of exploitation should not necessarily be interpreted, however, as a loss of agency. Koskela offers that these concepts themselves need to be re-operationalized in a sense that allows girls and young women the greatest possible agency. I embrace Koskela's framework to argue that when online spaces offer girls and young women more control over their online self-presentations, they more effectively promote agency than spaces that do not, and such spaces are therefore more liberating, regardless of the forms that these self-presentations may take.

For the sake of this chapter I operationalize control as the discursive ability to be cognizant of the exercise of power and, relatedly, to be able to freely decide whether to conform to enacted power or resist it; however, it is important to note that meanings of control are not universal and may change from agent to agent and context to context. Adopting a fluid, discursive framework for discussions of agency and liberation makes it possible to link these concepts to public self-presentations as well as private self-presentations, provided that both entail control on behalf of those whose content is being circulated. Framing control and agency in these ways can enable cyberfeminists to move forward to examine concepts such as online surveillance in terms that make it possible to associate these concepts with increased agency for girls and young women, rather than simply constrained agency. With this conceptualization of agency in mind, it is useful next to turn to specific discourses that could be refocused to recognize their potential for agency, rather than simply their potential for constraint.

Peer-to-peer surveillance in online spaces is gendered, with females more likely than males to engage in surveillance of self and of others.[50] While peer-to-peer surveillance can potentially constrain personal control by dictating the nature of online self-portrayals,[51] it can concurrently liberate girls and young women by allowing controlled self-portrayals to reach a broad group of online peers and by circulating self-images that online users have constructed themselves and want to see circulated. While users of social networking platforms are more or less likely to disclose certain personal information based on who is able to see them on line,[52] posting images and personal information can be an agential expression of self-control, where girls are empowered to explore various facets of identity and negotiate experimental selves.[53] Peer-to-peer surveillance can also provide a venue in which girls and young women are able to challenge normative standards of online gender expression and reach a wide audience while doing so, enabling resistance to patriarchal and heteronormative expectations of online gender performance. In this way, flouting privacy can be liberating, especially if girls gain other social capital by doing so.[54]

Allen asserts that in addition to surveillance by their peers, girls and young women on line – as well as women more generally – are "particularly vulnerable to privacy problems because they are perceived as inferiors, ancillaries, and safe targets."[55] Women on line can have their privacy "probed by others who implicitly assume that daughters, pregnant women, mothers and wives are more accountable for their private conduct than their male counterparts."[56] Online self-disclosure can also solidify patriarchal ideologies where men hold unrestricted access to the bodies of females. These risks, which are articulated in popular media and policy discourses stressing that girls should be more private online, can encourage girls and young women to limit self-disclosure while neglecting the empowering aspects of virtual self-exposure.[57]

Despite the plethora of constraints and risks articulated in mainstream discourses on gender and virtual expression, girls can also experience agency and liberation through online self-disclosure. Kelly, Pomerantz, and Currie, for example, "found girls bending and switching gender to improvise nonconformist femininities and learning to express parts of themselves that they had been made to feel were taboo offline."[58] This process of identity transformation can become a performance in itself, where girls display and publicly perform a somehow dysfunctional "old self," constructing the virtual exposure of private selves as paths to success and self-realization.[59] Queer, trans, and racial theorists are also beginning to consider the relationship between agency and online self-disclosure, where online self-disclosure has potential for minority subjects to contest normative standards situating gendered self-disclosure as more permissible when expressed by heterosexual,[60] Caucasian,[61] and cisgendered females.[62]

White contributes that by asserting control over when they are available and what can be seen on line, virtual actors can encourage spectators to "enter" into their personal environments and the posting of online content can be considered an assertion of personal agency,[63] countering the Western assumption that "what goes on inside the home is private."[64] Colley et al praise the potential of online disclosure to maintain positive relationships between girls and young women on line;[65] Gonzales and Hancock have similarly found that exposure to self-presentation on social networking sites can have a positive influence on self-esteem.[66] Applying critical feminist frameworks to surveillance and privacy studies shows promise to highlight these empowering aspects and encourage greater critical thought about culturally and socio-legally entrenched expectations of online gender performance,[67] building a cyberfeminist collective that can more feasibly work toward increasing agency for girls on line.

Authenticity vs. Inauthenticity: Body Image and Consumer-Media Culture

Various scholars have asserted that media representations of femininity can intersect with identity performance, often relaying conflicting messages about what it means to perform "girl" online.[68] Media representations can demonize perceived articulations of sexuality by girls and stress the importance of cautious, private, or ethically sensible self-portrayals on the one hand, while simultaneously emphasizing public engagement with celebrity culture, emulation of celebrity body image ideals, and consumption of appearance-focused media on the other hand.[69] These conflicting media representations are regulated by peer-to-peer surveillance in social networking, where girls and young women who do not conform to particular representations – and even those who conform particularly well – can be subject to negative judgment or harassment from other users.[70] Girls who perform privately, for instance, can be judged as prudish or uptight; women who perform publicly can be judged as attention seeking, superficial, or "slutty."[71] Since it can be impossible for girls and young women to adhere to both sets of media expectations for gender performance – to simultaneously be private and "responsible" as well as public and "mediatized" – in response they can self-censor or go offline, even at the expense of the increased social and economic opportunities associated with a greater online presence.[72]

Conflicting media representations of how to "properly" perform femininity within online spaces and the pressures they can exert upon young women frame another false dichotomy: online self-portrayals as either "authentic" or "inauthentic." Girls who self-portray "too privately" can be viewed as inauthentic because of their tendency to self-censor; however, those who portray "too publicly" can also be viewed as inauthentic, especially when their online profiles reflect appearance-focused media or celebrity culture.[73] Regardless of whether girls adhere to private or public media discourses on gender performance, then, they always face the critique that they are performing inauthentically, even if they are attempting to present a persona that represents aspects of an authentic self.[74] Further, since girls routinely use virtual technology to express parts of themselves they had been made to feel were taboo offline or to "try out" new or experimental identities, the boundaries between authentic and inauthentic self-portrayals are not distinct. Senft has described how girls perform different identities online, outlining that they may display particular character attributes without personally identifying with the roles they are playing. Girls may also engage in "deep acting," attempting to more strongly identify with feelings or images they are trying to project.[75] There are no clear lines distinguishing between authentic and inauthentic online self-portrayals; self-portrayals can be – and arguably always are – a mixture of both.

Related to debates about online authenticity and inauthenticity are intersectional discussions about the role of agency in authenticity, where inauthentic self-portrayals are usually operationalized as inagential. Rather than discussing agency in the context of whether or not online self-portrayals are authentic or inauthentic, however, it is more productive to discuss agency in the context of media pressures themselves and the gendered agency or lack of agency that they facilitate. Since agency is related to control over online self-portrayals, it does not necessarily matter whether portrayals are authentic or inauthentic. More important than authenticity is girls' ability to assert control over the way they are portrayed online and the external pressures that shape this ability. Since meanings of online performances are negotiated with audiences who interpret these performances and ascribe meaning to them, asserting this control also entails an ability to manage peers' processes of meaning-making relating to online portrayals, including their perceptions of these portrayals as authentic or inauthentic. Both self-portrayals themselves and their associated processes of audience meaning-making are impacted by a variety of media pressures. Since these pressures play such a considerable role in how girls self-present on line and how their online self-presentations are received by others,[76] it is important next to outline some of these pressures and examine their implications for girls' and young women's agency in more detail.

Numerous scholars identify a contemporary "consumer-media culture" that is primarily concerned with celebrity, sexually suggestive clothing, obesity, eating disorders, and overall body image, that has become a powerful influence upon self-formative processes, especially for adolescent females.[77] This consumer-media culture is underscored by a competitive discourse in advertising, where girls and young women are encouraged to conceptualize themselves as winning competitions with their peers, particularly in terms of attaining body ideals such as being prettiest or thinnest. This discourse is reflected not only in print media but across other forms of media as well,[78] including virtual and online social media.

Girls may rely upon media and consumer-media culture to gain authoritative knowledge to mark how young women are "supposed" to be, interpreting fictionalized gender portrayals as realities to which they should aspire; however, these portrayals are often unrealistic, resulting in idealized and internalized social roles that they typically are unable to fulfil.[79] Consumer-media culture perpetuates an unattainable "thin ideal," wherein "both women and men [overestimate] the thinness of body type preferred by others."[80] Girls who are aware of this thin, sexy ideal show tendencies to internalize it and believe that it is important to meet the expectations that it presents,[81] despite their potential to be judged by their peers as inauthentic, attention seeking or "slutty" for doing so.[82] The pressure to meet this unattainable thin ideal can constrain girls' and young women's online agency by rendering them unable to exert true control over their own body image portrayals. This pressure has been associated with potentially harmful consequences, including increased rates of eating disorders,[83] body dissatisfaction,[84] and relationship dissatisfaction.[85]

Online spaces are also venues in which girls may distance themselves from and bring themselves closer to aspects of celebrity, including how many hits a profile or webcam receives and how many friends a woman has on Facebook. Terri Senft notes that "On the web, popularity depends upon a connection to one's audience" and cites Jodi Dean's explanation: "Most people in technoculture know full well that they aren't really celebrities. ... In fact, this anxiety about not being known ... is a key component of the celebrity mode of subjectivization."[86] A relationship between intense celebrity worship and negative body image in adolescence has been noted; social networking–based quasi-social relationships with celebrities with "good" bodies have been found to contribute to negative body image and further reinforce unattainable thin ideals.[87]

The considerable constraints presented by media representations of girls and young women may partially explain why scholarly and policy discourse around empowering articulations of girls' and young women's sexuality, sexual agency, and sexual desire is limited. This dearth is troubling, since sexual agency has historically been accepted as a positive aspect of male sexual identity and a natural part of male sexual development.[88] Western discourses on girls' sexuality overwhelmingly conclude that "girls and women cannot hope to benefit from sexual self-presentations and representations, and that this will inevitably lead to an "unhealthy" sexuality."[89] Cyberfeminisms show promise to retool discourses on sexualized online self-presentations in new, more agential ways, affording girls a platform where they can benefit from empowering sexual online expression.

Sexuality can be depicted in an empowering way as a component of a broader social discourse that includes supportive and respectful interpersonal relationships, healthy self-conceptualization, and agency as control over self-depictions, regardless of whether or not they are sexualized. Girls can also potentially explore prospective sexual identities through transformative sexualities presented in sexualized media.[90] Royalle invokes Koskela by offering that sexualized images can be empowering when their working conditions permit individuals to be in control, for example, in images where young women are acting out their own fantasies as opposed to those of dominant men.[91] Azzarito likewise describes that sexualized media can be used to positively define and complement female bodies in opposition to specific, narrow, heteronormative male representations of femininity.[92] Agential sexualized online self-representations show promise to help contest these norms.

Cyberfeminisms are tasked with further exploring the relationship between media representations of gender and girls' online agency. In doing so, we must move beyond discourses focusing on binaries of online spaces and media discourses as simply being either risky or beneficial and either agential or inagential, recognizing that there are constraining and liberating factors that work simultaneously to frame girls' online experiences. We must also move away from discourses that focus on authenticity and inauthenticity and ultimately stifle young women's sexual expression and expand the scope of cyberfeminist discussions to encompass broader gendered media discourses. In doing so, we can build a more inclusive vision of virtual citizenship and media participation that allows girls greater opportunities for control and agential self-expression, ultimately achieving the goal of reducing gendered constraints upon agency.

Legal vs. Extralegal Regulation: Potential Responses to Online Gender Inequalities

That girls are cognizant of potential online risks and constraints upon agency and can independently enact strategies to manage them[93] stands in opposition to pop cultural discourses wherein young women are described as naïve virtual citizens who are in need of protection, censorship, or governance.[94] Legal initiatives attempting to deal with gender-related online risk are largely punitive, framing girls as either victims or perpetrators, and focusing on criminalization, "getting tough" on online harassment, or advocating that girls and young women not self-disclose on line.[95] These initiatives largely function on an individual as opposed to a collective level, attempting to identify characteristics of girls who are susceptible to online risk and subsequently "protect" them or punish their abusers.[96] In taking this approach, current legal responses neoliberally and patriarchically neglect to consider the root causes of online gender inequality, buying into uncritical pop cultural notions of what it means to be a female virtual citizen.

In this chapter, I have argued that it is prudent for regulatory responses to begin deconstructing uncritical binaries within prevailing media, policy, and cultural discourses that dictate socially accepted standards for the performance of femininity online. Simply aggregating the characteristics of individual young women in the name of "protection," or responsibilizing girls to self-protect, perpetuates false dichotomies of girls online as either victims or perpetrators, and either criminals or non-criminals. It also neglects to consider constraints upon girls' and young women's agency that are enacted by broader systemic frameworks, buying into the idea that online spaces are inherently risky and constraining and that gendered risks and constraints are inevitable. Cyberfeminist theoretical debate often focuses on a divide between legal and extralegal responses to online gender inequality, with theorists often rejecting one scheme in favour of the other.[97] As a result, yet another false binary has developed: the idea that online gender inequality can be addressed either by legal or by extralegal regulatory responses, but not by both. I conclude this chapter by briefly touching upon alternative policies and self-regulatory practices that could potentially address issues involving online gender inequality to better reflect cyberfeminist goals and move away from punitive responses that embrace dichotomous views of girls' online experiences.

While legal and policy responses to child pornography and sexting, for example, can implicate girls in child pornography offences, legal initiatives like Nova Scotia's *Cyber-safety Act*[98] and proposed amendments to the *Criminal Code*[99] have begun to address cyberbullying and online harassment. Using child pornography laws to address sexting has been criticized for potentially criminalizing those whom the law was supposedly intended to protect (including young women exploring their sexual agency),[100] for being unreasonably harsh or punitive,[101] and for constructing sexist narratives that generate stereotypes of girls and young women as self-exploitative, hypersexualized, or victims in need of patriarchal protection.[102] This sort of legal response continues the trend of punitiveness, responsibilization, and the policing of female sexuality, without disturbing the underlying context that may inform the behaviours addressed.[103]

Legal frameworks do, however, show some promise when it comes to dealing with issues related to constraints upon women's online agency. Karaian has outlined, for example, that education-based, macro-level legal responses that address issues of systemic inequality and underlying structural harms – rather than responsibilizing girls and young women to "act more safely" – could reduce girls' online inequality.[104] Hasinoff similarly argues that girls' online self-portrayals could be legally enshrined as an act of media authorship, where those who virtually self-disclose could invoke copyright law to control the information that they distribute on line.[105] Keats Citron has also suggested that rights relating to gendered respect and sexual agency could be enshrined in civil rights discourses, submitting that concepts like "respect for women" and "sexual agency" could be implemented as fundamental constitutional rights or within tort law, making it possible for those who have had their rights violated to sue those who have violated those rights.[106] These approaches would move punishment for gendered online harm out of the exclusive realm of "tough" criminal sanctioning (that can illogically catch young women in its dragnet), without undermining the empowering potential of young women's own consensual transgressions of constraining normative sexual morality.

In terms of extralegal and self-regulatory means of addressing online constraints on agency and gender equality, the promotion of feminist identity is promising. Feminisms can encourage the critical evaluation of women's work and politics; feminist young women tend to have more positive body images because of their greater ability to critique gendered cultural norms and consequently resist the unattainable thin ideal presented in contemporary media.[107] Feminism, respect for women, and promotion of gender equality can also be taught in schools, representing a macro-level solution to systemic patriarchy via the education system.[108]

Media literacy initiatives have been proposed as a possible way to promote greater media awareness,[109] higher long-term self-esteem, and the redefinition of female sexual norms, although immediate self-objectification has been forewarned of, as being a possible negative consequence of such interventions.[110] Media literacy initiatives could also encourage website designs that address girls and young women less as consumers or potential employees and more as emergent virtual citizens.[111] Finally, Welles suggests reconceptualizing ideas of sexuality and agency on a broad cultural level. As she writes, "Researchers suggest that a ... woman's ability to be conscientious about and fully present in her sexual experiences is correlated with her ability to act as an agent. The ability to make responsible and self-affirming sexual decisions is a crucial act of agency."[112] Such macro-level extralegal initiatives could work either alone or in tandem with legal responses that are comparatively more critically feminist in nature to address constraints upon girls' online agency and ensure that both online and offline gender inequality are ultimately reduced.

Conclusion:
Future Directions for Cyberfeminist Research

This chapter has begun to question some of the uncritical binaries that underscore mainstream political, theoretical, and media discourses on gender and virtual spaces, laying the groundwork for the deconstruction of oversimplified dichotomic conceptual lenses that impede cyberfeminisms from achieving greater online gender equality. These false binaries include (but are certainly not limited to) ideas of online vs. offline, cyberfeminisms vs. non-cyberfeminisms, cyberspatial environments as inherently utopian vs. dystopian, empowerment vs. vulnerability, risk vs. benefit, privacy vs. self-disclosure, online authenticity vs. inauthenticity, victimhood vs. blameworthiness, and regulatory responses to online gender inequality as legal vs. extralegal. If we look at these binaries more closely, it becomes clear that issues involving gender and virtual space are not, in fact, that simple: girls' virtual experiences are complexly nuanced and are not universal. This volume strives to continue deconstructing these and other related dichotomies in the interest of facilitating more productive cyberfeminist discussions by working toward common goals of decreasing virtual gender inequality and increasing girls' and young women's online agency.

I have suggested that a useful first step in deconstructing these dichotomies and ultimately achieving greater online gender equality is to consider online agency as "what, how and when [online content] is controlled by the person(s) whose images are circulated."[113] Doing so shows potential to reframe discourses on gender and online spaces to focus less on responsibilization, self-protection, and victim blaming, and more on the potential for liberation, acknowledging that agency rests in the ways that girls are able to control their online portrayals rather than their ability to comply with normative gendered standards of online self-presentation.

Future cyberfeminist initiatives, in addition to continuing to deconstruct uncritical binaries and engaging in more inclusive, agency-based discussions, must therefore begin to shift from micro-level discussions and punitive policy initiatives to those that function on a more collective macro-level. Potential constraints upon girls' agency cannot be reduced without widespread social involvement both at home and at the institutional level, for example, via educational or family-based initiatives that stress media literacy and the promotion of respect for all genders. It is important to abandon punitive patriarchal and neo-liberal discourses that identify characteristics of girls who are susceptible to online abuse and often responsibilize those who are "at risk" to self-protect against potential victimization. Such discourses accept gendered harm as natural and acceptable, perpetuating the notion that girls should not use virtual spaces to self-express and are blameworthy when online self-disclosure leads to victimization.

It is also important to begin to consider the positionality of marginalized young women within cyberfeminist discourses. Cyberfeminisms have far too frequently neglected the experiences of girls and women who are racialized, socio-economically under-privileged, from non-heterosexual sexual orientations, and/or lack access to virtual technology. As Fernandez and Wilding eloquently submit, "We do not support pan-capitalism. It is a predatory, pernicious and sexist system that will not change even if there was equal representation of gender in the policy-making classes. Our argument is that women need access to empowering knowledge and tools that are now dominated by a despicable 'virtual class'."[114] Cyberfeminisms must entail a commitment to the erasure of ideologies of colonial domination that run through Western culture. It is critical not only to ensure that discourse about cyberfeminisms is accessible to all girls and women – not only a privileged few – but also to recognize and reinforce the everyday cyberfeminist acts that girls and women engage in as they navigate an increasingly seamless online/offline existence.

In moving past problematic discourses, it is imperative that cyberfeminists begin to deconstruct prevailing media representations of gender and pop cultural expectations that dictate socially accepted standards for the performance of online femininity. Deconstructing these narratives on a macro scale can begin to challenge arbitrary normative standards of online gender performance and ultimately critique online spaces and current policy initiatives for how they entrench these sexist narratives. Most of all, it is crucially important to solicit girls' own perceptions and experiences – including the experiences and perceptions of those who are non-heterosexual, trans, racialized, or otherwise marginalized – and to use these intersectional insights to plot the course of future cyberfeminist initiatives. Working from the "ground up" to ensure that girls themselves have a voice in discourses on gender and virtual space is a key part of moving beyond patriarchal binary thought, increasing girls' online agency, and constructing virtual spaces that better reflect gender "e-quality."[115]

Notes

1   Donna Haraway, "A Cyborg Manifesto: Science, Technology and Socialist-Feminism in the Late Twentieth Century," in *Simians, Cyborgs and Women: The Reinvention of Nature*, ed. Donna Haraway (New York: Routledge, 1991), 150.

2   See, for example, Sadie Plant, "On the Matrix: Cyberfeminist Simulations," in *Cultures of Internet: Virtual Spaces, Real Histories, Living Bodies*, ed. Rob Shields (London: Sage, 1996), 170–183.

3   Sally Munt, *Technospaces: Inside the New Media* (London: Continuum, 2001).

4   Haraway, *supra* note 1; Plant, *supra* note 2.

5   Radhika Gajjala, "Internet Constructs of Identity and Ignorance: 'Third World' Contexts and Cyberfeminism," *Works and Days* 17 & 18:33/34, 35/36 (1999–2000): 117–137.

6   *Ibid.*, at 121.

7   *Ibid.*

8   Mary Flanagan & Austin Booth, "Introduction," in *Reload: Rethinking Women + Cyberculture*, eds. Mary Flanagan & Austin Booth (Cambridge, MA: MIT Press, 2002), 12.

9   Jessie Daniels, "Rethinking Cyberfeminism(s): Race, Gender and Embodiment," *Women's Studies Quarterly* 37:1/2 (2009): 101–124.

10   *Ibid.*, at 103.

11   Gajjala, *supra* note 5.

12   Eve Kosofsky Sedgwick, "Paranoid Reading and Reparative Reading; or You're So Paranoid, You Probably Think This Introduction is About You," in *Novel Gazing: Queer Readings in Fiction*, ed. Eve Kosofsky Sedgwick (Durham, NC: Duke University Press, 1997), 1–37.

13   Haraway, *supra* note 1.

14   *Ibid.*

15   Susanna Paasonen, "Surfing the Waves of Feminism," *Universidade de Brasília: Labrys Estudos Feministas* January/July (2005), para. 7, accessed 12 November 2014, <http://www.tanianavarroswain.com.br/labrys/labrys7/cyber/susanna.htm>.

16   Plant, *supra* note 2.

17   Chela Sandoval, "New Sciences: Cyborg Feminism and the Methodology of the Oppressed," *Cybersexualities* 23 (1995): 374–377.

18   Torin Monahan, "Editorial: Surveillance and Inequality," *Surveillance and Society* 5:3 (2008): 217–226.

19   Jane Bailey, "'Sexualized Online Bullying' Through an Equality Lens: Missed Opportunity in *AB v. Bragg*?," *McGill Law Journal* 59:3 (2014): 709–737.

20   Gajjala, *supra* note 5.

21   Faith Wilding, "Where is the Feminism in Cyberfeminism?" *N. Paradoxa: International Feminist Art Journal* 2 (1998): 6–13.

22   Steeves, Chapter VI. See also Terri M. Senft, *Camgirls: Celebrity and Community in the Age of Social Networks* (New York: Peter Lang, 2008).

23   Vili Lehdonvirta, "Virtual Worlds Don't Exist: Questioning the Dichotomous Approach in MMO Studies," *Game Studies* 10:1 (2010): para 4, accessed 12 November 2014, <http://gamestudies.org/1001/articles/lehdonvirta>.

24   T. L. Taylor, *Play between Worlds: Exploring Online Game Culture* (Cambridge, MA: MIT Press, 2006), 153.

25   Lehdonvirta, *supra* note 23.

26   Senft, *supra* note 22.

27   David J. Phillips, "Ubiquitous Computing, Spatiality, and the Construction of Identity: Directions for Policy Response," in *Lessons From the Identity Trail: Anonymity, Privacy and Identity in a Networked Society*, eds. Ian Kerr, Valerie Steeves & Carole Lucock (New York: Oxford University Press, 2009), 303–318.

28   "Top 50 Countries With the Highest Internet Penetration Rate," Internet World Stats, last modified 11 March 2014, <http://www.internetworldstats.com/top25.htm>.

29   Daniels, *supra* note 9; Flanagan & Booth, *supra* note 8.

30   Jane Bailey & Adrienne Telford, "What's So Cyber About It?: Reflections on Cyberfeminism's Contribution to Legal Studies," *Canadian Journal of Women and the Law* 19:2 (2007): 243–271.

31   Phillips, *supra* note 27; Robert Tokunaga, "Social Networking Site or Social Surveillance Site? Understanding the Use of Interpersonal Electronic Surveillance in Romantic Relationships," *Computers in Human Behavior* 27:2 (2011): 705–713.

32   Anita Allen, "Gender and Privacy in Cyberspace," *Stanford Law Review* 52:5 (2000): 1175–1200; Nicole S. Cohen & Leslie Shade, "Gendering

Facebook: Privacy and Commodification," *Feminist Media Studies* 8:2 (2008): 210–214.

33 Allen, *ibid.*; Cohen & Shade, *ibid.*

34 Angela McRobbie, *The Aftermath of Feminism: Gender, Culture and Social Change* (Thousand Oaks, CA: Sage, 2009); Shari Dworkin & Kari Lerum, "Bad Girls Rule: An Interdisciplinary Feminist Commentary on the Report of the APA Task Force on the Sexualization of Girls," *Journal of Sex Research* 46:2 (2009) 250–263; Amy Gonzales & Jeffrey T. Hancock, "Mirror, Mirror on my Facebook Wall: Effects of Exposure to Facebook on Self-Esteem," *Cyberpsychology, Behavior and Social Networking* 14:1/2 (2011): 79–83.

35 Allen, *supra* note 32; Shaheen Shariff & Leanne Johnny, "Cyber-Libel and Cyber-Bullying: Can Schools Protect Student Reputations and Free-Expression in Virtual Environments?," *Education & Law Journal* 16:3 (2007): 307–342.

36 Levina Clark & Marika Tiggemann, "Appearance Culture in Nine-to 12-Year-Old Girls: Media and Peer Influences on Body Dissatisfaction," *Social Development* 15:4 (2006): 628–643; Adriana Manago, Michael B. Graham, Patricia M. Greenfield & Goldie Salimkhan, "Self-Presentation and Gender on MySpace," *Journal of Applied Developmental Psychology* 29:6 (2008): 446–458; Fiona Brookes & Peter Kelly, "Dolly Girls: Tweenies as Artefacts of Consumption," *Journal of Youth Studies* 12:6 (2009): 599–613.

37 Senft, *supra* note 22; Shaheen Shariff, *Cyber-Bullying: Issues and Solutions for the School, the Classroom and the Home* (London: Routledge, 2008); Danielle Keats Citron, "Law's Expressive Value in Combatting Cyber Gender Harassment," *Michigan Law Review* 108:3 (2009): 373–415.

38 Shade, Chapter XVI.

39 Trevor Scott Milford & Ciara Bracken-Roche, "Social Surveillance: Feminist Implications for Online Privacy, Self-Disclosure and Gendered Agency," *Feminist Journal of Art and Digital Culture* 30.

40 Tokunaga, *supra* note 31.

41 Allen, *supra* note 32.

42 Gonzales & Hancock, *supra* note 34.

43 Allen, *supra* note 32; Shariff & Johnny, *supra* note 35.

44 Allen, *supra* note 32.

45 Senft, *supra* note 22; Shariff & Johnny, *supra* note 35.

46 Trevor Scott Milford, "Girls Milford, Agency: A Cyberfeminist Exploration," (master's thesis, University of Ottawa, 2013).

47 Jane Bailey, "Life in a Fish Bowl: Feminist Interrogations of Webcamming," in *Lessons From the Identity Trail: Anonymity, Privacy and Identity in a Networked Society*, eds. Ian Kerr, Valerie Steeves & Carole Lucock (New York: Oxford University Press, 2009), 283–301.

48   Hille Koskela, "Webcams, TV shows and Mobile Phones: Empowering Exhibitionism," *Surveillance and Society* 2:2/3 (2004): 211.
49   *Ibid.*, at 211.
50   Tokunaga, *supra* note 31.
51   Daniel Trottier, *Social Media as Surveillance: Rethinking Visibility in a Converging World* (London: Ashgate, 2012).
52   *Ibid.*
53   Senft, *supra* note 22; Phillips, *supra* note 27.
54   Bailey, *supra* note 47.
55   Allen, *supra* note 32 at 1178.
56   *Ibid.*
57   Milford & Bracken-Roche, *supra* note 39.
58   Dierdre M. Kelly, Shauna Pomerantz & Dawn Currie, "No Boundaries? Girls' Interactive, Online Learning About Feminities," *Youth Society* 38:3 (2006): 3–28.
59   Amy Dobson, "Femininities as Commodities: Cam Girl Culture," in *Next Wave Cultures: Feminism, Subcultures, Activism*, ed. Anita Harris (New York: Routledge, 2008), 128.
60   Mary Bryson, "When Jill Jacks In: Queer Women and the Net," *Feminist Media Studies* 4:3 (2004): 241.
61   Lisa Nakamura, *Digitizing Race: Visual Cultures of the Internet* (Minneapolis: University of Minnesota Press, 2008).
62   Marty Fink & Quinn Miller, "Trans Media Moments: Tumblr, 2011–2013," *Television & New Media* 15:7 (2013): 611.
63   Michele White, "Too Close to See: Men, Women and Webcams," *New Media & Society* 5:1 (2003): 7–28.
64   Bailey, *supra* note 47 at 292.
65   Ann Colley, Zazic Todd, Adrian White & Tamara Turner-Moore, "Communication Using Camera Phones Among Young Men and Women: Who Sends What to Whom?" *Sex Roles* 63:5–6 (2010): 348–360.
66   Gonzales & Hancock, *supra* note 34.
67   Milford & Bracken-Roche, *supra* note 39.
68   Senft, *supra* note 22; Clark & Tiggemann, *supra* note 36.
69   Milford, *supra* note 46; Senft, *supra* note 22; Clark & Tiggemann, *supra* note 36.
70   Milford & Bracken-Roche, *supra* note 39.
71   Jane Bailey, Valerie Steeves, Jacquelyn Burkell & Priscilla Regan, "Negotiating With Gender Stereotypes on Social Networking Sites: From 'Bicycle Face' to Facebook," *Journal of Communication Inquiry* 37:2 (2013): 91–112.
72   Keats Citron, *supra* note 37.
73   Bailey et al, *supra* note 71.

74 *Ibid.*

75 Senft, *supra* note 22.

76 *Ibid.*; Bailey et al, *supra* note 71; Milford, *supra* note 46.

77 Brookes & Kelly, *supra* note 36; Manago et al, *supra* note 36.

78 Elizabeth Heilman, "The Struggle for Self: Power and Identity in Adolescent Girls," *Youth & Society* 30:2 (1998): 182–208.

79 *Ibid.*

80 Sung-Yeon Park, Gi Woong Yun, Jacqueline McSweeney & Albert Gunther, "Do Third-Person Perceptions of Media Influence Contribute to Pluralistic Ignorance on the Norm of Ideal Female Thinness?" *Sex Roles* 57:7–8 (2007): 576.

81 Sarah Murnen, Linda Smolak, J. Andrew Mills & Lindsey Good, "Thin, Sexy Women and Strong, Muscular Men: Grade-School Children's Responses to Objectified Images of Women and Men," *Sex Roles* 49:9/10 (2003): 427–437.

82 Bailey et al, *supra* note 71.

83 Gemma Lopez-Guimera, "Influence of Mass Media on Body Image and Eating Disordered Attitudes and Behaviors in Females: A Review of Effects and Processes," *Media Psychology* 13:4 (2010): 387–416.

84 Brit Harper & Marika Tiggemann, "The Effect of Thin Ideal Media Images on Women's Self-Objectification, Mood and Body Image," *Sex Roles* 58:9–10 (2008): 649–657.

85 Eileen Zubriggen, Laura Ramsey & Beth Jaworski, "Self- and Partner-Objectification in Romantic Relationships: Associations with Media Consumption and Relationship Dissatisfaction," *Sex Roles* 64:7 (2011): 449–462.

86 Senft, *supra* note 22 at 26, citing Jodi Dean, *Publicity's Secret: How Technoculture Capitalizes on Democracy* (Ithaca, New York: Cornell University Press, 2002), 124.

87 John Maltby, David Giles, Louise Barber & Lynn McCutcheon, "Intense-Personal Celebrity Worship and Body Image: Evidence of a Link among Female Adolescents," *British Journal of Health Psychology* 10:1 (2005): 17–32.

88 Caitlin Welles, "Breaking the Silence Surrounding Female Adolescent Sexual Desire," *Women & Therapy* 28:2 (2005): 31–45.

89 Dworkin & Lerum, *supra* note 34 at 259.

90 Bailey, *supra* note 47.

91 *Ibid.*

92 Laura Azzarito, "Future Girls, Transcendent Femininities and New Pedagogies: Toward Girls' Hybrid Bodies?" *Sport Education and Society* 15:3 (2010): 261–275.

93 Shade, Chapter XVI

94 Catherine Arcabascio, "Sexting and Teenagers: OMG R U Going 2 Jail???" *Richmond Journal of Law and Technology* XVI:3 (2010): 1–42; John

Humbach, "'Sexting' and the First Amendment," *Hastings Constitutional Law Quarterly* 37:3 (2010): 433–485.

95 Keats Citron, *supra* note 37.

96 *Ibid.*

97 Keats Citron, *supra* note 37; Phillips, *supra* note 27.

98 *Cyber-safety Act: An Act to Address and Prevent Cyberbullying*, SNS, c.2, s.1., 2013 (first reading 25 April 2013).

99 Bill C-13, *An Act to Amend the Criminal Code, the Canada Evidence Act, the Competition Act and the Mutual Legal Assistance in Criminal Matters Act*, 2nd Sess, 40th Parl, 2013 (first reading 20 November 2013).

100 Jane Bailey & Mouna Hanna, "The Gendered Dimensions of Sexting: Assessing the Applicability of Canada's Child Pornography Provision," *Canadian Journal of Women and the Law* 23:2 (2011): 405–441.

101 Lara Karaian, "Lolita Speaks: 'Sexting', Teenage Girls and the Law," *Crime Media Culture* 8:1 (2012): 57–73.

102 Jane Bailey & Valerie Steeves, "Will the Real Digital Girl Please Stand Up?," in *New Visualities, New Technologies: The New Ecstasy of Communication*, eds. Hille Koskela & Macgregor Wise (Surrey: Ashgate, 2013); Karaian, *supra* note 101.

103 Bailey & Steeves, *ibid.* For an analysis of some the shortcomings of Bill C-13 (*supra* note 99), see Shariff & DeMartini, Chapter XI.

104 Karaian, *supra* note 101.

105 Amy Hasinoff, "Sexting as Media Production: Rethinking Social Media and Sexuality," *New Media & Society* 15:4 (2013): 449–465.

106 Keats Citron, *supra* note 37.

107 Senft, *supra* note 22.

108 Karaian, *supra* note 101. For an analysis of potential educational reforms in Canada, see Angrove, Chapter XII.

109 For analysis of potential media literacy initiatives, see Johnson, Chapter XIII.

110 Becky Choma, Mindi Foster & Eileen Radford, "Use of Objectification Theory to Examine the Effects of Media Literacy Intervention on Women," *Sex Roles* 56:9–10 (2007): 581–590.

111 Chad Raphael, Christine Bachen, Kathleen Lynn, Jessica Baldwin-Philippi & Kristen McKee, "Portrayals of Information and Communication Technology on World Wide Web Sites for Girls," *Journal of Computer-Mediated Communications* 11:3 (2006): 771–801.

112 Welles, *supra* note 88 at 31.

113 Koskela, *supra* note 48 at 211.

114 Faith Wilding & CAE, "Notes on the Political Condition of Cyberfeminism," in *First Cyberfeminist International Reader*, ed. Old Boys Network (Berlin: Old Boys Network, 1997), 23, quoted in Maria Fernandez and Faith Wilding, "Situating Cyberfeminisms," in *Domain Errors!*

Cyberfeminist Practices, eds. Maria Fernandez, Faith Wilding & Michelle Wright (New York: Autonomedia), 26.

115 Gajjala, *supra* note 5.

CHAPTER III

Thinking beyond the Internet as a Tool: Girls' Online Spaces as Postfeminist Structures of Surveillance

Akane Kanai

Introduction

Mary Celeste Kearney argues that girls' media studies scholarship, as part of its feminist underpinnings, understands girls to be "powerful agential beings."[1] Accordingly, it can be observed that within scholarship, internet technologies like social network sites (SNS) and blogs are optimistically constructed as a potential instrument by which girls control their identity[2] or a kind of territory that girls can claim as their own.[3] However, I suggest that this construction of "empowered girls" and its corollary of the internet as instrument to be wielded, can be productively called into question through further attention to the structures of surveillance, intimacy, and sociality when considering girls' identity online. More specifically, this chapter seeks to contribute to girls' media studies by building on its dialogue with feminist media scholarship of postfeminist identity that draws upon the Foucauldian notions of surveillance and discipline. I suggest that interrogating online spaces of sociality for girls as potentially disciplinary sites gives some explanatory power to common practices of identity by girls and young women with mainstream, regulatory postfeminist themes. My interest in doing so is not in order to contend that girls are *not* powerful, nor to speak for all girls; girls have demonstrated significant forms of resistance to mainstream gendered discourses through online activity such as in feminist blogs and other modes of digital organization.[4] However, I engage here with recurring, conventional themes identified in girls' self-presentation and suggest a reinvigoration of scholarly attention to the discursive social conditions of online production as a way forward for scholars of girls' media.

I begin with the context of feminist research aims in girls' media studies, and contemporary questions of control and autonomy in girls' identity-building online. I then foreground feminist Foucauldian scholarship in theorising how discipline and control have become constitutive elements of prevalent contemporary (post-feminist) femininities. Specifically, I draw on insights as to how post-feminist individuality harnesses the notion of constant discipline and self-surveillance as a means of success in a neo-liberal world, with the successful or "top" girl cast as the one who can produce herself as a successful postfeminist self-brand.[5] I then build on contributions of media scholarship to contend that the structures and participatory premises of interactive media can work to facilitate surveillance and monitoring. This paper thus seeks to disturb the conceptualization of the online space as a tool that girls are able to take up, by repositioning online spaces as complex, mediated sites of power within which girls' identities are implicated.

Media, Technology, and Feminist Scholarship

Media has constituted a complex and variegated site of inquiry for feminist scholars of identity. Feminist scholars have sought to understand how women have received, interpreted, and constructed media as a means of circulating meaning, connection, and power.[6] As media technologies have shifted and changed, arguably, so too have women's relationship to media and feminist theorisations of these. Initially, much second-wave feminist work in the 1970s and 1980s focused on mass broadcast media. Television, and the sexist representations to which women were subject, coincided with the theoretical predominance of a "'hypodermic" or technologically determinist view of the media. This view understood audiences to be directly influenced by media, in absorbing media messages.[7] Thus, the second-wave feminist push for "better" and more "realistic" representations of assertive, independent, and intelligent women in media,[8] perhaps, reflected the idea of women audiences as at risk of

passive acceptance of what was seen to be the broadcasting of feminine inferiority.[9] Later, with the "cultural turn" influenced by British
cultural studies, feminist media scholars began asking how women,
as active meaning makers, understood the media products they
were consuming.[10] Arguably, with the contemporary state of media
metamorphosis, the construct of the audience, the representation
contained in the media artifact, and the media producer have become
increasingly entangled and complex with associated transformations
in feminine identity. While concerns about sexist media representations and women's meaning-making are still relevant, I suggest that
one of the major changes that drives contemporary scholarship is
the significant shift in the assumptions about women's power over
their (re)presentation. The possibilities of self-representation open
up different questions about power and control in women's relationship to media.

The feminist underpinnings of girls' media studies are similarly
reflected in the desire to understand how girls are able to exploit self-
representative and user-based digital media for their own (beneficial)
identity development.[11] Scholars have viewed spaces where girls are
able to control, prune, and manage their identity as an important
part of an empowering identity-building trajectory.[12] Youth studies and girls' studies scholars often emphasize the possibilities of
online blogging and social networking, in particular, in providing
empowering spaces or tools that young people can use to negotiate
identity, connect, and grow.[13] Accordingly, characteristic research
questions ask whether girls can carve out their own individual identity by going online,[14] or how girls can claim space online as part of
a new online "public sphere" where they can air their issues and
concerns.[15] This involves asking how the internet can be used as a
tool by girls, or analyzing online spaces in terms of their *affordances*.[16]
As an example, Carla E. Stokes examines SNS NevaEvaLand to
understand how black girls in their online personas negotiate racist
and sexist discourses of their hypersexualization and deviance.[17] She
concludes that the girls' pages she considered were "influenced" by
norms of beauty and sexuality in commercial hip hop culture that
construct black women as (hetero)sexual accessories.[18] I suggest that
visible here is a subtextual premise, representative of the focus in
scholarship of youth online identity, that the online sphere presents
a neutral space where girls are able to potentially control or resist
outside or offline negative messages.

It is important, from a feminist standpoint, to valorize girls' exploration of online identity.[19] At the same time, I suggest that an emphasis on girls' power or agency in negotiating identity online needs to be carefully distinguished from elements of contemporary discourses of "Girl Power."[20] Girls' studies scholars such as Marnina Gonick have noted that "Girl Power" discourse is predicated on a binary, complementary twin discourse which emphasizes the ever-present proximity of girls to failure and danger. Drawing on the title of the best-selling 1994 book by psychologist Mary Pipher, *Reviving Ophelia: Saving the Selves of Adolescent Girls,* a high-profile example of this form of discourse, Gonick suggests that the discourse of *Reviving Ophelia,* together with Girl Power, participates in the psychological knowledge surrounding the neo-liberal girl subject.[21] Girls who fail to meet the problematic neo-liberal standard of the "self-determining individual" of "Girl Power" discourse are then at risk of personi-fication as the fragile and vulnerable Ophelia who populates the narratives of internet danger.[22] In media panics, the internet is often conceptualized as an unknown and dangerous space for girls *in par-ticular.*[23] This can be particularly seen in relation to accounts of girls' sexual identities online, which often take the form of reproducing sexist narratives: either "innocent" and vulnerable to sexual preda-tors; or precocious "vixens" whose overt sexuality is condemned.[24] In contradistinction to this, girls' studies scholarship constructs the internet as a space where girls experiment and learn.[25] However, I suggest that the construction of the girl as an *already* able internet "user" who is able to control her own construction, must be under-stood within the architecture of the online space concerned, which is always already situated within social discourses and relations.

In this chapter, I highlight the potential slippage of the notion of control over self-presentation as a means of girls' empowerment/Girl Power with postfeminist, neo-liberal discourses of identity. By post-feminism, I refer to the Western cultural sensibility that feminism, particularly second-wave feminism, is no longer relevant, rather than postfeminism epistemological rupture, third-wave of feminism, or as cultural backlash.[26] I also underline that it is a sensibility that dove-tails with hybrid and mobile neo-liberal rationalities[27] that construct and normalize the self-regulating, freely choosing and autonomous subject, erasing the social/political and the collective from the forma-tion of subjectivity.[28] As McRobbie notes, postfeminism requires girls and young women to come forward as aspiring economic agents, on the condition that they exploit traditional feminine traits and over-come (what are cast as) the individual obstacles of race and class.[29]

One might observe the correlation of postfeminism with major elements of Girl Power discourse, such as the emphasis on ambition, perfection, and individualism.[30] Evidently, the way these qualities fit into a successful neo-liberal subjectivity shows how neoliberalism animates both Girl Power and postfeminism. However, this is not to say that both discourses completely overlap. I suggest that one key distinction might be that postfeminism, as I have outlined, incor-porates second-wave feminism in order to repudiate its necessity. Accordingly, feminism and anti-feminism are inextricably entangled. However, critiques of the wide-ranging, diverse discourses which make up Girl Power related more to debates around Girl Power's relationship to feminism. In view of Girl Power's increasingly com-mercial dissemination of feminist-inflected ideas, *could* Girl Power be considered feminism, or was this a step too far?[31] One example of this debate coalesces in one of the major mainstream embodiments of Girl Power in the 1990s: the Spice Girls. Although signifying the commodification and (untenable) dilution of feminism to some, Driscoll suggests that the group's market accessibility produced a shift in broadening the possibilities of girlhood, even while dem-onstrating complicity with current systems of power and identity.[32] Though similar in many ways, Girl Power, then, can be understood as a varied set of discourses coming to prominence in the 1990s, which challenges the boundaries of what feminism might be, whilst postfeminism sets out clear ideas of what feminism constitutes, in order to dismiss its relevance.

Having said this, my primary concern here is with the overlap of neo-liberal individuality that both postfeminism and Girl Power offer, and with how postfeminism provides *techniques* of selfhood that further facilitate this individuality. Thus, in focusing on girls and power, this chapter builds on girls' media scholarship by particu-larly interrogating the individualistic, postfeminist and neo-liberal discursive context in which girls forge their identities. Taking up the idea that identity is made up of sets of processes and *practices* that are attached to socially and culturally constructed subject positions,[33] my aim is to analyze how girls' practices of identity can be understood by reference to the social and cultural discourses within which girls' identity-making is implicated. In particular, I turn my lens on the way that notions of surveillance, discipline, and control, as routes to empowered individuality, have arguably become formative in prevalent understandings of feminine identity.

Surveillance, Discipline, and Postfeminist Identity

In this section, I outline the way feminist scholars of contemporary postfeminist identity have drawn on Foucauldian notions of surveillance and discipline. One of the best known, earlier feminist articulations of feminine self-surveillance is found in Sandra Bartky's essay published in 1988, which connects panopticism to the production of disciplinary practices of femininity:

> The woman who checks her makeup half a dozen times a day to see if her foundation has caked or her mascara run, who worries that the wind or rain may spoil her hairdo, who looks frequently to see if her stockings have bagged at the ankle, or who, feeling fat, monitors everything she eats, has become, just as surely as the inmate of the panopticon, a self-policing subject, a self committed to a relentless self-surveillance.[34]

Bartky's theorization of control and self-surveillance as a *feminine* practice draws on Foucault's discussion of panopticism,[35] which conjures a "docile" subject, rendered disciplined through being aware of the potential of surveillance at all times. Foucault uses Jeremy Bentham's model prison order to illustrate the way in which this disciplinary power works. The panopticon, Foucault argues, was an exemplar of functional and hierarchical space, where prisoners were positioned in individual cells around the walls of a round building, and a surveillance tower, through which the surveyor was never visible, was located in the centre of the building. While the eye of the supervisor was unseen, prisoners were individually visible at all times, and aware of this visibility. In Foucault's articulation, consciousness of the *possibility* of the supervisor's gaze, given that the supervisor was never directly seen, normalizes and regularizes the prisoners; thus, it is not simply visibility, but visibility within an individualized and hierarchical system that produces docile, disciplined, and useful bodies.[36]

Bartky offers an important initial feminist theorization of the concept of discipline in connecting this self-surveillance with feminine practices of identity. This connection is manifested online with girls' documented preoccupation in SNS, in particular, with managing their appearance through practices such as ensuring that only "good" photos are uploaded,[37] and airbrushing one's photos.[38] However, this does not quite account for the diverse visual contexts and practices through which surveillance and self-surveillance occur in the contemporary context. I note in particular the tenor of "independence" that marks the self-presentation of girls online. Further, discipline and self-surveillance are now emphasized as *means* of empowerment or rather, individual feminine success.[39]

I argue that recent feminist work unpacking postfeminist media culture can serve as an inroad into understanding feminine identity practised through digital media. As I noted above, postfeminism can be understood as a sensibility which signals that feminism is no longer needed, which normalizes the self-regulating, autonomous subject.[40] McRobbie argues that the ideal postfeminist subject, the "top girl" operates from the (neo-liberal) understanding that her power stems from visibility of her own individual control of particular feminine domains.[41] Specifically, the top girl must exercise control over her (feminine) appearance, (hetero)sexuality, career or career potential, and independence. Each of these feminine domains is of importance, as one domain cannot be individually disentangled from the other domains. For example, an active (hetero)sexuality embodies the independence, individualism, and *control of one's body* in postfeminist aspiration. Thus, one can hedonistically engage in sex, but only on the basis that one does not procreate and one's body matches normative feminine ideals.[42] These interconnected domains can be understood as "luminous spaces" or "luminosities":

> The power they [the top girls] seem to be collectively in possession of, is "created by the light itself." These luminosities are suggestive of post-feminist equality while also defining and circumscribing the conditions of such a status. They are clouds of light which give young women a shimmering presence, and in so doing they also mark out the terrain of the consummately and reassuringly feminine.[43]

McRobbie's articulation of these spaces that illuminate "top girls," making visible and yet simultaneously circumscribing, suggests a powerful correlation with the panoptic prisoner of Foucault's imagining: highly visible, individualized, and confined. Indeed, these postfeminist girl subjects could be seen as exemplars of Foucault's articulation of discipline, given the high degree of self-surveillance associated with this visibility.

Alison Winch takes up the idea of the panopticon quite specifically in the "gynaepticon," as she terms it, as a means of conceptualizing the panoptic media, beauty, and lifestyle industries that purvey the idea of control of one's body as work that is never finished.[44] She cites as examples commercial bridal websites, such as confetti.co.uk and hitched.co.uk, which facilitate socializing by brides-to-be in order to build affective links to their websites.[45] The brides mutually confess their shame over their weight and bodies and express determination that they will achieve their ideal body weight for their "special day," providing regular updates to other members of the group.[46] Winch calls this labour an investment in "erotic capital," capital recognized by the other potential brides in their surveillance of each other in an intimate "girlfriend gaze."[47] Winch's example illustrates the way discipline, goal-setting, labour, and consumption in one's personal sphere are bound together in feminine achievement. Particularly, it illustrates how the luminous spaces that McRobbie articulates must in fact *work together* in order to denote "erotic capital": the body, the dress, and the aspiration are all mobilized to achieve a notion of ideal femininity. This reveals an intimate entanglement of femininity with norms of discipline, surveillance, and feminine sociality, imbricated within a commercial and consumerist setting.

While I suggest that Winch's case study is an illustrative example of digitally incited, mutually exercised feminine discipline, I am not suggesting that Foucault's panopticon is always directly transposable onto structures of SNS. Rather, my point is that, in drawing on this work on postfeminism, it is useful to more broadly consider the way structures of visibility, hierarchies, and social discourses work to create the conditions in which identity is made. For example, feminist work on spectatorship of the self-representative genre of reality television highlights features of *synoptic* regulation of others.[48] Thomas Mathiesen originally conceptualized synopticism as a key omission of Foucault's, arguing that the contemporary media context enabled social control through synoptic structures – where the masses saw the few, influential media personalities, as well as the (panoptic) unknown, bureaucratic halls of power that surveyed the masses.[49]

While synopticism has been critiqued for its top-down concep-tualization of social control and its focus on broadcast television in what is now a much more digitally convergent environment,[50] argu-ably a focus on *mutual* surveillance is still useful in thinking through postfeminist social regulation. Rather than Mathiesen's notion that seeing the few directly influenced the masses through their author-ity, reality television research indicates that seeing the few (aspiring reality stars) can catalyze *disciplinary* action by the viewing masses. For example, Daniel Trottier illustrates how the synoptic viewing structure of reality television works effectively to facilitate the mea-surement and comparison of where everyone is located on a "grid" of judgment — a "market" of personalities.[51] Indeed, feminist media research indicates that this invitation to disciplinary spectatorship is often taken up, with girls and women taking pleasure in judg-ing reality participants according to traditional gender criteria.[52] However, interestingly, Andrea Press's research on girls and young women of college age watching the reality show *America's Next Top Model* demonstrates that, while the young white women were quick to discipline both competitors and host Tyra Banks in traditionally gendered terms, the young black women in the study were more likely to note Tyra Banks's achievements, perhaps as a fellow black woman.[53] Further, the young women of college age in general were more critical than the middle school girls watching the show.[54] Thus, this raises questions as to how other, overlapping identities relat-ing to race and age might, in fact, counter postfeminist narratives of individuality and competition. The young white women in the study, rather than the girls or the young black women, were more primed to see the contestants and Banks in terms of gendered rivalry. Ultimately, neither synopticism nor panopticism as an individual lens will enable scholars to grapple with the intricacies of the ways in which girls or internet users in general produce online identity. Rather, they draw attention to different aspects of the social environ-ment of surveillance within which identity is practised. Accordingly, I suggest that having reference to varying and diverse configurations of postfeminist surveillance, discipline, and control, in keeping with structures of viewing and producing identity, can help to under-stand girls' practices of self-representation in online spaces, as well as in other self-representative contexts. Online, surveillance may be considered to intensify in two ways. First, the intensification occurs in the type of content that individuals share online. Increasingly "personal" content, by which I mean content that relates to ostensibly non-professional matters such as one's daily consumption, one's social circle, and one's family, is offered up to online contacts and friends through blogs and social networks.[55] Second, surveillance is intensified in relation to *time* spent online. As many-to-many broadcasting is facilitated through being able to both publish posts at any time and access someone's personal posts through a digital interface at any time, the period of time over which surveillance can be performed is also extended.[56]

Jessica Ringrose's ethnographic work on girls' digitized sexual identities on the SNS Bebo, gives an example of how girls' sexual self-representations online can be considered to be manifestations of postfeminist luminosities, performed under intensified surveillance in the school context.[57] Bebo, a site mainly used by adolescents, operates through the use of profiles that are interactive through the choice of a background "skin," and the ability to upload pictures, applications, and updates on the self. Ringrose's work involved male and female students aged 14 to 16 from two schools in the United Kingdom, one a high-achieving rural secondary school with low levels of socio-economic disadvantage, and the other an estate school in South London, with high levels of economic deprivation.[58] Through interviews and textual analysis of their profiles, Ringrose found that girls' profiles from both schools demonstrated significant "hypersexualized" and "pornified" content, where girls performed considerable sexual knowledge and desire. For example, the Playboy bunny was a popular feature on girls' skins, as were idealized images of youthful, slim, white feminine bodies in clothing revealing heteronormatively "sexy" features. Girls uploaded photobrushed pictures of themselves according to heterosexual conventions, with significant display of cleavage. Additionally, in their profiles, girls made public statements connoting knowledge and expertise in sex, referring to sexual positions but also talking about selling sex, one semi-humorous example being "Hi Im Denise And ii Like It UpThe Bum ... Just Like Your Mum! And I Suck Dick for £5'." However, Ringrose notes that while girls' profiles evinced a confident, explicit mainstream heterosexuality, channelling an impression of empowerment, offline girls told a different story. One respondent admitted she was in fact very self-conscious about her appearance and weight, though she frequently uploaded pictures of herself. Contradictions in how sexual confidence could be manifested and practised were common. In terms of relationships, girls were expected to wait for boys to approach them, according to contradictory social imperatives within the framework of school social relations. Though some girls attempted to appropriate terms such as "whore" and "slut" by using them affectionately between each other, Ringrose argues that the social microcosm within which this occurred prevented girls from being able to escape the shame of non-normative sexual behaviour. Being called a "fat slag," as one interviewee was, could indeed be used as a traditionally sexist and classist insult.[59]

Amy Dobson's investigation of young Australian women's sexual self-representations on MySpace also found evidence of post-feminist aspirations.[60] Aged between 18 and 21, the young women used similar methods to those employed by the girls in Ringrose's Bebo study to demonstrate an explicit heterosexual confidence and attractiveness. Though this representation appears to conform to dominant notions of young, feminine "sexiness," or "heterosexiness," as Dobson terms it, there are also clear aspirational messages from the young women about their individuality and autonomy, with mottos such as *"i am unattached, as free as a bird ... i don't depend on nobody and nobody depends on me,"* and *"individuality is everything."*[61] Further, this autonomy from (male) sexualization is expressed through representations of belonging to a strong pack of tight-knit, but exclusive, girlfriends: *"You're only as strong as The tables you dance on. The drinks you mix & the friends you roll with"*[62] and *"we're not sarcastic — we're hilarious; we're not annoying — we're just cooler than you; we're not bitches — we just don't like you;* and *we're not obsessed — we're just best friends."*[63]

I suggest Dobson's and Ringrose's work exposes some representative contradictions in the ways that sexuality is used to build online identity through a postfeminist rationale. The MySpace representations that Dobson investigated can be understood as part of a postfeminist compulsion to demonstrate heterosexiness as a form of independence, particularly given that the aspirational tone of the messages emphasizes personal autonomy. This feminine individuality, Dobson suggests, can also be seen as an outcome of the "girls can do anything" self-esteem discourse and strong internalization of neo-liberal discourses of individualization.[64] These young women evince an understanding of the postfeminist self as an ever-improvable project, within McRobbie's luminosity of upward mobility,[65] usually figured as career and education.[66] Thus, as Dobson observes, the profiles evince a strong need to demonstrate, somewhat ironically, to an outside audience that one does not need approval.[67]

I contend that reference to postfeminist discourses of identity can help us grapple with the contradictions presented in these girls' online profiles. Using this lens, this confident hypersexuality, performed independence and body visibility are recast as highly productive[68] *and* regulatory dimensions of femininity, particularly for adolescent girls and young women.[69] The examples of Ringrose's and Dobson's work highlight the normalization of postfeminist surveillance in the girls' production of identity, in the way that girls must manage contradictions in what empowerment must mean on a highly individual basis. As Girl Power emphasized the "personal power of individual girls to pursue an unlimited future,"[70] here, postfeminism appears as a context in which this "personal power" is derived through surveillance. Ringrose emphasized the role of intensified surveillance by the school peer group as the audience for whom the "heterosexiness" in profiles was produced.[71] The display of sexual confidence, heterosexiness, and availability online can in fact be understood as an expected, constitutive element of girls' self-*branding* within the school gender "market." Indeed, Ringrose and Barajas suggest that girls' hypersexualized presentations on Bebo correlate with Gill's insight that postfeminist empowerment requires one to always appear "up for it," while simultaneously, control of one's sexuality in the school context meant sexual *restraint*.[72] Thus, this performance can be understood as a manifestation of postfeminist regulation, shaped by a matrix of factors: the context of surveillance in Bebo, the social school environment, postfeminist discourses, and mainstream porn culture.

The young women on MySpace in Dobson's (2011) study could also be argued to be producing practices of exclusive and individualistic friendship under the "girlfriend gaze" elaborated by Winch. The girlfriend gaze signifies the way that postfeminist surveillance is extended through practices of feminine, homosocial friendship.[73] While Dobson notes the determinedly heterosexual tone of these representations,[74] suggestive of male (heterosexual) surveillance, the constant tributes to particular friends suggests that the same circle of friends use MySpace to connect and, indeed, to survey other friends. The intimate surveillance facilitated by the platform of MySpace here furthers and heightens the girlfriend gaze. Dobson notes that proclamations of enduring affection for one's girlfriends construct a world of satisfaction that is complete through this girlfriendship. However, these girlfriends are also *used* in these profiles within traditionally sexist terms, by constructing and disciplining "other women" and distinguishing oneself from the feminine masses.[75] Thus, the profiles can be seen to be regulative of others, while also manifesting the production of self through regulatory discourses. From these case studies, postfeminist surveillance for girls and young women can be seen to operate individually, practised on the self and through peers.[76] Surveillance operates and works ever more intensively, both within commercial sites and within female peer settings, where postfeminist narratives of discipline and control have been taken up and accepted within sites of *intimate* sociality like online forums.

Sites of Postfeminist Discipline and Surveillance: Interactive Media

I have discussed how feminist scholarship has identified the acceptance of self-surveillance and discipline in particular domains as a means of "empowerment," a vital part of postfeminist narratives. I now explore some structural aspects of interactive media that may intensify the call to girls to enact and embody postfeminist discipline, though this will differ across platforms.[77] By interactive media, I mean a broad range of media, including reality television and digital interfaces, which involve a "relational premise"[78] of interactivity and self-production.

I have argued that digital interfaces intensify surveillance in relation to the content of posts and extension of surveillance in terms of time. In constituting a means of intensified surveillance, interactive media arguably foregrounds the invitation to disciplined, regulatory production of individuality, as it requires the online participant to work on her recognizability in fitting into an existing visual/gendered economy of representation, for unknown numbers of watching others. Notably, Sarah Banet-Weiser suggests that "branded postfeminism has only intensified in the online era" in terms of the ways in which the self is constructed and represented, drawing attention to the way that self-branding on YouTube constructs a deliberate association of commercial products and names with feelings and relationships.[79] This, she argues, is due to two effects of the digital revolution: consumers can be said to be more in control of their own productions, but also increasingly under surveillance by media industries. Thus, discipline and control are intensified in the interactive online environment. When considering the interactivity of a platform, Banet-Weiser argues that scholars ought to consider the way that the practices of production and consumption play out. She considers YouTube an ideal means to construct the postfeminist self-brand, as it rewards the "contemporary interactive subject";[80] the mechanism of online feedback incites the continual shaping of the self-brand in structuring the relationship between creators and viewers as that of brand–consumer. Often, this feedback might be extremely harsh and overtly disciplinary;[81] though, as Winch argues, the girlfriend gaze can be as or more effective in furthering post-feminist discipline.[82] Girls are provided with gendered feedback on how best to improve their channel's popularity through increased numbers of "views."

I suggest that this structure of interactive surveillance offers particularly disciplinary forms of identity practice. The "star" of the reality show or a YouTube Channel offers a disciplinary visibility, as it imbricates the participant within a neo-liberal rationality; the "work of being watched"[83] actively encourages the commoditization of the self as a brand, as a process in the medium of self-represen-tation, and as an *end* in itself.[84] Though I contend that online spaces like SNS and blogs feature different structures of visibility and interactive, disciplinary feedback, attention to a context of heightened surveillance by others can assist in understanding how spectators or internet users adopt disciplinary practices. By participating in the relational premise[85] of watching "real people" at some level, the spec-tator or user is invited to take up a disciplinary position, comparing and measuring the participants.[86] Thus, interactivity facilitates the adoption of the logic of the self as brand; as participant, knowing one is seen by many, one must labour and control one's image to perfect the brand that is consumed.[87] As a reality television spectator, one understands that the participants of reality television are required to "sell themselves," thereby inciting disciplinary judgment on the part of the consumer. As I have indicated above, audience studies of girl and women spectators indicate that this invitation is often, though not always, taken up.[88]

I suggest that this feminine disciplinary appraisal is also reflected in the way that girls view the profiles of other girls on SNS, appraising choices of profile pictures and documentation of private leisure activities ranging from drinking to sport.[89] I note, however, that this appraisal is not necessarily malicious. Shade, for example, notes that while older girls in her focus group were critical of the SNS presentations of younger girls, criticism was expressed in terms of concern for the impressions given off by the younger girls that were susceptible to judgment by "others."[90] Thus, the older girls had already adopted disciplinary feminine standards in self-representation, and wanted to act in a "role model" capacity for younger girls. Criticism was a way of wanting to "help" younger girls in a disciplinary world. This echoes Winch's discussion of how "girlfriendship" operates to normalize and legitimate the monitoring of oneself in relation to appearance and bodily maintenance.[91] I point particularly to Winch's example of a bridal group based on forum members that sets a weight loss target, with other members supporting each other's "goals."[92] Winch notes that women often return to these groups even after they have been married, indicating the value of sociality, but also how intimacy is effectively built *through* the disciplinary narrative of feminine weight loss. Winch's discussion of these web forums demonstrates that, even as the ambient privacy of the internet furthers intimate feminine sociality, it also heightens the reach and intensity of postfeminist discipline through feminine surveillance. These web forums act to regulate and engender feminine norms even as individual women find support.

Though femininity is cast as a project that requires ever-more work and constant feedback in order to find acceptance in society at large, I note that the outcome of this labour is still stressed as being one's "true" self.[93] This requirement to ensure one's acts reflect one's "true" self arguably requires further labour and discipline. I suggest that this is the case *particularly* within sites of more intensified spaces of surveillance, like the online environment. This is arguably seen in the way the girls in Dobson's study frequently uploaded quotes expressing aspirational autonomy next to images of mainstream heterosexiness.[94] This upholds the postfeminist idea that one is sexy, but "for oneself" rather than for others, disavowing the possibility of societal structures as producing one's own practices.[95] The postfeminist luminosity of independence, entangled with these other domains of bodily appearance and sexuality, operates to legitimate feminine disciplinary practices and labour on oneself as part of one's "true" identity. However, this "authenticity" must be constantly proven by virtue of the nature of the online environment. Thus, a disciplined and controlled profile building a picture of one's "true" self must be regularly and consistently maintained and updated. While girls may be enabled to carefully construct a disciplined and controlled self-narrative through online tools, online contacts may have the potential to disrupt it. Interestingly, Rob Cover argues that the "friendship" regime of Facebook, while inciting the recording of a consistent and unified self, may be destabilized through the interaction and surveillance of online friends.[96] The work of discipline towards achieving postfeminist identity is thus ongoing and never quite achieved. Interactive media accordingly intensifies self-surveillance through not only inciting disciplined self-presentation for the appraisal of others, but requiring that this presentation be constantly and consistently maintained.

Three forms of repetitive disciplinary identity practice, then, can be observed to invite postfeminist identity performance in online spaces of sociality: a disciplined and controlled interactive media participant, or one who strives to achieve an authentic brand; the disciplinary judgment applied by the discerning consumer; and the internalized disciplinary eye of the spectator. These practices demonstrate girls working *within* a system of power, a system that operates to make girls visible, but often according to postfeminist understandings of empowerment through discipline and control over selected domains.

Concluding Thoughts

The idea of one's identity as ultimately controlled by oneself is arguably highly appealing, and speaks to desires for one's autonomy and independence. However, this need for control needs to be situated within a broader context of mediated gender cultures. I have argued that online spaces of interactive sociality, such as SNS and blogs, by inviting certain practices of discipline and control, and operating through conditions of heightened surveillance and/or intimacy, should be understood as sites of potentially intensified conditions of production and regulation of postfeminist femininity. I suggest that the interrogation of these social conditions of surveillance, whether this be a heterosexual adolescent peer-policing environment, or in the intimate setting of "girlfriendship," promises potential in the understanding of tensions in girls' production of self online. Discourses of Girl Power and postfeminism both provide a template for girls' agency, which emphasize individual rather than *social* power. However, postfeminism increasingly draws on the idea of the personal brand and surveillance as a route to power, at the *expense* of the social. Claims of girls' power, if not grounded in consideration of how technological, social, and cultural conditions shape the way that individuality and "power" itself can be performed, may not adequately address girls' lived experience.

I have drawn on feminist Foucauldian scholarship and girls' media studies scholarship to offer what I hope will be a useful theoretical contribution for thinking through girls' production of self in a complex, technologically varied, and mediated world. In doing so, my intention has not been to close down the possibility of resistance for girls using the online medium to construct identity. Rather, my aim has been to ask about the work done by online structures of surveillance and the discursive possibilities that are (unevenly) available to girls. My aim has also been to alleviate some of the implicit pressures on girls in feminist aspirations for their liberation; as Dobson notes, the girl as "sign" is heavily weighted as a symbol of (meritocratic) progress and potential.[97] My hope is that, in analyzing the way girls' digital identity is often enmeshed in broader postfeminist, neo-liberal narratives, we might be able to better understand the highly complex and fraught world that girls must negotiate and through which girls' practices are "produced." In doing so, we may be able to more empathetically and realistically appreciate the ways girls do identity, the meaning of which changes through discourse, technologies, and other forms of power.

Notes

1   Mary Celeste Kearney, "Girls' Media Studies 2.0," in *Mediated Girlhoods: New Explorations of Girls' Media Culture*, ed. Mary Celeste Kearney (New York: Peter Lang, 2011), 3.

2   Leslie Regan Shade, "Internet Social Networking in Young Women's Everyday Lives: Some Insights from Focus Groups," *Our Schools, Our Selves* (2008), <http://www.policyalternatives.ca/sites/default/files/ uploads/publications/Our_Schools_Ourselve/8_Shade_ internet_social_ networking.pdf>.

3   *Ibid.*; Niels van Doorn, Liesbet van Zoonen & Sally Wyatt, "Writing from Experience: Presentations of Gender Identity on Weblogs," *European Journal of Women's Studies* 14:2 (2007), <http://hal.archives-ouvertes.fr/ docs/00/57/13/02/PDF/PEER_stage2_10.1177%252F1350506807075819.pdf.>

4   Jessalynn Keller, "Virtual Feminisms: Girls' Blogging Communities, Feminist Activism, and Participatory Politics," *Information, Communication & Society* 15:3 (2011), <http://www.academia.edu/1364158/Virtual_Feminisms_Girls_blogging_communities_feminist_activism_and_participatory_politics>; Jessalynn Keller, "Fiercely Real?: Tyra Banks and the Making of New Media Celebrity," *Feminist Media Studies* 14:1 (2014), <http://www.academia.edu/2174890/Fiercely_Real_Tyra_Banks_and_the_Making_of_New_Media_Celebrity>.

5   Rosalind Gill, *Gender and the Media* (Cambridge: Polity Press, 2007); Angela McRobbie, *The Aftermath of Feminism: Gender, Culture and Social Change* (London: SAGE 2009), 56.

6   Charlotte Brunsdon, Julie D'Acci & Lynn Spigel, "Identity in Feminist Television Criticism," in *Feminist Television Criticism: A Reader*, ed. Charlotte Brunsdon (Oxford: Clarendon Press, 2008); Charlotte Brunsdon, "The Feminist, the Housewife and the Soap Opera," in *The Feminist, the Housewife, and the Soap Opera*, eds. Charlotte Brunsdon & John Coughie, (Oxford: Oxford University Press, 2011); Gill, *ibid.* note 5; Myra Macdonald, *Representing Women: Myths of Femininity in the Popular Media* (London: Edward Arnold, 1995).

7   Gill, *supra* note 5 at 4.

8   James Benet, "Conclusion: Will Media Treatment of Women Improve?" in *Hearth and Home: Images of Women in the Mass Media*, ed. Gaye Tuchman, Arlene Kaplan Daniels & James Benet (New York: Oxford University Press, 1978); Carol Lopate, "Daytime Television: You'll Never Want to Leave Home," *Feminist Studies* 3:3/4 (1976): doi:10.2307/3177728; Gaye Tuchman, "Introduction: The Symbolic Annihilation of Women by the Mass Media," in *Hearth and Home: Images of Women in the Mass Media*, ed. Gaye Tuchman, Arlene Kaplan Daniels & James Benet (New York: Oxford University Press, 1978).

9   Brunsdon et al, *supra* note 6; Brunsdon, supra note 6.

10   Ien Ang, *Desperately Seeking the Audience* (London and New York: Routledge, 1991); Brunsdon, supra note 6 at 23–26.

11   Kearney, *supra* note 1.

12   Deirdre M. Kelly, Shauna Pomerantz & Dawn H. Currie, "'No Boundaries'? Girls' Interactive, Online Learning About Femininities," *Youth & Society*, 38:1 (2006), <http://wenku.baidu.com/view/ec998d8a680203d-8ce2f2484.html>; Rodda Leage & Ivana Chalmers, "Degrees of Caution: Arab Girls Unveil on Facebook," in *Girl Wide Web 2.0: Revisiting Girls, the Internet and the Negotiation of Identity*, ed. Sharon Mazzarella (New York: Peter Lang, 2010).

13   danah boyd, "Why Youth (Heart) Social Network Sites: The Role of Networked Publics in Teenage Social Life," in *Youth, Identity and Digital Media*, ed. David Buckingham (Cambridge: The MIT Press, 2008); Koen

Leurs & Sandra Ponzanesi, "Gendering the Construction of Instant Messaging," in *Women and Language: Essays on Gendered Communication across Media*, ed. Melissa Ames & Sarah Himsel Burcon (Jefferson: McFarland, 2011); Susannah Stern, "Producing Sites, Exploring Identities: Youth Online Authorship," in *Youth, Identity and Digital Media*, ed. David Buckingham (Cambridge, Massachusetts: The MIT Press, 2008); Jacqueline Ryan Vickery, "Blogrings as Virtual Communities for Adolescent Girls," in *Girl Wide Web 2.0* (see note 12)

14   Michelle S. Bae, "Go Cyworld! Korean Diasporic Girls Producing New Korean Femininity," in *Girl Wide Web 2.0* (see note 12); Kelly et al, *supra* note 12; Shayla Marie Thiel, "'IM Me': Identity Construction and Gender Negotiation in the World of Adolescent Girls and Instant Messaging," in *Girl Wide Web: Girls, the Internet and the Negotiation of Identity*, ed. Sharon Mazzarella (New York: Peter Lang, 2008).

15   Anita Harris, "Young Women, Late Modern Politics, and the Participatory Possibilities of Online Cultures," *Journal of Youth Studies* 11:5 (2008): 5, doi:10.1080/13676260802282950.

16   boyd, *supra* note 13; Paul Hodkinson & Sian Lincoln, "Online Journals as Virtual Bedrooms?: Young People, Identity and Personal Space," *Young* 16:1 (2008), <http://www.paulhodkinson.co.uk/publications/hodkinsonlincoln.pdf>; Kelly et al, *supra* note 12; Sonia Livingstone, "Taking Risky Opportunities in Youthful Content Creation: Teenagers' Use of Social Networking Sites for Intimacy, Privacy and Self-Expression," *New Media & Society* 10:3 (2008), <http://eprints.lse.ac.uk/27072/1/Taking_risky_opportunities_in_youthful_content_creation_(LSERO).pdf>; Priscilla Regan & Valerie Steeves, "Kids R Us: Online Social Networking and the Potential for Empowerment," *Surveillance and Society*, 8:2 (2010), <http://library.queensu.ca/ojs/index.php/surveillance-and-society/article/view/3483/3437>.

17   Carla E. Stokes, "'Get on My Level': How Black American Adolescent Girls Construct Identify and Negotiate Sexuality on the Internet," in *Girl Wide Web 2.0* (see note 12), 47.

18   *Ibid.*, at 63.

19   Kearney, *supra* note 1.

20   Marnina Gonick, "Between 'Girl Power' and 'Reviving Ophelia': Constituting the Neoliberal Girl Subject," *NWSA Journal* 18:2 (2006), <http://go.galegroup.com/ps/i.do?id=GALE%7CA149460403&v=2.1&u=otta779 73&it=r&p=AONE&sw=w&asid=b34a2d730c564e3db5529594f24d99bf>; E. Riordan, "Commodified Agents and Empowered Girls: Consuming and Producing Feminism," *Journal of Communication Inquiry* 25:3 (2001), doi:10.1177/0196859901025003006.

21   Gonick, *supra* note 20 at 2.

22   *Ibid.*

23   Lynne Edwards, "Victims, Villains, and Vixens: Teen Girls and Internet Crime," in *Girl Wide Web: Girls, the Internet, and the Negotiation of Identity,* ed. Sharon Mazzarella (New York: Peter Lang, 2005); Sharon Mazzarella, "Introduction: It's a Girl Wide Web," in *Girl Wide Web* (see note 14).

24   Edwards, *ibid.*, at 13–30; Shayla Thiel-Stern, "Femininity out of Control on the Internet: A Critical Analysis of Media Representations of Gender, Youth, and Myspace.Com in International News Discourses," *Girlhood Studies* 2:1 (2009): doi:10.1177/1461444812459171.

25   Bae, *supra* note 14; Ashley D. Grisso & David Weiss, "What Are Gurls Talking About? Adolescent Girls' Construction of Sexual Identity on Gurl.Com," in *Girl Wide Web* (see note 14); Kearney, *supra* note 1; Kelly et al, *supra* note 12; Thiel, *supra* note 14; Vickery, *supra* note 13.

26   Gill, *supra* note 5 at 254.

27   Nikolas Rose, *Governing the Soul: the Shaping of the Private Self* (London: Free Association Books, 1999).

28   Rosalind Gill & Christina Scharff, "Introduction," in *New Femininities: Postfeminism, Neoliberalism and Subjectivity,* ed. Rosalind Gill & Christina Scharff (Basingstoke: Palgrave Macmillan, 2011).

29   Angela McRobbie, "Top Girls?: Young Women and the Post-Feminist Sexual Contract," *Cultural Studies* 21: 4–5 (2007): doi:10.1080/095023807 01279044.

30   Dawn H. Currie, Deirdre M. Kelly & Shauna Pomerantz, *Girl Power: Girls Reinventing Girlhood.* (New York: Peter Lang, 2009).

31   Catherine Driscoll "Girl Culture, Revenge and Global Capitalism: Cyber-girls, Riot Grrls, Spice Girls," *Australian Feminist Studies* 14:29 (1999), 178: doi:10.1080/08164649993425.

32   *Ibid.*, at 189.

33   Stuart Hall, "Who Needs Identity?" in *Questions of Cultural Identity,* ed. Stuart Hall & Paul du Gay (London: SAGE, 1996).

34   Sandra Bartky, "Feminism, Foucault and the Modernisation of Patriarchal Power," in *Feminism and Foucault: Reflections on Resistance,* ed. Irene Diamond & Lee Quinby (Boston: Northeastern University Press, 1988), 81.

35   Michel Foucault, *Discipline and Punish: The Birth of the Prison,* trans. Alan Sheridan. 2nd ed. (New York: Vintage Books, 1995).

36   *Ibid.*, at 200–202.

37   Malin Sveningsson Elm, "Exploring and Negotiating Femininity: Young Women's Creation of Style in a Swedish Internet Community," *Young* 17:3 (2009), <http://www.academia.edu/473916/Exploring_and_negoti-ating_femininity>; Adriana M. Manago, Michael B. Graham, Patricia M. Greenfield & Goldie Salimkhan, "Self-Presentation and Gender on MySpace," *Journal of Applied Developmental Psychology,* 29:6 (2008), <http://

www.cdmc.ucla.edu/Published_Research_files/mggs-2008.pdf>; Shade, *supra* note 2.

38   Jessica Ringrose, "Sluts, Whores, Fat Slags and Playboy Bunnies: Teen Girls' Negotiation of 'Sexy' on Social Networking Sites and at School," in *Girls and Education 3–16: Continuing Concerns, New Agendas*, ed. Carolyn Jackson, Emma Carrie & Emma Renold (Maidenhead: Open University Press, 2010).

39   Gill, *supra* note 5; McRobbie, *supra* note 5; McRobbie, *supra* note 29; Riordan, *supra* note 20; Estella Tincknell, "Scourging the Abject Body: Ten Years Younger and Fragmented Femininity under Neoliberalism," in *New Femininities: Postfeminism, Neoliberalism and Subjectivity*, ed. Rosalind Gill & Christina Scharff (Basingstoke: Palgrave Macmillan, 2011).

40   Gill & Scharff, *supra* note 28.

41   McRobbie, *supra* note 5.

42   McRobbie, *supra* note 29.

43   McRobbie, *supra* note 5 at 60.

44   Alison Winch, *Girlfriends and Postfeminist Sisterhood* (Basingstoke: Palgrave Macmillan, 2013), 5.

45   Though, arguably, these forums might also be considered to feature synoptic structures of surveillance in the mutual gaze.

46   Winch, *supra* note 44 at 187.

47   *Ibid.* at 191.

48   Andrea L. Press, "'Feminism? That's So Seventies': Girls and Young Women Discuss Femininity and Feminism in *America's Next Top Model*," in *New Femininities: Postfeminism, Neoliberalism and Subjectivity*, ed. Rosalind Gill & Christina Scharff (Basingstoke: Palgrave Macmillan, 2011); Beverley Skeggs & Helen Wood, *Reacting to Reality Television: Performance, Audience and Value* (London: Routledge, 2013).

49   Thomas Mathiesen, "The Viewer Society: Michel Foucault's 'Panopticon' Revisited," *Theoretical Criminology* 1:2 (1997), <http://core.roehampton.ac.uk/repository2/content2/subs/J.Lorent/J.Lorent1413/Mathiesen%20(1997)%20The%20viewer%20society.pdf>.

50   Aaron Doyle, "Revisiting the Synopticon: Reconsidering Mathiesen's 'the Viewer Society' in the Age of Web 2.0," *Theoretical Criminology* 15 (2011): doi:10.1177/1362480610396645.

51   Daniel Trottier, "Watching Yourself, Watching Others: Popular Representations of Panoptic Surveillance In Reality TV Programs," in *How Real Is Reality TV? Essays on Representation and Truth*, edited by David S. Escoffery (Jefferson: McFarland, 2006), 273–275.

52   Press, *supra* note 48; Skeggs & Wood, *supra* note 48.

53   Press, *supra*, at 129.

54   *Ibid.*, at 127.

55   Vincent Miller, "New Media, Networking and Phatic Culture," *Convergence: The International Journal of Research into New Media Technologies* 14:4 (2008), <http://www.academia.edu/176454/New_Media_Networking_and_Phatic_Culture>; Liesbet van Zoonen, "From Identity to Identification: Fixating the Fragmented Self," *Media, Culture & Society* 35:1 (2013), <http://mitp-webdev.mit.edu/sites/default/files/titles/content/9780262524834_sch_0001.pdf>.

56   Jodi Dean, *Blog Theory: Feedback and Capture in the Circuits of Drive* (Cambridge: Polity Press, 2010); Alexa Tsoulis-Reay, "Omg I'm Online … Again! MySpace, Msn and the Everyday Mediation of Girls," *Screen Education* 53 (2009).

57   Ringrose, *supra* note 38; Jessica Ringrose & Katarina Eriksson Barajas, "Gendered Risks and Opportunities? Exploring Teen Girls' Digitized Sexual Identities in Postfeminist Media Contexts," *International Journal of Media and Cultural Politics* 7:2 (2011): 121, <http://www.academia.edu/1472908/Gendered_risks_and_opportunities_Exploring_teen_girls_digital_sexual_identity_in_postfeminist_media_contexts>.

58   Ringrose & Barajas, *ibid.*, at 126.

59   *Ibid.*, at 170–179.

60   Amy Shields Dobson, "Bitches, Bunnies and Bffs (Best Friends Forever): A Feminist Analysis of Young Women's Performance of Contemporary Popular Femininities on MySpace," (PhD diss., Monash University, 2010); Dobson, "Hetero-Sexy Representation by Young Women on MySpace: The Politics of Performing an 'Objectified' Self," in *Outskirts* (2011), <http://www.outskirts.arts.uwa.edu.au.proxy.bib.uottawa.ca/volumes/volume-25/amy-shields-dobson>.

61   Amy Shields Dobson, "'Individuality is Everything': 'Autonomous' Femininity in MySpace Mottos and Self-Descriptions," *Continuum* 26:3 (2012): 375, doi:10.1080/10304312.2012.665835.

62   Amy Shields Dobson, "The Representation of Female Friendships on Young Women's MySpace Profiles: The All-Female World and the Feminine 'Other,'" in *Youth Culture and Net Culture: Online Social Practices,* ed. E. Dunkels, G. M. Franberg & C. Hallgren (Hershey, PA: IGI Global, 2011), 134.

63   *Ibid.*, at 141.

64   Dobson, *supra* note 62.

65   McRobbie, *supra* note 5.

66   See also Anthony Giddens, *Modernity and Self-Identity: Self and Society in the Late Modern Age* (Cambridge: Polity Press, 1991), 102, relating to the self as improvable project.

67   Dobson "Bitches, Bunnies and Bffs," *supra* note 60 at 63.

68   Productive in the Foucauldian sense of the word.

69 Judith Butler, *Gender Trouble*. 2nd ed. (New York: Routledge Classics, 2006); Gill, *supra* note 5; McRobbie, *supra* note 5.

70 Curry et al, *supra* note 30 at 20.

71 Ringrose, *supra* note 38; Dobson, *supra* note 61.

72 Ringrose & Barajas, *supra* note 57 at 124.

73 Winch, *supra* note 44.

74 Dobson, *supra* note 60.

75 *Ibid.*

76 Bartky, *supra* note 34.

77 Mark Andrejevic, *Reality TV: The Work of Being Watched* (Lanham: Rowman & Littlefield, 2004); Sue Collins, "Making the Most out of 15 Minutes: Reality TV's Dispensable Celebrity," *Television & New Media* 9:2 (2008): doi:10.1177/0163443711415746; Catherine Driscoll & Melissa Gregg, "Convergence Culture and the Legacy of Feminist Cultural Studies," *Cultural Studies*, 25 (2011), <http://www.academia.edu/1021401/Convergence_Culture_and_the_Legacy_of_Feminist_Cultural_Studies>; Laurie Ouellette & Julie Wilson, "Women's Work," *Cultural Studies* 25:4-5 (2011), <http://julieannwilson.files.wordpress.com/2011/06/womens-work-affective-labor-and-convergence-culture1.pdf>.

78 Dobson "Bitches, Bunnies and Bffs," *supra* note 60 at 7.

79 Sarah Banet-Weiser, "Branding the Post-Feminist Self: Girls' Video Production and Youtube," in *Mediated Girlhoods: New Explorations of Girls' Media Culture*, ed. Mary Celeste Kearney (New York: Peter Lang, 2011), 284.

80 *Ibid.*, at 278.

81 Kristyn Gorton & Joanne Garde-Hansen, "From Old Media Whore to New Media Troll," *Feminist Media Studies* 13:2 (2013), doi:10.1080/14680777.2012.678370; Camille Nurka, "Public Bodies," *Feminist Media Studies* (2013), <http://www.academia.edu/5892465/Public_Bodies>.

82 Alison Winch, "The Girlfriend Gaze: Women's Friendship and Intimacy Circles Are Increasingly Taking on the Function of Mutual Self-Policing," *Soundings* 52 (2012), <http://www.eurozine.com/articles/2012-12-04-winch-en.html>.

83 Andrejevic, *supra* note 77 at 6.

84 Collins, *supra* note 77.

85 Dobson, *supra* note 60 at 7.

86 Skeggs & Wood, *supra* note 48.

87 Banet-Weiser, *supra* note 79; Alison Hearn, "'John, a 20-Year-Old Boston Native with a Great Sense of Humor': On the Spectacularization of the 'Self' and the Incorporation of Identity in the Age of Reality Television," in *The Celebrity Culture Reader*, ed. P. David Marshall (New York: Routledge, 2006); Su Holmes, "When Will I Be Famous? Reappraising the Debate About Fame in Reality TV," in *How Real Is Reality TV: Essays*

on Representation and Truth, ed. David S. Escoffery (Jefferson: McFarland, 2006).

88   Press, *supra* note 48; Skeggs & Wood, *supra* note 48.

89   Manago et al, *supra* note 36; Ringrose, *supra* note 38; Shade, *supra* note 2.

90   Shade, *supra* note 2.

91   Winch, *supra* note 44.

92   Winch, *supra* note 44 at 25.

93   Gill, *supra* note 5.

94   Dobson, *supra* note 60.

95   Gill, *supra* note 5.

96   Rob Cover, "Performing and Undoing Identity Online: Social Networking, Identity Theories and the Incompatibility of Online Profiles and Friendship Regimes," *Convergence: The International Journal of Research into New Media Technologies* 18:2 (2012): 183, doi:10.1177/1354856511433684.

97   Dobson, *supra* note 60 at 376.

PART II

LIVING IN A GENDERED GAZE

The Internet and Friendship Seeking: Exploring the Role of Online Communication in Young, Recently Immigrated Women's Social Lives

Assumpta Ndengeyingoma

Introduction

Friendship seeking and relationship seeking are part of the developmental tasks that accompany adolescence. Several studies show the importance of these relationships for social and personal development.[1] The continuity of these relationships can be complex: friendships, dyads, or groups can develop from childhood, some of which can later become confidant relationships. Within the context of immigration, youth can become physically separated from their once-close friends. This can prevent friendship relationships from developing into confidant relationships, as these relationships are typically consolidated by physical presence.

The sociocultural contexts in schools in an immigrant child's host country offer the opportunity to develop friendships and romantic relationships. But racism, discrimination, prejudice, and stigmatization can also emerge in school environments. For example, native-born Canadians, immigrants from the same country as immigrant youth, or immigrants from different cultures and ethnicities can make intimidating comments aimed at immigrant youth regarding their ways of dressing, behaving, or speaking. This can occur face-to-face and also through online communication. All of these factors can constrain the ability of immigrant youth to make friends.

A trend has been observed where young immigrant women tend to seek friendships within online environments.[2] The aim of this chapter is to identify the factors associated with the use of the internet in friendship-seeking from the point of view of six teenage girls who immigrated to Canada's capital region. For the purposes of this paper, the "internet" refers to online social spaces used for communicative purposes, including social networking sites.

Context

Immigration is a key issue in modern societies. In the last five years, Canada has welcomed between 248,748 and 280,688 immigrants per year.[3] The reasons behind these immigration journeys are diverse. Some people migrate for economic reasons, others as part of government-managed family reunification programs, while others are refugees or migrate to join family members who have already established themselves in the new country. The immigration experience is often accompanied by considerable material, familial, and cultural losses for the immigrant, in addition to the stress of being confronted with new physical and social realities.[4] Newly immigrated people must rebuild their social networks to obtain the social support they need, but they may be faced with social exclusion in relation to their race, ethnicity, language, religion, or label as an immigrant. However, it should be noted that the immigration experience can have different impacts upon different people, depending on their age and social location.

As researchers such as Laursen, Wilder, Noack, and Williams point out,[5] a sense of belonging to a group that is separate from their parents is a priority for adolescents, allowing them to develop their own value systems, to define themselves, to identify goals, and to mature into adults. For youth between 12 and 18 years of age, interaction with peers is an important element contributing to social and cultural development.[6] Studies show that peer affiliation and peer acceptance present certain challenges for recently immigrated youth. These challenges can be related to relationships with peers or within the family dynamic. With regard to peer affiliation, the cultural diversity of a host country like Canada offers recently immigrated youth the opportunity to develop friendships with peers from all backgrounds. But Berry, Phinney, Sam, and Vedder also report that immigrant youth can face discrimination in a variety of host countries, including Canada.[7] Gariba conducted focus group interviews and survey questionnaires with Ghanaian and Somali youth residing in Toronto regarding their perceptions of barriers to labour market access. Participants reported a number of incidents in which they experienced discrimination.[8] Perceived discrimination also affected participants' feelings of community belonging, as well as feelings of belonging to society in general. Through surveys administered to Chinese American adolescents, Juang and Alvarez report that participants' perceived discrimination can lead to a variety of physical, social, and psychological consequences, including feelings of solitude, anxiety, and somatization.[9] Their analysis concluded that negative family interactions exacerbated the effects of perceived discrimination, while positive interactions buffered the effects of greater perceived discrimination.[10]

As noted, in addition to peer affiliation, family dynamics can also pose a challenge to friendship formation for newly immigrated youth, who can experience difficulty seeking out friendships due to family-related constraints. For example, Ahn, Kim, and Park's research with Korean American youth (90 percent of whom had parents born in Korea) revealed a child-parent gap in terms of adherence to traditional cultural values, which in turn related to parent/child conflict (particularly with respect to marriage and dating).[11] In Mexican American immigrant families, parental control in relation to friendships and socializing has been found to be accentuated for girls more than for boys.[12] This phenomenon can also be found within the general population, a finding that is often more pronounced in Eastern cultures than in Western cultures.[13]

Because of these factors, immigrant girls can find it hard to make friends. Searching for friendship online becomes a possible solution to the peer and family-related constraints that recently immigrated youth may face. While it is generally known that adolescents like using technology to communicate, specific challenges may be faced by some recently immigrated youths due to material or societal disadvantages.[14] Communication technologies could allow immigrant youth to reach out to their peers while bypassing potential challenges imposed by parental control and the social discrimination they may feel, as internet communication via online social media has unique characteristics such as cultural and linguistic diversity, interactivity, anonymity, and accessibility.[15] These potential advantages of online social communication can assist immigrant youth,[16] as well as youth in the general population[17] in articulating the various social challenges they may face.

The objective of this article is to identify the factors that lead to the use of the internet as a tool in searching for friends, as told by adolescent female youths using their migratory experiences as a starting point. A better understanding of neighbourhood, sociocultural, and familial barriers could contribute to reflections about the eventual role that people who interact with these youths, such as immigrant welcoming agencies, educators, health care workers, and parents, could play in supporting young women as they seek to establish themselves in Canada.

This article revisits data that was previously published in which I conducted semi-structured interviews, self-recordings and follow-up interviews with twelve refugee youth aged 13 to 18 years old, who had recently immigrated to Canada from five different countries in Sub-Saharan Africa and were living in the city of Gatineau, Quebec. The goals of this study were, first, to identify recently immigrated youths' perceptions of their migratory experiences and, second, to identify potential factors that could influence the development of their personal identities. This study employed Bronfenbrenner's Bioecological Systems Theory as a theoretical framework within which four dimensions of personal development were explored: proximal processes of social interaction; the person in development; the context of the person; and the factor of time.[18] In brief, the study concluded that immigrant youths' abilities to self-criticize, religious beliefs, complicated migratory trajectories, interactions with peers, family dynamics, and intercultural proximity facilitated the development of these youths' personal identities, although, in some cases, these factors also became restrictive to their development.[19]

Manesse's comparative concept analysis of experience was retained to operationalize the concept of a migratory experience within the context of this study. This philosophical conceptualization was selected because it regroups several characteristics of an experience. Thus, a migratory experience is operationalized as a mental as well as a physical activity, and is considered to be associated with an individual's personal signification to their perceptions as they express themselves from their own definition of their reality, lived or observed.[20] Unexpectedly, my participants brought up online communication repeatedly, indicating that there may be ways to support immigrant youth through social media and other forms of online community building. This chapter is an initial attempt to lay out my findings in this regard and suggest areas for further research.

Methodology

Participant Characteristics and Selection

This study took place in the Outaouais region, located in the southwest portion of the province of Quebec, which is part of the national capital region of Canada. According to the regionalization of immigration policy published by the Ministry of Immigration and Cultural Communities of Quebec, the Outaouais region places third in the list of Quebec regions that receive the most refugees who are selected and supported by the government.[21] Geographically speaking, this region offers the opportunity for recently immigrated adolescents to interact, whether through work or social or school activities, with youths in the neighbouring province of Ontario, whose principal language is often English. This reality can augment the challenges complicating immigrant youths' integration into their new cultural environments, as youths can perceive that they must adapt simultaneously to the cultures of both Quebec, which is more French, and Ontario, which is more English.

The six participants in this study were recruited through Accueil-Parrainage Outaouais (APO), a non-profit organization whose mission is to welcome immigrants and refugees who settle in the Outaouais region. Participants were selected through purposive sampling. Inclusion criteria specified that participants must identify as being teenage refugees who originated from Sub-Saharan Africa; be between the ages of 13 and 18; have lived in Canada for less than five years; be living in the Outaouais region; be able to speak, understand, and read French; and have parents who understand and read French. The diversity in the participants' regions of origin added to the richness of the data, making it possible to gather different migratory experiences.

For this specific study, all participants were female. Each had lived in refugee camps for between ten and fourteen years. Half of the participants currently lived with both of their parents, two participants resided with only their mother, and one participant lived with her older brother. Participants had between four and eight siblings. Ethical approval for this study was obtained through the research ethics committees at the Université du Québec en Outaouais and the Université du Québec à Trois Rivières. Informed consent was obtained from all participants and their parents.

Data Collection

This study used phenomenological methodology in order to take into account the natural context of the participants, their expression, and their frame of reference in relation to their experiences. The chosen data collection methods allowed the researcher to return to the participants to validate the meaning that the researcher gave to their experiences. This study used two different methods of data collection: (1) two types of interviews, including semi-structured interviews and semi-structured interviews based on the technique of meaning explanation (see below); and (2) self-recordings. These methods are complementary and can permit the understanding of different representations of a similar phenomenon,[22] as well as the comparison of participant perspectives and the triangulation of data.[23]

An initial semi-structured interview explored with participants their perceptions of their migratory experiences. In this study, individual face-to-face interviews lasted thirty to sixty minutes. Interviews were conducted in French and were carried out either in the home of the participant or in a research office. Five categories of questions were explored:

1. General data (e.g., do you work?).
2. Pre-migratory experiences (e.g., can you think of any experiences in or aspects of your country of origin that have impacted your life? If so, which ones? Do you share these events with anyone among your friends or family?).
3. Significance of the social context and its role in identity development, including questions about sense of belonging to Canada or Quebec, proximal community belonging, ethnic group belonging and family life (e.g., how do you find your neighbourhood? Can you describe it? Do you participate in activities related to your community of origin?).
4. Family life (e.g., are there situations where you think that your family members don't understand you? What do you do to make yourself understood in these situations?).

5. Feelings of unity and coherence in relation to adolescence, life objectives, personal power, and identity experimentation (e.g., what motivates you in life? Who is your favourite musical artist? Why? Do you use the internet to get to know other people? Are there ways that you learn through your friends when online?).

Audio self-recordings allowed participants to present and express their points of view and feelings relating to information they considered to be significant. Self-recording was explained to participants during the initial interview, and all participants were presented with the materials required for self-recording. The events could be from their home, school, or work environments. The events could be socially, culturally, academically, or emotionally significant, but they were not instructed that they must report a specific type of event. Rather, they were asked to identify information they considered significant, and to summarize and record these events over a four-day period, including two weekdays and two weekend days. They were asked to note their observations regarding these events, including the different ways in which these events can or could have been managed, and to provide an explanation of the course of action they took in order to deal with these events. As this method does not offer the possibility to engage in a deeper discussion to understand the reasoning behind participants' expressed emotions or actions, it was followed by a second individual interview.

This second semi-structured interview was based on the technique of meaning explanation (TME), which aims to explore more deeply participants' descriptions of their lived experiences.[24] In this study, the TME interview draws from the nine processes as proposed by Petitmengin: question raising; focusing attention; returning attention from "what" to "how"; moving from a general representation to a singular experience; retrospectively accessing a lived experience; drawing attention to the different dimensions of experience; deepening the description of a phenomenon to the level of accuracy required; deepening the description of characteristics other than those of a temporal nature of living; and encouraging the subject to describe phenomenon in his or her own words.[25]

Data Analysis

The analysis of conceptual categories was the method chosen to analyze the data gathered in this study. A conceptual category is defined as a textual production presenting itself in the form of a brief expression, permitting the identification a phenomenon that is apparent through a conceptual reading of research material.[26] Analysis of conceptual categories is carried out in two stages: vertical analysis, which is the analysis of all the data collected with one participant, and horizontal analysis, which is the comparative analysis of the data from all participants.[27]

Results

The results of this study demonstrate that recently immigrated youths describe the process of seeking friendship as part of a particular experience in a variety of well-defined contexts. This builds on previous qualitative research by the same author that demonstrated that seeking new friends is essential to the personal development of recently immigrated youths.[28] The three contextual categories identified in relation to friendship-seeking in this study are neighbourhood context, sociocultural context, and family context. Each of these contexts poses certain potential problems for immigrant girls seeking to make friends. Unexpectedly, all of the participants found online communication to be a valuable way to overcome the barriers encountered in each of these contexts, which are expanded upon below.

Neighbourhood Context within the Experience of Friendship Seeking

The results of this study demonstrate that immigrant youths living in comparatively quiet neighbourhoods associate these neighbourhoods with difficulties in forming ties with local youth because face-to-face contact is practically impossible in certain neighbourhoods. As explained by F1 (14 years old), who had lived in Canada for two years: "I arrived here in the month of November. You don't really see people. Here people are in their houses, I don't even know my neighbours."[29] The participants found that they must often stay inside their houses. The concept of staying at home and being confined to a defined space was very different from participants' lives in the countries where they lived prior to coming to Canada, where many participants were used to being outside most of the time.

The feeling of being confined to the house, reported by several participants in this study, was more often associated with exerted parental control than it was with the "quiet neighbourhood" phenomenon. Comparatively quiet neighbourhoods do not facilitate the development of friendships for recently immigrated girls because they offer fewer opportunities for social interaction, especially if the young girl comes from a country where winter does not exist. Without knowing how to practice any winter sports, these girls often end up staying indoors for approximately four months, which does not facilitate face-to-face interactions with other youths. This type of situation can lead to internet communication becoming the most viable option for socializing.

For some participants in this study, the fact that their schools were located far from their neighbourhoods also increased the difficulties they experienced in forging relationships. Living in Quebec was a decision made by their parents; to study in Ontario was a decision made by participants. Since their studies prior to their arrival in Canada had been in English, and Quebec laws (with very limited exceptions) require that youth studying in Quebec study at French-language institutions,[30] participants chose to study in Ontario rather than lose a year of schooling that would be required to adapt to a change in the language of their education. This situation resulted in fewer students living in the same neighbourhood as their school. Online communication was found to be a valuable way to overcome this physical barrier.

The participants in this study often described the school environment within the context of friendship-seeking. However, little was generally reported with regard to the geographical location of schools, how geographical barriers can impede the development of friendships, and how online spaces can help to overcome geographical barriers. The results of this study suggest that if the school is located far from the neighbourhood where the recently immigrated youth resides, then this may add to their difficulties in developing friendships, as there are fewer classmates living in their neighbourhood. Online communication may help youth to overcome physical barriers to communicate with school friends and other peer groups.

The participants indicated that communication within the experience of seeking friendship is facilitated by the frequency and ease of access to the internet. Prior to immigrating, none of the participants had had access to the internet and, at the time of the study, none of them reported owning a laptop or a smartphone. However, all of the participants said that they used the internet regularly. They had internet access at home, and there was a desktop computer either in their room or in their siblings' rooms. This accessibility allowed them to stay online in their bedrooms for a long time. The motives for using internet communication revolved most often around reinforcing real-life friendships, or searching for romantic relationships with people who shared the same values, as well as for advice as to the best course of action for different life situations.

Sociocultural Context within the Experience of Friendship Seeking

Sociocultural context is associated with participants' lived experiences in their school environments, as well as within their local neighbourhoods. As noted above, half of the participants reported living in the province of Quebec but studying in the province of Ontario, approximately twenty minutes away by bus. Participants reported that the school environment offered intercultural proximity, that is the opportunity to interact with peers from countries different from their own country of origin, and also intracultural proximity, that is interactions with peers from their country of origin.[31]

They therefore had the opportunity to develop friendships as well as romantic relationships with other immigrant peers. Several participants reported a sense of ease in making friends in such a multicultural environment. As stated by F3 (16 years old): "I have friends from several cultures: Romanian, Chinese, Mexican. I can learn a lot from their cultures."

Some participants also mentioned that they can face stigmatization on the basis of their countries of origin or the colour of their skin. As F5 (16 years old) recounted, "I am told that girls from my country boast too much and talk too much, but I tell them that I am not that type of girl." In order to avoid a discriminatory reaction, four participants stated that they do not reveal their country of origin most of the time, or that when they do reveal it, they specify that they grew up in another country. Often they choose to say that they are from lesser known countries. F6 (15 years old) explained, "I have African friends who say that they come from the Caribbean islands or that they are born in Europe. They don't like to say that they come directly from Africa because people will ask them if they have lived through war or poverty, etc."

The sociocultural contexts in schools also offered the opportunity for participants to develop romantic relationships. Four out of six participants mentioned that they would like a serious relationship with a boy from another culture; one said that she was currently in such a relationship and another said that she did not currently know what kind of relationship she wanted, as she was focused on finishing her secondary studies.

Several participants preferred intercultural romantic relationships, a preference that can potentially be related to participants' tendencies to question relationship- and gender-related customs and stereotypes from their countries of origin. All six participants described that they were generally unfamiliar with customs from their countries of origin because they had grown up elsewhere. F2 (15 years old) explained:

> In the culture of my country of origin, there are some very strange things that they call customs. For example, the women in my country of origin must stay at home and cook and clean while the man does nothing. Once they arrive here, the women must work, but they must also do all the house tasks alone, cooking, looking after the children and their homework, all while Mister does nothing, or watches television and says that it's their custom.

F4 (17 years old) stated:

> Culture from where I come from, I find it very difficult. The man tells you what to do and you must obey without discussion. If your husband dies, you must marry his brother. I do not want to enter into a relationship where I would have to apply these customs.

However, there were two participants who mentioned that, even if they would prefer an intercultural relationship, they would nonetheless enter a romantic relationship with a boy from their country of origin, provided that he was born or raised elsewhere and that his parents did not adhere to conservative cultural traditions or customs. The context behind this is that the participants in this study have virtually never lived in their country of origin because they were either born in a refugee camp or in a country that is not the country of origin of their parents. They used the internet and socializing with peers from the same cultural background as themselves to learn more about their culture, as well as observing their own family dynamics within that culture.

According to the participants of this study, maintaining an intercultural relationship is not easy. They reported being the targets of degrading statements from peers from their countries of origin who hold conservative belief systems and who reflect traditional cultural views regarding relationship-related customs, where intercultural relationships are often condemned or discouraged. Participants described being told face to face that they were sellouts or cowards for maintaining intercultural relationships; they also described receiving e-mails that threatened to reveal their relationships to their parents. In this instance, online communication opened girls up to judgement from their peers and was a means of monitoring their behaviour for the purposes of discipline/conformity to traditional cultural expectations of relationships. This intimidation can occur both online and in person. Since an intercultural relationship may be accompanied by intracultural intimidation, participants felt that belonging to a group was necessary for protection from such intimidations.

Just as participants recounted that their peers could condemn their intercultural relationships, they reported that their parents could similarly disapprove of these relationships. Because of this, most participants did not dare to reveal their relationships to their mothers. As F1 (14 years old) explained:

> I have a Jamaican boyfriend. My mother does not know it! She will tell me that I've lost my head, that I am young, that I must learn that trying to live in a culture that is not your own is very difficult. If she knew, she would never let me leave our house. It's my choice; I think that in life we need someone to listen to us, someone to love us.

Sometimes participants' parents approved of intercultural relationships, but with certain conditions attached. F2 (15 years old) said: "My parents may accept [an intercultural relationship], but not before 18 years old." F5 (16 years old) explained her own parents' conditions for acceptance of an intercultural relationship: "My parents may accept on condition that he does not spend the night at my house or myself at his house."

Intra- and intercultural proximity offers the possibility for friendship development within one's own culture or with other cultures. This is the case in certain schools in the city of Ottawa, such as those attended by the participants in this study. This proximity facilitates intercultural friendship seeking for recently immigrated youths, offering a context within which to compare one's own culture to others. While they did not report any discriminatory actions being taken against them, the participants described having interactions with immigrant and non-immigrant youth where they recounted hearing stereotyped or opinionated remarks aimed at devaluing the differences between their culture and other cultures. This is important to consider, since participants in this study expressed that they could face discrimination in relation to the application of traditional customs and cultural expectations for relationship and gender performance. When these forms of discrimination do not manifest in similar ways for members of the cultural majority, it is important to begin to more fully unpack the discrimination-related experiences of members of minority populations, including immigrant youth.

For the purposes of this chapter, it is important to note that my participants valued online communication because it gave them a way to participate in relationships that might not meet the approval of family members. At the same time, it opened them up to possible repercussions when peers used online communication to register their own discomfort with intercultural friendships and relationships, especially if peers intended to tell parents about relationships that the girls may have chosen to keep private.

Family Context within the Experience of Friendship Seeking

Participants described that family context could also facilitate or hinder their friendship and relationship seeking experiences. Conceptual categories that related to family context included the difficulty of communication with family members, liberty to socialize, and non-parental family relationships, which participants described as being helpful sources of advice when they felt less comfortable consulting their parents.

Participants perceived communication with their fathers to be difficult: as F1 (14 years old) outlined, "Fathers don't listen." F4 (17 years old) reported a similar experience, stating that fathers "either don't take you seriously or they tell you to go talk to your mother." F6 (15 years old) similarly recounted that fathers "are there only to tell you what's wrong or to set their expectations." Since they perceived communication with their fathers to be difficult, participants mentioned that they would find it difficult to talk to their fathers about online problems.

All participants found communication with their mothers to be easier than communication with their fathers, but noted that they could not speak freely with their mothers about all subjects, particularly if those subjects involved gender role expectations or social liberties:

> At home, I live like I was in Africa. My mother wishes to remain Africa[n], so I don't have a choice. I grew up like this. I think she says "no" before even listening to me. If I tell her that I'm going out with friends to a movie, she will tell me that I go out too often and that that is not good for a girl, that I must learn to stay home. (F4, 17 years old)

While participants found it easier to talk to their mothers, they did feel pressure to be model children in their mothers' eyes. A model child, participants suggested, would minimize her own suffering and not articulate problems such as online conflict that could potentially cause parents to feel stress or trauma. As F3 (16 years old) explained: "Immigrants who come from war-torn countries, the parents have suffered enough; we don't have to be adding to that." Other participants also reported that their parents have enough problems to manage, such as integrating into the Canadian workforce. In favour of not compounding the problems that they perceived their parents to be experiencing and to not disappoint their parents, participants often chose not to tell their parents about their problems. F2 (15 years old) noted that she understood her parents' hardships and that her recognition of these hardships was demonstrated by obedience and not augmenting these problems by adding her own: "It must be difficult for them to return to do studies, to look for work, to look after us, etc."

Participants in this study described that their parents often did not allow them to go out or socialize with friends. Online communications allowed some participants to bypass these restrictions placed upon their socialization, allowing them an opportunity to maintain friendships they did not have the freedom to maintain face to face. For example, F1 (14 years old) stated that, "Since I cannot go out often, at least I chat with my friends every night." It would appear that parents are aware that their teenage daughters are using online communication, as participants described having access to computers in their home; however, it is unclear whether parents are aware of the precise ways that their daughters are using these forms of communication. All of the participants mentioned that their parents had not had internet access in their country of origin, implying that their parents were not fully familiar with the intricacies and capabilities of online communication, as they were likely less experienced themselves with the use of these tools.

While participants did not feel like they could always speak freely with their parents, they did describe that other family members provided a family context wherein they could seek advice or support. All participants had found a comparatively young person, but older than themselves, within their immediate or extended family from whom they could seek advice. F1 (14 years old) detailed that, "I ask my sister because we're on the same level, we're both young"; other participants found similar confidants in siblings or cousins. However, participants mentioned that sometimes there were nonetheless things that they could not tell these confidants for fear of disappointing them.

It should also be noted that these reported family contexts are not specific to immigrant populations. Shearer, Crouter, and McHale, for example, have demonstrated that mothers generally know more than fathers about their teenagers' activities and are more likely than fathers to obtain new information, either by actively monitoring their adolescent or through voluntary disclosure of information by the adolescent.[32] What seems to be different in this current study is the cohesion within participants' non-parental family relationships that allowed for an influential role of an older sister or cousin, who served as a confidant or sounding board for problems that participants did not feel they could discuss with their parents. However, it should be noted (as above) that in order to avoid judgement or to avoid disappointing their sisters or cousins, there were certain limitations to topics that participants felt they could discuss with these family members, who were at times considered to be more like advisors and less like confidants.

In summary, the use of the internet as a method for friendship-seeking emerged as a commonly occurring conceptual category in this study, in both an empowering and a constraining manner. This suggests that further research is needed to explore the use of the internet for friendship seeking in neighbourhood contexts, sociocultural contexts, and family contexts.

Conclusion

In the female youth population in general, there are studies, such as the open-ended survey conducted by Reich and Subrahmanyam, which report that internet communication is used by some young women to fill the void that they perceive is left when they cannot see their friends in person.[33] My findings suggest that recently immigrated participants may also use online communication to bypass restrictions on leaving the house or to deflect the judgment from their peers and parents about their relationship choices. Further research is also needed to explore how internet communication is used by recently immigrated youth to reinforce real-life relationships, to seek out friendships with peers who share similar values, or to clarify one's point of view on a situation.

There are also important questions to ask about immigrant girls' experiences of online harassment. Communications between this study's participants and their parents already faced certain constraints, for example, when participants limited self-disclosure to parents for fear of disappointing them or compounding the hardships their parents experienced. This leads one to presume that a recently immigrated adolescent girl who is being cyberbullied because she is in an intercultural relationship will not be likely to report the bullying, as it will also reveal her relationship status to her parents. It is possible that intercultural cyberbullying could also lead to parents banning or monitoring the use of internet communication, compounding the isolation that recently immigrated young girls may feel.

The results presented in this study allowed for a discussion of the potential factors significant to the use of the internet in friendship seeking, as told by six adolescent female youths using their migratory experiences to Canada's capital region as a starting point. These exploratory results suggest three potential areas of focus for future research investigating the role of the internet in recent immigrants' social experiences, including neighbourhood contexts, sociocultural contexts, and family contexts. It would further appear that parents monitor online interactions less than they monitor offline social interactions. The role of the internet in the lives of this study's young, recently immigrated participants is highlighted, as it can act as a substitute for forbidden outings with peers and as a place for socialization or dating that may be discouraged by others from taking place.

Notes

1   Amrit Dhariwal, Jennifer Connolly, Marinella Paciello & Gian Vittorio Caprara, "Adolescent Peer Relationships and Emerging Adult Romantic Styles: A Longitudinal Study of Youth in an Italian Community," *Journal of Adolescent Research* 24 (2009): 594–595, doi:10.1177/0743558409341080; Julee P. Farley & Jungmeen Kim-Spoon, "The Development of Adolescent Self-Regulation: Reviewing the Role of Parent, Peer, Friend, and Romantic Relationships," *Journal of Adolescence*, 37:4 (2014): 436–437, <http://www.ncbi.nlm.nih.gov/pubmed/24793391>; Irene H. A. De Goede, Susan J. T. Branje, Marc J. M. H. Delsing & Wim H. J. Meeus, "Linkages Over Time between Adolescents' Relationships with Parents and Friends," *Journal of Youth and Adolescence* 38 (2009): 1312, <http://www.ncbi.nlm.nih.gov/pmc/articles/PMC2758153/>.

2   Mehra Bharat, Cecelia Merkel & Ann Peterson Bishop, "The Internet for Empowerment of Minority and Marginalized Users," *New Media & Society* 6 (2004): 781–802, <http://folders.nottingham.edu.cn/staff/zlizrb/2009_IC_NMW/Mehra_2004.pdf>; Nelly Elias & Dafna Lemish, "Spinning the Web of Identity: The Roles of the Internet in the Lives of Immigrant Adolescents," *New Media & Society* 11 (2009): 533-551, <http://www.israel-sociology.org.il/uploadimages/immigration25.pdf>.

3   Government of Canada, "Canada—Permanent residents by category, 2009–2013," <http://www.cic.gc.ca/english/resources/statistics/facts2013-preliminary/01.asp>.

4   Farah Ahmad, Angela Shik, Reena Vanza, Angela Cheung, Usha George & Donna E. Stewart, "Popular Health Promotion Strategies Among Chinese and East Indian Immigrant Women," *Women and Health* 40 (2004): 21–40, doi:10.1300/J013v40n01_02.

5   Brett Laursen, David Wilder, Peter Noack & Vickie Williams, "Adolescent Perceptions of Reciprocity, Authority and Closeness in Relationships with Mothers, Fathers and Friends," *International Journal of Behavioral Development* 24:4 (2000): 471, <http://jbd.sagepub.com/content/24/4/464.refs.html>

6   *Ibid.* at 470.

7   John W. Berry, Jean S. Phinney, David L. Sam & Paul Vedder, "Immigrant Youth: Acculturation, Identity and Adaptation," *Applied Psychology: An International Review*, 55 (2006): 316–317, <http://www.culturementalhealth.com/wp-content/uploads/2013/10/dwn46726.pdf>

8   Shaibu Ahmed Gariba, *Race, Ethnicity, Immigration and Jobs: Labour Market Access Among Ghanaian and Somali Youth in the Greater Toronto Area* (Toronto: Ontario Institute for Studies in Education of the University of Toronto, 2009), 222–229, unpublished dissertation, <https://tspace.library. utoronto.ca/bitstream/1807/19037/1/Gariba_Shaibu_A_200911_PhD_Thesis.pdf>.

9   Linda P. Juang & Alvin A. Alvarez, "Discrimination and Adjustment Among Chinese American Adolescents: Family Conflict and Family Cohesion as Vulnerability and Protective Factors," *American Journal of Public Health*, 100 (2010): 3–4, <http://www.ncbi.nlm.nih.gov/pmc/articles/ PMC2978186/>.

10   *Ibid.* at 5.

11   Annie J. Ahn, Bryan S. K. Kim & Yong S. Park, "Asian Cultural Values Gap, Cognitive Flexibility, Coping Strategies, and Parent-Child Conflicts Among Korean Americans," *Cultural Diversity and Ethnic Minority Psychology*, 14:4 (2008): 38–41, doi:10.1037/1099-9809.14.4.353.

12   Kimberly A. Updegraff, Melissa Y. Delgado & Lorey A. Wheeler, "Exploring Mothers' and Fathers' Relationships with Sons Versus Daughters: Links to Adolescent Adjustment in Mexican Immigrant Families," *Sex Roles* 60 (2009): 559–574, <http://www.ncbi.nlm.nih.gov/ pmc/articles/PMC2749271/>.

13   Marwan Dwairy & Mustafa Achoui, "Parental Control: A Second Cross-Cultural Research on Parenting and Psychological Adjustment of Children," *Journal of Child and Family Studies*, 19 (2010): 2, 21, <http:// link.springer.com/article/10.1007%2Fs10826-009-9334-2#page-1>.

14   Elias & Lemish, *supra* note 2 at 547.

15   *Ibid.*

16   *Ibid.*; Brendesha M. Tynes, Michael T. Giang & Geneene N. Thompson, "Ethnic Identity, Intergroup Contact, and Outgroup Orientation Among Diverse Groups of Adolescents on the Internet," *CyberPsychology & Behavior* 11 (2008): 463, <http://online.liebertpub.com/doi/abs/10.1089/ cpb.2007.0085>; Bharat et al, *supra* note 2 at 786.

17   Sonia Livingstone & Ellen Helsper, "Balancing Opportunities and Risks in Teenagers' Use of the Internet: The Role of Online Skills and Internet Self-Efficacy," *New Media & Society* 12 (2010): 13–14, <http://core.kmi.open. ac.uk/download/pdf/218744.pdf>; Kelly L. Schmitt, Shoshana Dayanim & Stacey Matthias, "Personal Homepage Construction as an Expression of Social Development," *Developmental Psychology* 44 (2008): 499–500, <http:// www.sovela.net/blogs/mestrado/wp-content/uploads/2011/06/doc8.pdf>; Patti M. Valkenburg & Jochen Peter, "Preadolescents' and Adolescents' Online Communication and Their Closeness to Friends," *Developmental Psychology* 43:2 (2007): 275, <http://dx.doi.org/10.1037/0012-1649.43.2.267>

18 Urie Bronfenbrenner, *The Ecology of Human Development: Experiments by Nature and Design* (Cambridge: Harvard University Press, 1979), 10; Urie Bronfenbrenner & Ann C. Crouter, "The Evolution of Environmental Models in Developmental Research," in *Handbook of Child Psychology, History, Theory and Methods*, 4th ed., eds. Paul Henry Mussen & William Kessen (New York: Wiley, 1983), 357–417; Urie Bronfenbrenner & Pamela Morris, "The Ecology of Developmental Process," in *Handbook of Child Psychology*, eds. William Damon & Richard M. Lerner (New York: John Wiley & Sons, 1998), 993–1028; Urie Bronfenbrenner & Gary W. Evans, "Developmental Science in the 21st Century: Emerging Questions, Theoretical Models, Research Designs and Empirical Findings," *Social Development* 9 (2000): 115–125, <http://onlinelibrary.wiley.com/doi/10.1111/1467-9507.00114/abstract>.

19 Assumpta Ndengeyingoma, Francine de Montigny & Jean-Marie Miron, "Development of Personal Identity among Refugee Adolescents: Facilitating Elements and Obstacles," *Journal of Child Health Care*, Epub (12 August 2013); doi:1367493513496670; Assumpta Ndengeyingoma, Francine de Montigny & Jean-Marie Miron, "Représentations de l'expérience migratoire d'adolescents africains immigrants avec leur famille au Québec," *Revue Québécoise de psychologie* 34 (2013): 114–115.

20 Laurence Manesse, "Autour du concept d'expérience chez Benjamin," *Revue Appareil* (2011): 7–8, <http://revues.mshparisnord.org/appareil/pdf/1172.pdf>.

21 Ministère de l'Immigration, de la diversité et de l'Inclusion, "L'immigration permanente au Québec selon les catégories d'immigration et quelques composantes 2009–2013," 66,<http://www.midi.gouv.qc.ca/publications/fr/recherches-statistiques/Portraits_categories_2009-2013.pdf>.

22 Michael Huberman & Matthew B. Miles, "Data Management and Analysis Methods," in *Collecting and Interpreting Qualitative Materials*, eds. Norman K. Denzin & Yvonna S. Lincoln (Thousand Oaks, CA: Sage, 2000), 220.

23 Norman K. Denzin, Yvonna S. Lincoln & Michael D. Giardina, "Disciplining Qualitative Research," *International Journal of Qualitative Studies in Education* 19 (2006): 778, <http://www.petajwhite.net/Uni/910/Legit%20and%20Representation/Representation%20Precis/Denzin%20Lincoln%20and%20Giardina.pdf>.

24 Pierre Vermersch, "Vécus et couches des vécus," *Expliciter* 66 (2006): 40–41, <http://www.academia.edu/7474892/V%C3%A9cus_etcouches_des_v%C3%A9cus._Questionner_le_d%C3%A9roulement_dun_entretien_V3>.

25 Claire Petitmengin, "Describing One's Subjective Experience in the Second Person, an Interview Method for the Science of Consciousness,"

Phenomenology and the Cognitive Sciences 5 (2006): 13–29, <http://espra. scicog.fr/Petitmengin%20Second%20person%20methods.pdf>.

26 Pascal Paillé & Adalgisa Battistelli, *L'Analyse qualitative en sciences sociales* (Paris: Armand Colin, 2003), 147–148.

27 *Ibid.*

28 Ndengeyingoma, de Montigny & Miron, *supra* note 19 at 114–115.

29 The interview transcripts, which were originally transcribed in French, were translated into English.

30 Commission Scolaire English-Montreal, "Registration" (Montreal: English Montreal School Board), subheading 4: <http://www.emsb.qc.ca/en/services_en/pages/registration_en.asp>.

31 Michael D. Reiter, Katherine Richmond, Amber Stirlen & Natalia Kompel, "Exploration of Intimacy in Intercultural and Intracultural Romantic Relationships in College Students," *College Student Journal* 43 (2009): 1080.

32 Cindy L. Shearer, Ann C. Crouter & Susan McHale, "Parents' Perceptions of Changes in Mother-Child, Father-Child Relationships During Adolescence," *Journal of Adolescent Research* 20:6 (2005): 662–684, doi:10.1177/0743558405275086.

33 Stephanie M. Reich & Kaveri Subrahmanyam, "Friending, IMing, and Hanging Out Face-to-Face: Overlap in Adolescents' Online and Offline Social Networks," *Developmental Psychology* 48 (2012): 361–365, doi:10.1037/a0026980.

CHAPTER V

"She's Just a Small Town Girl, Living in an Online World": Differences and Similarities between Urban and Rural Girls' Use of and Views about Online Social Networking

Jacquelyn Burkell and Madelaine Saginur

Introduction

This chapter examines the online social media experiences of girls (aged 15 to 17) and young women (aged 18 to 22) from rural and urban environments, focusing on the contrast between "small town" and "big city" participants in online social networks. Reasoning from a long history of social scientific research and thought, we anticipate that rural and urban girls and young women will report different experiences with online social media. We explore this possibility through a series of interviews and focus groups conducted with girls and young women residing in two communities (one small, one large) in southeastern Ontario, Canada.

The Urban/Rural Landscape in Canada

There is no question that Canadian society is moving toward urban living. In 1851, only 13 percent of Canadians lived in centres with populations of more than 1000; a hundred years later, the proportion was 62 percent, and by 2011, 81 percent of Canadians lived in population centres of 1000 residents or more.[1] In fact, the majority of Canadians now live in *large* urban centres: 2011 Census results indicate that 60 percent of Canadians live in urban centres with populations of 100,000 or more, 9 percent live in medium-sized population centres (populations of 30,000 to 99,999), and the remaining 31 percent live in rural areas and small centres with populations between 1,000 and 29,999.[2] These data highlight an unequivocal shift in the living situation of Canadians – a shift that mirrors the situation in the US and other countries around the world.[3]

The impact of urbanization of the North American population has been a focus of social scientific research since the early 1900s. Much of the research and discussion has revolved around the anticipated losses associated with the shift to an urban environment. In the early 1900s, for example, sociologist Georg Simmel noted that since urban dwellers come into contact with vast numbers of people each day, they conserve psychic energy by becoming acquainted with a far smaller proportion of people than their rural counterparts do, and by maintaining more superficial relationships even with these acquaintances.[4] Stanley Milgram, in his article "The Experience of Living in Cities," discussed how "the interposition of institutions between the individual and the social world" in cities "deprives the individual of a sense of direct contact and spontaneous integration in the life around him [sic]," simultaneously protecting and estranging the individual from their social environment.[5] Louis Wirth remarked on the "peculiar characteristics of the city as a particular form of human association,"[6] enumerating what he considered were the key characteristics of urban life: knowing a smaller proportion (though not necessarily a smaller number) of, and knowing less deeply, people whom individuals encounter; meeting each other in "highly segmented roles"; and having social relations characterized by "the superficiality, the anonymity, and the transitory character of urban social relations."[7] The notion of the urban environment as anonymous is echoed by Milgram, who explains that anonymity exists on a spectrum, with higher levels of anonymity associated with cities and lower levels associated with small town.[8] Thus, there was a general concern that urbanization would lead to less personal connection between people.

Support for this perspective, however, is not universal, and some scholars have taken issue with the view that urban life is qualitatively different from life in smaller communities, pointing out that, in many larger urban centres, neighbourhoods function as smaller "communities within communities." According to John Jakle, for example, the big city and small town have been stereotyped in the American experience as being at opposite ends of an imagined social gradient — the former more a place of cold impersonality in social relations and the latter more a place of warm personalized community. Assumptions about urban-based "mass society" largely blinded Americans through the twentieth century to the existence of, and importance of, locality-based community in big cities.[9]

Empirical investigations comparing rural to urban life reveal a small number of relatively stable predicted differences. In 1982, Claude Fischer published a study of personal networks of individuals living in towns and cities in northern California. The results suggest that those living in urban settings have fewer relatives in their social networks, and have social networks that are less densely connected; furthermore, individuals within the social networks of urban residents are less likely to share multiplex ties — that is, relationships that are based on multiple different types of connections (e.g., being family members, neighbours, *and* co-workers).[10] These results are consistent with more recent research findings that have found the social networks of rural residents to be smaller and more densely interconnected than those of urban dwellers.[11] These same studies reveal somewhat inconsistent results with respect to the homogeneity of social connections (e.g., in relation to age, gender, education, race/ethnicity, and religious affiliation), with rural residents generally (but not always) having less varied social networks; in addition, the social networks of urban residents include more non-kin ties.[12]

Fischer noted one other significant difference between rural and urban environments. According to his data, urbanization is related to a shift away from traditional values — thus, urban residents are more likely than rural residents to tolerate deviation from traditional strictures related to issues such as sexuality and religion.[13] While Fischer's data were collected in the late 1970s, and thus may have limited application to current society, more recent studies have found consistent results, demonstrating that rural Americans are in general more socially conservative than those living in urban or suburban areas, particularly with respect to religiosity, abortion, and same-sex relationships.[14] Recent international research indicates that tolerance — both of differences in general (e.g., neighbours of a different race or religion) and specifically of differences that are perceived as signalling threat (e.g., drug use by neighbours) – is positively related to community size: residents of larger communities show higher levels of tolerance.[15]

The "conditions of full acquaintance"[16] that are thought to characterize the rural environment, especially given the context of increased adherence to traditional values, wield a double-edged sword. As Milgram states, these conditions "offer security and familiarity, but they may also be stifling, because the individual is caught in a web of established relationships. Conditions of complete anonymity, by contrast, provide freedom from routinized social ties, but they may also create feelings of alienation and detachment."[17] Some empirical data support the notion that small town and rural environments are sites of unwelcome and indeed restricting social visibility, especially for adolescents. Health care providers who work in the sensitive areas of sexuality[18] and addiction services[19] suggest that confidentiality and anonymity are key issues for rural adolescents seeking health care, particularly when that care is associated with potentially stigmatized situations or conditions. Rural adolescents who identify as homosexual, for example, experience higher levels of distress than those living in urban environments.[20] The differences, however, are not large, and research on the experience of lesbian, gay, and bisexual adults living in rural environments reveals inconsistent results. Some data suggests that those living in rural areas fare better than those living in urban environments,[21] while other data suggest that lesbian, gay, and bisexual adults living in rural areas experience greater levels of heterosexist stigma.[22]

The Online World for Urban and Rural Canadians

In recent decades, the internet has provided an alternative – or additional – milieu for social life. Social media sites including MySpace, Facebook, Twitter, Pinterest, YouTube, and Instagram have provided an online environment for rich social interaction since the early 2000s. The online social environment is, in some ways, a curious hybrid of the characteristics that were traditionally associated with rural social life and those that were traditionally associated with urban social life. On the one hand, the architecture of online social networks facilitates the encountering of strangers that is typically associated with urban environments; at the same time, this same architecture impedes the ability to segment, a quality generally associated with rural environments. Online interactions may often be superficial and can be – and often are – anonymous; however, they are certainly not transitory. One salient aspect of online social networks is that they reduce (but do not eliminate) the effects of geographic distance.[23] In the online social environment, participants can and do maintain relationships with geographically distant friends and family, and establish new relationships with people they have never met in person – and indeed may never meet.

Although residents in rural areas have been slower to take up many online activities,[24] at least in part because they are less likely to have high-speed access,[25] home internet access is increasing in both rural and urban areas.[26] Canadian statistics reveal that in 2009, 68.4 percent of rural households had home internet access (compared to 79.7 percent of urban households), with the percentage even higher for those households that included unmarried children under 18 (84.6 percent of rural households compared to 90.1 percent of urban households).[27] According to the 2010 Canadian Internet Use Survey, 70 percent of rural residents have internet access, a figure significantly less than the 82 percent of Canadians living in urban areas who have that same access.[28] In the US, among those who have internet access, the majority (over 67 percent) use one or more social media sites (Facebook, Twitter, Instagram, Pinterest, or LinkedIn), and although there are some significant rural/suburban/urban differences in use, these are small in size (e.g., 70 percent of urban residents use at least one social networking site, compared to 61 percent of rural residents; note, however, there is no significant difference for Facebook use, which is 72 percent for urban residents and 63 percent for rural residents).[29] Recent Canadian data on the same question reveal that among those with internet access, 54 percent of those living in rural areas use online social networks compared to 58 percent of those living in urban areas: although there is a small difference between the groups, place of residence (rural/urban) is not a significant predictor of social networking site use.[30] Thus, it appears that while rural residents continue to experience a small deficit in terms of internet access, among those who do have access, the use of the internet for social networking is similar to that of their urban counterparts.

The advent of the internet has radically changed rural life, reducing the impact of geographic isolation and increasing access to services, information, and social connection.[31] In general, empirical research suggests that the size of social networks is increasing over time across the entire population (rural and urban alike), an effect that can be attributed at least in part to the increased capacity for online social interaction; this increase may be particularly important for rural residents, whose face-to-face social networks tend to be smaller.[32] "Some pundits have optimistically imagined that information and communication technologies such as the internet will reduce – and possibly even eliminate – 'the tyranny of space and distance.'"[33] Consistent with these predictions, in many respects the online social networks of urban and rural participants are similar, encompassing large numbers of geographically distributed connections.

Some data suggest that rural residents tend to wait longer to join online social networks, and their network of online connections tends to be slightly smaller, with connections more likely to be with people who live close by.[34] Overall, however, there are relatively few documented differences between the online social networks of rural and urban participants, a fact that may be explained by the relative independence of online social networks from geographic constraint, and the "friend of friend" linking that tends to characterize online social networks.[35] Online social networks provide opportunity to maintain existing relationships and forge new ones independent of geographic constraint. There is opportunity to identify and connect with like-minded others,[36] forming virtual communities with others who are widely distributed in real space. In many ways, these online social networks seem designed to minimize if not fully eliminate the rural/urban differences in social networks, potentially allowing those who live in rural areas a space to develop and maintain larger and less densely connected social networks with others who hold similar values. Thus, for rural residents, and particularly for rural adolescents and young adults, these networks may provide a welcome and indeed necessary space for identity development.

At the same time, the online social environment offers unprecedented opportunity for social surveillance[37] (characterized as interveillance,[38] participatory surveillance,[39] or lateral surveillance[40]) and control through

(1) watching and judging others;
(2) watching others watching oneself; and
(3) watching one's own online profile.[41]

Within the online social environment, "peers develop strategies for keeping track of one another, and those who write about new media might even go so far as to suggest that contemporary strategies for mutual monitoring merely rehabilitate, in technological form, the everyone-knows-everyone-else's-business world of traditional village life, undoing the anonymity of urbanized modernity."[42] Social network participants respond to various forms of social surveillance by limiting or controlling their own online presence to conform to prevailing norms.[43] Given the ubiquity of online surveillance and the ease with which surveillance can be accomplished, this raises the possibility that online social networks, rather than being a site where aspects of identity can be freely explored, instead become locales of increasingly restricted social expression. This could create increased pressure on rural social network participants, particularly if their smaller, more densely connected, and more multiplexed real-world social networks form a significant part of their online social worlds.

The eGirls Data

At this point in time, it remains an open question whether the online social environment is one that erases or exacerbates rural/urban differences in social experience. The current chapter addresses this question through data collected in a qualitative exploration of the online social experiences of girls and young women: The eGirls Project.[44]

In January and February of 2013 researchers with the eGirls Project held a series of interviews and focus groups with girls and young women between the ages of 15 and 22. All participants used interactive online media (such as social networking, blogging, and/or user-generated video sites) as a regular part of their social lives. Half of our sample resided in an urban Ontario setting and half resided in a rural Ontario setting.

We interviewed six girls aged 15 to 17 and six young women aged 18 to 22. An additional twenty-two participated in four focus group discussions, as follows: (1) seven girls aged 15 to 17 living in the urban setting; (2) five girls aged 15 to 17 living in the rural setting; (3) six young women aged 18 to 22 living in the urban setting; and (4) four young women aged 18 to 22 living in the rural setting. A professional research house recruited our participants on the basis of sex, age (either 15 to 17 or 18 to 22), and location of residence (urban or rural). While participants were not recruited on the basis of self-identification with regard to other aspects of their identities, such as race, ethnicity, gender identity, or sexual orientation, our participant group included members of racialized, linguistic, and various religious groups.

In the interviews and the focus groups, we explored, among other things, the types of visual and textual representations the participants used online to express their identity as young women, and the benefits and pitfalls they experienced on social media. We also asked for their views on the issues and policy responses focused on by policymakers (as identified in the review of federal parliamentary debates previously reported upon and summarized above).

With participant permission, the interviews and focus group were audiotaped and transcribed by our research assistants for analysis. All identifying information was removed from the transcripts, and pseudonyms were used to identify participants.[45]

In this chapter, we examine four themes that were salient in the interviews and focus groups:

1. awareness of and reflection on the urban/rural contrast;
2. the nature of online social networks;
3. freedom and constraint in online self-expression; and
4. managing conflict at the online-offline junction.

This chapter seeks to tease apart differences – and identify similarities – in how rural girls and young women versus urban girls and young women use social media and think about the associated benefits, risks and other issues.

I'm a "Small Town" Girl

One thing that became acutely evident from the data is that rural research participants are at least somewhat aware of their "ruralness," while urban research participants are oblivious to their own "urbanness." Four of the rural participants (two younger focus group participants, one younger interview participant, and one older interview participant) spontaneously noted the impact of small-town life on their online experience, but not one of the urban participants remarked on the importance of the urban nature of their lives. This discrepancy makes sense if we consider the representativeness of each of these living environments: according to the 2011 census, approximately one in three Canadians lives in rural areas or centres with 10,000 or fewer residents, while over half live in large urban centres with populations of over 100,000. Thus, our rural participants are decidedly different, in their living environment, than the majority of Canadians with whom they are likely to compare themselves.

The nature of the differences attributed to the rural/urban divide differed across respondents. Chelsea (17, rural) identified her community as safer than urban environments, remarking that while some [presumably rural] girls are "naïve" about the risk of encountering a sexual predator online, she didn't "find a lot of them in [town] because we are a small town." Cassandra, 19, attributed the appeal of online "drama "[46] to the lack of other available activities in her community: "small town, nothing to do." Sixteen-year-old Nicole contrasted the online presence of "rural girls" with that of "city girls," noting that city girls appeared "flawless" and "perfect" in their online photos, generating acknowledgement in the form of many "likes." She goes on to discuss how these online photographs are "photoshopped" to make the girls appear more attractive, since in person these apparently "flawless" girls are less attractive, looking just like "typical" girls. According to Nicole, city girls are more likely than their rural counterparts to "amp" themselves on the internet through practices such as the photoshopping of images because in small towns "everyone knows each other," implying that in such densely connected real-world networks it is more difficult to successfully present an online look that is different from your real-life appearance. Using concepts introduced by Goffman,[47] the densely connected social networks of rural girls make it more difficult for them to maintain a "back stage/front stage" separation, and breaches of this distinction create greater complexity for impression management. Nicole also commented on the multiplexed nature of rural social networks:

> Nicole: My sister, the other night this guy is coming over and she told me his last name, and I heard about his brother and he's just, you know, one of those guys that's into drugs and stuff. And I'm like "he shouldn't come over," and she's like "just because you think you know him doesn't mean he's a bad guy," but obviously everything that happens gets around town.

This issue is also reflected in the comments of a fourth participant, Paula, 17, whose account illustrates the impact of multiple interconnections in a small rural community:

> Paula: And I think it's different living in a small town, 'cause you just really know everyone on Facebook. Like, you actually know them, and they live on your street, or they're your cousin, or they go to your school … Or your cousin goes to your school. Happens to all of us … for example, like, I think if I lived in Toronto and [Beth, another rural girl in the focus group] lived in Toronto and I saw her post all that stuff and she went to my school, I'd think, "Oh, she's different." But I know [Beth], because I live in [name of town] and it's a small town. So you've built more of a relationship than social media … I think some people post things on Facebook, but I know that's not really how they are, because I've actually interacted with them not using the internet.

Her comments reflect an experience of dense and multi-stranded real-world social networks that blend seamlessly with social networks in the online environment. Her perspective, consistent with that of a number of other rural participants, is that the multi-stranded online and offline connectedness that characterizes her social world is *different* from the social reality experienced by girls living in urban environments. Urban girls and young women, who also describe this overlap between face-to-face and online environments, might disagree: but whether or not the difference is borne out in experience, our rural participants *believe* that their online social experience is different from that of girls and young women living in urban environments.

Rural/Urban Contrast in Online Networks

All of the girls and young women participating in this research described their online social networks as large and geographically dispersed, composed both of individuals with whom they have significant real-world interaction and others with whom they are connected only online. Parents and even employers were identified as part of the online social networks of many of the interview and focus group participants, although some reported restricting content or access to content for these groups, and others indicated that they explicitly excluded parents and/or employers from their online social networks. While some online interactions represented extensions of face-to-face activities (e.g., online negotiation of plans for the evening), in other cases online interactions were identified as a way of maintaining relationships with connections that were more geographically distant (e.g., family/friends who had moved away, or were more distant because the participant had themselves moved). In addition, many of the girls and some of the young women reported online connections with no "real world" component: online acquaintances and even friends whom they had never met in person and were not planning to meet in the future.[48]

One might anticipate that the observed differences in real-world rural and urban social networks would translate into the online environment in one of two ways: either rural participants would describe online networks that were denser and more multiplex than those described by urban participants, or rural participants would be more likely to befriend or otherwise interact with strangers online to satisfy a desire for a broader, more diverse social network than what is available to them in the physical world. Neither of these hypotheses was supported by the data. In their spontaneous discussion of their online networks, our respondents demonstrate no such difference: with respect to their discussion of the size and nature of their online social networks, our rural and urban respondents are indistinguishable. We cannot rule out the possibility that a detailed quantitative analysis of network size, density, or multiplexity would reveal rural/urban differences. In their discussions, however, our participants do not signal any salient differences; moreover, although rural participants identify various ways in which their online experience differs from that of their urban counterparts, the nature of their online social networks is *not* an identified difference.[49] Finally, there are indications in our data that rural and urban girls and young women are in fact linked in their social networks, a situation that likely arises from the "friend of friend" connections that give rise to many social network invitations: for example, Trish (rural, 18) revealed that "half" of her friends "added" her boyfriend from Montreal as a connection, thus creating a link between people living in her rural community and those living in the urban centre of Montreal. This suggests (but again does not confirm) that those living in geographically separate urban and rural environments may in fact share online community.

Free to Be Me (or Not)

Evidence suggests that the internet provides an environment where young people can explore alternative identities, a function that might be particularly important, and valuable, for rural girls and young women, whose self-expression could be more limited by their social environment.[50] At the same time, the online social world is not entirely distinct from the face-to-face social environment, and there is every reason to suspect that events and activities in one milieu would spill over to the other, potentially limiting online self-expression for fear of real-world consequences. We reasoned that this concern might affect rural girls and young women — with their densely interconnected and multiplexed real-world social networks — more than it affected those living in an urban environment. Surprisingly, neither expectation was reflected in our data.

Most of our participants (rural and urban, younger and older) agreed that online profiles are not "real" profiles, but instead are carefully crafted to promote a particular image. Thus, they do not identify online social spaces as spaces of individual self-expression, but instead experience these as spaces of socially enforced conformity. Profiles are characterized as "real but limited" (Abby, urban, 17), and what is posted online is identified as "a way of hiding yourself" (Paula, rural, 17), providing "an idea of what they're like, but not the whole idea" (Courtney, rural, 17). Girls and young women, both rural and urban, typically create online profiles to "fit in," posting information "that's not really how they are" (Paula, rural, 17), and sometimes even getting caught up in this manufactured online image: "they get so caught up with it that they have to post pictures all the time of their 'other' image or who they wanna be and forget about who they really are. That's not good" (Vicky, urban, 17).

With respect to this enforced conformity, there appeared to be no difference between our urban and rural participants, and their descriptions of the "right" kind of online image, and the need to present such an image, were effectively indistinguishable and interchangeable.

Both urban and rural participants noted the importance of presenting the "right" image online, to parents, employers, and male and female peers. Several discussed limiting or editing content to conform to this image. In particular, overly sexualized images and images of drinking were considered as potentially problematic, since they could upset parents, negatively affect employment, and result in being labelled as "slutty" by male and female classmates. Many participants refrained from including these kinds of images in their online profiles. At the same time, appropriately sexy images were identified by a number of participants as necessary for popularity with girls and desirability to boys. In some cases, parents and/or employers were excluded from online social networks in order to restrict access to content that might be considered problematic, and one respondent went so far as to maintain, for a period of time, a "clean" parallel online profile intended only for close family.

Participants were also concerned about the "small world" problem, whereby information posted to a social network profile could "leak" to unintended audiences. One rural participant, for example, remarked that her mother was concerned that other members of their church would see the "party" photographs of her daughter, thus engendering judgment of both mother and daughter:

> Amelia (rural, 18): We're a Christian family, so we go to church … but I will go out and, um, I will go out and have some drinks with some friends … I've had a couple of, I guess argue, well not arguments, but talks with my parents about how, um, my mom doesn't want pictures of me drinking on Facebook just because I'm friends with people who are from, just like the church community, and she said "I just don't want people seeing that and making judgments" … I said, "why are you so worried about what people will think when it's not what they think of you, it's what they think of me," but she explained it to me … "you are my child, I've raised you a way and I don't want people to make judgments about me from your actions."

While the question of judgment *vis-à-vis* traditional values *might* be specific to the rural environment, the issue of overlapping social groups certainly is not. Alessandra (urban, 21), discussing conflict over a photograph in which she appeared with the ex-boyfriend of a Facebook contact, noted "we have small social circles, I can't escape it if your boyfriend is at the same bar as me," while Cindy (urban, 20) noted that the notoriety that could be associated with a compromising photograph would easily travel between the three high schools in the city through social connections between students.

Thus, it appears that rural and urban participants share an experience of online social networks as spaces for tightly constrained social display that is limited both by peer group expectations and by the concern that posted information might "leak" across social groups and into offline environments. We observed no evidence of differences in the expectations or experiences of rural and urban participants: in particular, rural participants appeared no more likely to use online social spaces as sites of exploration, nor did they exhibit higher levels of concern about information reaching unintended audiences.

Managing Online/Offline Connections

"Drama" is a common aspect of online social experience,[51] played out in full view of social network members through status lines, posts, and comments on photographs. As Regan and Sweet note, online drama serves three interrelated functions: social aggression, monitoring and evaluating the behaviour of others, and amusement/leisure.[52] Although both girls and young women described "drama" in their online social environments, the issue was particularly relevant for the younger participants, and some of the young adults, when discussing online drama, identified it as something that happened "in high school." There were few identifiable differences between the discussions of rural and urban participants. All indicated that drama is often triggered by photographs and played out in terms of traded comments visible to the entire social network; that drama usually starts between two people, but others often join the fray; and that people not involved follow the online drama just to see what is happening (a form of entertainment).

While much drama is born and carried out in the online environment, both rural and urban participants described some occasions when offline drama moved online (e.g., when conflicts over relationships played out in the online environment). Reports of these experiences of interlaced real-world and online conflict were characteristic of the reports of both urban and rural participants, though more common for the girls than for the young women. In addition, most incidents that were described by participants were conducted in full view of the online social network, through tweets, Facebook timeline posts, or comments on photographs that were available to all online "friends" in the interconnected social network. In fact, this semi-public nature was intrinsic to much online drama, allowing initially uninvolved others to join and even take sides, and allowing those choosing to remain uninvolved to watch the drama from the sidelines as it unfolded.

The vast majority of participants appeared aware of the "hot-house" atmosphere of the online environment that can exacerbate online conflict. Both rural and urban participants seemed to be aware that face-to-face communication simply *works* better in these situations, and thus might be preferable to online interaction in order to minimize conflict. Monica (rural, 16) put it this way: when communicating face-to-face, "you can kind of see their reactions, and know how they're speaking to you." Monique (urban, 16) provides a very similar perspective:

> There's so much more happening when you're talking to someone face to face, you know your tone and body image and just everything else. It's so much easier to have those miscommunications over the internet, and so when you're talking about something serious, or you know if there's a fight going on … it should be done in person because you know you never really know what exactly, like because the words are taken out of their context [and] it's hard to really know how to react to that ….

There is some awareness that online communication can lead to mis-understanding: Chelsea (rural, 17) said that she doesn't joke around in written comments because "it might be taken the wrong way, and I've had it done. And I'm like, whoa, I didn't even mean it like that. And I'm like, okay, I'm not even touching my phone [for text messaging] for the rest of the day."

However, rural girls tended to react quite differently to being the target of negative online comments or bullying. All of the rural girls who were interviewed individually and some of the rural girls in the focus group stated that they had or they would talk face to face to someone who insulted or attacked them online. The rural girls were also more likely to comment on, and report attending to, the possibility that online drama could lead to breakdown of real-world relationships. Monica (rural, 16), for example, stated that, if she learned that she had been sitting at home alone on a night when friends were hanging out together, she would deal with the issue in person rather than starting drama online by posting a sarcastic status line about her friends. Another rural girl, Lynda (17), indicated that she would choose a face-to-face confrontation with anyone bullying her online rather than continuing the online interaction. A third rural girl, Nicole (16), said that in response to problematic comments on Facebook or twitter, she would text the person and say "let's not put it on Twitter or Facebook 'cause no one else needs to know our problems, you know?" These and other rural girls appeared to value private (and typically face-to-face) interaction as a way of settling (or at least not escalating) online conflicts.

Rural girls indicated that face-to-face interaction was preferable because it gave them better opportunity to assess, and limit, the impact of their comments or responses. One rural girl indicated that she would simply refrain from posting negative commentary on someone's online photo because, "you kind of have to put yourselves in their shoes, you never know how they're feeling that day, you never know what's going on in their life, and some things are enough to push someone over the edge" (Monica, rural, 16). Another rural girl, Chelsea (17), acknowledged that while she was able to "brush off" anonymous "hate messages" on Tumblr, these messages might "upset" others.

Despite acknowledging that face-to-face communication has the advantage of helping to avoid miscommunication and therefore encouraging dispute resolution, *none* of the urban girls indicated that they would move an online conflict to the offline context. The urban girls appeared to prioritize "winning" the argument over resolving it amicably. For example, Alicia (urban, 17) said it was easier to put an online bully "in her place" over MSN because, "she can't really see me." All the urban girls in the focus group agreed, "it's easier to say what you think [online] because your face isn't attached to it." Lauryn (urban 17) can't imagine *anyone* taking an online conflict offline because it precludes a "public" victory in the dispute:

> No one would actually go up to someone and be like "hey can we talk about this in private," and then go somewhere in private and be like "hey I don't like what you're doing, I don't like what you're saying, and stuff," but it seems like people want it, like want the attention, want everyone to see that they're tough.

None of the urban girls raised emotional reactions – their own or those of others in their social network – as a reason to move from online to face-to-face interaction.

One potential explanation for this difference is as follows: all of the girls want to have friendships in the offline world, and all of the girls want to put forward a good, powerful, popular image online.

However, when these two things come into conflict, their relative importance is different for urban and rural girls. For rural girls, with their smaller, more interconnected offline networks, offline relationships are of primary importance. We suggest that for rural girls, because there are fewer possibilities for offline friendships, maintaining an offline relationship is more valuable than "winning" an online conflict. For urban girls, with wider, more dispersed offline networks and many more possibilities for meeting new people, it appears to be the opposite: online image is ultimately given more weight. As a number of urban girl focus group participants explain:

> Jacquelyn (urban, 17): Yeah, everyone wants to prove, I don't know, everyone wants to prove that they can, like, they can outdo the other person or, like, show them that they're better than the other person and they want everyone else to see.
> Abby (urban, 17): Intimidate.
> Jacquelyn (urban, 17): Like, intimidate them.
> Researcher: How come, like, why is that a good thing?
> Eve (urban, 16): I just, like, it's power, you know, it's a feeling and you want more.

Interestingly, this distinction appeared significantly less apparent among the older group of participants. The rural young women, like their younger counterparts, tended to prefer face-to-face interactions to address conflict that originated online, and this tendency was also demonstrated among the urban young women. One urban young woman recounts an incident that occurred to her:

> Mackenzie (urban, 20): Um, I've really only seen one, I guess [stumbles over words] …. It wasn't a catfight between two girls, but it was like two girls seriously bad-mouthing a third friend, and you just don't want to get into that, because you're, like, I know that if I say anything, even just to say I'm not involved in this … that automatically makes me involved in this somehow …. So I just [pause] didn't put anything on Facebook, but I did go them the next day and was like, "hey, still friends with this person. Not a bad person. So going to say straight up from here, you guys may have a problem with her, but I do not."

Another urban young woman, Cindy (20), clearly states that conflict should be resolved privately and not on Facebook. This shift for urban participants — from a focus on "online power" as girls toward a preference for resolving conflict offline — could be a maturational effect. We noted less focus on "drama" among *all* young women in the study when compared to the girls who participated, as well as a relaxation of the need to appear "cool," or "popular," or "powerful."

Conclusion

There can be no doubt that small-town life is changing. Not only are fewer and fewer people living in rural areas or small urban centres, but the nature of the residents has also changed. In the US, for example, immigration has changed the demographic profile of small-town residents,[53] many small towns have become "bedroom" communities for nearby larger urban centres, and wealthier urbanites move (full- or part-time) to smaller urban or rural centres for a different way of life.[54] At the same time, it remains true that "everyone in a small town knows everyone else's business."[55]

The focus of this paper is the contrast between the online experiences of girls and young women living in rural (small town) versus urban environments. Our primary finding is that there are in fact very few reported differences in online experiences between these two groups. Although some rural participants identify their "ruralness" as having an impact on their online social lives, the discussions of rural and urban participants are virtually indistinguishable with respect to the nature of their online social networks and the character of their online social activities. For the most part, rural and urban participants describe their online networks in very similar terms, with these networks including family, relatives, close friends, and acquaintances (including those developed online) from both nearby and more distant geographic locations. Their descriptions of social surveillance from online and offline connections are, similarly, virtually indistinguishable, and rural and urban participants report similar social constraints on the content of their online profiles.

Our data do suggest one interesting difference. "Drama" was salient in the online experiences of almost all of our participants, and in the majority of cases it played out online and was visible to an audience that included all members of the online social networks of the participants. Indeed, in some cases, "audience" members commented on and even joined in the online drama, encouraged by the original participants as part of a process of establishing friendship or social value. Young women, both urban and rural, reported less "drama," and described it in similar ways. Rural and urban girls, however, demonstrated a difference. While rural girls described "drama" in terms similar to those used by their urban counterparts, they differed in one way: for rural girls, taking drama "offline" or at least to private communication appeared to be, in at least some circumstances, a preferable alternative. When rural girls described moving a semi-public online conflict to a private and often offline context, they offered two rationales: first, that face-to-face interaction offered the opportunity for clearer communication; second, that they were better able to assess the impact of communication and limit the degree to which they were inflicting emotional pain when communicating face-to-face. This privileging of face-to-face relationships makes sense, given the smaller real-world communities in which rural girls live: in a town of ten thousand compared to one of one million, there are simply far fewer alternatives for everyday real-world social interaction, and girls and young women living in small towns can ill afford to alienate large numbers of friends and acquaintances. No matter how large, rich, and indeed engrossing the online social world is for these girls and young women, real-world social interaction remains of primary importance, and when there are few real-world relationships to choose from, it is important that those relationships be maintained.

This finding warrants further exploration. We observed this difference in participants recruited for a qualitative research study examining the online experiences of rural and urban girls and young women, and additional research is required to determine if the differences generalize to other populations. If, upon further research, this distinction appears to hold, it would be an important factor to consider when designing policy and educational responses to issues, such as cyberbullying, that are raised by online social interaction. The finding suggests that rural and urban girls might be responsive to different educational interventions, with urban girls more likely to respond to an intervention that unpacks the online power dynamic involved in cyberbullying, and rural girls more likely to respond to an intervention that focuses on the emotional impact of cyberbullying. Educational and policy responses should take into account the different perspectives uncovered by this research, and build both into their approaches to new media education and policy.

Notes

1   Statistics Canada, "Population, Urban and Rural, by Province and Territory (Canada)," <http://www.statcan.gc.ca/tables-tableaux/sum-som/l01/cst01/demo62a-eng.htm>.
2   Statistics Canada, "Distribution of Population by Size of Population Centre, 2006 and 2011 Censuses," <http://www.statcan.gc.ca/pub/92-195-x/2011001/geo/pop/tbl/tbl10-eng.htm>.
3   United Nations Department of Economic and Social Affairs, Population Division, "World Urbanization Prospects, the 2014 revision," <http://esa.un.org/unpd/wup/>.
4   Georg Simmel, *The Sociology of Georg Simmel*, ed. K.H. Wolff (Macmillan: New York, 1950).
5   Stanley Milgram, "The Experience of Living in Cities," *Science* 167:3924 (1970): 1462, <http://www.cl.cam.ac.uk/~dq209/others/experience.pdf>.
6   Louis Wirth, "Urbanism as a Way of Life," *American Journal of Sociology* 44:1 (1938): 4, <http://www.sjsu.edu/people/saul.cohn/courses/city/so/2768119[1]Wirth.pdf>.
7   *Ibid.*, at 12. Milgram includes notes that Wirth was criticized for not noting that cities are made up of neighbourhoods that function like small towns and he cites by way of example, H. J. Gans, *People and Plans: Essays on Urban Problems and Solutions* (Basic Books: New York, 1968); Jane Jacobs, *The Death and Life of Great American Cities* (Random House: New York, 1961); and others.
8   Milgram, *supra* note 5 at 1462.
9   John A. Jakle, "America's Small Town/Big City Dialectic," *Journal of Cultural Geography* 18:2 (1999): 1, doi:10.1080/08873639909478302.
10   Claude S. Fischer, *To Dwell Among Friends* (The University of Chicago Press: Chicago, 1982).
11   J. J. Beggs, V. A. Haines & J. S. Hurlbert, "Revisiting the Rural-Urban Contrast: Personal Networks in Nonmetropolitan and Metropolitan Settings," *Rural Sociology* 61:2 (1996): 306–325, doi:10.1111/j.1549-0831.1996.tb00622.x; K. J. C. White & A. M. Guest, "Community Lost or Transformed? Urbanization and Social Ties," *City & Community* 2 (2003): 239–259.
12   White & Guest, *ibid.*
13   Fischer, *supra* note 10.

14   Michele Dillon & Sarah Savage, "Values and Religion in Rural America: Attitudes Toward Abortion and Same-Sex Relations," *The Carsey Institute at the Scholars' Repository* 1 (2006), <http://scholars.unh.edu/carsey/12/>.

15   Christopher M. Huggins & Jeffrey Debies-Carl. "Tolerance in the City: The Multilevel Effects of Urban Environments on Permissive Attitudes," *Journal of Urban Affairs* (2014), doi:10.1111/juaf.12141.

16   Milgram, *supra* note 5 at 1466.

17   *Ibid.* at 1464.

18   Ruth Garside, Richard Ayres, Mike Owen, Virginia A.H. Pearson & Judith Roizen, "Anonymity and Confidentiality: Rural Teenagers' Concerns when Accessing Sexual Health Services," *The Journal of Family Planning and Reproductive Health Care* 28 (2002): 23–24, <http://jfprhc.bmj.com/content/28/1/23.long>.

19   Catherine T. Baca, Dale C. Alverson, Jennifer Knapp Manuel & Greg L. Blackwell, "Telecounseling in Rural Areas for Alcohol Problems," *Alcoholism Treatment Quarterly* 25:4 (2007): 31–45, doi:10.1300/J020v25n04_03.

20   Tracy J. Cohn & Valerie S. Leake, "Affective Distress Among Adolescents Who Endorse Same-Sex Sexual Attraction: Urban versus Rural Differences and the Role of Protective Factors," *Journal of Gay & Lesbian Mental Health* 16:4 (2012): 291–305, doi:10.1080/19359705.2012.690931.

21   Chris Wienke & Gretchen J Hill, "Does Place of Residence Matter? Urban-Rural Differences and the Wellbeing of Gay Men and Lesbians," *Journal of Homosexuality* 60:9 (2013): 1256–1279, <http://www.tandfonline.com/doi/full/10.1080/00918369.2013.806166#.VDBAuildVUg>.

22   Eric Swank, Breanne Fahs & David M. Frost, "Region, Social Identities, and Disclosure Practices as Predictors of Heterosexist Discrimination Against Sexual Minorities in the United States," *Sociological Inquiry* 83:2 (2013) 238–258, <http://www.breannefahs.com/uploads/1/0/6/7/10679051/2013_sociological_inquiry_swank_fahs_frost.pdf>.

23   Jessica L. Collins & Barry Wellman, "Small Town in the Internet Society: Chapleau Is No Longer an Island," *American Behavioral Sciences* 53:9 (2010): 1344, doi:10.1177/0002764210361689; In our data, this quote from Laura, 18 (from Belgium, but living in a small town in Canada for the year) illustrates the point: "For me I find so [connecting online makes real space friendships stronger], because they're so far away now. So it's nice to keep in contact, to know that they're still, like, thinking about me, and, like, that they say, like, that they miss me or that they miss the things we used to do, like, last year. So I know that they're still there and they will still be my friend next year. Because that's one of the things that can happen if you're not keeping in contact, then maybe you could lose just the friendship. So that's why Facebook's pretty good, or email."

24   Statistics Canada, "Canadian Internet Use Survey, Internet Use at Home, by Internet Activity, Urban or Rural Distribution," <http://www5.statcan.

gc.ca/cansim/a26?lang=eng&retrLang=eng&id=3580130&pattern=358013
0&csid=>.

25 Canadian Radio-television and Telecommunications Commission,
    Canadian Radio-television and Telecommunications "Availability and
    Adoption of Digital Technologies," <http://www.crtc.gc.ca/eng/publica-
    tions/reports/policyMonitoring/2013/cmr6.htm>.

26 *Ibid.* at table 6.1.3 and figure 6.1.6.

27 Statistics Canada, *supra* note 24.

28 Michael Haight, Anabel Quan-Haase & Bradley A. Corbett, "Revisiting
    the Digital Divide in Canada: The Impact of Demographic Factors on
    Access to the Internet, Level of Online Activity, and Social Networking
    Site Usage," *Information, Communication & Society* 17:4 (2014): 503–519,
    doi: 10.1080/1369118X.2014.891633.

29 Maeve Duggan & Joanna Brenner, "The Demographics of Social Media
    Users — 2012," *Pew Research Center's Internet & American Life Project*, 14
    February 2013, <http://www.pewinternet.org/files/old-media/Files/
    Reports/2013/PIP_SocialMediaUsers.pdf>; see also Maeve Duggan
    & Aaron Smith, "Social Media Update 2013," *Pew Research Centre*, 20
    December 2013, <http://www.pewinternet.org/files/2013/12/PIP_Social-
    Networking-2013.pdf>.

30 Haight et al, *supra* note 28.

31 Collins & Wellman, *supra* note 23 at 1344.

32 Hua Wang & Barry Wellman, "Connectivity in America: Changes in
    Adult Friendship Network Size from 2002 to 2007," *American Behavioral
    Scientist* 53:8 (2010), 1148–1169, <http://groups.chass.utoronto.ca/netlab/
    wp-content/uploads/2012/05/Social-Connectivity-in-America-Changes-
    in-Adult-Friendship-Network-Size-from-2002-to-2007.pdf>.

33 Collins & Wellman, *supra* note 23, citing Edward J. Malecki, "Digital
    Development in Rural Areas: Potentials and Pitfalls," *Journal of Rural
    Studies* 19 (2003): 201.

34 Eric Gilbert, Karrie Karahalios & Christian Sandvig, "Network in the
    Garden: Designing Social Media for Rural Life," *American Behavioral Sci-
    entist* 53 (2010): 1367–1388, <http://www-personal.umich.edu/~csandvig/
    research/The_Network_in_the_Garden_ABS.pdf>.

35 Collins & Wellman, *supra* note 23 at 1344; Jilin Chen, Werner Geyer,
    Casey Dugan, Michael Muller & Ido Guy, "Make New Friends, but Keep
    the Old: Recommending People on Social Networking Sites," (paper pre-
    sented at SIGCHI Conference on Human Factors in Computing Systems,
    Boston, Massachusetts, 2009): 201–210, <http://files.grouplens.org/papers/
    paper1165-chen.pdf>; Adriana M. Manago, Tamara Taylor & Patricia M.
    Greenfield, "Me and My 400 Friends: The Anatomy of College Students'
    Facebook Networks, their Communication Patterns, and Well-Being,"

Developmental Psychology 48 (2012): 369–380, <http://dx.doi.org/10.1037/a0026338>.

36 Slane, Chapter X.

37 Alice Marwick, "Public Domain: Surveillance in Everyday Life," *Surveillance & Society* 9:4 (2012): 378–393, <http://library.queensu.ca/ojs/index.php/surveillance-and-society/article/view/pub_dom/pub_dom>.

38 Miyase Christensen & André Jansson, "Complicit Surveillance, Interveillance, and the Question of Cosmopolitanism: Toward a Phenomenological Understanding of Mediatization," *New Media & Society* (2014): 8, <http://phdtree.org/pdf/47109679-complicit-surveillance-interveillance-and-the-question-of-cosmopolitanism-toward-a-phenomenological-understanding-of-mediatization/>.

39 Anders Albrechtslund, "Online Social Networking as Participatory Surveillance," *First Monday* 13:3 (2008), <http://firstmonday.org/article/view/2142/1949>.

40 Mark Andrejevic, "The Discipline of Watching: Detection, Risk, and Lateral Surveillance," *Critical Studies in Media Communication* 23:5 (2006): 391–407, doi:10.1080/07393180601046147.

41 Christensen & Jansson, *supra* note 38 at 8.

42 Mark Andrejevic, "The Work of Watching One Another: Lateral Surveillance, Risk, and Governance," *Surveillance & Society* 2:4 (2005): 481–482, <http://www.surveillance-and-society.org/articles2(4)/lateral.pdf>.

43 Daniel Trottier & David Lyon, "Key Features of Social Media Surveillance," *Internet and Surveillance: The Challenges of Web 2.0 and Social Media,* eds. Christian Fuchs, Kees Boersma, Anders Albrechtslund, & Marisol Sandoval (Routledge: New York, 2012), 89.

44 Bailey & Steeves, Introduction. See also http://egirlsproject.ca.

45 Our rural adult focus group included Catlin (19), Laura (18), Trish (18), and Brianne (20). Our rural minor focus group included Courtney (17), Chelsea (17), Paula (17), Beth (16), and Josie (16). Our urban adult focus group included Keira (21), Donna (19), Jill (20), Andrea (22), Ashley (18), and Kathleen (20). Our urban minor focus group included Vicky (17), Eve (16), Abby (17), Jacquelyn (17), Lauryn (17), Monique (16), and Jane (16). Our rural adult interviewees were Cassandra (19), Becky (19), and Amelia (18). Our rural minor interviewees were Monica (16), Lynda (17), and Nicole (16). Our urban adult interviewees were Alessandra (21), Mackenzie (20), and Cindy (20). Our urban minor interviewees were Alicia (17), Clare (16), and Josée (15).

46 Regan & Sweet, Chapter VII.

47 Erving Goffman, *The Presentation of Self in Everyday Life,* (New York: Anchor Books, 1959).

48 Reported connection to strangers appeared to be linked to age. Girls were more likely than young women to report online connections to

people unknown offline, and among those who did not connect with strangers offline, many said that they used to interact with strangers online when they were younger, e.g., Jane, 16 stated " … I look back now and I think it's really stupid, but yeah at the time it's fun."

49 Where rural participants *do* identify a difference in social networks, it is related to offline connections.

50 Patti M. Valkenburg, Alexander P. Schouten & Peter Jochen, "Adolescents' Identity Experiments on the Internet," *New Media & Society* 7:3 (2005): 383–402, <http://www.sagepub.com/rpc2study/articles/Chapter08_Article01.pdf>.

51 *Supra* note 46.

52 *Supra* note 46.

53 Kyle E. Walker, "Immigration, Local Policy, and National Identity in the Suburban United States," *Urban Geography* 35 (2014): 508–529, doi: 10.1080/02723638.2014.890423; Justin Peter Steil & Ion Bogdan Vasi, "The New Immigration Contestation: Social Movements and Local Immigration Policy Making in the United States, 2000–2011," *American Journal of Sociology* 119 (2014): 1104–1155, <http://papers.ssrn.com/sol3/papers.cfm?abstract_id=2433132>.

54 Lyn C. Macgregor, *Habits of the Heartland: Small-Town Life in Modern America* (Cornell University Press: Ithaca, 2010).

55 *Ibid.* at 5.

CHAPTER VI

"Pretty and Just a Little Bit Sexy, I Guess": Publicity, Privacy, and the Pressure to Perform "Appropriate" Femininity on Social Media

Valerie Steeves

When McRobbie and Garber first coined the term "bedroom culture" in 1976, they were attempting to create a theoretical framework to explore girls' resistance to restrictive cultural tropes around gender.[1] Subculture studies of the time largely ignored girls, and instead focused on the ways that boys resignified public spaces for their own cultural purposes. As a corrective, McRobbie and Garber located girls' cultural practices in the private space of the bedroom, and argued that girls were free there to pursue their cultural goals by reading magazines, talking to each other on the phone, trying on clothes, listening to music, and fantasizing about pop idols.[2]

By locating resistance in the privacy of the bedroom, McRobbie and Garber were challenging the assumption that equality cannot be advanced in the private sphere,[3] particularly because privacy too often shields abusive men from public accountability for violence against women.[4] However, girls in the 1970s had less access to the public sphere than their male peers because, as girls, they were subjected to a higher degree of parental control.[5] The bedroom therefore provided an alternative space where girls could access mainstream cultural products and communications technologies (like radios) in private, and use them to construct potentially more empowering identities.[6] Conceptualizing the bedroom as a resistive space accordingly put privacy and communications into dialogue with equality in productive ways. Privacy could promote equality by providing a boundary that enabled girls to enjoy a personal, personalized, and intimate socio-technical space,[7] where they could retreat from the pressure of the public sphere, produce their own cultural meanings, and potentially challenge restrictive stereotypes.

When Lincoln revisited McRobbie and Garber's work in the early 1990s, she argued that the bedroom continued to be one of the few places where girls could enjoy this sense of "a room of one's own,"[8] Lincoln's research participants – much like McRobbie and Garber's – went there to chat with friends, talk about romantic relationships, and experiment with clothes, makeup, and hairstyles. In this regard, the bedroom was still a private place to which girls could retreat to find "respite from the public world" and play with the cultural capital available to them to experiment with their identities. However, Lincoln argued that the bedroom of the 1990s had become a hybrid space, with attributes of both the private and the public spheres, and that this hybridity was ultimately empowering for girls because it increased their access to publicity.

Lincoln supported this conclusion with two lines of reasoning. First, she suggested that the technologies of the day made the boundaries around the bedroom more permeable. Personal televisions, music players, mobile phones, and the internet provided girls with a way to "cross over" into the public sphere and access an "immense" range of cultural choices from which to "pick and mix" as they went about the business of identity construction.

Second, since girls enjoyed more access to the public sphere than their counterparts in the 1970s, they used photos and other memorabilia of their participation in parties, concerts, and other events to record their "cultural interests … biographically on their bedroom walls." In this way, the bedroom became an important site where they could "document their 'coolness' through active participation in the public sphere of the pub or club." Lincoln concluded that the public and private spheres accordingly "interact[ed] simultaneously as bedroom culture," and that this intermingling made it possible for girls to take a more active role in the shaping of their "social- and cultural-life worlds."[9]

As the variety of personal networked media have grown, a number of other feminist scholars have also celebrated the emancipatory potential of technologies that blur the lines between the private sphere and the public sphere, in the hope that this blurring will create liminal spaces where girls can increasingly control their visibility[10] and break discriminatory stereotypes.[11] The promise, as Reid-Walsh and Mitchell articulate, is that these "semi-private places of creativity and sociality [will become] sites of 'virtual bedroom culture'"[12] that are "separate, private and safe" and under the control of the girls themselves.[13] Moreover, unlike the girls of the 1970s, who largely consumed pre-packaged media products, today's girls can, it is hoped, become media producers and distributers in their own right, "subverting the public/private binary that has historically limited girls' experiences."[14] From this perspective, the potential for resistance is amplified by networked technologies because the virtual bedroom is no longer relegated to the private sphere so long associated with repression; indeed, the benefit is that these technologies provide girls with unrestricted access to the public sphere. As Kearney concludes, by creating and posting media content, "contemporary female youth are not retreating to private spaces; they are *reconfiguring* such sites to create new publics that can better service their needs, interests, and goals.[15]

In this chapter, I explore the qualitative findings of the eGirls Project to test these assumptions against the lived experiences of girls and young women living in Ontario, Canada. When the eGirls Project was initiated, one of the aims was to map the variety of ways that girls could perform emancipatory identities on social media. However, the findings identify a complex and contradictory set of affordances and constraints that open up some opportunities and shut down others. This has further complicated the already complex task of creating and inhabiting emancipatory feminine identities, because mainstream stereotypes are now embedded by commercial interests into the sociotechnical spaces that girls inhabit. This makes it more difficult for girls to retreat into a private sphere where they can try on a variety of identities with few or no social consequences. I conclude that equality can be better promoted by protecting the privacy of the virtual bedroom from commercial interests that seek to replicate the kinds of stereotypes that constrain girls' enjoyment of the public sphere, and providing girls with more tools to control who has access to the virtual traces of themselves that they leave on social media.

Methodology

In January and February of 2013, researchers with the eGirls Project held a series of interviews and focus groups with girls and young women between the ages of 15 and 22. All participants used interactive online media (such as social networking, blogging, and/or user-generated video sites) as a regular part of their social lives. Half of our sample resided in an urban Ontario setting and half resided in a rural Ontario setting.[16]

We interviewed six girls aged 15 to 17 and six young women aged 18 to 22. An additional twenty-two participated in four focus group discussions, as follows: (1) seven girls aged 15 to 17 living in the urban setting; (2) five girls aged 15 to 17 living in the rural setting; (3) six young women aged 18 to 22 living in the urban setting; and (4) four young women aged 18 to 22 living in the rural setting. A professional research house recruited our participants on the basis of sex, age (either 15 to 17 or 18 to 22), and location of residence (urban or rural). While participants were not recruited on the basis of self-identification with regard to other aspects of their identities, such as race, ethnicity, gender identity, or sexual orientation, our participant group included members of racialized, linguistic, and various religious groups.

In the interviews and the focus groups, we explored, among other things, the types of visual and textual representations the participants used online to express their identity as young women, and the benefits and pitfalls they experienced on social media. We also asked for their views on the issues and policy responses focused on by policymakers (as identified in the review of federal parliamentary debates previously reported upon and summarized above).

With participant permission, the interviews and focus groups were audiotaped and transcribed by our research assistants for analysis. All identifying information was removed from the transcripts, and pseudonyms were used to identify participants.[17]

Life in the Virtual Bedroom

The findings indicate that social media have indeed provided girls with opportunities to shape the identities they inhabit in the public sphere in emancipatory ways. All of the participants reported using profiles on various sites (e.g., Facebook, Twitter, Pinterest, Tumblr) to extend their networks, and to pursue their professional or political goals. A social media presence was universally seen as a useful way to cultivate professional relationships with (prospective) employers and clients. For example, 19-year-old Cassandra used a Facebook page to promote her new aesthetics business, providing detailed descriptions of the products and services she offered to solicit clients. Other girls used social media for social and political activism, and a number indicated that certain sites, like Twitter, were an easy way to keep informed about the issues of the day. Accordingly, the hybridity inherent in networked technologies gave the participants a window into the public sphere, and a door through which to enter that sphere for their own purposes.

For a few of the participants, social media were also a satisfying outlet for the type of creative expression that Kearney described.[18] Again, the hybridity of the space was key here. The pleasure came not only in using media tools to produce their own content, but also in sharing with others what they created in private. For example, 16-year-old Clare indicated that she frequently videotaped her hands while she played her own arrangements of rock songs on the piano and posted the videos on YouTube. Because she played by ear, a number of people contacted her to comment on the arrangements and ask her for the music she had composed. Fifteen-year-old Emily was very proud of a graphic art logo she created to help promote an online campaign against social injustice. And Cassandra posted pictures of ceramics she painted. The ceramics were so popular that friends and family asked for particular pieces and began to commission her work for pay. Reflecting on this, she noted, smiling," ... On my other profile, like my normal profile [for family and friends], every day, I've pictures of the canvases I paint; I've pictures of drawings that I drew. All the artsy fartsy things I do to my room."

Although most of the participants saw themselves as consumers of media content rather than as producers, all but two of them posted photos on a regular basis and all had either frequently commented on others' photos or had others comment on theirs. This activity spanned platforms and most participants had ongoing access to their profiles through portable devices, like smartphones and tablets. Again, the hybridity of these spaces meant that this experience could be very satisfying. Watching videos on YouTube, listening to music, and following their own "random" interests (from celebrities and fashion to pets, food, and dancing cats) on social media provided our participants with an opportunity to privately collect cultural capital with which to experiment. They would then appropriate elements of this cultural capital to "try on" new, less child-like identities, and then publicly display them to friends through the photos they posted. When friends responded positively, the publicity afforded by social media increased their confidence. As 17-year-old Alicia noted, "It's nice to know that, like, people actually, like, care type of thing and like, they wanna know, like, stuff [about your life]." Accordingly, photos posted on social media played a central role in the task of becoming a teenager and adult, and posting and perusing photos was by far participants' favourite online activity.

However, when participants mentioned posting photos of themselves, a surprising number of them immediately placed a *caveat* around this practice, expressly indicating that they did post photos, *but* they did not post anything "bad," "inappropriate," "crazy," "rough or greasy," "trashy," "sleazy," or "scandalous." Rather than opening up space for new performances of femininity, social media came with a clear and vigorously enforced set of social rules about acceptable ways of being a girl.[19] Alicia's comments were typical: when asked about her photos, she responded by saying:

> There's usually nothing … bad [laughter] … I'd be like, oh, make sure I'm appropriate when I'm speaking, but I'm usually, like, I'm not bad … I don't know, like cleaner, type of thing.… . no, my pictures are usually good. So … well, like, it's usually just like a face shot of, like, me and people or, um, like nature or, like, the weather or, like, my family, so like, it's never anything that bad.

This juxtaposition between "good" photos and "bad" photos resonated strongly with all of our participants. There was also a real consensus about what constituted a "bad" photo. The 15- to 17-year-old girls who participated in the urban focus group put it this way:

> Lauryn: … the classic, like, girl, like, pictures at your webcam and you're bending over like this just to see, you can see right down your shirt ….
> Eve: … girls are, like, squishing their boobs together or something [group laugh]. And like, bending over and they're, like, I don't know, trying to turn sideways or whatever 'cause it looks bigger this way [group laugh]. Yeah.

Lauryn: Or like taking a picture and people being like, oh, like, I like your hair, and they'll take it from behind, but in reality you know they're doing it so you can see their butt ….

Photos of girls involving alcohol, smoking, or drugs were also seen to be problematic. Although many of the participants indicated that they did drink or smoke, they were very careful about posting any photos that showed them doing so, to avoid being "trashy" (Amelia, age 18). Young women 18 and older, in particular, were careful to keep their profile pictures "neutral," and would use privacy controls such as untagging photos in which they were dancing or behaving in a sexual manner (Jill, age 20) in an attempt to control the flow of those images beyond a trusted circle of friends and/or family. Accordingly, although social media gave them access to the public sphere, they were very careful about how they represented themselves there, to avoid being seen as "bad" girls, replicating the traditional divide between "good" girls, who do not act in overtly sexual ways or engage in male pastimes like drinking or smoking, and "bad" girls, who do. They also saw it as their responsibility to police their image – and often the images of other girls – to ensure that photos conformed to highly gendered behavioural norms.

The most restrictive regulation involved the display of the feminine body. "Too much" exposure was universally recognized as "inappropriate"; this included "cleavage" (Alicia), photos without "a lot of clothes" (Clare), that are "way too revealing" (Nicole, age 16), "sexual pictures" (Emily, age 15), or pictures of a girl "pose[d] in suggestive ways" (Clare). Alicia illustrated the difference between "good" and "bad" photos by drawing a finger across her chest, literally encoding the difference on her body:

Clothing-wise, like, I don't know, like I feel right now, well I'm not really showing anything but like, um, my friend, like, I'm pretty sure she would just use this blue shirt [drawing a line close to her nipples] and I put this top underneath [drawing a line at the top of her cleavage].

When I asked her what was "bad" about showing so much cleavage, she indicated it was "something people could take in the wrong way."

This taking things in the "wrong way" was highly gendered. Whereas boys were free to post shirtless photos or show off their abs, photos displaying a girl's body would be read differently:

> … Girls, we have to, like, um, cover ourselves more than guys, so, like, I find that, like, um, if you were to look at a picture of a girl, like, um, with just like, uh, like a crop top or something and then a guy with no top, I don't know, they're kind of similar but the way you would look at it would be different … people will talk. (Alicia).

All the participants indicated that they paid a great deal of attention to selecting appropriate photos to post because the talk generated by a poor display was often incredibly harsh, especially among the teenagers. Girls who exposed too much skin were quickly labelled "sluts," "whores," and "trash." Even girls who admitted they posted these kinds of pictures tended to judge themselves harshly. Cindy (age 20), who indicated that the "duck face" (a particularly reviled pose where a girl turns her face sideways and sucks in her cheeks) was "totally my go-to," burst out laughing when she talked about posting pictures of her boyfriend and said, "I'm one of those girls. I hate it. I'm one of those girls … I hate it when girls post [those kinds of pictures]." She later qualified, "But I don't go too, too overboard." For example, she described photos taken of her wearing lingerie as part of a modelling photo shoot as "not scandalous by any means … Like, nothing was showing, you know, but I wouldn't put that one on Facebook …. That's just way too much."

To complicate things further, girls were not judged by their male and female peers solely on the basis of what they displayed, but also on their presumed motivations for posting the photo. Again, the conversation among the 15- to 17–year-olds in the urban setting is illustrative:

> Monique: There's a difference between, like, flaunting it and, like, actually just ….
> Abby: Being yourself.
> Monique: Having it there because you have boobs [group laugh], like we all have boobs, but yeah. But there's a difference between wanting to show them to the whole world and you can still be respectful to yourself, you know ….

Lauryn: … you can, like, totally tell when someone's doing it on purpose or it just so happens to be the picture [others agree]. Yeah, like, you can tell by like the angle, like, they're taking the picture, if you're constantly taking all your profile pictures from up here so you can see down your shirt, like, you can tell, like, you know which girl's, like, doing it on purpose and which girls aren't.

Girls who did it "on purpose" were variously described as "insecure," "self-absorbed," "annoying," "conceited," "bragging," "desperate," or "attention whores."

At the same time, "good" photos were often marked by features that also showed up in "bad" photos. A "good" photo was described as one in which a girl's hair and makeup were perfect, and her body was displayed to emphasize her breasts or lips and to make her look thinner. Girls who trashed the duck face in one moment would later talk about various duck face photos they had posted of themselves in the past, because "it makes your cheeks look thinner and your lips look bigger" (Cindy, Jill).

There was a similar ambiguity about sexualized photos. Although photos that went "too far" opened a girl up to harsh judgment, a "good" photo was one in which a girl looked "pretty and just a little bit sexy, I guess. That's it" (Kathleen, age 20). "Not like a stripper, like" (Monica, age 16) but thin, attractive, and fit: "Personally, I mean, if I have a crappy smile and if I'm standing the wrong way and I have a bulge hanging over somewhere, I'm not going to — it's vain, but I'm not going to put that up on Facebook" (Emily, age 15).

Accordingly, the line between "good" photos and "bad" photos was often a very hard one to define, and the fact that a photo would be seen by others on social media increased the potential for a harsh judgment. As Monica (age 16) summarized, "Well, some people are fine, just put whatever on there. And it's like if you don't like it, don't look at it. But other people are very conscious of their, like, worry that they'll get crap or something."

"Getting crap" was not limited to girls who transgressed the line between "good" and "bad" photos. It also included girls and young women who did not fit within the idealized norm of feminine beauty or behaviour. For example, 17-year-old Lynda indicated that a photo of a girl who was not thin would attract "something rude." She spoke of a friend who posted a photo on social media and was told, "'I understand why you're so self-conscious about your weight. If I looked like you, I would be too.' That's horrible." She went on to explain:

> Lynda: Like, if a girl puts a picture up without makeup on or something, people could attack her, like, that even people she doesn't know could see it.
> Researcher: What do they say?
> Lynda: I don't know. Some people would call her ugly or something if you don't wear makeup. Or they'll just attack her for that.... They could attack their appearance, or the way you act or relationships with guys, being with guys.... Like, they could say the way you look in general or, like, clothes you wear or lack of clothes you wear.

Keira (age 21) spoke of a girl in high school who did not follow the crowd, who was "just bash[ed]" by a boy on social media:

> I think it was about how she looks. What she was wearing. She had a very authentic look, and she was never really scared to say what she wants or act in any way that she wants. But—oh, man, I think it was mostly about her looks, maybe what she normally wears.... Anyway, it was just bizarre.

Simply posting too much information about herself could open a girl up to judgment, especially if she violated traditional feminine norms around passivity and privacy. Interestingly, even though social media has a public-ness about it, girls who failed to maintain a certain degree of privacy online were subjected to criticism by their peers. Jill's comment exemplifies this:

> I used to have this girl on Facebook, and she'd just write every-thing. "Off to the mall, then going for a nap," "Just woke up from the nap, off to the bathroom," just totally personal. And I knew I wasn't the only one who thought this. I had to delete her; it was just, like, so annoying. It was like, why do you feel the need to write these things on Facebook? I don't need to know that you left your house …. if you're posting, like, extremely specific little details, like, personal things: "Off to get my hair cut," "Off to do my nails," things like that. It's just a little too much.

In like vein, Nicole posted a photo on Ask.fm, a site that she described as "probably the most horrible thing I've ever seen in my life." The questions she received were mostly telling her she was pretty and nice, but some asked her, "Why are you so attention seeking?" As she pondered her experience, she indicated, "I have never thought of myself as attention seeking compared to some other girls … it just sets you apart from other people. 'Cause to me, attention seeking is that one person who's on Facebook 24/7, putting pictures of themselves and is just searching for things they can do to hear their name more, you know …. But I never thought of myself as that."

This kind of self-reflection was common among the participants. They described social media as a place where they faced an incredible amount of judgment and pressure, especially about their bodies: a place where girls are open to criticism because they are too fat, too made up, not made up enough, expose too much cleavage (and are therefore "sluts"), don't expose enough cleavage, have too many friends (and are therefore "desperate"), and/or don't have enough friends (and are therefore "losers"). The oppressive need for attention to detail, to present that "just right" image, was often exhausting, especially for high school students. As Cindy notes, "Being made fun of, high school is brutal, I hated high school for all the cattiness and, uh, the judgment."

Even though the participants were quick to judge girls who posted "bad" photos on social media, they also had an empathetic understanding of why "other" girls would do so. They all commented on the pressure created by the unrealistic representations of beauty that are embedded throughout mainstream media. Emily described it this way:

> Barbie, that's pretty, that's the perfect example that everyone uses. So like Barbie, top models, and everything, we all see — we always see those kind of [people], they're all amazing, … [on] magazines or television and stuff like that, it's mostly really, really awesome people and, like, they're really pretty and really like skinny and everything, they're perfect.

Moreover, they are also uniformly underweight. As Monica noted, "Well, magazines and stuff, it's like weight loss is the whole idea of 'get into your bikini bod by the summer'. That's all they support. They don't support anything else. Not everybody in the world is

ninety pounds kind of thing." Clare agreed: "Um, uh, in like the tab-
loids, I guess, they like kind of freak if somebody gains five pounds.
It's kind of ridiculous."

Cassandra argued that "everything in ads is more directed
towards girls" and girls are encouraged to buy products to look like
"all those beautiful women who have all these professional people
doing their hair." Cassandra went on to say that girls are told, "'If I
get this, I'll look like Halle Berry.' And you get this, you're like, 'Oh
my God, I'm not looking like Halle Berry.' So you're trying everything
…. So I don't know, girls are just … I don't know … just have to look
good …. It's just the way we work, I guess …. "

Again, this pressure is highly gendered. Participants argued
that girls are not only subjected to more messages about their bodies
than boys are, they are also taught to compete with each other for
male attention. And the way to win the competition is to emulate
the kinds of femininity that they see performed in media. As Emily
noted:

> Emily: There's more pressure for the girls [than] for the guys,
> um, there's a lot of pressure which is put on the girls, and we
> often see it on the television and everything like that ….
> Researcher: Television and what else? What else is "everything
> like that"?
> Emily: So, uh, and us girls, we're trying to be like that because
> we know guys are more interested in those kind of people and
> everything, um. So we're really more, like, aware of that, but
> also the guys, the guys, they – them, um, then it's, um, I don't
> know, they're more at ease about themselves.

Alessandra (age 21) pointed the finger at music videos, movies,
television shows, and magazines. For example, music videos "have
a man, who is perhaps fully clothed or maybe has his shirt off, he's
rapping and then next to him are women in bikinis. OK. So the
women are just objects, they're just complementary, he's the centre
focal point and the women are just ornaments around him." In like
vein, Alessandra also said:

> What does Cosmo tell you about being a woman? That your
> whole, that being a woman is about how well you can please
> guys. Like, uh, how to look beautiful in the summer, how to

please your man, 101 ways to I don't even wanna mention it. You know, so I'm thinking that, OK, to be a good woman I need to know how to do all these disgusting acts, I need to know how to be beautiful, I need to know how to lose weight, that's a big important one, if you're not skinny then no one is going to love you, that's what every magazine is about, "'oh she gained ten pounds'."

Interestingly, participants indicated that social media only makes the pressure to be "beautiful" worse. The "like" function means that each image they post is judged by their peers, and certain images are more likely than others to receive positive attention, especially from boys. Being "pretty" and "a little sexy" will attract a certain level of approval, but girls who post revealing or highly sexualized images are likely to receive the most likes: "I used to think, oh cool, I got ten likes and then you look at the girls who look revealing and they have fifty [from guys] and you're, like, oh I wonder why" (Nicole).

The peer surveillance they experienced also taught them to look for external male validation, and the easiest way to attain that validation was to conform to gendered stereotypes. This was best illustrated by their discussion of confidence. When asked why girls would take the risk of harsh judgment by posting a lingerie shot or some other sexualized pose, the response was universal – it was because the girl was "confident." But when their understanding of confidence was probed, they explained that once a girl posts a shot like that, she will typically watch it closely. If it receives at least ten likes in the first ten minutes, then the girl is confident. If it does not, then she immediately removes the photo and feels humiliated.

However, even when girls successfully attract male attention, the attention itself often sets them up for conflict with other girls. As Cassandra explained:

They are going to get feedback like, "Wow, you're hot." Definitely from guys. "Wow, you're sexy!" "Damn, what I would do if I was there," and, like, all that kind of stuff. And from girls, you're gonna get, um … from their best friends, probably, "Oh my God, you look gorgeous! You look so skinny!" And you're gonna get from girls that don't like her, "Wow, you're a slut!" you know, like, "You're nothing but a whore!" like, "Put some clothes on!" So like, it's different. It depends on who's gonna comment.

Jill illustrated how this could easily escalate into conflict:

> "A girl, let's say she's, I don't know, with a bunch of guys in a sexual pose, or … has tons of booze around her, or something. Someone will write a comment that will be, like, kind of subtle but showing that it's inappropriate, and a lot of people will join in, and you can get, like, up to seventy-five comments and everyone's joining in and fighting."

This competition between girls can be intense and highly personal. When Cassandra was in high school, for example, she was "desperate" to be friends with the group of people she considered to be the most popular, and did "everything" — paying close attention to selecting fashionable clothes, carefully applying makeup, and mimicking fashionable hairstyles — to fit in. A schoolmate posted a comment on a photo of her on the social media page of one of the popular girls, saying "Hahaha, love having friends that make you look good." When she asked the popular girl what it meant, she was told, "Oh, I have you around to make me look good because you're bigger than me and you're uglier than me." Cassandra, who was 14 years old at the time, was so devastated that she "struggled with depression … started cutting, that kind of stuff."

The presence of "more girls everywhere … trying to put, like, the prettiest girls on magazines and stuff" (Lynda) on social media also increases the pressure to conform to the stereotype. Monica noted, "I don't know, sometimes, it'll make you feel like crap. It's like, just again setting in, why can't I look like that? Why can't I be like that? Why don't I have these friends? Why am I not popular? And just drains everybody else." Even when the image is "fake," the public approval garnered through a high "likes" count engenders insecurity: " … [T]here's [city] girls on Facebook … they'll have like five hundred likes on some of their pictures and … I'll sit there and like notice it at first and be, like, this person has to be fake 'cause they're so pretty and they're so Photoshopped … but whenever you see them on Facebook you're, like, oh my God, they are so flawless."

Cindy indicated that that kind of "perfection" is discouraging because "you're like, oh man, I don't look like that. Um, but I could someday, you know, but you just, you don't right now. So you might get down on yourself because of that." She felt that the ubiquitous presence of diet ads, weight loss tips, and other "beauty aids," on social media, as well as pages posted by models and clothing companies, created an overwhelming desire to "change my body." Cindy was particularly upset when she found this type of content on Pinterest. For her, "it's a page where you can post things you wish you could have or you wish you could do or places you wish you could go to, so it's, it's great. But it's awful at the exact same time … also kind of sad because a Pinterest page is for a diet and weight loss." She concluded, "I think social media is great at giving girls this fantasy world but at the same time I think it's also really easy to sort of make them feel really bad about themselves."

Revisiting Privacy, Publicity, and Equality in the Virtual Bedroom

The eGirls findings suggest that girls' experiences on social media are complex and contradictory, in ways that both reflect and reiterate themes raised by Milford and Kanai in earlier chapters in this volume. At first blush, the participants' descriptions of their profiles resonate strongly with Lincoln's description of the bedroom as "a haven of memorabilia"[20] that "tell[s] stories of a teenage girl's youth cultural interests and, ultimately, cultural identity."[21] In addition, the hybridity that Lincoln celebrates enables girls to project a carefully constructed self-image into the public sphere. The emancipatory potential of this hybridity is most easily realized in the world of work; our participants were confident about their ability to use social media to present themselves as (potential) employees and entrepreneurs. This is a particularly encouraging use of social media, especially given the fact that in 2012 there were 950,000 self-employed women in Canada[22] and just under half of all small to medium-sized enterprises were entirely or partly owned by women.[23]

However, when the eGirls participants stepped out of the role of economic actor and sought to express themselves and interact socially as *girls becoming women*, the crossover between the private and public domains in the virtual bedroom opened them up to harsh judgment if they failed to conform to a very narrow performance of a sexualized – but not too sexualized – female body. The participants' preoccupation with the gendered body and sexuality is "unsurprising, as gender and sexuality to some degree determine our conception of adolescence."[24] As Levy-Warren points out, the work of middle adolescence in particular is to integrate the change from a relatively ambiguous body to a post-puberty body that is unmistakably shaped in a gendered way.[25]

Their interest in popular culture is also unsurprising; it is well established in the literature that "media and popular culture offer social discourses that play a key role in [adolescent] identity construction."[26] However, the harsh judgment the participants were exposed to in the public sphere was not mitigated by networked access to the sphere, or the fluidity between the private bedroom and the public social media site. I would suggest that the easy flow between private and public amplified the potential for conflict and constraint, for two reasons.

First, the crossover is not limited to the girls themselves. The relative privacy of the early days of the internet provided girls with liminal spaces where they could avoid surveillance and the appropriation of voice, primarily because adults did not think to look for them there.[27] However, through a confluence of policies that promote the commercialization of online spaces and policies that seek to "protect" girls from online risks, girls are now subjected to high levels of online surveillance.[28] This surveillance, especially on the part of parents and school administrators, constrains the kinds of identity experimentation available to them on social media,[29] particularly because the corporate design of the sites makes it increasingly difficult to control which audience sees which performance.[30] In other words, the hybrid nature of the space makes it easy for adults to ignore the "Do Not Enter!" sign on the virtual bedroom door, especially in the name of safety, and invisibly watch girls as they go about the business of identity play. This shuts down the potential for transgressive and resistive performances because girls are unable to obtain the privacy they need to individuate.[31]

Second, although social media do provide girls with easy access to a wide range of popular culture products, they also provide commercial producers and marketers with easy access to the girls themselves. Intense commercial surveillance appropriates the cultural products girls publish there and uses the insight they provide into girls' insecurities and dreams to steer social interaction on the site[32] through commercial practices like native advertising and behavioural targeting. This not only reproduces the mainstream media stereotypes that are linked to poor body image[33] and the sexualization of girls,[34] it embeds these stereotypes directly into girls' sociotechnical environment. This constrains girls' ability to "pick and mix"[35] the cultural images to bring to the bedroom, and instead enables the corporation housing the social media site to wallpaper the images of its choosing directly onto the bedroom wall. This is particularly troubling because the power of these stereotypes may be amplified on social media since girls are encouraged to inhabit them there, much as they do the virtual avatars in video gaming that have been linked to lower self-efficacy[36] and higher acceptance of rape myths.[37]

The eGirls participants were well aware of the negative effects of media stereotypes and sought to avoid gendered conflicts by walking the fine line between "a little bit sexy" and "slut." However, as Durham notes, adolescent girls are under a high degree of social pressure to conform to "the norms of femininity" and typically judge themselves through the lens of peer acceptance.[38] It is accordingly

> … unreasonable to expect adolescent girls—who are develop-
> mentally at a life stage in which social and peer approval are
> of paramount importance—to be able to produce individually
> oppositional readings of media messages that would translate
> into a coherent and robust lived opposition. Isolation is the ulti-
> mate terror in girls' lives: peer approval plays an inordinately
> important role in their socialization.[39]

To avoid this isolation, a number of our participants chose to leave social media—especially Facebook—for extended periods of time. By reasserting the firm boundaries around the bedroom as a site of private creativity and reflection, they were able to tone down the "drama" and avoid both the surveillance and the ridicule[40] that marked their experiences in online spaces. In many ways, going off line re-establishes the conditions of Lincoln's bedroom as a space where "the teenager can exert control over what level of 'the public' can filter into the bedroom space"[41] through zones "oriented by the social activities that take place within the space."[42]

When this retreat is a conscious rejection of the politics of the public sphere, it can be emancipatory in its own right. As Harris writes:

> Rather than seeing young women's retreat back into the private
> as a simple failure of access to or possibilities within the public,
> I would suggest that this has been an active choice on the part of
> young women refusing to participate in particular constructions

of girlhood. Specifically, they are rejecting the commodification and depoliticization of girl culture.[43]

However, we can also expand the potential for resistance by regulating the corporations that design, control, and mine the sociotechnical spaces that girls inhabit. Requiring corporations to provide girls with better technical tools that allow them to control the lines between their multiple audiences will help them better manage the fluid movement of cultural capital between the private sphere of creativity and identity play and the public sphere of performativity and resistance. Restricting native advertising and behavioural targeting on social media will help insulate girls from the negative effects of media stereotyping and push back against commercial surveillance. But perhaps most importantly, we need to create non-commercial sociotechnical spaces where girls can express themselves and project resistive identities into the public sphere.

The lessons of the virtual bedroom remind us of the resilience of both patriarchal restrictions and girls' ability to challenge those restrictions. Simple access to the public sphere has not been a complete corrective, because the commodification of online spaces privileges a narrow performance of "appropriate" femininity in order to be recognized in a "visual/gendered economy of representation for unknown numbers of watching others."[44] By focusing on empowering girls to control when they move from the private sphere to the public sphere and carving out commercial-free zones, we may be better able to realize the potential of the virtual bedroom to position girls as resistive media producers and distributors.

Notes

1　Sian Lincoln, "Teenage Girls' 'Bedroom Culture': Codes Versus Zones," in *After Subculture: Critical Commentaries in Contemporary Youth Culture*, eds. Andy Bennett & Keith Kahn-Harris (Basingstoke: Palgrave, 2004), 95; Jacqueline Reid-Walsh & Claudia Mitchell, "Girls' Web Sites: A Virtual 'Room of One's Own'?," in *All About the Girl: Culture, Power and Identity*, ed. Anita Harris (New York: Routledge, 2004), 175.
2　Angela McRobbie & Jenny Garber, "Girls and Subcultures," in *Resistance through Rituals: Youth Subcultures in Post-War Britain*, eds. Stuart Hall & Tony Jefferson (London: Harper Collins Academic, 1976), 112.

3   Anita Harris, "Revisiting Bedroom Culture: New Spaces for Young Women's Politics," *Hecate* 27:1 (2001): 131.

4   Jena McGill, "What Have You Done for Me Lately? Reflections on Redeeming Privacy for Battered Women," in *Lessons from the Identity Trail: Anonymity, Privacy and Identity in a Networked Society*, eds. Ian Kerr, Valerie Steeves & Carol Lucock (New York: Cambridge University Press, 2008), 165.

5   Reid-Walsh & Mitchell, *supra* note 1 at 175. There are indications that girls continue to be subjected to more parental control than boys when it comes to accessing networked media (see Johnson, Chapter XIII). Navigating parental control with respect to media may be particularly challenging for girls from some immigrant families (see Ndengevin-goma, Chapter IV).

6   Angela McRobbie & Jenny Garber, "Girls and Subcultures," in *Feminism and Youth Culture: From Jackie to Just Seventeen*, ed. Angela McRobbie (Boston: Unwin Hyman, 1991), 112.

7   Lincoln, *supra* note 1 at 95.

8   It is, however, interesting to consider, whether, and if so, how, the "postfeminist discipline through feminine surveillance" that Kanai suggests in Chapter III frames girls' self-representations online was also operational in the less mediated bedroom space theorized by McRobbie & Garber, and later by Lincoln, *supra* note 1.

9   Lincoln, *supra* note 1 at 95–103.

10 Michele White, "Too Close to See: Men, Women and Webcams," *New Media & Society* 5:1 (2003): 8.

11 Teri Senft, *Camgirls, Celebrity and Community in the Age of Social Networks* (New York: Peter Lang, 2008), 84; Krista Scott-Dixon, "Turbo Chicks: Talkin' 'bout My Generation: Third Wave Feminism Is Comfortable with Contradiction Because That's the Only Way the World Makes Sense," *Herizons* 16:2 (2002): 16; Hille Koskela, "Webcams, TV Shows and Mobile Phones: Empowering Exhibitionism," *Surveillance and Society* 2:2/3 (2004): 211.

12 Reid-Walsh & Mitchell, *supra* note 1 at 174.

13 *Ibid.,* at 174.

14 Mary Celeste Kearney, "Productive Spaces: Girls' Bedrooms as Sites of Cultural Production," *Journal of Children and Media* 1:2 (2007): 127.

15 *Ibid.,* at 138, emphasis in original. For further analysis of these claims, see Milford, Chapter II and Kanai, Chapter III.

16 For a rural/urban comparative analysis, see Burkell & Saginur, Chapter V.

17 Our rural adult focus group included Catlin (19), Laura (18), Trish (18), and Brianne (20). Our rural minor focus group included Courtney (17), Chelsea (17), Paula (17), Beth (16), and Josie (16). Our urban adult focus

group included Keira (21), Donna (19), Jill (20), Andrea (22), Ashley (18), and Kathleen (20). Our urban minor focus group included Vicky (17), Eve (16), Abby (17), Jacquelyn (17), Lauryn (17), Monique (16), and Jane (16). Our rural adult interviewees were Cassandra (19), Becky (19), and Amelia (18). Our rural minor interviewees were Monica (16), Lynda (17), and Nicole (16). Our urban adult interviewees were Alessandra (21), Mackenzie (20), and Cindy (20). Our urban minor interviewees were Alicia (17), Clare (16), and Josée (15).

18   Kearney, *supra* note 14 at 138.

19   A finding remarkably similar to those discussed in Kanai, Chapter III.

20   Lincoln, *supra* note 1 at 102.

21   Lincoln, *supra* note 1 at 96.

22   Statistics Canada, "Labour Force Survey," (Statistics Canada, 2012).

23   Sonya Gulati, "Canada's Small and Medium-Sized Business Owners: Diverse Society in a Microcosm," *TD Economics Special Report* (2012).

24   Meenakshi Gigi Durham, "Constructing the 'New Ethnicities': Media, Sexuality and Diaspora Identity in the Lives of South Asian Immigrant Girls," *Critical Studies in Media Communication* 21:2 (2004): 142.

25   Marsha H. Levy-Warren, *The Adolescent Journey: Development, Identity Formation, and Psychotherapy* (New York: Jason Aronson, 1977), xvii.

26   Durham, *supra* note 24 at 141.

27   Harris, *supra* note 3 at 132; MediaSmarts, *Young Canadians in a Wired World, Phase I: Parent and Youth Focus Groups* (Ottawa: MediaSmarts, 2000), 23; MediaSmarts, *Young Canadians in a Wired World, Phase II: Focus Groups* (Ottawa: MediaSmarts, 2004), 15.

28   Valerie Steeves & Jane Bailey, "Will the Real Digital Girl Please Stand Up?," in *New Visualities, New Technologies: The New Ecstasy of Communication*, eds. Hille Koskela & John Macgregor Wise (Surrey, UK: Ashgate, 2013), 43; see also Bailey, Chapter I; Milford, Chapter II; Kanai, Chapter III.

29   Valerie Steeves, *Young Canadians in a Wired World, Phase III: Talking to Youth and Parents about Life Online* (Ottawa: MediaSmarts, 2012), 4.

30   Valerie Steeves, *Young Canadians in a Wired World, Phase III: Online Privacy, Online Publicity* (Ottawa: MediaSmarts, 2014), 36.

31   Valerie Steeves, "Swimming in the Fishbowl: Young People, Identity and Surveillance in Networked Spaces," in *Digitizing Identities*, eds. Irma van der Ploeg & Jason Pridmore (London: Routledge, 2015, in press).

32   Valerie Steeves, "It's Not Child's Play: The Online Invasion of Children's Privacy," *University of Ottawa Law and Technology Journal* 3:1 (2006): 174; Valerie Steeves, "The Watched Child: Surveillance in Three Online Playgrounds," in *Rights of the Child: Proceedings of the International Conference, Ottawa 2007*, eds. Tara Collins, Rachel Grondin, Veronica Pinero, Marie Pratte & Marie-Claude Roberge (Montreal: Wilson & Lafleur, 2008), 118.

33 Shelly Grabe, Monique L. Ward & Janet Shibley Hyde, "The Role of the Media in Body Image Concerns Among Women: A Meta-Analysis of Experimental and Correlational Studies," *Psychological Bulletin* 134:3 (2008): 460.

34 Rebecca L. Collins, "Content Analysis of Gender Roles in Media: Where Are We Now and Where Should We Go?," *Sex Roles* 64:3–4 (2011): 295.

35 Lincoln, *supra* note 1 at 98.

36 Elizabeth Behm-Morawitz & Dana Mastro, "The Effects of the Sexualization of Female Video Game Characters on Gender Stereotyping and Female Self-Concept," *Sex Roles* 61:11–12 (2009): 808.

37 Jesse Fox & Jeremy N. Bailenson, "Virtual Virgins and Vamps: The Effects of Exposure to Female Characters' Sexualized Appearance and Gaze in an Immersive Virtual Environment," *Sex Roles* 61:3–4 (2009): 148.

38 Meenakshi Gigi Durham, "Articulating Adolescent Girls' Resistance to Patriarchal Discourse in Popular Media," *Women's Studies in Communication* 22:2 (1999): 222.

39 *Ibid.*

40 Kandy James, "'I Just Gotta Have My Own Space!': The Bedroom as a Leisure Site for Adolescent Girls," *Journal of Leisure Research* 33:1 (2001): 74.

41 Lincoln, *supra* note 1 at 96.

42 Lincoln, *supra* note 1 at 97.

43 Harris, *supra* note 3 at 133.

44 See Kanai, Chapter III.

CHAPTER VII

Girls and Online Drama: Aggression, Surveillance, or Entertainment?

Priscilla M. Regan and Diana L. Sweet

Introduction

Drama as a concept is difficult to define. For most scholars and individuals, it generally includes some heightened emotional behaviour or words, some aggressive "lashing out" or attempt to involve others in what is occurring, and some connection to or interpretation of everyday events or words. Drama may include "spreading rumors, social exclusion, and threats of withdrawal of acceptance and love."[1] Drama is often used, especially for young people, as shorthand for what they regard as indirect, relational, and social aggression. According to Coyne et al, relational aggression can best be understood as the behaviour of individuals that intentionally hurts others; however, it can also be understood as inadvertent, with the goal being not to hurt others but to draw attention to oneself.[2] The increasing degree to which internet-connected technologies are incorporated into young people's lives has broadened the sphere within which drama takes place. Not only are the lines blurred between online and offline life in the classroom, but the same has happened in their personal lives. As difficult as the concept has been to define, drama on networked platforms creates new challenges and opportunities for new research.

The goal of this chapter is to query the meaning and purpose of online drama in the lives of young women and girls in order to provide an understanding of online drama that can inform policy discussions. We use as our data the interviews and focus group discussions from the eGirls Project discussed in other chapters in this volume.[3] In January and February of 2013, researchers with the eGirls Project held a series of interviews and focus groups with girls and young women between the ages of 15 and 22. All participants used interactive online media (such as social networking, blogging, and/ or user-generated video sites) as a regular part of their social lives. Half of our sample resided in an urban Ontario setting and half resided in a rural Ontario setting.[4] We interviewed six girls aged 15 to 17 and six young women aged 18 to 22. An additional twenty-two participated in four focus group discussions, as follows: (1) seven girls aged 15 to 17 living in the urban setting; (2) five girls aged 15 to 17 living in the rural setting; (3) six young women aged 18 to 22 living in the urban setting; and (4) four young women aged 18 to 22 living in the rural setting. A professional research house recruited our participants on the basis of sex, age (either 15 to 17 or 18 to 22) and location of residence (urban or rural). While participants were not recruited on the basis of self-identification with regard to other aspects of their identities, such as race, ethnicity, gender identity, or sexual orientation, our participant group included members of racialized, linguistic, and various religious groups. Participants agreed to the audiotaping and transcription of the interviews and focus groups, with use of pseudonyms and deletion of all identifying information.[5]

The topic of drama was prevalent in all the interviews and the focus groups. Our participants were acutely aware of instances of drama, were concerned about its negative effects on other individuals and on the social group itself, were intrigued by the various ways in which individuals responded to drama, and were puzzled by the connections between drama online and offline. The distinction between drama and gossip is an important one to address up front. We conceptualize gossip as one potential manifestation of drama, but we do not intend to conflate their meanings. This point will be addressed in greater detail throughout the paper as necessary.

We use three different conceptual lenses or frameworks for analyzing the drama we find in the eGirls focus groups and interviews—the frame of social/relational aggression, the frame of surveillance, and the frame of entertainment—in order to better understand the dynamics and meaning of these dramatic interactions among girls and young women. We chose and created the three separate frames based on the evidence present in the transcripts. The way the young women used, spoke of, and related to drama seemed to largely fit under these separate conceptualizations. As will be discussed throughout the chapter, they all touch upon different aspects and thus tease out nuances and richness that have their own policy implications. The chapter first examines the connections, as well as the similarities and differences, between online and offline drama; second, briefly reviews the literature regarding drama in the lives of girls and young women through the three conceptual lenses noted above; third, provides evidence from our data that reflects each framework; and finally, concludes with a discussion of how each framework increases understanding of what is occurring when girls and young women engage in (and are exposed to) online drama and corresponding policy implications as we see them.

Online and Offline Overlaps and Disconnects

Drawing lines between online and offline activities generally (and drama in particular) has become more difficult and may soon be impossible. Initially some scholars and commentators envisioned the internet as a "place" separate from the physical world, as reflected in terms such as "meatspace" and "cyberspace." Rheingold reflected on both the positive and negative possibilities of a "virtual community" that contained the prospect of a separate existence from that of one's physical community and offered individuals ways of transforming their identities.[6] Turkle suggested that "life on the screen" offered individuals a space in which to play with different identities, personal styles, and behaviours.[7] Over time it became clear that the online and offline worlds are less parallel universes than ones that intersect and now may be totally integrated, given the ubiquity of online devices and their multiple uses. The advent of the social networking sites, where people connect mostly with offline acquaintances and other people with whom they already share some kind of relationship, means that people expect to see "true" representations.

The fluidity between the online space and other social environments seems to escalate the drama that occurs in one environment and then quickly moves to the other. While one might expect that online personas will now generally depict accurate representations of the offline self, the online version now also has to adapt and contend with technological and emotional limitations in how one can display and interpret content and their meanings, as illustrated below:

> Brianne (Age 20): Because you spend the whole—if you're in school with them and you're there and in all your classes, you're already talking to them all day, then you go home and you're still talking to them all day, then it's like, somebody says one thing and takes it wrong, or they're trying to make a funny comment and you don't think it's funny, then the next thing you know, it's like, you're in this big fight. So sometimes you just have to separate, like, your alliances—like, who do you talk to on Facebook or, like, who to chat with. And who to, just, not.

Our respondents, especially the older respondents,[8] were frustrated by the fluidity of drama across the online and offline worlds and identified a desire to separate the two because "there's no proper emotions displayed through Facebook because a lot of things can be very vague and misinterpreted, and that kind of thing I don't like, so generally I try to stay away from serious conversation on Facebook and try to leave it to in person" (Becky, age 19). The key problem in the online environment was the room for misinterpretation and misunderstanding, whereas, "I can look at a person I can see how they act emotionally when I say something verbally and I can catch the mistake right then and there" (Becky, age 19).

Moreover, our respondents noted that the interpersonal filtering that occurs in the offline world gets lost in online spaces, as individuals do not seem compelled to adhere to the same type of social graces that are expected in offline experiences. As Caitlin (age 19) notes, "Like my friend, she is the worst person on Facebook. She'll be so mean to you on Facebook, but the second she sees you face-to-face, everything's perfect …. " Unlike talking about someone behind their back in offline spaces, such comments on Facebook are generally visible to wider audiences, and the audience—or possibility of an audience—may play a role in the online drama.

Conceptual Lenses

In order to better understand the role, meaning, and implications of online drama for girls and young women, and informed by our focus group and interview data, we use three different conceptual lenses. Each lens highlights somewhat different elements of drama and casts drama in slightly different ways, which we maintain are all important. As noted above, the three lenses are social/relational aggression, surveillance, and entertainment. We view our analysis as compatible with Marwick and boyd's definition of drama as "performative, interpersonal conflict that takes place in front of an active, engaged audience, often on social media."[9] Each of our lenses taps a component of their definition with the "mean girls" lens focused on the "interpersonal conflict"; the surveillance lens focused on the "in front of," in that a choice is made to actively watch (or put something "in front of" you); and the entertainment lens focused on the "engaged [but sometimes passive] audience." We believe that disaggregating these separate components will help to better understand the phenomenon of online drama and thereby to craft better policy responses.

The social/relational aggression lens is often associated with the "mean girls" construction, which casts drama as interpersonal, even while categorizing it as a particular kind of social phenomenon. As Ringrose argues, the preoccupation with female adolescent relational aggression reflects a postfeminist response to feminist critiques of notions of girls as vulnerable and to critiques of male-biased models of developmental psychology, which resulted in a focus on "mean girls" as the representation of girls' aggression. "Mean girls" bully, gossip, manipulate, exploit, and lead victims to feel ostracized and, in some cases, driven to suicide. Ringrose notes that the result of this line of thinking has been to view girl power and girl aggression in pathological ways based on white, middle-class expectations, and solutions to such meanness also reflected in liberal thinking about preserving white, middle-class femininity.

The surveillance lens takes a broader approach to online drama, seeing it as an instance of general social curiosity, monitoring, and norm-setting, which is facilitated by the architecture of the online world. Online drama involves watching others and watching oneself for purposes of checking on someone in order to hold them accountable or to judge their behaviour.[10] The surveillance lens highlights both the "stalking" that occurs as friends and others actively watch those on social networking sites, as well as the self-presentation and identity formation that involves one watching and judging oneself online.

Finally, the entertainment lens views online drama as something to be watched for its emotive draw or appeal. Uses and gratifications theory from communication literature illuminates the importance of the role of individual motivations for using social media. One of the main directions of current research employing the uses and gratifications theory focuses on the "effectiveness of different media (or content) to meet an individual's needs."[11] Of the many other gratifications sought by individuals, one is entertainment. In this case, girls and young women literally watch the dramatic unfoldings of their peers' lives and comment on them in much the same way as they would a TV show or movie—for the enjoyment or pleasure it brings. This is sometimes referred to as "stalking," but following someone's activities for entertainment is passive, somewhat akin to "rubbernecking" or watching a fight in a school cafeteria. "Stalking" for surveillance purposes is more intentional and active. Another key aspect of the entertainment lens is the link to gossip. As Fine and Rosnow note, entertainment is one of the main functions of gossip, especially when a friendly relationship already exists between parties.[12]

Once these three frames were conceptualized, we re-analyzed the transcripts and found that each lens drew our attention to different elements of what the girls and young women termed online drama. In the sections that follow, we demonstrate what we found as we turned each lens back to our data. In the final section we compare the frameworks, provide preliminary thoughts on how each lens may add to and better qualify our understanding of online drama, and consider how these different lenses might similarly or differently inform policy discussions.

Social/Relational Aggression Frame

This lens is the one that is most often used in discussing both online and offline emotionally charged interactions of girls and young women. The term itself highlights both the gendered and also the "adolescent" character of the interactions. The term does, however, also convey the sense that such interactions are intended to be harmful or critical—and that there is a target whom one wants to marginalize. The somewhat typical logic is reflected in this exchange in one of our focus groups:

> Abby (age 17): Girls are just so good at pointing out what people are just so insecure about, and feel bad about, like.
> Eve (age 16): We get in your head, we know.
> Abby (age 17): Psychological pain [laughing].

Eve (age 16): I don't know, we know how to get into each other's head, it's weird, but like we just know.

Jacquelyn (age 17): 'Cause we know what would affect us.

The nature and intensity of the social/relational aggression also seem to vary somewhat by the online site itself, some of which is dependent upon specific affordances and limitations of the architecture.[13] For example, in a focus group, one girl (Lauryn, age 17) noted that "a lot of the time, like, on Twitter it will be more like people attacking like your character, like saying like you're so over dramatic or you're such a dummy, you're so like stupid, more stuff like that. Where if it's on Facebook, it's more pictures. It's going to be a lot more, you're fat, you're ugly. It really depends on the situation that you're in." The other girls in the focus group elaborated on this type of interaction:

Abby (age 17): Yeah, like if someone puts up a picture and they're all dressed up and they have their makeup done, and you put, why are you trying, you just killed, like, their whole ….

Eve (age 16): Like she felt so happy about those pictures, like, oh, my hair ….

Abby (age 17): Yeah, like you put the effort in and you think you'll get something good out of it, then they put, why you are trying, for no reason like.

Lauryn (age 17): But, then no one says anything about it, "why are you trying" and no comments under that.

Abby (age 17): Because then it looks like you're on the person's side.

There is a distinct power relationship that is being negotiated in these interactions, as this quote from one of our interviews illustrates:

Eve (age 16): In general, even girls can be like, you know, power-seeking people, when you're like, in a position when you can get more, you're going to go for it, and if you know that you can get into that person's face to get more, you're still going to go for it. Some people will do anything just to go, go push them out of the way or anything. So just to be that tough person you're going, you know, [to] put that other person down and like, push them aside and show them that you, you're tougher.

The power and social aggressive elements of these interactions are related to behaviour that school administrators and policies call cyberbullying. While the parallels are clear, the social/relational aggression frame is meant to help us better understand elements of this behaviour beyond the capacity of most definitions of cyberbullying alone. Through interviews and surveys, a study by Lenhart et al provides evidence that the vast majority of students witness "mean or cruel behaviour on social media."[14] In a recent report by MediaSmarts on young Canadians in the Internet age, 37 percent of students report having been the object of online mean or cruel behaviour, while only 23 percent admit to having done or said something mean to someone else online.[15] Moreover, the report highlights inconsistencies with generally accepted principles about the gendered aspect of online mean and cruel behaviour, stating that boys take part in such behaviour more often than girls. Marwick and boyd point out the ways that young people distinguish "drama" or "punking and pranking" from bullying.[16] They find that the dichotomous and protagonist/antagonist nature and labels that coincide with the latter may be too clear-cut for students. By sticking with terms like drama, punking, and pranking, young people are able to maintain a certain level of ambiguity and avoid prescriptive, adult labels of "bully" or "victim."[17]

With specific regard to the behaviour portrayed by girls, some scholars have also argued that in participating in aggression that is indirect or less obvious, girls avoid being labelled as deviant.[18] Related to this, Oppliger surveys the vast number of typical "mean girl" characters who permeate through TV serials.[19] The TV shows and characters exhibit an element of norm-setting by demonstrating possible models of acceptable behaviour. Our respondents similarly viewed social/relational aggressive behaviour in an explanatory social context, such as advertising and beauty ideals or competition for male attention. They were indeed aware of this as gendered behaviour, positioning and competing for male attention.[20] Regarding gendered responses to interpersonal drama, Paula (age 17) concludes that "boys are a little more direct about it. Like, it's just more, like childish stuff, but girls get more, like mean about it, like, talk about personal stuff online." Others from the focus group agree that girls "backstab" other girls on Facebook, whereas boys will publicly call for offline solutions (possibly altercations) to online drama.

Another reason that our respondents appear to avoid the cyberbullying label is that it seems related to a phase of adolescent development, while drama itself seems to occur across different age cohorts. One of our interviewees (Becky, age 19) explained it as follows:

> like my sister, when she was younger she was cyberbullied, and I'm sure when I was younger, too, I was cyberbullied. You know the reason why I say that is 'cause like, when we were younger, it's because there's generally a lot more drama on Facebook. And [it] has to do back with high school, and if you really don't like somebody, it's easier to say it on Facebook than say it straight to their face .... And with, um, because everybody is so uneducated at that young age, I would say because everybody is more ignorant, they're going to not know to walk away from it, like, they continue to fuel the fire.

What does appear to be different in the online world is that the architecture of the sites plays an important role in how girls and young women engage in drama. As noted above, in one focus group, Lauryn (age 17) drew a distinction between Twitter, where words were the currency, and Facebook, where pictures were more often used to depict the drama. In an interview, Amelia (age 18) pointed out that, on Facebook, making fun of someone or starting a rumour will occur, but that would not be posted on Twitter; instead, on Twitter "you don't see the actual hurt, like, happening but you'll see the effect of it afterwards." The limit on characters confines the role of Twitter in young people's social lives. Although requiring an authentic identity, Facebook allows more freedom in engaging with both friends and acquaintances in a more visual and blatant manner. How open one is, and how much of an overlap one allows between close friends and others, depends on how one sets one's privacy settings. Interestingly, we did not find the girls and young women in our study talking about permissions and privacy settings in the context of their discussions about online drama as much as we expected.[21]

One might expect that the online architecture would be more individually – and identity-wise – based than in the offline world, but as Monique (age 16) noted, groups are able to challenge that by having "a whole group of girls formulating this one text or tweet or whatever. Um, it's a lot more having to do with social standing and positioning, so you want your friends to be supporting you … we need that support, that social sort of assurance."

Another challenge posed by online architecture is that one might not be communicating with the person one thinks one is communicating with. For example, Cassandra (age 19) noted, "Me and my friend Mariah got into a fight, and she stole my friend Celine's phone and she was texting me off my friend Celine's phone bitching at me, and I'm thinking Celine is mad at me, but it's my other friend."

The girls and young women we talked to identified two ways of dealing with certain kinds of online drama. The first is the quite traditional method of "going to the principal," supplemented by removing oneself from Facebook or unfriending someone. In a MediaSmarts report, students found cyberbullying easier to deal with because it left behind an easy-to-follow trail so often absent in face-to-face bullying.[22] A focus group participant, Keira (age 21), for example, recalled an instance of an online fight where a student printed out an entire conversation in order to bring it and show the high school principal. Unfortunately the MediaSmarts report also noted that students felt that the schools (teachers and other authorities) took many of the general interactions among young people and redefined them as bullying.[23]

Another of our interviewees reported a similar instance when two girls had a "big long fight on Facebook" and printed off the Facebook pages and "ended up taking them to the principal because she was threatening her and threatening to, you know, do things like stab her with a knife if she ever came close." The conflict stopped, not necessarily because the principal intervened, but because "they blocked each other from Facebook … [and] took out the social media aspect" (Becky, 19). The second way of dealing with online drama is also similar to offline methods, that is, by establishing a boundary — "to make it private" (Monica, age 16) by texting or talking face-to-face. This instance of boundary-setting also demonstrates another way in which young people are focused on the importance of audiences. A different MediaSmarts report on online privacy showcases how young people actively block friends more often than family members.[24]

Similarly, after two close friends drifted apart somewhat after going to college, one misinterpreted a subsequent online posting, and the friends resolved it by taking each other off Facebook — as relayed in the following:

Cassandra (age 19): Um … the situation before college was, I was in college for about a month, and I kind of lost, you know, contact with friends here, you know, busy doing my own thing. And my friend posted something, "Wow, it's amazing how people go off to college and totally forget about their best friends." And I thought it was about me, so I commented, like, I sent her a private message, and I was like, "Is that comment about me because like, you know, why don't you just tell me straight up?" She's like, she didn't comment back. I was like, whatever, I'm gonna delete [her] because I'm not gonna deal with that. And then it just started a big fight.

Researcher: Now was that a really super close friend?

Cassandra: Yeah. She, she's my best friend.

Researcher: Is she still your best friend?

Cassandra : Yeah. We're, we're friends again.

Researcher: Yeah.

Cassandra : But we don't have each other on Facebook.

The social/relational aggression frame emphasizes both the passive and active elements of online drama. As the next sections will demonstrate, this conceptual lens may miss other aspects of online drama.

Surveillance Frame

An expanding literature seeks to understand the nature, degree, and consequences of surveillance activities in online environments, and specifically on social networking sites (SNSs). Scholars, like Koskela, have demonstrated how the traditional panopticon can translate into surveillance of urban spaces and then of cyberspace as well.[25] In the case of online spaces, surveillance is not only practiced by authorities, by those in power or seeking power, but it is also performed by the majority of members of SNSs. In fact, young people talk about Facebook "stalking" as an everyday occurrence. Lampe et al presented a study in which college freshman were surveyed regarding their use of Facebook.[26] After keeping in touch with high school friends, respondents indicated that looking at profiles of individuals they met in offline social situations was the second most frequent reason to use Facebook. This behaviour has been called Facebook stalking, with this type of surveillance constraining the capacity of girls and young women to fully participate online, due to the possibility of unknown observers and unintended consequences.[27] The surveillance activities described by the respondents include social curiosity, the desire to remain up to date, norm-setting, and identity formation and self-presentation.

The surveillance can be between family members, friends, current or former romantic partners, acquaintances, and so on. The interviews and focus groups most frequently brought up issues of peer surveillance. To a large extent, peer surveillance was based on curiosity. For example, Courtney (age 17) reported, "when you see your boyfriend liking, like, naked girl photos and stuff like that. That's another drama thing to do with photos, is when you can actually see when people like something, and you're like, 'Ohhhh. They like that?'"

This curiosity has been defined by Hartung and Renner as the "desire for new information and knowledge," thus encapsulating a benign element to the behaviour.[28]

Another important motivator in peer surveillance was to be up to date: "Yeah, like, at my locker, my friends will be like, 'Did you hear what this person said to this person last night on Facebook?' and then I'll go on Facebook and check it out" (Paula, age 17). Being up to date also enabled one to check the veracity of what was being talked about: "So I know what's going on. Who's saying what, make sure nobody … so I know the story kinda too, so. When they're explaining back to me, I'll be like, um, you actually said that" (Monica, age 16).

Peer surveillance appears to play an important role in norm-setting amongst a group. For example, Jill (age 20) reported: "A girl, let's say she's — I don't know, with a bunch of guys in a sexual pose, or drinking a lot — has tons of booze around her, or something. Someone will write a comment that will be, like, kind of subtle but showing that it's inappropriate, and a lot of people will join in …. " The judging that is enabled through peer surveillance can be somewhat harsh without the larger context in which to place it, as Lauryn (age 17) reports:

> Everything on the internet is so easy to judge. Like, if you see, like, a girl, like a picture of a girl, and she's not really wearing that much makeup, like not that much clothes, but automatically in your head you want to think, oh, she's a slut. But in reality, if you get to know her, she might be one of the nicest girls, she may not be a slut at all. Maybe she's just comfortable taking a

picture like that, so it's like, I think that, like, people, like, judge it a lot, and they stereotype a lot and you don't know that. Just because a girl is taking a picture in a slutty outfit doesn't mean that she's not doing good things in her life …. Like, I wouldn't want people to judge me at high school just off one picture, just 'cause like, you can see some of my boobs. Like, I don't want people to be, like, oh she's such a slut.

Peer surveillance is also related to girls and young women engaging online mechanisms in their identity formation and self-presentation.[29] While it was not originally the case in the 1990s, the majority of well-known and well-used SNSs now require a certain amount of authenticity, thus limiting the degree to which an individual can "try on" new identities.[30] There is, however, a chance to be selective in the information and the identity that is presented on such SNSs. This is relevant for networking sites like LinkedIn that focus on professional identities as opposed to social and personal connections. Similarly, individuals can be selective in the information they share on the sites themselves. If an individual chooses to keep certain details private, the identity may be authentic but not complete. Our respondents, who were clearly conscious of their evolving identities and the appropriateness of conveying different images to different audiences, used such boundary-setting as a way of controlling parental surveillance, in order to restrict their parents' knowledge of the drama in their lives and even their parents' ability to add more drama by their reactions. This is reflected in the two quotes below:

> Beth (age 16): Well, both my parents have Facebook. They never go on it, but they both tried to add me. Well, my mum hasn't, but my dad is pretty cool. But, still, I wouldn't want him seeing … not what I post, but what people post on my wall. 'Cause, like, my family is really tight in that way, and they'd try to, like, do something about it. And I can handle myself. So it's just – I don't really want them getting themselves into something that is my battle.

And:

> Becky (age 19): Um, mine is, it'll show some more than others, because I did modelling and some of the photos I posted

are boudoir and, ah, I had negative criticism from my mother. Everybody else loved it, but my mother thought it was light porn in her opinion, and I, I understood that if she didn't want to see that, that was fine.

The architectures of the sites allow surveillance to occur in ways that increase the likelihood or intensity of online drama. For example, many sites provide a feature by which you can monitor whether others have read your post/update:

> Catlin (age 19): And they can see when you read it too, now. It used to be, like, you couldn't tell, and now it says "seen" and it tells you what time they saw your message at. So you know if they're ignoring it or not.

Most of our respondents agreed that they "hated" this feature. As another focus group member noted:

> Paula (age 17): … And, like, I hate the new "seen it at 11:some-thing" [feature on Facebook that tells you at what time some-thing has been read], because then you're, like, and then they're going to get mad, if you've just read it and you don't answer.

Some take this feature into account in deciding how to communicate with someone, also allowing opportunities for more drama. One young woman (Jill, age 20), who wanted to wish her ex-boyfriend happy birthday "sent him a short little message on Facebook, so I'd know if he'd read it or not. Because if it was in a text, you never know if it goes through; text is kind of unreliable. And he did read it, and he never responded. And yeah, it kind of hurt to see that he read it and didn't take the time to respond." Another girl who sent a friend several messages about getting together could tell that her friend had read the messages and ignored them but the message sender (Andrea, age 22) noted that "it's good to know, sometimes, how stupid people are [laughter]."

The surveillance lens highlights the ways in which policing what people are doing, or whether they are responding, or how they are responding can accentuate and intensify what is occurring online. One can use the architecture or technical capacities of online sites to manipulate online drama in ways not easily possible offline. The policy perspective associated with this lens would logically focus, not on the behaviour of girls and young women, but instead on the policies of the online sites and how much control they afford the user in use of these technical capacities. The next section offers a third frame for viewing online drama—with yet another policy perspective.

Entertainment Frame

An individual's motivation for media use can in part be seen to drive each of the three lenses and the type of drama and the ways they are involved in drama. This may be especially the case when delving into the entertainment lens. In a study looking at Facebook gratifications specifically, Zhang et al identified entertainment as one of the most important.[31] Their study, however, characterized Facebook entertainment as a way of killing time, escaping from work or pressure, or enjoyment through playing games and other applications. In this respect, the present study underlines the need for future research to include aspects of audience engagement and a more well-rounded concept of entertainment in the understanding of online drama.[32] Enjoyment from watching drama unfold may be a way to either kill time or escape work or pressure, but being interested in the dramatic lives of others is specific in a way not well examined in the literature up until now. After watching drama unfold, spectators then have something to talk about further. As pointed out above, gossip is considered entertaining, especially when the parties all know each other.[33] Furthermore, it should be noted that while gossip is so often associated with girls, recent scholarship demonstrates the tendency to gossip remains high across one's lifespan regardless of gender.[34]

Our respondents describe how they glance or browse through posts on social networking sites to see what others are doing. This seems similar to "channel-surfing," not targeted or looking for something specific, but flipping through to see what might be of interest. In this way, they are looking for what is entertaining, and acting as an online spectator, as indicated by the passage below:

> Chelsea (age 17): If it's really hardcore drama, like, I will sit there and wait 'til it ends, because I'm, like, sitting there with my bowl of popcorn, I swear to you. It's happened before. But there are just some nights that I'll look at it and I'm like, I just move on. But then there are other nights when I'm like, "Ooh, look at this." Researcher: And what kind of stuff catches your eye like that?

> Chelsea : It's, like, mostly, like, the people I know or the people, like, acquaintances … like, I know them by face, and I'm like, "Oh my God, I can't believe they're saying that." Like, it's not complete strangers; that's just not fun. Like, I don't know them; I don't know their story. So it's more likely, like, just friends. Or not friends, or if they're friends the next day, or what they're doing.

The fact that young girls and women have large numbers of friends or followers on their social networking sites has not gone unnoticed and is sometimes criticized by peers.[35] But the entertainment lens highlights a somewhat different aspect of the extent of one's friends or followers. As one of our respondents observed, it is not uncommon for students to have friended every other student in their grade. Our interviews and focus groups indicate that the motivation behind having so many friends may be in part due to the passive entertainment these friends provide the user. One of the main reasons girls may find online drama as entertaining as they do is because they are often only loosely affiliated with the persons involved. The same may happen in offline spaces when a fight breaks out and students gather around. Those who are invested in the situation, or are close friends, will likely step in and get involved. The passive spectators will want a good view of what is happening and the entertainment value is enough to remain connected to certain figures online:

> Andrea (age 22): Like, okay. Sometimes on Facebook—I was actually talking with my friends about this the other day, too. There are, like, those people that when you're looking at your newsfeed, you're not friends with them in person, but you think they're really entertaining on Facebook, so you keep them. And kudos if they do that to you too, but they'll post something really funny … they keep their Facebook really updated with what their life is. And that's kind of … it's like, oh, it's awful that I'm saying this, but it's like a reality show, like, on your Facebook. And you can see, like, what's going on. And it's sadly interesting.

Again, we see the theme of Facebook "stalking" as entertainment:

> Cassandra (age 19): Yeah, in college, I added them on Facebook, you know, do the whole Facebook stalking, look at their pictures, you know, check out their main page, whatever.

Researcher: And what's the point of all that?

Cassandra : I don't know. You're bored. You just like stalking ….

Researcher: Entertainment again?

Cassandra : Yeah. Entertainment, like, I don't know, 'cause everybody forgot what outdoors is. So, or picking up the phone.

While the majority of people would value entertainment as a passive activity, there are also those individuals who are entertained by being a part of the activity. Starting drama out of perceived boredom was also an underlying theme throughout some of the interviews.

Cassandra (age 19): All my friends. All my friends flip out publicly. They, I don't know ….

Researcher: That's gotta be a lot of drama ….

Cassandra : Very.

Researcher: Why do you think they like it [drama]?

Cassandra : Small town, nothing to do. You know, like, if you're not in a club, if you're not on the internet, if you're not in school, if you're even doing something you shouldn't be doing. So like, drama keeps them entertained.

The entertainment lens reveals that, although our respondents may be using language that evokes surveillance images, for example, voicing a desire to "keep up with" certain drama, the respondents are acting more as spectators of people and events, and are watching more passively for their own entertainment. The following exchange well illustrates this:

Researcher: [Laughter] So what kind of things would like, what sort of things do you feel you need to be kept in the loop about?

Amelia (age 18): Um, gossip, like, what's happened on the weekend, like, usually for the past little while I haven't been able to go, uh, 'cause I've had car troubles, so I have been, haven't been out. So like I'll use Twitter for, as in, fill me in with what's going on at parties or something, if there's been drama or if somebody breaks up or [laughter] something, just stupid small town gossip kind of stuff.

Researcher: [Laughter]

Amelia : Just like teenagers, it's pretty ridiculous, but that's what it is.

Researcher: But it's fun?

Amelia: Yeah.
Researcher: And, and so um, what, are you comfortable giving an example of a recent drama that you heard about on Twitter?
Amelia: Um yeah. There's typically, it's a lot of, kinda relationship stuff. Like there's couples who break up and get back together all the time and it's just, it's ridiculous. [laughter] Um, usually that's like, they'll like just, like, post something about, like, oh why do you do this to me like. Blah, blah, blah, like breaking up, and just kind of small things, where they're complaining about it and then, you know, maybe a day later or two days later they'll post something like, oh I love you so much, like.

The entertainment lens highlights the seemingly more benign aspects of online drama where usually the spectator is involved only passively. In this sense drama serves the same purpose that gossip often does — what's happening now, or did you hear what so and so said or did. Online drama is fodder for speculation, analysis, and discussion among spectators who are participating in what they see as an engaging, enjoyable pastime, sometimes without consideration of the potential impact on the people who are under observation.

Discussion

Each of the lenses highlights a distinct aspect of online drama and reveals the complexity of the intentions and interactions of those involved in such drama. Online drama is not merely social aggression. Nor is it simply monitoring and evaluating one's own or others' behaviour or personae. Nor is it only for amusement or leisure. In this respect, all three lenses are able to better inform our nuanced understanding of how young women engage in online drama and offer some guidance as to possible policy responses and consequences of those responses.

The three lenses also draw attention to the gendered elements girls and young women see in online drama, and how they talk about online drama. Our participants tend to describe other girls in stereotypical ways, sometimes applying the "mean girl" label while letting male aggression go uncontested as just "boys being boys." They also identified meanness as being associated with social power, the high school clique that excludes and operates in both online and offline settings. The surveillance lens is similarly described in gendered terms – parents and others judging behaviour or pictures based on stereotypes or expectations, with drama usually being a negative reaction if a girl strays from the norm. The entertainment lens also engages with stereotypical elements of female behaviour and interests, with links to gossip and the passive enjoyment that comes from drama.

Comparing what is emphasized as one focuses each lens on our participants' discussions about online drama reveals not only the nuances of each lens but the contrasting policy implications. As discussed earlier, the social/relational aggression lens emphasizes elements of power and antagonism – behaviour that is generally accepted as needing to be prevented or deterred in order to protect those who might be targets. But as the MediaSmarts report points out, there is a tendency in schools and policy discussions to define most dramatic interactions among youth as bullying.[36] Similarly, the earlier research of Barron and Lacombe on the media and policy responses to the murder of Reena Virk in 1997 and the resulting "moral panic" about the "nasty girl" point to the policy tendency to see a need for social control and repressive measures.[37] This frame may be the default for policy discussions because it is relatively easy to understand, as it relies on familiar stereotypes[38] and it addresses the potential negative effects that such behaviour might have on others. But it is a paternalistic and punitive response that assumes the behaviour is "bad" and that not only involves regulation by authorities but also puts responsibility on girls and young women to regulate themselves.[39]

As we analyzed the comments of girls and young women using the surveillance lens, it became clear that the surveillance they were talking about was less that of authority figures, parents, and teachers, and more "peer surveillance" or "lateral surveillance"[40] that serves social purposes for both small group formation and cohesion, and for self-development. In general, a surveillance definition of the policy problem emphasizes policy solutions involving the technical capacities of online architectures, as well as notices featuring what to do under certain circumstances and outlining conditions under which one should be cautious. The surveillance definition also shifts attention to surveillance by those with a more controlling or self-interested intent than the curiosity we find motivating peer surveillance. Our analysis leads us to conclude that if we use the surveillance lens to inform public policy, policies need to recognize that the architecture itself creates new opportunities for drama, as well as intensifying drama already taking place, and that policy should be directed not to the motivations of the girls and young women who are watching or being watched, but to the practices of the companies designing and hosting the sites.

Finally the entertainment lens — curious spectators observing online drama as they would a TV show — appears at first to reveal rather benign reasons and effects of online drama, with little justification for policy intervention. However, the parallels between online drama and reality TV are hard to miss. The lure of online drama seems to be encouraged by the celebrities of reality TV, as the "housewives" of wherever TV shows illustrate.[41] If this is indeed the case, then the entertainment lens may provide a justification for a policy response, which draws attention to the need for the media to show greater responsibility and leadership on these issues. In general, however, the entertainment lens reveals that girls' and young women's somewhat passive browsing of online drama is primarily a social mechanism for gathering information about how those in or close to their social group think, feel, and are behaving — a realm where policy intervention would not be justified.

Our analysis overall provides evidence that the online drama that girls and young women engage in and observe is not merely a simple, one-dimensional phenomenon. Instead it is a complex social activity that intersects with offline lives, evolves over time as participants mature, and serves personal, interpersonal, and group purposes. Policy discussions need to take the various lenses into account and not default to what may be considered a somewhat simplistic view of online drama as "mean girls" or social aggression.

Notes

1   Sarah Coyne, Jennifer Linder, David Nelson & Douglas Gentile, "'Frenemies, Fraitors, and Mean-em-aitors': Priming Effects of Viewing Physical and Relational Aggression in the Media on Women," *Aggressive Behavior* 38 (2012): 141, <http://onlinelibrary.wiley.com/doi/10.1002/ab.21410/abstract>.

2   *Ibid.*

3   See Steeves, Chapter VI; Bailey, Chapter I; Burkell & Saginur, Chapter V; Heath, Chapter XIV.

4   For a rural/urban comparative analysis, see Burkell & Saginur, Chapter V.

5   Our rural adult focus group included Catlin (19), Laura (18), Trish (18) ,and Brianne (20). Our rural minor focus group included Courtney (17), Chelsea (17), Paula (17), Beth (16), and Josie (16). Our urban adult focus group included Keira (21), Donna (19), Jill (20), Andrea (22), Ashley (18), and Kathleen (20). Our urban minor focus group included Vicky (17), Eve (16), Abby (17), Jacquelyn (17), Lauryn (17), Monique (16), and Jane (16). Our rural adult interviewees were Cassandra (19), Becky (19), and Amelia (18). Our rural minor interviewees were Monica (16), Lynda (17), and Nicole (16). Our urban adult interviewees were Alessandra (21), Mackenzie (20), and Cindy (20). Our urban minor interviewees were Alicia (17), Clare (16), and Josée (15).

6   Howard Rheingold, *The Virtual Community: Homesteading on the Electronic Frontier* (Reading: Addison-Wesley, 1993).

7   Sherry Turkle, *Life on the Screen: Identity in the Age of the Internet* (New York: Simon & Schuster, 1997).

8   We also noted that rural girls were more likely to try to resolve issues offline than online: Burkell & Saginur, Chapter V.

9   Alice Marwick & danah boyd, "'It's Just Drama': Teen Perspectives on Conflict and Aggression in a Networked Era," *Journal of Youth Studies* 17:9 (2014): 5, <http://research.microsoft.com/pubs/228265/It's%20just%20drama.pdf>.

10   Deborah G. Johnson & Priscilla M. Regan, *Transparency and Surveillance as Sociotechnical Accountability: A House of Mirrors* (London: Routledge, 2014).

11   John Raacke & Jennifer Bonds-Raacke, "MySpace and Facebook: Applying the Uses and Gratifications Theory to Exploring Friend-Networking Sites," *CyberPsychology & Behavior* 11:2 (2008): 170, <http://online.liebertpub.com/doi/pdf/10.1089/cpb.2007.0056>.

12   Gary Alan Fine & Ralph L. Rosnow, "Gossip, Gossipers, Gossiping," *Personality and Social Psychology Bulletin* 4:1 (1978), 163, doi: 10.1177/014616727800400135.

13   See Bailey, Chapter I.

14   Amanda Lenhart, Mary Madden, Aaron Smith, Kristen Purcell, Kathryn Zickuhr & Lee Rainie, "Teens, Kindness and Cruelty on Social Network Sites," *Pew Research Center cruelty on social network sites,* 9 November 2011, <http://www.pewinternet.org/2011/11/09/teens-kindness-and-cruelty-on-social-network-sites>.

15   Valerie Steeves, *Young Canadians in A Wired World, Phase III: Online Privacy, Online Publicity* (Ottawa, Media Awareness Network, 2014), 11, 25, <http://mediasmarts.ca/sites/mediasmarts/files/pdfs/publication-report/full/YCWWIII_Online_Privacy_Online_Publicity_FullReport.pdf>.

16   Marwick & boyd, *supra* note 9 at 14.

17   *Ibid.* at 11.

18   Rachel Simmons, *Odd Girl Out: The Hidden Culture of Aggression in Girls* (Boston: Houghton Mifflin Harcourt, 2011).

19   Patrice A. Oppliger, *Bullies and Mean Girls in Popular Culture* (Jefferson: McFarland, 2013) 95.

20   See Steeves, Chapter VI, and Bailey, Chapter I.

21   See Bailey, Chapter I and Heath, Chapter XIV, for a discussion of technical architectures facilitating conflict.

22   Lenhart et al, *supra* note 14; MediaSmarts, *Young Canadians in a Wired World, Phase III: Talking to Youth and Parents about Life Online Executive Summary* (Ottawa, Media Awareness Network, 2012), 5, <http://mediasmarts.ca/sites/mediasmarts/files/publication-report/summary/ycwwiii-youth-parents-summary.pdf>.

23   Lenhart et al, *supra* note 14 at 37.

24   Valerie Steeves, *Young Canadians in A Wired World, Phase III: Online Privacy, Online Publicity*, (Ottawa, Media Awareness Network, 2014), 26, <http://mediasmarts.ca/sites/mediasmarts/files/pdfs/publication-report/full/YCWWIII_Online_Privacy_Online_Publicity_FullReport.pdf>.

25   Hille Koskela, "'Cam Era' – The Contemporary Urban Panopticon," *Surveillance & Society* 1:3 (2002): 293, <http://www.surveillance-and-society.org/articles1(3)/camera.pdf.

26   Cliffe Lampe, Nicole Ellison & Charles Steinfield, "A Face(Book) in the Crowd: Social Searching vs Social Browsing," in *Proceedings of the 2006 20th Anniversary Conference on Computer Supported Cooperative Work* (New York: ACM, 2006): 167–170, <https://www.msu.edu/~nellison/lampe_et_al_2006.pdf>.

27   Jane Bailey, Valerie Steeves, Jacquelyn Burkell & Priscilla Regan, "Negotiating with Gender Stereotypes on Social Networking Sites: From 'Bicycle Face' to Facebook," *Journal of Communication Inquiry* 37:2 (2013): 108, <http://digitalmediafys.pbworks.com/w/file/fetch/69691259/Bailey_Jane2013GenderStereotypes.pdf>.

28   Freda-Marie Hartung & Britta Renner, "Social Curiosity and Gossip: Related to but Different Drives of Social Functioning," *PLoS ONE* 8 (2013): 7, <http://www.plosone.org/article/info%3Adoi%2F10.1371%2Fjournal.pone.0069996>.

29   Priscilla Regan & Valerie Steeves, "eKids R Us: Online Social Networking and the Potential for Empowerment," *Surveillance & Society* 8 (2012) <http://library.queensu.ca/ojs/index.php/surveillance-and-society/article/view/3483/3437>.

30   Alice Marwick, "Online Identity," in *A Companion to New Media Dynamics*, eds. John Hartley, Jean Burgess & Axel Bruns (Malden: Wiley-Blackwell, 2012).

31 Yin Zhang, Leo Shing-Tung Tang & Louis Leung, "Gratifications, Collective Self-Esteem, Online Emotional Openness, and Traitlike Communication Apprehension as Predictors of Facebook Uses," *Cyberpsychology, Behavior and Social Networking* 14:12 (2011), doi:10.1089/cyber.2010.0042.

32 See Kanai, Chapter III for a discussion of spectators of reality TV interacting in a disciplinary role as judges of the participants.

33 Raake & Bonds-Raake, *supra* note 11 at 163.

34 Hartung & Renner, *supra* note 28 at 8.

35 Steeves, *supra* note 24; Bailey et al, *supra* note 27.

36 Valerie Steeves, *Young Canadians in a Wired World, Phase III: Cyberbullying: Dealing with Online Meanness, Cruelty and Threats*, (Ottawa: Media Awareness Network, 2014), 10, <http://mediasmarts.ca/sites/mediasmarts/files/pdfs/publication-report/full/YCWWIII_Cyberbullying_FullReport.pdf>.

37 Christie Barron & Dany Lacombe, "Moral Panic and the Nasty Girl," *The Canadian Review of Sociology and Anthropology* 42:1 (2008): 52, <http://mike.rivait.net/Files_Otober1_2008/Moral%20Panic%20and%20Nasty%20Girls.pdf>.

38 Jane Bailey & Valerie Steeves, "Will the Real Digital Girl Please Stand Up?: Examining the Gap Between Policy Dialogue and Girls' Accounts of their Digital Existence," in *New Visualities, New Technologies: The New Ecstasy of Communication*, eds. Hille Koskela & Macgregor Wise (London: Ashgate , 2010).

39 It is also out of step with MediaSmarts' recent findings that, in fact, boys are more likely than girls to say or do mean things online: Steeves, *supra* note 36 at 3. For further discussion of the gendered, raced, and classed implications of the "mean girls" discourse, see: Meda Chesney-Lind & Katherine Irwin, *Beyond Bad Girls: Gender, Violence and Hype.* (New York: Routledge, 2008).

40 Mark Andrejevic, "The Work of Watching One Another: Lateral Surveillance, Risk and Governance," *Surveillance and Society* 2:4 (2005) <http://www.surveillance-and-society.org/articles2(4)/lateral.pdf>; Regan & Steeves, *supra* note 29.

41 L. Monique Ward & Corissa Carlson, "Modeling Meanness: Associations Between Reality TV Consumption, Perceived Realism, and Adolescents' Social Aggression," *Media Psychology* 16:4 (2013), doi:10.1080/15213269.2013.832627.

CHAPTER VIII

BBM Is Like Match.com: Social Networking and the Digital Mediation of Teens' Sexual Cultures

Jessica Ringrose and Laura Harvey

Introduction

Mobile digital technologies cannot be treated like some additional feature in young people's lives. The mobile phone is often more like a limb, rather than a separate object from the posthuman cyborg body.[1] These technologies are "actants" that dramatically re-shape the agentic possibilities of relating between (post)humans.[2] They are radically transforming "cultures of connectivity" with temporal and material effects.[3] Consider, for instance, how these 15-year-old girls discuss the mobile phone in their daily rhythms:

> Interviewer: So how much are you using your [mobile] phone do you think in an average day?
> Monique: Like all the time.
> Kylie: I use it to wake myself up, then I use it to phone Riley or you to see where you are to meet each other in the morning, and then when I get on the way to school I will be texting people from school ... I use my phone every second of the day. If I am not using it I feel a bit weird.
> Monique: I use it to go to sleep with my music on.
> Tracy: I talk on my phone all day long.

These technologies are deeply attached to young people's sense of self. Indeed, life could be unthinkable without them. As Jodie (13) put it, "I would die without my Blackberry."[4] Adam (15) explained that once most of his group of friends at his school had Blackberries in 2011, "everyone" had to get one in order to communicate, and it mostly replaced texting and Facebook because it was "portable … always in your pocket," did not require an internet connection, and was more "secret," thus less easily monitored by adults. The technologies of choice change rapidly and are also overlapping, with mobile phone, text, Facebook, BBM, Twitter, Tumblr, Instagram, Skype, Snapchat, and others variously in use. Unsurprisingly, this multiplication of "24/7" technological plugging in forges new bonds and intense degrees of connection:

> Kylie: My boyfriend, he got me to call him the other day, he stayed on the [mobile] phone for like three hours. That is like half my minutes gone, and then he fell asleep … But do you know what the weirdest thing is, once he fell asleep, I couldn't hang up, because I wanted to listen to him breathing …. What we do is, we drop in and out of sleep.

Staying up all night on your personal mobile phone with your boyfriend, reports of young people keeping Skype on for long durations to be visibly and aurally "in touch," or discussions of ongoing snapchatting photo exchanges throughout the day with one another are just a few examples of the radical or hyper-connectivity[5] of unlimited texts, mobile minutes, and broadband that extend the temporal duration of intimate relations.[6] For example, 15-year-old boys explained how they went about initiating hook-ups with girls on BBM through instant messaging via the "Broadcaster," and Kylie said:

> But, like, our phones play a massive part in relationships. Like phone calls until late hours. Texting, not as much because now we have got BBM. BBM is like Match.com basically, you have got everyone there and it is, like … and people send broadcasts over BBM. Like, there will be a smiley face and then next to the smiley face there will be something like, "Would you have sex with me?" "Would you do this, would you do that?" and then by sending that broadcast, like, the boy will answer it and then you will start talking to them …. Like the question will be, like,

"Would you have sex with me lights on/lights off. Socks on/socks off. What position? To what song? Condom or no condom?" Stuff like that.

Kylie refers to BBM as like Match.com, and Facebook as "Baitbook":

Everyone calls Facebook Baitbook, because basically Bait is like everyone can see it, so it is like, if someone was getting like, told, "I'm going to batter you," on Facebook, like, they can print screen it.

These new hybrid terms point to how technological processes are re-shaping and re-mediating teen sociality, connectivity, and sexuality – friendship, dating, intimacy, and conflict.

This chapter specifically explores how these new digital affordances of social media are transforming the gendered and sexual relationalities of networked teens. danah boyd's[7] work has consistently illustrated how much young people "heart" social networking and find digital connections, including flirtation and sexual communication, "dramatic," exciting, and fun.[8] boyd makes tentative suggestions about how youth relationships online are shaped by gender, suggesting that the escalation of "drama" or conflict online is typically viewed as "girls' work."[9] Sexualized rules around representation also involve girls' concerns about looking "slutty" online.[10] However, as Van Doorn notes, social networking research on young people has "largely neglected the gendered and sexual dimensions of SNS participation."[11] This is particularly evident in the neglect of the intersections between three research areas: (1) networked, digital cultures; (2) age, and young teen cultures; and (3) gender and sexual cultures. Exceptions to this neglect are found in research exploring how social media use shapes young people's gender and sexual cultures, such as C. J. Pascoe's research on how platforms like SMS and Myspace mediate gender, sexual, and racial power hierarchies in young people's relationship cultures; De Ridder and Van Bauwel's research on gendered and sexual interactions in teenagers' (age 14 to 18) comments on Facebook; and research on teens' (age 13 to 16) performances of sexualized femininity and masculinity across social networking platforms such as Bebo, Facebook, and BBM by Ringrose and Erickson Barajas in 2011 and Ringrose and Harvey in 2014.[12]

We aim to contribute to these intersecting areas of research by exploring how the technological affordances of mobile media are mediating the gender and sexual cultures of networked teens. Drawing on Kember and Zylinska's work, we approach mediation not as a "transparent layer or intermediary between independently existing entities" such as young people, their Blackberries, and their Facebook profiles, but rather as a vital, temporal process, in which technologies, media, and lives are intimately entangled.[13]

Our analysis combines this understanding of mediation with recent work on the affordances of digital technologies, examining these affordances, not as separate entities, but as part of what Kember and Zylinska term the "lifeness of media — that is, the possibility of the emergence of forms always new, or its potentiality to generate unprecedented connections and unexpected events."[14] boyd summarizes how mobile digital media platforms are characterized by common elements of "Persistence: the durability of online expressions and content; Visibility: the potential audience who can bear witness; Spreadability: the ease with which content can be shared; and Searchability: the ability to find content."[15] To take just a few examples we discuss in the chapter: the new visibilities around performing gender and sexuality online include the ability to display one's relationship status in a variety of ways, for instance, through a profile image of an engagement ring. Being visibly tagged in "sexy" images can be both affirming and anxiety provoking, for example, when an unknown older girl tags herself in a sexualized image she posts on your Facebook wall. The sharing or "spreadability" of sexual images works in highly gendered ways.[16] Sexually "suggestive" images of teens' bodies can operate as commodities, but girls' bodies are treated very differently than boys' bodies in the networked peer group. The searchability of contact information for forging new intimate relations (flirting/dating/hooking up) can be seen as fun and exciting, but also as risky and threatening in gender-specific ways that extend into offline experience.[17] The "persistence" or duration of online talk and images can also be highly gendered and sexualized: one can come to "regret" posting a range of content; we show how sexually explicit content shapes teen peer relationships long after the moment of sharing online.[18]

Methodology

We draw on a research project that mapped experiences of digital sexual communication among economically and racially marginalized young people in London.[19] The project worked in depth with a total of thirty-five young people aged 13 to 15 in two school communities in inner city, multicultural, London schools in 2011. Our methodology included conducting initial focus groups, where we asked young people to "walk us through" their online and mobile phone practices. Young people were then invited to "friend" our Facebook research account.[20] We conducted weekly observations of account activity on selected Facebook profiles for three months. Finally, we returned for in-depth individual interviews with twenty-two case studies.

Below, we explore four of these case studies in detail, examining how social networking practices enable new flows of connectivity[21] and new mediated temporalities.[22] We demonstrate that these flows are constituted through gendered and sexual discourses of performing idealized forms of masculinity and femininity. We explore the power relations in play where digital practices mediate binary and hierarchical forms of gendered and sexual differences.[23] As we have noted, however, it is critical that online and offline are not understood as distinct arenas, following Van Doorn's argument that

> it is becoming increasingly difficult to separate bodies, gender and sexuality from the technological networks that give them form and meaning. Conversely, media technologies cannot be apprehended without accounting for the embodied and gendered use cultures that imbue them with significance by mobilizing them within larger everyday networks both virtual and concrete.[24]

Kylie

Kylie is a 15-year-old white British girl in Year 10[25] at Ashburton High School, which is located in a mixed borough with both high-income and low-income catchment (area from which students can attend the school). One of the first things that struck us about Kylie was that her Facebook profile image was of her engagement ring, which did an enormous amount of "visibility" work signalling the sought after, concrete heterosexual commitment she had with Jake, her boyfriend. As with many teen relationships, the issue of when to "have sex" was paramount in Kylie's discussion in the interview, and she proudly recounted Jake saying "With you I don't need it, like you entertain me in other ways" and "Like with them [other girls] he says, 'It was all about sex, with you I could wait like 100 years.'" Kylie placed Jake's waiting and commitment to her in explicit contrast to weaker girls who "love attention" and give boys mixed messages:

> And a lot of girls get touched up when they don't like it because over BBM or Facebook or something they will be, like, "Oh when I see you I will do this" and they don't ever do what they say they are going to do. So a lot of boys get annoyed and they are just like, "Oh but you said −" and it is just like "Yeah, but now she is saying no sort of thing" but you can understand where they are coming from, why they are getting angry … I think what boys are on now is how many girls they can do this with and how many girls … it is like the porn on the phones again, it is all a competition. It is the same as how many girls they can get … there is a girl in Year 7, she used to get touched up a lot, but she loved the attention, so it was like the boys always used to do this game, where they would see, like, what parts of her body they could touch. So it started off with, like, bending her over and slapping her bum, and then now it is like terrible, they will like pull her backwards and touch her vagina and that and, like, she just sits there and laughs and I am like, I go all red in the face, because I get all embarrassed for her ….

This dialogue indicates the complex intermeshing of how being in touch online and what gets said on BBM or Facebook relates to "touching up" in the corridors at school. Kylie suggests that there are some girls that are saying they will do things online, which gets boys "annoyed" when they "say no." Kylie also says these aspects are a competitive game for boys in her peer group, going on to discuss an example where Jake's friend Dwayne shows them an image of a girl's breasts:

> When he showed Jake he was like … "I don't see the point in them doing that," and he is like, "I would never ask Kylie for

a picture," because he is like, "Why am I going to put it on my phone so then when my friends go through my phone they see my girlfriend?" And I was like "exactly" and then Jake's friend is like, "Oh no, come on man that would be live, like showing everyone," and I was just standing there and I was like, "No." The boys, like, they don't hide nothing, they will talk about it in front of you, and they will talk about having sex with a girl, they will tell you everything, they will be, like, "Oh yeah she was dirty, she didn't wash," like they proper don't care what they say in front of you. And it is just like giving the girl a bad name, and then the really bitchy girls in my year will go back and tell her, "Oh you're a tramp, you don't wash," and stuff like that. And it is just like, but you first have to sit there and think, did he actually have sex with her?

Here we can see how technology enters into and mediates a set of material and affective gender relations in local and specific peer cultures, travelling back and forth between online and offline spaces. Jake is negotiating pressure around having images of Kylie's body to show to other boys, something constituted as more "live" than the flesh-and-blood Kylie "standing there." Kylie also talked about how popular boys could have "20-30" images on their phone, but her distress centres more on the culture of hostile slut-shaming[26] around girls' sexual activity (connected to and implicated within the photos). She discusses boys calling girls "dirty," which would circulate (spreadability) and how "bitchy'" girls will call those girls "tramps." This narrative complicates boyd's discussion of online conflict as "girls work" (implying that girls are the primarily bitchy agents). Rather, we see much more complex sexual culture and gendered power relations where digital images sought after by boys create a range of competitive and relational issues around sexually appropriate femininity and aggressive and "protective" masculinity. This is not to undermine the findings that girls were understood to be "really bitchy'" to each other (online and offline). But boys' involvement in stimulating competitive heterosexualized feminine aggression through open discussions of girls' bodies, sexual encounters, and collecting and comparing digital images of girls' bodies (as well as professional porn, etc.) adds greatly to our understanding of teen "drama" through an understanding of the performances of masculinity and femininity online.[27]

Kylie also described Jake and his friends monitoring what girls could wear offline:

> Kylie: Yeah, because like, today I have come in with a skirt on. Like, if you look, my skirt is not even short, but because I haven't got no tights on, one of his friends is like, "Oh look at your chick, what's she doing?" He [Jake] come over to me and he is like, "Couldn't you have worn tights?" and I was like, "No, it's hot, why do I have to wear tights, I'm wearing shorts." He is like, "Let me see," and I lifted it up to show him and he is like, "What are you doing man? Pull your skirt down," and I was like, "But I've got shorts on there," and he was like, "Yeah but all my boys can see" … And he gets all moody …
> Interviewer: What would that mean for the other boys? They would think you were a …
> Kylie: They would be like, "Oh she's a little slag," and then he would end up getting angry and having a fight with one of them …. [Jake] thinks he is possessive, like everyone is like, "No you're not, you are just protective," and I tell him, "You are not possessive" … but when he is feeling down and upset, like, he will be, like, "Yeah but I tell you what not to wear and stuff like that" … I do feel that he loves me back and that so … if he don't like my skirt, I won't wear it for him, because I don't want him to feel uncomfortable, sort of thing.

Kylie narrates a form of masculine regulation and "possession" over girls' bodies, suggesting that anger and control are signs of love.[28] Jake's version of masculinity is a "protect and shield your body" from others' view: he does not want his girlfriend to display her body online in images or offline at school. This operates against and in relation to a predatory version of masculinity performed by Jake's friend Dwayne, where the capture and display of girls' bodies through digital images/video become commodities to be possessed, traded (spread) amongst boys for homosocial reward or "ratings,"[29] described further by Kylie:

> Basically with the boys it is a competition, who can get the most revealing picture or the biggest breast girl … and the girls send them as like, "Oh if you go out with me we could probably have sex or I could do stuff" … a lot of girls in this neighbourhood

don't have respect for their self …. I don't defend boys, yeah, because of what they do at times, they exploit girls and that, but if a girl is telling you, you can put this picture up if you want and then sends it, then obviously the boy is going to like … because she is one of the most popular girls … if I have got a picture of Jenny (13) it is like they have completely won the competition sort of thing.

Kylie suggests boys compete in ways that "exploit" girls, but she also defends boys through a sexual double standard where girls who put up pictures are read as not "respecting" themselves. Kylie went on to say she was sick of boys' "messing with our heads," which gave girls "low self-esteem," although she positioned younger girls like Jenny as more vulnerable to older boys' mind games than the more seasoned 15-year-olds. Kylie positioned younger boys as the most desperate to get an image because of hormones and their "excitement" over girls' "developing" body parts. We want to continue exploring these age-specific understandings of how teen boys attempt to intra-act with girls' bodies through social media and at school, turning next to a 13-year-old girl's accounts of these practices.

Cherelle

Cherelle is a Black British 13-year-old girl. She is living in an economically deprived area surrounding Langthorpe College, a school that is gated with security cameras and high barbed-wire fencing. As we have been discussing, BBM was the dominant social media environment that the young people were using in 2011 in the research schools, and Cherelle related multiple times how much she loved BBM as a way to stay in touch with friends and to make new friends, saying she couldn't "put her phone down." With Blackberry you have a profile image like Facebook, but contacts are added by circulating a pin number, along with a description to the user's friend network, suggesting they add them: this is called a pin "broadcast," which is interesting because it requires some type of description of the user to be broadcast around the network. Cherelle described the importance of the body parts and the physical appearance of Black girls in particular as being big tits, big bum, working through digital media practices[30] in the descriptions that circulated on BBM:

> If it is a boy and a girl told a boy to BC their pin, then they will say, "Oh she has big tits and a big bum and she's fit[31] and if you get to know her, she's nice" ... It's mad.

She went on to mention the idea of "linking up" or meeting the people she's made contact with online, depending on their "personality" and whether they are "nice":

> If the person can't see your picture properly, they say "Can you send me a picture of your face, so I can see you clearly?" and sometimes they can be very nasty, saying, "Can I have a picture of your tits?" or stuff like that, and yeah, sometimes they will get upset and overact and maybe delete you. But that's alright, but when you are linking someone, they want to know what you want to do when you link. But most boys will say, "We are gonna lips and hug and stuff," and, yeah, just go to the park and do stuff and, yeah, that's what most people do.

Cherelle relates interactions with boys around being asked for images and discussions of meeting to "lips" (kiss) and hug, in ways that imply fun banter. She also describes how sometimes conflicts emerge over "nasty" photo requests. She was particularly concerned around issues of "searchability" through locatable "facts" about her being posted:

> When I lost my BBM, there is some girl in Year 10 and I told her to BC my pin ... she put lots of facts about me ... so I had lots of adds, and then for example, a boy, he said, "Oh you're peng" that means, oh you're pretty and stuff, and, "where do you live?" I said, "[area] but I hang around [other area]." They said, "Oh I live in [area]." "Okay, so what school do you go to?" they said [X school] and then he was all like, "Oh do you want to link?" I was like, "Maybe," and he said, "What would you do if we linked?" and I said, "I dunno," and then he said, "Oh would you give me blows?" that means suck my dick? and I was like, "No not really," and then he said, "Why?" and I said, "Because I'm not like that," but he became furious .... I just ended up deleting him because of what he is saying ... boys get really serious because they just get really angry at the time and say, "Do it,

there's nothing to it. Oh you are pissing me off, I know where you live you know," and they will try for it in any type of way, even if they don't even know you.

Cherelle felt that too much location information had exposed her in relation to a sexually aggressive boy who asked her "would you give me blows" and threatened her "I know where you live," a form of masculine aggression she discussed further:

> Cherelle: Well, I know lots of times I've been asked, and some-times I will say, "No," and they will say, "Okay," and they will be, like, nice to you, and then they will ask again, and then they will put pressure on you and stuff like this, and I will just be, like, "I'm sorry I don't want to," and they will say, "Why?" and I will say, "I just don't want to," and they will say, like, "There's nothing wrong, like, all you need to do is just suck on it," and I will be like, "But I don't want to do that," and just keep going and put the angry face on BBM and dedicate their status to you in a negative way.
>
> Interviewer: Like, say what kind of thing?
>
> Cherelle: Like, "Oh this girl is pissing me off."
>
> Interviewer: And do they say it to you, or do you just kind of know?
>
> Cherelle: You know, you can tell ... I just delete them.
>
> Interviewer: Okay, and do they ask you in person? ...
>
> Cherelle: Oh, people in our school? ... Some boys would say, oh whatever, and sometimes they would just get your head and go like that [motion to push down head], but like you come up quick and just say, "Get off me," but yeah, that is as far as it goes.

The relations between being online and asked to perform a blow job and having boys post something negative about the refusal is greatly complicated here by knowing the contact as part of the wider peer group at school. Cherelle describes being physically approached on the playground and her head being pushed down towards the boys' groin. Despite saying "that is as far as it goes," Cherelle recounted other stories of boys "rushing" (running up to) girls and pushing them over, "touching them up" on their "tits" and "bum," and "dag-gering" them (dry humping them from behind or front):

Interviewer: So do you really feel concerned about them, or do you just think, no, they are not really going to do anything to me?

Cherelle: I feel concerned most of the time, because I'm okay with the boys now, because before, if I said something on BBM or Facebook and they got upset, I just like got into little arguments, like they would say, "Watch tomorrow, gonna rush you," and this stuff. And tomorrow they will just floor you and kick and run, all this. But yeah ….

Interviewer: They do. So you have been beaten up by a boy?

Cherelle: Yeah, not like really hard and stuff, but like they will kick me, I have got punched quite a lot of times and yeah …. Like they [boys] rush people. Like they beat them up for no reason and just loud and, yeah … you walk past and, like, a boy will pass, and they will squeeze your bum or something, and like, just touch your tits ….

What is critical here is the impotency of "deleting" a known contact if they are also part of your school peer group. The issue is not simply online searchability, persistence, or duration of information, since the complex gendered and sexual relations of the peer group bleed into the material, physical offline material space of school:

Cherelle: Like when Kamal first started school, he used to hang around with Veronica and me, so I became good friends with Kamal, because he was quiet then, but then he met the boys in our year group who are popular and stuff, and then he started hanging around with them and he became the same and worse.

Interviewer: Like how, like what do they do?

Cherelle: Like every boy that I have on BBM, well not everyone, but most have put nasty pictures … a girl naked or on top of a boy. The pictures, what you will find on a dirty boy's display picture, is either of him or his penis and a girl sucking it, or a girl naked or a dirty cartoon, things like that …

Interviewer: Oh yeah, dirty cartoon. I wanted to ask you about this one. So this one is from Kamal?

Cherelle: Oh gosh …

Interviewer: Because you commented on it [on Facebook] … I was just wondering what you thought about that?

Cherelle: I was looking through his pictures and then I saw that, and I was like, that is disgusting. I was talking to him about most of his pictures on the phone, and yeah, and he said, "Oh why are you acting like it's all that and stuff," and I was like, "It's disgusting and it's on your Facebook," and he was like, "Yeah, and?" … But most boys just don't think that is, they don't take it seriously, they take it like it is just normal.

Interviewer: It is interesting because you said, "LOL ouch," and he says, "Cherelle knows," and then you realize that and you said, "Shut up," right?

Cherelle: … Like we was really close, but that was then … when he started to change, that is when I saw this picture.

Cherelle mentions a friend in her year group (Kamal) and discusses boys' nasty, dirty pictures online. The interviewer then brings up a sexually explicit cartoon image on Kamal's Facebook page that Cherelle had commented on. The image was of a naked black man entering a white, blonde haired woman from behind who is crying. The comments on the photo were mostly "Lool" and "wooooow," but Cherelle said "O:Lord," to which Kama replied "Cherelle knows," and Cherelle replies "LOL shut up, Kamal." Cherelle suggests the digital image is connected to how she felt Kamal "started to change." To continue discussing these relationship dynamics we turn next to Kamal.

Kamal

Kamal is a Black British boy (14), who transferred recently to Langthorpe College. As a newcomer to the school, Kamal was negotiating his relationship with different peer groups and worked hard in the focus groups and the individual interview to perform a kind of "older," "popular," hard masculinity. As part of this bravado, he proudly displayed his topless body on Facebook, saying about one image of his back muscles that got forty-two likes on Facebook: "wow this picture is good I think it should go on Facebook!" Kamal is negotiating the "visibility" of displaying his own developing body. Posting and tagging images of girls' bodies was also part of performing popular masculinity. Recall that Kylie mentioned some boys had up to thirty images of girls on their phones as signalling high popularity. Kamal claims to have thirty such images, also positioning the images as part a competition:

Kamal: Because sometimes when you and your friend could have a competition of how many girls you can get and … just compare how much pictures you get.

Interviewer: So then do you go to your mates, "Look at this, I've got thirty pictures."

Kamal: No. I go, "I've got bare pictures of girls here," and then when they say, "How much?" I will tell them how much, but I won't really show them.

Interviewer: You won't really show them?

Kamal: No, I will show them, but like, where they will, like, hold my phone and look at it and try to go through the next ones, which might have a girl's face in it, for example … I won't let it out of my possession … I wouldn't want them to know who the girl was, because like, I would only do it for someone I didn't like, and I wouldn't have a picture of someone I didn't like, so yeah.

We interpret Kamal as performing a heteronormative, desirable, and conquering masculinity through making a show of possessing such images. But Kamal also describes a kind of "heroic" masculinity code of honour working through new media practices here. By not revealing the faces of the images of the girls he's been sent, he is attempting to demonstrate a form of power to "expose" or reveal a girl's identity online.[32] However, it is not clear whether Kamal does know the girls in the images. For instance, Kamal's BBM profile image was an image of a girl's breasts, which he claims is his girlfriend, but then says no one actually knows who it is because it is "just her bra without her head." Images are deployed to construct an older and knowing form of masculinity in conditions that are less certain than possibly claimed. Kamal also talked about tagging himself in the images of girls on Facebook:

Kamal: If I like the picture I could tag myself in it, and then it will come to my profile. I could make it my profile picture … it all leads to ratings, because he's got that girl on Facebook and she's nice and how did he get her, they just want to find out, things like that.

Interviewer: And what do the girls think if you tag yourself in their pictures?

> Kamal: Nothing, sometimes they will un-tag you, if they don't want you to tag them. But by the time they get to know that you are tagged in it, you could have made it your profile picture already. They can un-tag you from it, but then you have still got the picture.

Tagging allows for connectivity and digital attachment to other girls' profiles, although Kamal suggests it is not usually girls he is friends with offline whose images he tags himself in. It is thus not clear if the thirty images he claims he has on his phone have been sent to him or he has simply saved them to his phone. Kamal explains how the negotiation of asking for images from girls you know is actually quite difficult and complex:

> Kamal: Well, you only get pictures from girls that like you or your girlfriend, yeah. That is like mostly the only time you will get pictures ...
> Interviewer: Do some people say "No, I'm not sending you a picture"?
> Kamal: Yeah.
> Interviewer: And do you say, go on go on go on, or do you just go away?
> Kamal: No, I will ask why first. And if they don't give me a good reason then I can see that they don't really want to talk about it, so I just change the subject.
> Interviewer: What counts as a good reason?
> Kamal: Like when they go, like for example, they will go, "Because you are not my boyfriend," then that means that some people will do a wink face ... and that is like okay, she wants you to move to her, like she wants you to be her boyfriend. Because she doesn't trust you as a friend, but she trusts you as a boyfriend, if that makes sense?

Kamal suggests that girls want to have some sort of trust in you as a boyfriend before they will send an image to you, which is actually a much harder negotiation to sustain. These discussions all point to the discrepancy between having images on your phone and actually having a known girlfriend in the peer group. While Kamal's Facebook wall had many interactions with girls, and images of him posing for photos with girl friends, recall that Cherelle has challenged Kamal's physical harassment and his posting of "dirty" pictures on Facebook and Blackberry, positioning this as linked to a negative change in their friendship. The complex relations entangled with such images became apparent when we discussed the sexually explicit cartoon on his Facebook page. Kamal became defensive, saying at first that it was just funny and "boys' sense of humour is better than girls'," but when the interviewer presses him about why it is funny, because the woman is crying, Kamal said "I don't know" four times and cracked his chewing gum. Later the interviewer returned to the cartoon image:

> Interviewer: Do you think about that person and image, them being a person, or like what do you think? What do you think she is thinking?
> Kamal: She is enjoying it. It is a way of expressing feelings, yeah …. Like people get hurt, yeah, but that like, they enjoy getting hurt, because they know how it will feel next time or like see, erm, like they enjoying it. Not like they were enjoying getting hurt the next time, but next time they will know what it feels like and they will like be prepared.
> Interviewer: So like just generally like sex being painful then, like that prepares them for that?
> Kamal: Yeah.
> Interviewer: Do you feel that as a picture that is really realistic, as a picture of sex?
> Kamal: No.
> Interviewer: Why don't you think it is?
> Kamal: Well, for one, it is a cartoon, two, the people don't look real, like, yeah. It just looks unreal, but then it looks funny, but real at the same time. Do you get what I'm saying?
> Interviewer: Yeah, I get it. But I'm still not entirely sure what is funny about it. Maybe it is just because, as you were saying, not quite sure.
> Kamal: Because people just find other people's pain funny. They find things like that funny.

This cartoon is just one of many forms of sexualized (and other) images that circulate in teens' social media networks which have a "disgust," "shock," or "gross out" joke factor.[33] On the one hand, the image is not real and this is part of what is suggested makes it humorous. On the other hand, Kamal's comments that girls are preparing for pain in sex seem to imply a connection to "real" life. The relation between fantasy and reality in sexual images (e.g., in animated, professional, peer-produced pornography) is an important space for further discussion around gendered power in youth sexual cultures.[34] Given it is a black man on top of a white woman, there are also complex racialized, sexualized power dynamics at work in discussing this representation in a research encounter, which need to be understood in the context of wider discourses of racism and "othering" of Black masculinity and sexuality. The interview was conducted by a white woman, in the context of a school in which there were high levels of digital surveillance, including disciplinary processes around sexualized content accessed at school. This raises complicated and difficult questions about the power dynamics of a white woman researcher discussing this particular image with a Black teen boy. Our focus in this chapter, however, is how the image works in relation to the girls in his school-based friendship group. Recall that Cherelle said the image was nasty and changes her feelings for him, in concert with the sexual aggression he displays in the school space, something Kamal also defends as a "funny" aspect of male ratings that girls don't mind:

Interviewer: Yeah, so does that happen quite a bit, like people just getting touched up in the corridor?
Kamal: Yeah.
Interviewer: What is going on there?
Kamal: Like boys just touch girls' breasts and their bums and that.
Interviewer: And what do the girls reckon about that?
Kamal: Nothing, most girls don't mind it.
Interviewer: How can you tell which girls mind it and which don't?
Kamal: Because say, for example, I touch a girl's breasts, if she doesn't say like stop or don't touch me, then she doesn't mind it …
Interviewer: How does it work?
Kamal: It is like for example, my friend and my girlfriend, yeah. My friend will do that to my girlfriend, yeah. My other friends would rate him for that, because it is my girlfriend and I am

going out with her. So obviously like I won't get angry, but I will go and do the same thing to his girlfriend.
Interviewer: Okay, what do the girlfriends think about all of this?
Kamal: Nothing, they just think it is funny.

The interview illustrates a pattern across the 13-year-old boys, where having access to girls' bodies both online and offline is normalized into a humorous aspect of "lad culture."[35] There is a homosocial[36] exchange where touching up of girlfriends is a jokey form of rivalry between the boys, as they navigate entry into competitive hierarchical masculinity with unclear boundaries around embodied (sexual) consent.[37] Many young people were critical of the practice and girls were often angry, but they also made excuses, such as Kylie and others who said it was the Year 8 boys' "crazy" hormones. Next, however, we explore some of the differences in how these relations of power manifest with older participants, considering the case of popular older boy, Kaja.

Kaja

The final case study we want to explore is Kaja, a 15-year-old boy also from Langthorpe College, whose family emigrated from a South Eastern European country[38] before he started school. Kaja described himself as "known" and popular and, like other boys, discussed how ratings came from being seen as brave and able to cope with violence. For instance, Kaja discussed having been robbed once for his phone, and talked about the importance of being "known" and confident in avoiding such situations. For Kaja, like Kamal, being able to display hard muscularity and sexual prowess was also key to being powerful, describing himself as "beautiful" and sought-after by girls. For instance, after Kaja's BBM pin was broadcast, a 21-year-old young woman added him on Facebook and started sending him pictures of her breasts. Also like Kamal, Kaja discussed having a folder of around thirty pictures of girls' breasts on his phone:

Interviewer: And what are they — like what is, like, the purpose of keeping them all?
Kaja: I don't know, they are just on my phone. But I don't watch them unless I am showing someone …

Interviewer: So, like, you have got them on your phone and so, that is just so that you can say, "I've got thirty pictures on my phone"?

Kaja: Kind of, like say other people they are like, "Oh I got this girl to do this," I will be like, "Look at my phone" …

Interviewer: So do you keep it on your phone so you can just go …

Kaja: Evidence. Yeah.

The need for "evidence" related to systems of popularity in which proof of sexual desirability and experiences could be materialized in images, which could be shared with other boys:[39]

Kaja: … if they ever say I'm a virgin I will just prove it to them.

Kaja: We all get ratings. It is stupid, but I don't know. We are going to grow up then.

The images are a type of visibility and persistence that form a commodity, directly related to proving sexual activity and getting "ratings," which are desired as part of the peer economy of gendered value, despite the claim that they are immature and "stupid." Kaja positions ratings, and the images, as a youth cultural practice, bounded to a particular moment, but powerful nonetheless in terms of the requirement to provide "proof." All images were not equally capable of providing such proof, however. As we saw earlier, the value of the image relates to the popularity of the girl:

Kaja: Well, say if I got a popular girl to do it, that looks like one of those girls who wouldn't do it, then it would make me look even better. But …

Interviewer: How would she look like a girl that wouldn't do it?

Kaja: Just the way she acts and that, innit.

Interviewer: So, you have got to spell it out for me.

Kaja: The way she dresses, the way she talks to boys.

Interviewer: So what way of dressing and talking to boys would mean you wouldn't think she would normally do it?

Kaja: Like girls in this school, yeah, their skirts are really high, so you would know, that would give you a hint that they want attention …

Interviewer: So if someone was wearing short skirts she would be more likely to send you a picture?
Kaja: Yeah, from my opinion.

Kylie described how girls' skirts are monitored and evaluated as codes of sexual appropriateness, with sexual "easiness" read onto displaying more legs as a sign of sluttiness. Kaja says a girl with a short skirt is more likely to send an image, but those seen as less "attention seeking" would be more highly valued conquests. Images exchanged between people already in a relationship were much more acceptable, since Kaja said that "random" girls who sent images to boys they were not "going out with" would get called "slags." However, Kaja also went on to explain how he explicitly did ask for images from girls he was not in a relationship with:

Kaja: If I think a girl has got a nice body, yeah, I will just flirt with her and say, "Yeah you should write my name," or something like that, yeah. But if she does trust me, if she will do it for me, she will just say at the start, "Don't expose me."
Interviewer: And is she right to trust you then?
Kaja: Yeah.
Interviewer: Because you are not going to expose her?
Kaja: No.
Interviewer: Like but don't you have to show the pictures to get ratings?
Kaja: But she don't know that. My friends are not the type of people — they see the picture — but it is not like I'm going to send it to them or anything. It is not published, I'm not going to show it to the whole school.

This passage illustrates how Kaja feels it is acceptable to ask a girl to trust him and send an image to him, despite being clear that he will show his friends on his phone, although he is not sending it around or "publishing" or "exposing" it to the whole school. To "expose" a girl's image online is a form of digital "visible," "spreadable" and "searchable" sexual "stigma" that can be attached to images of teen girls' bodies, thus mediating gendered relations and "sexual double standards" in new ways.[40]

Even if girls posted the images themselves, they were subject to the possibility of shaming around the images. Recall the 21-year-old who started sending Kaja images of her breasts. Two similar images from another "older girl" were displayed on Kaja's Facebook page. One image is a close-up of a girl pushing her cleavage together with "Kaja owns" written on it in marker pen, and his friends responded by saying it was a "fat man." There was a second image with the breasts in greater relief to show the size and waist, which got positive responses from his friends. Kaja was concerned, however, about being tagged in the image because he said the girl lived far away and was older, and also because the breasts were potentially undesirable (seen as a fat man rather than female breasts):

> Kaja: So she put the picture up [on Facebook] and tagged me. But she is from far, like she has no shame. I don't even know where she lives, she says she lives far.
> Interviewer: In London far?
> Kaja: No, out of London.
> Interviewer: So does it matter if she tags you. Is that, like, good?
> Kaja: I don't really care. It is nothing that I ain't seen before.

The way that Kaja defends against association with the image is to call the girl "shameless," implying her lack of sexual respectability. But also it seems part of the construction of heteronormative popular masculinity of collecting images that he must follow a conquest dynamic where boys solicit the images. Girls who aggressively express their own sexual interest by self-posting and tagging are less valuable than "innocent," "respectable" girls, whom Kaja places into the category of "friend" and potential "girlfriend":

> Interviewer: And like so, do you have friends that are girls that you are not flirting with and stuff?
> Kaja: Yeah, a lot of friends …
> Interviewer: And you wouldn't ask them for pictures?
> Kaja: Nah.
> Interviewer: So like what is different with those?
> Kaja: They respect theirselves.
> Interviewer: So do you think, then, the girls that are sending the pictures don't respect themselves, then?
> Kaja: They can't be respecting themselves if they are taking pictures of their body and whatever, naked.

> Interviewer: What makes you say that? Could they like looking at a picture of themselves? Because you posted a picture up of your six pack right on Facebook, what is different about it?
> Kaja: That's a good question. I don't know. It's just different.
> Interviewer: Different because they are a girl?
> Kaja: Yeah, different because they are a girl.
> Interviewer: So what does respecting yourself look like for a girl?
> Kaja: [Embarrassed laugh] Dress appropriately, act appropriately.

There are several paradoxes here. Kaja draws distinctions between the shameless girls out there and the girls that he is "friends" with and respects. Kaja wants to ask (good-looking) girls for images, yet a girl needs to already be in a relationship for a picture to be more acceptable. Kaja seems aware of some of the contradictions around naming what makes girls "respectable." An unknown girl who takes a naked image and sends an image of herself to Kaja is read very differently from Kaja asking a girl he likes for an image, which emerges again when Kaja describes another older girl sending an image with "Have sex with me" on her body:

> Interviewer: So like how do you feel when somebody sends you that picture?
> Kaja: Just makes me even more big-headed …
> Interviewer: Does it make you think, do you look at that and think, right I'm going to have sex with her?
> Kaja: Yeah, kind of.
> Interviewer: Because that seems like a request?
> Kaja: Yeah, I can have sex with her, but I wouldn't. She has probably had sex with a lot of people.
> Interviewer: And that bothers you?
> Kaja: Yeah, I don't want to catch nothing. I wouldn't risk it …
> Kaja: She don't respect her body. People's, a lot of stuff has been in her and that is just …

Kaja seems to be negotiating a set of complex, defensive relations around the image. On the one hand he says it makes him feel "big-headed" and he later says he likes getting the image. Indeed, the image, made especially (and labelled personally) for him, signifies his personal desirability in a different way from the images Kamal discusses tagging on girls' Facebook pages above. However, despite this bravado, being tagged in images with sexual propositions from an older woman may be actually discomfiting for Kaja, who is operating with a more traditional form of morality around sexual activity, femininity, and masculinity, given he condemns the girl who sexually propositions him through an image as likely diseased, someone he could never have a relationship with:

> Kaja: Not all girls, but see girls like that, yeah, if I had sex with them, [pause] I wouldn't want to go out with them again … say, if I am out with her … people would be, like, "Oh, that is the girl I had sex with, she sent me this," and I will be like, "What?" And you have just got to know these things, innit.
> Interviewer: So it is more likely what other people think, kind of thing?
> Kaja: Yeah, yeah. But girls like this, I wouldn't love. I don't know why, I just wouldn't love. I wouldn't have respect for them.

For Kaja, the digital image implying sex marks the girl as easy, slutty, and unable to garner respect and love. As we saw with Kamal, these same rules are not applied to boys' topless images, however: thus we see how the images mediate newer formations of older formations of sexual double standards around feminine sexual activity and respectability and masculine prowess via the circulation and relative reward and/or judgements of social media images.

Conclusion

This chapter has explored how new digital affordances of new media and social networking practices are mediating and reassembling youth sexual cultures. Many of the examples are reminiscent of older patterns of sexualized (and racialized) difference making and gendered power relations in teen peer cultures.[41] Perhaps what is "new" about new media is how the digital affordances add more layers—extra temporal, spatial, affective, and performative dimensions—to how gendered and sexual power relations, embodiment, and identity work in teens' now networked peer cultures. Kylie's (15) case study underscored issues of new visibility in negotiating and performing her relationship with her boyfriend online and offline. We discussed having to manage desires for photos of girls' bodies, which would render the girl more "live," in line with Kember and

Zylinska's[42] arguments about the new forms of liveness and vitality emergent through new media practices. We also looked at how the enduring inequitable gender relations of sexual control over girls' bodies played out through dynamics of protective vs. predatory masculinity *vis-à-vis* this technology. Possessive "boyfriend" is now performed in relation to whether or not or how you display sexualized images of girls and your girlfriend online and judging and monitoring girls in the schoolyard as well.

Our data with Cherelle (13) allowed us to foreground how new practices of performing feminine desirability are emergent in being asked for images of your body through social media platforms. These negotiations were often fun, yet this was blurred by risks,[43] given that some broadcasts and requests led to lack of control over personal information, and to a material and embodied threat of being found in your neighbourhood. Moreover, e-safety policies about "deleting" online contacts are not helpful for coping with problems of being "touched up," as well as sexually harassed at school via social media from known boys in the peer group.

Kamal's (14) case study showed how popular masculinity is performed (or attempted) via the ambiguous possibilities of digital tagging (connecting) and collecting images of girls' bodies (visibility with material affective force as commodities that persist) afforded by new media technologies. We also explored how the persistence of Kamal's pornographic cartoon image, as well as how his attitude to ownership and access to "touching up" girls' bodies offline shaped his friendship with girls in his peer group like Cherelle.

Kaja's (15) case showed the digital affordances of being able to "expose" girls' images as sexually stigmatizing (a practice that combines online visibility and spreadability). Kaja performs a traditional form of masculinity by carefully negotiating his relationship to explicit images and texts from older girls, defending against attachment to un-"known" girls through sexual shaming. What is new is that it is the image itself that marks the girl as slutty through codes that imply sexual intent – older norms of female sexual respectability[44] are re-mediated through this technology – rules about online display that were not applied to boys' body images.

Thus, this chapter has begun a discussion of how digital affordances shape the possibilities of connectivity and relationality in young people's gender and sexual cultures. There remains, however, great scope for exploring how the new affordances of visibility, searchability, spreadability, and persistance of social media may also present spaces for reworking age-old gender and sexual inequalities in ways as yet unforeseen.

Notes

1   Donna Haraway, "A Cyborg Manifesto: Science, Technology, and Socialist-Feminism in the Late Twentieth Century," in *Simians, Cyborgs, and Women: The Reinvention of Nature* (New York: Routledge, 1991), 180, <http://cstpr.colorado.edu/students/envs_5110/siamanscyborgs.pdf>.

2   Bruno Latour, *Reassembling the Social: An Introduction to Actor-Network-Theory* (New York: Oxford University Press, 2005).

3   José van Dijck, *The Culture of Connectivity: A Critical History of Social Media* (New York: Oxford University Press, 2013).

4   Sarah Kember & Joanna Zylinska, *Life after New Media: Mediation as a Vital Process* (Cambridge: MIT Press, 2012).

5   Barry Wellman, "Physical Place and Cyberplace: The Rise of Personalized Networking," *International Journal of Urban and Rural Research* 25:2 (2001): 230, <http://www.itu.dk/people/khhp/speciale/videnskabelige%20artikler/Wellman_2001%20-%20%20personalized%20networking.pdf>.

6   Van Dijck, *supra* note 3.

7   danah boyd, "Why Youth (Heart) Social Network Sites: The Role of Networked Publics in Teenage Social Life,"*Youth, Identity, and Digital Media*, ed. David Buckingham (Cambridge, MA: MIT Press, 2008).

8   Alice Marwick & danah boyd "The Drama! Teen Conflict in Networked Publics," paper presented at the Oxford Internet Institute Decade in Internet Time Symposium (22 September 2011), <http://ssrn.com/abstract=1926349>.

9   danah boyd, *It's Complicated: The Social Lives of Networked Teens* (London: Yale University Press, 2014), 139.

10   Jane Bailey, Valerie Steeves, Jacquelyn Burkell & Priscilla Ryan, "Negotiating with Gender Stereotypes on Social Networking Sites: From 'Bicycle Face' to Facebook," *Journal of Communication Inquiry* 37:2 (2013): 107, <http://digitalmediafys.pbworks.com/w/file/fetch/69691259/Bailey_Jane2013GenderStereotypes.pdf>.

11   Niels Van Doorn, "The Ties that Bind: The Networked Performance of Gender, Sexuality and Friendship on MySpace," *New Media and Society* 12:4 (2010): 584.

12   C. J. Pascoe, "Resource and Risk: Youth Sexuality and New Media Use," *Sexuality Research and Social Policy* 8:1 (2011); Sander De Ridder & Sofie Van Bauwel, "Commenting on Pictures: Teens Negotiating Gender and Sexualities on Social Networking Sites," *Sexualities* 16:5–6 (2013),

doi:10.1177/1363460713487369; Jessica Ringrose & Katarina Eriksson Barajas, "Gendered Risks and Opportunities? Exploring Teen Girls' Digital Sexual Identity in Postfeminist Media Contexts," *International Journal of Media and Cultural Politics* 7:2 (2011), <https://www.academia. edu/1472908/Gendered_risks_and_opportunities_Exploring_teen_ girls_digital_sexual_identity_in_postfeminist_media_contexts>; Jessica Ringrose & Laura Harvey, "Boobs, Back-Off, Bits and Blows: Mediated Body Parts, Gendered Reward, and Sexual Shame in Teens' Networked Images," *Continuum* [forthcoming].

13   Kember & Zylinska, *supra* note 4 at xv.

14   *Ibid.* at xxvi.

15   boyd, *supra* note 9 at 11.

16   Henry Jenkins, *Spreadable Media: Creating Value and Meaning in a Networked Culture* (New York University Press, 2013), 3.

17   Sonia Livingstone & Leslie Haddon, *EU Kids Online: Final Report* (London: LSE, 2009), 16, <http://www.lse.ac.uk/media@lse/research/eukidsonline/eu%20kids%20i%20(2006-9)/eu%20kids%20online%20i%20reports/ eukidsonlinefinalreport.pdf>.

18   Rebecca Brown & Melissa Gregg, "The Pedagogy of Regret: Facebook, Binge Drinking and Young Women," *Continuum* 26:3 (2012), 357–369.

19   Jessica Ringrose, Rosalind Gill, Sonia Livingstone & Laura Harvey, *A Qualitative Study of Children, Young People and 'Sexting'* (London: NSPCC, 2012), <http://www.lse.ac.uk/media@lse/documents/MPP/Sexting-Report-NSPCC.pdf>.

20   Libby Brockman, Dimitri Christakis & Megan Moreno, "Friending Adolescents on Social Networking Websites: A Feasible Research Tool," *Journal of Interaction Science* 2:1 (2014), <http://www.journalofinteraction-science.com/content/2/1/1>.

21   Van Dijck, *supra* note 3.

22   Richard Grusin, *Premediation: Affect and Mediality after 9/11* (New York: Palgrave, 2010).

23   Rosi Braidotti, *Nomadic Subjects: Embodiment and Sexual Difference in Contemporary Feminist Theory*, 2nd ed. (New York: Columbia University Press, 2011); Jessica Ringrose, *Postfeminist Education? Girls and the Sexual Politics of Schooling* (New York: Routledge, 2013).

24   Niels Van Doorn, "Digital Spaces, Material Traces: How Matter Comes to Matter in Online Performances of Gender, Sexuality and Embodiment," *Media, Culture and Society* 33:4 (2011): 531–547.

25   Year 10 in the UK system is equivalent to Grade 9 in Canada [editor's note].

26   Jessica Ringrose & Emma Renold, "Teen Girls, Working-Class Femininity and Resistance: Retheorising Fantasy and Desire in Educational Contexts of Heterosexualised Violence," *International Journal*

of Inclusive Education 16 (2012), <https://www.academia.edu/632774/ Ringrose_J._and_Renold_E._2012_Teen_girls_working_class_femininity_and_resistance_Re-theorizing_fantasy_and_desire_in_educational_contexts_of_heterosexualized_violence>.

27   See Laura Harvey & Jessica Ringrose, "Sexting, Ratings and (Mis)recognition: Teen Boys' Performing Classed and Racialised Masculinities in Digitally Networked Publics," in *Children, Sexuality and 'Sexualisation'*, eds. Emma Renold, Jessica Ringrose & Danielle Egan [forthcoming] for a fuller discussion of boys performing classed and racialized heteromasculinity in networked publics. For a discussion of teen "drama," see boyd, *supra* note 9.

28   Christine Barter & Melanie McCarry, "Love, Power and Control: Girls' Experiences of Partner Violence and Exploitation," in *Violence against Women: Current Theory and Practice in Domestic Abuse, Sexual Violence & Exploitation*, eds. Nancy Lombard & Leslie McMillan (London: Jessica Kingsley, 2012), 103–124.

29   "Ratings" is a complex system of value and recognition, in which boys could gain by being "hard," brave, sexually active, etc. For a more detailed discussion see Harvey & Ringrose, *supra* note 27; Ringrose & Harvey, *supra* note 12.

30   Debbie Weekes "'Get Your Freak On': How Black Girls Sexualise Identity," *Sex Education* 2:3 (2002): 251–262.

31   UK slang for sexually attractive [editor's note].

32   Diane Reay, "Shaun's Story: Troubling Discourses of White Working Class Masculinities," *Gender and Education* 14:3 (2002): 221–234.

33   Monique Mulholland, *Young People and Pornography: Negotiating Pornification* (New York: Palgrave, 2013).

34   Polly Haste, "Sex Education and Masculinity: The 'Problem' of Boys," *Gender and Education* 25 (2013): 515–527, doi:10.1080/09540253.2013.789830.

35   Vanita Sundaram, *Preventing Youth Violence: Rethinking the Role of Gender and Schools* (London: Palgrave, 2014).

36   Eve Kosofsky Sedgwick, "Between Men: English Literature and Male Homosocial Desire, rev. ed." (New York: Columbia University Press, 1992), 1.

37   Anastasia Powell, *Sex, Power and Consent: Youth Culture and the Unwritten Rules* (Melbourne: Cambridge University Press, 2010).

38   We have not included the name of the country to protect the participants' anonymity.

39   See Ringrose & Harvey, *supra* note 12, for a more detailed discussion of the relationship between sexual experiences, ratings, and images.

40   Daniel Trottier, *Identity Problems in the Facebook Era* (London: Routledge, 2012), ii.

41   Weekes, *supra* note 30; Reay, *supra* note 32.

42   Kember & Zylinska, *supra* note 4.

43   Livingstone & Haddon, *supra* note 17.

44   Beverley Skreggs, *Formations of Class and Gender: Becoming Respectable* (London: SAGE, 1997), 47.

PART III

DEALING WITH
SEXUALIZED VIOLENCE

CHAPTER IX

Rape Threats and Revenge Porn: Defining Sexual Violence in the Digital Age

Jordan Fairbairn

*Definitions of violence against women continue to evolve as
the breadth and harm of these experiences becomes known.*[1]

*J**ust ignore the trolls. Don't share personal information. Go offline.* These
mantras pervade discussions of digital communication and the
abuse and harassment that occur online. Although often well meaning, these statements contain problematic assumptions about whose
responsibility it is to prevent harassment and how seriously we
take certain forms of abuse. These statements also contain insights
into how we relate the online interactions to the physical world, or
what is often referred to as "in real life." However, this is changing.
Like sexual harassment and domestic violence in previous decades,
advocates and activists are rejecting the notion that online abuse
and harassment is an unfortunate but inevitable feature of girls' and
women's existence. This notion is being replaced by a growing understanding that much abuse and harassment online is a manifestation
of broader social ills such as misogyny, racism, and homophobia, and
should therefore be taken seriously. For example, Canadian women's
rights advocate Julie Lalonde writes,

> To believe that what happens online is of no consequence to the
> offline world is incredibly naïve. Just ask Anita Sarkeesian, who
> started a Kickstarter campaign to create videos about gender

stereotypes in video games and received countless threats to her life as a result. Or you can ask Jill Filipovic, a blogger, columnist and attorney, who recently wrote about her experience of having an online troll show up at her door. Or Amanda Hess, who recently wrote a lengthy piece detailing her experiences of online threats and quoted her friends, Lindy West and Jessica Valenti, whose personal safety was threatened by the same people we keep collectively deeming as harmless. The list goes on and on. Women, particularly women of colour, queer women and women with disabilities, are continuously threatened and harassed online.[2]

Emerging research is also highlighting and forging stronger linkages between sexual violence and online spaces.[3] The right to safe participation in online spaces is a driving force of this movement, with rape threats, slut shaming, and so-called revenge porn and/or nonconsensual sharing of intimate images drawing particular attention.

In this chapter I argue that how violence is defined and operationalized matters for addressing sexual violence in digital spaces. To consider how definitions of violence shape our understanding of sexual violence against women and girls online, I draw from several areas relevant to social policy development, including advocacy work (Take Back the Tech), data collection practices (Statistics Canada General Social Survey), and media (news coverage of revenge porn). I approach so-called revenge porn as a form of violence against women and girls and take the position that violence is not a universal constant but, rather, a constructed understanding of socially defined harms resulting from aggression and abuse of power. Thus, definitions of sexual violence are historically, socially, and politically located and are presently evolving among activists, scholars, and advocates to capture harms associated with online violence. As a result of this evolution, the widespread but narrow understanding of violence as physical assault is not sufficient for current digital contexts.

Violence against Women and Girls as a Framework of Understanding

Language matters. In particular, it matters when new understandings of social phenomena are being shaped. In this chapter, I am applying a framework of violence against women (VAW) to online sexual violence for two reasons: first, to narrow the field of study to a more manageable focus; and second, but more importantly, this terminology places this analysis within broader feminist work that draws attention to the way that systems of gendered inequality enable and support physical, sexual, and psychological violence against women and girls worldwide. Although the umbrella terminology VAW is most frequently used in research and advocacy, in this chapter I will also use violence against women and girls (VAWG). This offers an alternative to generic terms such as "cyberbullying" that are used to describe a plethora of behaviours in ways that fail to meaningfully distinguish between materially different activities that merit distinctive analyses and responses.[4] The term *VAWG* is also in keeping with the youth-focused nature of this collection more broadly, while signalling recognition that girls may experience violence very differently from the ways in which women experience it.[5]

VAW exists in many forms and all areas of society. The 1993 United Nations Declaration on the Elimination of Violence against Women defines violence as any act that results in, or is likely to result in, physical, sexual, or psychological harm or suffering to women, including threats of such acts, coercion, or arbitrary deprivation of liberty, whether occurring in public or private life.[6] This declaration is particularly significant because it was the first internationally agreed upon definition of violence "as it pertained to women's experiences."[7] In specifically addressing violence against women, the declaration speaks about violence occurring in three spheres: the family, the community, and the state. Table 1 summarizes these areas.

Table 1: United Nations Definition of Violence against Women

Arena	Includes
Family	Physical, sexual, and psychological violence, including battering; sexual abuse of female children in the household; dowry-related violence; marital rape; female genital mutilation and other traditional practices harmful to women; non-spousal violence and violence related to exploitation.
Community	Physical, sexual, and psychological violence, including rape; sexual abuse; sexual harassment and intimidation at work, in educational institutions, and elsewhere; trafficking in women and forced prostitution.
State	Physical, sexual, and psychological violence perpetrated or condoned by the state, wherever it occurs.

In exploring the intersections with online abuse and harassment, this chapter focuses primarily on sexual violence against women and girls. Definitions of sexual violence vary in specifics, but generally acknowledge that sexual violence is about exerting power and aggression (not sexual desire) over someone else in order to undermine an individual's sexual or gender integrity.[8] Table 2 presents sample definitions of sexual violence.

Table 2: Definitions of Sexual Violence

Source	Definition of Sexual Violence
World Health Organization (WHO)	Any sexual act, attempt to obtain a sexual act, unwanted sexual comments or advances, or acts to traffic, or otherwise directed against a person's sexuality using coercion by any person regardless of their relationship to the victim, in any setting, including but not limited to home and work.[9]
Centres for Disease Control and Prevention (CDC)	Any sexual act that is perpetrated against someone's will. Sexual violence encompasses a range of offenses, including a completed non-consensual sex act (i.e., rape), an attempted non-consensual sex act, abusive sexual contact (i.e., unwanted touching), and non-contact sexual abuse (e.g., threatened sexual violence, exhibitionism, verbal sexual harassment).[10]
Ontario Sexual Violence Action Plan	Any violence, physical or psychological, carried out through sexual means or by targeting sexuality. This violence takes different forms, including sexual abuse, sexual assault, rape, incest, childhood sexual abuse, and rape during armed conflict. It also includes sexual harassment, stalking, indecent or sexualized exposure, degrading sexual imagery, voyeurism, cyber harassment, trafficking, and sexual exploitation.[11]

The WHO definition is broad, yet specifies that sexual violence includes psychological violence and sexual harassment. The CDC's is more specific and notes that threatened and/or verbal sexual violence fall under the umbrella definition of sexual violence. More locally, the Government of Ontario's Sexual Violence Action Plan provides many examples of sexual violence, and includes specific reference to cyber harassment as part of this continuum. The Ontario Coalition of Rape Crisis Centres (OCRCC) also uses this definition of sexual violence.[12]

Since these various definitions of sexual violence already widely recognize psychological and verbal abuse as part of the spectrum of violence, it is arguably unnecessary to specifically state that sexual violence can be cyber based. However, as we continue to draw and re-draw boundaries around various forms of abuse online (revenge porn, non-consensual sexting, cyberbullying), it is, in fact, necessary to be clear about defining online sexual violence *as* sexual violence. Based on the above definitions, we see that international human rights organizations and sexual assault service providers recognize sexual violence as something that involves multiple dimensions of violence. If this is to be widely relevant in our digital era, it is important to understand what sexual violence against women looks like in emerging media contexts.

Sexual Violence and Digital Spaces

In addition to emerging research,[13] the Association for Progressive Communications' Take Back the Tech campaign is perhaps the most large-scale, comprehensive, and targeted advocacy effort to currently focus on VAWG online. Take Back The Tech is a collaborative campaign that takes place each year during the 16 Days of Activism against Gender-Based Violence (November 25 to December 10). It acts as "a call to everyone – especially women and girls – to take control of technology to end violence against women."[14] This campaign is important for conceptualizing digital technology and VAWG because of its understanding of the multi-faceted significance of digital technologies. That is, Take Back the Tech approaches digital technologies as tools and arenas that can be engaged for prevention work that are also woven into violence and power relations in various spheres.[15] Table 3 summarizes these key relationships.[16]

Table 3: Examples of Harms Related to Online Sexual Violence

Area of Harm	Connections to Digital Spaces
Sexual violence (physical)	Using social media to gain trust and/or arrange to meet in physical space and commit sexual assault; posting personal/location information and encouraging others to perpetrate sexual assault; recording and/or distributing images of sexual assault.
Sexual violence (psychological)	Sexual threats; sending repeated and unwanted sexual communication; using social networking sites to promote sexual violence or vilify survivors of sexual assault; stealing, coercing, and/or non-consensual sharing of sexually explicit images.

Table 3: (Continued)

Area of Harm	Connections to Digital Spaces
Communication rights infringement	Includes not only the freedom of opinion and expression but also areas such as the right to information, privacy, democratic governance, participation in culture, language, creativity, education, peaceful assembly and self-determination. Creation of hostile digital spaces infringes on these rights.

Source: Association for Progressive Communications

Although Table 3 distinguishes between physical sexual violence and psychological sexual violence for illustrative purposes, this is a blurry and often artificial distinction. For example, physical sexual violence frequently results in psychological harms for survivors, and psychological sexual violence can result in physical injuries such as self-harm or suicide. Take Back the Tech, like much anti-violence work, considers sexual harassment to be a form of sexual violence. Beyond its many concrete objectives and activities, the campaign also offers a valuable theoretical framework for weaving together an understanding of sexual violence and communication rights infringement where it is understood that "fear plays a significant role in arranging spatial relations."[17] Online harassment is understood as a form of sexual violence in part because of the emotional distress and breach of an individual's sense of safety. Moreover, when people's safety and integrity is compromised online, they are marginalized and/or pushed out of these spaces. When this happens repeatedly based on gender identity and/or sexual orientation (among other factors, including racism), these patterns of discrimination exclude certain social groups from full participation in society.

In the definitions provided earlier (Table 1), we see that in addition to physical violence, sexual violence and psychological violence are included in each category of family, community, and state violence. Online violence could occur in all spheres, but perhaps falls most readily under community violence, including "sexual harassment, threats, and intimidation at work, in educational institutions and elsewhere."[18] Remember that online spaces are, for many, deeply integrated with work and/or educational experiences and institutions, as well as social relationships generally, and the boundary between offline and online is increasingly artificial.

Efforts to categorize online sexually violent threats and non-consensual sharing of intimate photos, for example, as sexual violence are working against a strong social current of resistance (e.g., "But he wasn't actually going to rape her"). This reluctance reveals important social attitudes, and in fact tells us a great deal about how well equipped we feel as a society to deal with the complications that arise from taking online sexual violence seriously. In this context, two questions are important to keep in mind. First, what other forms of violence were once considered inevitable (and even acceptable) for many women? Marital rape, domestic violence, and the sexual harassment of women and girls in the workplace and in schools were all once socially acceptable, and attitude changes took time (and are still underway).[19] Second, whose interests lie in maintaining the status quo, where online sexual violence is often trivialized? Defining something as violence is a call to action, a way to explicitly convey that certain behaviours are (1) an abuse of power; (2) harmful; and (3) unacceptable.

International campaigns such as Take Back the Tech exemplify the ongoing work being done to evolve definitions of violence. In Canada, recent initiatives, such as the thirty-five recommendations made by West Coast LEAF around legal responses to gendered hate and harassment online[20] and the Status of Women Canada's funding for projects that address cyber and sexual violence,[21] are indicative of a growing awareness among various sectors that online sexual violence must be addressed. Campaigns such as Take Back the Tech highlight that power and control are complex and multi-faceted within digital spaces. Not only does online sexual violence harm those targeted, it creates a culture where sexual abuse and harassment is expected, tolerated, and/or encouraged, and women and girls are held responsible for their safety and blamed for their victimization. These conditions are now widely characterized as rape culture,[22] and online environments are part of this culture. As boundaries between online and offline become increasingly blurred and our online presence increasingly integrated with professional and personal existence, it is imperative that we find ways to define, document, and prevent violence in all spaces, and to support the work of those undertaking this challenging task. In the remainder of this chapter, I will briefly consider how data surrounding online sexual violence could be drawn from the national victimization survey data and explore media coverage of revenge porn to consider how seriously we take this form of online sexual violence.

Counting Sexual Violence: The General Social Survey
The General Social Survey (GSS) was established in 1985 as a series of independent, annual, cross-sectional surveys that explores six areas in depth.[23] The GSS (Victimization) has been conducted every five years since 1988 and explores criminal victimization and spousal violence. It is the only national survey of self-reported victimization in Canada.[24] Police, all levels of government, victim and social service agencies, community groups, and university researchers use GSS data to understand and respond to victimization, including sexual violence.[25] As noted in Angrove's chapter in this volume, we know from the GSS that women experience significantly higher rates of sexual violence compared to men. Specifically, women are eleven times more likely than men to be a victim of sexual offences and three times as likely to be the victim of criminal harassment (stalking).[26] Sexual violence is also one of the most underreported crimes: a majority of incidents (approximately 88 percent) are not reported to police.[27] We know that girls between the ages of 12 and 17 are eight times more likely than boys of the same age to experience sexual assault or another type of sexual offence.[28] This is also an age group whose lives are frequently embedded in digital contexts. In order to contribute to and build on the work of advocacy campaigns and legal analysis, it is important to explore the role and potential of core data collection practices.

How might information on online sexual violence be compiled from current GSS data? Table 4 presents select definitions from questions related to sexual violence, stalking, and cyberbullying that are used in the most recent version of the GSS (Victimization) survey questionnaire, the GSS 2014 (Cycle 28).[29]

Table 4: General Social Survey Question Categories to Consider for Online Sexual Violence Data Collection

Category	Definition
Sexual violence	Forced or attempted to force into unwanted sexual activity, by threatening, holding down, or hurting in some way; unwanted touching or grabbing, kissing, or fondling; sexual activity to which you were not able to consent (drugged, intoxicated, manipulated, or forced in other ways than physically).

Table 4: (Continued)

Category	Definition
Stalking	Repeated and unwanted attention that caused you to fear for your safety or the safety of someone known to you. Includes: repeated, silent, or obscene phone calls; unwanted messages through email, text, or social media; followed or spied on you either in person or through an electronic tracking device; posted inappropriate, unwanted, or personal information about you or pictures on a social media site.
Cyberbullying	Use of the Internet to embarrass, intimidate, or threaten someone. Includes: threatening or aggressive emails, instant messages, or comments directed at you; circulating or posting pictures that embarrassed you or made you feel threatened; use of your identity to send out or post embarrassing or threatening information.
Hate crimes	Crimes motivated by the offender's hatred of a person's sex, ethnicity, race, religion, sexual orientation, age, disability, or language.

Source: General Social Survey Cycle 28 Questionnaire

In comparison to the more comprehensive definitions of sexual violence presented earlier in this chapter (see Table 2), these GSS questions present a more narrow understanding of sexual violence that more closely corresponds to legal definitions of sexual assault. While this definition focuses on physical acts of violence, online sexual violence data could be gleaned from additional GSS categories. For example, the stalking category includes receiving threatening messages and/or having inappropriate, unwanted, or personal information or pictures posted on a social media site. The cyberbullying group of questions, however, is less helpful for assembling data on online sexual violence. Although the questions encompass online aggression, the specific nature of the abuse (i.e., whether or not is sexual abuse) is not captured by the term "cyberbullying." A broad umbrella term, "cyberbullying" is used to describe many forms of abuse and harassment, including online sexual violence. Because this term is widely used, it may be that GSS respondents, if they report sexual harassment online at all, will report this harassment as cyberbullying rather than as sexual violence (which does not ask about non-physical violence) or stalking (a term not widely used to describe online rape threats and/or non-consensual sharing of photos, for example).

Finally, it is possible that data from hate speech questions could be useful to understanding sexually violent vitriol directed at women online. However, because this category asks specifically about crimes, it is likely that many acts of online sexual violence as defined in this chapter would not be captured under the current design. To prevent sexual violence against girls and young women in a cultural context where online sexual violence is not widely understood as violence, understanding the frequency and nature of online sexual violence requires additional detail and context in data collection practices. We need to think about what we know about sexual violence prevention and how this applies to digital spaces, rather than getting caught up in overly specific constructed categories. An example of such a category, which I will spend the rest of this chapter unpacking in relation to VAWG, is so-called revenge porn.

Revenge Porn and VAWG

Revenge porn is generally described as the practice of someone (usually a man) sharing intimate photos in order to humiliate an ex-partner (usually a woman).[30] The photos are often thought to have been taken consensually initially (though this is often not the case), but are then used by the "spurned lover" for revenge when the relationship ends. Revenge porn, as a social phenomenon, came into the spotlight during 2012 and 2013 primarily through the identification and arrest of an American man named Hunter Moore. Moore created and ran the site isanyoneup.com, where he encouraged men to share naked photos of women, along with their names, age, location, and links to their various social media profiles. Although he was previously immune to criminal charges because he was said to be only sharing third-party material, in 2012 Moore was charged for his role in hacking into people's email accounts to steal photos. In December 2013 Moore was indicted on felony charges that included identity theft and conspiracy.[31] While legal scholars such as Danielle Keats Citron acknowledge that Moore's prosecution is a step in the right direction, they also argue that it does not indicate that existing laws are sufficient to address revenge porn.[32]

So-called revenge porn is an important piece of evolving discussions about defining VAWG for three central reasons. First, it is a very recently labelled type of victimization. Second, there are gendered biases in both the effects of revenge porn as well as the criminal justice (non)response to victims.[33] And third, although not often explicitly identified or discussed as a form of VAWG, as noted in Shariff and DeMartini's chapter in this volume,[34] discursive tendencies surrounding revenge porn are similar to those surrounding sexual violence generally, such as victim blaming ("What was she thinking taking that photo?") and viewing men as inevitable perpetrators ("Of course he shared it, what did you expect?"). Because of this, identifying revenge porn (or non-consensual disclosure of intimate images, as it is referred to in recent Canadian legislation[35]) as a form of VAWG is important to help shifting definitions of violence better address current digital contexts.

What can news media coverage tell us about current understandings of revenge porn as a form of VAWG? To answer this question, I read all online articles on revenge porn from the *Toronto Star* (N=4), the *Globe and Mail* (N=8), the *New York Times* (N=5), and *CNN* (N=7). This sample, collected from November 2011 to March 2014, was therefore small (24 articles) but exhaustive, as it contained all revenge porn online news coverage from these particular publications.[36] The average article length was 618 words, and ranged from 44 to 1,007 words. What is clear from the publication dates of these articles is that the emergence of news media use of the term "revenge porn" is much more recent than the broader practice of digital non-consensual sharing of intimate photos. Of the 24 articles found containing the term revenge porn, 22 were published between 15 June 2013 and 11 February 2014 (one article per year was published in 2011 and 2012).

Before discussing the findings in more detail, it is useful to provide a sense of the news themes. I found that news coverage of revenge porn fell into three general categories: (1) event/case; (2) legislation; and (3) victimization. The event/case group focuses on describing what revenge porn is by describing charges laid in two separate cases (both in California). Next, the legislation group discusses proposed laws in California and in Canada to address cyberbullying and revenge porn. The final category, victimization, focuses on the harms that victims of revenge porn experience, and connects the phenomenon of revenge porn to sexual harassment more broadly. Table 5 provides a summary of these categories and an example quotation to illustrate the type of coverage found in that category.

Table 5: News Media Coverage of Revenge Porn

Article Focus	Number of Articles	Example Quotation
Event/Case	13	"Federal prosecutors allege Moore operated the website, where he posted, 'nude or sexually explicit photos of victims.' The pictures, prosecutors added, were submitted without the victim's permission 'for purposes of revenge.'" (*Toronto Star*, 23 January 2014)
Legislation	7	"Bill C-13 criminalizes the distribution of 'intimate images' without consent – including so-called 'revenge porn' – and offenders risk up to five years in prison …. The bill should deter anyone from texting, posting or emailing such images without consent." (*Toronto Star*, 24 November 2013)
Victimization	4	"The effects can be devastating. Victims say they have lost jobs, been approached in stores by strangers who recognized their photographs, and watched close friendships and family relationships dissolve. Some have changed their names or altered their appearance." (*New York Times*, 23 September 2013)
	Total: 24	

In reading the articles, I was interested in two questions: Do these articles use the term "violence" in relation to revenge porn? What harms is the victim portrayed as experiencing? I will consider each of these questions in relation to the three news themes.

Article Focus: Event/Case

The first group of articles identifies non-consensual sharing of intimate photos as the core element of revenge porn, described as something done by an ex-partner (usually male) with intent to humiliate the victim. Several articles indicate that the site isanyoneup.com sparked such public outrage not only because the photos were posted without consent, but because they were personalized: that is, victim's photos were linked to their social media accounts and, in some cases, their phone numbers and home addresses. For example, one article from the *Globe and Mail* states that "[The site] allowed users to submit nude photos of people (submitted by jilted exes, angry friends and hackers) and listed their names, locations and social media profiles – the latter a particularly cruel addition in an age dominated by Google search results."[37]

No articles in this category use the term "violence" (e.g., "sexual violence") to describe the situation. One article uses the term "extortion" to describe how the accused allegedly charged victims between $250 and $350 to have their photos removed from his site.[38] This category of articles generally conveys the view that revenge porn is despicable but does not discuss specific harms experienced by victims. For example, one article states, "There aren't any laws against being a grade A jerk or hosting extremely harmful and non-consensual pornography."[39] Another notes that "so far only two states have restricted this humiliating, reputation-killing practice."[40]

Article Focus: Legislation

Of the seven articles focusing on proposed legislation, four focus on Canadian legislation and three discuss California legislation. The Canadian articles focus on revenge porn as a form of cyberbullying, and repeatedly reference the high-profile cases of Amanda Todd and Rehtaeh Parsons as context for the proposed bill.[41] The articles are generally quite critical of the legislation. For example, one article reads:

> Bill C-13 touches upon cyberbullying in an almost cursory manner. It makes it a crime to share an intimate image without the consent of the person depicted in that image – a reasonable provision – but much else in the bill seems tacked on simply to increase police powers to investigate our online activities.[42]

As with the event/case group, articles discussing the proposed legislation also do not use the term "violence." One article uses "harassment" to describe women's experiences, including those of two teen girls: "After the deaths of Rehtaeh Parsons and Amanda Todd, teens who were harassed online by their peers...."[43] Sexual violence experienced by these young women and others are often simply described as cyberbullying: "We know the results of cyber bullying [sic] – we have heard about children who took their own lives because they could not cope with the humiliating consequences that befell them."[44]

Although arguably empathetic, the fact that what happened to these young women is described as humiliation, but not violence, is significant. It does not have to be one or the other. Part of sexual violence is humiliation and degradation, is violating a person's dignity and sense of well-being. But humiliation does not adequately capture the extensive trauma, isolation, and fear experienced by those who are targets of sexual violence.

Article Focus: Victimization

This small category of articles prioritizes stories of women who have experienced revenge porn, and links these stories to the broader context of sexual violence. Notably, legal scholars wrote two of the four articles in this group, including an in-depth piece by Danielle Keats Citron, who has explored online harassment in her work. Although only one article actually contains the term "violence," this group of articles discusses revenge porn in the context of a larger culture of sexual harassment (including slut shaming) and as inflicting significant harms to women who experience it. For example, one article states, "The effects can be devastating. Victims say they have lost jobs, been approached in stores by strangers who recognized their photographs, and watched close friendships and family relationships dissolve. Some have changed their names or altered their appearance."[45] Another article maintains that legislation against revenge porn could be a short-term solution to fixing the larger culture of sexual harassment: "It makes sense to use the criminal law to deal with some of the more worrying or immediately harmful effects of a slut-shaming culture while we undertake the larger task of changing the culture itself."[46] Keats Citron further explains,

> Revenge porn is a harmful form of bigotry and sexual harassment. It exposes victims' sexuality in humiliating ways. Their naked photos appear on slut shaming sites. Once their naked images are exposed, anonymous strangers send e-mail messages that threaten rape. Some have said: "First I will rape you, then I'll kill you."[47]

Revenge porn is not gender neutral. Sexual double standards are widely applied to women's and men's sexual activity in society (e.g., slut/stud), and attitudes and beliefs that women's behaviour provokes sexual violence are deeply ingrained.[48] Thus, the nature and consequences of revenge porn are more severe for women than men. When drawing boundaries between what is violence and what is not, it is important to draw from the expertise that tells us that power and control are central to violence in all spaces. In digital spaces, personal and technological boundaries are blurred and converging. Of course, not all conflict online is violence; it is important to look at power, consent, the presence of hate speech pertaining to gender, race, sexual orientation, etc., and what threats are made. But telling someone, "I will rape you and then kill you" is violence, whether uttered in person, in a letter, on the phone, or online.

Shifting Definitions

Widespread recognition of sexual violence as a social problem did not happen organically. Dedicated research, survivor, and advocacy work built a conversation in legal arenas, social services, and research practice to provide a framework to talk about rape. The first rape crisis hotline was established in Washington in 1972,[49] and the first rape crisis centre in Canada (Vancouver Rape Relief and Women's Shelter) opened in 1973.[50] In Canada, the 1980s rape law reform campaign and subsequent passage of the 1983 sexual assault legislation, led by women's organizations and feminist lawyers, resulted in a dramatic increase in awareness of sexual violence as a political issue.[51] By the early 1980s, sexual violence and domestic violence had come to be viewed as symbols of women's oppression and therefore central to feminist attention and activism.[52] As Johnson and Dawson explain,

> In the past four decades, numerous achievements can be attributed to the tireless efforts of those involved in the violence against women movement. The definition of violence has been broadened to include those victimized by marital and non-marital partners and to recognize the equally detrimental effects of psychological, verbal, and financial abuse along with physical and sexual violence.[53]

Although research and advocacy efforts are advancing awareness of online activity and abuse, initial efforts to define and prevent violence online have been hindered by a lack of conceptual clarity about what it is we are working to prevent.[54] This is not unlike sexual violence prevention more broadly, where, as Holly Johnson explains, "a problem that has plagued prevention efforts is the inability to achieve consensus about what behaviours constitute violence."[55]

Thus, clear definitions are needed to address violence against women and girls in all forms.

Revenge porn and other forms of online sexual violence are about much more than humiliation, harm to reputation, and privacy violation. These acts marginalize and hinder individual public participation based on gender and sexuality. Though campaigns such as Take Back the Tech reflect this growing awareness, our prevailing definitions of violence, including many laws, policies, and government data collection practices have a ways to go. The 2013 *Report to the Federal/Provincial/Territorial Ministers Responsible for Justice and Public Safety: Cyberbullying and the Non-Consensual Distribution of Intimate Images* acknowledges that existing criminal offences "do not adequately address the harm that is caused by the non-consensual sharing of intimate images."[56] However, the report does not discuss this harm as violence nor the gendered nature of the targeted offences.[57] Furthermore, it contains specific assumptions about harms resulting from non-consensual sharing of intimate images: "The result of this type of conduct is usually embarrassment or humiliation caused by the breach of privacy, but not necessarily a fear for one's safety."[58]

Without a great deal more research to include the perspectives of those who experience sexual violence online, it is difficult to say to what extent they fear for their physical safety.[59] Additionally, by continuing to understand safety as primarily physical, and breaches of privacy as embarrassment, law and policy ignore the complexity of our social world. For example, women have had to change their identities, and have lost jobs and job opportunities due to online violence.[60] Isolation and poverty are important factors in women's health and safety, and so it is misguided to conclude that online sexual violence has no impact on physical well-being.

It is also important that conversations about how to define violence look beyond individual situations to consider how abuse and harassment occurs based on gender, racialization, sexuality, ability, class, and other social forces. Sylvia Walby argues that "the sociological analysis of violence requires the development of an appropriate ontology of violence; defining the concept and elucidating the nature of the relationship between violence and other social forces."[61] As we work to define violence in the digital age, we need to identify and interrogate pathologies within our ontology of violence. For example, Keats Citron explains that society has historically marginalized harms that uniquely affect women.[62] She argues that we must break down myths pertaining to online harassment, including the idea that online harassment represents innocuous teasing; that women can address the harassment on their own; and that online abuse is part of the Internet's unique norms. Keats Citron maintains, "Just as society ultimately rejected the argument that law should ignore domestic violence and sexual harassment because families and workplaces had their own norms, federal and state law make clear that offline institutions can be brought to bear in cyberspace."[63]

Further to this, when deciding how to define violence we must consider the question, what are the consequences when we define violence in very specific ways? Holly Johnson and Myrna Dawson highlight the costs of defining sexual violence too narrowly: "Widespread myths and stereotypes severely limit what constitutes 'real rape' and prevent women from naming their experience as violence, even when they suffer injuries and trauma."[64] Myths and stereotypes also contribute to a culture of victim blaming. If we assume that online violence can be ignored, walked away from,[65] and/or is something that people cause or deserve, then we will continue to hold people responsible for the abuse and harassment they experience. Alternately, if we understand that violence online cannot just be ignored or dismissed because of the real psychological or emotional harm that it causes, perhaps we will be able to develop victim/survivor supportive approaches that take this violence seriously within a spectrum of harmful behaviours.

Of course, it is also important that we consider potential unintended consequences of shifts in defining violence. For example, after 1980s rape law reform, at least some research suggests that respondents viewed offences that were labelled as sexual assault as less serious that the same scenarios defined as rape.[66] The point here is to take violence more seriously, not less. We should not think about "lowering" our bar of what constitutes violence, but expanding our field of attention and responsiveness. In that regard, law and policy have important symbolic roles to play.[67] Violence is an abuse of power that hinders a person's ability to be physically and emotionally safe in the world. This world includes the Internet. In one television interview, Hunter Moore responded to critics by saying that if he had not monetized revenge porn, someone else would have. He told victims it was their fault for taking intimate photos in the first place, saying, "It's 2012, what did you expect?" For decades, those working to address violence against women have been fighting an uphill battle against beliefs that violence, particularly sexual violence, is inevitable for women in certain marginalized groups (e.g., Indigenous women) and who engage in certain behaviours (e.g., drinking, walking alone at night). Much progress has been made, and there is much more work to be done. Moving forward, listening to survivors, advocates, and emerging research, I hope that our answer to Moore's question will be: we expect better. Understanding multiple dimensions of violence is a critical part of developing a strong theoretical framing and research base surrounding sexual violence and digital media, and this understanding is imperative to garnering public and policy support for anti-violence work in all spheres.

Notes

1   Holly Johnson & Myrna Dawson, *Violence Against Women in Canada: Research and Policy Perspectives* (Don Mills, ON: Oxford University Press Canada, 2011), 2.

2   Julie S. Lalonde, "Online Harassment Isn't Melodrama, but Serious Abuse," Canada.com, 24 January 2014, <http://o.canada.com/technology/internet/online-harassment-isnt-melodrama-but-serious-abuse>.

3   See Danielle Keats Citron, "Law's Expressive Value in Combating Cyber Gender Harassment," *Michigan Law Review* 108 (2009); Anastasia Powell, "Configuring Consent: Emerging Technologies, Unauthorized Sexual Images and Sexual Assault," *Australian & New Zealand Journal of Criminology* 43 (2010); Jane Bailey & Mouna Hanna, "The Gendered Dimensions of Sexting: Assessing the Applicability of Canada's Child Pornography Provision," *Canadian Journal of Women and the Law* 23:1 (2011); Nicole Bluett-Boyd, Bianca Fileborn, Antonia Quadara & Sharnee Moore, *The Role of Emerging Communications Technologies in Experiences of Sexual Violence: A New Legal Frontier?*, Research Report No. 23 (Melbourne, Australia: Australian Institute of Family Studies, 2013), <http://www.aifs.gov.au/institute/pubs/resreport23/rr23.pdf>; Michael Salter, "Justice and Revenge in Online Counter-Publics: Emerging Responses to Sexual Violence in the Age of Social Media," *Crime Media Culture* 9 (2013), doi:101177174165901349391.

4   Jane Bailey, "Time to Unpack the Juggernaut?: Reflections on the Canadian Federal Parliamentary Debates on 'Cyberbullying'," *Dalhousie Law Journal* 35 [forthcoming], archived at Social Sciences Research Network, <http://papers.ssrn.com/sol3/papers.cfm?abstract_id=2448480>.

5   While there is limited research on differences between women's and girls' experiences of online harassment, we can draw from research on how girls may experience violence more broadly. For example, issues

of consent, sexual exploitation, and abuses of power related to sexual violence have historically been a key area of focus for those under 18. Additionally, research has found that societal acceptance of violence is a major issue facing girls, and that self-esteem, self-image, peer pressure, self-harm (suicide, eating disorders), and the internalization of stereotypes and negative images of girls are significant issues of concern. Yasmin Jiwani, Kelly Gorkoff, Helene Berman, Gail Taylor, Glenda Vardy-Dell & Sylvie Normandeau, *Violence Prevention and the Girl Child: Final Report* (Ottawa: The Alliance of Five Research Centres on Violence, 1999), <http://fredacentre.com/wp-content/uploads/2010/09/Jiwani-et-al-1999-Violence-Prevention-and-the-Girl-Child-.pdf>.

6   General Assembly, "United Nations General Assembly, Declaration on the Elimination of Violence against Women," United Nations General Assembly 48/104 (NY: United Nations, 20 December 1993), <http://www.un.org/documents/ga/res/48/a48r104.htm>.

7   Johnson & Dawson, *supra* note 1.

8   Government of Ontario, *Changing Attitudes, Changing Lives: Ontario's Sexual Violence Action Plan* (Toronto: Queen's Printer for Ontario, March 2011), 5, <http://www.women.gov.on.ca/owd/docs/svap.pdf>.

9   Rachel Jewkes, Purna Sen & Claudia Garcia-Moreno, "Sexual Violence," in *World Report on Violence and Health*, eds. Etienne G. Krug et al, (Geneva: World Health Organization, 2002), 149, <http://whqlibdoc.who.int/hq/2002/9241545615.pdf>.

10   "Sexual Violence: Definitions," Centres for Disease Control and Prevention (CDC), <http://www.cdc.gov/violenceprevention/sexualviolence/definitions.html>.

11   Government of Ontario, *supra* note 8 at 6.

12   The Ontario Coalition of Rape Crisis Centres (OCRCC) explains that "any definition must acknowledge that while the majority of sexual violence is committed by men against women and children, it is also experienced by people in same sex relationships, by Trans people and by some men." <http://www.sexualassaultsupport.ca>.

13   *Supra* note 3.

14   "Take Back the Tech," *Take Back the Tech*, <https://www.takebackthetech.net/page/about-campaign>.

15   Take Back the Tech defines VAW as "any act the results in harm or disproportionately affects women," and the campaign works by looking at how both technology and VAW affect people's capacity to fully enjoy human rights and fundamental freedoms. The campaign uses a broader lens of "information communication technologies" (ICTs) rather than only focusing on the internet. According to Take Back the Tech, ICTs, broadly refer to tools and platforms that we use for our communication and information needs. Some examples include radio, mobile telephones,

television broadcasts, and the internet. <https://www.takebackthetech. net>.

16   Jac Sm Kee, "Cultivating Violence through Technology? Exploring the Connections between Information and Communication Technologies (ICT) and Violence against Women (VAW)," (Melville, SA: APC, 2005), <www.genderit.org/sites/default/upload/VAW_ICT_EN.pdf>. Take Back the Tech discusses six core areas of violence: domestic violence, sexual harassment, sexual violence, trafficking of women, conflict situations, and communication rights. Given space limitations and the specific focus of this chapter, I am focusing here on only part of the work that Take Back the Tech does in this area.

17   *Ibid.*, at 23.

18   However, domestic violence involving electronic and digital media is also well documented. For example, see Joanne Belknap, Ann T. Chu & Anne P. DePrince, "The Role of Phones and Computers in Threatening and Abusing Women Victims of Male Intimate Partner Abuse," *Duke Journal of Gender Law & Policy* 19 (2012), <http://scholarship.law.duke.edu/cgi/viewcontent.cgi?article=1232&context=djglp>.

19   Of course, there is still much work to be done in these areas. For example, research suggests sexual harassment of girls is pervasive and starts early. See Helene Berman, Katherine McKenna, Carrie Traher Arnold, Gail Taylor & Barbara MacQuarrie, "Sexual Harassment: Everyday Violence in the Lives of Girls and Women," *Advances in Nursing Science* 22:4 (2000): 32–46, <www.crvawc.ca/documents/Sexual%20Harassment%20Everyday%20Violence.PDF>. Furthermore, factors such as racism and ableism increase the severity and nature of the sexual harassment that girls experience at school. Harilyn Rousso, "Sexual Harassment in School: Invisible Issues for Girls and Young Women with Disabilities," Gender, Diversities and Technology Institute (Newton, MA: 2009, <www2.edc.org/GDI/publications_SR/publications/CRicaPub/RoussoEnglish.pdf>

20   "#CyberMisogyny: Using and Strengthening Canadian Legal Responses to Gendered Hate and Harassment Online," West Coast LEAF, <www.westcoastleaf.org/userfiles/file/Cyber%20Misogyny%20Report.pdf>.

21   Status of Women Canada, "Cyber and Sexual Violence: Helping Communities Respond," <http://www.swc-cfc.gc.ca/fun-fin/cfp-adp/2013-2/index-eng.html>.

22   See Emile Buckwald, Pamela R. Fletcher & Martha Roth, *Transforming a Rape Culture* (Minneapolis: Milkweed Editions, 1993); Tanya Horek, "#AskThicke: 'Blurred Lines,' Rape Culture, and the Feminist Hashtag Takeover," *Feminist Media Studies* 14:6 (2014): 1105–1107, doi:10.1080/14680777.2014.975450.

23 The current topics for the independent surveys are, caregiving, families, time use, social identity, volunteering, and victimization. Statistics Canada, "The General Social Survey: An Overview," 2013, <http://www.statcan.gc.ca/pub/89f0115x/89f0115x2013001-eng.htm>.

24 *Ibid.*

25 Statistics Canada, "General Social Survey: Victimization," October 2014, http://www23.statcan.gc.ca/imdb/p2SV.pl?Function=getSurvey& SDDS=4504.

26 See Angrove, Chapter XII; Maire Sinha, *Measuring Violence Against Women: Statistical Trends* (Ottawa: Canadian Centre for Justice Statistics, 2013), 8, <http://www.statcan.gc.ca/pub/85-002-x/2013001/article/11766-eng.pdf>.

27 Maire Gannon & Karen Mihorean, *Criminal Victimization in Canada, 2004* (Ottawa: Canadian Centre for Justice Statistics, 2005), 25.

28 Statistics Canada, *supra* note 25.

29 The 2014 GSS data will be released in 2015. According to Statistics Canada, this cycle will reintroduce questions on stalking, which were initially introduced in the 2004 Victimization Survey but were not part of the 2009 survey.

30 Danielle Keats Citron & Mary Anne Franks, "Criminalizing Revenge Porn," *Wake Forest Law Review* 49 (2014): 345.

31 *Ibid.*

32 *Ibid.*

33 Michael Salter, "Responding to Revenge Porn: Gender, Justice and Online Legal Impunity," paper presented at Whose Justice? Conflicted Approaches to Crime and Conflict, University of Western Sydney, Sydney (27 September 2013).

34 Shariff & DeMartini, Chapter XI.

35 See the discussion of Bill C-13, *infra* note 42.

36 Four additional articles were excluded from the sample because they mentioned "revenge porn" only in passing. For example, one article overviewed topics from that week's daytime television lineup and noted that "revenge porn" had been discussed, but did not elaborate further.

37 Emma Woolley, "When a Revenge Porn Kingpin Is Busted, Does It Matter Why?" *Globe and Mail*, 11 February 2014, <http://www.theglobeandmail.com/technology/digital-culture/when-a-revenge-porn-kingpin-is-busted-does-it-matter-why/article16776273/>.

38 Associated Press, "California: Man Is Charged in 'Revenge Porn' Case," *New York Times*, 10 December 2013, <http://www.nytimes.com/2013/12/11/us/california-man-is-charged-in-revenge-porn-case.html?_r=0>.

39 Woolley, *supra* note 37.

40   Editorial Board, "Fighting Back Against Revenge Porn," *New York Times*, 12 October 2013, <http://www.nytimes.com/2013/10/13/opinion/sunday/fighting-back-against-revenge-porn.html>.

41   Amanda Todd was a 15-year-old student in Port Coquitlam, British Columbia who committed suicide following months of online sexual exploitation, blackmailing, and bullying. Rehtaeh Parsons was a 17-year-old Nova Scotia high school student who committed suicide after months of digital harassment related to her sexual assault.

42   Tabatha Southey, "Bill C-13 is About a Lot More Than Cyberbullying," *Globe and Mail*, 6 December 2013, <http://www.theglobeandmail.com/globe-debate/columnists/maybe-one-day-revenge-porn-will-be-have-no-power/article15804000/>.

43   Editorials, "Cyberbullying Law Sneaks in Measures on Police Snooping," *Toronto Star*, 24 November 2013, <http://www.thestar.com/opinion/editorials/2013/11/24/cyberbullying_law_sneaks_in_measures_on_police_snooping_editorial.html>.

44   Sean Fine, "Tory 'Revenge Porn' Bill Touches on Terrorism, Cable Theft," *Globe and Mail*, 20 November 2013, <http://www.theglobeandmail.com/news/politics/tories-wide-ranging-crime-bill-cracks-down-on-distributing-intimate-images/article15533521/>.

45   Erica Goode, "Victims Push Laws to End Online Revenge Posts," *New York Times*, 23 September 2013, <http://www.nytimes.com/2013/09/24/us/victims-push-laws-to-end-online-revenge-posts.html>.

46   Michael Plaxton, "Canadian Women Deserve More Than a 'Revenge Porn' Law," *Globe and Mail*, 22 November 2013, <http://www.theglobeandmail.com/globe-debate/canadian-women-deserve-more-than-a-revenge-porn-law/article15560839/>.

47   Danielle Keats Citron, "Revenge Porn Should Be a Crime in U.S.," *CNN*, 16 January 2014, <http://edition.cnn.com/2013/08/29/opinion/citron-revenge-porn/>.

48   Helen Benedict, *Virgin or Vamp? How the Press Covers Sex Crimes* (New York: Oxford University Press, 1992).

49   Michelle Wasserman, "Rape: Breaking the Silence," *The Progressive* 37 (1973).

50   Joanna Den Hertog, "Herstory: Johanna Den Hertog – A Founding Member Keynote Speech at Rape Relief 35th Anniversary," 2008, Vancouver Rape Relief and Women's Shelter, <http://www.rapereliefshelter.bc.ca/about-us/herstory/herstory>.

51   Maria Los & Sharon E. Chamard, "Selling Newspapers or Educating the Public? Sexual Assault and the Media," *Canadian Journal of Criminology* 39 (1997): 293–328.

52   *Ibid.*

53   Johnson & Dawson, *supra* note 1 at 188.

54 Bluett-Boyd et al, *supra* note 3.

55 Holly Johnson, "Preventing Violence against Women: Progress and Challenges Volume," *Revue de l'IPC Review* 1 (2007): 73, <https://www. ncjrs.gov/App/Publications/abstract.aspx?ID=241584>.

56 CCSO Working Group, *Report to the Federal/Provincial/Territorial Ministers Responsible for Justice and Public Safety: Cyberbullying and the Non-consensual Distribution of Intimate Images* (Ottawa: Department of Justice, 2013), 16, <http://www.justice.gc.ca/eng/rp-pr/other-autre/cndii-cdncii/pdf/cndii-cdncii-eng.pdf>.

57 For example, the report contains only six instances of the word "violence," none of which are referring to the specific behaviours under debate.

58 Johnson, *supra* note 55 at 16.

59 Carissima Mathen, "Crowdsourcing Sexual Objectification" *Laws* 3:3 (2014): 529–552, doi:10.3390/laws3030529.

60 Associated Press, "'Most Hated Man on the Internet' Charged over Plot to Post Stolen Nude Photos," *Toronto Star*, 24 January 2014, <http://www. thestar.com/news/world/2014/01/24/most_hated_man_on_the_internet_charged_over_plot_to_post_stolen_nude_photos.html>.

61 Sylvia Walby, "Violence and Society: Introduction to an Emerging Field of Sociology," *Current Sociology* 61 (2012): 101, doi:10.1177/0011392112456478.

62 Danielle Keats Citron, "Law's Expressive Value in Combating Cyber Gender Harassment," *Michigan Law Review* 108 (2009), <http://www. michiganlawreview.org/assets/pdfs/108/3/citron.pdf>.

63 *Ibid.* at 401.

64 Johnson & Dawson, *supra* note 1 at 103.

65 Indeed, as noted in Shariff and DeMartini, Chapter XI, certain cyberbullying programs unrealistically advocate that targets should "walk away."

66 Julian V. Roberts, "Sexual Assaults in Canada: Recent Statistical Trends," *Queen's Law Journal*, 21 (1996): 395–421.

67 Tang Kwong-leung, "Rape Law Reform in Canada: The Success and Limits of Legislation," *International Journal of Offender Therapy and Comparative Criminology* 42 (1998), doi:10.117710306624X9804200307.

CHAPTER X

Motion to Dismiss: Bias Crime, Online Communication, and the Sex Lives of Others in *NJ v. Ravi*

Andrea Slane

In 2010, first-year Rutgers University student Dharun Ravi surreptitiously used his webcam to observe his roommate, Tyler Clementi, having a sexual encounter with another man in the dorm room they shared. Criminal charges laid against Ravi included four counts of invasion of privacy, each enhanced by bias intimidation on the basis of Clementi's sexual orientation.[1] He denied all charges and refused a plea deal, publicly insisting that he did not harbour any prejudice against gay people.[2] As the case proceeded to court, the defence filed a series of motions attempting to have the case dismissed, arguing that the evidence did not support the charges—especially those regarding bias. This motion record contains a large quantity of online communications evidence. This chapter elaborates on legal arguments put forward by the defence in relation to the bias intimidation charges, focusing on how the online communications evidence operates in relation to the parties' efforts to deny or affirm a finding of bias intimidation. That evidence provides a rich opportunity to consider how online communications and associated offline behaviours challenge legal understandings of what constitutes criminal activity, and, in particular, what should count as bias-motivated criminal activity online.

Bias intimidation offences are unusual sorts of criminal offences in that they do not stand alone, but are always linked to a predicate offence. They are designed to more harshly punish defendants who are motivated to commit another criminal offence against a particular victim as a result of their bias against that victim's identifiable membership in a target group. In the Ravi case, the underlying offence was invasion of privacy (i.e., voyeurism, arising from using the webcam to observe sexual activity, publicizing its availability to others, and attempting to do so a second time). The bias intimidation charges claimed that each of these acts was integrally linked to either Ravi's negative views of Clementi's sexual orientation, or, as elaborated below, to Clementi's feeling intimidated because of these acts.

It is tempting to think of this case as one about the tragic consequences of "cyberbullying," as was common in media reports about the incidents[3] – that is, about the often relentless and cruel abuse and harassment of gay youth and girls, as other contributors to this volume have explored, that can play a role[4] in leading some victims to commit suicide.[5] However, the incidents themselves, as well as the attitudes and behaviours of Ravi and the other inhabitants of the dorm, do not support approaching the case this way, at least not straightforwardly. While, tragically, Clementi did commit suicide shortly after the incidents – no doubt fuelling public speculation that he was driven to do so by the cruelty of his peers – this assumption is not based on any factual evidence. In any case, the suicide is not relevant to the criminal case against Ravi.[6] Instead, the charges Ravi faced implicate far more complex social interactions, some of them inflected with prejudice against gays, but none of them bearing the marks of overtly mean-spirited and relentless targeting of an individual for his difference.

The analysis I present here is situated in socio-legal studies, so it cannot directly explore the motivations behind Ravi's actions or Clementi's reactions: it will only do so indirectly through examining the online communications evidence submitted in court, and its relationship to the aims of the parties (to affirm or deny that Ravi was biased, or that Clementi was intimidated, in relation to the incidents). To more finely focus on defence strategies denying bias, I will limit my analysis to the motion record in the first motion to dismiss, which is the legal process by which the defence can attempt to have a case thrown out, and where the burden of proof falls on the defence rather than its usual location with the prosecution.[7] That motion record reveals how the defence's interpretation of online communications suggests there is a continuum of speech that ranges from common forms of social interaction that may raise social justice concerns about tolerance and acceptance, to forms of speech that meet the stringent requirements of criminal liability. While Clementi's state of mind (whether he felt "intimidated" in a legal sense) is more difficult to determine given his tragic absence as a witness, the available evidence as a whole reveals a complex interplay between online communication and shifting social norms regarding homosexual identity and gay sex, including from Clementi's perspective. My analysis supports further consideration of context, complexity, and nuance in interpreting youth online interactions, especially where the stakes for young people who may be convicted of criminal offences are extremely high.

Analysis of the Motion Documents and Online Communications Evidence

Before examining the motion record in depth, I will present some uncontested facts, mingled with contested ones. In September 2010, Clementi started a sexual relationship with an older man he met online. He had one sexual encounter with this man (M.B.) on September 16 in his dorm room, while his roommate (Ravi) was out.[8] On September 19, he asked Ravi, to whom he had been randomly assigned to share a dorm room by the university, if he could have exclusive use of the room for a few hours. Ravi agreed, but for reasons that are contested, went directly across the hall and called his computer, knowing it was set to automatically answer and activate his webcam.[9] Through his own webcam, Ravi and another student (Molly Wei) were able to view Clementi and M.B. becoming intimate, and they shut down the call after a few seconds. Ravi posted news of the event to his public Twitter feed: "Turned on iChat and saw my roommate making out with a dude. Yay." He and Wei also alerted dorm mates and friends, both in person and via online communications. A small group of young women, led by Wei, opened the webcam connection again for another few seconds, though Ravi was not present. Afterward, Clementi saw Ravi's tweet, but did not talk to him about it. Two days later Clementi asked for exclusive use of the room again, and again Ravi agreed. He put out another public tweet: "Anyone with iChat, I dare you to video chat me between the hours of 9:30 and 12. Yes it's happening again." Upon seeing this tweet, Clementi filed a formal complaint with the residence assistant and requested a room change. He also powered off Ravi's computer, so no one could access the webcam during his encounter with M.B. on

21 September. Ravi claimed to have disabled the webcam feature as well, though whether he did so is contested.[10]

These bare facts leave significant room for interpretation as to what role bias against Clementi's sexual orientation might have played. Surely, as other contributors to this volume explore, sexism and homophobia are strong forces in online interactions, especially in situations where peers use information about sexuality or sexual activity to instil shame in the target and bring on shaming judgments by others.[11] The Ravi case does not appear to have been about bringing shame upon Clementi, however. Instead, as this chapter goes on to show, it may be more about the role that a not purely benign curiosity about gay sex played in the social dynamics of a dorm occupied primarily by young people who did not know one another well. Further, issues raised by the case are more specifically about how the social dynamics impacted Clementi as an openly gay member of that dorm community. Clementi appeared to be unconcerned about others knowing he was gay and actively pursuing sexual contacts, but he also had difficulty relating to his peers more generally.[12]

These complex social dynamics do not fit straightforwardly into the mould of bias intimidation crimes. While there has been significant scholarly debate about the essential components of bias crime, most scholars require hostility or at least the perception of hostility toward the target group.[13] However, some sociologists argue that sexual orientation–based bias has changed in character as a result of the successes of the LGBTQ rights movement, such as the inclusion of sexual orientation as a recognized ground of bias in hate crimes. They suggest that at least some young people are living in a "post-homophobic" culture, where blatant hostility toward homosexuality is no longer acceptable.[14] This means that while negative associations with gay identity and gay sexuality persist, they are not necessarily consolidated into an overriding rejection of homosexuality, and negative associations formerly connected to sexual object choice may be used more generally as denigrating terms, with a broad range of intended meanings.[15] Homophobic language often serves to regulate gender conformity among peers, rather than sexuality itself.[16] This means that being called "gay" or "fag" can be about failure to display a narrow band of masculine behaviours and traits, without reference to sexuality, and can be used aggressively or playfully between men, depending on the context. These shifts complicate the relationship between homophobic language and the kind of animus against sexual minorities that the law has typically recognized in bias crimes. The defence in the Ravi case consequently sought to emphasize the mismatch between the defendant's views on homosexuality (typical of the persistent but milder forms of negative social associations with homosexuality) and the pernicious disgust-based forms of homophobia that are more straightforwardly the subject of bias intimidation offences.[17]

In order to proceed to trial, the State of New Jersey in the Ravi case had to present evidence to a grand jury in an indictment hearing, trying to demonstrate that it had sufficient grounds to carry forward with the prosecution.[18] Indictment hearings differ considerably from trials: the prosecution presents its preliminary case on a fairly low standard – namely, merely to show that it has "probable cause to believe that a crime occurred" and if so, then that there is "sufficient evidence to connect the accused to that crime," not proof beyond a reasonable doubt as is required at trial.[19] An indictment returned by a grand jury (that is, permission to proceed to trial) is difficult to overturn, since at this point legal process prefers to see a case fully tried. If the defence seeks to dismiss an indictment, it must show a blatant error of law or that patently insufficient or misleading evidence was led, so that the burden of proof to dismiss an indictment is the opposite of what it will be at trial (where the burden of proof falls entirely on the prosecution).[20] In other words, it is not enough for the defence just to raise a reasonable doubt at this stage. The motion record submitted by the defence at this point in the Ravi case therefore provides a unique opportunity to analyze an alternative narrative put forward affirmatively by the defence regarding the meaning of the online actions and interactions of the defendant, the victim, and their peers.

New Jersey's bias intimidation offences are broader than those of most other US states, in that they include three variants: (1) committing the underlying crime intending to intimidate the victim because of his or her group membership; (2) doing so knowing that the victim would be intimidated on that basis; or (3) that the victim was in fact intimidated by the underlying offences, in circumstances where it was reasonable for him or her to assume that he or she was targeted because of his or her group membership.[21] As Ravi was charged with all three variants, online communications evidence aiming to support or negate any of these three circumstances is relevant to the case.[22]

In strongly arguing that these charges were inappropriate to the facts, the defence submitted evidence of electronic communications from two time periods: (a) when the defendant and victim were first introduced to one another (indirectly and directly); and (b) at the time of the first invasion of privacy incident. During the first period, Ravi engaged in peer data mining to uncover whatever online information he could about his future roommate, and reacted to those discoveries in conversations with friends and in performative acts of self-presentation via social media. Clementi, meanwhile, discussed his future roommate online with friends, including his difficulties talking to him after they met. Evidence from the second time frame illustrates the role of social media and other forms of online communication in spreading social news pertaining to a peer's sexual activity. This evidence included Ravi's use of Twitter as a mode of self-presentation, while Clementi appeared to use online communications as a primary locus of support, both from friends and from gay online forums.

The defence argued a particular interpretation of the evidence, countered by the prosecution's interpretation. Of the two interpretations, the defence interpretation relied more heavily on social context to interpret Ravi's words, while the prosecution tended to argue for the meaning of words at face value. The defence strategy aimed to soften and recast Ravi's words and online actions by offering an alternative interpretation of Ravi's motivations for talking about Clementi the way he did, and for using social media to announce and frame his experiences at university.

However, the defence did not use the same level of contextual interpretation when it came to Clementi's online communications. Instead, the defence pointed to instances where Clementi made light of Ravi's attitudes and deeds in online conversations, and read these comments literally. The prosecution strategy continued to rely on its own straightforward reading of Clementi's words as well, but focused on different points in conversations where Clementi spoke of feeling violated. The lines of argument pertaining to whether Clementi was intimidated merely highlighted different segments of conversations, each side selectively choosing which words should be taken as most revealing of Clementi's reactions to Ravi's misdeeds. These literal strategies lack the capacity to grasp the nuances of online social interactions, and so are unlikely to accurately capture Clementi's reactions to the social dynamics surrounding these incidents.

I will next analyze how the evidence operated to support the parties' arguments, especially the defence, in each of the relevant time frames. Overall, I argue that a more contextual approach to interpreting the online communications evidence is necessary to determine what sorts of online communications appropriately serve as evidence of criminal bias intimidation.

Peer Data Mining, Judgmental Commentary, and Online Self-Presentation

A key aspect of the defence's argument focused on Ravi's various conversations and pronouncements – mostly online – about his future roommate's characteristics and interests, including his sexuality, in the days *before* they moved in together at Rutgers. The defence also submitted evidence of Clementi's instant message conversations about Ravi from this time frame, and additional ones discussing his awkward relationship with Ravi shortly after their initial meeting.

Different Homophobias and Their Role in Heterosexual Male Self-Presentation

Rutgers University provides incoming students living in dorms with the first name and last initial of their assigned roommate, along with an email address. The defence submitted a conversation log in which Ravi (using the username "goodyearsoles") chatted online with a friend using the name "bigeaglefan75" as they together searched for and shared information about their roommates based on the information the university provided. The defence recounted this conversation and sequence of events as follows:

> Early after learning T.C.'s first name and email address, Defendant searched the internet to learn some things about him, a fairly common occurrence these days when you meet someone new. One of the searches led defendant to a gay-themed website.
> Defendant then decided to learn a little more. He came upon a Facebook profile of an individual who had the same first name as T.C., was starting Rutgers in the fall, and was openly gay. Assuming this was his roommate, Defendant started looking through the young man's public profile. Defendant chatted with friends online about the information he was finding, including impressions about how flamboyant the person

appeared to be regarding his homosexuality. He and his friends
privately made some juvenile jokes about it (hardly shocking
behavior for an 18-year-old boy), and expressed some apprehension about living with someone whose lifestyle is so different
from his.

But his attitude appeared to be summed up by his comment, "I'm not really ... angry ... or sad ... Idc [I don't care)]."

Defendant was asked by this friend, "What if he wants
you ... wont that get [awkward]"?

Defendant responded, "He [probably] would ... Why
would it be [awkward] ... He'd want me ... I wouldn't want him
... I do that with girls who want me but it's not mutual."

Nevertheless, however, Defendant learned that it was all a
strange mistake. Upon learning that his roommate was actually
T.C., Defendant commented that his real roommate was "also
gay but regular gay."[23]

This excerpt reveals how the defence set up its argument that there
is a distinction between the kind of homophobia that it alleged can
correctly be identified as capable of inspiring a bias crime, and the
kind of casual prejudice that Ravi (and his friends) displayed in
their discussion of the "wrong Tyler." The defence normalized Ravi's
response to this other Tyler's sexual identity as "hardly shocking
behavior for an 18-year-old boy." Further, it argued that Ravi was
not concerned about being the object of gay sexual interest, implicitly
suggesting that disgust at this thought is a necessary feature of the
kind of homophobia that inspires bias crimes. Once the misidentifica-
tion had been corrected, Ravi showed even less concern about having
a roommate who was "also gay but regular gay." The defence thus
argued that even if Ravi was somewhat prejudiced in a common sort
of way against "flamboyant" gays by making them the brunt of his
"juvenile jokes," he was not disturbed by being in close proximity to
gay sexuality generally and so was not capable of a bias crime on the
basis of homosexuality, especially toward someone who is "regular"
gay. The defence went on to accuse the prosecution of mischaracter-
izing Ravi's words as uniformly expressing "concern" about having
a gay roommate.[24]

This kind of argument is supported by some scholarship about
contemporary changes in negative attitudes about homosexuality,
especially in social environments where thoroughgoing homophobia

has become an unacceptable form of prejudice. In these environments, expressions of disgust for homosexuality tend to reflect negatively on the speaker, so many young people in these contexts explicitly disavow being homophobic, even if they continue to use expressions that cast some ways of "being gay" negatively.[25]

The defence submitted an online conversation as evidence to support this more nuanced framing of Ravi's attitudes toward homosexuality. An excerpt from this conversation (between Ravi and bigeaglefan75) began with the following sequence of short statements in which Ravi summed up what he knew about his future roommate: "So far/This kid is Gay/ Tries to be good with computers and fails/ he's poor/ and makes ugly tshirts/ He's the literal opposite of me."[26] His discovery of Clementi's homosexuality was thus embedded in the discovery of other "unflattering" characteristics, apparently pointing to Clementi being uncool: that is, not computer savvy, not artistically talented, not well-off, and not socially confident (all unlike Ravi himself). In other words, it appears that Clementi being gay in itself was not the issue – rather, it was being gay in combination with these other non-identity-based differences that led Ravi to see his own social status improved by ridiculing his future roommate for all of these characteristics.[27]

The profile of Clementi that Ravi developed from his internet data mining makes distinctions based on other personality characteristics: notions of what is geeky or flamboyant serve to modify "gay," contrasting these more precise markers of different ways to "be gay" with other more favourable ones like "regular" gay, or even cool gay, in the case of a gay friend.[28] For the purposes of the defence, these nuances themselves were not of interest and are not elaborated: they were simply submitted to demonstrate that Ravi did not have an overriding problem with homosexuality itself, which the defence implicitly suggests is the only kind of homophobia that could substantiate a bias intimidation charge.[29]

Another line of argument for the defence was that Ravi did not have a general problem with gay sex, even though joking about proximity or exposure to gay sex is a standard part of Ravi's online repertoire. According to evidence submitted by the defence, Ravi first discovered Clementi's sexuality by tracing his email address to a forum on Just Us Boys, a gay-themed website. Ravi immediately shared this discovery with bigeaglefan75 by sending him a link to the site without telling him where the link will take him. Bigeaglefan75 responded with "WAIT WTF" and "is that him" and a series of "OMG," "LMAO," and "LMFAO" before Ravi responded with "No it's not lol."[30] Bigeaglefan75 carried on with "OH," "WELL FUCK YOU," and "why am I looking at a penis," to which Ravi replied, "You likes it." Bigeaglefan75 wrote "LOL no" and "wait so how did you find your roommates post on that site with just his email" and Ravi replied, "I'm a pro."[31] Visiting a gay website was clearly titillating, unnerving, and also humorous, and Ravi mostly seemed to relish having brought his friend there unexpectedly, and for a "legitimate" non-sexual purpose (finding out information about his future room-mate).[32] While it is not clear whether this helps the defence argument that Ravi did not harbour the kind of homophobia that would make him capable of intentionally or recklessly intimidating Clementi, it does point to a common performative practice, in keeping with Ravi later using exposure to live gay sex (via his webcam) as a foil for his own brand of humorous online interactions with his ostensibly straight friends.

The exchange with bigeaglefan75 also includes indications that Ravi regularly engaged in quippy public pronouncements on Twitter, which were mainly designed to augment his public persona as cool and funny. He and his friend demand of each other to "Look at my twitter" or "check my twitter" after posting something they find humorous.[33] These duelling performative Twitter posts illustrate how Ravi used Twitter to project his own sense of a confident, funny, socially dominant self, sometimes by denigrating others, to his networked public, which, as some sociologists have pointed out, is likely a much more precisely imagined audience than merely the vast public of the internet at large.[34] The legal status of this perception – that a forum that does not bar anyone from seeing it may be public to varying degrees – is still unsettled however.[35] For the most part, courts consider a public forum to address the world at large unless there are barriers to entry. Such a simple approach to the intended audience for online forums is not appropriate for criminal proceedings that rely on a factual determination of intentions, however, as bias intimidation does.[36]

The evidence regarding Ravi's performative use of Twitter lends some insight into why Ravi would later use Twitter to broadcast the news that his roommate was in their room "making out with a dude. Yay." That is, Ravi was augmenting his cool status by reporting to his larger friendship circle that something ironically uncool was happening to him. The online communication evidence from August 2010 thus both directly and indirectly supports the defence's argument that both the content of Ravi's comments and his use of online communications media did not rise to the level of criminal bias. Instead, so the defence argument goes, they merely reflected the common social practices of a certain mode of young heterosexual masculinity – that is, "juvenile jokes," which primarily serve to reflect favourably on the sort of confident, ironic, masculinity Ravi considered himself to embody. Setting aside the social harms of these kind of attitudes, the indirect function of this line of argument appears to be that Ravi did not intend to intimidate, nor even did he know his actions would intimidate Clementi even if unintentionally, mostly because Ravi was entirely self-absorbed and so did not consider the potential impact of his actions on Clementi at all.

The prosecution characterized these sorts of conversations very differently: given the low standard of proof required at the indictment hearing stage, it merely insisted that Ravi's online conversations "document his concern and displeasure, if not alarm" over the discovery that his future roommate was gay.[37] The prosecution singled out particularly inflammatory words or statements from a conversation Ravi had with another friend, such as "F—K MY LIFE. He's gay," "he'd be a chick in a gay relationship," "fag," and "what if I catch him with a dude in my room."[38] However, the actual instant message chat log submitted, if read contextually, embeds these statements in a larger conversation. That conversation positions homosexuality in relation to what Ravi and his friend clearly agree are other unflattering interests (violins, fish tanks, gardening, and lack of computer savvy), or as banter during which friends teased each other about viewing gay porn while maintaining a firm grasp on their mutual heterosexuality.

In sum, the defence argued that the evidence demonstrated that Ravi did not display the sort of homophobia – read as intent to do harm to gay people – that would make him capable of a bias intimidation crime. In contrast, for the prosecution, even this fairly ordinary version of homophobia – bound up as it is with other forms of adolescent judgment and prejudice – was sufficient to indicate that Ravi was at least inclined to be indifferent to the harmful effects of his actions toward Clementi. The legal question then is whether insensitivity to the impact of the words and actions of one's self-serving online persona is sufficient grounds for conviction for intention to intimidate or knowledge that one's actions would intimidate, on the basis of sexual orientation.

Gay Youth Making Light of Homophobia

The third version of the bias intimidation charges focuses entirely on the victim (requiring proof that he was intimidated and reasonably assumed he was targeted for being gay). Here, the primary defence strategy in the first time frame was to argue that Clementi was not intimidated by Ravi to the degree that should be required for a bias intimidation conviction.

The defence tried to use online communication evidence to show two things. First, Clementi also made some mild negative comments about Ravi (based on his ethnicity), which the defence argued illustrated how common and not necessarily indicative of bias such comments are. Second, the defence argued that while Clementi clearly felt that Ravi exhibited some discomfort about his sexuality, for the most part Clementi took these indicators in stride and sometimes even found them amusing and joked about them with friends.

With regard to the first argument, the defence provided the following excerpt from a text conversation Clementi had with his friend H.Y. shortly after he and Ravi moved in together, in which Clementi remarked "his [family] is sooo indian/first gen americanish … just like … first son off to college … his rents defs owna dunkin [donuts]."[39] Based on these comments, the defence argued, "In other words, just like Defendant, T.C. was evaluating his roommate based on superficial characteristics, because that was all he knew of him at the time. It was *not* suggestive of T.C. being prejudiced about Indians, any more than Defendant's private jokes were indicative of homophobia."[40] In other words, the defence argues that because Clementi exhibited milder forms of racism toward Ravi, he would not have been disturbed by Ravi exhibiting milder forms of homophobia toward him. This sort of racism and homophobia is therefore cast by the defence as normal, and so not capable of serving as evidence of a criminal level of bias.

As to the second line of argument, the defence submitted an excerpt from a second conversation with another friend, S.C., arguing that Clementi "became aware that Defendant likely knew that he was gay. He could tell Defendant was uncomfortable, because he observed Defendant changing his clothes in the closet. T.C. was amused by the awkwardness of it, but was not upset with Defendant as a roommate at this point."[41] The defence argued that this conversation illustrates that Clementi was generally satisfied with Ravi as a roommate, as "he noted that Defendant was 'considerate' and 'perceptive' about T.C. wanting to be left by himself. At one point, T.C. commented that Defendant was 'way too considerate of me.' T.C. also said that he 'wouldn't mind if [Defendant] found me with a guy."[42] Here, the defence was arguing that in order to be "intimidated" in the sense required by a bias intimidation offence, Clementi would have had to fear his roommate, and the defence concluded that on the facts he clearly did not.

The defence did not choose to emphasize broader contextual cues about Clementi's relationship with his roommate, however, even where it may have served to further support the defence argument that Clementi did not feel intimidated by Ravi. Within the evidence submitted are indicators that Clementi's awareness of his roommate's discomfort with his sexuality was part of a larger problem. The two roommates appeared unable to connect with one another on many levels, not just in relation to Clementi's sexuality, which may have reduced the impact of some statements highlighted by the prosecution. The defence submitted the following conversation between Clementi and S.C., for instance:

[S.C.]: hows living w ur roomie
[TC]: its k/he's never in the room lolz/oh but hehe he knows I'm gay/ and wow/ he changes his pants/ inside his closet/ hehe-hehehe/ soooo funny/ its like the most awk thing you've ever seen/ but oh well
[S.C.]: hahaha
[TC]: yah he's pretty fine all around/ a lil bit messy/ but so far so good[43]

The conversation continued with S.C. asking how Ravi knew Clementi was gay. Clementi described accurately how Ravi figured it out, which he knew from Ravi's own Twitter feed, not from any direct conversation with Ravi: "he did some internet investigating lolz/ he googled the first part of my email address/ and it turns out I used that as a screen name on some site/ and so he just naturally assumes/ And idk/ I'm out to a whole bunch a people."[44] S.C. replied, "interesting/ well I bet ur roomie help," to which Clementi queried "how so? help how?" and S.C. explained, "he probably told ppl [people]."

Clementi replied, "oh haha/ yah/ he tweeted about it/ hehehe/." S.C. replied, "lol," and Clementi continued, "but yah/ I would say I'm out/ oh but about roomie/ I don't think I've actualy ever talked to him heheh/ we kinda just ignore ea other."[45] At this point (i.e., prior to the invasion of privacy incidents), Clementi appeared to see humour in Ravi's awkwardness about his sexuality, even as he also expressed some anxiety to another friend, H.Y., about not being able to talk to Ravi about even ordinary roommate things like where to place furniture or whether to open or close the blinds.[46]

Embedded in these exchanges is evidence that Clementi actually did not appear to be very concerned about his sexual hookups being noticed or even inadvertently witnessed. While not in itself relevant to the case, the record notes that Clementi had a sexual encounter with M.B. in the dorm room once prior to the incidents, which Ravi did not know about as he wasn't home. After this encounter, Clementi discussed the complications of short-term rentals of motel rooms with S.C. and noted how privacy is hard to come by in a dorm, and that he would likely "get a reputation" anyway, even if Ravi didn't walk in "while I'm getting fucked haha" because "you have to walk through the lounge in order to get to my room ... /there are always people around/ Bringing a 25 year old guy/ into my room/ who leaves like 3 hrs later/i mean ... / somebody had to notice."[47]

These exchanges seem to support several of the defence's purposes, even though they are not explicitly pointed to in the arguments. First, they show that Clementi was not worried about being "outed" as gay, nor particularly concerned about people in the dorm knowing that he was having sex with a man in his room. The defence offers a contextual reading of these statements in the days leading up to the incidents, designed to lessen the strength of the prosecution argument that Clementi was intimidated by information about his sexual activity being broadcast via Ravi's Twitter feed or discussed among dormmates – though this strategy does not address any possible distinctions between sexual information and the capacity to actually view Clementi having sex with his date. Second, the exchanges also reveal that Clementi was keen on having a regular place to bring his date to for sex, and had difficulty talking to Ravi. The defence suggests that these exchanges might then provide an alternative explanation for Clementi's request for a single room following the incidents, and so raise doubt as to whether his request resulted from intimidation specific to the incidents.[48]

Peer Surveillance and Social News Broadcasting

With regard to the time frame immediately surrounding the webcam incidents themselves, the defence submitted further online communication evidence, as well as excerpts from witness interviews with investigators, to continue the strategy of distancing Ravi's actions from homophobic intentions. For example, the defence tried to frame Ravi's discussions of the webcam incidents as merely reactions to (and capitalizing on) a novel experience (that is, glimpsing and being in close proximity to live gay sex) as opposed to being motivated by intention to intimidate Clementi based on his sexual orientation. The defence also tried to frame Clementi's distress and outrage following the incidents as resulting from invasion of privacy itself, rather than specific to feelings of intimidation on the basis of his sexual orientation.

Gaining Social Status via Creating Social Buzz

Immediately after seeing Clementi and his date "making out" through the webcam, Ravi and Wei generated significant social buzz about their actions and what they had seen, both in the dorm itself and among a broader friendship circle. Within the dorm itself, this social news broadcasting was mostly done in person, and the defence submitted excerpts from police interviews with witnesses from the dorm, none of whom reported having heard Ravi "say anything negative about homosexuals" or being a "homophobic person."[49] These excerpts support and continue the defence's argument regarding Ravi's online comments about Clementi before the incident—that to be sufficiently homophobic to commit a bias crime, one must have an overriding animosity toward gay people as a whole, which Ravi did not. This argument, supported by the witness statements that share this point of view, recasts milder forms of homophobia as something not appropriate for punishment by the criminal law.[50]

The defence characterized Ravi and Wei's use of social media as follows:

> Both were stunned, as they had never personally observed anything like this before. Defendant posted to his Twitter feed, "Turned on iChat and saw my roommate making out with a dude. Yay." Wei and Defendant started messaging friends to check out Defendant's Twitter. Their friends replied with some

crude jokes, often making fun of Defendant for having a gay roommate.[51]

While not explicitly saying so, the defence's argument was that this sort of peer surveillance and subsequent social news broadcasting was merely a normal reaction by heterosexual youth who found themselves in close proximity to gay sex, which is cast as distinct from homophobia toward gay people. The defence suggests that by broadcasting this kind of news, Ravi and Wei were merely attempting to improve their social status.[52] Inviting others to partake in the experience of seeing live gay sex (even if only for a few seconds) was not, the defence argued, fuelled by homophobia per se, but rather by a quest to socially capitalize on a novel experience. Again, this argument relied heavily on distinguishing between the kind of homophobia that the defence claimed inspire criminal intentions, and the kinds of homophobia that makes seeing gay sex shocking and titillating to those who haven't seen it before.

If we extend the defence's implicit argument regarding the use of Twitter as a vehicle for Ravi's self-presentation, then Ravi's decision to publicize having stumbled upon his roommate having gay sex becomes similar to his pronouncements about having a geeky gay roommate (i.e., "isn't it funny/ironic that this is happening to *me*"). This entirely self-absorbed practice continues then with the tweet regarding the second attempted invasion of privacy incident two days later: "Anyone with iChat, I dare you to video chat me between the hours of 9:30 and 12. Yes it's happening again." [53] According to the defence, this second tweet was intended as another in the series of sarcastic comments by Ravi about the irony of the situation, and was not meant to actually inspire anyone to check out the webcam, nor to particularly engage in ridicule of Clementi. In other words, the defence was willing to admit that Ravi was immature and insensitive, but argued that he should not be held to have a criminal level of bias against Clementi.

Further, the defence argued that Ravi did not use his public Twitter account to address the world at large: it argued that he did not intend Clementi to see the Twitter post and never drew the post to his attention. In other words, Ravi was essentially addressing his own friendship circle, those he knew to be following his Twitter feed.[54] A central argument of the defence then was that bias intimidation requires a defendant to *directly* intimidate the victim, not indirectly expose the victim to negative social consequences by others (which the defence also argued were in any case not intended either).[55]

In contrast, the prosecution emphasized the negative tone of these tweets, and argued that a heterosexual encounter would not have generated the same level of interest, and therefore that Clementi could reasonably assume that he was targeted because of his sexual orientation.[56] The prosecution stressed that Ravi's tweets were set to be public, and thereby were accessible by anyone (including Clementi).[57] It argued that the public nature of the second tweet "clearly establishes the defendant's intent on September 19 and again on September 21 – to expose T. C.'s sexual orientation to others to embarrass, humiliate and intimidate him."[58]

This raises an important legal issue regarding whether bias intimidation must be directed specifically at the victim, or whether (as argued by the prosecution) simply putting the content out there for the victim to discover or otherwise exposing a victim to intimidation (including by others) is sufficient.[59] It also raises two further issues regarding interpretation of "public" online communications that are not directly addressed in the case: whether privacy settings alone determine the intent of a party for communications to be read widely (which runs contrary to how many users subjectively consider their online communications); and whether mentioning a person's sexual orientation or the fact of their same-sex sexual activity alone is sufficient to infer an intent to humiliate or embarrass, especially where the subject is fairly open about his sexuality and active sex life, as was the case here.[60]

Again, the defence's interpretation of online communications suggests there is a continuum of speech that ranges from common forms of social interaction, that may raise social justice concerns about tolerance and acceptance, to forms of speech that meet the stringent requirements of criminal liability. In this case at least, a more contextual approach appeared to provide the defence with support for its argument that Ravi's online behaviour should not fall within the bias intimidation offence.

Feeling Violated vs. Feeling Intimidated

To argue that Clementi did not feel intimidated, the defence focused on excerpts from Clementi's online conversations with his friend H.Y., in which he characterized the first webcam incident as another amusing example of how awkward Ravi felt about his sexuality. It noted that Clementi "found the incident 'sooo funny,'" and that he commented, "it's not like he left the cam on or recorded anything/ he just like took a five sec peep lol."[61] With regard to Ravi's tweet, the defence cited Clementi's comments, "When I first read the tweet/ I defs felt violated/ But then/ When I remembered what actually happened ... / Idk ... /Doesn't seem soooo bad lol"[62] and "I'm really excited to see what the next tweet will be/ heehee/ tomoro night lol/maybe."[63] Further, the defence referred to how Clementi explicitly dismissed the action as a hate crime: after H.Y. suggested that "it could be interpreted as a hate crime," Clementi responded "hahaha a hate crime lol/ that would be so funny/ white people never get hated/ hee hee" to which H.Y. responded "you're gay ...."[64] The defence summarized this exchange as indicating that "T.C. regarded the incident on the 19th as 'not so bad,' that he expressed amusement over it, and that he laughingly dismissed the idea of a 'hate crime.'"[65]

The defence's characterization of Clementi's state of mind as far from intimidated relies in part on the frequent "laughing" indicators in his online speech, expressions like "hehe," "haha," and "lol." However, a contextual reading of these expressions would show that Clementi's online conversations are virtually all peppered with such expressions, regardless of the seriousness of the subject matter. Some scholars have noted a common social tendency to make light of unpleasant situations on social media, in order to portray an online persona who is happy and hence "likeable."[66] While it would have helped the prosecution's case, the prosecution did not raise this contextual interpretation of Clementi's online speech patterns in reply to the defence either.

The second argument put forward by the defence argued that Clementi's statement that he "defs felt violated" was not specifically related to his sexual orientation, but rather that the reaction would likely have been the same regardless of the motivation behind the privacy invasion. The defence provided additional excerpts from online conversations Clementi had on a Just Us Boys forum a few hours after filing his room change request, in which he "described Defendant's behaviour as 'obnoxious,' and described his level of annoyance as 'kinda pissed' but 'aside from being an asshole from time to time, [Defendant is] a pretty decent roommate.'"[67] The defence concluded, "there is no evidence that T.C. actually was intimidated by the Defendant .... There was evidence that he felt violated, though that is inherent in the Invasion of Privacy charge. But he never expressed fear."[68]

A fundamental legal question is whether the third variant of the New Jersey bias intimidation offence (feeling intimidated in circumstances where it is reasonable for victims to assume that they were targeted because of their group membership) requires *fear* on the part of the victim, or whether outrage about being targeted because of sexual orientation would be sufficient. If outrage is sufficient, it may be relevant that Clementi chose to voice his strongest feelings of violation about the incidents on a specifically gay online forum.[69] However, the prosecution did not address these contextual distinctions.

Finally, the defence also raised the question of whether any violation or outrage Clementi felt was due to his reasonable conclusion that he was targeted for being gay, or whether it was more generally related to having his sexual privacy invaded. Invasion of privacy is a sexual offence, involving observing or recording a person whose intimate parts are exposed or who is engaged in sexual penetration or sexual contact. The defence therefore raised a valid question that the prosecution did not address, preferring instead to continue to assume that, in effect, whenever a gay person's sexual privacy is invaded, it follows that any reaction he or she experiences results from feeling targeted for being gay.

By failing to address the particular type of targeting that Clementi could reasonably assume, the prosecution argument runs into the legal territory that plagues the application of both gender and sexual orientation bias offences to sexual crimes. In many jurisdictions, New Jersey included, gender bias is excluded as a ground for bias offences linked to sexual crimes, in part because of the difficulty in separating out the kind of gender bias that should qualify for harsher punishment as a bias crime, from other gender dynamics at play more generally in sexual offences.[70] While many legal scholars have made a convincing case for including gender bias as a ground in relation to sexual violence against women, especially where there is evidence of animus against women as a group, the case for including gender bias as a ground in relation to non-violent sexual crimes like invasion of privacy has not been fully developed.[71] This makes the prosecution's job of building a solid argument for applying sexual orientation bias to non-physical sexual crimes all the more crucial, because doing so could help lay important groundwork for recognizing when gender bias should apply to similar situations.

The rub lies in that both women and gay people could reasonably assume they were targeted for a sexual crime because of their group membership, precisely because of the sexual nature of the crime. If such a reasonable assumption is a foregone conclusion, however, then a key source of justification for bias crimes — recognizing enhanced harm to the target group — is lost, since it is generalized.[72] A more convincing approach would be to prove that the victim reasonably assumed he or she was targeted *for a bias crime* because of his or her sexual orientation or gender, rather than only for the underlying non-physical sexual offence. This would help clarify the nature and degree of bias the victim must reasonably perceive, and might help forge a pathway for recognizing gender bias as an appropriate ground as well.

Conclusion

The defence's motion to dismiss was ultimately unsuccessful, and the case did proceed to trial as planned, where the defence and prosecution continued to argue many of the same points as described above. While much more evidence was presented at trial, including several weeks of witness testimony, in the end, Ravi's conviction on the bias intimidation offences relied only on the third variant: Clementi was found to have been intimidated under circumstances where he reasonably assumed he was targeted because of his sexual orientation. In other words, the jury was not convinced beyond a reasonable doubt that Ravi intended to intimidate Clementi, or knew that he would cause Clementi to feel intimidated as a result of his actions. The jury seemingly agreed with the defence's argument that Ravi "showed poor, but not criminal, judgement."[73] However, the jury was also convinced beyond a reasonable doubt that Clementi felt intimidated to the required degree and reasonably assumed he was targeted for his sexual orientation.

Reflecting on the motion record and the arguments put forth by the parties, this result acknowledges that some negative comments about gay identity, and some negative reactions to being in proximity to gay sexual activity, do not substantiate an intent to intimidate that rises to the level of a criminal offence. However, a finding of guilt on the third variant of bias intimidation based on Clementi's perceptions of events is more problematic in the absence of more contextual consideration of both Clementi's comfort with public knowledge of his sexual activity and how he spoke more generally in online contexts.[74] Since Ravi received a lighter sentence than would normally be imposed by a bias intimidation conviction, the judge clearly was also not comfortable with a straightforward application of a bias offence to this type of crime. The judge stated during the sentencing hearing, "I do not believe [Ravi] hated Tyler Clementi. He had no reason to, but I do believe he acted out of colossal insensitivity."[75] The prosecution has appealed this light sentence; and the defence has appealed the conviction.[76]

This was a difficult case: the bias intimidation charges were an ongoing issue for Ravi, who denied hating gays all along.[77] His conviction on invasion of privacy charges is relatively uncontroversial, but the bias intimidation conviction has inspired much debate about whether these laws are appropriately applied to this type of offence, and especially to this type of online conduct. Much of the debate about the appropriateness of Ravi's bias intimidation charges has centred on whether bias intimidation charges should ever be applied to non-physical predicate crimes, an argument that too handily discounts psychological harm.[78] A thornier issue is whether bias intimidation charges are appropriate tools for addressing common non-physical forms of sexual *prejudice* in the context of sexual crimes, as opposed to statements that are clearly intended to cause a victim to feel threatened (psychologically or physically). On the other hand, this case further raises important questions about the limitations of requiring proof that a victim feels a high level of threat or danger. Imposition of such a standard would seem to preclude redress for bias-motivated acts against victims who are not ashamed of public exposure of their sexual identity or activities, as well as those who eschew displaying their feelings of intimidation, but who are nonetheless disturbed by the criminal conduct maliciously directed at them because of their sexuality (or gender).[79]

At the same time, the case raises important cautions about the criminalization of online communication conduct, and in particular the uneven levels of sophistication that parties use to argue about the interpretation of online evidence. Bias intimidation is a unique offence that requires adjudicators to delve into and pass judgment on the states of mind of the perpetrator and victim. Informed contextual analysis of online communications evidence in these cases is essential to arriving at an appropriate determination of what kinds of online statements and actions serve as reliable indicators of a criminal level of bias motivation and impact. Our legitimate concerns about the emotional health and well-being of LGBTQ youth online (and girls, as more directly examined throughout this volume) requires that we strive to understand the complexities of how information about the sex lives of others operates in the social ecology of young people, and to incorporate these complexities into legal arguments both for and against criminal convictions for particular online acts. Moreover, closer examination of the heteronormative masculinity at play in the case raises questions about the ways that stereotypes and prejudices operate to shape and constrain the gender and sexual performances available to all youth in online communication.

Notes

1   Superior Court of New Jersey, Middlesex County, *Indictment of Dharun Ravi*, Ind. No. 11-04-00596, File No. 10002681, Filed 20 April 2011 (photocopies obtained from Superior Court of New Jersey, Middlesex County).

2   Mark Di Ionno, "Exclusive Interview with Dharun Ravi: 'I'm Very Sorry about Tyler,'" *Star-Ledger*, 22 March 2012, <http://blog.nj.com/njv_mark_diionno/2012/03/exclusive_interview_dharun_rav.html>. "I'm never going to regret not taking the plea," Ravi said emphatically. "If I took the plea, I would have had to testify that I did what I did to intimidate Tyler and that would be a lie. I won't ever get up there and tell the world I hated Tyler because he was gay, or tell the world I was trying to hurt or intimidate him because it's not true."

3   Michael Koenigs & Ian T. Shearn, "Tyler Clementi Cyberbullying Trial Begins Today," *abcNews*, 21 February 2012, <http://abcnews.go.com/US/tyler-clementi-bullying-trial-begins-today/story?id=15752236>.

4   While cyberbullying may be a contributing factor in some suicide cases, a simple or direct causal relationship should not be assumed. See Jane Bailey, "Time to Unpack the Juggernaut? Reflections on the Canadian Federal Parliamentary Debates on 'Cyberbullying,'" *Dalhousie Law Journal* 37:2 [forthcoming]: 38–39, archived at Social Sciences Research Network, <http://papers.ssrn.com/sol3/papers.cfm?abstract_id=2448480>.

5   The term "cyberbullying" is used to describe peer harassment centrally involving online communication technologies. One widely accepted general definition considers it to consist of "willful and repeated harm inflicted through the medium of electronic text," involving a power imbalance between the perpetrator and the victim. Justin Patchin &

Sameer Hinduja, "'Bullies Move Beyond the Schoolyard: A Preliminary Look at Cyberbullying," *Youth Violence and Juvenile Justice* 4:2 (2006): 152.

6   Several scholars have noted that Clementi's suicide played a prominent role in formulating public discussion about cyberbullying of gay youth and the emotional toll it can take. Much of the discussion, however, was based on false assumptions about what Ravi did. Andrew Gilden, "Cyberbullying and the Innocence Narrative," *Harvard Civil Rights – Civil Liberties Law Review* 48 (2013), <http://papers.ssrn.com/sol3/papers.cfm?abstract_id=2208737>; Jeffrey W. Cohen & Robert A. Brooks, *Confronting School Bullying: Kids, Culture, and the Making of a Social Problem* (Boulder, CO: Lynne Rienner, 2014); Jasbir K. Puar, "The Cost of Getting Better: Suicide, Sensation, Switchpoints," *GLQ: A Journal of Lesbian and Gay Studies* 18 (2012), doi:10.1215/10642684-1422179.

7   *State of New Jersey v. Dharun Ravi* (10 August 2011) Pros. File #10002681 (Superior Court of New Jersey, Middlesex County, Law Division – Criminal Part) On Motion to Dismiss the Indictment and Compel Discovery, Brief on Behalf of Defendant Dharun Ravi (photocopies obtained from Superior Court of New Jersey, Middlesex County).

8   *Ibid.*, at 5.

9   *Ibid.*, at 5–6. Ravi's motivation for turning on iChat immediately upon leaving his room, according to the defence, was because he was concerned about having a "strange older man" in his room where he had left his iPad. He claims he did not expect to see any sexual activity.

10   *Ibid.*, at 21.

11   Jane Bailey, Valerie Steeves, Jacquelyn Burkell & Priscilla Regan, "Negotiating with Gender Stereotypes on Social Networking Sites: From 'Bicycle Face' to Facebook," *Journal of Communication Inquiry* 37 (2013), <http://digitalmediafys.pbworks.com/w/file/fetch/69691259/Bailey_Jane2013GenderStereotypes.pdf>; Robyn M. Cooper and Warren J. Blumenfeld, "Responses to Cyberbullying: A Descriptive Analysis of the Frequency of and Impact on LGBT and Allied Youth," *Journal of LGBT Youth* 9 (2012), <http://www.partnershipsjournal.org/index.php/ijcp/article/viewFile/72/57>. See also Mary Ann Franks, "Unwilling Avatars: Idealism and Discrimination in Cyberspace," *Columbia Journal of Gender and Law* 20 (2011), <http://papers.ssrn.com/sol3/papers.cfm?abstract_id=1374533>.

12   Gilden, *supra* note 6.

13   Valerie Jenness, "The Hate Crime Canon and Beyond: A Critical Assessment," *Law and Critique* 12 (2001), doi:10.1023/A:1013774229732.

14   Mark McCormack, *The Declining Significance of Homophobia: How Teenage Boys Are Redefining Masculinity and Heterosexuality* (Oxford: Oxford University Press, 2012).

15   V. Paul Poteat & Craig D. DiGiovanni, "When Biased Language Use Is Associated with Bullying and Dominance Behavior: The Moderating Effect of Prejudice," *Journal of Youth and Adolescence* 39 (2010), doi:10.1007/s10964-010-9565-y.

16   C. J. Pascoe, "Notes on a Sociology of Bullying: Young Men's Homophobia as Gender Socialization," *QED: A Journal of GLBTQ Worldmaking* 1 (inaugural issue; 2013): 87–104, <http://msupress.org/wp-content/themes/press/jfileviewer.php?id=50-21F-7105&art=yes>.

17   Associated Press, "Dharun Ravi Sentence in Rutgers Webcam Case Renews Hate Crime Law Debate," *Washington Post*, 22 May 2012, <http://www.washingtonpost.com/national/dharun-ravi-sentence-in-rutgers-webcam-case-renews-hate-crime-law-debate/2012/05/22/gIQAuioDiU_story.html>; Lila Shapiro, "Dharun Ravi Appeals Highlight the Continued Hate-Crime Law Debate," *Huffington Post*, 13 June 2012, <http://www.huffingtonpost.com/2012/06/13/dharun-ravi-appeals-hate-crime_n_1594320.html>.

18   An indictment hearing would be called a preliminary hearing in Canada.

19   *State of New Jersey v. Dharun Ravi* (13 August 2011) File #10002681(Superior Court of New Jersey, Middlesex County, Law Division – Criminal Part) State's Response to Motion to Dismiss the Indictment and Compel State to Produce Discovery, Brief Submitted on Behalf of State of New Jersey (photocopies obtained from Superior Court of New Jersey, Middlesex County), at 11.

20   At trial, the *prosecution* must prove the defendant's guilt beyond a reasonable doubt. On a motion to dismiss an indictment, the *defence* must show that the indictment hearing was "manifestly deficient or palpably defective." *State v. Hogan* (1996) 144 N.J. 216, <http://leagle.com/decision/1996360144NJ216_1229.xml/STATE%20v.%20HOGAN>, 676 A.2d 533 at 228–29.

21   N.J.S.A 2C:16-1(a)(1), (2), and (3) <ftp://www.njleg.state.nj.us/20002001/AL01/443_.PDF>.

22   At trial, Ravi was convicted of all of the privacy offences, but only the third variant of bias intimidation. He also received a light sentence, incommensurate with what would normally be expected of a bias intimidation conviction. Ravi was sentenced to three years probation, thirty days in county jail, three hundred hours of community service, counselling on "cyberbullying and alternative lifestyles," and a $10,000 fine. The contents of the counselling are not specified. Kashmir Hill, "Dharun Ravi Gets off Easy in Rutgers Spying Case: Month in Jail and $10,000 Fine," *Forbes*, 21 May 2012, <http://www.forbes.com/sites/kashmirhill/2012/05/21/dharun-ravi-gets-off-easy-in-clementi-case-month-in-jail-and-10000-fine/>.

23 *Supra* note 7 at 2. Note that the motion documents provide clarification of some colloquialisms used in online communications – such as replacing "awk" with "[awkward]" – but many of the grammatical peculiarities of the online text record are left as is.

24 *Ibid.* at 3.

25 Joseph Burridge, "'I Am Not Homophobic *but...*': Disclaiming in Discourse Resisting Repeal of Section 28," *Sexualities* 7 (2004), doi:10.1177/1363460704044804.

26 *Supra* note 7, Volume I Appendix at DA 1.

27 The practice of improving your own social status by ridiculing and denigrating others is a common adolescent behaviour. David Johnson & Geraldine Lewis, "Do You Like What You See? Self-Perceptions of Adolescent Bullies," *British Educational Research Journal* 25 (1999), doi:10.1080/0141192990250507.

28 Ravi states that one of his "closest friends" is gay in a text he sent Clementi after being informed of the room change request. *Supra* note 7 at 1.

29 Some public commentary also supported this point of view. See J. Bryan Lowder, "Did Dharun Ravi Really Commit a Hate Crime?" *Slate*, 20 March 2012, <http://www.slate.com/blogs/xx_factor/2012/03/20/did_dharun_ravi_really_commit_a_hate_crime_.html>; Emily Bazelon, "Make the Punishment Fit the Cyber-Crime," Opinion, *New York Times*, 19 March 2012, <http://www.nytimes.com/2012/03/20/opinion/make-the-punishment-fit-the-cyber-crime.html?_r=0>.

30 All grammatical and spelling appear as they are in the original text. Common online acronyms include WTF (what the fuck); OMG (Oh my God); LMAO (laughing my ass off); LMFAO (laughing my fucking ass off); and LOL (laughing out loud).

31 *Supra* note 7, Volume I Appendix at DA 1–2.

32 There are, of course, a variety of theories about why heterosexual men might be attracted to gay sexual materials. See, for instance, Brian P. Meier, Michael D. Robinson, George A. Gaither & Nikki J. Heinert, "A Secret Attraction or Defensive Loathing? Homophobia, Defense, and Implicit Cognition," *Journal of Research in Personality* 40 (2006), doi:10.1016/j.jrp.2005.01.007.

33 *Supra* note 7 at DA 1.

34 Alice E. Marwick & danah boyd, "I Tweet Honestly, I Tweet Passionately: Twitter Users, Context Collapse, and the Imagined Audience," *New Media & Society* 13 (2010), <http://www.tiara.org/blog/wp-content/uploads/2010/07/marwick_boyd_twitter_nms.pdf>.

35 Woodrow Hartzog & Frederic Stutzman, "The Case of Online Obscurity," *California Law Review* 101:1 (2013), <http://papers.ssrn.com/sol3/papers.cfm?abstract_id=1597745>.

36   Helen Fenwick & D. Fenwick, "The Changing Face of Protection for Individual Privacy Against the Press: Leveson, the Royal Charter and Tort Liability," *International Review of Law, Computers & Technology* 27:3 (2013), <http://www.tandfonline.com/doi/pdf/10.1080/13600869.2013.797 203>.

37   *Supra* note 19 at 1.

38   *Ibid.* at 4.

39   *Supra* note 7 at 3–4, referencing evidence in Appendix 1 at DA 14–15.

40   *Ibid.* at 4.

41   *Ibid.* at 4–5.

42   *Ibid.*

43   *Ibid.*, at Volume I Appendix at p. DA 25.

44   *Ibid.*

45   *Ibid.*

46   *Ibid.* at DA 20–21.

47   *Ibid.* at DA 31.

48   The prosecution, in contrast, did not submit any evidence in their response pertaining to Clementi's state of mind prior to the incidents.

49   *Supra* note 7 at 55. Witness Scott Xu (described by the defence as having been friends with the defendant since seventh grade) stated to investigators, "he's not in any way a homophobic person." *Supra* note 7 at Appendix IV at DA 335.

50   This is not to say that all negative associations with homosexuality are the same. As Lawrence Blum has suggested regarding racism, the term *homophobia* may have lost some coherence in the wake of social change. Lawrence Blum, *I'm Not a Racist but …* (Ithaca, NY: Cornell University Press, 2003).

51   *Supra* note 7 at 6.

52   danah boyd, "Streams of Content, Limited Attention: The Flow of Information through Social Media," *Educause Review* (2010), <https://net.educause.edu/ir/library/pdf/ERM1051.pdf>.

53   *Supra* note 7 at 64.

54   Some scholars have noted that people don't necessarily use publicly accessible social media with the intent of worldwide exposure. Instead, they often have more particularized social audiences in mind for the social news or status updates that each platform addresses. See danah boyd, *It's Complicated: The Social Lives of Networked Teens* (New Haven: Yale University Press, 2014).

55   *Supra* note 7 at 39–40.

56   Some commentators have thought of circumstances where a heterosexual sexual encounter *would* inspire interest in order to counter this assumption. Richard Cohen, "Tyler Clementi and the Questionable Wisdom of Hate Crime Laws," *Washington Post*, 19 March 2012, <http://www.

washingtonpost.com/blogs/post-partisan/post/tyler-clementi-and-the-questionable-wisdom-of-hate-crime-laws/2012/03/19/gIQAlpaENS_blog.html>.

57 *Supra* note 19 at 22.

58 *Ibid.*

59 This same legal issue has come up in relation to "revenge porn," when an ex-lover posts an intimate image without the consent of the victim without alerting her to having done so, but with the obvious intent to harass her indirectly. Danielle Keats Citron & Mary Anne Franks, "Criminalizing Revenge Porn," *Wake Forest Law Review* 49 (2014): 345, <http://papers.ssrn.com/sol3/papers.cfm?abstract_id=2368946>.

60 Gilden, *supra* note 6.

61 *Supra* note 7 at 8, citing evidence submitted in Appendix III at DA 191.

62 *Ibid.*

63 *Ibid.*, at 8–9.

64 *Ibid.*, citing DA 195.

65 *Ibid.* at 24.

66 Kathryn R. Brown, "The Risks of Taking Facebook at Face Value: Why the Psychology of Social Networking Should Influence the Evidentiary Relevance of Facebook Photographs," *Vanderbilt Journal of Entertainment and Technology Law* 14 (2012): 367, <http://www.jetlaw.org/wp-content/journal-pdfs/Brown2.pdf>.

67 *Supra* note 7 at 9.

68 *Ibid.* at 40.

69 *Out Online: The Experiences of Lesbian, Gay, Bisexual and Transgender Youth on the Internet,* (New York: GLSEN, 2013), <http://glsen.org/press/study-finds-lgbt-youth-face-greater-harassment-online>.

70 NJ Rev Stat § 2C:16-1 (2013); Jessica P. Hodge, *Gendered Hate: Exploring Gender in Hate Crime Law* (Boston: Northeastern University Press, 2011).

71 Beverly A. McPhail, "Gender-Bias Hate Crimes: A Review," *Trauma, Violence, & Abuse* 3 (2002), doi:10.1177/15248380020032003; Hannah Mason-Bish, "Examining the Boundaries of Hate Crime Policy: Considering Age and Gender," *Criminal Justice Policy Review* 24 (2011), doi:10.1177/0887403411431495; Mark Austin Walters & Jessica Tumath, "Gender 'Hostility,' Rape, and the Hate Crime Paradigm," *The Modern Law Review* 77 (2014), doi:10.1111/1468-2230.12079.

72 Heidi M. Hurd & Michael S. Moore, "Punishing Hatred and Prejudice," *Stanford Law Review* 56 (2004): 1081–1146.

73 *Supra* note 7 at 29.

74 While it is beyond the scope of this chapter, the defence made a considerable effort to obtain disclosure of evidence of Clementi's state of mind related to his suicide, including the writings he left behind. The judge consistently denied these requests, supporting the prosecution

argument that Ravi was not being charged with causing the suicide and so this evidence was not relevant to the case.

75   Associated Press, *supra* note 17.

76   Kate Zernike, "Judge Defends Penalty in Rutgers Spying Case, Saying It Fits Crime," *New York Times*, 30 May 2012, <http://www.nytimes.com/2012/05/31/nyregion/judge-defends-sentence-imposed-on-dharun-ravi.html?pagewanted=all&_r=0>.

77   Di Ionno, *supra* note 2.

78   The defence submitted a statement by Marc R. Poirier, for instance, who provided an academic argument as to why New Jersey's bias intimidation offences should not apply to what Ravi did, which included (a) that only violent crimes should serve as predicate crimes; (b) that even where non-violent crimes are found to be appropriate underlying crimes, the sentencing enhancements set out in the legislation are only appropriate for violent crimes; and (c) that Ravi's biases were at most "generally customary, though offensive, behaviours." Marc R. Poirier, "Statement on Predicate Crimes for Bias Intimidation," 2 May 2012 at 6, submitted in *State of New Jersey v. Dharun Ravi* (May 3, 2012) Pros. File #10002681(Superior Court of New Jersey, Middlesex County, Law Division – Criminal Part) Sentencing Memorandum on Behalf of Defendant Dharun Ravi.

79   Gilden, *supra* note 6 at 360.

CHAPTER XI

Defining the Legal Lines: eGirls and Intimate Images

Shaheen Shariff and Ashley DeMartini

Introduction

The objective of this chapter is to address the nuanced complexities relating to sexting in the context of sexualized cyberbullying among youth, and related legal and educational dilemmas in public policy. We focus on key societal and legal issues to address why recent legislative proposals and legal responses to sexualized cyberbullying are misguided. To provide the context behind the legalities, we first highlight the scholarly discourse around the dynamics of rape culture to draw attention to the fact that sexting, and the non-consensual distribution of intimate images among youth, is not a new online phenomenon created by teens. Rape culture concerns the way societal attitudes condone, minimize, and/or normalize sexual violence against women through social institutions, communities, and individuals.[1] Thus, when we discuss the advent of sexualized cyberbullying among teens, we also argue that it belongs to pre-established social norms embedded in and perpetuated by adult society. What has changed is the rapid pace at which various forms of expression, including offensive and demeaning photographs and images, can be distributed and shared online, and the hurdles involved in having such content removed. We present this context by highlighting three disturbing trends:

1. Patterns in social media communication and popular culture that suggest a misogynist backlash against influential women and girls.
2. The gendered dimensions and perceptions of harm, responsibility, and culpability regarding sexting, and the non-consensual distribution of intimate images, as they emerge in popular culture and research involving children and teens aged 9 to 18.
3. Concerns regarding reactive legislative and public policy responses to sexting and cyberbullying among children and youth.

We draw on existing scholarly literature to address the behaviour of slut shaming as an expression of victim blaming,[2] along with well-publicized cases of sexualized cyberbullying. We then turn to explore the degree to which slut shaming and rape culture surfaced in research findings from two overlapping research projects on youth and sexting undertaken in Dr. Shariff's Define the Line projects at McGill University (the DTL research). Drawing from this research, we conclude that meaningfully responding to sexualized cyberbullying (including non-consensual distribution of intimate images) will require multi-pronged strategies that incorporate proactive educational initiatives. We examine the shortcomings of Canada's most recent reactive legislative response: criminalization of the non-consensual distribution of intimate images in the controversial Bill C-13.

We conclude our chapter with recommendations for a re-thinking of legal responses that pay more attention to human rights and educational initiatives. We argue that rather than looking solely to criminal law, which is punitive and reactive, constitutional and human rights frameworks offer a proactive approach that might allow for greater consideration of the complex and nuanced online social contexts we highlight here. As some scholars suggest, the "big stick sanctions"[3] that criminalize children fail to directly address the deeply embedded systemic forms of misogyny in greater society. We suggest that given the current policy vacuum resulting from unprecedented dilemmas arising from digital technologies, thoughtful, proactive, and non-arbitrary responses (as opposed to reactive and arbitrary ones) show greater promise for addressing problems arising from sexting and sexualized forms of cyberbullying.

To that end, we recommend that a practical starting point would be to enhance public legal education and critical media literacy. In 1973, then–Chief Justice of Canada Bora Laskin argued that public legal literacy was long overdue,[4] but little has been done to address that gap in public knowledge across Canada. As society becomes increasingly immersed in online communication, it is essential that people should be better apprised of their legal rights and responsibilities, and of the emerging legal risks to their privacy and safety. As we present our discussion of rape culture and slut shaming in this chapter, it will become quickly apparent to readers why it is particularly important for all members of society to become better informed about the legal rights of girls and women, both online and offline. Legal literacy could, for example, play a key role in raising young people's awareness about issues of consent in cases of sexting. If legal responses continue to ignore issues of misogyny, homophobia, sexism, racism, and other forms of discrimination within society, and their influence on perpetuating cyberbullying and sex-related online offences, the policy vacuum will continue to prevail.

Backlash Against Influential Women Online

The prevalence of sexist and misogynist attitudes online is well documented.[5] These attitudes are not new to North American society, but online forums amplify and intensify the spread and coverage such attitudes receive.[6] In this section, we set the stage for understanding how sexist and misogynist attitudes enable rape culture to thrive online and offline. Women and girls can encounter these views daily, both directly and indirectly, and it is glaringly evident when women attempt to assert their views online. In short, when women claim space that challenges the traditional and underlying assumption that public space is male space – and heterosexual at that – misogynist attitudes surface through various forms of online abuse. Similarly, Shariff has noted that when women in positions of cultural or political influence use their agency to express informed opinions and/or when they assert feminist perspectives, they often threaten insecure males, leading to (often sexualized) attacks.[7] We outline below a handful of high-profile examples.

Amanda Hess, a prominent journalist and frequent tweeter, received death threats on her social media pages for writing about issues around sex. She encountered a barrage of tweets, which ranged from attacks on her appearance, "I see you are physically not very attractive," to physical threats on her life, "happy to say we live in the same state. I'm looking you up, and when I find you, I'm going to rape you and remove your head."[8] Hess has suggested that similar disturbing forms of misogyny too often happen to women. Anita Sarkeesian, feminist pop culture critic, had her Wikipedia page hacked repeatedly with obscenities and pornography after the launch of her campaign that examines the sexist and misogynistic portrayals of women in video games. One man even went so far as to create a video game that allowed players to beat up and inflict black eyes and cuts on a virtual Sarkeesian.[9] Blogger and programmer Kathy Sierra received death threats too, which caused her to cancel a public appearance and freeze her blog.[10] These forms of harassment can be devastating, and the humiliation can affect women's health, academic success, and careers.[11] The examples discussed above point to the insidious backlash against women in positions of influence, who may or may not express feminist views, yet can become targets of extreme sexual harassment and online ridicule simply by asserting themselves in public online spaces.

The integration of online and offline sexism has become increasingly transparent in recent incidents on Canadian university campuses. For example, in early 2014, the University of Ottawa's female student council president was targeted in an online exchange between some of her male colleagues. Below is a pseudonymized excerpt from that exchange as reported in the blog, The Belle Jar:[12]

> A [a non-elected [male] student]: Let me tell you something right now: the "tri-fluvienne" [nickname for someone from Trois-Rivières, Quebec] president will suck me off in her office chair and after I will fuck her in the ass on [a third party's] desk.
> B [male VP Social for the Criminology Student Association]: Someone punish her with their shaft.
> C [male member of the board of directors of the Student Federation of the University of Ottawa]: Well Christ, if you fuck [female student council president's name] I will definitely buy you a beer.

The excerpt illustrates the glorification of heteronormative vio-lence – a kind of violence that polices sexuality and gender roles, and hinges on the assertion of the sexual dominance of the alpha, hetero male.[13] Other recent Canadian university examples include frosh chants endorsing non-consensual sex at the University of British Columbia and St. Mary's University, which were reported in mainstream media in the fall of 2013.[14] These events further highlight the depth of the internalization of rape culture, given that the video in the St. Mary's incident shows young women chanting these violent lyrics alongside their male counterparts. Rape culture affects not only relationships between males and females, but also between members of the same sex. For example, in 2005, senior members of McGill University's football team used a broomstick to sexually assault a male freshman player.[15] This latter incident speaks to the functions of rape culture: the assertion and maintenance of heteronormative male power and dominance. According to Pascoe, there is peer pressure among young males to prove their heterosexuality to their peers,[16] which can lead to acts of sexual harassment of females and homophobic harassment among males.[17] Although the definition of rape culture in our introduction defines it as sexual violence that specifically targets women and, while we recognize that rape culture disproportionately affects females,[18] the discussion above seeks to address its pervasiveness as it functions to reinscribe gender norms and inequality. In so doing, we emphasize the fact that both adolescent girls and boys must navigate this corrosive environment.

Situating the Gendered Dimensions of Sexting within the Context of Slut Shaming and Rape Culture

Social media has introduced new avenues for communication and expression of one's identity. The extent to which social media has shifted behavioural norms and boundaries is only beginning to be understood, but these changes are well-reflected in some of the attitudes and behaviours of adolescents who live a seamlessly integrated online/offline existence.[19] One of these behaviours is the practice of sexting. Adolescents exploring their sexuality are doing so in an online era; many, but not all, even choose to express these personal explorations through digital technologies such as smartphones, tablets and laptops – as though these are extensions of their corporeal selves.[20]

Sexting is typically used to refer to the sending and/or receiving of sexual or sexually suggestive images or videos, nude or semi-nude, through cellphones and social media apps.[21] Snapchat has become one of the social media applications favoured as a forum for sexting amongst adolescents. This app allows users to take images, record videos, and send them to recipients with a limited time to view. One concern is that the platform might lead adolescents to believe they can act without worrying about creating a lasting record when, in fact, their actions are traceable. Although Snapchat deletes the files from the recipient's as well as the application's server, recipients can take a screenshot of the image sent. In a matter of seconds, images intended to be privately communicated can be widely disseminated online.

Snapchat was involved in a November 2013 situation in which ten boys between the ages of 13 and 15 were arrested in Laval, Quebec. Media reports indicated that the boys had convinced several female classmates to use Snapchat to send them intimate photographs. One news media report describes the girls' actions as "flirty-fun,"[22] assuming that the girls did not realize that Snapchat did not guarantee the absence of a digital record. The boys reportedly took screenshots of the girls' nude and intimate images, and distributed them via social media. They were subsequently charged with distribution and possession of child pornography. Two of the boys face additional charges of production of child pornography. All await court hearings.[23]

While some statistics suggest that girls and boys are equally likely to send sexts,[24] the potential consequences of sexting are deeply gendered, exposing girls to greater risks of shaming and humiliation that are tied to a sexual double standard.[25] Young girls who have trusted male peers and sent sexualized images online have sometimes paid the heavy price of public humiliation, ruined reputations, and blame for bringing it on themselves through slut-shaming.[26] In the result, we suggest that the gendered dimensions of sexting need to be understood within the broader contexts of slut shaming, sexualized stereotyping in media, and rape culture.

Slut Shaming and Sexualized Sterotyping in Media

Slut shaming tends to target females when they express their sexual agency beyond what society deems culturally appropriate for women and girls.[27] For the purposes of this chapter, we define sexual agency as purposeful decisions made by women or girls to express their sexuality on their own terms (versus ways in which society pressures them to express it). At the same time, we also acknowledge later in this section that feminist scholarship has taken issue with the way that neo-liberal market forces are usurping women's notions of sexual agency and spinning them as choices to self-objectify.[28] Slut shaming reveals that women and men do not enjoy the same privileges when it comes to the expression of sexuality, pointing to the entrenched gender inequality within North American society.[29] Slut shaming's foray onto the internet provides a context for opinions to spread rapidly and widely, intensifying and amplifying the shame of targeted girls and women, even though slut shaming itself is certainly not a new phenomenon.

In the mid-seventeenth century, men who employed female domestics reportedly used the term "slut" as both an affectionate and condescending term.[30] Female domestics often had to navigate sexual harassment by the males in the households where they worked. By the late eighteenth century, middle-class women appropriated the term to pejoratively refer to female domestic servants. In this way, the term became a means for women of higher socioeconomic status to distinguish themselves from women of lower socioeconomic status, while also allying themselves with men.[31] The term functioned to draw class (and in some cases race) lines between the "morality" and "purity" of the middle class and the "impurity" of the lower-class female servants. In many cases, the term rendered sexually exploited domestic servants as "a source of filth and became a prelude to their dismissal."[32] While the term has continued to morph and shift in its etymology, one thing that has remained disturbingly consistent is how often women use it to police one another.[33] Internalization of heteronormative male-dominated narratives about the limits of female sexual agency by both men and women facilitates the production and reproduction of rape culture within society.[34] These problems are compounded by approaches to online behaviours such as cyberbullying that focus largely on the outward behaviours of youth from developmental perspectives and that fail to take environment into account, rather than targeting confusing and conflicting media messages around sexuality and misogynistic and homophobic attitudes among adults.

Contemporary examples of slut shaming abound online, from a viral Tumblr post, "Hey Girls. Did You Know?", that paired photos of women's exposed breasts with the phrase, "Hey Girls. Did You Know … that uhm, your boobs go inside your shirt," and resulted in other posts, including, "Hey Girl. Did you know? That you spread Nutella

... not your legs,"[35] to the online posting of images of two teenaged Steubenville boys raping a 16-year-old girl at a party[36] that resulted in online attacks on the victim, including, "Shouldn't they charge the lil' slut for underage drinking?" or, "I honestly feel sorry for those boys in that Steubenville trial, the whore was asking for it."[37]

Slut shaming, like other exercises of power, whether engaged in by men or women, needs to be understood as a mechanism to police and govern societal norms.[38] Slut shaming polices the extent to which women, and especially adolescent girls, can freely express their sexual agency before enduring scorn from society; hence, creating a double standard and marking female sexuality as deviant.[39] Further, slut shaming helps to shape social understandings of rape. As Poole has noted, "peers, adults, media and courts all give attention to how much make-up a girl uses, the type of clothing she wears, how late she stays out, and how she acts towards males."[40] Notwithstanding the policing of the sexual agency of women and girls that is deeply entrenched in North American society, popular culture in North America regularly confronts female adolescents with quite contradictory messages about sexuality; a conflict that Attwood appropriately describes as the archetypal "Madonna-Whore binary."[41]

On the one hand, women and girls are encouraged to take on leadership roles and positions of power traditionally held by males. On the other hand, popular culture also suggests that women's power flows from performances that push conventional social boundaries around female sexuality and publicly represent strong messages of sexual independence.[42] The marketization of the modern woman – strong and sexually assertive – dominates popular culture storylines across the music, film, advertising, and television industries.[43] Suddenly, "high-heeled shoes are emblematic of confident, powerful femininity."[44] As Gill notes, marketers have (re)packaged and incorporated a non-threatening neo-liberal version of feminism in their advertising in order to sell products, rather than to liberate women from traditional subjugated positions.[45] Where adolescents are concerned, since the 1990s, ideas of "Girl Power" have led to the proliferation of images of overtly sexualized women in mass media, offered as proof of women's empowerment and agency.[46] These marketing tactics spin the notions of agency and independence as a part of a sexually liberated woman's choice to voluntarily self-objectify.[47] Music videos glamorizing female stripper-pimps and a naked young woman swinging on a wrecking ball can be understood as marketing mechanisms for a heteronormative economy through which adolescent girls are socialized[48] to understand women's bodies "as the primary source of woman's capital."[49]

Girls and young women (as well as boys and young men), then, face conflicting and confusing[50] messages that on the one hand depict sexualized self-representations as a primary source of agency and empowerment for females and on the other hand can result in renewed efforts to control them through sexual violence, embarrassment, and slut shaming.[51] As Steeves notes[52], girls are thus left to negotiate an unspoken line in teen digital culture in relation to expressions of their sexuality. Too much and they are perceived to be "sluts." Too little isolates them from the popular peer group.[53] Patterns, behaviours, and risks related to sexting must be understood and evaluated in light of this context. Otherwise, we will miss important opportunities to proactively mitigate the risks of gendered harms currently disproportionately borne by women and girls. Through critical media literacy education, for example, we can assist girls (and boys) to recognize that sexualized celebrity culture is a business that is not only occurring within a larger economy that positions power, pleasure, and agency in relation to heterosexual relationships, but also, streamlines what kind of bodies (read race and body type) are seen as beautiful.[54]

Rape Culture: Gang Rapes, "Up for It," and "Asking for It" on Social Media

In the sections above, we defined rape culture as both an individual and systemic response to sexual violence against women that functions to condone, normalize, and/or minimize these sexually violent behaviours and attitudes.[55] We considered the pervasiveness of rape culture in order to contextualize how both females and males navigate, internalize, and perform these violent societal norms in online spaces. While we maintain that rape culture disproportionately affects women and girls, the emergence of rape culture online presents a disturbing new trend of concern to all.

Over the past couple of years, another dimension of rape has emerged; that is, some adolescent boys have begun to post videos and images of gang rape on social media forums, such as Facebook. This iteration of sexually violent acts online re-victimizes girls every time the videos of their physical and sexual abuse are distributed, viewed, saved, and reviewed on e-mail, smartphones, and social media. Recent mediatized examples include cases in Maple Ridge, Steubenville, Nova Scotia, and Chicago. In the Maple Ridge case, the female victim was drugged and gang-raped at a rave party while a 16-year-old male watched the rape, videotaped the incident, and passed it to an older friend to post on Facebook.[56] In Chicago, three teenaged boys raped and sodomized a 12-year-old girl, after luring her into one boy's home, and days later posted the act on Facebook.[57]

The cases cited above also involved public backlash against the victims, which we suggest reflects the insidious impacts of rape culture. For example, in the Maple Ridge case, once the video went viral, there was significant discussion on social media as to whether the girl who was raped had "asked for it" and whether the images in the video made it look as though she "enjoyed" it.[58] Similarly, in the Steubenville rape, discussion over social media forums contained comments that blamed the victim by naming her a "slut" and "whore," as though she was "asking for it."[59] We will return to this notion of "asking for it" momentarily, as it also provides an occasion to think about rape culture and its relationship to adolescent males. First, we return to our earlier discussion on the neo-liberal constructions of femininity and depictions of the modern, sexually empowered woman within popular culture and advertising. In doing so, we not only begin to understand how adolescent females are negotiating their identities within a society saturated with contradictory messages, but also, we can begin to discuss how adolescent males are negotiating their understandings of female sexuality amidst North American society's sexist and misogynist portrayals of women and girls. In the last decade, Gill notes, a new figure of femininity has been constructed within media and advertising: "a young, attractive, heterosexual woman who knowingly and deliberately plays with her sexual power and is always 'up for it' (that is, sex)."[60]

Moreover, to think about the ways popular culture and advertising construct this new femininity, is to also think about the ways that male sexual fantasy perpetuates this notion of the sexually insatiable female figure. Or, as Evans, Riley and Shankar note, this "up for it" femininity[61] that some suggest is reflected in the emergence of pole-dancing classes or the popular re-emergence of burlesque dance classes.[62] Gill suggests that the neo-liberal transformation of feminist ideals of sexual agency and empowerment has turned feminism into a sexy kind of "feminism lite" — a form of feminism that poses no threat to the patriarchal norms that govern political and economic relations within mainstream society.[63] This kind of "feminism lite" creates a market (from pop icons to car advertisements) that cultivates a popular belief among consumers that women live in an era where feminism is no longer relevant. However, Gill argues that hetero male sexual fantasy, and its widespread production, "made real" these sexually assertive females as role models for women of the millennium by guising and selling it to women as if these attitudes were "authentically owned by women."[64] It is important to note that our examination of women does not presume them to be passive, but as active subjects that are also subjected to intricate belief systems and norms that are sexist and misogynist. Perhaps a weakness in Gill's analysis, as Evans, Riley, and Shankar point out, is her homogeneous portrayal of women's engagement with neo-liberal marketization of the modern women.[65] Even as we discuss the ways in which sexist views intertwine with popular culture, we must keep in mind that women's experiences of these trends depend on their varying positionalities within society.

Gill's work is influenced by Turner's examination of how "straight porn" has moved from the realm of fantasy to mainstream society, conveniently coinciding with the emergence of the "up for it" female figure in popular culture and advertising. As Turner has put it:

> Once porn and real human sexuality were distinguishable. Not even porn's biggest advocates would suggest a porn flick depicted reality, that women were gagging for sex 24/7 and would drop their clothes and submit to rough, anonymous sex at the slightest invitation. But as porn has seeped into mainstream culture, the line has blurred. To speak to men's magazine editors, it is clear they believe that somehow in recent years, porn has come true. The sexually liberated modern woman turns out to resemble — what do you know! — the pneumatic, take-me-now-big-boy fuck-puppet of male fantasy after all.[66]

One potential problem of the marketing of the "up for it" female stereotype to hetero male consumers is that male youth may draw their understandings of female sexuality from sources in popular culture, normalizing male sexual violence against girls. Herein lies the toxic, destructive force of rape culture: its impact on youth culture and its incorporation into sexual exploration.

Issues around slut shaming and rape culture memes around "asking for it" also arose in the findings of the DTL Research Project related to sexting.

Define the Line: DTL Research

Methodology

In 2012, DTL conducted one online survey with 1,088 North American students between the ages of 9 and 18. The age range was further broken down into two groups: pre-Facebook age (9 to 12) and Facebook age (13 to 17) – the latter indicative of the legal age at which adolescents can obtain a Facebook account. The results of this study were previously published on the Define The Line website[67] as well as in Shariff's book.[68] Since most participation on Facebook involves posting of images, comments, and messages, the online survey was designed to present participants with hypothetical case studies to analyze and gauge their responses to what took place.[69] One of these scenarios is discussed in more detail below.

In addition to the survey, twenty focus groups of four to eight students were also conducted at participant schools in Montreal, Vancouver, and Seattle. The data were coded and analyzed in 2013, using NVivo software to derive patterns from the open-ended questions and focus group discussions. The goal of the study was to learn more about how students in these age groups perceive or define the line between what they consider to be harmless teasing, joking, and sarcasm or bantering among friends on social media, and harmful or illegal conduct. Among other things DTL researchers sought to determine

- the extent to which these participants recognized the legal risks involved in sexting;
- the forms of discrimination that informed their attitudes such as sexism and homophobia, and;
- their perceptions regarding privacy and ownership of content once it is posted online, especially as it pertains to sexting and the non-consensual distribution of intimate images.

Slut Shaming and "Asking for It"

In the focus group sessions, participants viewed videos entitled "The Cell Phone" and "La Photo" on the Define the Line website, (www. mcgill.ca/definetheline.ca). In both video- vignettes a teenage girl is coerced into sending a nude photograph of her breasts to a male classmate under the pretence that he would maintain its confidentiality. He then promptly distributes the photograph online. A lack of empathy for the female victim in the videos was evident in some of the reactions to the actors, with some participants assigning more blame to the girl who sent the original photo than to the boy who passed it to his friends. As one participant put it, "I think it's 60 percent the girl's fault and then 40 percent the guy's fault, because she starts the whole process of it being sent to everyone." Another participant also seemed to empathize with the male perpetrator in terms of the photo spreading, noting: "Sometimes it just spirals out of control."

The "asking for it" meme may also help to explain some of DTL's online survey findings with the older adolescents aged 13 to 17. As reported in DTL's recent "Facebook Report,"[70] all participants were presented with two hypothetical situations to analyze:

- The first involved the story of Dana and Louise. Dana passed out drunk at Louise's party, prompting Louise to take a picture of her and share it with others online.
- The second considered the story of Brian and Angee. Angee sent Brian a sexually explicit photo, which he later sent on to others.

The difference in responses to the two scenarios is very interesting. In the first case, participants were asked to check one or the other:

- Dana had a right to object to Louise posting her photo online without her permission; or
- Dana does not have the right to object because the photo was taken at Louise's party where others saw Dana.

Of the 530 youth in the Facebook Age group (aged 13 to 17) who responded to the questions, 522 (99 percent) responded that Dana did have the right to object, whereas only six (1 percent) responded that she did not have the right to object to her photo being posted online without her permission. That the vast majority responded in favour of Dana's right to object may suggest an element of empathy for Dana in light of the situation.

In the second scenario, participants were asked to check one or the other:

- Angee has the right to object to her photo being shared online without her permission; or
- Angee does not have the right to object to her photo being shared online because she sent it to Brian and so now Brian can do whatever he wants with it.

In this particular case, only 311 out of 581 participants (54 percent) of participants stated that Angee did have a right to object to her sexually explicit photo being shared. The disturbing aspect of our findings is that 270 out of 581 participants (46 percent) of the participants felt that Angee did not have a right to object, because she sent the photograph to Brian. These kinds of results may shed light on the highly publicized news media cases in which youths have non-consensually forwarded intimate images. In this study, almost half of the participants believed it was acceptable to non-consensually distribute intimate images sent to you by another person. These respondents would appear to have attached very little accountability or responsibility to the person who breaches trust.

These very different answers to the two questions create an interesting discrepancy. What motivated the vast majority of participants to find Dana had a right to object while almost half felt Angee did not? While further qualitative research to follow up more specifically on this kind of difference is needed, it may be that this difference reflects less empathy for the target of the sexualized attack, but perhaps also that almost half of respondents felt that by "consenting" to Brian seeing her naked photo, Angee should be taken to have consented to his distributing it. Alternatively, it may be that participants were simply confused about consent altogether. However, when the recipient of an intimate photo passes it on, or it ends up on Facebook's timeline, it can have devastating effects.

These kinds of findings, together with the research relating to slut shaming and rape culture, must be taken into account when we consider how best to respond to non-consensual distribution in light of public pressure on governments to address the too numerous and tragic teen suicides, most of them by high school girls who were exploited online. Unfortunately, issues such as slut shaming and rape culture have not been well attended to in Canada's most recent response to cyberbullying – Bill C-13, the *Protecting Canadians from Online Crime Act*.[71]

A Reactive Legal Approach

Policymakers have come under significant pressure to develop and implement stronger legislation and harsher punishment for young offenders who engage in cyberbullying and, in particular, non-consensual distribution of intimate images. While police in a number of US jurisdictions initially responded by using child pornography laws to arrest and detain youth, Canadian authorities were slower to do so.[72] However, there have been a few recent instances of Canadian teens being charged with child pornography offences, including two boys in Nova Scotia and a teen girl in British Columbia.[73] US court rulings confirm opinions expressed by many American judges that applying these laws to children's behaviour is like attempting to "fit a square peg in a round hole."[74] While child pornography laws were created to protect children from sexual exploitation, these laws (and Canada's obscenity laws) have been used to charge Canadian youths in connection with instances of non-consensual distribution (including in relation to online postings of alleged sexual assaults).[75]

Canada's Controversial Cyberbullying Legislation: Bill C-13

The Canadian Department of Justice touts Bill C-13 as a "cyberbullying law." However, it has been vigorously criticized as one that has little to do with cyberbullying, and everything to do with surveillance and infringement of Canadians' privacy rights.[76] Here, we highlight the sections on Non-Consensual Distribution of Intimate Images (Non-Consensual Provisions) in order to assess the degree to which they can meaningfully respond to underlying environmental factors such as rape culture and slut shaming that the research discussed above suggests is so heavily informing sexting and related forms of non-consensual distribution among youth.

    While the Non-Consensual Provisions would offer an alternative to charging youth with child pornography offences that were originally designed to protect youth, and may also address a gap in protecting against violations of adult women's privacy rights,[77] we remain concerned about four fundamental issues.

1. The Non-Consensual Provisions will do little to undermine the rape culture and slut shaming that inform non-consensual distribution of intimate images among youth.

The Non-Consensual Provisions react by punishing non-consensual distribution, but offer no proactive strategy for addressing underlying misogynistic attitudes that render teen girls vulnerable in the first place. "Big stick sanctions"[78] are unlikely to change youth behaviour without evidence-based educational supports to help young people understand the lines between harmless and harmful forms of online expression and to understand the rights and entitlements of others.

While the federal government has supported some educational programs, one of the few programs it has chosen to finance is disappointing. The WITS program (Walk Away, Ignore, Talk it out, Seek Help) has received government funding as an educational support for Bill C-13.[79] The fundamental premise of this program is out of touch with young people's digital reality. It advocates "walking away" from the abuse, but most social media participants would agree that it is impossible for victims of cyberbullying and non-consensual distribution to "walk away" when their nude or intimate images appear across the internet. The 24/7 nature of the online/offline world confirms how impossible it is to ignore the overwhelming number of online insults and hateful "slut-shaming" comments.[80] As some of the research discussed above suggests, some youth may believe that anyone who sends intimate images to another is "asking for" non-consensual forwarding by the recipient.

Furthermore, Shariff's earlier research confirms that young people often do not report their own victimization for fear of further retaliation and/or having their online privileges revoked.[81] Therefore, the WITS program suggestion to "seek help" by reporting may be unrealistic. Further, the suggestion to "talk it out" seems quite unhelpful in the case of sexualized attacks: how likely is a target to feel safe discussing the situation with a perpetrator who is slut shaming her? It is equally disappointing that when so many well-researched and evidence-based anti-cyberbullying programs are available and were presented to the Standing Senate Committee on Human Rights, taxpayers' money is spent on programs that are so out of touch with young people's reality.[82] Ultimately, without effective educational programs, the Non-Consensual Provisions under Bill C-13 seem unlikely to effect the kind of real change that is needed in order to address sexualized forms of cyberbullying.

2. C-13 does nothing to support youth in defining the line between joking and harmful behaviour.

As noted above, young people are navigating complex terrain in terms of proving their strength and status in a digital and online social network and often make decisions premised on the misogynistic and homophobic assumptions represented in the world around them. As a result, they may have difficulty defining the line between jokes and harmful behaviour. While C-13 would react by criminalizing those who non-consensually distribute intimate images of others, it offers nothing to assist youth in decoding the discriminatory messages around them or in learning how to make decisions that are respectful of the rights of others or empathetic to the situation of others.

3. Policy should proactively address rape culture and misogyny, not just its symptoms.

As we have explained earlier in this chapter, girls and young women are both encouraged by media to represent certain forms of sexuality, but are also at risk of slut shaming for doing so. The meaning and consequences of cyberbullying and sexting must be understood in the context of systemic forms of discrimination that disempower women and girls in particular. Addressing the symptoms of disrespect for the rights of girls and women, without proactively addressing the discriminatory roots of that disrespect are unlikely to yield meaningful lasting results.

4. Engage youth in policy development.

As we have shown above, youth are navigating a complex environment that is not necessarily well understood by adults.[83] For that reason, policy processes regarding online issues such as cyberbullying and non-consensual distribution, which so directly affect youth, must also incorporate the voices of youth. As Bailey argues in Chapter I,

engaging youth in policy development permits them to take ownership and gain agency in understanding how the law impacts their
online communication.

Conclusion

The contextual issues raised in this chapter suggest that the Canadian
public needs improved knowledge regarding the social challenges
and mixed messages young people receive from adults through popular culture and modelled behaviours. We examined these contentions
through patterns in social media communication and popular culture
that suggest a misogynist backlash against influential women and
girls, which is also reflected in misogynistic attacks online. Moreover,
the gendered dimensions and perceptions of harm, responsibility,
and culpability regarding sexting create an uneasy relationship
between female expressions of sexuality and societal expectations
around the female body. As also indicated in the findings of the
eGirls Project,[84] women and girls are simultaneously encouraged
to be both sexy and pure, and those who do not carefully negotiate
these invisible lines risk slut shaming and victim blaming even when
their images are non-consensually redistributed. It is imperative to
enhance public legal education relating to all forms of law, including
criminal, human rights, constitutional, and private law. As noted in
our introduction, there is currently an over emphasis on punitive
legal responses, which criminalize children, and which have also
been described by scholars as "big stick sanctions" that don't work.[85]
It is therefore essential to question what other legal frameworks, such
as human rights, constitutional, tort law, and emerging provincial
education legislation,[86] might more effectively respond to cyberbullying. Reactive criminal legislation alone does not respond to the
underlying environmental problems at the root of non-consensual
distribution and other forms of sexualized cyberbullying. We need
to work towards proactive educational initiatives that incorporate
critical media and legal literacy[87] aimed at addressing rape culture,
among other things. We need to especially raise the level of respect
for the equality and privacy rights of girls and women. Otherwise, we
will always only be dealing with symptoms, and not the foundational
problems of sexualized cyberbullying.

Notes

1   Although difficult to pinpoint, the origins of this term surfaced some-
time during the 1970s. In 1975, Lazarus and Wunderlich produced the
film, *Rape Culture*, which through the perspectives of its interviewees
outlined the operatives of this culture in North American society. See
Judy Norsigian, "Women, Health, and Films," *Women and Health* 1 (1975):
29–30, doi:10.1300/J013v01n01_07; Nicola Henry & Anastasia Powell (eds.),
*Preventing Sexual Violence: Interdisciplinary Approaches to Overcoming a
Rape Culture* (London, UK: Palgrave Macmillan, 2014); Anastasia Powell,
"Rape Culture: Why Our Community Attitudes to Sexual Violence Matter," *The Conversation* (2014), <http://theconversation.com/rape-culture-
why-our-community-attitudes-to-sexual-violence-matter-31750>. For
further discussion, see Fairbairn, Chapter IX.

2   For the evolution of the term "slut," its usage, and the practice of slut
shaming, see Feona Attwood, "Sluts and Riot Grrls: Female Identity
and Sexual Agency," *Journal of Gender Studies* 16:3 (2007): 233–247; Clare
McCormack & Nevena Prostran, "Asking for It: A First-Hand Account
from SlutWalk," *International Feminist Journal of Politics* 14:3 (2012):
410–414.

3   Sally M. Kift, Marilyn A. Campbell & Desmond A. Butler, "Cyberbullying in Social Networking Sites and Blogs: Legal Issues for Young People
and Schools," *Journal of Law, Information and Science* 20:2 (2010): 60–97.

4   Bora Laskin, "The Function of the Law," *Atlanta Law Review* 11 (1973):
118–122.

5   Danielle Keats Citron, *Misogynistic Cyber Hate Speech* (University of
Maryland: Francis King Carey School of Law, 2011), <http://works.
bepress.com/danielle_citron/31>.

6   *Ibid.*

7   Shaheen Shariff, *Sexting and Cyberbullying: Defining the Line on Digitally
Empowered Kids* (New York: Cambridge University Press, 2014).

8   Amanda Hess, "Why Women Aren't Welcome on the Internet,"
Pacific Standard, 6 January 2014, <http://www.psmag.com/navigation/
health-and-behavior/women-arent-welcome-internet-72170/>.

9   Oliver Moore, "Woman's Call to End Video Game Misogyny Sparks
Vicious Online Attacks," *Globe and Mail,* 11 July 2012, <http://
www.theglobeandmail.com/news/world/womans-call-to-end-video-
game-misogyny-sparks-vicious-online-attacks/article4405585/>.

10   BBC News, "Blog Death Threats Spark Debate," *BBC News Technology,*
27 March 2007, <http://news.bbc.co.uk/2/hi/6499095.stm>.

11   Keats Citron, *supra* note 5.

12   The Belle Jar, "Rape Culture at the University of Ottawa," The Belle Jar (blog), 28 February 2014, <http://bellejar.ca/2014/02/28/rape-culture-at-the-university-of-ottawa>.

13   We want to thank Jailyn Hanson, an undergraduate student from the University of Winnipeg, for bringing our attention to this idea of heteronormative policing of sexualities when she spoke insightfully about her experience as a trans person living in the midst of cis-privilege.

14   CBC News British Columbia, "UBC Investigates Frosh Students' Pro-Rape Chant: Chant Condoned Non-Consensual Sex with Underage Girls," 7 September 2013, <http://www.cbc.ca/news/canada/british-columbia/ubc-investigates-frosh-students-pro-rape-chant-1.1699589>; CBC News Nova Scotia, "Saint Mary's University Frosh Chant Cheers Underage Sex: Frosh Week Leaders, Student Union Executive Sent to Sensitivity Training," 4 September 2013, <http://www.cbc.ca/news/canada/nova-scotia/saint-mary-s-university-frosh-chant-cheers-underage-sex-1.1399616>.

15   John Kryk, "Target in 2005 McGill Hazing Horror Speaks Out," Toronto Sun, 9 November 2013, <http://www.torontosun.com/2013/11/09/target-in-2005-mcgill-hazing-horror-speaks-out>.

16   C. J. Pascoe, Dude, You're a Fag: Masculinity and Sexuality in High School (Berkeley: University of California Press, 2007).

17   B. W. Frank, "Masculinities and Schooling: The Making of Men," in Systemic Violence: How Schools Hurt Children, eds. J. R. Epp & A. M. Watkinson (London: Falmer Press, 1996), 113; Geoff Bender, "Resisting Dominance? The Study of a Marginalized Masculinity and Its Construction Within High School Walls," in Preventing Violence in Schools: A Challenge to American Democracy, eds. Joan N. Burstyn, Geoff Bender, Ronnie Casella, Howard W. Gordon, Domingo P. Guerra, Kristen V. Luschen, Rebecca Stevens & Kimberly M. Williams (New Jersey: Lawrence Erlbaum, 2001), 61–77; Nan Stein, "Sexual Harassment in School: The Public Performance of Gendered Violence," Harvard Law Review 65 (1995): 163–173.

18   Eliana Suarez & Tehany M. Gadalla, "Stop Blaming the Victim: A Meta-Analysis on Rape Myths," Journal of Interpersonal Violence 25:11 (2010): 1–26.

19   Valerie Steeves, Young Canadians in a Wired World, Phase III: Sexuality and Romantic Relationships in the Digital Age (Ottawa: MediaSmarts, 2014), <http://mediasmarts.ca/sites/mediasmarts/files/pdfs/publication-report/full/YCWWIII_Sexuality_Romantic_Relationships_Digital_Age_Full-Report_0.pdf>.

20   Ibid.

21   Nicole Poltash, "Snapchat and Sexting: A Snapshot of Bearing Your Bare Essentials," Richmond Journal of Law and Technology 19 (2013): 14.

22   Karen Seidman, "Child Pornography Laws 'Too Harsh' to Deal with Minors Sexting Photos without Consent, Experts Say," National Post,

16 November 2013, <http://news.nationalpost.com/2013/11/16/child-pornography-laws-too-harsh-to-deal-with-minors-sexting-photos-without-consent-experts-say/>.

23 CBC News Montreal, "Child Porn Charges Laid against 10 Laval Teens – Police Allege Boys Traded Screen Grabs of Girlfriends' Explicit Snapchat Photos," 14 November 2013, <http://www.cbc.ca/news/canada/montreal/child-porn-charges-laid-against-10-laval-teens-1.2426599>.

24 Steeves, *supra* note 19.

25 Jane Bailey & Mouna Hanna, "The Gendered Dimensions of Sexting: Assessing the Applicability of Canada's Child Pornography Provision," *Canadian Journal of Women and the Law* 406 (2011): 405–441; Jane Bailey & Valerie Steeves, "Will the Real Digital Girl Please Stand Up?," in *New Visualities, New Technologies: The New Ecstasy of Communication,* eds. Hille Koskela & Macgregor Wise (London: Ashgate, 2013), 41–66; Michele Ybarra, Kimberly Mitchell, Janis Wolak & David Finkelhor, "Examining Characteristics and Associated Distress Related to Internet Harassment: Findings from the Second Youth Internet Safety Survey," *Pediatrics* 118 (2006): 1169–1177.

26 In this instance, we are thinking about some of the adolescent girls, such as Amanda Todd, who endured the humiliation and backlash from their communities, and beyond, as their images spread online. For further discussion on the media's treatment of the Amanda Todd case, see Shariff, *supra* note 7 at 39–40.

27 Emily Poole, "Hey Girls, Did You Know? Slut-Shaming on the Internet Needs to Stop," *University of San Francisco Law Review* 48 (2013): 221–260.

28 Eva Chen, "Neoliberalism and Popular Women's Culture: Rethinking Choice, Freedom and Agency," *European Journal of Cultural Studies* 16:4 (2013): 440–452; Rosalind Gill, "Empowerment/Sexism: Figuring Female Sexual Agency in Contemporary Advertising," *Feminism & Psychology* 18:1 (2008): 35–60.

29 *Ibid.*

30 Bonnie Blackwell, "How the Jilt Triumphed over the Slut: The Evolution of an Epithet, 1660–1780," *Women's Writing* 11:2 (2004): 141–161; Attwood, *supra* note 2.

31 Attwood, *supra* note 2.

32 *Ibid.,* at 234.

33 While for the purposes of our discussion we examine how society uses the term "slut" to shame young female adolescents, Attwood, *supra* note 2, gives a well-rounded examination as to how the term as been (re)appropriated by some feminist scholarship and activism as well as within the gay and bisexual communities.

34 As described in further detail below, we believe that education can play an important role in cultivating media and human rights awareness

amongst adolescent girls and boys as they come of age exploring their sexual identities in an era of social media and cellphones.

35 See Shariff, *Confronting Cyberbullying: What Schools Need to Know About Misconduct and Legal Consequences* (Cambridge: Cambridge University Press, 2009).

36 Andrew Welsh-Huggins, "Ohio Football Players Guilty in Rape of 16-Year-Old Girl, Face Year-Plus in Jail," *National Post*, 17 March 2013, <http://news.nationalpost.com/2013/03/17/ohio-football-players-guilty-in-rape-of-16-year-old-girl-face-year-plus-in-jail/>; Meghan Murphy, "The Steubenville Rape Case: This Is Masculinity," *Feminist Current*, 19 March 2013, <http://feministcurrent.com/7339/the-steubenville-rape-case-this-is-masculinity/>.

37 M. Binder, "If you thought these unbelievable reactions to Steubenville would just peter out, I guess you can say you were pretty, pretty wrong," comment on Tumblr, 19 March 2013, <http://publicshaming.tumblr.com/day/2013/03/19>.

38 Gill, *supra* note 28.

39 Attwood, *supra* note 2.

40 Poole, *supra* note 27 at 242.

41 Attwood, *supra* note 2 at 234.

42 Here we are thinking of celebrity examples such as Lady Gaga, Rihanna, Madonna, Miley Cyrus, and Beyoncé.

43 Chen, *supra* note 28.

44 Gill, *supra* note 28 at 37.

45 *Ibid.* at 35–60.

46 Chen, *supra* note 28.

47 *Ibid.*

48 Yuanyuan Zhang, Travis L. Dixon & Kate Conrad, "Female Body Image as a Function of Themes in Rap Music Videos: A Content Analysis," *Sex Roles* 62:11–12 (2010): 787–797; Meredith Levande, "Women, Pop Music and Pornography," *Meridians: Feminism, Race, Transnationalism* 8:1 (2007): 293–321; Chen, *supra* note 28.

49 Gill, *supra* note 28 at 42.

50 Ryan Grenoble, "Amanda Todd: Bullied Canadian Teen Commits Suicide After Prolonged Battle Online and in School," *Huffington Post*, 10 November 2012, <www.huffingtonpost.com/2012/10/11/amanda-todd-suicide-bullying_n_1959909.html>; Bob Cook, "Lesson From Steubenville Trial: How Jock Culture Morphs Into Rape Culture," *Forbes*, 17 March 2013, <www.forbes.com/sites/bobcook/2013/03/17/lesson-from-steubenville-rape-trial-how-jock-culture-morphs-into-rape-culture>; Shariff, *supra* note 7; Shaheen Shariff, *Facebook Report* (9 April 2014).

51 Jessica Ringrose & Emma Renold, "Slut-Shaming, Girl Power and 'Sexualisation': Thinking Through the Politics of the International

SlutWalks With Teen Girls," *Gender and Education* 24 (2012): 333–343; Celeste Hirschman, Emily A. Impett & Deborah Schooler, "Dis/Embodied Voices: What Late-Adolescent Girls Can Teach Us about Objectification and Sexuality," *Sexuality Research & Social Policy* 3:4 (2006): 8–20; Poole, *supra* note 27; Rebecca Holman, "She's a Homewrecker: The Website Where Women Expose 'Infidelity'. The Internet Just Ate Itself," *The Telegraph*, November 15, 2013, <http://www.telegraph.co.uk/women/womens-life/10452482/Shes-A-Homewrecker-the-website-where-women-slut-shame-each-others-infidelity.-The-internet-just-ate-itself.html>; Olga Khazan, "The Evolution of Bitchiness," *The Atlantic*, 20 November 2013, <http://www.theatlantic.com/health/archive/2013/11/the-evolution-of-bitchiness/281657/>.

52   See Steeves, Chapter VI.

53   Shariff, *supra* note 50.

54   Gill, *supra* note 28.

55   Powell, *supra* note 1.

56   Shariff, *supra* note 7.

57   Mary Elizabeth Williams, "Horrifying New Trend: Posting Rapes to Facebook," *Salon*, 20 May 2013, <http://www.salon.com/2013/05/20/worst_horrifying_new_trend_posting_rapes_to_facebook/>; Liam Ford, "Prosecutors: 3 Teens Posted Taped Sex Assaults of Girl, 12, on Facebook," *Chicago Tribune*, 17 May 2013, <http://www.chicagotribune.com/news/local/breaking/chi-3-teens-posted-taped-sex-assaults-of-girl-12-on-facebook-20130517-story.html>.

58   Shariff, *supra* note 7.

59   Binder, *supra* note 37.

60   Gill, *supra* note 28 at 41.

61   Adrienne Evans, Sarah Riley & Avi Shankar, "Technologies of Sexiness: Theorizing Women's Engagement in the Sexualization of Culture," *Feminism & Psychology* 20:1 (2010): 114–131.

62   *Ibid.*

63   Ratna Kapur, "Pink Chaddis and SlutWalk Couture: The Postcolonial Politics of Feminism Lite," *Feminist Legal Studies* 20:1 (2012): 1–20.

64   Gill, *supra* note 28.

65   Evans et al, *supra* note 61.

66   Janice Turner, "Dirty Young Men," *The Guardian*, 22 October 2005, <http://www.theguardian.com/theguardian/2005/oct/22/weekend7.weekend3>; also cited in Gill, *supra* note 28.

67   Shaheen Shariff, "Define the Line: Clarifying Boundaries between Cyberbullying and Socially Responsible Digital Citizenship," Define the Line, April 2014, <www.mcgill.ca/definetheline>.

68   Shariff, *supra* note 7.

69   *Ibid.*

70   Shariff, *supra* note 50.

71   Julia Nicol & Dominique Valiquet, *Bill C-13: An Act to Amend the Criminal Code, the Canada Evidence Act, the Competition Act and the Mutual Legal Assistance in Criminal Matters Act* (Ottawa: Library of Parliament, 2014), <http://www.parl.gc.ca/Content/LOP/LegislativeSummaries/41/2/c13-e.pdf> .

72   Daniel Schwartz, "The Fine Line between 'Sexting' and Child Pornography: Criminal Code May Be Too Blunt an Instrument to Stop the Practice of Young People Sharing Sexually Suggestive Images," *CBC News*, 13 August 2013, <http://www.cbc.ca/news/canada/the-fine-line-between-sexting-and-child-pornography-1.1367613>.

73   Stephen Kimber, "Why Are We Using Child Pornography Laws to Charge Children?," *Rabble.ca*, 14 January 2014, <http://rabble.ca/blogs/bloggers/skimber/2014/01/why-are-we-using-child-pornography-laws-to-charge-children>.

74   Re: C.S., 2012 CP-39-JV-447-2012, <http://www.krautharris.com/documents/In-re-CS.pdf>.

75   Louise Dickson, "Vancouver Island 'Sexting' Case Sparks Challenge over Charging Youth with Child Pornography," *Vancouver Sun*, 18 September 2013, <http://www.vancouversun.com/technology/Vancouver+Island+sexting+case+sparks+challenge+over+charging+youth+with+child+pornography/8928731/story.html>.

76   It is not within the scope of this chapter to address details of the lawful access clauses and their harmful potential in terms of privacy breaches. For a fuller analysis of these aspects of the bill see Jane Bailey (supported by Professors Faye Mishna, Wayne MacKay & Andrea Slane), "Submission to the House of Commons Standing Committee on Justice and Human Rights Regarding Bill C-13," 26 May 2014, available at: <http://egirlsproject.files.wordpress.com/2014/06/submission-c-13-baileymishnamackayslane2.pdf>.

77   Carissima Mathen, "Crowdsourcing Sexual Objectification," *Law.* 2014 3:3 (2014): 529–552, doi:10.3390/laws3030529.

78   Kift et al, *supra* note 3.

79   Nicol & Valiquet, *supra* note 71.

80   Standing Senate Committee on Human Rights, *Cyberbullying Hurts: Respect for Rights in the Digital Age* (Ottawa: Parliament of Canada, 2012), <http://www.parl.gc.ca/Content/SEN/Committee/411/ridr/rep/rep09dec12-e.pdf>.

81   Shaheen Shariff & Andrew H. Churchill (eds.), *Truths and Myths of Cyber-Bullying: International Perspectives on Stakeholder Responsibility and Children's Safety* (New York: Peter Lang, 2010).

82 Examples of such programs include those by EGALE, Define the Line, Kids Help Phone, and SafeTeen: Standing Senate Committee on Human Rights, *supra* note 80 at 111–116.

83 See Slane, Chapter X, for an analysis of the importance of contextualized understandings of youth's online communications practices in criminal cases.

84 See, for example, Steeves, Chapter VI, and Bailey, Chapter I.

85 Kift, Campbell, & Butler, *supra* note 3; see Milford, Chapter II, for further discussion of the limitations of criminal law responses.

86 See Angrove, Chapter XII, for further discussion of equality-based education law responses.

87 See Johnson, Chapter XIII, for further discussion of critical media literacy and digital citizenship initiatives.

"She's Such a Slut!": The Sexualized Cyberbullying of Teen Girls and the Education Law Response

Gillian Angrove

Introduction

Sexualized Cyberbullying and the Canadian Context

On 27 September 2012, the Supreme Court of Canada released *A.B. v. Bragg Communications Inc.*,[1] in which a teenage girl "sought to unmask her cyberbullies"[2] in order to pursue a defamation action, while still protecting her own anonymity. In 2010, A.B. discovered that someone had created a fake Facebook profile using her picture, a slightly modified version of her name, and other identifying particulars.[3] In addition to the photo, the creator of the profile had included "unflattering commentary about the girl's appearance along with sexually explicit references."[4]

At issue in the case was a balance between the freedom of the press and open court principles on the one hand, and the privacy and protection of children from sexualized cyberbullying on the other.[5] Further, A.B. argued that unless her privacy was protected, "young victims of sexualized cyberbullying like her would refuse to proceed with their protective claims," and therefore be "denied access to justice."[6] Justice Abella, writing for the Court, commented on A.B.'s privacy interests in the case, and observed, "it is not merely a question of her privacy, but of her privacy from the relentlessly intrusive humiliation of sexualized online bullying."[7] She further reasoned that:

> If we value the right of children to protect themselves from bullying, cyber or otherwise, if common sense and the evidence persuade us that young victims of sexualized bullying are particularly vulnerable to the harms of revictimization upon publication, and if we accept that the right to protection will disappear for most children without the further protection of anonymity, we are compellingly drawn in this case to allowing A.B.'s anonymous legal pursuit of the identity of her cyberbully.[8]

Less than two weeks after the decision in *A.B. v. Bragg* was released, 15-year-old Amanda Todd committed suicide in British Columbia. Prior to her death, Amanda posted a video on YouTube to tell her story of taking a nude image of herself via a webcam, and the subsequent blackmail, stalking, and harassment that followed by tormentors in cyberspace and in the schoolyard.[9] In Amanda's case, she was deeply affected by both the aggressive cyberbullying and bullying conducted at the hands of her peers, and the deliberate sexual extortion, or "sextortion,"[10] by unknown online predators.[11]

Officials at the school districts where Amanda spent her final months say they employed strategies such as preventative action, restorative justice, and mediation to stop "bullying" – but they admitted to having "limited reach beyond the schoolyard."[12]

In April 2012, 17-year-old Rehtaeh Parsons passed away after an attempted suicide. In November 2011, Rehtaeh was allegedly sexually assaulted by four perpetrators while attending a house party. A cellphone photo of the sexual assault was shared repeatedly by students at her school and across social media sites.[13] Subsequently, Rehtaeh was subjected to relentless sexualized bullying and cyberbullying.[14] Leah Parsons, Rehtaeh's mother, has explained "she was never left alone ... boys she didn't know started texting her and Facebooking her asking her to have sex with them. It just never stopped."[15]

The administration at Rehtaeh's school, Cole Harbour High School, knew of the allegations that four boys (who also attended Cole Harbour High) had sexually assaulted her, but "did not step in to question those involved or address bullying."[16] Halifax regional school board spokesman Doug Hadley said the school administration "didn't want to interfere with the police investigation."[17]

Sexualized cyberbullying is a troubling and complex problem that in particular affects teen girls across the country. In *The Report of the Nova Scotia Task Force on Bullying and Cyberbullying* ("the *Nova*

Scotia Task Force Report"), Professor Wayne MacKay explains that the struggle against cyberbullying "must be waged on many different fronts," including prevention education, criminal legislation and tort liability, and restorative approaches.[18] Although a holistic approach to cyberbullying is ideal, in large part, Canadian policymakers, the media, and the public have assigned responsibility of the so-called "cyberbullying problem"[19] to our schools and the education system.[20] Only more recently have other sorts of specific criminal law and tort-based statutory approaches begun to emerge.[21] To the extent that we have framed cyberbullying as an education — and education law — issue, there are challenges and opportunities. This framing influences the way we collectively perceive the problem and how we collectively respond. Although education law cannot provide exact solutions to the many challenges in addressing cyberbullying, it can provide a useful framework within which students, teachers, administrators, policymakers, and society can begin to find ways to meet the challenges.[22]

Whether or not we agree with categorizing cyberbullying as an education issue, an essential role of schools is to "teach good citizenship and basic values," including equality.[23] Teachers are "well placed to promote equality" and to act as exemplars for their students.[24] There is significant, and relatively untapped, potential for preventing and responding to sexualized cyberbullying through education law. This potential can be realized if equality is the "driving force" behind education legislation. That is, equality in education legislation cannot just be an "add-on,"[25] but it must be "the substance behind creating safe schools."[26] Equality as the substance behind education law will help facilitate and encourage the development of schools with inclusive and equality-driven approaches; and schools with inclusive and equality-driven approaches may foster students' empathy, respect for peers, self-esteem, and sense of belonging to the school community and larger society.[27]

Equality-driven education legislation that allows for and facilitates inclusive schools may also enable students, teachers, and administration to understand, identify, question, and stand up against different forms of oppression and discrimination — for only with "such understanding is it possible to work together to build a more just society."[28]

Therefore, this paper will investigate the sexualized cyberbullying of teen girls at secondary schools in Canada and the current education law response. Specifically, provincial education law in British Columbia, Ontario, and Nova Scotia will be examined to ascertain whether equality is a "driving force" behind the legislation – and how, if at all, the law responds to or prevents sexualized cyberbullying.[29]

Applying a Substantive Equality Lens to Education Law

In order to fully comprehend the implications of sexualized cyberbullying, I have chosen to apply an equality lens to all facets of the discussion. An equality lens insists on equal treatment and equal opportunity for all, regardless of gender and other intersecting forms of oppression. An equality lens also acknowledges that the impacts of sexualized cyberbullying and sexualized violence affect girls and women differently than they do boys and men. That is, if we truly want to understand the impacts of sexualized cyberbullying, we must question exactly *who* is likely to be victimized and how. We must also consider the systemic inequalities that disproportionately expose Canadian women and girls to sexualized violence. An equality lens will locate sexualized cyberbullying within these systemic inequalities, and will guide my consideration of the appropriate education law response. This lens is essential because much of the current literature and legislation pertaining to cyberbullying is gender "neutral"; however, the risks of sexualized cyberbullying and sexualized violence are unevenly borne by girls and women (and also by members of the LGBTQ community).[30]

Women and girls experience systemic inequality in myriad forms, including sexual targeting, domestic violence, and sexual abuse.[31] According to a 2013 Statistics Canada report, women had a much higher rate of police-reported violence than men in Canada.[32] Women are eleven times more likely than men to be sexually victimized, three times as likely to be stalked, and twice as likely to be the victim of indecent and harassing phone calls.[33] MacKinnon argues that women are sexually assaulted "not individually or at random, but on the basis of sex."[34] Accordingly, sexualized violence can be understood as "an indication and a practice" of sex inequality that both "symbolizes and actualizes" women's "subordinate social status to men."[35]

Importantly, the women who remain further disproportionately affected by sexualized violence are women of colour and Indigenous women, trans people, women with disabilities, non-status women,

women with addictions, and women living in poverty.[36] For example, approximately 40 percent of women with disabilities in Canada will be assaulted, sexually assaulted, or abused throughout their lifetime.[37] Aboriginal women are 3.5 times more likely than non-Aboriginal women to experience incidents of violence.[38] Arguably, this reality is "the product of the racist, colonialist, ableist, ageist, capitalist, misogynist system within which our society exists."[39] Therefore, in order to respond to the sexualized cyberbullying of girls, we should also aim to understand the interconnectedness of gender, race, and class and other oppressions.[40]

In the context of bullying and cyberbullying, much of the gender "neutral" education legislation focuses on naming, prohibiting, and punishing certain types of behaviour. This approach is problematic because it tends to misunderstand equality. Professor Donn Short has written extensively about the bullying of sexual-minority youth in Canada and the necessary response from schools. He argues that in order to prevent bullying of sexual-minority youth, education law should "allow for" and "facilitate" an equitable school culture. Although Short's argument is located in the lived experiences of sexual-minority youth and argued through an equity lens, its conceptual foundation should apply equally to the misogynistic and racist underpinnings of the sexualized cyberbullying of teen girls. That is, education law should not be restricted to solely naming, prohibiting, and punishing sexualized cyberbullying, but it should actively facilitate a school culture predicated on principles of equality. MacKinnon has stated that "law has a choice" – it can either inscribe misogyny on society, or it can dynamically move against inequality by promoting equality.[41] School cultures are a microcosm of societal culture – and if our schools are rooted in and facilitate equality, perhaps we may begin to tear down some of the structural inequalities that disproportionately expose Canadian women and girls to sexualized violence.

Defining the Terms: Cyberbullying and Sexualized Cyberbullying
In order to effectively respond to the challenges of sexualized cyberbullying, it is critical to define the seemingly basic terms that are at the heart of this paper. Although cyberbullying is a term that most Canadians are relatively familiar with, "a universal definition of cyberbullying does not yet exist" and the "concept itself is actually hard to define."[42] For example, from a legal perspective, if the

definition contains too many elements it could make establishing a violation very difficult; however, from a school administrator perspective it is important to have enough detail to distinguish "bullying" from other forms of school violence.[43]

How, then, can education law define "cyberbullying" so that the rights and expectations of victims are respected, while at the same time ensuring that the definition does not serve as a catch-all for every unwelcome behaviour? The *Nova Scotia Task Force Report* proposed a definition specifically for the purposes of education legislation that seeks to achieve this balance:

> Bullying is typically a repeated behaviour that is intended to cause, or should be known to cause, fear, intimidation, humiliation, distress or other forms of harm to another person's body, feelings, self-esteem, reputation or property.
>
> Bullying can be direct or indirect, and can take place by written, verbal, physical or electronic means, or any other form of expression.
>
> Cyberbullying (also referred to as electronic bullying) is a form of bullying, and occurs through the use of technology. This can include the use of a computer or other electronic devices, using social networks, text messaging, instant messaging, websites, e-mail or other electronic means.
>
> A person participates in bullying if he or she directly carries out the behaviour or assists or encourages the behaviour in any way.[44]

This definition is "conceived broadly" and also "includes the role of bystanders and others who may encourage such behaviour."[45]

The definition of "sexualized cyberbullying" as a form of cyberbullying has received less attention. "Sexualized bullying" is a term that has been used to describe bullying of a sexual nature. It has been defined as "unwanted sexual attention that makes the recipient feel uncomfortable, demeaned or humiliated."[46] Further, it is "usually directed against females" and can include obscene gestures or communication, remarks about a person's body, sexual demands, and can also include criminal offences such as unwanted sexual touching, assault, and rape.[47]

The Scope of the Problem

There are statistical inconsistencies on the prevalence of cyberbullying in Canada. However, there is a growing body of research and commentary that demonstrates that girls and women are more likely to experience sexualized cyberbullying.[48] The sexualized cyberbullying of teen girls may manifest itself in numerous ways, including: slut shaming, threats of sexual violence, harassment, cyber stalking, exclusion, and "outing" (revealing that someone is LGBTQ), and can "extend to highly sexual comments and visual pornography that dehumanizes women."[49]

The Effects of Sexualized Cyberbullying on Teen Girls

The immediacy and prevalence of electronic communications and social networking websites have intensified sexualized cyberbullying.[50] Cyber-insults are now so common that many teens downplay the incidents as digital "drama."[51] Unfortunately, the lived experiences of too many Canadian girls have proven that sexualized cyberbullying and its effects are not always just drama.[52]

The personal characteristics of the victim, her surrounding environment,[53] and her exposure to repeat victimization[54] can affect the severity of the impact of cyberbullying. Potential effects include academic difficulties, anxiety, depression, low self-esteem, and physical symptoms (including headaches, stomach pains, back pains, and dizziness),[55] as well as self-harming behaviours such as self-mutilation and eating disorders.[56] Less obvious, but potentially equally serious effects include internalized oppression, harmful impacts on self-identity, and distorted attitudes about one's gender group.[57]

Further, sexualized cyberbullying affects girls' perception of self, and inhibits their participation online.[58] For girls who are concerned about their peers' approval, "checking Facebook provides a barometer about how much they are liked or how appealing they are."[59] As demonstrated in the eGirls Project findings reported by Professors Bailey and Steeves in their chapters in this volume, girls' online presentations of self also "involve complex negotiations" between "online self-exposure" and the "gendered risk of harsh judgment" that goes along with slut shaming.[60] In a hypersexualized online world where girls are taught to walk a fine line between "sexy" and "slut," it is likely that girls may, and often do, confuse sexualized cyberbullying with "the acceptance they seek from others."[61]

The effects of sexual bullying/assault and cyberbullying can be exacerbated when a student seeks out help and the school fails to effectively respond.[62] For example, in Australia, a 15-year-old girl approached her school principal to request a meeting with a counsellor after being sexually assaulted by a peer. The principal responded by telling her that the counsellor "did not have time for such petty things."[63] Again, in Rehtaeh Parsons' case, the administration at Rehtaeh's school "did not step in to question those involved or address bullying."[64]

Given the seemingly commonplace nature of cyber-insults, and the potentially tragic consequences associated with sexualized cyberbullying, how can our education law and schools respond effectively?

The Role of Education Law and Its Application in Nova Scotia, Ontario, and British Columbia

Education Law as a Response to Sexualized Cyberbullying

If cyberbullying is predominately framed as an "education issue," schools, school boards, teachers, and ministries of education may be deemed the appropriate actors to respond to the issue.

It is worthwhile to pause and consider the complex and varying roles faced by today's teachers and school administrators. They are often required to act "not only as a parent but also as a police officer, social worker, and professional educator," and as such find themselves "confused and frustrated" with the multiple roles and jurisdictions assigned to them.[65] For example, many teachers and administrators may find it difficult to intervene in cases involving sexualized cyberbullying, given that much of it occurs off school-grounds. School administrators often cite the lack in education law of explicit authority to act in regards to off-school conduct as the reason for failing to intervene.

Despite the numerous roles and jurisdictions assigned to teachers and school administrators, both are well placed to promote, educate, and exemplify equality.[66] Further, ambiguities in legislation may be overcome if there is clear and equality-based education law. In order to truly achieve "safe schools," education law must engage equality as a substantial part of how "safety" is conceptualized.

Indeed, effective education law should "conceptualize safety broadly in order to give voice" to equality and social justice "as proactive components of the goal of constructing safe schools."[67] Professor Short emphatically argues that education law should actively "facilitate" an equitable school culture. He suggests that to "prevent" bullying and cyberbullying, and not just respond to it, a cultural transformation is needed – that is, "a conception of safety that includes and proactively pursues" equality and social justice should "not only be a worthy idea but also a reality."[68]

Short identifies the need for curriculum change to include queer content and to recognize queer families in order to ensure that social justice is not just an idea but a reality. However, he notes that the curriculum will not change "unless education ministries direct it to change" and unless "queer youth are reconstructed legally as full citizens within schools."[69] Similarly, if education law is to ensure equality and prevent the sexualized cyberbullying of girls, it needs to facilitate a culture where children and youth are taught to identify discrimination and the effects of discrimination, and how to respond effectively.

That is, education law should serve as a catalyst and motivator for teachers, administrators, and students to foster a culture in which understandings of concepts like safety are rooted in a deep understanding of equality. Wayne MacKay has argued that law is a "lighthouse of equality" that can guide "educators through the fog of educating in a complex society."[70] Education law can "provide a useful framework" within which those on the front lines of education can respond to inherently complex challenges such as sexualized cyberbullying.[71] MacKay further explains that the concept that schools should be "discrimination free zones" and have a positive duty to promote equality originates from the Supreme Court of Canada in *Ross v. New Brunswick Board of Education No 15.*, where Justice La Forest writes:

> The school is an arena for the exchange of ideas and must, therefore, be premised upon principles of tolerance and impartiality so that all persons within the school environment feel equally free to participate. As the Board of Inquiry stated, a school board has a duty to maintain a positive school environment for all persons served by it.[72]

Importantly, if education law enables schools to develop safe and equality-based cultures that promote "qualities such as trust, mutual respect, caring and consideration for others, then bullying is more likely to be marginalized."[73]

The next three subsections analyze existing public secondary school education law in British Columbia, Ontario, and Nova Scotia to determine which of these provinces have taken the lead on equality-based education law, and which, if any, have fallen behind. I have chosen to focus on these three provinces because "cyberbullying stands apart as the foremost topic of discussion" within these jurisdictions.[74] In addition, I believe these provinces in particular will represent a diverse range of education law responses.

Preventing and Responding to Sexualized Cyberbullying in British Columbia Education Law

In British Columbia (BC), education is governed by the *School Act*.[75] The statute does not contain a provision that defines or addresses bullying or cyberbullying; nor does the statute assign responsibility to school boards, schools, or staff to create safe or equality-based environments at schools. The preamble to the legislation states, *inter alia*:

> WHEREAS it is the goal of a democratic society to ensure that all its members receive an education that enables them to become literate, personally fulfilled and publicly useful, thereby increasing the strength and contributions to the health and stability of that society;
>
> AND WHEREAS the purpose of the British Columbia school system is to enable all learners to become literate, to develop their individual potential and to acquire the knowledge, skills and attitudes needed to contribute to a healthy, democratic and pluralistic society and a prosperous and sustainable economy.[76]

In *Chamberlain v. Surrey School District No 36*,[77] Chief Justice McLachlin explained that the message of this preamble is "clear" and that "the British Columbia school system is open to all children of all cultures and family backgrounds. All are to be valued and respected."[78] With respect to Chief Justice McLachlin, although the preamble may be "clear," the subsequent provisions are less emphatic with regard to school values and respect. The only provisions in the *School Act* and

School Regulation that allude to student safety refer to the installation and operation of surveillance cameras,[79] and the development of and compliance with school rules and codes of conduct. For example, sections 85(1.1) and 168(2)(s.1) of the *School Act* make it mandatory for boards of education to establish codes of conduct and to ensure that schools within their school district implement the codes. Section 6(1) of the *School Act* states:

> 6(1) A student must comply
> (a) with the school rules authorized by the principal of the school or Provincial school attended by the student, and
> (b) with the code of conduct and other rules and policies of the board or the Provincial school.[80]

Further, section 4(1)(c) of the *School Regulation* states:

> 4(1) The duties of a teacher include the following:
> [...]
> (c) ensuring that students understand and comply with the codes of conduct governing their behaviour and with the rules and policies governing the operation of the school.[81]

These provisions conceptualize "security" as the "primary focus of ensuring a safe school environment."[82] When education law focuses on physical security, measures can include "surveillance cameras, dress policies, security guards, and an emphasis on containing or, if unsuccessful, responding to violent behaviours."[83] Within this approach schools "perceive their own students as the threat to certifying the safety of the school."[84]

The *School Act* is problematic because the statute does not affirmatively enable students, teachers, and administrators to pursue goals of equality and social justice. The legislation does not distinguish between on- and off-school conduct, it does not define in-person or online behaviour that is unacceptable, nor does it encourage affirmative measures that require equality-enhancement, such as curriculum development. Incorporating equality into education law in BC should encourage a "proactive approach in which justice is looked for in the school environment and sought in the larger community as well."[85] That is, a focus on equality in the legislation may empower students to seek out justice and therefore stand up against the sexualized cyberbullying of their peers.

Although the "hard" education law in BC is relatively silent in regards to safe and equality-based schools, the province's Ministry of Education has addressed "safe, caring and orderly schools."[86] In 2002, the Minister of Education appointed a Safe Schools Task Force to meet with parents, students, and educators across BC to identify ways to address violence in schools,[87] and in 2003, the task force's report contained a number of recommendations for improving school safety, which led to the development of *British Columbia's Safe, Caring and Orderly Schools Strategy* ("the Strategy").

According to the Strategy's guide ("the Guide"), BC schools use efforts to "build 'community,' fostering respect, inclusion, fairness and equity," and "set, communicate and consistently reinforce clear expectations of acceptable conduct."[88] The Guide suggests some practices for achieving caring schools, including that the environment of a school should be "inviting and welcoming, fostering feelings of acceptance and belonging for members of the school community"; that members of the school should "relate to one another in supportive ways"; and that regular opportunities are offered "to learn about and celebrate human rights, diversity in the community and other key elements of caring schools."[89] However, the guide does not explicitly discuss how to facilitate an equality-driven school culture, nor does it provide any empirical data to suggest whether this is being achieved in practice.

The provincial standards for codes of conduct at schools in BC are set out in subordinate legislation in the *Provincial Standards for Codes of Conduct Order* ("the Ministerial Order")[90] which were issued according to sections 85(1.1) and 168(2)(s.1) of the *School Act*. These standards set out process and content elements that must be addressed in the development of all codes of conduct at schools. Some of the process elements include involving students, parents, and staff in the development and review of codes of conduct; ensuring that there is clear knowledge of the code of conduct; and keeping codes of conduct current and relevant.[91] The content requirements are set out in section 6 of the Ministerial order, and include:

> 6. Boards must ensure that the following elements are included in their codes of conduct:

(a) one or more statements that address the prohibited grounds of discrimination set out in the BC Human Rights Code in respect of discriminatory publication and discrimination in accommodation, service and facility in the school environment;

(b) a statement of purpose that provides a rationale for the code of conduct, with a focus on safe, caring and orderly school environments;

(c) one or more statements about what is

i. acceptable behaviour, and

ii. unacceptable behaviour, including aggressive behaviours such as bullying behaviours while at school, at a school-related activity or in other circumstances where engaging in the activity will have an impact on the school environment;

(d) one or more statements about the consequences of unacceptable behaviour, which must take account of the student's age, maturity and special needs, if any;

(e) an explanation that the board will take all reasonable steps to prevent retaliation by a person against a student who has made a complaint of a breach of a code of conduct.[92]

BC has also produced a companion document to the Ministerial Order and the Strategy, titled *Developing and Reviewing Codes of Conduct: A Companion* ("Code of Conduct Companion"). The document explains that codes of conduct have great potential, specifically that:

Codes can be used to teach and model socially responsible behaviour, and the language and concepts of the codes reinforced through teaching and student leadership. A sense of pride in the code should be part of students' experience. We want every student to feel a sense of belonging and pride in his or her school, that people in the school community are respectful and fair, and that they feel safe.[93]

Importantly, the Code of Conduct Companion also provides content suggestions for codes of conduct in BC. Some of these suggestions address conduct that occurs off school property, and provide definitions of "bullying behaviour" and "cyberbullying" for schools to use in their respective codes of conduct. The document states that boards *may* wish to include statements in their codes that explain school responsibilities in regards to student conduct that occurs off the school grounds. Further, the definitions of bullying and cyberbullying provided for use in codes of conduct are also discretionary.[94]

Although these content suggestions for codes of conduct are a step in the right direction, they remain *suggestions*. Content components that have the potential to address sexualized cyberbullying are not mandatory, and therefore some schools in BC may not have the appropriate tools via the code of conduct to effectively prevent or respond to incidents of sexualized cyberbullying. It is unclear why the government in BC has yet to amend its *School Act* to include mandatory safe school provisions. However, in 2012 the BC government opted to invest in a $2 million, 10-point strategy to address bullying in schools and "ensure students feel safe, accepted and respected."[95] The strategy is based on a "policy-to-action" formula, and includes the development of an anonymous online reporting tool for students, stronger codes of conduct for schools, online resources for parents, and dedicated safe school co-ordinators in every school district.[96] Obviously, the contribution of financial resources to prevent and address bullying and cyberbullying is valuable; however, BC should also amend its *School Act* to include an equality lens in order to demonstrate that equality-based and safe schools are a priority within the province.

Preventing and Responding to Sexualized Cyberbullying in Ontario Education Law

In Ontario, the *Education Act*[97] governs the operation of schools and delivers education throughout the province. Ontario has taken the lead in developing education law with equality as its "substance" with the *Accepting Schools Act*,[98] which amended the *Education Act*. As a result, the *Education Act* is comprehensive, and includes the rights and responsibilities of teachers, schools, school boards, and ministries in regards to preventing and intervening in bullying and cyberbullying. At the forefront of the legislation is the *prevention* of bullying and cyberbullying, and an equality and gender-based lens, with part of the preamble stating:

The people of Ontario and the Legislative Assembly:
[...]
Believe that all students should feel safe at school and deserve a positive school climate that is inclusive and accepting, regardless of race, ancestry, place of origin, colour, ethnic origin, citizenship, creed, sex, sexual orientation, gender identity, gender expression, age, marital status, family status or disability;
Believe that a healthy, safe and inclusive learning environment where all students feel accepted is a necessary condition for student success;
[...]
Recognize that a whole-school approach is required, and that everyone – government, educators, school staff, parents, students and the wider community – has a role to play in creating a positive school climate and preventing inappropriate behaviour, such as bullying, sexual assault, gender-based violence and incidents based on homophobia, transphobia or biphobia.[99]

Unfortunately, although part of the Preamble states that all students should feel safe at school "regardless of race," there is no mention of racialized violence in the paragraph that requires a whole-school approach to preventing inappropriate behaviour, including "bullying, sexual assault, gender-based violence and incidents based on homophobia, transphobia or biphobia."[100] This absence is troubling, given that racialized and Indigenous girls and women are disproportionately affected by violence.

The *Accepting Schools Act* also amended the *Education Act* to include a definition of cyberbullying, and the legislation states that for the purposes of the definition of "bullying," cyberbullying is included.[101] Perhaps more striking is the amendment of section 8(1) (29.1), which allows the Minister to "require boards to develop and implement an equity and inclusive education policy."[102] Further, section 303.1(1)(a) states that every board shall support students who want to establish and lead activities and organizations that promote a safe and inclusive learning environment, including "activities or organizations that promote gender equity."[103]

Section 301(1) allows the Minister to "establish a code of conduct governing the behaviour of all persons in schools."[104] The purposes of the code of conduct include promoting "responsible citizenship by encouraging appropriate participation in the civic life of the school community" and to "prevent bullying in schools."[105]

The need for *intervention* in sexualized cyberbullying is also stressed. For example, section 301(7.1) states that the Minister shall establish policies and guidelines with respect to bullying prevention and intervention in schools, including training for all teachers and other staff; resources to support students who have been bullied; resources to support students who have engaged in bullying; procedures for responding appropriately and in a timely manner to bullying; and matters to be addressed in bullying prevention and intervention plans established by the board.[106]

The *Education Act* also extends the right to discipline to include actions that occur off school property and outside school activities where engaging in the activity will have an impact on the school climate.[107] Eric M. Roher has explained that "under [the] Ministry of Education policy, the term 'school climate' is defined as 'the sum total of all personal relationships within a school' and in accordance with Ministry policy, a positive climate exists when all members of the school community feel safe, comfortable and accepted."[108] However, the *Education Act* itself does not define "school climate," nor do its regulations. Roher further explains that the courts and administrative tribunals have determined that in order to discipline for off-school conduct, there needs to be a direct and causal link or nexus to the school.[109] However, it is not made clear what evidence is needed to establish that nexus.

The Ministry of Education first released the Provincial Code of Conduct ("PCC") as a result of Bill 212, the *Education Amendment Act (Progressive Discipline and School Safety)*.[110] It was further amended by the *Accepting Schools Act* to include the prevention of bullying in schools under the purposes of the PCC. Under the PCC, school boards have a responsibility to develop effective intervention strategies and respond to all infractions related to the standards for respect, civility, and safety.[111] Under the "leadership of their principals," teachers and other staff are expected to "hold everyone to the highest standard of respectful and responsible behaviour."[112] Teachers and school staff uphold these high standards when they "help students work to their full potential and develop their sense of self-worth" and by empowering "students to be positive leaders in their classroom, school and community."[113] Further, "students are to be treated with respect and dignity" and in return, they must "demonstrate respect for themselves, for others, and for the responsibilities of citizenship through acceptable behaviour."[114]

According to Ministry policy, the PCC sets "clear provincial standards of behaviour."[115] The standards of behaviour in codes of conduct specific to Ontario school boards must be consistent with, and include, the standards stated by the PCC. Further, if a school board requires a principal to develop codes of conduct specific to their school, the code must set out "clearly" what is "acceptable and what is unacceptable behaviour" for all members of the school community.[116] Clear standards are fundamental in order to ensure consistent application and enforcement of the PCC across the province.

The explicit references to bullying, sexual assault, gender-based violence, and equity in Ontario's *Education Act* are laudable and should be replicated in other jurisdictions. Unfortunately, while the legislation gives voice to equality, equity, and social justice, it falls short of *requiring* curriculum that teaches and pursues equality in schools. However, the Ontario Ministry of Education has announced a revised health and physical education curriculum to go into effect in September 2015, which moves toward active facilitation of an equality-based school culture.[117] While incorporating educational initiatives aimed at alerting students to risk and ways of protecting themselves from risk,[118] the revised curriculum also specifically incorporates units for elementary students on understanding and challenging media stereotypes, developing healthy relationships, and respect for diversity,[119] and content for secondary students on consent and sexual limits, and factors affecting gender identity and sexual orientation (including unrealistic and exclusionary media bias and stereotyping and how to challenge them).[120] While not necessarily explicitly teaching children and youth the meaning of equality, development of these kinds of skills academically may well contribute to a "growing recognition of the gender-specific consequences of cyberbullying," and hopefully, a more effective means of prevention and intervention.[121]

Preventing and Responding to Sexualized Cyberbullying in Nova Scotia Education Law

Nova Scotia is actively responding to cyberbullying with the appointment of the Nova Scotia Task Force on Bullying and Cyberbullying, the *Task Force Report*, and subsequent legislation: the *Promotion of Respectful and Responsible Relationships Act*[122] and the *Cyber-safety*

Act.[123] Through the *Task Force Report,* Nova Scotia has "overtly recognized the heightened vulnerability of girls in the context of cyberbullying," and has explicitly discussed the "sexualization of girls and/or young women in the media ... as a contributing factor to the problem of cyberbullying."[124]

In Nova Scotia, the primary piece of education legislation is the *Education Act.*[125] In the Preamble, the *Education Act* references "equitable participation" in the education system. The *Promotion of Respectful and Responsible Relationships Act* further amended the Preamble to state that all members of a school community share responsibility for creating a school-wide approach that maintains a positive and inclusive school climate.[126] The Preamble also states that students must be held accountable for their actions, and that "responsibility and accountability can be fostered through preventative, proactive and restorative approaches."[127]

The *Promotion of Respectful and Responsible Relationships Act* also amended the *Education Act* to establish a Provincial school code of conduct policy that considers cyberbullying.[128] Section 141(1)(ja) of the *Education Act* now states:

> 141(1) The Minister may
> [...]
> (ja) establish a Provincial school code of conduct policy with respect to promoting school and student safety that includes a Provincial school code of conduct and provisions regards student conduct and consequences for disruptive behaviour and severely disruptive behaviour, including incidents of bullying and cyberbullying;[129]

In 2013, Nova Scotia enacted the *Cyber-safety Act.* This legislation creates a tort of cyberbullying, creates a protection order for victims of cyberbullying, and establishes a Cyber SCAN investigative unit to investigate cyberbullying throughout the Province. The *Cyber-safety Act* also defines "cyberbullying" as:

> 3(1) In this Act,
> [...]
> (b) "cyberbullying" means any electronic communication through the use of technology including, without limiting the generality of the foregoing, computers, other electronic devices,

social networks, text messaging, instant messaging, websites and electronic mail, typically repeated or with continuing effect, that is intended or ought reasonably [to] be expected to cause fear, intimidation, humiliation, distress or other damage or harm to another person's health, emotional well-being, self-esteem or reputation, and includes assisting or encouraging such communication in any way.[130]

This definition is also included in the Regulations to the *Education Act*.[131] Both the definition and the *Cyber-safety Act* have received mixed responses. Critics have asserted that the law has "sweeping parameters,"[132] that it "essentially makes 'being mean' against the law,"[133] and that it "makes bullies of us all."[134] On the other hand, some academics were encouraged by the definition of cyberbullying, noting that judges will work with the definition and "apply it in a way that's effective without getting overly broad."[135]

The *Cyber-safety Act* also amended the *Education Act* to provide that the principal may apply the school code of conduct for incidents that occur off school grounds and outside school activities where the behaviour "significantly disrupts the learning climate of the school."[136] In the *External Review of the Halifax Regional School Board's Support of Rehtaeh Parsons*, authors Debra Pepler and Penny Milton explain that regardless of this amendment, "it is unclear how principals may investigate off-school activities; whether the principal should investigate allegations that are under police investigation; and how to deal with situations in which the school has no direct knowledge."[137] Any ambiguity in the *Education Act* regarding when a school can intervene is problematic and should be clarified. Nova Scotia has already experienced first-hand the effects of ambiguous legislation, given that in Rehtaeh Parsons's case the "school was unsure whether it should take further action because of the criminal investigation."[138]

The current Provincial School Code of Conduct has not been updated since the *Promotion of Respectful and Responsible Relationships Act*. The document currently states the standards of behaviour for school members, including respecting the "diversity of all school members regardless of their race, culture, ethnicity, religion, gender, sexual orientation, age, or ability"; exhibiting "behaviour that avoids all forms of intimidation, harassment, racism, and discrimination"; and using information and communications technology, including the internet and e-mail communication, in a responsible and appropriate manner consistent with the Nova Scotia Public School Network Access and Use Policy.[139]

The Provincial School Code of Conduct also categorizes bullying, sexual harassment, sexual assault, and racial and/or discriminatory misconduct as "behaviour that is serious enough to significantly disrupt the learning climate of the school, endanger the well-being of others, or damage school property."[140] However, the document is relatively silent in terms of equality, cyberbullying, or the gendered impacts of cyberbullying.

Although Nova Scotia is actively responding to cyberbullying, there is more to be done, including a greater focus on student empowerment and equality in the *Education Act*. For example, this could be achieved in part by a provision that requires curriculum that enables students to understand, prevent, and respond to oppression and discrimination. Further, any ambiguities in the legislation should be clarified to ensure that it is consistently and effectively applied.

Effective Implementation of Education Law and the "Unofficial" Codes of Conduct

Of course, developing equality-based education law is only half of the battle. As was previously stated, the law must be clear and consistently applied so that schools are able to commit to the promotion of a safe and inclusive culture. Education legislation and provincial codes of conduct must be free from ambiguity, and must affirmatively promote equality, while maintaining meaningful consequences for those who breach the standards.

In order to ensure consistent application and enforcement of education law, it is essential to define within the legislation the responsibilities of school administration and teachers when it comes to intervening in sexualized cyberbullying. In her testimony to the Senate Standing Committee on Human Rights, Elizabeth Meyer noted:

> Teachers feel they have very limited influence and authority in school settings, especially related to cyberbullying. However, they are often the ones tasked with tackling these complex and difficult issues because they have the most direct contact with the students ... conflicting legal decisions leave schools with no

clear guidance on how to respond. Teachers and administrators feel insecure and powerless to intervene. Schools need clear jurisdiction to be able to address incidents that take place off-campus but clearly impact students' feelings of safety at school and, by extension, in their community.[141]

School administrators, teachers, and students must be empowered and given the appropriate tools to prevent sexualized cyberbullying. It is clear that when teachers and administrators feel "insecure and powerless to intervene," there is a greater risk that victims of sexualized cyberbullying will continue to be isolated from support systems.[142]

It may also be worthwhile to consider the "unofficial codes of conduct" that govern secondary schools. Donn Short has stated that there are "hidden and informal practices that are inevitably positioned in schools" and that the effectiveness of equality policies are "negatively impacted not by structural obstacles to their implementation but by the presence of other interacting normative regimes that complicate the effectiveness of policies."[143] He further explains that the literature thus far on bullying and cyberbullying has not investigated the overlap between "formal state law" (education acts, provincial codes of conduct) and the "normalizing culture of the daily life of schools with respect to gender, sexuality, and other norms … which complicates and interacts with formal law."[144] It is important to question whether "formal state law" can ever fully address sexualized cyberbullying if it fails "to account for the perpetuation of social norms within youth culture."[145]

Of course, "laws, policies, and procedures can only do so much."[146] Laws and policies do not ensure an equality-based normative regime between students at schools. Nor do they "guarantee good relationships."[147]However, "good relationships" and inclusive "unofficial codes of conduct" can be created through positive school climates, which can have a significant impact on eliminating instances of cyberbullying.[148] Developing a positive school climate with equality as its "substance" may be a challenge; however, "progress can be made by recognizing that everyone in the broader school community is an equal participant in fostering change."[149] In his testimony to the Standing Senate Committee on Human Rights, William Gardner explained:

> The response we advocate in terms of cyberbullying for schools is something we call the whole-of-school-community approach. This reiterates some of what the previous witnesses were saying about the school reaching beyond the school gate .... There is a role for everyone within this community in preventing and responding to cyberbullying, and we want to engender that approach when we talk about cyberbullying in schools.[150]

Education law "is certainly not the only tool for reform."[151] The *Task Force Report* stresses that "partnering and networking among the many stakeholders, educating the various audiences and implementing preventative measures" are all crucial aspects to reducing sexualized cyberbullying.[152] However, education law is a key vehicle that reflects "our core values and principles and indicate[s] what we stand for as a society."[153] In that context, education law should serve as the "lighthouse of equality," guiding administrators, teachers, and students to equality, safety, and inclusivity.[154]

Conclusion

One goal of education in Canada is to promote "equality, respect and tolerance."[155] As stated in the seminal United States case *Brown v. Board of Education of Topeka*, "education is perhaps the most important function of state and local governments ... it is the very foundation of good citizenship."[156] The Supreme Court of Canada has explained, "education awakens children to the values a society hopes to foster and to nurture."[157] However, education can only do this if our schools are equality-based, inclusive, and safe. Effective education law can and should serve as a catalyst for change amongst administration, teachers, and students to ensure an equal and inclusive environment. With equality as its foundation, education law can give a voice to those who have experienced sexualized cyberbullying – and will ensure that the experiences of too many girls, including Rehtaeh, Amanda, and A.B., lead to positive change.

Acknowledgements

I was inspired, in part, to write this paper after reading Donn Short's book *Don't Be So Gay! Queers, Bullying, and Making Schools Safe*,[158] and after conversation with Jane Bailey, who highlighted the value in examining the impacts of cyberbullying on teen girls from the perspective of an equality lens. I would like to thank the participants of the eGirls Project workshop, and Jane Bailey, Val Steeves, Ben Bisset, Wayne MacKay, Glen Canning, and Leah Parsons for their thoughtful comments.

Notes

1   *A.B. v. Bragg Communications Inc.*, 2012 SCC 46, <https://scc-csc.lexum.com/scc-csc-scc-csc/en/item/10007/index.do>, [2012] 2 S.C.R. 567.
2   Kalen Lumsden, "Bullying and Balancing Rights in *A.B. v. Bragg Communications*," IP Osgoode, 16 November 2012, <http://www.iposgoode.ca/2012/11/bullying-and-balancing-rights-in-ab-v-bragg-communications/>.
3   *A.B. v. Bragg*, *supra* note 1 at para 1.
4   *Ibid.*
5   Lumsden, *supra* note 2.
6   *A.B. v. Bragg*, *supra* note 1 at para 10.
7   *Ibid.*, at para 14.
8   *Ibid.*, at para 27.
9   Gillian Shaw, "Amanda Todd's Mother Speaks Out about Her Daughter, Bullying," *Vancouver Sun*, 13 March 2013, <http://www.vancouversun.com/news/Amanda+Todd+mother+speaks_about+daughter+bullying+with+video/7384521/story.html>.
10 "The Sextortion of Amanda Todd," Documentary, *The Fifth Estate*, CBC, 2013.
11 Jennifer Dunning, "Amanda Todd, Sextortion and Cyberbullying," CBC, 13 November 2013, <http://www.cbc.ca/newsblogs/yourcommunity/2013/11/amanda-todd-and-sextortion.html>.
12 Tara Carman, "Amanda Todd: School Districts Have Limited Reach with Anti-bullying Tactics," *Vancouver Sun*, 16 October 2012, <http://www.vancouversun.com/news/Amanda+Todd+School+districts+have+limited+reach+with+anti+bullying+tactics/7394300/story.html>.
13 Jordan Venton-Rublee, "Rehtaeh Parsons' Father Speaks at McGill," *McGill Daily*, 7 October 2013, <http://www.mcgilldaily.com/2013/10/rehtaeh-parsons-father-speaks-at-mcgill/>.
14 "Rehtaeh Parsons, Canadian Girl, Dies after Suicide Attempt; Parents Allege She Was Raped by 4 Boys," *Huffington Post*, 9 April 2013, <http://www.huffingtonpost.com/2013/04/09/rehtaeh-parsons-girl-dies-suicide-rape-canada_n_3045033.html>.
15 *Ibid.*

16   Frances Willick & Sherri Borden Colley, "School Administration Didn't Probe Incident," *Chronicle Herald*, 9 April 2013, <http://www.thechronicle-herald.ca/metro/1122506-school-administration-didn-t-probe-incident>.

17   *Ibid.*

18   Task Force on Bullying and Cyberbullying, *Respectful and Responsible Relationships: There's No App for That: The Report of the Nova Scotia Task Force on Bullying and Cyberbullying* (Nova Scotia: The Task Force, 2012) at 48.

19   Framing "cyberbullying" as an "education issue" also influences the terminology we use. Academics have criticized the term "cyberbullying" for being over broad, and have argued it is "an umbrella term for a wide variety of issues and behaviours." Others suggest that the term may be too "soft" for the actual consequences experienced by victims. See Jane Bailey, "Bill C-13: The Victims of 'Cyberbullying' and Canadians Deserve More", The eGirls Project, 28 November 2013, <http://www.egirlsproject.ca/2013/11/28/bill-c-13-the-victims-of-cyberbullying-and-canadians-deserve-more/>; Donalee Moulton, "Parrying Thrusts of the Cyberbully," *Lawyers Weekly*, 13 January 2012, <http://www.lawyer-sweekly.ca/index.php?section=article&articleid=1568>. For the purposes of this contribution, I use the term "cyberbullying" but do agree that in many circumstances the preferred terminology should include "sexual violence," "assault," "intimidation," and "harassment."

20   Designating cyberbullying as an "education issue" is demonstrated in part by lawsuits filed by parents against school boards for failing to address bullying. For example, in 2011 four claims were filed in Ontario against the Bluewater School Board for failing to protect students from bullies. Similar lawsuits have also appeared in Vancouver, Winnipeg and Ottawa. See Stephanie Findlay, "Bullying Victims Are Taking Schools to Court," *Maclean's*, 14 September 2011, <http://www.macleans.ca/news/canada/taking-schools-to-court/>.

21   See *Cyber-safety Act*, SNS 2013, c. 2, <http://www.nslegislature.ca/legc/bills/61st_5th/3rd_read/b061.htm> and Bill C-13, *Protecting Canadians from Online Crime Act*, 2nd Sess, 41st Parl, 2014. The inadequacy of a purely criminal law approach is addressed in Shariff & DeMartini, Chapter XI.

22   A. Wayne MacKay, "Safe and Inclusive Schooling = Expensive/Quality Education = Priceless/ For Everything Else There are Lawyers," *Education & Law Journal* 18 (2008): 21, ISSN: 0838-2875.

23   *Ibid.*

24   A. Wayne MacKay, Lyle Sutherland & Kimberley D. Pochini, *Teachers and the Law: Diverse Roles and New Challenges,* 3rd ed. (Toronto: EMP, 2013), 115.

25   Tim McCaskell, *Race to Equity: Disrupting Educational Inequality* (Toronto: Between the Lines, 2005), 182.

26 Donn Short, *Don't Be So Gay! Queers, Bullying, and Making Schools Safe* (Vancouver: UBC Press, 2013), 38.

27 New Brunswick, *MacKay Report on Inclusion, Inclusion: What is Inclusion Anyway?* (New Brunswick: MacKay Report, 2007).

28 McCaskell, *supra* note 25 at 230–231.

29 For the purposes of this paper, I chose to focus on education legislation specific to public schools.

30 Jane Bailey, "'Sexualized Online Bullying' Through an Equality Lens: Missed Opportunity in *A.B. v. Bragg?*," *McGill Law Journal* 59 (2013–2014): 709.

31 Catharine MacKinnon, "Reflections on Sex Equality Under Law," *Yale Law Journal* 100:5 (1991): 1298, doi:0.2307/796693.

32 Statistics Canada, *Measuring Violence against Women: Statistical Trends ed.* *Maire Sinha,* (Ottawa: StatCan, 2013), < http://www.statcan.gc.ca/pub/85-002-x/2013001/article/11766-eng.htm >.

33 *Ibid.*

34 MacKinnon, *supra* note 31 at 1301.

35 *Ibid.,* at 1302.

36 See for example: Maggie Macaulay, "Is Critique of 'Rape Culture' Enough? Waving the Feminist Arms in the Academy," *Rabble* (September 2013), <http://www.rabble.ca/blogs/bloggers/campus-notes/2013/09/critique-rape-culture-enough-waving-feminist-arms-academy>; Government of Newfoundland & Labrador, "Violence Against Aboriginal Women Fact Sheet," 2013, <http://www.gov.nl.ca/vpi/facts/VAW_EN_Fact%20Sheet_Aboriginal_Women.pdf>; DAWN Canada, "Women with Disabilities and Violence," DAWN January 2014, <www.dawncanada.net/main/wp-content/uploads/2014/03/English-Violence-January-2014.pdf>.

37 Government of Newfoundland & Labrador, "Violence Against Women with Disabilities Fact Sheet," 2013, <http://www.gov.nl.ca/VPI/facts/violence_against_women_with_disabilities_fs.pdf>.

38 Government of Newfoundland & Labrador, *supra* note 36.

39 Toronto Anarchist Bookfair, "Sexual Assault and Consent Policy Statement," *Toronto Anarchist Bookfair (blog)*, July 2014, <http://www.toronto-anarchistbookfair.wordpress.com/sexual-assault-and-consent-policy/>.

40 Jo-Anne Lee, "Amanda Todd, More Than Bullying," *Antidote,* November 2012, <http://www.antidotenetwork.org/2012/11/amanda-todd-more-than-bullying-part-1>.

41 MacKinnon, *supra* note 31 at 1306; Short, *supra* note 26.

42 Senate Standing Committee on Human Rights, *Cyberbullying Hurts: Respect for Rights in the Digital Age* (Canada: December 2012), 8–9, <http://www.parl.gc.ca/content/SEN/committee/411/ridr/rep/rep09dec12-e.pdf>.

43 *Nova Scotia Task Force Report, supra* note 18 at 40.

44   *Ibid.*, at 42–43.

45   *Ibid.*, at 43.

46   Keith Sullivan, *The Anti-Bullying Handbook,* 2nd ed. (Ireland: National University of Ireland, 2011), 54.

47   *Ibid.*

48   See for example: Danielle Keats Citron, "Law's Expressive Value in Combatting Cyber Gender Harassment," *Michigan Law Review* 108 (2009), ISSN: 0026-2234: 373; Jane Bailey Valerie Steeves, Jacquelyn Burkell & Priscilla Regan, "Negotiating with Gender Stereotypes on Social Networking Sites: From 'Bicycle Face' to Facebook," *Journal of Communication Inquiry,* doi:10.1177/0196859912473777. Moreover, a recent Canadian survey reveals that "girls are twice as likely as boys to see online threats as a serious problem," see Valerie Steeves, *Young Canadians in a Wired World, Phase III: Cyberbullying: Dealing with Online Meanness, Cruelty and Threats* (MediaSmarts: 2014), 3, <http://mediasmarts.ca/sites/mediasmarts/files/pdfs/publication-report/full/YCWWIII_Cyberbullying_FullReport.pdf>.

49   Susan O'Neil, *Bullying by Tween and Teen Girls: A Literature, Policy and Resource Review, Ecole Heather Park Elementary,* <http://hpar.sd57. bc.ca/~sfleck/HPES_Behavior/bullying/female_relational_agression. pdf>; Keats Citron, *supra* note 48; Bailey et al, *supra* note 48.

50   O'Neil, *ibid.*

51   *Nova Scotia Task Force Report, supra* note 18 at 14. See also Regan & Sweet, Chapter VII, reporting on online drama in the context of the eGirls Project findings.

52   Alice Marwick & danah boyd, "The Drama! Teen Conflict, Gossip and Bullying in Networked Publics, paper presented at Oxford Internet Institute's "A Decade in Internet Time: Symposium on the Dynamics of the Internet and Society," Oxford, 22 September 2011, <http://www. academia.edu/2672673/The_Drama_Teen_Conflict_Gossip_and_Bullying_in_Networked_Publics>. Distinguishing between situations in which comments made are simply drama without material negative effects and those which lead to serious harm is a key challenge to developing meaningful policy responses, see Steeves, *supra* note 48 at 8.

53   Senate, *supra* note 42 at 42.

54   *Ibid.*

55   *Ibid.*, at 47.

56   *Ibid.*

57   For example, see Karen D. Pyke, "What Is Internalized Racial Oppression and Why Don't We Study It? Acknowledging Racism's Hidden Injuries," *Sociological Perspectives* 53:4 (2010): 551, for a discussion of internalized oppression and internalized racism. Arguably, internalized oppression in the context of sexualized cyberbullying may have similar deleterious effects as the internalization of racist hate speech.

58   Keats Citron, *supra* note 48.
59   Laura Choate, *Adolescent Girls in Distress: A Guide for Mental Health Treatment and Prevention* (New York: Springer, 2013), 15.
60   Bailey et al, *supra* note 48 at 18. See Bailey, Chapter I; Steeves, Chapter VI.
61   Choate, *supra* note 59 at 24.
62   Sullivan, *supra* note 46 at 55.
63   *Ibid.*
64   Willick & Borden Colley, *supra* note 16.
65   MacKay et al & Borden Colley , *supra* note 24 at 10.
66   *Ibid.*, at 115.
67   Short, *supra* note 26 at 101.
68   *Ibid.*, at 103.
69   *Ibid.*, at 236.
70   MacKay, *supra* note 22 at 23.
71   *Ibid.*
72   *Ross v. New Brunswick School District No 15*, [1996] 1 SCR 825, <https://www.canlii.org/en/ca/scc/doc/1996/1996canlii237/1996canlii237.html> [1996] canLII 237 (SCC).
73   Sullivan, *supra* note 46 at 18.
74   Claire Feltrin, "Girls Online – Canadian Provinces Policy Review," The eGirls Project, May 2013, <http://egirlsproject.files.wordpress.com/2013/09/canada-provinces-policy-review-2013.pdf>.
75   *School Act*, R.S.B.C. 1996, c. 412, <http://www.bced.gov.bc.ca/legislation/schoollaw/revisedstatutescontents.pdf>.
76   *Ibid.*
77   *Chamberlain v Surrey School District No 36*, 2002 SCC 86, <http://www.scc-csc.lexum.com/scc-csc/scc-csc/en/item/2030/index.do>, [2002] 4 S.C.R. 710.
78   *Ibid.*, at para 23.
79   *School Act, supra* note 75, at s. 74.01.
80   *Ibid.*, at s. 6.
81   *School Regulation, B.C. Reg. 265/1989*, at s. 4, <http://www.bced.gov.bc.ca/legilsation/schoollaw/d/bcreg_265-89.pdf>.
82   Short, *supra* note 26 at 96.
83   *Ibid.*
84   *Ibid.*
85   *Ibid.*, at 96.
86   British Columbia, Ministry of Education, *Safe, Caring and Orderly Schools: A Guide (BC: 2008)*, <http:///www.bced.gov.bc.ca/sco/guide/scoguide.pdf>.
87   *Ibid.*
88   *Ibid.*, at 9.
89   *Ibid.*, at 31.

90 *Provincial Standards for Codes of Conduct Order, Ministerial Order 276/07,* (2007), *(School Act).*

91 British Columbia, Ministry of Education, *Developing and Reviewing Codes of Conduct: A Companion* (BC: 2007), <http:///www.bced.gov.bc.ca/sco/resourcedocs/facilitators_companion.pdf>.

92 *Provincial Standards for Codes of Conduct, supra* note 90.

93 *Developing and Reviewing Codes of Conduct, supra* note 91.

94 *Ibid.* The definition of bullying behaviour, and cyberbullying does not address sexualized cyberbullying.

95 Dirk Meissner, "Amanda Todd's Legacy: A Look at Canada's Anti-Bullying Efforts a Year after Her Death," *CTV News,* 9 October 2013, <http://www.ctvnews.ca/canada/amanda-todd-s-legacy-a-look-at-canada-s-anti-bullying-efforts-a-year-after-her-death-1.1490889>.

96 ERASE Bullying, "Policy to Action," <http://www.erasebullying.ca/policy/policy.php>.

97 *Education Act,* R.S.O. 1990, c. E.2, <http://www.e-laws.gov.on.ca/html/statutes/English/elaws_statutes_90e02_e_htm>.

98 *Accepting Schools Act,* S.O. 2012, c. 5, <http://ontla.on.ca/web/bills/bills_detail.do?locale=en&BillID=2549>.

99 *Education Act, supra* note 97.

100 *Ibid.*

101 *Ibid.,* at s. 1.

102 *Ibid.,* at s. 8.

103 *Ibid.,* at s. 303.

104 *Ibid.,* at s. 301.

105 *Ibid.,* at s. 301.

106 *Ibid.,* at s. 301.

107 *Ibid.,* at ss. 306 and 310. These sections were amended as a result of the *Education Amendment Act (Progressive Discipline and School Safety)* S.O. 2007, c. 14, <http://www.e-laws.gov.on.ca/html/source/statutes/English/2007/elaws_src_s07014_e.htm>.

108 Eric M. Roher, "Dealing with Off-school Conduct: Cyberbullying, Drug Dealing and Other Activities Off School Property," *Education & Law Journal* 21 (2012): 91, ISSN: 0838-2875.

109 *Ibid.*

110 Education Act, *supra* note 97.

111 Ontario, *The Provincial Code of Conduct, Policy No 128,* 2012, <http://www.edu.gov.on.ca/extra/eng/ppm/128.pdf>.

112 *Ibid.,* at 6.

113 *Ibid.*

114 *Ibid.*

115 *Ibid.,* at 2.

116 *Ibid.,* at 3.

117 Canadian Press, "What Ontario's New Sex Ed Curriculum Teaches in Grades 1 through 12" *Global News*, 23 February 2015, <http://globalnews.ca/news/1845754/what-ontarios-new-sex-ed-curriculum-teaches-in-grades-1-through-12/>.

118 For example, students in elementary school will learn about "how to assess risk, respond to dangerous situations, and protect themselves from a variety of social dangers [including] … bullying … violence, and technology-related risks," while secondary school students will learn about "responding to bullying/harassment (including sexual harassment, gender-based violence, homophobia and racism)," *The Ontario Curriculum Grades 1–8: Health and Physical Education* (Ontario Elementary, 2015): 127; *The Ontario Curriculum Grades 9 to 12: Health and Physical Education* (Ontario Secondary, 2015): 38.

119 Ontario Elementary, *supra* at 82, 127.

120 Ontario Secondary, *supra* at 101, 104, 159.

121 Feltrin, *supra* note 74.

122 *Promotion of Respectful and Responsible Relationships Act*, SNS 2012, c. 14, <http://www.nslegislature.ca/legc/PDFs/annual%20statutes/2012%20Spring/c014.pdf>. Nova Scotia Task Force Report, *supra* note 18.

123 *Cyber-safety Act, supra* note 21.

124 Feltrin, *supra* note 74.

125 *Education Act, SNS 1995-96, c. 1*, <http://www.nslegislature.ca/legc/statutes/education.pdf>.

126 *Ibid.*

127 *Ibid.*

128 CCSO Cybercrime Working Group, *Cyberbullying and the Non-Consensual Distribution of Intimate Images* (Ottawa: Department of Justice Canada, 2013), <http://www.justice.gc.ca/eng/rp-pr/other-autre/cndii-cdncii/pdf/cndii-cdncii-eng.pdf>.

129 *Education Act, supra* note 125 at s. 141.

130 *Cyber-safety Act, supra* note 21 at s. 3.

131 *Ministerial Education Act Regulations*, N.S. Reg. 80/97, s. 47, <http://www.novascotia.ca/just/regulations/regs/edmin.htm>.

132 Robyn Urback, "Nova Scotia Cyber Law Turns Bullied into Bullies", *National Post*, 8 September 2013, <http://fullcomment.nationalpost.com/2013/09/09/robyn-urback-nova-scotia-cyber-law-turns-bullied-into-bullies/>.

133 *Ibid.*

134 Jesse Brown, "Nova Scotia's Awful Cyber Abuse Law Makes Bullies of Us All," *Maclean's*, 8 August 2013, <http://www.macleans.ca/society/technology/nova-scotias-awful-cyber-abuse-law-makes-bullies-of-us-all>.

135 Patricia Brooks Arenburg, "Legal Experts Question Haste of Rehtaeh's Law," *Chronicle Herald*, 16 August 2013, <http://www.thechronicleherald.ca/novascotia/1148032-legal-experts-question-haste-of-rehtaeh-s-law>.

136 *Education Act, supra* note 125 at s. 122.

137 Debra Pepler & Penny Milton, *External Review of the Halifax Regional School Board's Support of Rehtaeh Parsons*, (Nova Scotia, 2013), 10, <http://www.ednet.ca/files/reports/External%20Review%20of%20HRSB%20Final.pdf>.

138 *Ibid., at 11.*

139 Department of Education, *Provincial School Code of Conduct and School Code of Conduct Guidelines*, (Nova Scotia, 2008), <http://www.studentservices.ednet.ca/sites/default/files/provincial_school_code_of%20conduct.pdf>.

140 *Ibid., at 5.*

141 Senate, *supra* note 42 at 64.

142 *Ibid.*

143 Short, *supra* note 26 at 178.

144 *Ibid.*

145 Short, *supra* note 26 at 178. The importance of addressing problematic social norms through digital literacy and digital citizenship initiatives is addressed in detail in Johnson, Chapter XIII.

146 Pepler & Milton, *supra* note 137 at 12.

147 *Ibid.*

148 Senate, *supra* note 42 at 59.

149 *Ibid.*

150 *Ibid.*

151 *Nova Scotia Task Force Report, supra* note 18 at 48.

152 *Ibid.*

153 *Ibid.*

154 MacKay, *supra* note 22.

155 *Ross, supra* note 73 at para 82.

156 *Brown v. Board of Education of Topeka, 347 US 483* (1954) at 493.

157 *Ross, supra* note 73 at para 82.

158 Short, *supra* note 26.

PART IV

eGIRLS, eCITIZENS

Digital Literacy and Digital Citizenship: Approaches to Girls' Online Experiences

Matthew Johnson

Towards a Digital Citizenship Approach to Education

Often efforts to educate young people about digital technology have focused primarily on teaching them to protect themselves online. This focus on "online safety" has been tremendously influential for a number of reasons: first, many educational programs have been provided by or developed in collaboration with law enforcement agencies;[1] second, the content of these programs has accorded with a perception, largely a result of media reporting, that digital environments are particularly risky compared to offline spaces;[2] third, a cultural tendency towards "juvenoia" — a term coined by David Finkelhor of the Crimes Against Children Research Center to describe "an exaggerated fear about the influence of social change on children and youth"[3] — is currently pervasive. This response manifests itself both as fear *for* children and fear *of* children, and, as the earlier "predator panic" has been supplemented with alarm over cyberbullying, the two have essentially merged.

MediaSmarts' research project Young Canadians in a Wired World found that adults and youth have absorbed the internet safety message. Parents in our focus groups spoke often of feeling pressured to take any steps they could to keep their children safe, including subjecting them to constant monitoring;[4] almost half of the students in our quantitative survey felt that the internet was an unsafe place for them, and almost three-quarters agreed with the statement "I could be hurt if I talk to someone I don't know online."[5] These figures become even more striking when we look at the gender breakdown: significantly more girls than boys (49 percent compared to 39 percent) felt that the internet was an unsafe space for them, and 82 percent of girls—compared to just 63 percent of boys—feared they could be hurt if they talked to someone they didn't know online. This may not be surprising: Genevieve Bell, director of Intel Corporation's Interaction and Experience Research, points out that "moral panic … is always played out in the bodies of children and women,"[6] an observation supported by our findings that more girls (52 percent) than boys (44 percent) felt their parents were worried that they can get online.[7]

Leaving aside other criticisms of the online safety model (such as the fact that it is based on incorrect assumptions of the actual risks facing youth),[8] it is clear from this data that it has a particularly negative impact on girls, who may be deprived of opportunities online due to exaggerated safety concerns. They may also be particularly disadvantaged in their acquisition of digital skills, including (ironically) the ability to manage online risk: research suggests that more restrictive approaches based on the online safety model produce students who are less able to keep themselves safe online and are generally less confident and capable users of digital technology.[9] As well, the narrow focus of the online safety approach prevents educators from addressing many issues of key importance to girls, such as the effects of digital media on body image. For this reason, we argue that the online safety model be discarded in public awareness campaigns, classrooms, and curricula and replaced with a focus on digital literacy and digital citizenship.

MediaSmarts has been a pioneer in promoting media literacy, digital literacy, and digital citizenship in a Canadian context.[10] With a primary focus on parents and teachers of youth in the K–12 sector, the organization produces resources such as tip sheets, lesson plans, professional development packages, and interactive classroom tutorials that prepare adults in children's lives to help them to face the challenges they will face in mass media and the digital environment and to take advantage of the opportunities they will encounter. As well as its efforts in education and public awareness, MediaSmarts periodically conducts a research project titled *Young Canadians in a Wired World*; the latest iteration, Phase III (conducted between 2011 and 2013), gives a snapshot of what Canadian youth are doing online, their opinions about and experiences in the digital realm, and what digital literacy skills they are learning and from whom. The data gathered is an invaluable resource in developing MediaSmarts' approach to digital literacy and digital citizenship education.

Both "digital literacy" and "digital citizenship" are terms that lack fully agreed upon definitions, so it will be useful to define them here. MediaSmarts uses a definition of digital literacy organized around three main areas of competency – *use, understand,* and *create:*

> 1. *Use* represents the technical fluency needed to engage with computers and the internet. Skills and competencies that fall under "use" range from basic technical know-how – using computer programs such as word processors, web browsers, email, and other communication tools – to the more sophisticated abilities for accessing and using knowledge resources, such as search engines and online databases, and emerging technologies such as cloud computing.
>
> 2. *Understand* is that critical piece – it's the set of skills that help us comprehend, contextualize, and critically evaluate digital media, so that we can make informed decisions about what we do and encounter online. These are the essential skills that we need to start teaching our kids as soon as they go online.
>
> *Understand* includes recognizing how networked technology affects our behaviour and our perceptions, beliefs and feelings about the world around us.
>
> *Understand* also prepares us for a knowledge economy as we develop – individually and collectively – information management skills for finding, evaluating, and effectively using information to communicate, collaborate, and solve problems.
>
> 3. *Create* is the ability to produce content and effectively communicate through a variety of digital media tools. Creation with digital media is more than knowing how to use a word processor or write an email: it includes being able to adapt what we produce for various contexts and audiences; to create and communicate using rich media such as images, video, and sound; and to effectively and responsibly engage with Web 2.0 user-generated content such as blogs and discussion forums, video and photo sharing, social gaming, and other forms of social media.

> The ability to create using digital media ensures that Canadians are active contributors to digital society. Creation — whether through blogs, tweets, wikis or any of the hundreds of avenues for expression and sharing online — is at the heart of citizenship and innovation.[11]

What is most important about this model is that it is concerned with developing skills rather than with producing an end result such as safety. Because it is focused exclusively on skills, however, some feel that it needs to be supplemented with education in digital citizenship. This is another disputed term,[12] but what's useful about the concept is that it recognizes that youth can act as full citizens of online communities in a way that they often cannot fully act as citizens in their offline lives, and as a result have rights and responsibilities (though digital citizenship programs often emphasize the latter at the expense of the former, and may be used to "rebrand" online safety narratives). Young people's online citizenship may also serve as a bridge to getting them involved in causes or communities offline. Digital citizenship also recognizes that the main risks to youth are from youth, whether themselves or their peers, but, unlike anti-cyberbullying programs that are based on the online safety model, the emphasis is on encouraging youth to be aware of what they can achieve online and to use that ability responsibly, rather than deterring unwanted behaviour through the threat of punishment. Another reason that digital citizenship is an important supplement to digital literacy is that while it focuses on the online context, the attributes that digital citizenship education seeks to develop originate outside of that context and are applicable to all parts of a person's life. These attributes can be summarized as empathy, ethics, and activism.

Empathy is an essential element of citizenship in its broadest sense as participation in society. We tend to think of empathy as an attribute, something we either have or do not have, but we actually choose, mostly unconsciously, whether or not to feel empathy in a particular context. That choice can be influenced by a number of factors,[13] and the online context has a number of features that may inhibit empathy: in particular, some or all of the things that trigger empathy in us — a person's tone of voice, body language, and facial expression[14] — are often absent when we interact with them online.

Ethics and empathy are closely linked because the first steps in making an ethical decision are to identify the situation as a moral issue (rather than a strictly practical one) and to understand the issue emotionally.[15] Unfortunately, youth often don't view their online actions and experiences in ethical terms,[16] but MediaSmarts' *Young Canadians in a Wired World* research suggests that teaching young people ethical decision making can play a significant role in their online behaviour: in most cases, for instance, the presence of a household rule has a strong relationship with whether or not youth engage in risky or problematic behaviour.[17] More specifically, the presence of a rule about treating people with respect online – which requires youth to exercise both empathy and ethical thinking – had a strong relationship with a lower rate of being mean or cruel to someone online.[18]

The third element of digital citizenship is activism. Though this term has become politicized, in a context of citizenship it simply means taking an active role in the affairs of one's state or community. Online activism may involve using digital media to engage with issues in the local community or state politics, and may be as broadly focused as tuition rates[19] or as narrow as the quality of school lunches.[20] Our research found that 35 percent of Canadian youth had joined or supported an activist group online at least once.[21] Activism may also focus specifically on influencing online communities, such as campaigns aimed at improving the climate of social media.[22] Because of the corporate nature of nearly all online environments frequented by youth (only one of the top ten websites among Canadian youth, *Wikipedia*, is not owned by a for-profit corporation),[23] it is also important to include consumer activism in our definition of digital citizenship. Consumer activism involves a recognition of the corporate nature of most online "communities" and "public spaces" as well as an understanding of what rights youth possess as consumers and how to exercise them, including using complaint mechanisms and organizing public pressure campaigns (such as the effort to get Facebook to be more responsive to complaints about hate material).[24]

Finally, media literacy is also a key element of both digital literacy and digital citizenship. This is partly because an understanding of the key concepts of media literacy, such as recognizing that both traditional and digital media are largely commercial products and that they have social and political implications,[25] is needed to be able to critically engage with online content or understand and exercise one's rights as a digital citizen.

Media Literacy–Based Approaches to Girls' Online Issues

Many of the issues that youth face online affect girls in ways that are different from and sometimes disproportionate to the ways they affect boys. For that reason, it is important that digital literacy and digital citizenship programs consider girls' particular experiences online. At the same time, it is also important that boys not be left out of discussions of "girls' issues" in order to shift the narrative away from "girls' need to protect themselves" to *all* youth need to be responsible, ethical, and active digital citizens.

Young people constantly face decisions about privacy while online, both how to manage their own privacy and what to do with others' content. Our research shows that young Canadians do have strong notions of privacy, and many take positive steps to manage it, such as keeping contact information private, disguising their online identities, deleting online content they have created, and using social network blocking tools to determine which audiences see particular content.[26]

Youth also rely on social norms around online privacy: nine out of ten students expect a friend to ask before posting a bad or embarrassing photo of them, and just over half expect friends to ask before posting a good photo as well. Social strategies are also preferred when it comes to dealing with a loss of control over privacy. The most popular strategies for dealing with unwanted photos being posted online are to ask the person to take the photo down (80 percent of all students said they would do this) and to untag the photo, which 40 percent of students said they would do. (Though untagging is a technical measure, it is also a social one because there's nothing preventing the photo from being re-tagged with your name; a key part of untagging, therefore, is communicating to the person who posted the photo that you do not want it to be tagged with your name.)[27]

While social means were overall the most popular responses, they were more popular among girls than boys; responses that involved taking direct action (such as logging into the poster's account and taking the photo down) or appeals to authority (such as teachers, school principals, or the social media provider itself), which were much less popular overall, were more popular among boys than girls. Girls were more likely to turn to parents, but since parents – unlike school staff or social media providers – are unable to take direct action, appealing to them can be seen as more of a social strategy.[28] Perhaps further research could explore whether or not girls are setting the social norms for how to deal with privacy and identity issues online, and whether or not boys prefer approaches that do not involve direct communication and social negotiation.

Given that the most popular strategies rely on social negotiation, it makes sense for educators to, as John Dewey put it, "meet the child where he or she is ... and encourage that child to take the next step" by teaching privacy management in terms of respecting and acting within social norms on privacy.[29] Our interactive resource "MyWorld," for instance, presents students with privacy dilemmas within a social context, such as the correct response to having an embarrassing photo of you posted and what to do when you receive.[30] Our findings also show the importance of promoting positive social norms about respect for others' privacy among youth, which is a key element of our resource and professional development series "Stay on the Path: Teaching Kids to Be Safe and Ethical Online." This resource helps parents, teachers, and other adults who care for young people understand how children's moral and emotional development influences the decisions they make and informs the best ways to help them see the digital environment through an ethical framework and to develop their personal morality. It explores the question of privacy by examining the reasons why youth may share their and others' personal material and provides guidance for helping youth deal with accidental or intentional "oversharing."[31]

Social expectations may also influence decisions on sharing sensitive content. Some youth may have difficulty in opting out of the "sexual banter, gossip, discussion" that happens online, and while this pressure may lead both girls and boys to send sexts, the same pressure can also push boys in particular to share sexts they receive with their peers to win social approval – or to avoid the social risks that can come from refusing to do so.[32] There is little evidence that sending sexts is by itself a risky act. For example, in one study, American university students reported positive experiences.[33] Where harm is most likely to occur is when sexts are shared or forwarded. While a sext that is only ever seen by the original recipient is unlikely to cause any harm, the risks caused by sexts that are seen by other recipients are obvious. Contrary to widespread perceptions that sharing of sexts is rampant, our research found that it is far from common behaviour: of the 24 percent of students in grades 7 to 11 with cellphone access who have received a sext directly from the sender, just 15 percent (or 4 percent of all students in grades 7 to 11 with cell phone access) have forwarded one to someone else. Our research suggests that those sexts that are forwarded, however, may reach a fairly wide audience: one in five students say that they have received a sext that was forwarded to them by a third party.[34]

There has been little research into identifying which youth are more likely to forward sexts that they receive, but our research on the effect of household rules on students' behaviour provides an interesting insight. While we found a strong connection between household rules and student behaviour in general – and, in particular, that the presence of a household rule on treating others with respect online has a strong association with not being mean or cruel online[35] – there is no relationship between the presence of such a rule and whether or not students forward sexts.[36]

Having a sext of oneself forwarded, of course, has particular consequences for girls: though sexts sent by boys are actually more likely to be forwarded,[37] girls who send sexts are often subject to greater social disapproval than boys.[38] Our qualitative research suggests that girls who send sexts are seen as having transgressed appropriate gender roles and, therefore, given up the right to expect that their images will not be shared or forwarded.[39] Gender roles may also contribute to sharing sexts being seen as a positive act, both as a sanction on inappropriate behaviour by girls and as something that is rewarded by status among boys (some studies have shown that boys gain status by sharing and forwarding sexts that were sent to them.)[40] While the public understanding of cyberbullying has become somewhat more nuanced, advice to parents and youth on sexting still draws heavily on the online safety model.[41] As a result, the advice focuses on how potential senders of sexts can protect themselves from negative consequences rather than on the ethical responsibility of those who receive them. A digital literacy approach, on the other hand, goes beyond simply telling girls not to send sexts to helping all youth to recognize and deal with unhealthy relationships. One study suggests that youth who are coerced or pressured into sending sexts are three times more likely to experience negative consequences than those who send them willingly.[42] This approach encourages young people to think through the ethical ramifications of forwarding sexts they receive – both of which are major components of our youth tip sheet *Think before You Share*.[43]

Much of the harm that comes from sexting seems to be related to gender-related double standards that portray girls both as innocent guardians of their sexual innocence and, if they should stray from that role, as being responsible for any consequences they might suffer as a result of their actions.[44] Research has found that these stereotypes are found even in educational anti-sexting campaigns, another way in which poorly considered interventions may cause more harm than good.[45] Because these gender norms are often communicated and reinforced by mass media, media literacy must be a part of any program that aims to mitigate the possible risks of sexting. MediaSmarts' many lessons on media and gender – from "Girls and Boys on Television" for grades 3 to 6 to "Gender Messages in Alcohol Advertising" for grades 7 to 10[46] – provide teachers with tools for deconstructing gender norms, while parent tip sheets like *Talking to Kids about Gender Stereotypes* and *Little Princesses and Fairy Tale Stereotypes* help parents talk about the issues with their children.[47]

While youth are most concerned about controlling their personal information, particularly photos, there are other dimensions to privacy. To be active and engaged digital citizens – especially when participating in online communities that exist to make a profit for corporations – youth need to have an understanding of data privacy as well. Unfortunately, our research shows that Canadian youth have received very little information on this aspect of privacy from either parents or teachers. While 82 percent of students reported that they had learned about using privacy settings from some source (including being self-taught from online sources), just 66 percent have learned anything about how corporations collect and use personal information online. Moreover, 65 percent of students have never had anyone explain a privacy policy or terms of service to them, which may explain why 68 percent of them mistakenly believe that all privacy policies guarantee that the site will not share their personal information. Girls are somewhat more likely to say that they have never learned about data privacy, though boys and girls are equally likely to overestimate the protection afforded by privacy policies.[48]

However, these findings should not be interpreted as evidence of a lack of young people's interest in the subject: 75 percent of students said they would like more control over what companies do with the content they post online, and 36 percent of students would like to learn more about how companies collect and use personal information. Considering the popularity of social networks among

Canadian girls,[49] a clear understanding of how corporations use their personal information – as well as what contractual rights they have and how they can influence corporations through collective action – are essential. MediaSmarts resources on this topic start with the educational game *Privacy Pirates*, which teaches children aged 7 to 9 that their personal information has commercial value.[50] The lesson "Online Marketing to Kids: Protecting Your Privacy" (grades 6 to 9) introduces students to the ways in which commercial websites collect personal information and to the issues surrounding children and privacy on the internet, while high school students are invited to consider the trade-offs we all make on a daily basis between maintaining our privacy and gaining access to information services in the lesson "The Privacy Dilemma."[51]

One of the most heavily gendered digital issues, from young people's point of view, is cyberbullying. This term, as has been noted elsewhere, is not one that youth see as relevant to their experience: teens, in particular, are more likely to define it as being anything *other* than what they do themselves, referring to their own behaviour with less loaded terms like "pranking"[52] or "drama."[53] What is interesting about these alternate terms is that they are very specifically gendered: pranking is defined as what boys do and drama is what girls do,[54] even if they refer to the same behaviour. Although the term "drama" implies spreading and responding to rumours, our research found that boys and girls were equally likely to have spread rumours about someone online. However, other forms of cyberbullying are more gendered: girls are more likely to post or share an embarrassing photo or video, while boys are more likely to make fun of someone's race, religion, or ethnicity, or to harass someone in an online game.[55]

The reasons given by students for cyberbullying are gendered as well, in ways that suggest that interventions may need to be better differentiated: while boys were most likely to say that they had been mean or cruel online because they were "just joking" (64 percent of boys compared to 45 percent of girls, and at 55 percent the top reason overall), they were also more than twice as likely as girls (20 percent compared to 8 percent of girls) to say that they had done it because they were bored. Girls, on the other hand, were more likely than boys to say they had been mean to get back at someone for what they had said or done to them (52 percent of girls, 45 percent of boys) or to a friend (34 percent of girls, 29 percent of boys). They also were more likely to have been mean or cruel because they were angry (29 percent of girls, 21 percent of boys) and because they simply "did not like" the other person.[56] While there are several anti-bullying programs that focus on developing empathy,[57] the empathy-building approach may be most effective in making youth less likely to bully others as a way of entertaining themselves, perform for peers, or alleviate boredom, all of which are more common motivations among boys. For interventions to be more effective for girls, however, they may need to focus more heavily on emotional self-regulation than empathy. Elizabeth Englander has noted that repeated exposure to materials that trigger an emotional reaction can "prime" people to feel negative emotions more strongly, so that a back-and-forth of texts or Facebook comments between two or more people could quickly intensify feelings of anger. According to Englander, "girls seem to be more likely than boys to experience this phenomenon."[58] Advice for witnesses to bullying (both online and offline) has to become more nuanced as well, since evidence suggests that unless youth are encouraged to feel an ethical and moral duty toward all other people, they interpret "stand up to bullying" as meaning "stand up for your friends"[59] – which, as noted above, is the third most common reason given for being mean or cruel online. Accordingly, teaching youth how to manage their emotions and how to make wise choices about what to do when they witness cyberbullying are key elements of MediaSmarts' resource package "Stay on the Path: Teaching Kids to Be Safe and Ethical Online"[60] and our upcoming interactive classroom tutorial for elementary students.

Girls are also somewhat more likely to experience online meanness and cruelty than boys, and more likely to say that it was a serious problem for them.[61] Online relationship violence is similarly gendered. This may include behaviours such as using digital technology to make threats; accessing a partner's online accounts without permission; harassing a partner's online contacts; expecting a partner to "check in" routinely via texts or GPS; pressuring a partner for sexual photos or using digital technology to pressure them for sex; or embarrassing a partner publicly using digital media. Girls are twice as likely as boys to have experienced online relationship abuse that is sexual in nature; they are also more likely to have engaged in non-sexual online relationship abuse.[62] As with sexting, these numbers underline the need to teach youth about healthy relationships, and also serve as a reminder that we have to consider both sexes as possible targets *and* perpetrators of online relationship abuse.

Girls do not only face harassment online from partners, of course, and in this area the numbers are much less equivocal. As noted above, girls are less likely to see the internet as a safe space than boys (though they are just as likely to feel they can keep themselves safe,)[63] and one reason for this may be the frequent and often public attacks on women online. Some attacks may be high profile, such as those experienced by feminist media critic Anita Sarkeesian after she launched an online campaign to fund a series of videos looking at sexism in video games,[64] but women who aren't public figures attract online hostility as well: over a third of Canadian students in grades 7 to 11 encounter sexist or racist content online at least once a week.[65] Girls are much more likely than boys to feel hurt when a racist or sexist joke is made at their expense (57 percent of girls compared to 34 percent of boys) while boys, in keeping with their attitudes towards cyberbullying, are much more likely to say they and their friends "don't mean anything by it" when they say racist or sexist things online and to not speak up against such content because "most of the time, people are just joking around."

While girls may be most affected by encountering this content, it seems likely that interventions will have to focus on boys, who are much more likely than girls to sexually harass someone online or to make fun of their religion, ethnicity, or sexual orientation.[66] Many of the online spaces frequented by boys – particularly multiplayer games – are characterized by highly aggressive and frequently racist, misogynist, and homophobic discourse.[67] One study found that playing *Halo 3* with a female voice and a female-identifying name led to three times more negative comments than playing with a male voice and male-identifying name or no voice and a gender-neutral name.[68] There has also been a rise of online hate material specifically targeting women,[69] and, like other forms of hate, this rhetoric can influence the culture of more mainstream spaces.[70] While most online misogyny is not connected to what may often be thought of as "traditional" hate groups (for example, white extremist groups), it relies on the same "ideologies" of hate such as othering and dehumanizing the target group and casting the hate group as a victim,[71] and appeals in a similar way to youth – particularly boys and young men – who feel alienated from society.[72] Young people need to be equipped with the media and digital literacy skills to recognize hate content when they encounter it – for example, an understanding of the markers of an argument based on hate – and to recognize and decode the various persuasive techniques hate groups use to build group solidarity and recruit new believers, such as employing misinformation,[73] denialism and revisionism,[74] and pseudo-science.[75] Youth also need to be empowered to speak out against hate, especially when they encounter it in mainstream spaces such as online games or social networks. MediaSmarts' "Media Diversity Toolbox" includes a resource package called "Facing Online Hate," a suite of professional development material, lesson plans, and interactive tutorials that show the ways in which online hate material does harm and provide teachers and students with the media literacy skills and digital activism tools needed to recognize, decode, and confront it.[76]

Another issue where there is a significant overlap between digital and media literacy is body image. While this is a concern for an increasing number of boys as well,[77] girls are most affected by body image concerns influenced by media and, in particular, by digital media. These concerns fall into three main areas: the distorted body ideals created by digital photo manipulation; the sense of constantly being judged and the need to be always "camera-ready" caused by social media as evidenced in the eGirls Project findings;[78] and the risks from online communities that promote eating disorders.

Retouching photos in this way raises a number of concerns. One is that the already unrealistic bodies youth are exposed to, are presented in ways that make them literally impossible: models frequently have collarbones, ribs, and even hips erased to make them look thinner.[79] Exposure to digitally altered images of women's bodies has been shown to increase body dissatisfaction in young women.[80] In 2011 the American Medical Association urged governments and industry bodies to stop retouching models, warning "we must stop exposing impressionable children and teenagers to advertisements portraying models with body types only attainable with the help of photo editing software."[81] A 2011 study found that 84 percent of British young women knew what photo manipulation was and how it was used, and the same number agreed that using it to change models' bodies should be unacceptable.[82] Unfortunately, just knowing that images are manipulated doesn't defuse their effects. As Dr. Kim Bissell, founder of the Child Media Lab at the University of Alabama, puts it, "We know they're Photoshopped, but we still want to look like that."[83]

Girls and young women often use photo manipulation software to retouch their own photos. Connie Morrison, in her book *Who Do*

They Think They Are? Teenage Girls & Their Avatars in Spaces of Social Online Communication, says, "Girls understand that the images on television and in magazines are manipulated, and for some this understanding seems to lead to an expectation that they can (or should) be doing the same."[84] As one of the girls she interviews puts it, "It makes me more comfortable ... when my profile picture is something that looks flawless and 'pretty' even though I know it's fake."[85] Even when images are not altered, however, many girls have expressed a need to always be "camera-ready" to avoid having an unflattering photo taken.[86] Use of social networks such as Facebook has been connected to higher levels of body image concerns among girls, an issue that has only grown as social networks devoted specifically to photo sharing such as Instagram, as well as photo-sharing apps like Snapchat, have become popular.[87]

While youth primarily use social networks to keep in touch with their offline friends, digital technology also makes it easier to contact people around the world who share the same interests. Although connections of this kind can often be very positive, particularly for those who live in small or isolated communities, these online communities can also reinforce negative attitudes toward body image. Most notorious are the "pro-anorexia" or "pro-ana" communities, which consist of websites, blogs, blogrings (blogs linked by a particular topic), and even discussion groups on virtual worlds such as *Stardoll*, that provide photos, tips, testimonials, and sometimes videos encouraging eating disorders.[88] Content analysis of these communities has shown that while they do provide social support for girls suffering from eating disorders, they nevertheless reinforce the behaviours associated with anorexia or bulimia as part of the social norms of the online community.[89]

Media literacy education has been shown to be one of the most successful interventions for eating disorders and body image issues.[90] Effective literacy programs are long-term; focus on critical thinking, questioning, and discussion; invite active involvement through activities, rather than direct instruction; and teach key concepts of media literacy.[91] These are elements of many of MediaSmarts' resources on body image, such as our parent tip sheet *Talking to Kids about Body Image*, which encourages adults to start the conversation about how women's bodies are represented in digital and traditional media – and how girls represent themselves – as early as possible.[92]

The State of Digital Literacy and Digital Citizenship Education in Canada

Considering the importance of digital literacy and digital citizenship in addressing the issues that girls face online, it is important to know just what education they are receiving in these areas and from whom. While our research found that nearly all girls have access to the internet outside of school, not all are receiving the same education in using digital devices. The digital literacy skill that students most often reported having learned was how to find information online. Roughly the same number of girls (7 percent) as boys (8 percent) said they had learned this from any source, and similar numbers had learned from their parents (46 percent of boys, 49 percent of girls) and friends (28 percent of both boys and girls). Girls, however, were much more likely to have learned about the topic from teachers (53 percent compared to 38 percent of boys) and less likely to be self-taught from online sources (16 percent compared to 26 percent of boys). Though somewhat fewer students overall have learned about authenticating online information (80 percent overall; 82 percent of boys, 78 percent of girls), the same pattern recurs when we look at where they learned it: friends and parents are roughly equally common as sources, while girls are more likely to learn from teachers (52 percent compared to 38 percent of boys) and boys are half again as likely to have learned from online sources (21 percent compared to 14 percent of girls).[93]

There are two reasons to be concerned about this pattern. The first is that since girls rely heavily on parents and (compared to boys) teachers as sources of digital literacy education, they are less likely than boys to learn some key skills: just 62 percent of girls have learned anything about how corporations collect and use personal information online, compared to 70 percent of boys, and the difference seems to be almost entirely due to boys' use of online sources. While the number of boys and girls who learned from parents, teachers, and friends is almost the same, almost twice as many boys as girls learned about this topic from online sources (25 percent compared to 15 percent). However, boys' greater likelihood of learning about this topic did not translate into a greater practical understanding, as they were just as likely to overestimate how much privacy policies limited sites' use of their data.[94]

Perhaps more significant than the fact that boys are more likely than girls to get their digital literacy education from online sources is that they're less likely to get it from teachers. Each province and territory has an official curriculum that all of the teachers in that jurisdiction are expected to follow. Thus, while we might expect the number of students who have learned about various topics from teachers to vary by province (depending on the content of that province's curriculum), it should not vary by gender. The fact that it does suggests that digital literacy has not yet been integrated into the curricula of most provinces or territories in Canada and, in the cases where it has been, that curriculum is not being implemented in all schools and classrooms. Instead, digital skills are only available to students whose teachers have a special interest in the subject or to students who have the interest and agency to ask for them. In keeping with Angrove's recommendation for educational reform that incorporates respect for diversity and equality,[95] it is also clear that what is needed to ensure that girls are able to engage with both the challenges and opportunities facing them online is a comprehensive digital literacy and digital citizenship program that will not just make sure that these topics are included in provincial and territorial curricula but provide teachers with the resources and professional development they need to bring them into their classrooms. A comprehensive curriculum is also required to ensure that the broad range of skills that make up digital literacy – from media literacy skills to emotion regulation, online ethics, and active citizenship – are all included, and that teachers receive the training they need to be able to teach them effectively. Standardizing curriculum will also make it possible to formally evaluate digital literacy programs and materials to ensure that schools are using those that are most effective.

Notes

1   Lisa M. Jones, Kimberly J. Mitchell & Wendy A. Walsh, *Evaluation of Internet Child Safety Materials Used by ICAC Task Forces in School and Community Settings, Final Report* (Durham, NH: Crimes Against Children Research Center, 2012), <https://www.ncjrs.gov/pdffiles1/nij/grants/242016.pdf>.

2   Steven Roberts & Aziz Douai, "Moral Panics and Cybercrime: How Canadian Media Cover Internet Child Luring," *Journal of Canadian Media Studies* 10 (2012), <http://cjms.fims.uwo.ca/issues/10-01/DouaiRoberts.pdf>.

3   David Finkelhor, *The Internet, Youth Safety and the Problem of "Juvenoia"* (Durham, NH: Crimes Against Children Research Center, January 2011), last modified January 2011, <http://www.unh.edu/ccrc/pdf/Juvenoia%20 paper.pdf>.

4   Valerie Steeves, *Young Canadians in a Wired World, Phase III: Talking to Youth and Parents about Life Online* (Ottawa: MediaSmarts, 2012), <http:// mediasmarts.ca/sites/default/files/pdfs/publication-report/full/YCWW III-youth-parents.pdf>.

5   *Ibid., at* 29.

6   Bell cited in Ben Rooney, "Women and Children First: Technology and Moral Panic," *TechEurope* (blog), *Wall Street Journal,* 11 July 2011, <http://blogs.wsj.com/tech-europe/2011/07/11/women-and-children-first-technology-and-moral-panic/>.

7   Steeves, *supra* note 4 at 29.

8   Sonia Livingstone, "Online Risk, Harm and Vulnerability: Reflections on the Evidence Base for Child Internet Safety Policy," *Zer* 18:35 (2013): 13–28, <http://www.ehu.es/zer/hemeroteca/pdfs/zer35-01-livingstone. pdf>.

9   Office for Standards in Education, Children's Services and Skills (Ofsted), *The Safe Use of New Technologies* (Manchester, UK: 2010), <http:// webarchive.nationalarchives.gov.uk/20141124154759/http://www.ofsted. gov.uk/resources/safe-use-of-new-technologies>.

10 "History," MediaSmarts, <http://mediasmarts.ca/about-us/history>.

11 "Digital Literacy Fundamentals," MediaSmarts, <http://mediasmarts. ca/digital-media-literacy-fundamentals/digital-literacy-fundamentals>.

12 Anne Collier, "Why Digital Citizenship's a Hot Topic," *NetFamily-News.org,* (blog), 23 September 2010, <http://www.netfamilynews.org/ why-digital-citizenships-a-hot-topic-globally>.

13 Albert Bandura, "Social Cognition Theory of Moral Thought and Action," in *Handbook of Moral Behavior and Development: Volume 1: Theory,* eds. William M. Kurtines & Jacob L. Gewirtz (Hillsdale, NJ: Lawrence Erlbaum, 1991), 45–103.

14 Christina Regenboen, Daniel A. Schneider, Andreas Finkelmeyer, Nils Kohn, Birgit Derntl, Thilo Kellerman, Raquel E. Gur, Frank Schneider & Ute Habel, "The Differential Contribution of Facial Expressions, Prosody, and Speech Content to Empathy," *Cognition & Emotion* 26 (2012): 995–1014, doi:10.1080/02699931.2011.631296.

15 James R. Rest, *Moral Development: Advances in Research and Theory* (New York: Praeger, 1986).

16 Carrie James with Katie Davis, Andrea Flores, John M. Francis, Lindsay Pettingill, Margaret Rundle & Howard Gardner, "Young People, Ethics, and the New Digital Media: A Synthesis from the Good Play Project,"

GoodWork Project Report Series, No. 54. Project Zero (Cambridge, MA: Harvard Graduate School of Education, 2008.)

17   Steeves, *supra* note 4.

18   *Ibid.*

19   Micah L. Sifry, "Children's Crusade: A Primer on How Britain's Students Are Organising Using Social Media," *TechPresident* (blog), 29 November 2010, <http://techpresident.com/blog-entry/childrens-crusade-primer-how-britains-students-are-organising-using-social-media>.

20   Greg Toppo, "Kids Upload and Unload on School Cafeteria Lunches," *USA Today*, 2 December 2013, <http://www.usatoday.com/story/news/nation/2013/12/02/school-lunch-photos/3784625/>.

21   Steeves, *supra* note 4.

22   Megan Boldt, "Osseo High-Schooler Battles Taunts with Tweets," *Pioneer-Press*, 9 September 2012, <http://www.twincities.com/education/ci_21656149/osseo-high-schooler-battles-taunts-tweets>.

23   Steeves, *supra* note 4.

24   Soraya Chemaly, Jaclyn Friedman & Laura Bates, "An Open Letter to Facebook," *HuffPost Tech* (blog), 21 May 2013, <http://www.huffingtonpost.com/soraya-chemaly/an-open-letter-to-faceboo_1_b_3307394.html>.

25   "Media Literacy Fundamentals," MediaSmarts, <http://mediasmarts.ca/digital-media-literacy-fundamentals/media-literacy-fundamentals>.

26   Steeves, *supra* note 4.

27   *Ibid.*

28   *Ibid.*

29   John Dewey, *How We Think (Boston: D. C. Heath, 1910)*.

30   "MyWorld: A Digital Literacy Tutorial for Secondary Students," MediaSmarts, <http://mediasmarts.ca/game/myworld-digitial-literacy-tutorial-secondary-students>.

31   "Stay on the Path: Teaching Kids to be Safe and Ethical Online Portal Page," MediaSmarts, <http://mediasmarts.ca/stay-path-teaching-kids-be-safe-and-ethical-online-portal-page>.

32   Jessica Ringrose, Rosalind Gill, Sonia Livingstone & Laura Harvey, *Qualitative Study of Children, Young People and "Sexting": A Report Prepared for the NSPCC* (London: NSPCC, 2012), <http://www.nspcc.org.uk/preventing-abuse/research-and-resources/qualitative-study-sexting/>.

33   Tara Culp-Ressler, "Study Finds That Sexting Doesn't Actually Ruin Young Adults' Lives," *ThinkProgress* (blog), 10 September 2013, <http://thinkprogress.org/health/2013/09/10/2599811/study-sexting-college/>.

34   Steeves, *supra* note 4.

35   *Ibid.*

36   Culp-Ressler, *supra* note 33.

37   *Ibid.*

38 Jessica Ringrose, Laura Harvey, Rosalind Gill & Sonia Livingstone, "Teen Girls, Sexual Double Standards and 'Sexting': Gendered Value in Digital Image Exchange," *Feminist Theory* 14 (2013): 305–23, <http://www.academia.edu/3581896/Ringrose_J._Harvey_L_Gill_R._and_Livingstone_S._2013_Teen_girls_sexual_double_standards_and_sexting_Gendered_value_in_digital_image_exchange_Feminist_Theory>.

39 Steeves, *supra* note 4.

40 Ringrose et al, *supra* note 38.

41 *Ibid.*

42 Elizabeth Englander, *Low Risk Associated with Most Teenage Sexting: A Study of 617 18-Year-Olds*, MARC Research Reports Paper 6 (Bridgewater, MA: Massachusetts Aggression Reduction Center, 2012), <http://webhost.bridgew.edu/marc/SEXTING%20AND%20COERCION%20report.pdf>.

43 *Think before You Share*, MediaSmarts, <http://mediasmarts.ca/sites/default/files/pdfs/tipsheet/TipSheet_Think_Before_You_Share.pdf>.

44 Ringrose et al, *supra* note 38.

45 *Ibid.*

46 "Girls and Boys on Television," MediaSmarts, <http://mediasmarts.ca/lessonplan/girls-and-boys-television>; "Gender Messages in Alcohol Advertising," MediaSmarts, <http://mediasmarts.ca/sites/mediasmarts/files/pdfs/lesson-plan/Lesson_Gender_Messages_Alcohol_Advertising.pdf>.

47 *Talking to Kids about Gender Stereotypes*, MediaSmarts, <http://mediasmarts.ca/sites/default/files/pdfs/tipsheet/TipSheet_Talking_Kids_Gender_Stereotypes.pdf>; *Little Princesses and Fairy Tale Stereotypes*, MediaSmarts, <http://mediasmarts.ca/backgrounder/little-princesses-and-fairy-tale-stereotypes>.

48 Steeves, *supra* note 4.

49 *Ibid.*

50 *Privacy Pirates: An Interactive Unit on Online Privacy (Ages 7–9)*, MediaSmarts, <http://mediasmarts.ca/game/privacy-pirates-interactive-unit-online-privacy-ages-7-9>.

51 "Online Marketing to Kids: Protecting Your Privacy – Lesson," MediaSmarts, <http://mediasmarts.ca/lessonplan/online-marketing-kids-protecting-your-privacy-lesson>; "The Privacy Dilemma: Lesson Plan for Senior Classrooms," MediaSmarts, <http://mediasmarts.ca/lessonplan/privacy-dilemma-lesson-plan-senior-classrooms>.

52 Steeves, *supra* note 4.

53 danah boyd, *It's Complicated: The Social Lives of Networked Teens* (New Haven: Yale University Press, 2014).

54 Alice Marwick & danah boyd, "The Drama! Teen Conflict, Gossip, and Bullying in Networked Publics." Paper presented at A Decade in Internet

Time: Symposium on the Dynamics of the Internet and Society, Oxford, UK, 21 to 23 September 2011.

55   Steeves, *supra* note 4.

56   *Ibid.*

57   David Bornstein, "Fighting Bullying with Babies," *Opinionator* (blog), *New York Times*, 28 November 2010, <http://opinionator.blogs.nytimes. com/2010/11/08/fighting-bullying-with-babies/>.

58   Elizabeth Kandel Englander, *Bullying and Cyberbullying: What Every Educator Needs to Know* (Cambridge, MA: Harvard Education Press, 2013), 76.

59   Silvia Diazgranados Ferráns, Robert L. Selman & Luba Falk Feigenberg, "Rules of the Culture and Personal Needs: Witnesses' Decision-Making Processes to Deal with Situations of Bullying in Middle School," *Harvard Educational Review* 82 (2012): 445–470, < http://her.hepg.org/ content/4u5v1n8q67332v03/fulltext.pdf>.

60   MediaSmarts, *supra* note 31.

61   Steeves, *supra* note 4.

62   Janine M. Zweig, Meredith Dank, Pamela Lachman & Jennifer Yahner, *Technology, Teen Dating Violence and Abuse, and Bullying* (Washington, DC: Urban Institute, 2013), <https://www.ncjrs.gov/pdffiles1/nij/grants/243296. pdf>.

63   Steeves, *supra* note 4.

64   Antonia Zerbisias, "Internet Trolls an Online Nightmare for Young Women," *Toronto Star*, 18 January 2013, <http://www.thestar.com/news/ insight/2013/01/18/internet_trolls_an_online_nightmare_for_young_ women.htm>.

65   Steeves, *supra* note 4.

66   *Ibid.*

67   K. L. Gray, "Deviant Bodies, Stigmatized Identities, and Racist Acts: Examining the Experiences of African-American Gamers in Xbox Live," *New Review of Hypermedia and Multimedia* 18:4 (2012): 261–276, doi:10.1080/13614568.2012.746740.

68   Jeffrey H. Kuznekoff & Lindsey M. Rose, "Communication in Multi-player Gaming: Examining Player Responses to Gender Cues," *New Media & Society* 15:4 (2013): 541–556, doi:10.1177/1461444812458271.

69   Southern Poverty Law Center, "Misogyny: The Sites," *Southern Poverty Law Center Intelligence Report* 145 (Spring 2012), <http://www.splcenter. org/get-informed/intelligence-report/browse-all-issues/2012/spring/ misogyny-the-sites>.

70   Phyllis B. Gerstenfeld, Diana R. Grant & Chau-Pu Chiang, "Hate Online: A Content Analysis of Extremist Internet Sites," *Analyses of Social Issues and Public Policy* 3:1 (2003): 29–44, <http://floodhelp.uno.edu/uploads/ Content%20Analysis/Gertstenfeld.pdf>.

71 Robert C. Rowland & Kirsten Theye, "The Symbolic DNA of Terrorism," *Communication Monographs* 75 (2008): 52–85, doi:10.1080/03637750701885423.

72 Randy Blazak, "From White Boys to Terrorist Men: Target Recruitment of Nazi Skinheads," *American Behavioral Scientist* 44 (2001): 982–1000, <http://www.sagepub.com/martin3study/articles/Blazak.pdf>.

73 Priscilla Marie Meddaugh & Jack Kay, "Hate Speech or 'Reasonable Racism?' The Other in Stormfront," *Journal of Mass Media Ethics* 24 (2009): 251–268, <http://journalismethics.info/JMME%20-%20Hate%20Speech%20or%20Reasonable%20Racism.pdf>.

74 Lacy G. McNamee, Brittany L. Peterson & Jorge Peña, "A Call to Educate, Participate, Invoke and Indict: Understanding the Communication of Online Hate Groups," *Communication Monographs* 77 (2010): 257–280, doi:10.1080/03637751003758227.

75 Rowland & Theye, *supra* note 71.

76 "Facing Online Hate: Portal Page," MediaSmarts, <http://mediasmarts.ca/facing-online-hate-portal-page>.

77 Moss E. Norman, "Embodying the Double-Bind of Masculinity: Young Men And Discourses of Normalcy, Health, Heterosexuality, and Individualism," *Men and Masculinities* 14 (2011): 430–449, doi:10.1177/1097184X11409360.

78 See Bailey, Chapter I: Steeves, Chapter VI.

79 Cheryl, "May *Vogue* Visits the Future and the Future Is Missing a Clavicle," *Jezebel*, 6 May 2008, <http://jezebel.com/387701/may-vogue-visits-the-future-and-the-future-is-missing-a-clavicle>.

80 Marika Tiggemann, Amy Slater & Veronica Smyth, "'Retouch Free': The Effect of Labelling Media Images as Not Digitally Altered on Women's Body Dissatisfaction," *Body Image* 11 (2014): 85–88, http://www.sciencedirect.com/science/article/pii/S1740144513001083.

81 Dr. Barbara McAneny cited in "AMA Adopts New Policies at Annual Meeting," American Medical Association, last modified 21 June 2011, <http://www.ama-assn.org/ama/pub/news/news/a11-new-policies.page>.

82 Erin Anderssen, "In an Airbrushed World, How Do You Define What's Truly Hot?" *Globe and Mail*, 1 March 2012, last updated 6 September 2012, <http://www.theglobeandmail.com/life/parenting/in-an-airbrushed-world-how-do-you-define-whats-truly-hot/article550540/?page=all>.

83 Deidre Stalnaker, "On the Cover, in the Mirror," *Research Magazine*, 21 January 2010, <http://research.ua.edu/2010/01/on-the-cover-in-the-mirror/>.

84 Connie Morrison, *Who Do They Think They Are? Teenage Girls & Their Avatars in Spaces of Social Online Communication* (New York: Peter Lang, 2010).

85   *Ibid.*

86   Randye Hoder, "For Teenage Girls, Facebook Means Always Being Camera-Ready," *Motherlode: Living in the Family Dynamic* (blog), *New York Times*, 7 March 2012, <http://parenting.blogs.nytimes.com/2012/03/07/for-teenage-girls-facebook-means-always-being-camera-ready/?_php=true&_type=blogs&_r=0>.

87   Marika Tiggemann & Amy Slater, "NetGirls: The Internet, Facebook, and Body Image Concern in Adolescent Girls," *International Journal of Eating Disorders* 46:6 (2013): 630–633, <http://www.adelaide.edu.au/hda/news/T1_Slater.pdf>; Steeves, *supra* note 4 at 29; Mark Hoelzel, "New Study Shows Instagram and Snapchat Beating Twitter among Teens and Young Adults," *Business Insider*, 13 March 2014, <http://www.businessinsider.com/instagram-and-snapchat-are-more-popular-than-twitter-among-teens-and-young-adults-sai-2014-3>.

88   Alex Cohen, "Countering the Online World of 'Pro-Anorexia,'" 27 February 2009, <http://www.npr.org/templates/story/story.php?storyId=101210192>.

89   Stephanie Tom Tong, Daria Heinemann-LaFave, Jehoon Jeon, Renata Kolodziej-Smith & Nathaniel Warshay, "The Use of Pro-Ana Blogs for Online Social Support," *Eating Disorders: The Journal of Treatment and Prevention* 21 (2013): 408–422, <ttp://www.ncbi.nlm.nih.gov/pubmed/24044597>.

90   Zali Yager & Jennifer A. O'Dea, "Prevention Programs for Body Image and Eating Disorders on University Campuses: A Review of Large, Controlled Interventions," *Health Promotion International* 23:2 (2008): 173–189, <http://heapro.oxfordjournals.org/content/23/2/173.abstract>.

91   Niva Piran, Michael P. Levine & Lori M. Irving, "GO GIRLS! Media Literacy, Activism and Advocacy Project," *Healthy Weight Journal* 14 (2000): 89–90, <http://www.moreofmetolove.com/resources/article/go-girls-media-literacy-activism-and-advocacy-project/>.

92   MediaSmarts, *supra* note 47.

93   Steeves, *supra* note 4.

94   *Ibid.*

95   Angrove, Chapter XII.

CHAPTER XIV

Security and Insecurity Online: Perspectives from Girls and Young Women

Sarah Heath

Introduction

Participation in the online world is often contingent on one's ability to disclose and share personal information about one self.[1] Such disclosure can have positive implications. Critical scholars have noted that disclosure can deepen existing relationships, allow participants to express themselves, experiment with their identities, and seek authenticity, as well as validate themselves to others.[2] Governing discourses often draw attention to the negative consequences of this disclosure.[3] In particular, it has been noted that users may inadvertently experience a loss of privacy as a result of participating in online social networks, which may lead to the use of one's personal information for impersonation and harassment.[4] As Bailey notes,[5] the safety and security of children and youth online has been discussed in parliamentary debates in the context of child luring, sexual assault, child pornography, sexting, and cyberbullying,[6] all of which can result in physical, emotional, psychological, and/or moral harm.

Girls and young women, in particular, have been characterized by policy makers as potential victims of online security threats. In their analysis of legislative debates, Bailey and Steeves[7] note that policy solutions (i.e., increased surveillance, censorship, self-monitoring, and criminalization) portray girls and young women as all-knowing and comfortable on the internet but naïve and vulnerable in relation to how they view their personal security and the security of their information.[8] It appears that policy makers have conceptualized insecurity primarily as a function of the risk that children and youth create themselves (i.e., their personal, intellectual, developmental, moral, and sexual traits). Although policy makers have also drawn some associations between online risks and the architecture of social networking sites (SNS; specifically the consequences of anonymity and a lack of accountability online), internet service providers, and societal messages around sexualization and objectification, the actions of children and youth remain paramount. Bailey,[9] however, suggests that girls' and young women's description of online risks in general, and the recommendations they propose to reduce those risks in particular, differ drastically from those depicted by policy makers. She instead identifies how the technical infrastructures of SNS organize girls and young women in ways that promote conflict.

What is particularly interesting are the gaps between how girls and young women, critical scholars, and policy makers have each described threats to security (or insecurity) and the kinds of responses each suggests are needed to minimize or regulate these threats. While policy makers argue that security risks are an inevitable result of online self-disclosure, such a perspective fails to recognize the presumptive controls initiated by users to protect and maintain their security online. These presumptive controls and the expectations with regards to their use were discussed by the girls and young woman who were interviewed as part of the eGirls Project.

In January and February of 2013, researchers with the eGirls Project held a series of interviews and focus groups with girls and young women between the ages of 15 and 22. All participants used interactive online media (such as social networking, blogging, and/or user-generated video sites) as a regular part of their social lives. Half of our sample resided in an urban Ontario setting and half resided in a rural Ontario setting.[10]

We interviewed six girls aged 15 to 16 and six young women aged 18 to 22. An additional twenty-two participated in four focus group discussions, as follows: (1) seven girls aged 15 to 17 living in the urban setting; (2) five girls aged 15 to 17 living in the rural setting; (3) six young women aged 18 to 22 living in the urban setting; and (4) four young women aged 18 to 22 living in the rural setting. A professional research house recruited our participants on the basis of sex, age (either 15 to 17 or 18 to 22), and location of residence (urban or rural). Although participants were not recruited on the basis of self-identification with regard to other aspects of their identities, such as race, ethnicity, gender identity, or sexual orientation, our participant group included members of racialized, linguistic, and various religious groups.

In the interviews and the focus groups, we explored, among other things, the types of visual and textual representations the participants used online to express their identity as young women, and the benefits and pitfalls they experience on social media. We also asked for their views on the issues and policy responses focused upon by policy makers (as identified in the review of federal parliamentary debates discussed by Bailey in Chapter I of this volume). With participant permission, the interviews and focus group were audiotaped and transcribed by our research assistants for analysis. All identifying information was removed from the transcripts, and pseudonyms were used to identify participants.[11] The interview and focus group transcripts were then coded for major themes. One major theme that appeared in the data was the use of security controls by participants on SNS.

The objective of this chapter is to explore girls' and young women's perspectives regarding the threats to security (or insecurities) they encounter through their participation on SNS. This will advance the discussion about how to build an online environment that supports and encourages positive experiences for girls and young women.[12] I begin with an overview of how the eGirls participants used security controls as a way to secure their online communications and their expectations in this regard. Specifically, I explore how the presence of certain features on a SNS, including aspects that girls and young women viewed as indicators of security (e.g., control of personal content, consistency, ease of updating, and management of privacy settings), influenced how they participated on the site. For SNS perceived to be "insecure," participants managed their privacy and security by employing risk-reducing strategies through the use of security controls. These included the triage of online requests, the deployment of exclusionary techniques (blocking users, hiding profiles, creating groups, etc.), and the use of privacy settings. I then discuss these strategies, as well as the concerns expressed by participants that such strategies cannot fully ensure that they can assert control over their online interactions.

Situating (In)Securities within Broader Discussions of Online Safety and Privacy

For regulators, educators, and parents, online safety concerns generally focus on the protection of youth from sexual predation and harassment through parental supervision,[13] awareness and responsibilization[14] on the part of the child,[15] and abstinence from sharing of information.[16] In addition, policy makers rarely use the term "security" in relation to the use of online social media; instead, they discuss the issues in terms of risks and harms, especially risks to and harms associated with personal and moral safety (i.e., the corruption of an individual by exposing them to something they would not otherwise be exposed to). These kinds of harms, however, are highly unlikely to occur and the interventions adults rely on to protect youth from them are often at odds with the experiences of young people.[17] Youth tend to be more concerned about online privacy and the security of their personal information more generally.[18] Privacy refers to an individual's ability to control the sharing and dissemination of their personal information, including how it will be used and manipulated.[19] From youths' perspective, the loss of privacy is often deemed to be a loss of security and online risks to privacy create insecurities that they must navigate.[20] The loss of privacy and control over personal information may also result in safety concerns, which creates a blurring of these two concepts (i.e., security and safety).

Scholarship addressing young people's perspective of online security suggests that even though children disclose personal information online, they generally think about and are concerned with the protection of their privacy.[21] Moreover, Burkell, Steeves, and Micheti report that the children they interviewed did not necessarily disclose personal information online willingly, but often saw disclosure as a compromise that was required in order to participate in social activities online.[22] Youn found that the promise of additional benefits from an online forum correlated with greater disclosure by youth, even when the information was not required in order to participate on the site.[23] But young people still identify a variety of perceived insecurities, including the inability to limit information to "just friends" or to change default settings that maximize exposure, and the ability of corporations, education institutions, and law enforcement officers to access information marked as private.[24]

In response to these insecurities, children have developed risk reduction strategies. For example, a 2013 survey conducted by MediaSmarts on the social media use and privacy practices of Canadian children revealed that 90 percent of grade 4 students refrained from posting their contact information online.[25] Many teenagers reported altering their behaviour to protect their privacy, by "falsifying information, providing incomplete information, or going to different websites that do not ask for personal information."[26] Forty-seven percent of Canadian students aged 9 to 17 also indicated that they had represented themselves as someone else to protect their privacy online.[27] Children noted other strategies, such as deleting comments and photos where they were tagged (which 97 percent of students reported doing).[28] Youth, in addition, reported using privacy settings to restrict the disclosure of their information.[29] These self-help strategies are particularly noteworthy, given the fact that privacy policies are often incredibly difficult to interpret and the privacy options offered by SNS are often limited, both of which combine to constrain the flexibility youth need to handle privacy dilemmas online.[30]

Moreover, some youth believe the ability to access information does not necessarily mean it should be accessed by corporations, educational institutions, parents, and law enforcement, as youth may still deem this material "private" (regardless of its accessibility in a public place).[31] This flies in the face of privacy regulations that typically assume individuals will protect their privacy by limiting what they disclose online.

These research findings have focused on the online experiences of youth as a whole. However, girls' online experiences, as described by Bailey and Bailey and Steeves, suggest that girls' and young women's experiences on SNS are highly gendered.[32] Regan and Steeves have also highlighted "gendered differences in patterns of online communication among children and youth, especially with regard to privacy protective behaviours," where girls are less likely to disclose characteristics because they are girls.[33] This is further complicated because the structure of the online environment reinforces "media stereotypes and the commodification of girls' sexuality."[34] Marketing messages embedded within SNS encourage a certain type of consumption, especially by girls, and legitimate a certain kind of sharing.[35] Coercive marketing techniques built into the architecture of the site also persuade youth to disclose information, which is collected for marketing purposes, often with-out their knowledge.[36]

This means that girls are in a unique situation. On the one hand, they are attracted to SNS because of their desire to control the presentation of their online self and to be seen positively in the online world.[37] On the other hand, the gendered nature of their vis-ibility "creates a sense of fear among policy makers precisely because it allows girls to step beyond the constraints they experience in real space."[38] Girls are therefore seen as in need of regulation, both to protect them from harms and to ensure they perform a particular type of femininity.

However, as the eGirls data demonstrates, the nature of those harms remains highly contested, especially because safety and security are typically understood as two separate concepts. Safety addresses the risk of harm to oneself, as opposed to security, which focuses on the risk of harm to one's personal information. The distinction between the two blurs in relation to the online world, where one's personal information is easily accessible and risks to the protection of one's personal information can be associated with risks to one's safety. For example, in the case of cyberbullying, one's profile picture, which is personal information, can be accessed by anyone due to the technical architecture of the SNS, and can expose the poster to various forms of harassment, potentially resulting in a variety of harms (e.g., physical, emotional, psychological, and/or moral harm).

SNS Insecurities and Security Controls from the Perspectives of Girls and Young Women

Just as the term "security" was rarely used by policy makers, the girls and young women who participated in the eGirls Project rarely used the term "security" in relation to the use of online social media. Instead, they talked about risks and harms. However, whereas policy makers focus on risks that implicate personal and moral safety (i.e., the corruption of an individual by exposing them to something they would not otherwise be exposed to), the eGirls participants talked more about technical risks to their information and possible impli-cations for their physical safety. Nonetheless, the former concerns were paramount. Although the girls discussed stranger danger,[39] particularly in the context of unsafe things they may have done in the past, they were primarily concerned about the security of their personal information because of its permanency online. They complained when pictures of them were shared because a friend or family member uploaded them online without their consent. They were also concerned that information posted about them could possibly be retrieved by others (potentially undesirable others) and used to inhibit their opportunities in the future, such as career prospects.

The girls and young women also described their concerns regarding the requirement that they must provide personal information in order to participate on most SNS. Specifically, they were worried that unknown individuals would obtain their information and use it to impersonate them online, or to contact them, or to do other things that would harm or violate them (psychologically or physically). They also noted how the design and structure of the SNS meant they shared more information. For example, when asked if there is any information participants do not include in their profile, Amelia (18) noted, "I used to have my cellphone number in there. I took that off though, umm, cause people were texting me who, you know, I was like, I don't really want you to have my number type thing." And when asked about privacy and the various platforms, she continued to say,

> Twitter, I think you, you don't post a lot of personal information. Like you don't post, um, really very much cause if you go to someone's profile, [it] just gives you the layout and it just gives you the picture and your name. Um, and then it'll have, you can write a little blurb about yourself type of thing but, like, in that you don't, you don't have to put anything like, you don't even have to put anything in that so you could just have your picture, your name and just all your tweets. So you could really be whoever you wanted to be. You would, could keep stuff out of it that you didn't want people to know really easily. Um whereas in Facebook, I think because you go on Facebook and then you can edit your file and it will give you all these options that you can add to, right, like you can add your name and your number and your address and like where you're from and there's apps like, um, I went to high school with you type thing. Like it's going to connect you back to who you are and you might get connected to things that you didn't want to be connected to. So I think more so with Twitter, you're free to be absolutely like,

who like, whoever you wanted to be, whether that's a negative or a positive thing because you could really like, somebody else could be pretending to be someone who they're totally not. Um, so, I mean I don't know, it's a positive and a negative, right, just depends on how they're using it ... But I think Facebook definitely more so. There, you feel more obligated to include like, all your information, because they put it there and they label it, right, whereas Twitter, they don't.

Some participants likewise acknowledged that they were unaware that SNS collected their information or knew what those companies did with that information; further, most of the participants were disgruntled by the fact that their information was being used for other nefarious purposes (e.g., data mining, marketing, advertising, business planning, etc.) than what they intended, which was limited to their own social participation. For example, when asked if they had a sense of what Facebook and other sites did with their information, focus group participants responded as follows:

> Donna (19): Yeah. I know that they use some of your information to post, like, advertisements that are directly related to you, which I find kind of creepy. Like, I was actually kind of – not worried, but more just surprised to find that out, that they can just go through my stuff and find their way around and find a way to post something they think I'll find interesting.
> Ashley (18): Yeah, I hate that.
> Researcher: And you said that's creepy?
> Donna (19): I don't know if creepy's the right word.
> Andrea (22): I'd say creepy.
> Donna (19): The fact that they're going through all of my information and can specifically – Like, I'll have advertisements for university, advertisements for gym memberships, like, stuff that's directly related to, like, my age group of people. I don't know, I was really surprised when I found that out. I thought they just post stuff ... And they don't tell you what they're accessing. They just say, "Can I access your information?"
> Andrea (22): At any time. Any day. I'm like, "What?"

The primary source of these kinds of security risks was rooted in the pressure girls and young women felt to participate in networked communications. Indeed, in responding to the risks posed by participation online, some girls and young women suggested that the best approach to remove such risks was to abstain from participating altogether: to "not connect with the outside world" (Brianne, 20), or "if you're really worried about something being on the internet or if you don't, if you're so afraid of someone else seeing it, don't post it, don't sign up, don't put your name on it" (Cindy, 20).

However, abstaining from connection with the outside world (as suggested by Brianne) was described as impossible by other girls and young women. They noted that they felt pressure from friends, community groups, and family members both to actively participate on SNS and to include friends, community group members, and family members in their online communities. Clare (16) suggested that even girls who experience online harassment might find it hard to disconnect: "[Bullying is] harder to stop unless the person deletes their account and for some reason a lot of kids don't like to do that even if they are being bullied. So I guess, I don't know, they don't really take responsibility for it. They don't realize it can escalate into bigger things. But also it's harder to do I guess."

Along with this social pressure to participate in SNS comes the need to share personal details with numerous people as a result of having a plethora of friends or followers on various SNS. However, several girls and young women explained that the greater number of people associated with your various profiles, the more likely it is that the security of your information will be reduced. For example, Jill (20) reported,

> I feel like, as people grow up, they do, like, cleanups of their friends on Facebook. It drops by, like, 200 people, because they realize as they're getting older that, like, they're more mature and it's less about having so many friends on Facebook. And they're realizing that their security is more at risk. I feel like I dropped [pause] I was at, like, almost 600 friends, then I went down to, like, 350. And I couldn't even [pause] It's just so difficult to delete friends on Facebook, as it is now … 'cause, when I got my Facebook, I was a lot more young, younger. And I'd comment on a lot more people's photos, who I'm not really friends with now, and I felt, like, I don't really need that comment there. Or, like, a conversation I had with a friend once on Facebook, I didn't find it necessary. So instead of going to delete, like, all

my comments that I'd made, I just figured I would delete my Facebook; deactivate it. And then I think it was the entire summer, I didn't have Facebook. Then when I went back to school in the fall, I got it again. 'Cause you really feel, like, shunned out sometimes, because everything happens on Facebook. Like, party updates, or events.

The participants also alluded to the complexity of privacy policies and privacy settings on several of the SNS. This complexity was deemed to be the cause of some of the insecurity they experienced online. Indeed, the complexity of privacy settings, and the requirement to enter significant amounts of personal information on particular platforms online, was seen as a direct threat to their ability to control the disclosure of their information and, subsequently, their security. Participants noted that they did not trust Facebook's privacy settings as they made it hard to keep personal information private. Even if they set their settings to "private" (meaning that their information was only available to their "friends"), the settings were often changed without them knowing, and the complexity of the settings made it hard to see how they could restrict their information to a smaller audience. Some participants felt that this increased the likelihood that their information would be collected and used for unintended purposes by unknown users, institutions, and corporations. For example, Catlin (19) said,

> Like, Facebook privacy settings, they change all the time, and you have to keep on, like, updating your privacy settings and a whole bunch of other stuff. But Google, like, it just stays, it stays the same. And they have way more security. Like, no one can search me on my Google account. It's just for pictures, so absolutely no one can. But Facebook, they'd be able to.

Other participants similarly noted that the technical platforms of SNS combined with other technologies in their life made keeping their personal information private even more difficult, as they experience a loss of control over how (and if) their information is shared. Catlin (19) continued,

> But, like, the only thing bad about the Google account I have is that every time I take a picture on my phone, it automatically

uploads it to my Google account. Automatically. It doesn't matter how many times I try to delete it, because I can't even delete it off my phone. It's so hooked up to my Google account. 'Cause when you first get an Android, you have to get a Google account. So now everything gets uploaded to my Google account.
Researcher: And what bothers you about that?
Catlin (19): Well, just, like, I don't want all of my pictures on my Google account. Like, I should be able to decide what pictures I want. But it automatically uploads it. Like, if I go to take, like — I had to take a picture of … I work at [a retail store] and I took a picture in the break room of my schedule. And it uploads it to Google. And I don't want that on my Google account.

This need to post more personal information (rather than less) and accumulate more friends (rather than fewer) was attributed to the profit-seeking focus of these SNS. Some participants discussed their distaste for the use of their personal information for marketing purposes or for the generation of corporate profits, but felt that it was inevitable and not unexpected since they were using a "corporate tool," such as Facebook.

This visibility was complicated by the perceived anonymity of other users who could peruse their profiles; and some participants saw this as a key cause of the various insecurities they experience online. Many identified the anonymity of online participation as posing a risk for interactions as people can say and do things that that they may not be accountable for, making online communication more dangerous and "unsafe":

Brianne (20): It's like, I don't really care. They'll use, like, language that you've never used in front of your parents, or they'll say something they'd never say … so I don't know, I find it's almost like you have a split personality disorder. You have a Facebook person and you have a human person.
Laura (18): It makes it more open, on Facebook.
Brianne (20): Because you can hide behind the screen, you can say whatever you want.
Researcher: So what tends to be … what tend to be the differences between your Facebook … if the person's behaving differently, the difference between the Facebook …

Catlin (19): On Facebook, I find, you're more willing to state what you're actually thinking.

Laura (18): Yeah.

Catlin (19): Like, my friend, she is the worst person on Facebook. She'll be so mean to you on Facebook, but the second she sees you face-to-face, everything's perfect; everything's fine. Yeah.

Participants spoke about several strategies to reduce risks associated with this insecurity, including deleting content, blocking people, or limiting real information (e.g., posing as a boy). This discussion was typical:

Researcher: Okay. And so, have you ever had a friend request from somebody you didn't know?

Josie (16): Yeah. You just delete the comment, kind of thing.

Paula (17): Yeah. My Instagram is blocked, because I post a lot of pictures of my house and stuff, that I don't want people to see. But my Twitter isn't blocked; I think I should lock that.

Beth (16): Yeah, I block mine. I don't want other people to see my stuff.

Researcher: Alright.

Chelsea (17): Well, I don't have anything blocked. 'Cause I don't post ... like, I don't have my real name on, like, any site. I normally just use "First Name, Last Name," because that's my mother's maiden name.

Researcher: Do you ever think about using a name that doesn't identify you as a girl?

Courtney (17): [jokingly] Yeah. Fred.

Chelsea (17): Fred. [Laughter]

Other strategies involved talking to one's parents, exiting areas where they were more likely to encounter a stranger (e.g., chat rooms), or ignoring "friend" requests. But the principle strategy discussed by the participants was the use of a triage process. This process involved thinking about how a certain profile could harm them or reflect poorly on their associated friends and family. Monica described it this way:

Researcher: What did you think you knew? What would you tell the thirteen-year-old self?

Monica (16): Uh, just be careful what you post. Anyone could get your information. If you're not careful with it, just be conscious of what you're posting, what you're doing, how you wanna be portrayed on the internet.

Participants also spoke about investigating the profile of someone who was unknown to them, but who had sent a request to become an online "friend."

Although the participants outlined a variety of instances that led to feelings of insecurity online, each instance involved the use of their personal information by an unknown person for an unintended purpose. For example, some girls and young women spoke about receiving a "friend" request from someone they did not know. They also referred to incidents where they were contacted by someone with whom they did not have a previously established relationship. They typically considered these online requests to be "creepy," "inappropriate," or "wrong," so they would ignore, delete, or block the person:

Andrea (22): I have a story, when I first got Facebook I was moving to Ottawa; I was on the Ottawa group because you used to have the location if you were part of a group. And I was like, "Oh, I'm moving to Ottawa," and some guy is asking me where I work and what my age is, so he could pick me up from the airport. And I'm like, "I'm pretty sure I'm coming with my family." [Laughter] He's asking what school I'm going to go to, I'm like, "Fuck."

Jill (20): Yeah, I've had, like, random people just message me and be like, "Hey, nice picture," like via inbox, like, private messages or whatever. Just "Nice picture; add me on Facebook." No.

Jill (20): Yeah. Somebody sent me such a weird message once. Like, the picture was, like, me and my friend and we were both wearing, like, the same outfit and doing, like, the same post, like, mirror images of each other. So he sent me a message, and it was so creepy, because, like, he was commenting on how our smiles were different. He was like, "You and the other girl, the only thing different is your smile." That was his comment.

Researcher: This was someone, like, a perfect stranger?

Jill (20): Yeah. And I was like, "Thank you for this. Go away." [Laughter]

The participants also discussed the importance of having someone to talk to if they needed advice about what to do in a particular situation, such as receiving a request that made them feel uncomfortable. It was in these instances that access to friends, family, teachers, community members, and non-governmental organizations (NGOs), such as the Kids Help Phone[40] and MediaSmarts,[41] became important. They did not expect these parties to preach or to scold the person going through the incident, or to force them into pursing a formal legal action. Instead, the participants felt that these parties should provide youth with opportunities to discuss any threats to their safety or security online and provide online tools to help girls better control the collection of their personal information. They additionally expressed a desire to have someone to converse with if they were unsure about whether something was appropriate or inappropriate or what the consequences of a particular action might be.

When asked about existing and proposed legislation regarding criminalized perpetrators of luring, assault, and pornography (including sexting), the majority of the participants favoured the use of criminal offences to discourage future events; however, in the discussion of texting legislation, which may criminalize victims as well as perpetrators, some participants were concerned with the further trauma the victim and the perpetrator would experience as a result of criminal justice involvement:

> Amelia (18): I don't think … [charging girls who sext with child pornography is a good idea] because well, I don't know, it depends on circumstances. I think, if she's getting pressured into it, I don't think having that charge of child pornography is a good thing because that's going to make her feel even worse if she actually had you know a charge for it type thing. Um, whereas if she's doing it for her own, like, if she's doing it cause she wants to, I think maybe yeah you should like, it doesn't really have as much as an effect type thing, so it, I, it depends on the circumstances.

Many participants felt that such actions would not address the underlying issues (i.e., mainstream stereotypes, architectural constraints, etc.). For example, Lauryn (17) explains,

I [think] having a law against it is kinda like, I don't know, it's kinda like, like, as long as, like, got the awareness out to girls our age, saying, like, look, if you put this picture up here this is what can happen, and like, people, like, your picture can be sent to anybody, you don't know who's going to see it, maybe you put something on technology you can't get rid of it, maybe you can delete it off your phone but you can't delete it off of everyone else's phone, I think that would be a lot more helpful 'cause, like getting the awareness out, and then if they still chose to do it like, they chose to do it but like it's different then. I don't know. I think like more awareness about what could happen about it would be more beneficial than just saying you can't do it cause it it's get people a better idea of what can actually happen.

In addition to using various online tools to selectively share information, participants also actively removed undesirable pictures or sought to control the emailing or texting of particular pictures to certain others. For example, in a discussion on sexting, Andrea (22) noted the difficulty in controlling the distribution of one's personal pictures online, even if the original intention was not to disclose them to a wider public audience:

"But I think the moment the picture is out there, it's, like, everyone's picture now, on the internet …. It should be your picture. Model pictures, porn, that's one thing. But our own pictures distributed like that is so unfair. But I think, I talked to somebody about this, and they said it would be hard to charge, find, and charge everybody who distributed those pictures."

Discussion: Comprehending SNS Insecurities and Controls

Although the participants frequently spoke about the loss of privacy and the collection and use of personal information by SNS, they had strategies to help them obtain control over their information and to minimize insecurities. They expressed concerns primarily about the permanency of the information they shared online, and particularly how that could pose a challenge to them in the future (i.e., when applying for jobs). Similarly, the girls and young women took issue with the collection of personal information online, which resulted in a loss of their anonymity and their ability to distance themselves from the offline world.[42]

In contrast to policy makers who attributed these insecurities to be a result of the actions of children and youth,[43] the girls and young women we spoke to commonly assessed security risks when they were interacting online and attempted to keep control of their information. In particular, they frequently made judgments about whether something they either did or encountered on SNS was right or wrong, appropriate or inappropriate, and creepy/strange or familiar. Because of the potential consequences of their actions, they then acted accordingly by blocking or deleting users, censoring themselves, or disengaging from conversations. Although girls and young women were portrayed in policy as being unaware, or not considering the consequences of their actions online, the participants clearly expressed discomfort regarding the need to share (so much of) their personal information and were concerned with what corporations sought to do with that information. This finding is consistent with previous research that determined that girls and boys were uncomfortable with the amount of personal information corporations collected from them, and, as a result, likened such corporations to stalkers.[44] This concern for privacy also extended to family members, as children are careful to guard their activities from family members.[45] In particular, control over image and self-presentation was important to girls and young women.[46]

The eGirls participants instead attributed the insecurities they experienced online to the online environment, as opposed to their own specific actions (i.e., those within their control). The large number of people they interacted with online, and the complexity of privacy settings and online forum structures, were viewed as increasing the sharing of (permanent) information in ways that the user could not control and could not reasonably understand or predict. Control appears to be a significant issue as protection of one's privacy is dependent on one's ability to reduce or minimize the likelihood that that information is used in unknown ways.[47] It is, therefore, understandable that the participants noted feeling like they had to be a "defensive user" in today's online environment, as they were expected to understand and foresee potential incidents in a complex and ever-changing environment.

These insecurities were also linked to the pressure on girls and young women to participate with friends, family members, schools (e.g., teachers), and community organizations (e.g., Girl Guides, sports activities, community groups, etc.) online. Through all of these offline interactions, girls and young women were also expected to create and maintain mutual and respectful online interactions. This contrasts with policy makers' attribution of risks to the extensive use girls make of social media, since people within the individual's offline world are expecting and demanding that use and, in some cases, participating in online social media on their behalf (e.g., parents' pictures and videos of their children).

Moreover, the commercial nature of digital spaces and the profit associated with the trade in personal information not only promote but also require insecurity, in many cases. The emphasis to include more friends, messages, notes, posts, personal information, and pictures, rather than less, is consistent with a business model that encourages the disclosure and sharing of information on the part of many users who are visibly linked to each other through "tagging" each other in comments and pictures.[48] The sharing of personal information that results from these SNS features often occurs without the express consent and knowledge of the user until after the fact. Deleting and removing oneself from these comments and photographs is often difficult and time consuming. Accordingly, even when one intends to limit the disclosure of one's information and reduce insecurities, these insecurities still result.[49]

Girls and young women both attributed the cause of some insecurity to the nature of the online environment due, in large part, to the perceived anonymity of other users and the resulting lowering of inhibitions. This is in sharp contrast to policy makers, who tend to privilege the actions of these companies, while requiring children and youth to act in certain proscribed ways to avoid risks that have been created by the design of the environment itself.[50] Current policies accordingly constrain the privacy of youth and children and their ability to use technology for exploration, self-expression, relationship building, and social validation. In some cases, these constraints have resulted in the criminalization of those who such laws were originally designed to protect. As Bailey and Steeves note, "corporate and policy practices often simultaneously ignore and constrain girls' online agency."[51]

In terms of responding to online insecurities, although girls and young women were generally in agreement with the response of policy makers to criminalize perpetrators, they also noted the potential impact the criminal justice system would have on girls as victims. As a result, the participants were focused on responses that included providing advice and assistance to girls and young women who were inexperienced in using social media. They were also focused on providing them with opportunities to learn about social media and the importance of certain (defensive) practices and strategies online, in order to develop resiliency with respect to threats to security.[52]

These practices included the use of false information to ensure anonymity.[53] Other strategies included the use of a triage process to provide an opportunity to think about the potential consequences of how their information appeared, whether it could be used by unknown others, and how that use may reflect on or be seen by their friends and family. This demonstrates what Karaian refers to as a broadening of the scope of responsibilization where girls and young women are "often understood as both victim and perpetrator" of their own and others' demise.[54] As Karaian notes in her examination of sexting campaigns, "girls are responsibilized for managing not only their own risks but also the risks, such as criminalization, faced by their peers"; that is, "by abstaining from sexting these girls can prevent the criminalization of their peers who, presumably, would not have re-posted or further disturbed their images had the girls not created them in the first place."[55] And since one's ability to secure one's information is constrained by the architecture of SNS themselves, the ability of girls and young women to prevent these instances is likely an illusion. The constraints placed on girls ironically force them to "lose the calculating subjectivity that is necessary for governing oneself"[56] in an online environment shaped by privacy laws that seek to commodify the information they post there.

Conclusion

As Bailey notes, policymakers are implicitly asking and expecting children and youth to respond to infrastructural challenges that they themselves have no control over. As a result, refraining from participation in SNS appears to be the most effective response to these challenges.[57] However, because SNS are so essential to the social interactions of children and youth, such action is not possible. We need to make available safer ways to participate in SNS that do not threaten the security of one's personal information.[58] For example, more control over one's privacy settings in a clear and understandable manner appears to be one way to improve the experiences of girls and young women online.[59] In addition, alternatives to the law, such as the promotion of societal values and mechanisms that reshape social media into an encouraging and learning environment for girls, may also assist in the creation of positive online experiences.

Notes

1   Jane Bailey & Valerie Steeves, "Will the Real Digital Girl Please Stand Up?: Examining the Gap Between Policy Dialogue and Girls' Accounts of their Digital Existence," in *New Visualities New Technologies: The New Ecstasy of Communication*, eds. Hille Koskela & Macgregor Wise (London: Ashgate, 2013), 1–36; D. Buhrmester & K. Prager, "Patterns and Functions of Self-Disclosure during Childhood and Adolescence," in *Disclosure Processes in Children and Adolescents*, ed. K. Rotenberg (New York: Cambridge University Press, 1995), 10–56; Patti M. Valkenburg & Jochen Peter, "Social Consequences for the Internet for Adolescents," *Current Directions in Psychological Science*, 18 (2009): 1, doi:10.1111/j.1467.

2   Bailey & Steeves, *supra* note 1; Helen Adams, "Social Networking and Privacy: A Law Enforcement Perspective," *School Library Media Activities Monthly* 23 (2007): 33, as cited in Priscilla Regan & Valerie Steeves, "Kids R Us: Online Social Networking and the Potential for Empowerment," *Surveillance & Society* 8:2 (2012), <http://library.queensu.ca/ojs/index.php/surveillance-and-society/article/view/3483/3437>; Ilene R. Berson & Michael J. Berson, "Challenging Online Behaviors of Youth," *Social Science Computer Review* 23:1 (2005), 29–38, <http://www.abuse-watch.net/Challenging%20Online%20Behaviors%20of%20Youth%20Berson%20and%20Berson.pdf>; Sonia Livingston & Magdalena Bober, *UK Children Go Online: Surveying the Experiences of Young People and Their Parents* (London: Economic and Social Research Council, 2004); Kelly Mendoza, "'WATZ UR NAME?' Adolescent Girls, Chat Rooms, and Interpersonal Authenticity," Working Paper No. 403, (Media Education Lab, 2007), <http://mediaeducationlab.com/sites/mediaeducationlab.com/files/403_WorkingPapers_Mendoza.pdf>; Leslie Regan Shade, "Internet Social Networking in Young Women's Everyday Lives: Some Insights from Focus Groups," *Our Schools/Ourselves* (Summer 2008): 65–78, <http://www.policyalternatives.ca/sites/default/files/uploads/publications/Our_Schools_Ourselve/8_Shade_internet_social_networking.pdf>.

3   Bailey & Steeves, *supra* note 1.

4   Sandra Petronio, *Boundaries of Privacy: Dialectics of Disclosure* (New York: State University of New York Press, 2002).

5   Bailey, Chapter I.
6   For a list of the relevant bills being debated at the time of discussion, see Hannah Draper, "Canadian Policy Process Review 1994–2011," 5 March 2012, The eGirls Project, <http://egirlsproject.ca/research/research-memos-backgrounders/2013-policy-discourses-jurisdictions/>.
7   Bailey & Steeves, *supra* note 1.
8   *Ibid.*
9   Bailey, Chapter I.
10 For a rural/urban comparative analysis, see Burkell & Saginur, Chapter V.
11 Our rural adult focus group included Catlin (19), Laura (18), Trish (18), and Brianne (20). Our rural minor focus group included Courtney (17), Chelsea (17), Paula (17), Beth (16), and Josie (16). Our urban adult focus group included Keira (21), Donna (19), Jill (20), Andrea (22), Ashley (18), and Kathleen (20). Our urban minor focus group included Vicky (17), Eve (16), Abby (17), Jacquelyn (17), Lauryn (17), Monique (16), and Jane (16). Our rural adult interviewees were Cassandra (19), Becky (19), and Amelia (18). Our rural minor interviewees were Monica (16), Lynda (17), and Nicole (16). Our urban adult interviewees were Alessandra (21), Mackenzie (20), and Cindy (20). Our urban minor interviewees were Alicia (17), Clare (16), and Josée (15).
12 See also Bailey, Chapter I.
13 Valerie Steeves & Cheryl Webster, "Closing the Barn Door: The Effect of Parental Supervision on Canadian Children's Online Privacy," *Bulletin of Science, Technology & Society* 28:1 (2008), doi:10.1177/0270467607311488.
14 The notion of "responsibilization" derives from the work of O'Malley. The concept refers to the process whereby government agencies provide individuals with tools to govern themselves by modifying their behaviour and taking precautions in order to decrease the likelihood that they become victimized through decreased exposure to crime. P. O'Malley, "Responsibilization," in *The SAGE Dictionary of Policing*, eds. A. Wakefield & J. Fleming (London: SAGE, 2009), 277–279. In her analysis of the Respect Yourself campaign, Lara Karaian argues that slut shaming is used to responsibilize teenage girls in order to prevent sexting harms to themselves and potential perpetrators. Lara Karaian, "Policing 'Sexting': Responsibilization, Respectability and Sexual Subjectivity in Child Protection/Crime Prevention Responses to Teenagers' Digital Sexual Expression," *Theoretical Criminology* 18:3 (2014): 284.
15 Karaian, *supra* note 14 at 284.
16 Valerie Steeves, Trevor Milford & Ashley Butts, *Summary of Research on Youth Online Privacy* (Ottawa: The Office of the Privacy Commissioner of Canada, 2010), <https://www.priv.gc.ca/information/research-recherche/2010/yp_201003_e.pdf>.

17 *Ibid.*

18 Sonia Livingstone, "Taking Risky Opportunities in Youthful Content Creation: Teenagers' Use of Social Networking Sites for Intimacy, Privacy and Self-Expression," *New Media and Society* 10 (2008): 393–411, <http://eprints.lse.ac.uk/27072/1/Taking_risky_opportunities_in_youthful_content_creation_(LSERO).pdf>.

19 Susan Barnes, "A Privacy Paradox: Social Networking in the United States," *First Monday* 11 (2006), <http://firstmonday.org/article/view/1394/1312>.

20 Esther Dyson, "Reflections On Privacy 2.0," *Scientific American* 299 (2008): 50–55, <http://libserver.wlsh.tyc.edu.tw/sa/pdf.file/en/e080/e080p042.pdf>.

21 Valerie Steeves, *Young Canadians in a Wired World, Phase II: Trends and Recommendations* (Ottawa: MediaSmarts, 2005), 17, <http://mediasmarts.ca/sites/mediasmarts/files/pdfs/publication-report/full/YCWWII-trends-recomm.pdf>.

22 Jacquelyn Burkell, Valerie Steeves & Anca Micheti, *Broken Doors: Strategies for Drafting Privacy Policies Kids Can Understand* (Ottawa: Office of the Privacy Commissioner of Canada, 2007): 2, <http://www.idtrail.org/files/broken_doors_final_report.pdf>.

23 Seounmi Youn, "Teenagers' Perceptions of Online Privacy and Coping Behaviors: A Risk-Benefit Appraisal Approach," *Journal of Broadcasting & Electronic Media* 49 (2005): 86, <http://beta.orionshoulders.com/Resources/articles/26_22338_%20().pdf>.

24 Priscilla Regan & Valerie Steeves, "eKids R Us: Online Social Networking and the Potential for Empowerment," *Surveillance & Society* 8 (2012), <http://library.queensu.ca/ojs/index.php/surveillance-and-society/article/view/3483/3437>; Youn, *supra* note 23; Kate Raynes-Goldie, "Aliases, Creeping and Wall Cleaning: Understanding Privacy in the Age of Facebook," *First Monday* 15 (2010), <http://firstmonday.org/htbin/cgiwrap/bin/ojs/index.php/fm/article/view/2775/2432>.

25 Valerie Steeves, *Young Canadians in A Wired World, Phase III: Online Privacy, Online Publicity* (Ottawa: Media Awareness Network, 2014): 2, <http://mediasmarts.ca/sites/mediasmarts/files/pdfs/publication-report/full/YCWWIII_Online_Privacy_Online_Publicity_FullReport.pdf>

26 Regan & Steeves, *supra* note 24 at 156.

27 *Ibid.*

28 *Ibid.*

29 Matthew J. Hodge, "Comment: The Fourth Amendment and Privacy Issues on the 'New' Internet: Facebook.com and Myspace.com," *Southern Illinois University Law School Journal* 31 (2006): 111–112, <http://pdf.aminer.org/000/244/151/privacy_issues_on_the_internet.pdf>; Regan & Steeves, *supra* note 24.

30 Jim Rapoza, "'Privacy Policy' as Oxymoron: Current United States (US) Law Prevents Real Progress in the On-Line Privacy Push," *eWeek*, 20 October 2008, 48, cited in James P. Lawler & John C. Molluzzo, "A Study of the Perceptions of Students on Privacy and Security on Social Networking Sites (SNS) on the Internet," *Journal of Information Systems Applied Research* 3:12 (2010), <http://proc.conisar.org/2009/3732/CONISAR.2009.Lawler.pdf>; Sören Preibusch, Bettina Hoser, Seda Gürses & Bettina Berendt, "Ubiquitous Social Networks: Opportunities and Challenges for Privacy-Aware User Modelling," (Berlin: Impressum, 2007), <http://www.diw.de/documents/publikationen/73/diw_01.c.59994.de/dp698.pdf>.

31 Barnes, *supra* note 19; Steeves, *supra* note 25; Steeves at al, *supra* note 16.

32 Bailey, Chapter I; Bailey & Steeves, *supra* note 1.

33 Regan & Steeves, *supra* note 24 at 152.

34 Bailey & Steeves, *supra* note 1 at 4.

35 Steeves et al, *supra* note 16 at 7.

36 Clay Clavert, "Sex, Cell Phones, and the First Amendment," *The Catholic University of America CommLaw Conspectus* 18 (2009), <http://firstamendment.jou.ufl.edu/pubs/SexCellPhonesPrivacyArticle.pdf>.

37 Steeves et al, *supra* note 16 ; Bailey & Steeves, *supra* note 1; Shade, *supra* note 2.

38 Bailey & Steeves, *supra* note 1 at 25.

39 Bailey, Chapter I.

40 Kids Help Phone is a free, anonymous, and confidential phone and online professional counselling service for youth. For more information, please visit:http://org.kidshelpphone.ca/en.

41 MediaSmarts is an educational website containing a wide range of copyright-cleared resources to help teachers integrate media literacy and web literacy. For more information, please visit:<http://mediasmarts.ca/>.

42 Amy Dobson, "Performative Shamelessness on Young Women's Social Network Sites: Shielding the Self and Resisting Gender Melancholia," *Feminism & Psychology* (2013): 411, doi:0959353513510651.

43 Bailey & Steeves, *supra* note 1. Also see Bailey, Chapter I, for further discussion.

44 Bailey & Steeves, *supra* note 1 at 4; Burkell et al, *supra* note 22; Amanda Lenhart & Mary Madden, *Teens, Privacy and Online Social Networks* (Washington, D.C.: Pew Internet & American Life Project, 2007).

45 Livingstone & Bober, *supra* note 2; Steeves, *supra* note 21.

46 Bailey & Steeves, *supra* note 1 at 1.

47 *Ibid.*, at 26.

48 Burkell et al, *supra* note 22; Regan & Steeves, *supra* note 24.

49 Bailey & Steeves, *supra* note 1 at 2.

50 *Ibid.*, at 25.

51 Bailey & Steeves, *supra* note 1.
52 Valerie Steeves, "Young People on the Internet," in *The Routledge Handbook of Surveillance Studies*, eds. David Lyon, Kevin Haggerty & Kirstie Ball (New York: Routledge, 2012).
53 Regan & Steeves, *supra* note 24.
54 Karaian, *supra* note 14 at 289.
55 *Ibid.*
56 Dawn Moore & Mariana Valverde, "Maidens at Risk: 'Date Rape Drugs' and the Formation of Hybrid Knowledges," *Economy and Society* 29 (2000): 526, cited in Karaian, *supra* note 14.
57 Bailey, Chapter I.
58 Jacquelyn A. Burkell, Alexandre Fortier, Lorraine Wong & Jennifer Lynn Simpson, "The View From Here: User-Centered Perspectives on Social Network Privacy," *FIMS Library and Information Science Publications*, Paper 25 (2013), <http://ir.lib.uwo.ca/cgi/viewcontent.cgi?article=1027&context=fimspub>.
59 See Bailey, Chapter I, for further discussion and a detailed description of the ways in which technical infrastructures set girls up for conflict online.

CHAPTER XV

Transformative Works: Young Women's Voices on Fandom and Fair Use

Betsy Rosenblatt and Rebecca Tushnet

Introduction

Media fandom is a worldwide cross-cultural phenomenon. Although fandom as a concept has far-reaching and diverse historical roots, this chapter focuses on a particular variety of media fandom that includes as a significant focus the creation of "fan-works," new creative works based on existing media. These works include fanfiction, fanart, and "vids," which are montages of images from media sources, often set to music, that tell a story or highlight particular themes or characters. Outside media fandom, fanworks are often lumped in with other forms of remix culture because they mix elements of existing media, such as characters, settings, or images, with each other and with new ideas or material. This brand of fandom is a mostly online activity, and most participants are female.[1]

Much fanwork creation relies on copyright laws that authorize creators to copy, remix, and derive their creations from copyrighted works without prior permission under certain circumstances. These laws generally include among their considerations whether the new work is non-commercial and whether it transforms the purpose or meaning of the original.[2] Non-commerciality and transformativeness are central to fan remix and the creation of fan communities. Many scholars have considered the relationships between fans, fandom, and law. This chapter contributes to that scholarship by presenting empirical examples of the transformative impact of copyright fair use and fair dealing laws on the lives of individual fanwork creators, especially young women.

This chapter draws principally on fans' responses to a call by the US-based non-profit Organization for Transformative Works (OTW) for personal accounts of how creating fanworks has influenced fans' lives.[3] The responses indicated that fandom and fanwork creation provide unique opportunities for young women and girls to develop selfhood, emotional maturity, and professional skills. Broad understandings of fair use, fair dealing, and other laws permitting the creation of non-commercial derivative works not only promote individual expression by often marginalized speakers, but also offer those speakers benefits that are not readily available through other means.

Methodology

The OTW is a non-profit organization established in 2007 with the aim of promoting the acceptance of non-commercial fanworks as legitimate creative works, to preserve the history of fan culture, and to protect and defend fanworks from commercial exploitation and legal challenge. Among other things, the OTW conducts legal advocacy and operates the Archive of Our Own (AO3), a non-profit website that hosts users' fanworks. The OTW "represents a practice of transformative fanwork historically rooted in primarily female culture," and while the organization explicitly welcomes and includes fans of all genders and sexual identities, it also values its "identity as a predominantly female community with a rich history of creativity and commentary."[4]

In the course of its legal advocacy work, the OTW reached out to its members and users for their own stories regarding why they remix and how participating in remix culture has helped them. In October 2013, the OTW distributed the call via the OTW's news blog and social media outlets, including Twitter and Tumblr:

> The OTW's Legal Advocacy project has stood up for fans' rights to create and share, helping individual fans with legal questions and making fans' collective voices heard in court cases.
>
> Recently, our Legal Committee asked for fans to help by providing either media stories or personal stories of takedown

requests and actions that have made fans hesitant to create or share fanworks.

> Your help is needed again! … The Legal Committee is thus looking for stories of how fandom has helped fans in day-to-day life. We need you to share your individual stories with concrete examples. For example, perhaps being in fandom has helped you to learn a language, helped you in school, or helped you improve skills that you use elsewhere – skills such as writing, video editing, coding websites, audio editing, or anything else. We don't need personal information from you, but the more specific the story, the better.[5]

Respondents sent their personal narratives to the OTW via email. Over a one-month period, the OTW received 107 responses. The sampling described here identifies trends in those responses, relying heavily on quotations to share the voices of those who responded, since much public discussion about fans (and young women) discounts their own understandings and experiences. These quotations illustrate potential synergies between copyright law and fanwork creation in the personal development of girls and women.

We note that, because of the electronic nature of these responses, we cannot independently verify the age or gender of each respondent. Compounding this uncertainty, many fans use pseudonyms that might obscure their genders. For those reasons, we have depended on cues in the responses that indicate that the they are indeed from girls or women describing their youth, such as references to high school, entering college, living with parents, or choosing a career path. Respondents are identified herein by the names they used in their responses, many of which are likely not the names they use in non-fandom contexts.

Fandom and Self-Actualization

The responses overwhelmingly described how both fanwork creation and participation in fan communities helped girls and young women find their own voices, explore and understand themselves, and gain skills that served them later in life. As described below, fandom provides opportunities that other activities may not because fandom encourages generative discourse – that is, each fan builds on others' work while contributing her own insights. The discursive nature of fandom permits fans to connect with others like themselves despite geographic distance.

Fanworks Help Young Women Understand Themselves

Individual fanwork creators often say that participating in fandom changed their lives. Adria, one of the respondents, wrote, "Fanfiction literally saved my life. Not only could I read and watch the stories I loved, but I could write them, get that pain and hopelessness out in characters and worlds that I knew as well as my own." This characterization of fandom as rescuer was not uncommon. For many, fanworks represent an opportunity to meet personal emotional needs through engagement with familiar, even beloved, source material. Fans reported feeling unique – able to contribute creatively to fandom – but not alone. Amanda M. explained how remix provided a path toward emotional health:

> I started drawing fanart, though I had only a vague interest in art before that point. I ended up drawing nearly every day and improving quickly, motivated to draw for and contribute to the fandom I had joined. I made friends. I got better. I no longer felt inferior in my family situation, as I had discovered something unique I could throw my all into ....
>
> Producing and consuming fan-created media has remained a constant for all of these years. I'm not saying that they've been easy ones, but the community has helped me through. On my darker days, I'm able to funnel my negativity through art rather than through violence, and it has been five years since I last took a blade to my own skin. I can't say I'm one of the people who would not be alive today without fandom, but I certainly would not be the same person.

Through fan remix, young women learn that they can be makers, and that their expression is valuable because it is their own.[6] Libitina began in fandom as a consumer of fanworks, and became a creator, and doing so allowed her to "gain ... confidence in her opinions." Soon, she was "producing essays – proper collegiate essays – with ease." She explained that fandom allowed her to discover her own writing style: "letting myself have my own voice, and having the time, space, and encouragement to find that voice – is what fandom gave me."

Fandom also creates an opportunity for creators who do not see themselves and their interests represented in popular culture to create and share a version of that culture that reflects their own priorities and concerns. New technologies allow individuals with limited financial means, including youth dependent upon parents for support, to talk back to mass culture,[7] and fan communities allow individuals to find, support, and get support from others with similar interests. By rewriting and rearranging the portions of mass media that speak to them, fans explore and create a sense of themselves as autonomous individuals.

For example, a common trope in fandom is the "Mary Sue," a power fantasy in which a female character representing the author joins the main characters and proves to be the best of them all. This type of rewriting "offers a partial antidote to a media that neglects or marginalizes certain groups. Victims of prejudice often internalize its claims …. Mary Sues help the writer claim agency against a popular culture that repeatedly denies it."[8] Given the social science evidence on the importance of representations, Mary Sue remixes can help combat the toxic effects of stereotyping and underrepresentation:

> Many Mary Sues comment on or criticize the original, while at the same time creat[ing] something new. They highlight the absence of society's marginal voices in the original works, the stereotyped actions or inactions of certain characters, and the orthodoxy of social relationships in the original.[9]

Fanworks also permit young women to explore issues of gender and sexuality. Women have been the primary producers of "slash" fanworks, which take characters who are usually shown in official texts as heterosexual and portray them in same-sex relationships.[10] This practice challenges mainstream gender norms and stereotypes, allowing fans to explore alternative sexualities and gender roles. By rewriting official texts, slash writers reimagine what is possible. "In the process, they not only escape the inequalities of the real space marketplace of speech, but they create a new world — one in which the gender of the author plays a minimal role in the construction of the marketplace of expression."[11] Slash can "negate the uneven power balance afforded to women and men by simply removing 'gender as a governing and determining force in the love relation-ship.'"[12] As Lauren S. explained, "fanworks were and are vitally important to my acceptance of my queer sexuality, as they provide a world where non-heterosexuality is accepted and celebrated." Lillian K. had a similar experience, encountering asexuality through fandom:

> The availability of non-heteronormative narratives in mainstream media is, rather unfortunately, slim. As I was going through puberty, I relied on fanfiction to give me these queer storylines and explore as proxy the spectrum of sexuality and gender .... It is through fanfiction that I first learned the term "asexual," which, after further research, I now identify as. It is through fanfiction that I lost that unfamiliar-idea-uneasiness regarding non-heterosexual, non-cisgender identities and people, which made me a better, more accepting person.

Because of its ability to look beneath the surface of conventional characters, remix can challenge not only conceptions of gender and sexual identity but also of race and disability. Tea F.'s experience highlights how remix creation empowers girls and young women of colour to move beyond traditional underrepresentation. Tea F. ran a fanfiction-based roleplaying site, where she encountered a fourteen-year-old girl, C:

> One day, C contacted me, very distraught, to tell me she would no longer be allowed to use my website, because she was getting Ds in English class, and had to pull her grades up. I was shocked — C was an exceptionally talented writer for her age, and wrote several hundred words a day on my website. She was exactly the kind of young woman whom I expected to be getting As in her English classes. I talked to C and her father at length about the problem.
>
> It turned out that she was getting frustrated in English class because, as a female Chinese-American immigrant, she couldn't relate to the readings in class, that were mostly written by and featuring European-American men. She much preferred writing fanfiction where she could explore other Chinese-American girl characters, rather than writing about characters and authors who had nothing in common with her and bored her to tears.

Tea F. spoke with C's teacher, and came to an agreement that allowed C to receive extra credit for writing fanfiction. C learned to love English. Now, "seven years later, C is a senior in college double-majoring in English and photography." Similarly, Medellia's story explains how *X-Men: First Class* fandom exposed her to new visions of disability that she, as a wheelchair user, could identify with, and how participation in fan community prompted her own creativity:

> There are relatively few stories in pop culture about people with disabilities, fewer where they're main characters, even fewer in genre fiction ... In that little corner of the internet, I found more depictions of a wheelchair user having power, respect, love and adventures than I've ever seen in "real" entertainment. Even seeing [an *X-Men* character] as a future wheelchair user was a comfort I had been missing .... It wouldn't have worked the same for us to individually make up stories for original characters; that's lonely work and we never would have come together if not for our interest in characters we knew and loved.

The connections enabled by shared interest in a mainstream text, combined with the freedom to remix it, create spaces for diversity of all kinds. Amanda B.'s story is very different from Medellia's, but it similarly emphasizes the uniqueness of non-commercial remix culture:

> I can honestly say that fandom helped me survive my teenage years. Because fanfiction is written mostly by amateurs, it is largely based on how the writers are feeling and the kinds of experiences they are familiar with. This gives fanfiction an unparalleled amount of honesty and allows the reader to emo-tionally connect with the characters' situations like I have never found to be true in any other type of media — and I have been reading my entire life. I am an aromantic, asexual autistic with an anxiety disorder and I knew *none* of that throughout nearly my entire high school career .... Fanfiction truly, honestly, was the only thing that got me out of bed some days. When I was so angry I couldn't speak, I went to fanfiction. When I was so depressed I wanted to die, I went to fanfiction. When I was so ecstatically joyous that I felt like multicolored sparks of light were zipping around my insides, ricocheting off the prison of my

skin—it was probably because of fanfiction. Fandom has allowed me to connect with three of the best friends I have ever had in my life and I absolutely believe it has made me a better person. It has given me, an autistic woman who cannot read faces or body language, cannot hold a conversation, cannot stand to be touched, a way to feel less alone.

The variety and freedom of non-commercial remix allows for these kinds of engagements, and many others, as Ashley's story demonstrates:

> I was born with a physical disability called Cerebral Palsy …. When I discovered fandom in the seventh grade, with it came, for the first time in my life, honest-to-God friends, who just wanted to be around me because we all enjoyed the same book series …. Because of our shared fandom, for once, somebody was looking at me, and not my *body*.
>
> As the years went by and I joined other fandoms, created work and finally get the nerve to post it where anyone could see it, I gained other friends. Friends whose only connection to me was their usernames, their own fanfiction profiles and stories, and the way we all messaged and encouraged one another to write. I learned that it wasn't okay for my family to think I was sick and wrong … just for being bisexual and not homophobic; I learned that if a dedicated writer could overcome dyslexia (like one of my friends), then it wasn't so far-fetched to try and apply that to myself and my CP; … and I learned what it felt like to be surrounded by a community that could accept me for myself.

These stories only scratch the surface of the diversity of remix cultures, and the incomparable benefits they provide to those who love them. Fanworks are often dismissed as nothing more than trivial, derivative foolishness. But this derision is often bound up with negative attitudes towards feminine pursuits and particularly negative attitudes towards young women's attempts to find their own identities. As one commenter put it:

> The teen fic writer is finding her literary voice, learning to comment on mainstream fictions, finding a way to express her sexuality that's not entirely about recreating herself as a visual

object for others' consumption. She is rarely a very good writer, because she's usually a very new one .... She has an intellectual life, even if it's sometimes more potential than realized.[13]

As the next section details, fandom can help develop that intellectual life in ways that pay off both inside and outside fan communities.

Remix Cultures Teach Important Skills

Remix encourages young women to develop skills they will use later in life. Seeing other creators just like them – ordinary, nonprofessional – gives new creators the confidence to try making works of their own. Relatedly, remix offers participants unique access to an audience that is engaged with the subject matter, conversant in the fine details of the relevant art form, and eager to offer feedback. The skill benefits of non-commercial remix culture are widespread and powerful, and they reach across multiple media: language skills, writing, visual art, video, and other technical fields.

Rebecca Black's empirical research has revealed that young writers using online fan fiction sites can effectively learn English, as well as different cultural perspectives.[14] Love of the original source motivates people to spend hours writing and reviewing in English, and audience members, even strangers, volunteer to help creators improve linguistically because they want more commentary on their favourite sources.[15] This is borne out in the responses the OTW received. Nadja R.'s experience was typical:

> I am not a native speaker of English, yet today, at 27, I am doing my PhD in English Literature. This is largely due to the fact that I have been reading and writing in English ever since I was about 13 years old. What have I been reading and writing? Fanfiction .... Most of it, especially the high quality works, were in English, so I was highly motivated to hone my English skills until I was capable of writing in this foreign language. As a result, my grades in English were always straight As. My teachers wondered how someone with no English relatives who had never been to the US or the UK could possibly develop such a large vocabulary .... I can honestly say that without fanfiction, I wouldn't be where I am now, career-wise!

The same phenomenon works in the other direction. A number of respondents described translating non-English source material or fanworks into English for English-speaking fans, which gave them experience that allowed them to be hired as translators.

Fanwork creation also builds fans' skills in their native languages. Sarah D. explained that reading and writing fanfiction improved her storytelling skills, vocabulary, and critical thinking:

> I believe that the huge volume of well-written fics that I read was responsible for my perfect score on the reading part of the SAT. Reading fanfiction gave me more confidence in my own writing — when I read fics especially by new authors I could see how their abilities improved the longer the story went on. This impressed on me the importance of practice and learning from past mistakes. In the same vein, when I posted my first fics on fanfiction.net I was able to get a lot of constructive criticism on my writing. I would not have had access to such constructive criticism had I posted only original works. I know this because when I posted my original writing on fanfiction.net's sister site, I received one comment whereas my fic would get at least 20. The resources available to fanfiction writers are amazing — from beta readers to peer reviews. Those who participate in fandom are invested in the fics, because everyone wants good fics to read. In a way, a fic writer can get more personal attention than a student in English class.

Samantha C. emphasizes the particular value of fandom's community feedback to adolescents:

> Fanworks … are an outlet for adolescents in an unstable and shifting time in their lives when they are discovering themselves. Adolescence is generally when people reach the developmental stage where they come to question what they have learned and begin to think critically …. Fanfiction is an arena where writers can try everything, good or bad, and learn to write better. It's a self-teaching tool …. No matter what fandom I was interested in writing for, someone was there to read it and tell me they enjoyed it. I wasn't used to that sort of confidence boost. You can't walk around school offering people copies of your most recent writing and ask for opinions.

Nicky found that analytical skills developed in remix culture paid dividends in her school and career:

> One of fandom's greatest strengths is that it … has complicated, important conversations about gender, sex, race and class that equal and exceed most of the discussions I had in college. Because they are taking place online, their audience and participants are huge and hugely varied, and it was easy for a newcomer like me to catch up on the basics. When I walked into my first gender studies course in college, I was miles ahead of the curve … [which] led to an internship with one of my publishing heroes and my first post-college job.
>
> While more abstract academics are important too, fandom works more accessibly, analyzing media that 16-year-old me was invested in, and it kept records in places I didn't need college admission or a journal subscription to get to. Our culture is saturated with images, with advertising, with media of every kind, and as a young woman, having the tools to describe and deconstruct the flood was invaluable.

Tassos found in her youthful experiences with fan remix the confidence to start a new career as an adult:

> I've always loved making up stories, but I never had that kick in the pants to start really writing and *finishing* stories till I found fandom. *Farscape* was my first fandom when I was 16, and I wrote my first fic then too. Writing in fandom was both work and play. Work because writing is hard; play because I got to experiment with different ideas, different styles, got instant feedback both good and bad, write stories that failed, write stories that succeeded, learn about my own process, became part of a community where I could do all that and where my off the wall ideas and enjoyment of fandom was valued.
>
> Fast forward ten years. I'm 25, in my first job after college as a science major working in a university lab as a lab tech and manager. I hate my job …. I hear about science journalism as a possible career path, and one of the big reasons my depressed self doesn't talk myself out of this big huge change in direction is because I know I can write. I have the confidence from having

written fic for ten years that I can make it and get paid to write
for a living in a very competitive field.

Fans also gain skills in visual art and develop technological prowess through remix creation. The vidding community has been particularly valuable as a "female training ground," teaching technical
skills to women: web design, coding, video and image editing, and
filmmaking.[16] A school semester offers only a few opportunities to
evaluate each student's creative work, while a fan community has
almost limitless capacity to respond to fanworks. According to Ania,
"I got more practice with video- and audio-editing doing Sherlock
fanvids than I did at uni, even though my studies are related to that
(telecommunication with focus on audio processing)." Isabel H's
story was similar. She taught herself how to use increasingly complex
video-editing programs and techniques in order to make vids: "Now,
I'm at the Columbus College of Art and Design in pursuit of a degree
in Cinematic Arts so I can be a professional film editor. All because
that roughly 6 years ago, I got into the *Teen Titans* fandom .... I feel
most myself when editing videos."[17]

Others reported gaining web-based skills through fandom. For
Kristen, for example, creating her first fan site at age seventeen "led
to an ongoing love of web design." She taught herself several web
design programs and techniques, which she implemented on her
fannish websites, and reported that "as an adult, I have used these
skills in every job I've ever had." These experiences are consistent
with the research literature indicating that video remix develops
digital literacy – the ability to communicate persuasively with audio-
visual materials.[18]

Synergies with the Law

Since remix often involves copying and transforming copyrighted
materials, it relies for its legality on fair use and fair dealing doctrines. US law analyzes the legality of fanworks according to a
general doctrine of fair use; Canadian law incorporates both a fair
dealing doctrine and an exception to copyright infringement for
non-commercial user-generated content (UGC).[19] Although the
nations' laws differ from each other, both laws tend to favour non-
commerciality and promote transformativeness, either of meaning,
purpose, or both. In both countries, non-commerciality is a core

consideration,[20] and non-commercial remixes are especially likely to constitute fair or non-infringing use, even when the result is minimally transformative.[21]

Transformativeness is implicit in both countries' laws. Although fair use under US law does not explicitly demand transformativeness, the US Supreme Court has explained in *Campbell v. Acuff-Rose Music* that transformative works "lie at the heart of the fair use doctrine's guarantee of breathing space within the confines of copyright."[22] For that reason, even substantial copying in the service of transformation can be fair, as long as it results in a new meaning, message, or creative vision.[23] Similarly, Canada's UGC exception does not explicitly demand transformativeness but does require that the new work not be a substitute for the existing one.[24]

As fan remixes tend to be both transformative and non-commercial, the two factors work together to create space for fanworks and fan communities in ways that are particularly beneficial to fans' self-expression without causing financial harm to — and often providing financial support for — markets that copyright holders have a right to control. Likewise, the fact that these doctrines do not require advance permission for transformative, non-commercial copying is essential to their role for young women and girls, who often would not ask for permission or would be ignored if they did.

Both nations' doctrines have uncertainties that may undermine these synergies between law and creative practice. Because US law depends on a flexible set of factors to determine whether a particular use is fair, fanwork creators remain vulnerable to unpredictable legal challenges from rights holders even for fanworks that are likely to constitute fair use.[25] Canadian law provides what appears to be a more certain copyright regime by incorporating a statutory safe harbour for non-commercial remix, but may still leave fanwork creators vulnerable to challenge based on rights holders' moral rights or allegations that fanworks have a "substantial adverse effect, financial or otherwise," on exploitation of the existing work.[26] In addition, because Canada's UGC exception is a recent and relatively untested legal development, it remains to be seen how much certainty it will actually provide for fanwork creators. Notwithstanding these potential uncertainties in Canada's regime, the element-based structure of the UGC exception provides greater facial predictability than the factor-based structure of US fair use law.

Non-Commerciality

The non-commercial nature of fandom makes it particularly condu-
cive to self-expression by young women and girls. Because fan communities create a built-in audience, fanwork creators need not cater to
the commercial market in order to find an audience for their works.
And because fanworks are free to consume, young women and girls
can experience them and become a part of their communities despite
limited resources. Nadja R. learned English through fan fiction
because "fanfiction was free, it was about things that I, as a teenager,
loved passionately, and most of all, it meant that I could participate
and have an audience of my own." By contrast, copyright-incentiv-
ized works invariably seek to appeal to more consumers. Even when
they target niche markets, they will target markets—people who can
pay for something specialized.[27] Not incidentally, people who can pay
are less likely to be young, female, relatively poor, or otherwise part
of culturally devalued groups, since cultural and economic power
are often related.[28] As Medellia, whose participation in *X-Men: First
Class* fandom helped her deal with her disability, explained, she knew
that stories about disability

> wouldn't sell a big-budget movie, but it doesn't have to in fan-
> fiction, because fanfiction is a hobby and a social outlet, not a
> moneymaking venture …. I enjoy the participation as much
> as the finished project. I have friends and allies who share my
> interests, and we can tell the stories and make the art we want
> to see, for each other.

Instead of money, fans provide other fans support and feedback,
which generates a culture of giving and learning.[29] As Nicky wrote,
"fandom's gift based economy and penchant for sharing expertise
profoundly shaped my creative process."

Non-commercial creative uses, precisely because they are not
motivated by copyright's profit-based incentives, are also more likely
to contain content that the market would not produce or sustain.[30]
As media scholar Catherine Tosenberger argues, non-commercially
generated works are often "unpublishable," which

> frees [fanwork creators] to tell the stories they want to tell. You
> can do things in fanfiction that would be difficult or impossible
> to do in fiction intended for commercial publication, such as

experiments with form and subject matter that don't fit with prevailing tastes …. It's a way of asserting rights of interpretation over texts that may be patriarchal, heteronormative, and/or contain only adult-approved representations of children and teenagers.[31]

This is reflected in Elisa D.'s story of how fan remix helped her overcome depression: "Freed from the constraints of publication, etc., I was able to write stories again …. Most readers are not interested in traditional serial-fiction. But fan fiction lovers adore serials."

Non-commerciality also promotes community building. As sociologist Viviana Zelizer has explained, defining an activity as non-commercial, even if it takes place in spaces where other people are making money (such as YouTube), changes how people feel and reason about it. "Earmarking" – treating value differently depending on the social context in which it is exchanged – is pervasive, not just for money but for everything from "tokens and commercial paper to art objects, and even including kitchen recipes or jokes – anything, in fact, that is socially exchangeable." Earmarking is an excellent way of "[e]stablishing or maintaining individual or group identity."[32] Authors who think of themselves as creating for free – for the joy of sharing with other people – will think differently about their works than authors who hope to sell their output in the open market. And their works, as a result, will be systematically different from works produced by copyright's incentives.[33] Thus, fandom's non-commercial nature creates the close-knit, interactive fan communities that support young women's personal growth. This social benefit is one reason that copyright law should treat non-commercial remix with special solicitude.

Transformativeness

Likewise, the fact that fan remix transforms rather than supplants pre-existing media content both promotes self-expression by girls and young women who might not see themselves in more mainstream media products and encourages them to talk back to the media. Remixes demonstrate that there is no single, necessary story and that everyone has a right to offer an interpretation.[34] Thus, "rewriting the popular narrative becomes an act of not only trying to change popular understandings, but also an act of self-empowerment."[35] Historically, remix comes disproportionately from minority groups:

women;[36] gay, lesbian, bisexual, transgender, and queer people;[37] and racial minorities of all sexes and orientations.[38] As fan N.J.B. wrote to the OTW,

> Fanfiction is the supportive, creative space for blacks who after seeing a movie in which all the main characters are white, thinks, "I would do it differently, and here's how." Fanfiction is for the girls who read a comic book in which the heroes are all men, and imagines herself as Captain America. Fanfiction is for all those who watch/listen/read to a story and cannot empathize with the characters as they are, but see potential in tweaking, recreating, and re-imagining the story to fit and resonate with their own lives. Finally, fanfiction is for all groups of people misrepresented in our mass media, and it gives them a space to create alternatives which are as empowering for the producer as the consumer.

This process is reflected in the story of Alice Randall, whose retelling of *Gone with the Wind* from the perspective of the slaves on the estate ultimately led to an important US fair use decision.[39] Well before the internet made so much fan creativity easily findable, she began her imaginative career as a girl remixing *Batman*:

> When I was a girl of six or seven I fell in love with the television series Batman. And like many loves, there was something I hated in it too: I hated the fact that no one who looked like me was in the story. For two weeks after that awareness I was frustrated. The third week I wrote myself in. I literally began to write out Batman scripts and write a part for me into them, a Bat Girl part. My Bat Girl wasn't a sidekick; she was a catalyst; every time I wrote her into a story, she changed its ending. When they took Batman off the air, I made my first long-distance phone call. I wanted to save the show.[40]

Randall's story illustrates the way in which young people who find they have something to say about what's left out of mass media can transform themselves into creators as they transform the source works.

Benefits of Not Requiring Permission

That fair use and fair dealing doctrines do not require advance permission for transformative, non-commercial copying is essential to their role for young women and girls. First, it permits young women to use underlying media sources as they wish to, not as rights holders wish them to. Second, it is particularly valuable for those who, like young women and girls, may be conditioned not to even try to seek permission if it is required.

It is well established that licensing breeds censorship. Existing licensing options for user-generated content (other than Creative Commons) always retain the option to censor.[41] Official fan communities want fans to "celebrat[e] the story the way it is,"[42] not to explore ways in which it might be different. Nor could rights holders reasonably be expected to applaud uses of their works that transform characters and critique themes as fan remix often does. The most transformative and self-actualizing fanworks – for example, those that identify gaps and flaws in a work's representation, or challenge characters' sexualities – are the same ones that rights holders would be least likely to permit, if they were given the opportunity to approve or disapprove.[43]

Likewise, creativity is often spontaneous and unpredictable.[44] If someone has to take a license before writing five hundred words about Harry Potter, they will make other plans. This is especially true for younger (and less experienced) writers. Given the small scale and limited resources of these individuals, "anything that raises their innovation costs can ... have a major deterrent effect."[45] Not only might they fear denial of permission, but even more perniciously, they might not even think to ask.

Members of marginalized groups are already likely to be nervous about expressing themselves, and barriers to expression can silence them before they even start.[46] Female vidders, for example, have historically been reluctant to step up and claim cultural legitimacy, and legal uncertainty hinders both production of transformative works and remixers' ability to achieve mainstream recognition.[47] The OTW routinely receives queries from young women who are afraid to post their fanworks online, for fear that in doing so they may draw legal action from rights holders. In contrast, the queries that the OTW receives from men more frequently request assistance in opposing challenges by rights holders to already-existing fanworks. If they have to seek permission to create, young women and girls – who already feel unrepresented in the system, something they turn to fanworks to remedy – are less likely to seek permission. This phenomenon not only emphasizes the importance of permission-free fair use and fair dealing systems, but also strongly counsels against the sort of "take down first and ask questions later" approach permitted by the US Digital Millennium Copyright Act (DMCA),[48] since underrepresented speakers are also less likely to push back when their works are challenged.[49] Permission-free use is a crucial element of fandom's role in promoting young women's self-actualization through fan remix.

Conclusion

Together, the non-commerciality of fan communities and transformative potential of fan remix work together to create a space where young women and girls can experience the self-discovery and skill building discussed above. It is no surprise that fanwork production is a female-dominated form in North America. While female content producers are underrepresented in commercial spheres, the non-commerciality of fandom frees girls and young women to create and consume works that represent their own lives and interests.

Neither today's technologies nor the practices surrounding the use of those technologies can be fully understood without attention to the role of law. US and Canadian law both favour non-commercial remix, but differ in that US fair use law relies on a flexible set of factors, while Canadian law defines fair dealing broadly and adopts a statutory safe harbor for non-commercial remix.[50] Although non-commercial, transformative works generally fall soundly within the ambit of US fair use, the OTW still receives a steady stream of inquiries from girls and young women who are concerned that by posting their fanworks, they may run afoul of US copyright law. To the extent that legal uncertainty and risk aversion may lead girls or young women to refrain from participating in fan remix communities, Canada's UCG exception may provide a model for US copyright reform, but only if that UGC exception actually results in greater legal certainty for fanwork creators.[51] Regardless, as the responses to the OTW's call for comments demonstrate, the benefits of a system that favours non-commercial, transformative remix for those young women and girls who elect to participate in fan remix are undeniable.

Notes

1   United States, U.S. Copyright Office, *Public Hearings: Exemption to Prohibition on Circumvention of Copyright Protection Systems for Access Control Technologies 0108.20-0111.15* (Washington, DC: Library of Congress, 2009), <http://www.copyright.gov/1201/hearings/2009/transcripts/1201-5-7-09.txt>; Abigail Derecho, "Gender and Fan Culture (Round Eight, Part One): Abigail Derecho and Christian McCrea," *Confessions of an Aca-Fan*, 26 July 2007, <http://henryjenkins.org/2007/07/gender_and_fan_culture_round_e.html> ("[O]nline fanfic ... was the invention of white American women [most of them were white, most of them were women, not all]"); Jaime Warburton, "Me/Her/Draco Malfoy: Fangirl Communities and Their Fictions," in *Girl Wide Web 2.0: Revisiting Girls, the Internet, and the Negotiation of Identity*, ed. Sharon R. Mazzarella (New York: Peter Lang, 2010).

2   For US fair use law, see 17 U.S.C. § 107, <http://www.law.cornell.edu/uscode/text/17/107>; for Canadian fair dealing law see *Copyright Act* (R.S.C., 1985, c. C-42), § 29.21, <http://laws-lois.justice.gc.ca/eng/acts/c-42/page-19.html#h-27>.

3   The authors both serve on the Legal Committee of the OTW.

4   "What We Believe," Organization for Transformative Works, <http://transformativeworks.org/about/believe>.

5   The OTW posted the call on its news blog and Tumblr account on 3 October 2013. For the full text of the call, see <http://transformativeworks.org/news/your-personal-fandom-stories-are-urgently-needed>; on Twitter, the OTW linked to that post with the following tweet, sent on 3 October, 2014 at 9:53 a.m.: "Our legal team needs YOUR fandom stories ASAP to help them argue for fans' rights to create & share http://bit.ly/1c9dS2Z #copyright #NTIA."

6   Francesca Coppa, "An Editing Room of One's Own: Vidding as Women's Work," *Camera Obscura* 26 (2011): 124 ("A vidder can tailor-make her media to be as she likes it, and can convey her preferred reading of a text by showing us exactly what and how she sees."); Erik Jacobson, "Music Remix in the Classroom," in *DIY Media: Creating, Sharing and Learning with New Technologies*, eds. Colin Lankshear & Michele Knobel (New York: Peter Lang, 2010), 32 ("Remix, as a particular form of [the principle that you don't have to be a virtuoso or have a band to make music], teaches people that anybody can comment on or interpret already existing music. Finally, as with punk, the expectation is not that you are remixing to secure immortality. The idea is that doing it yourself (DIY) is a worthwhile activity in and of itself.").

7   Rebecca Tushnet, "I Put You There: User-Generated Content and Anti-Circumvention," *Vanderbilt Journal of Entertainment and Technology Law* 12

(2010): 903–905, 930, n168; Marcus Boon, *In Praise of Copying* (Cambridge, MA: President and Fellows of Harvard College, 2010), 147, <http://www. soundsphenomenal.org/projects/rootmap/resources/Boon_text_final. pdf> (montage "is a poor people's art," based on limited resources).

8   Anupam Chander & Madhavi Sunder, "Everyone's a Superhero: A Cultural Theory of 'Mary Sue' Fan Fiction as Fair Use," *California Law Review* 95 (2007): 609, <http://scholarship.law.berkeley.edu/cgi/viewcontent.cgi? article=1228&context=californialawreview>.

9   *Ibid.*, at 613.

10   Sonia K. Katyal, "Performance, Property, and the Slashing of Gender in Fan Fiction," *Journal of Gender, Social Policy, and the Law* 14 (2006): 467, <http://www.wcl.american.edu/journal/genderlaw/14/katyal3.pdf> (discussing the role of slash in making queer meanings).

11   *Ibid.*, at 489.

12   *Ibid.*, at 486 (citation omitted).

13   Comment by thesmallmachine on Laura Miller, "Middle-Earth According to Mordor," *Salon*, 15 February 2011, <http://www.salon. com/2011/02/15/last_ringbearer/#postID=2042021&page=0&comment= 1986322>.

14   See, e.g., Rebecca W. Black, "Access and Affiliation: The Literacy and Composition Practices of English Language Learners in an Online Fanfiction Community," *Journal of Adolescent and Adult Literacy* 49 (2005), <https://resources.oncourse.iu.edu/access/content/user/miku-leck/Filemanager_Public_Files/L750%20Electronic%20Lang%20and%20 Lit/Instruction/Fanfiction%20_%20English%20Lang%20Learners.pdf>; Rebecca W. Black, "Language, Culture, and Identity in Online Fanfiction," *E-Learning* 3 (2003), <http://www.wwwords.co.uk/pdf/validate.asp ?j=elea&vol=3&issue=2&year=2006&article=5_Black_ELEA_3_2_web>.

15   Black, "Access and Affiliation," *supra* note 14 at 123–124.

16   Jesse Walker, "Remixing Television," *Reason Magazine*, August/September 2008, <http://reason.com/archives/2008/07/18/remixing-television>.

17   See also Michele Knobel, Colin Lankshear & Matthew Lewis, "AMV Remix: Do-It-Yourself Anime Music Videos," in *DIY Media: Creating, Sharing and Learning with New Technologies*, eds. Colin Lankshear & Michele Knobel (New York: Peter Lang, 2010), 205 (AMV remix is a cultural practice that aids effective learning and fosters high levels of personal involvement and motivation in learning, and whose lessons can be brought into the classroom); Scully1121, "There is Hope for Vidders," *LiveJournal*, 16 November 2011, <http://vidding.livejournal.com/275168o. html> (describing how fan's youthful remix experience allowed her to build skills she later used to earn work for a television show).

18   See, e.g., Kyle D. Stedman, "Remix Literacy and Fan Compositions," *Computers and Composition* 29 (2012), doi:10.1016/j.compcom.2012.02.002.

19 US fair use law, *supra* note 2; *Copyright Act, supra* note 2.

20 *Ibid.*

21 *Sony Corp. v. Universal City Studios*, 44 U.S. 417 (1984): 449, <http://www. law.cornell.edu/copyright/cases/464_US_417.htm> (holding that non-commercial uses are presumptively fair); *Copyright Modernization Act*, S.C. 2012, c. 20, <http://laws-lois.justice.gc.ca/eng/annualstatutes/2012_20/ FullText.html>, s. 29.21 (creating exception for non-commercial user-generated content); Graham Reynolds, "Towards a Right to Engage in the Fair Transformative Use of Copyright-Protected Expression," in *From "Radical Extremism" to "Balanced Copyright": Canadian Copyright and the Digital Agenda*, ed. Michael Geist (Toronto: Irwin Law, 2010), 395.

22 *Campbell v. Acuff-Rose Music, Inc.*, 510 U.S. 569, <https://supreme.justia. com/cases/federal/us/510/569/case.html>, 579 (1994).

23 See generally, e.g., *Seltzer v. Green Day, Inc.*, 725 F.3d 1170 (9th Cir. 2013, use of entire image in music video that gave image new, religious meaning was transformative and fair); *Cariou v. Prince*, 714 F.3d 694, at p. 705–8 (2d Cir. 2013, because an audience could readily find new meaning and message in Prince's artworks, they constituted fair use regardless of amount copied or intent toward the original).

24 *Copyright Act, supra* note 2.

25 Cf. Matthew Sag, "Predicting Fair Use," *Ohio St. L. J.* 73 (2012), <http:// moritzlaw.osu.edu/students/groups/oslj/files/2012/05/73.1.Sag_.pdf> (assessing the predictability of fair use outcomes in litigation); Pamela Samuelson, "Unbundling Fair Uses," *Fordham Law Review* 77 (2009), <http://papers.ssrn.com/sol3/papers.cfm?abstract_id=1323834> (identifying policy-based clusters in fair use jurisprudence); Barton Beebe, "An Empirical Study of U.S. Copyright Fair Use Opinions, 1978–2005," *U. Pa. L. Rev.* 158 (2008), <https://www.law.upenn.edu/journals/lawreview/ articles/volume156/issue3/Beebe156U.Pa.L.Rev.549(2008).pdf> (identifying predictable patterns in fair use jurisprudence).

26 *Copyright Act, supra* note 2, at s. 14.1, s. 28.1, s. 28.2, s. 29.21.

27 Neil Weinstock Netanel, "Copyright and a Democratic Civil Society," *Yale Law Journal* 106 (1996): 362, <http://ecohist.history.ox.ac.uk/readings/ ip/netanel.htm> ("[E]xpansive copyright owner control over existing expression may exacerbate the problem of market- based hierarchy. Given authors' needs to draw on the existing images, sounds, and texts that make up our cultural milieu, conglomerate control over existing expression would continue to subvert the democratization of public discourse even in a digital age in which many authors no longer rely on conglomerates to market and distribute new works.").

28 Henry Jenkins, "Gender and Fan Studies (Round Five, Part Two): Geoffrey Long and Catherine Tosenberger," *Confessions of an Aca-Fan*, <http:// henryjenkins.org/2007/06/gender_and_fan_studies_round_f_1.html>("[I]

ssues of gender, race, class, sexuality ... have affected who has *access* to that institutional approval .... Fandom is a space where people who have historically been denied access to institutional narrative creation have said, 'Well, then, we'll tell this story *our way.*' ... The Internet has exacerbated fandom's anarchic tendencies, and all those old cultural hierarchies – creator/consumer, male/female, straight/queer, art/crap – are getting shaken up .... In fandom, you don't have to be anointed by the Official Culture Industry to be an artist, to share your work and have it be appreciated.").

29   Two of the most popular fan fiction archives, for example, ban commercial appeals on their sites but leave opportunities for readers to comment upon a work. See "Fanfiction," last modified 5 March 2009, <https://www.fanfiction.net/tos/>; "Archive of our Own," <archiveofourown.com/tos>.

30   Rebecca Tushnet, "User-Generated Discontent: Transformation in Practice," *Columbia Journal of Law & The Arts* 31 (2008): 506, <http://scholarship.law.georgetown.edu/cgi/viewcontent.cgi?article=1068&context=fwps_papers> ("by its very independence from the incentives of formal markets, non-commerciality signals the presence of expression tied to a creator's personhood "); Rebecca Tushnet, "Economies of Desire: Fair Use and Marketplace Assumptions," *William and Mary Law Review* 51:513 (2009): 531–536, <http://scholarship.law.georgetown.edu/cgi/viewcontent.cgi?article=1021&context=facpub> (expanding upon the relationship between non-commerciality of transformative works and their propensity to express a creator's personhood).

31   Catherine Tosenberger, "Potterotics: Harry Potter Fanfiction on the Internet," PhD diss., University of Florida, 2007, 34–35, <http://ufdc.ufl.edu/UFE0019605/00001/pdf> ("Fandom is a space where freedom to read and write whatever one wants are felt in a much more concrete way than in more 'official' spaces .... Fanfiction is, in many ways, given life by what other spaces don't allow."); Liz Gannes, "NTV Predictions: Online Video Stars," *Gigacom*, 30 December 2007, <http://gigaom.com/2007/12/30/ntv-predictions-online-video-stars/> ("Fans, operating outside of the commercial mainstream, have the freedom to do things which would be prohibited [to] those working at the heart of a media franchise – explore new stories, adopt new aesthetics, offer alternative interpretations of characters, or just be bad in whatever sense of the word you want. And much of the online video content thrives because it is unpublishable in the mainstream but has strong appeal to particular niches and subcultures." Quoting Henry Jenkins; alteration in original); Timothy B. Lee, "Ars Book Review: 'Here Comes Everybody' by Clay Shirky," review of *Here Comes Everybody* by Clay Shirky, *Ars Technica*, 3 April 2008, <http://arstechnica.com/articles/culture/book-review-2008-04-1.ars/3> (interview

with Clay Shirky discussing valuable group productions whose transaction costs mean that they can only take place voluntarily, outside the market and the firm).

32 Viviana A. Zelizer, "The Social Meaning of Money: 'Special Monies'" *The American Journal of Sociology* 95 (1994), <http://cas.umkc.edu/econ/economics/faculty/wray/631Wray/Zelizer.pdf>.

33 Mark S. Nadel, "How Current Copyright Law Discourages Creative Output: The Overlooked Impact of Marketing," *Berkeley Technology Law Journal* 19 (2004): 797–803, <http://community-wealth.org/sites/clone.community-wealth.org/files/downloads/article-nadel.pdf>.

34 See also Robert S. Rogoyski & Kenneth Basin, "The Bloody Case that Started from a Parody: American Intellectual Property and the Pursuit of Democratic Ideals in Modern China," *UCLA Entertainment Law Review* 16 (2009): 258 (Remix allows average citizens who lack political power under China's authoritarian regime to "appropriate and democratize their own cultural benchmarks, encouraging the kind of cultural participation that is vital to the development of 'a just and attractive society.'" Citation omitted).

35 Chander & Sunder, *supra* note 8 at 619–620.

36 Kristina Busse, "In Focus: Fandom and Feminism: Gender and the Politics of Fan Production," *Cinema Journal* 48 (2009): 105–106, <http://queergeektheory.org/InFocus48-4.pdf>; Francesca Coppa, "A Fannish Taxonomy of Hotness," *Cinema Journal* 48 (2009), <http://www.yalelawtech.org/wp-content/uploads/Coppa_In_Focus.48.4.pdf>; Micole, 29 August 2007 (11:15 EST), "Women's Art and 'Women's Work,'" *Ambling Along the Aqueduct*, <http://aqueductpress.blogspot.com/2007/08/womens-art-and-womens-work.html>.

37 Julie Levin Russo, "User-Penetrated Content: Fan Video in the Age of Convergence," *Cinema Journal* 48 (2009): 126 ("In many cases, [fan videos] render queer dimensions of these sources visible by telling stories of same-sex romance (known as 'slash') through sophisticated viewing and editing techniques." (Citation omitted); see Katyal, *supra* note 10 at 468–469 (discussing the role of slash in making queer meanings).

38 Olufunmilayo B. Arewa, "From J.C. Bach to Hip Hop: Musical Borrowing, Copyright and Cultural Context," *North Carolina Law Review* 84 (2006): 561, 622, <http://www.cs.northwestern.edu/~pardo/courses/eecs352/papers/sampling%20and%20copyright.pdf>; K. J. Greene, "'Copynorms,' Black Cultural Production, and the Debate over African-American Reparations," *Cardozo Arts & Entertainment Law Journal* 25 (2008): 1186, <http://www.cardozoaelj.com/wp-content/uploads/2013/03/Green.pdf>.

39 *Suntrust Bank v. Houghton Mifflin Co.*, 268 F.3d 1257 (11th Cir. 2001), <http://www.yale.edu/lawweb/jbalkin/telecom/suntrustbank%28appeal%29.pdf>.

40 "A Conversation with Alice Randall," Houghton Mifflin Harcourt, <http://www.hmhbooks.com/readers_guides/wind_done_gone/index2.shtml#conversation>.

41 YouTube's Content ID system always provides copyright owners the option to block content for any reason, as does Amazon's Kindle Worlds. "How Content ID Works," Google Support: YouTube, <https://support.google.com/youtube/answer/2797370?hl=en>; "Content Guidelines and Review Process," Kindle Worlds, <https://kindleworlds.amazon.com/faqs?topicId=A2W2IF5J2WZDKT>; *Bloodshot*, Kindle Worlds <https://kindleworlds.amazon.com/world/Bloodshot?ref_=kww_home_ug_Bloodshot> (along with standard bans on "erotica" and "offensive content," requiring characters to be "in-character," and banning "profane language," graphic violence, "references to acquiring, using, or being under the influence of illegal drugs," and "wanton disregard for scientific and historical accuracy").

42 Amy Harmon, "'Star Wars' Fan Films Come Tumbling Back to Earth," *New York Times*, 28 April 2002, B28, <http://www.nytimes.com/2002/04/28/movies/film-star-wars-fan-films-come-tumbling-back-to-earth.html>.

43 Chander & Sunder, *supra* note 8 at 623 ("While DC Comics produced an alternative strip featuring an evil Batman, it issued a cease and desist letter to an artist depicting Batman and Robin as lovers [sometimes explicitly]. An evil Batman, it seems, is more palatable than a gay one." Citation omitted).

44 Julie Cohen, "Creativity and Culture in Copyright Theory," *UC Davis Law Review* 40 (2007): 1151, <http://scholarship.law.georgetown.edu/facpub/58/>.

45 Andrew W. Torrance & Eric A. von Hippel, "Protecting the Right to Innovate: Our 'Innovation Wetlands,'" MIT Sloan Research Paper no. 5115–13, 9 October 2013: 18, <http://ssrn.com/abstract=2339132>.

46 Library of Congress Rulemaking Hearing Section 1202, Testimony of Francesca Coppa 0119.4–0120.4, 7 May 2009, <http://www.copyright.gov/1201/hearings/2009/transcripts>.

47 *Ibid.*, at 0120.5–0120.17.

48 US fair use law, *supra* note 2 (providing copyright safe harbor for internet service providers that comply with notice-and-takedown procedures).

49 United States, United States Patent and Trademark Office, *Department of Commerce Private Meeting: Copyright Policy, Creativity and Innovation in the Digital Economy* (Washington, DC: 2013), 192, <http://www.uspto.gov/ip/global/copyrights/121213-USPTO-Green_Paper_Hearing-Transcript.pdf> ("[P]eople who are most likely to create non-commercial remix are

disproportionately women, disproportionately minorities of various kinds, and they already feel unwelcome in the larger system, and I can see this in my own practice. When a guy who makes a Stargate remix gets a takedown from YouTube, he writes me, even though we've never met. You know, he finds me, and he says I'm just going to counter-notice. This is fair use. Women, if they find me, then we call—I have a long conversation with them, we talk it over in great detail, and hopefully I convince them that they can counter-notify when they have a valid fair use defense, which by the way is often.").

50 *Supra* note 2.

51 See Lawrence Lessig, *Remix: Making Art and Commerce Thrive in the Hybrid Economy* (New York: Penguin Press, 2008), 254 (arguing for exemptions for non-commercial use).

CHAPTER XVI

I Want My Internet! Young Women on the Politics of Usage-Based Billing

Leslie Regan Shade

Stop right now, thank you very much, I need my internet to
  download stuff
Hey you, Mister ISP, we don't want to pay any usage-based fee
Do-do-do-do-do-do-do-do-do … we got to work together …
Ba-da-ba-da-ba-da-da-da-da … the internet's forever …

Stop right now, we have had enough, the internet belongs to all of us …
Hey you, trying to charge me more, checking my Facebook shouldn't
  make me poor …
Do-do-do-do-do-do-do-do-do … we got to work together.…
Ba-da-ba-da-ba-da-da-da-da … the internet's forever …

(The Site Girls, 2011)

Based on the bouncy song, "Stop" by the popular mid-1990s girl-power band The Spice Girls, the Site Girls' music video rendition remixes the Motown-influenced song and catchy chorus to argue for the curtailing of usage-based billing by internet service providers. The four campily dressed Site Girls (two men, two women) vamp and sing in a university library amongst rows of books and computer terminals. One of the Site Girls is a stern Mr. CRTC, who warns the other Girls to

*Slow it down, read the sign, we're going to make you pay for your
    time online.
Got to keep it down, baby. We're metering you time.
Your freedom of expression doesn't match your bottom line.*

Posted on YouTube in 2011, the music video was created by university students in response to the Stop The Meter campaign, initiated by the Canadian digital rights group OpenMedia. The campaign's goals were to persuade the Canadian Radio-Television and Telecommunications Commission (CRTC), the minister of industry, and large telecoms to put an end to the practice of usage-based billing (UBB), a system that allows internet service providers (ISPs) to calculate how much data their users upload or download to the internet, and to charge them according to their usage. Under UBB, higher monthly internet costs impact "heavy" internet users—for instance, those uploading or downloading large data and video media, and innovative content creators who depend on fast and fulsome internet connections. Critics against UBB cited as concerns the challenge of small ISPs to compete in an oligopolistic telecom market, the high costs of internet access in Canada compared to other countries, and a resultant negative impact on the average internet consumer whose monthly fees could exceed their ability to pay, thus leading to continued concerns of digital divides.

This chapter examines the Stop the Meter campaign and in particular focuses on how young women used YouTube as a site for speaking out against UBB and for urging their viewers to sign OpenMedia's online petition against UBB. The actions of these young women personify what Lance Bennett, in his analysis of digital rights activism, describes as "easily embraceable personal action frames."[1] Personal action frames, often crowdsourced, use social media to enable individuals to become "catalysts of collective action processes as they activate their own social networks."[2]

This example of youth digital activism is situated within a model of digital policy literacy, which emphasizes how the effective use of digital media involves learning and negotiating the policy processes, political economic parameters, and infrastructural affordances that shape information and communication technologies.[3] The first element of the model, policy processes, is particularly apt, as it considers structures that enable and constrain citizen and youth involvement in making policy decisions around digital communication.

Structures of policy participation include diverse modes of policy activism and intervention within, or outside, official policy-making processes. The Stop the Meter campaign illustrates the vibrancy of citizen-generated activism to effectuate the public interest in telecom policy, and, as well, the surprising viral nature of the campaign that catalyzed many young women to take to YouTube and speak out about the importance of the internet in their everyday lives.

Young People and Social Media: "Connected and Confident"

MediaSmarts' Young Canadians in a Wired World, Phase III research project (2014) surveyed just over five thousand Canadian students in grades 4 to 11 about their use of the internet and mobile technologies, asking a series of questions related to ethics, privacy, digital literacy, bullying, and commercialization. The report found that youth were "highly connected,"[4] using a variety of platforms, with 99 percent having access to the internet outside of school. Portable devices – tablets, laptops, smartphones – are common. Social media included Facebook, where, in grades 7 to 11, equally 83 percent of young women and young men had an account; yet young women surpassed young men in having personal accounts on other popular social media sites: Twitter (53 percent young women, 41 percent young men), Instagram (55 percent young women, 32 percent young men), Pinterest (22 percent young women, 4 percent young men), and Tumblr (41 percent young women, 16 percent young men).[5] "Confident and enthusiastic"[6] characterizes young Canadians' use of the internet for sociality, information, and education.

For young people, social media generates what danah boyd calls "networked publics": "an important public space where teens can gather and socialize broadly with peers in an informal way."[7] While specific social media platforms wane in popularity (for instance, Facebook – because more adults and parents have joined) and others, such as Pinterest and Tumblr, are used to curate specific content for different audiences,[8] boyd's observations that "teens' mediated interactions sometimes complement or supplement their face-to-face encounters"[9] ring true with the MediaSmarts' findings, as well as with the findings of the eGirls Project reported in this volume.[10]

Relevant to this chapter is whether and how young Canadian women use the internet for civic and political activism, and what their knowledge is about digital policy issues. In their findings,

MediaSmarts reports that only a small proportion of students participate in online public debate and activism.[11] Thirty-five percent of youth have joined or supported activist groups online (examples cited include Free the Children, Greenpeace, Students against Bullying), but not in a sustained fashion. There are no significant gender differences, although youth in higher grades are more likely to join online groups.[12] And while YouTube was the most popular website for 75 percent of youth, most young people watch content rather than create, post, and distribute their own content online; only 36 percent of young men and 30 percent of young women have posted video or audio files.[13]

Civic and Political Participation by Youth

Although there is an emerging literature on civic and political participation by youth, in general few studies have yet specifically addressed political uses that young women in particular make of new information and communication technologies. The general scholarship on young people and political engagement suggests that youth have in many instances eschewed traditional forms of citizen participation, such as voting (if they are of the majority age), political party membership, and reading mainstream news media. However, these forms of "dutiful" citizen participation are generationally situated, and instead young people engage in other "non-traditional" modes of engagement, such as volunteering, consumer activism, and engagement in networked media.[14]

As Kahn and his collaborators wrote, for youth there is "more emphasis on lifestyle politics, influencing business practices through boycotts and buycotts, and expressive acts tied to popular culture."[15] Participatory forms of politics-driven participation include blogging and sharing or discussing perspectives on social media, which can "foster offline engagement by increasing individuals' political interest and thus their motivation to be involved, by developing civically relevant digital skills, and by placing participants in contexts where recruitment is more likely."[16]

Noted alongside the popular use of social media by young people is its increasing use for civic and political engagement. "[Networking young citizens]," writes Brian Loader, "are more project orientated; they reflexively engage in lifestyle politics; they are not dutiful but self-actualizing; their historical reference points are less likely to be those of modern welfare capitalism but rather global information networked capitalism and their social relations are increasingly enacted through a social media networked environment."[17]

Similar to Bennett, Emily Weinstein[18] found that youth's expression of their politics and civic engagement is characterized by the personalization of their message and their politics. Tactics youth deploy for civic engagement are diverse, but as Elisabeth Soep cautions, these can challenge social inclusion as these literacies are evolving.Practices tend to be learned through peer engagement, by "geeking around," and in non-formal educational settings.[19] Soep proposes that young people need a combination of social and technical skills: social, to learn how to effectively manage the interpersonal dynamics of their social networks and learn how to engage in public awareness; and technical, learning digital and creative skills by designing tools and platforms, understanding the nuances of remix and appropriation.

Much research on youth and civic and political participation online tends not to differentiate by gender, a point noted earlier by Anita Harris,[20] who also demonstrates that feminist theory is attending to cultural and digital sites wherein young women enact various forms of cultural "resistance." (One recent example is Megan Boler's work on young adult women's labour in the Occupy Movement.)[21] This is echoed by Caroline Caron,[22] who proposes that scholars in both girlhood studies and political theory need to pay more attention to girls' cultural production and media-making activities and how their practices and discourse can be integrated into, and contribute towards, theorizations of citizenship. Martha McCaughey also argues that we need more research and information on whether young women's active use of social media is creating new forms of political consciousness "that will ultimately lead to new definitions of activism and of feminism, and new theories of social change."[23]

Digital Policy Activism

Many young Canadians are increasingly savvy about their rights as digital users and eager to contest digital policy. Copyright reform has been of particular interest to both young men and women, as they voiced their concerns through social media (the early popularity of

Facebook was used to great effect for the first phase of copyright reform activism in 2007).[24] Openmedia and other groups championed net neutrality activism, with youth participating in a rally on Parliament Hill. One successful intervention was instigated by University of Ottawa law students, with the support of the Canadian Internet Policy and Public Interest Clinic, in a complaint filed to the Office of the Privacy Commissioner, alleging various violations of Canadian privacy laws by Facebook under the *Personal Information Protection and Electronic Documents Act*.[25] Facebook was asked to make remedies, and Canada became the first country in the world to issue legally binding recommendations to the popular site whose global membership at that time topped 300 million.[26]

UBB

Usage-based billing also elicited activism by young people, who avidly took to YouTube to voice their concerns. Before a discussion of the texture of their responses, a brief description of UBB and the regulatory debates is provided.

UBB refers to a mechanism wherein ISPs charge their subscribers based on how much bandwidth they are using within a monthly billing period. Some ISPs contend that this practice is necessary to manage their network congestion, which has increased because of the prevalence of online multimedia content, internet streaming services such as Netflix, and the frequency of downloading. In Canada, the large telecom firms such as Bell Canada and Rogers control both wholesale access to the internet and subscriber's homes through the "last mile". They are in turn obligated to provide internet access to smaller independent ISPs at wholesale rates; the smaller ISPs thus rent network access from the larger telecoms and package their own retail internet services to their subscribers, often as unlimited monthly bandwidth packages.

The debates around UBB surfaced in the spring of 2010 when the CRTC approved Bell Canada's application to bill wholesale and retail internet customers based on their bandwidth usage.[27] In the fall the CRTC issued a call for comments on UBB.[28] In November OpenMedia launched a petition, StopTheMeter, to persuade Tony Clement (then Minister of Industry), the CRTC, and other stakeholders to put an end to UBB. Within 24 hours, over one thousand people signed the petition.

In January 2011 the CRTC rendered its decision on UBB. It ruled that large ISPs may determine the rates they charge to small ISPs for user bandwidth, but in turn small ISPs must get a 15 percent discount when they buy wholesale.[29] Steve Anderson, executive director of OpenMedia, responded to the decision by saying that, "It is deeply disappointing that the Commission has decided to give a few companies a free hand to engage in economic discrimination and crush innovation. Now is the moment for forward-looking visionary policy-making – not half measures and convoluted compromises with the companies trying to kill the open internet. This decision is a step in the right direction, but it is clear to me that Canadians are going to have to continue to speak out on this issue".[30]

By mid-January 2012 the Stop the Meter petition was signed by 25,000 people, and by the end of February over 160,000 people, energized by widespread media coverage of the issue and the campaign, signed the petition. Wading into the debate, Minister of Industry Clement himself tweeted his displeasure at the CRTC ruling. Prime Minister Stephen Harper also tweeted his concerns and ordered a review of the decision.[31] Opposition parties (the Liberals and NDP) also spoke out against the decision.

The CRTC quickly announced a review of the decision, solicited online comments, held a public hearing in July at CRTC headquarters in Gatineau, Quebec, and rendered its compromise decision in November. During these six months even more consumers, public interest groups, and businesses were galvanized by the UBB debates, and by the end of April 400,000 had signed the OpenMedia petition, and by early summer half a million people had signed.

The CRTC's November decision proscribed a wholesale billing model based on capacity; it ruled that large ISPs may charge independent ISPs a flat monthly rate, or a rate based on capacity and the number of users. Under this decision, independent ISPs were thus tasked with managing their network capacity by determining in advance the amount they need to serve their retail customers.[32] Pleased with the decision, OpenMedia wrote that it was a "step forward for the open and affordable internet," with Anderson applauding the consumer activism: "It is truly rare for people to outmaneuver Big Telecom's army of lobbyists, but together Canadians did it".[33]

Youth and UBB

What galvanized young Canadians to react against the somewhat arcane and seemingly not exciting topic of UBB? OpenMedia catalyzed debate with its campaign and online petition Stop The Meter. As a national, non-profit, and nonpartisan media reform organization, OpenMedia's membership consists of a network of civil society; consumer, labor and media advocacy organizations; grassroots activists; and academics. Initiated by Steve Anderson when he was an MA student at Simon Fraser University (SFU) in Vancouver, and initially called the Campaign for Democratic Media, OpenMedia's goals are to increase public awareness and informed participation in Canadian media, cultural, information, and telecommunication policy formation. Campaigns prior to UBB included Stop Big Media, to influence the 2007 CRTC Diversity of Voices hearing on media concentration, the Save Our Net campaign on net neutrality, and the 2010 petitioning of the CRTC for licensing of the English-language service of the Al Jazeera international television news network.[34]

Run by a slim staff of young people (paid staff, at the time of UBB policy debates all young women; unpaid interns; volunteers; and a board of directors), and dependent on modest financial support from member organizations and donations, OpenMedia's creative use of social media, blunt messaging, and home-base in Vancouver (resident to a healthy media-activist community characterized by a successful series of annual Media Democracy Days) was recognized by local and national media, citizens, consumers, corporations, industry, and government regulators. Indeed, following a very robust and successful campaign against Bill C-30, the federal government's proposed "lawful access" surveillance legislation,[35] OpenMedia's "youthful team of leaders" was awarded the 2013 British Columbia Civil Liberties Association (BCCLA) Youth Activism Award.[36]

With the Stop the Meter campaign, OpenMedia was successful in crowdsourcing through its website and in its use of Twitter, listserv messages, humorous short videos, and a national "day of action" in February with rallies against UBB across the country, to maintain the persistence of the issue in mass media – public and private broadcasters, local and national print media.

Humour played a key role in the public discourse about UBB. Two videos in particular virally spread on YouTube, through listservs, Facebook, and on websites. These were situated amongst a growing use of social media for satirical and critical commentary, prominent in the 2011 federal election,[37] which transpired as the CRTC decision was under reconsideration in the spring. One video featured the popular CBC comedian Rick Mercer, from his weekly television show, in a spoof of the *Heritage Minutes* (historical dramatizations of key events in Canadian history inserted in between shows broadcast on CBC and CTV).[38] Titled "Our Gouge-Based Heritage," the video features Mercer in four distinct moments in time:

> 1892: as a telegraph operator chastised by his boss, "Don't use Morse Code so extravagantly – who do you think we are? America?!"
> 1956: as a telephone salesman, chastised by his boss, "These long distance calls are killing us!"
> 1973: as a tele-facsimile operator chastised by his boss, "Our phone bills are going through the roof!", and,
> 2011: as an office worker typing on his internet–enabled computer, chastised by his boss, "Didn't you get the memo about the unlimited bandwidth? Clue in …rates are going up!"
> The tagline: "Paying way more for communications – a part of our gouge-based heritage."[39]

The oft-remixed Hitler "Downfall" video was also used for comedic effect. In this instance, Hitler and his troops have over-extended their monthly cap on Rogers and have been cut off; seething, Hitler screams "Monthly Usage Caps! What good is Netflix if I can't even watch it?!? What am I to do? I refuse to sit at Second Cup and leech their WiFi like some grad student."[40]

In the winter of 2011 when the campaign was ramping up (after the initial CRTC decision and before and during the time when the government ordered the CRTC to reconsider its decision), young people posted short videos on YouTube. Using their webcams to record themselves, in what looks to be their bedrooms, living rooms, or their parent's rec rooms or basements, they described what impact UBB would have on their uses, such as for online gaming, video production, communicating with friends and family, and school research. Through their short messages, youth displayed "easily embraceable personal action frames"[41] about the potential impact of UBB on their personal use of the internet, and the importance of the internet for their generation. There were at least a dozen videos posted by young people, but at the time of this writing, most of these videos have been taken down or made private by their owners. This ephemerality speaks to the ability of young people to fluidly use social media for various phases of their identity formation and political identities, and to be able to "forget" their online traces (when they have not been replicated elsewhere by others) when they become passé or, perhaps, embarrassing.

For many youth, vlogging (video blogging) on YouTube is an accessible space to display and debate issues of social and civic importance; this aligns with their affiliation in using social media to connect with their "networked publics." Purchased by Google for US$1.65 billion in 2006,[42] YouTube has since transitioned from a platform populated by amateur videos to one where Google seeks a variety of monetization schemes, the development of premium content, and specialized and sponsored content channels.[43]

In her ethnographic study of how young people use YouTube, Patricia Lange presents a reticulated model of civic participation that emphasizes "social connections, shared interests, and interactions around particular social and place-based attachments," which are focused around "technical affiliations, technologized identities, and affective ties that diffusely propagate shared values."[44] This is a useful framework to consider UBB youth activism.

Lange describes a US teenager named Frank, who took to YouTube to voice his support for network neutrality. Addressing the camera directly, he displays his technical affiliation as a networked and "geeky" teen, joins a wider public discourse debating the issue (which at that time was being deliberated at the Federal Communications Commission), and aligns himself with a concerted movement for net neutrality, spearheaded by the public interest group Free Press and its widespread Save the Internet campaign.

Similar to the example of Frank, UBB activism by youth was comprised of a model of reticulation. Youth were exposed to the issue through a shared interest and passion for the internet; the issue of UBB thus "operates from a socio-emotional starting point."[45] Knowledge and interest in UBB was spurred on by public discourse through OpenMedia, the SFU OpenMedia Club, OpenMedia interns, and print and broadcast coverage in technology, business, and national news sections. This type of "flash activism"[46] involved forwarding, linking, and liking slogans, events, campaigns, petitions, news articles, and videos.

In their accounts of their internet use, their knowledge of UBB, and the potential impact of UBB on their continued internet use, young women's vlogs addressed several concerns: the personal economic impact of not being able to use the internet to its full potential; the social ramifications of not being online; and the consequences for Canadian identity and citizenship in having haphazard, non-robust, and expensive internet connections. Three videos produced by young women (based on the context of the videos, they are estimated to be undergraduates in postsecondary institutions) are next examined to highlight these concerns. The videos were posted to YouTube in early 2011 and, at the time of the writing of this chapter in mid 2014, were all still publicaly available on YouTube. The names of the young women are anonymized in the descriptions, below, but the quotes remain theirs.

Economic Concerns

OpenMedia's Stop the Meter campaign messaging repeatedly emphasized the high cost of internet service under a UBB scenario: "Canadians will have no choice but to pay much more for less Internet." The petition asked the CRTC, industry minister, and prime minister to "stand up for consumer choice and competition in the Internet Service market. I want affordable access to the Internet." The culprits? "Big phone and cable companies," whose motivations are to "gouge Canadians, control the Internet market, and ensure that we continue to subscribe to their television services."[47]

Grace, a young Asian-Canadian woman, narrated a fairy-tale-like script over colorfully hand-drawn stick images. In the fairy tale, set in the far away land of Canada, the internet kings Rogers and Bell were known in their kingdom for charging high rates, and "because they were kings of the internet, they basically had everyone by the balls." Enter the brave knight, an independent ISP named TekSavvy, offering low internet prices and no bandwidth limits. While the kings colluded and tried to influence the small ISP to join their ways to impose a meter, to no avail, the commoners became weary of the "monopoly power of the two kings," proclaiming, "we have the right to give them the finger and have the internet with no meter at reasonable rates." Grace's narrative then cuts to herself as she directly addresses the camera: "Seriously guys, this may sound corny, but unity is the answer." She entreats her viewers to attend a local Stop the Meter rally, sign the petition at StopTheMeter.ca, and visit her "failed" website for more detail.

In a video made as a class project, several young women describe UBB as what occurs when consumers exceed their monthly internet subscription limit, causing overages to get expensive. "It's really not fair," they say, and cite the negative impact for households, businesses, and university students.

Caitlin read a three-and-a-half-minute letter addressed to then–Minister of Industry Tony Clement about UBB – "an issue that is dear to my heart and will effect each and every Canadian in just a few short weeks ... it is far more dramatic and wide sweeping than I had originally imagined." Seated on a couch, with a handmade pastel patchwork quilt tossed over its back, she talks about the variations in bandwidth speed and pricing across Canadian provinces and, looking directly at the camera, sincerely says, "I hope you will realize what barriers this will place on people."

Social Concerns

UBB was also expressed as an impediment to sociality, communication, and entertainment pursuits. Interviewing themselves, the students in the class video project described their use of the internet: for research ("I've never been to the library"); to maintain family ties abroad ("I'd be so homesick if I didn't have Skype or MSN Messenger"); for entertainment and "to pass the time," through Facebook, YouTube, or downloading movies and music ("it saves me a lot of money"). If the internet became unaffordable, the young women said they would listen to the radio more; go to the library "at least once in my life," or a place with "free WiFi like Starbucks"; in lieu of Skype, they would write letters more. They would also watch more TV, do more homework, rent movies, go to movie theatres, and buy albums.

For Caitlin, the internet was envisioned as "open, accessible and a hub of cultural learning and collaboration," enshrined in some government constitutions as an "inalienable human right." Positioning herself as a digital native, she spoke of the intrinsic elements of the internet that constitute it as "a home – an abstract place where every individual has equal rights and power to express themselves – to find information and truth and to learn and better themselves regardless of gender, ethnicity, and most importantly, socio-economic status."

Canadian Identity

Stop the Meter campaign messaging stressed that a UBB system would "crush innovative services, Canada's digital competitiveness, social progress, and your wallet." It positioned the battle as pitting the large incumbent telecommunication firms (Bell, Rogers) against the small independent ISPs across the provinces. Oligopolistic power was positioned as evil and detrimental to Canadian communication rights and cultural sovereignty. Caitlin pronounced the internet as a space imbued with Canadian values; if diminished, she would be "personally crushed" and "enormously disappointed in my country."

Referring to the recurrent issue regarding the brain drain of Canadian talent and accompanying lure of more attractive jobs in other countries, especially the United States, Caitlin directly related a UBB system as a reason that she might be forced to move to more "innovative" countries so that she could pursue her future career which would be undoubtedly dependent on the internet. "I don't want to choose between being employed and being Canadian," she proclaimed.

Despite the amateur quality of their video production, Lange's reticulated model of civic participation is evident in these young women's commentaries and observations about the impact of UBB on themselves and their peers. As they emphasize, their everyday communication is reliant on an accessible and affordable internet, and redolent in their commentaries is the personal – and collective – right to be connected. Their uses are imbued with "technical affiliations" (the internet is ubiquitous and an intrinsic facet for young Canadians); "technologized identities" (the internet is a positive and necessary tool for self-actualization); and, through a public concern with the issue of UBB, the young women create "affective ties that diffusely propagate shared values."[48]

UBB as Digital Policy Literacy

The attention to usage-based billing by young women serves as a useful example of digital policy literacy. Digital policy literacy involves an understanding of policy processes, the political economy of media systems, and knowledge of digital infrastructures. A model of digital policy literacy was developed to serve as an intervention expanding the core elements of media and digital literacy, and to explicitly situate digital policy as a key literacy attribute.[49] By foregrounding digital policy, the model expands upon the tenets of media and digital literacy with their focus on critical reflections on media content that analyzes aesthetics, production, and ideology[50] and how people "engage proactively in a media world where production, participation, social group formation, and high levels of nonprofessional expertise are prevalent."[51]

The following table outlines the characteristics and areas of enquiry for the three elements of digital policy literacy – policy processes, political economy, and infrastructures – related to the young women's literacy around usage-based billing.

Table 1: Digital Policy Literacy Model and UBB

Digital Policy Literacy Elements	Characteristics and Areas of Enquiry for Each Element	Digital Policy Literacy Related to UBB
Policy processes	How is policy constituted?	Gaining an understanding of CRTC regulatory functions, processes, and policies.
	What are structures of participation in policy making?	Gaining an understanding of the role of Industry Canada in telecom policy and its interventions in regulatory matters.
	What are effective modes of activism and intervention to shape policy?	Exercising civic participation through petitions, rallies, and media discourse; social media engagement; "flash activism;" and video creation.
Political economy	What are the socio-political relations surrounding the ownership, production, distribution, and consumption of media?	Gaining an understanding of telecom ownership in Canada and the dominance of Bell and Rogers, and the economic challenges of independent internet service providers.
	How do they reinforce, challenge or influence social relations of class, gender, and race?	Gaining knowledge of wholesale and retail cost structures for internet access and how this can impact affordability and access for many Canadians, especially those with low income and students.

Table 1: (Continued)

Digital Policy Literacy Elements	Characteristics and Areas of Enquiry for Each Element	Digital Policy Literacy Related to UBB
Infrastructures	How do technological affordances and design activate or inhibit online interactions?	Gaining knowledge of the practice of monthly internet subscriptions and the cost of data.
	What is their impact on ownership of content, privacy protection, access, and communication?	Gaining knowledge of how over-ages and high costs can inhibit internet communication for many Canadians, especially those with low income and students.

There is much to applaud in the spirited responses of young women who spoke out against UBB. In questioning the power of big telecom and the actions of regulators, and in expressing concern about access to and affordability of internet services, these young women displayed an awareness of the "public interest" necessity of the internet. But did the framing of the issue from OpenMedia and these young women focus more on their rights as *consumers* of communication services and obscure a more important, yet related, focus on their role as *citizens* using communication services? How are notions of "digital citizenship" and "digital consumership" intertwined? Strategically, media reform organizations and digital policy advocacy organizations such as OpenMedia are savvy to align their messaging towards the consumer impact of policies in order to attract wider public appeal for their campaigns. This consumer orientation is an example of "easily embraceable personal action frames."[52] In the case of UBB, the framing also fed into the dominant governmental policy discourse of marketization, as emphasized in the 2010 consultation paper on the digital economy.[53]

Contemporary telecommunication regulation and services are governed by a regime of market-generated rules for consumers that can often obscure a tradition of ensuring universality for citizens. Policy discourse tosses the terms citizen and consumer interchangeably, and as Sonia Livingstone and Peter Lunt write (in the context of UK policy): "Is 'consumer' taking over from 'citizen' in the communications sector, as suggested by the ubiquitous discourse of choice and empowerment? Does the 'citizen' have a voice in regulatory debates, or is this subordinated to the market?"[54]

As the first frame in the digital policy literacy model suggests, policy processes involve a nuanced understanding of the structures of participation in various forms of policymaking. In the case of the CRTC, it is not an easily comprehended organization, and indeed, for many Canadians and industry, it is a reviled organization precisely because of its regulatory function in the broadcasting and telecommunications sphere. Participating in the policy functions of the CRTC as an intervenor or interested citizen can require a modicum of knowledge of "the rules of engagement" in responding to calls for public participation. Academic advocacy in regulatory realms can be challenging because of academic reward systems favoring peer-reviewed outputs, and negotiation with non-profit and community-based advocacy organizations.[55] Recognizing the need for more fulsome public input, the CRTC has recently published a citizen's guide to participating at the CRTC.[56] Nonetheless it can be difficult for citizens to garner the expertise and the resources to compete on an equal footing with industry interests, who have at their disposal vast resources (legal advice, funds, and dedicated staff) to devote to the detailed public hearings. Tensions can arise then, about how citizens respond to telecommunications policy issues: as digital citizens or as digital consumers. This tension, I might suggest, is indeed a constructive dialogical space for young Canadians to further their knowledge of the complexity of digital policies, and how they might effectively intervene and perhaps shape policy outcomes.

This example of young women engaged in discussing a salient (yet obscure) digital policy issue in thoughtful and creative ways is indeed inspiring. Their knowledge of a technical and policy issue runs counter to how many young women are using YouTube. For instance, Sarah Banet-Weiser has described and critiqued the post-feminist self-brand, wherein gender empowerment is equated with heightened consumer sovereignty.[57] She analyzes how young girls brand themselves using YouTube as a platform; their amateur videos display their engagement with popular culture, dancing, and lip-synching to popular music, and performing femininity in fanciful play-acting. As discussed in further detail by Kanai,[58] important to this self-branding is the feedback loop — the number of views and comments received validate the video and the importance of the self-brand. In a case study looking at "Am I Pretty?" YouTube videos where young women present confessional portraits of their physicality, Banet-Weiser argues that these videos epitomize gendered neoliberal brand culture, showcasing vulnerable young women and packaging them within the commercialized self-esteem market.[59]

In a converged media culture that encourages the commodification of sexuality, recent research exploring how young women are taking to social media for civic and political participation is encouraging. Jessalynn Keller highlights how blogging as a practice has been embraced by many young feminists who have created vibrant communities to discuss contemporary social and political issues; Keller points out that young feminists "are establishing public selves that challenge gender norms and ageist assumptions that youth are uninterested in social change."[60] Likewise Julia Schuster argues that online activism is very important for young feminists to participate in political activities but that because there are generational divides in the use of social media, older people may perceive younger women to be less politically active.[61] And, in a distressingly increased climate of misogyny, Carrie Rentschler describes heightened social media activism by young women against rape culture using mobile media apps such as Hollaback!, which documents and maps street-level harassment; a tactic that Rentschler characterizes as "response-ability": "the capacity to collectively respond to sexual violence and its cultures of racial, gendered and sexuality harassment."[62]

In their use of social media to express their thoughts on political and social issues, chronicle their lives, showcase their creative work, and increasingly to market and brand themselves for future careers in various sectors, a type of labour that Tamara Shepherd describes as "apprenticeship labour,"[63] young people need to know about the policies and politics of the social media platforms they use. In MediaSmart's findings, youth awareness of digital policy issues, in that instance privacy, was variable. The researchers found that there were negligible differences between what young men and young women reported about their knowledge of online privacy policies: 39 percent of young men and 38 percent of young women stated that social media companies are not interested in what they do online, and 67 percent of young men and 68 percent of young women assumed that a privacy policy meant that a company would not share their personal information with others.[64] However, youth were aware of how to use privacy settings to manage their interpersonal relationships, suggesting that for many young people, "privacy is linked to self-presentation and the management of social relationships."[65] (Notably, Sarah Heath reports similar findings from the eGirls Project with respect to privacy and online security in this volume.[66] MediaSmarts recommends that digital literacy education consider the commercial impact of corporately owned social media and the limitations of privacy policies, as well as provide a more nuanced understanding of how young people consider and manage their online privacy.

These concerns echo the framework for digital policy literacy, described earlier in this chapter, and point to a continued need to work with young women to understand how they use social media for education, entertainment, socialization, and civic participation, and to further unpack their knowledge of digital policy issues, such as privacy, surveillance, intellectual property, the terms of service that govern the use of social media, and the regulatory conditions around telecommunication services. As this small case study of activism against UBB reveals, young women are passionate about their use of the internet for their everyday lives and recognize its necessity for their current studies and for their future employment. Importantly, they acknowledge the importance of the internet and robust public interest policies for Canadian identity and citizenship, seeing access to the internet as a basic right.

Postscript

Much has been written in internet studies about the ethical uses of public internet content in research, and indeed the delineation between what should be considered public and private content.[67] The Association of Internet Researchers has compiled a guide to internet ethics, outlining questions to consider regarding ethical practice.[68] In this chapter, with respect to data collection of the production, presentation, and performance of internet content, an expectation of privacy by the creators is not assumed, as the vlogs were posted on a public site with an expectation that they would be viewed and commented on by third parties; in fact, by entreating viewers to sign the OpenMedia petition, the young women all expected to have an audience for their vlogs. According to YouTube's Terms of Service for the period of time when the vlogs were created (the terms of service are from 2007), parent company Google holds a wide-ranging license over this content, including rights to make it available to third parties.[69]

Acknowledgements

Thanks to the Social Sciences and Humanities Research Council (SSHRC) for the funding of the research project Young Canadians, Participatory Digital Culture, and Policy Literacy.

Notes

1   W. Lance Bennett, "The Personalization of Politics: Political Identity, Social Media, and Changing Patterns of Participation," *Annals of the American Academy of Political and Social Science* 644 (2012): 29, <http://sciencepolicy.colorado.edu/students/envs_5720/bennett_2012.pdf>.

2   *Ibid.*, at 22.

3   Leslie Regan Shade, "Towards a Model of Digital Policy Literacy," paper presented at the iConference, Toronto, Ontario, 7–10 February, 2012, <http://dl.acm.org/citation.cfm?id=2132176>; Leslie Regan Shade & Tamara Shepherd, "Youth and Mobile Privacy: Applying a Model of Digital Policy Literacy," *First Monday* 18 (2013) <http://firstmonday.org/ojs/index.php/fm/article/view/4807/3798>.

4   Valerie Steeves, *Young Canadians in a Wired World, Phase III: Life Online* (Ottawa: MediaSmarts, 2014), 2, <http://mediasmarts.ca/sites/mediasmarts/files/pdfs/publication-report/full/YCWWIII_Life_Online_Full-Report.pdf>.

5   *Ibid.*, at 21–24.

6   *Ibid.*, at 3.

7   danah boyd, *It's Complicated: The Social Live of Networked Teens* (New Haven: Yale University Press, 2014), 5.

8   Mary Madden, "Teens Haven't Abandoned Facebook – Yet," *Pew Research Internet Project*, 15 August, 2013, <http://www.pewinternet.org/2013/08/15/teens-havent-abandoned-facebook-yet/>.

9   *Supra* note 7 at 5.

10 See also Bailey, Chapter I; Burkell & Saginur, Chapter V; Steeves, Chapter VI; Regan & Sweet, Chapter VII; Heath, Chapter XIV.

11 Valerie Steeves, *Canadians in a Wired World, Phase III: Experts or Amateurs? Gauging Young Canadians' Digital Literacy Skills* (Ottawa: MediaSmarts, 2014), 6, <http://mediasmarts.ca/sites/mediasmarts/files/pdfs/publication-report/full/YCWWIII_Experts_or_Amateurs.pdf>.

12 *Ibid.*, at 33.

13 *Ibid.*, at 31.

14 W. Lance Bennett, "Changing Citizenship in the Digital Age," in *Civic Life Online: Learning How Digital Media Can Engage Youth*, ed. W. L. Bennett (Cambridge, MA: MIT Press, 2008), 1–24; Michael Xenos, Ariadne Vromen & Brian D. Loader, "The Great Equalizer? Patterns of Social

Media Use and Youth Political Engagement in Three Advanced Democracies," *Information, Communication & Society* 17 (2014), doi:10.1080/1369 118X.2013.871318.

15   Joseph Kahne, Nam-Jin Lee & Jessica T. Feezell, "The Civic and Political Significance of Online Participatory Cultures among Youth Transitioning to Adulthood," *Journal of Information Technology & Politics* 10 (2013): 13, doi:10.1080/19331681.2012.701109.

16   *Ibid.*, at 4.

17   Brian D. Loader, Ariadne Vromen & Michael A. Xenos, "Introduction: The Networked Young Citizen: Social Media, Political Participation and Civic Engagement," *Information, Communication & Society* 17 (2014): 145, doi:10.1080/1369118X.2013.871571.

18   Emily C. Weinstein, "The Personal is Political on Social Media: Online Civic Expression Patterns and Pathways among Civically Engaged Youth," *International Journal of Communication* 8 (2014), <http://ijoc.org/index.php/ijoc/article/view/2381>.

19   Elisabeth Soep, *Participatory Politics: Next-Generation Tactics to Remake Public Spheres* (Cambridge, MA: MIT Press, 2014), <http://mitpress.mit.edu/books/participatory-politics>.

20   Anita Harris, "Introduction: Youth Cultures and Feminist Politics," in *Next Wave Cultures: Feminism, Subcultures, Activism*, ed. Anita Harris (New York: Routledge, 2008).

21   Megan Boler, Averie MacDonald, Christina Nitsou & Anne Harris, "Connective Labor and Social Media: Women's Roles in the 'Leaderless' Occupy Movement," *Convergence: The International Journal of Research into New Media Technologies* 20 (2014), doi:10.1177/1354856514541353.

22   Caroline Caron, "Getting Girls and Teens into the Vocabularies of Citizenship," *Girlhood Studies* 4 (2011), <http://dx.doi.org/10.3167/ghs.2011.040206>.

23   Martha McCaughey, "Technology Is My BFF: What Are New Communication Technologies Doing to/for Girls?," *Media Report to Women* 41 (2013): 10–11, <http://mediareporttowomen.com/issues/411.htm>.

24   Blayne Haggart, "Fair Copyright for Canada: Lessons for Online Social Movements from the First Canadian Facebook Uprising," *Canadian Journal of Political Science/Revue canadienne de science politique* 46 (2013), doi:10.1017/S0008423913000838.

25   Lisa Feinberg, "Facebook: Beyond Friends," *Our Schools/Our Selves* 17 (2008), <http://www.policyalternatives.ca/sites/default/files/uploads/publications/Our_Schools_Ourselve/9_Feinburg_facebook_beyond_friends.pdf>.

26   "Backgrounder: Facebook Investigation Follow-up Complete," Office of the Privacy Commissioner of Canada, last modified 22 September 2010, <http://www.priv.gc.ca/media/nr-c/2010/bg_100922_e.cfm>; Elizabeth

Denhem, *"Privacy and the World Wide Web: How the OPC Investigation of Facebook Made Worldwide Waves, Remarks at the IAPP KnowledgeNet Session"* (Ottawa: Office of the Privacy Commissioner of Canada, 2009), <http://priv.gc.ca/speech/2009/spd_20091007_ed_e.cfm>.

27 "Telecom Decision CRTC 2010-255. Bell Aliant Regional Communications, Limited Partnership and Bell Canada – Applications to Introduce Usage-Based Billing and Other Changes to Gateway Access Services," Canadian Radio-Television and Telecommunication Commission (CRTC), last modified 1 April 2011, <http://www.crtc.gc.ca/eng/archive/2010/2010-255.htm#archived>.

28 "Usage-Based Billing for Gateway Access Services and Third-Party Internet Access Services: 8661-C12-201015975," Canadian Radio-Television and Telecommunication Commission (CRTC), last modified 3 February 2011, <http://www.crtc.gc.ca/PartVII/eng/2010/8661/c12_201015975.htm>.

29 "Telecom Decision CRTC 2011-44. Usage-Based Billing for Gateway Access Services and Third-Party Internet Access Services," Canadian Radio-Television and Telecommunication Commission (CRTC), last modified 25 January 2011, <http://www.crtc.gc.ca/eng/archive/2011/2011-44.htm>.

30 Steven Anderson, "Spark 136 – January 30 & February 2: Usage-Based Billing, Part 1," interview by Nora Young, *Spark*, CBC, 28 January 2011, <http://www.cbc.ca/spark/2011/01/spark-136-january-30-february-2-2011/>.

31 CBC News, Science & Technology, "CRTC's Internet Billing Decision Faces Review," CBC News, last modified 1 February 2011, <http://www.cbc.ca/news/technology/crtc-s-internet-billing-decision-faces-review-1.1080216>.

32 "CRTC Supports Choice of Internet Services," Canadian Radio-Television and Telecommunication Commission (CRTC), last modified 15 November 2011, <http://www.crtc.gc.ca/eng/com100/2011/r111115.htm>.

33 "Regulators Pull Back from Usage-Based Billing after Half-a-Million Canadians Speak Out," OpenMedia, last modified 15 November 2011, <https://openmedia.ca/news/regulators-pull-back-usage-based-billing-after-half-million-canadians-speak-out>.

34 "About Us," OpenMedia, <https://openmedia.ca/about-us>.

35 Jonathan A. Obar & Leslie Regan Shade, "Activating the Fifth Estate: Bill C-30 and the Digitally-Mediated Public Watchdog," in *Strategies for Media Reform: Communication Research in Action*, eds. D. Freedman, R. W. McChesney & J. A. Obar (New York Fordham University Press, forthcoming), <http://papers.ssrn.com/sol3/papers.cfm?abstract_id=2470671>.

36 "Liberty Awards 2013 Recipients," British Columbia Civil Liberties Association, <http://bccla.org/2013-liberty-awards-gala/liberty-awards-gala/2013-awards/>.

37   Ian Reilly, "'Amusing Ourselves to Death?' Social Media, Political Sat-
      ire, and the 2011 Election," *Canadian Journal of Communication* 36 (2011),
      <http://www.cjc-online.ca/index.php/journal/article/view/2508/2259>.

38   Katarzyna Rukszto, "History as Edutainment: *Heritage Minutes* and the
      Uses of Educational Television," in *Programming Reality: Perspectives
      on English Canadian Television,* eds. Zöe Druick & Aspa Kotsopoulos
      (Waterloo, ON: Wilfrid Laurier Press, 2008).

39   Rick Mercer: "Our Gouge-Based Heritage," YouTube posted by
      TheOpenmedia, 17 February 2011, <https://www.youtube.com/
      watch?v=qoZGkqQvAVw>.

40   "Hitler Gets Netflix and Hits the Internet Cap," YouTube posted by
      FightingInternet, 8 February 2011, <http://www.youtube.com/watch?v=y-
      Mg6pq33Zc>. See also Christopher J. Gilbert, "Playing with Hitler:
      Downfall and Its Ludic Uptake," *Critical Studies in Media Communication*
      30 (2013), doi:10.1080/15295036.2012.755052.

41   *Supra* note 1 at 29.

42   Andrew Ross Sorkin & Jeremy W. Peters, "Google to Acquire YouTube
      for $1.65 Billion," *New York Times,* 9 October 2006, <http://www.nytimes.
      com/2006/10/09/business/09cnd-deal.html>.

43   John Seabrook, "Streaming Dreams: YouTube Turns Pro," *New Yorker,*
      16 January 2012, <http://www.newyorker.com/reporting/2012/01/
      16/120116fa_fact_seabrook?currentPage=all>.

44   Patricia G. Lange, *Kids on YouTube: Technical Identities and Digital Literacies*
      (Walnut Creek, CA: Left Coast, 2014), 98.

45   *Ibid.,* at 121.

46   Jennifer Earl & Katrina Kimport, *Digitally Enabled Social Change: Activism
      in the Internet Age* (Cambridge, MA: MIT Press, 2011).

47   "Stop Telecom Price Gouging," OpenMedia, <https://openmedia.ca/
      meter>.

48   Lange, *supra* note 44 at 98.

49   Shade, *supra* note 3; Shade & Shepherd, *supra* note 3.

50   Patricia Aufderheide, *National Leadership Conference on Media Literacy,
      Conference Report* (Washington, DC; Aspen Institute, 1983); Renee Hobbs
      & Amy Jensen, "The Past, Present, and Future of Media Literacy Educa-
      tion," *Journal of Media Literacy Education* 1 (2009), <http://digitalcommons.
      uri.edu/cgi/viewcontent.cgi?article=1000&context=jmle>.

51   James Paul Gee, *New Digital Media and Learning as an Emerging Area
      and "Worked Examples" as One Way Forward* (Cambridge, MA: MIT
      Press, 2010), 36, <https://mitpress.mit.edu/sites/default/files/titles/free_
      download/9780262513692_New_Digital_Media.pdf>.

52   Bennett, *supra* note 1 at 29.

53 "Shaping Canada's Strategy for the Digital Economy," Industry Canada, last modified March 24, 2011, <http://www.ic.gc.ca/eic/site/ich-epi.nsf/eng/02090.html>.

54 Sonia Livingstone & Peter Lunt, "Representing Citizens and Consumers in Media and Communications Regulation," *Annals of the American Academy of Political and Social Science* 611 (2007): 53, <http://core.kmi.open.ac.uk/download/pdf/92940.pdf>.

55 Tamara Shepherd, Gregory Taylor & Catherine Middleton, "A Tale of Two Regulators: Telecom Policy Participation in Canada," *Journal of Information Policy* 4 (2014) <http://jip.vmhost.psu.edu/ojs/index.php/jip/article/view/163/106>.

56 Canadian Radio-television and Telecommunications Commission, It's Your CRTC: "Here's How to Have Your Say! A Five-Minute Guide to Understanding and Participating in Our Activities," (Gatineau, QC: CRTC, 2014), <http://www.crtc.gc.ca/eng/info_sht/g10.htm>.

57 Sarah Banet-Weiser, "Branding the Post-Feminist Self: Girls' Video Production and YouTube," in *Mediated Girlhoods: New Explorations of Girls' Media Culture,* ed. Mary Celeste Kearney (New York: Peter Lang, 2011), 281.

58 Kanai, Chapter III.

59 Sarah Banet-Weiser, "'Am I Pretty or Ugly?' Girls and the Market for Self-Esteem," *Girlhood Studies* 1 (2014), <http://dx.doi.org/10.3167/ghs.2014.070107>.

60 Jessalynn Marie Keller, "Virtual Feminisms: Girls' Blogging Communities, Feminist Activism, and Participatory Politics," *Information, Communication & Society* 15 (2012): 429, 444, doi:10.1080/1369118X.2011.642890.

61 Julia Schuster, "Invisible Feminists? Social Media and Young Women's Political Participation," *Political Science* 65 (2013), <http://pnz.sagepub.com/content/65/1/8.full.pdf>.

62 Carrie A. Rentschler, "Rape Culture and the Feminist Politics of Social Media," *Girlhood Studies* 7 (2014): 68.

63 Tamara Shepherd, "Young Canadians' Apprenticeship Labour in User-Generated Content," *Canadian Journal of Communication* 1 (2013): 47, <http://www.cjc-online.ca/index.php/journal/article/view/2598/2361>.

64 Valerie Steeves, *Canadians in a Wired World, Phase III: Online Privacy, Online Publicity* (Ottawa: MediaSmarts, 2014), 37. <http://mediasmarts.ca/sites/default/files/pdfs/publication-report/full/YCWWIII_Online_Privacy_Online_Publicity_FullReport.pdf>.

65 *Ibid.,* at 26.

66 Heath, Chapter XIV.

67 For a summary of considerations for internet qualitative research see Claire Hewson, "Qualitative Approaches to Internet-Mediated Research: Opportunities, Issues, Possibilities," in *The Oxford Handbook of Qualitative*

Research, ed. Patricia Leavy (Oxford: Oxford University Press, 2014): 423–454.

68   Annette Markham & Elizabeth Buchanan, *Ethical Decision-Making and Internet Research: Recommendations from the AoIR Ethics Working Committee* (Version 2.0), Association of Internet Researchers, 2012, <http://aoir.org/reports/ethics2.pdf>.

69   See "Google Terms of Service," 17 April 2007, at para 11.1 and 11.2, <https://www.google.com/intl/en/policies/terms/archive/20070416/>; for the latest terms of service see, "Google Terms of Service" dated 14 April 2014, <https://www.google.com/intl/en/policies/terms/>.

Conclusion: Looking Forward

Jane Bailey and Valerie Steeves

eGirls, eCitizens reveals the complexity and nuances of girls' and young women's networked lives. Not only does it challenge early euphoric predictions that networked communications platforms would facilitate the overthrow of patriarchy, it also calls into question more recent dystopian policy rhetoric premised on various caricatures of girls as hapless victims whose greatest challenge is stranger danger. Indeed, as Part III of the book demonstrates, many girls and young women have strategies for addressing their own perceptions of online risk, and are eager to access tools that facilitate and enhance their online participation in cultural production, self-exploration, and political protest. Far from being hapless victims, many girls and young women actively participate in the digital environment that policymakers in Canada and elsewhere have chosen to make the centerpiece of economic and social policy. In exercising their participatory rights in networked public and private spaces, they demonstrate strength, ingenuity, and resilience.

And yet, many chapters underscore the ways in which the sociotechnical environment can limit and complicate girls' and young women's equal participation in the digital society. These elements include all-too-familiar discriminatory identity markers relating to gender, race, gender identity, immigrant status, and sexual orientation, as well as other aspects of girls' diverse existences (such as urban vs. rural living). They also address new forms of social interaction that are structured by the commodification of the social world and the commercial agenda that drives the design of networked spaces. Clearly young women participate in digitally networked social spaces to make friends, to enhance and maintain existing relationships, to engage in gender performance, and to explore their sexuality. However, enjoyment of these affordances is constrained by the surveillant force of a gendered gaze that too often subjects them to harsh judgment both for mirroring and for failing to mirror the stereotypical, racialized, and heteronormative representations of femininity and masculinity embedded in networked spaces. Their equal participation is also too often limited by the humiliation and shaming associated with online sexualized violence and harassment.

Paying attention to girls' and young women's own accounts of these affordances and constraints creates an opportunity to develop policy and educational approaches that can potentially reshape sociotechnical spaces in ways that reflect and respect girls' and young women's own understanding of their lived experiences. If technology is indeed as "plastic" as Lessig imagined, and policymakers remain committed to prioritizing digitized networks as primary vehicles for reaching our socioeconomic and cultural goals, we owe it to girls and young women to ensure that that "plastic" is shaped to create spaces in ways that recognize and facilitate their equal right to participate. To do that, we need to move beyond simplistic, reactive policy responses aimed at individual punishment and surveillance toward proactive approaches that critically address the ways in which technical and market forces combine with discriminatory social norms to undermine girls' and young women's equal online participation.

From this perspective, it is important to interrogate the commercial structures underlying the internet. The work of the eGirls Project strongly suggests that the mainstream commercial stereotypes embedded in networked spaces combine with social norms to set girls up for conflict and harassment. Replication of other kinds of stereotypes and biases steeped in discriminatory structures (such as racism, homophobia, and colonialism) can interlock with sexism to further complicate the experiences of girls and young women targeted by intersecting axes of oppression. Arguably, these embedded structures disproportionately expose all youth, especially those belonging to marginalized groups, to conflict in ways that limit their right to equal participation in the digital society.

So what are the next steps? In order to better understand how underlying commercial structures interact with discriminatory social norms in this context in ways that undermine equal online participation by all youth, it will be essential to know more about the commercial structures themselves, and about the impact of intersecting axes of oppression on youth engagement. Clearly, the research we have done in the eGirls Project suggests that the economic model behind e-commerce (i.e., disclosure of information in exchange for services) creates a bias in favour of disclosure. Youth are key to understanding the privacy implications of this model, because, as early adopters of online media, they drop terabytes of data (often unknowingly) as they go about their daily lives, and this data is processed to target them with behavioural marketing to shape their attitudes and behaviours. Moreover, the marketing analytics sort youth into categories that often reproduce real-world patterns of discrimination. This creates a feedback loop that reinforces mainstream stereotypes: online architectures encourage certain kinds of identity performances (e.g., highly stereotypical white, heteronormative sexualized performances of girl and "feminine" beauty), and combine with social norms to open youth up to discrimination and harassment (e.g., slut shaming, homophobia).

Equality-based research on our digital society must unpack these commercial practices and their connection to and perpetuation of systemic discrimination, with the goal of developing policy and educational approaches grounded in and respectful of the diverse lived experiences of youth affected by interlocking axes of oppression and marginalization. Research founded on an intersectional human rights approach will enable us to better understand the impact of stereotypes embedded in the online commercial model on youth vulnerable to identity-based harassment, and deepen our knowledge of how online harassment is experienced in different ways by differently situated groups. This will help us "unpack the warm human and institutional choices that lie behind" the technical infrastructures[1] that shape the lived experiences of youth online, and work to create a digital environment in which girls and young women can flourish.

Notes

1   Tarleton Gillespie "The Relevance of Algorithms," in *Media Technologies: Essays on Communication, Materiality and Society*, eds. Tarleton Gillespie, Pablo J. Boczkowski & Kirsten A. Foot (Cambridge, MA: MIT Press, 2014), 167–194.

Bibliography

Adams, Helen. "Social Networking and Privacy: A Law Enforcement Perspective." *School Library Media Activities Monthly* 23 (2007): 33.

Ahmad, Farah, Angela Shik, Reena Vanza, Angela Cheung, Usha George, and Donna E. Stewart. "Popular Health Promotion Strategies Among Chinese and East Indian Immigrant Women." *Women and Health* 40 (2004): 21–40. doi:10.1300/J013v40n01_02.

Ahn, Annie J., Bryan S. K. Kim, and Yong S. Park. "Asian Cultural Values Gap, Cognitive Flexibility, Coping Strategies, and Parent–Child Conflicts Among Korean Americans." *Cultural Diversity and Ethnic Minority Psychology* 14:4 (2008): 38–41. doi:10.1037/1099-9809.14.4.353.

Albrechtslund, Anders. "Social Networking as Participatory Surveillance." *First Monday*, March 3, 2008. http://firstmonday.org/article/view/2142/1949.

Allen, Anita. "Gender and Privacy in Cyberspace." *Stanford Law Review* 52:5 (2000): 1175–1200. http://scholarship.law.upenn.edu/faculty_scholarship/789.

Anderson, Steven. "Spart 136 — January 30 & February 2: Usage Based Billing, Part 1." *Spark,* CBC, January 28, 2011, http://www.cbc.ca/spark/2011/01/spark-136-january-30-february-2-2011/.

Anderssen, Erin. "In an Airbrushed World, How Do you Define what's Truly Hot?" *The Globe and Mail*, March 1, 2012. http://www.theglobeandmail.com/life/parenting/in-an-airbrushed-world-how-do-you-define-whats-truly-hot/article550540/?page=all.

Andrejevic, Mark. "Discipline of Watching: Detection, Risk, and Lateral Surveillance." *Critical Studies in Media Communication* 23 (2006): 391–407. doi:10.1080/07393180601046147.

———. "The Work of Watching One Another: Lateral Surveillance, Risk, and Governance." *Surveillance & Society* 2 (2005): 481–82. http://www.surveillance-and-society.org/articles2(4)/lateral.pdf.

———. *Reality TV: The Work of Being Watched.* Lanham: Rowman & Littlefield Publishers, 2004.

Ang, Ien. *Desperately Seeking the Audience.* London and New York: Routledge, 1991.

Aqua. "Barbie Girl." http://www.azlyrics.com/lyrics/aqua/barbiegirl.html.

Arcabascio, Catherine. "Sexting and Teenagers: OMG R U Going 2 Jail???" *Richmond Journal of Law and Technology* XVI:3 (2010): 1–42. http://jolt.richmond.edu/v16i3/article10.pdf.

Archive of our Own. "The Archive of Our Own is a place for fanworks, including fan fiction based on books, TV, movies, comics, other media, and real-person fiction (RPF)." http://www.archiveofourown.com/tos.

Arenburg, Patricia B. "Legal experts question haste of Rehtaeh's law." *The Chronicle Herald,* August 16, 2013. http://www.thechronicleherald.ca/novascotia/1148032-legal-experts-question-haste-of-rehtaeh-s-law.

Arewa, Olufunmilayo B. "From J.C. Bach to Hip Hop: Musical Borrowing, Copyright and Cultural Context." *North Carolina Law Review* 84 (2006): 547–645, archived at Social Sciences Research Network: http://papers.ssrn.com/sol3/Delivery.cfm/SSRN_ID633241_code542089.pdf?abstractid=633241&mirid=1.

Associated Press. "Dharun Ravi Sentence in Rutgers Webcam Case Renews Hate Crime Law Debate." *The Washington Post,* May 22, 2012. http://www.washingtonpost.com/national/dharun-ravi-sentence-in-rutgers-webcam-case-renews-hate-crime-law-debate/2012/05/22/gIQAuioDiU_story.html.

Attwood, Feona. "Sluts and Riot Grrls: Female Identity and Sexual Agency." *Journal of Gender Studies* 16 (2007): 233–247. doi:10.1080/09589230701562921.

Aufderheide, Patricia. *National Leadership Conference on Media Literacy, Conference Report.* Aspen Institute, Washington D.C., 1983.

Azzarito, Laura. "Future Girls, Transcendent Femininities and New Pedagogies: Toward Girls' Hybrid Bodies?" *Sport Education and Society* 15:3 (2010): 261–275. doi:10.1080/13573322.2010.493307.

Baca, Catherine T, Dale C Alverson, Jennifer Knapp Manuel, and Greg L Blackwell. "Telecounseling in Rural Areas for Alcohol Problems." *Alcoholism Treatment Quarterly* 25 (2007): 31–45. doi:10.1300/J020v25n04_03.

Bae, Michelle S. "Go Cyworld! Korean Diasporic Girls Producing New Korean Femininity." In *Girl Wide Web 2.0: Revisiting Girls, the Internet, and the Negotiation of Identity,* edited by Sharon Mazzarella, 91–116. New York: Peter Lang, 2010.

Bailey, Jane, and Adrienne Telford. "What's So Cyber About It?: Reflections on Cyberfeminism's Contribution to Legal Studies." *Canadian Journal of Women and the Law* 19:2 (2007): 243–271. doi:10.1353/jwl.0.0005

Bailey, Jane, and Mouna Hanna. "The Gendered Dimensions of Sexting: Assessing the Applicability of Canada's Child Pornography Provision." *Canadian Journal of Women and the Law* 23:2 (2011): 405–441. doi:10.3138/cjwl.23.2.405.

Bailey, Jane, and Valerie Steeves. "Will the Real Digital Girl Please Stand Up?" In *New Visualities, New Technologies: The New Ecstasy of Communication,* edited by Hille Koskela and Macgregor Wise, 41–66. London: Ashgate Publishing, 2013.

Bailey, Jane, Valerie Steeves, Jacquelyn Burkell, and Priscilla Regan. "Negotiating With Gender Stereotypes on Social Networking Sites: From 'Bicycle Face' to Facebook." *Journal of Communication Inquiry* 37: 2 (2013): 91–112. doi:10.1177/0196859912473777.

Bailey, Jane. "'Sexualized Online Bullying' Through an Equality Lens: Missed Opportunity in *AB v. Bragg?" McGill Law Journal* 59: 3 (2014): 709–737. http://lawjournal.mcgill.ca/userfiles/other/49414-Article__5___Bailey__Case_Comment_.pdf.

——— . "Bill C-13: The Victims of "Cyberbullying" and Canadians Deserve More." *The eGirls Project,* November 28, 2013. http://www.egirlsproject.ca/2013/11/28/bill-c-13-the-victims-of-cyberbullying-and-canadians-deserve-more.

———. "Life in a Fish Bowl: Feminist Interrogations of Webcamming." In *Lessons From the Identity Trail: Anonymity, Privacy and Identity in a Networked Society,* edited by Ian Kerr, Valerie Steeves and Carole Lucock, 283–301. New York: Oxford University Press, 2009.

———. "Submission to the House of Commons Standing Committee on Justice and Human Rights Regarding Bill C-13 (Protecting Canadians from Online Crime Act)." http://egirlsproject.files.wordpress.com/2014/06/submission-c-13-baileymishnamackayslane2.pdf.

———. "Time to Unpack the Juggernaut?: Reflections on the Canadian Federal Parliamentary Debates on 'Cyberbullying.'" (2014–2015) Dal LJ [forthcoming], unpublished, archived at Social Sciences Research Network. http://papers.ssrn.com/sol3/papers.cfm?abstract_id=2448480.

Bandura, Albert. "Social Cognition Theory of Moral Thought and Action." In *Handbook of Moral Behavior and Development: Volume 1: Theory,* edited by William M. Kurtines and Jacob L. Gewirtz, 45–103. Hillsdale: Lawrence Erlbaum Associates, Inc, 1991.

Banet-Weiser, Sarah. "'Am I Pretty or Ugly?' Girls and the Market for Self-Esteem." *Girlhood Studies* 7:1 (2014): 83–101. doi:10.3167/ghs.2014.070107.

———. "Branding the Post-Feminist Self: Girls' Video Produciton and You-Tube." In *Mediated Girlhoods: New Explorations of Girls' Media Culture*, edited by Mary Celeste Kearney, 277–194. New York: Peter Lang, 2011.

Barber, Terry. "Young People and Civic Participation: A Conceptual Overview." *Youth and Policy* 96 (2007): 19–39. http://www.youthandpolicy.org/wp-content/uploads/2013/07/youthandpolicy96.pdf.

Barlow, John P. "Declaration of the Independence of Cyberspace." https://projects.eff.org/~barlow/Declaration-Final.html.

Barnes, Susan. "A Privacy Paradox: Social Networking in the United States." *First Monday* 11:9–4 (2006). http://firstmonday.org/article/view/1394/1312.

Barron, Christie, and Dany Lacombe. "Moral Panic and the Nasty Girl." *The Canadian Review of Sociology and Anthropology* 41 (2008): 51–69. doi:10.1111/j.1755-618X.2005.tb00790.x.

Barter, Christine, and Melanie McCarry. "Love, Power and Control: Girls' Experiences of Partner Violence and Exploitation." In *Violence Against Women: Current Theory and Practice in Domestic Abuse, Sexual Violence & Exploitation*, edited by Nancy Lombard and Leslie McMillan, 103–124. London: Jessica Kingsley Publications, 2012.

Bartky, Sandra. "Feminism, Foucault and the Modernisation of Patriarchal Power." In *Feminism and Foucault: Reflections on Resistance*, edited by Irene Diamond and Lee Quinby, 61–86. Boston: Northeastern University Press, 1988.

Bazelon, Emily. "Make the Punishment Fit the Cyber-Crime" (Opinion) *New York Times*, March 19, 2012. http://www.nytimes.com/2012/03/20/opinion/make-the-punishment-fit-the-cyber-crime.html?_r=0.

BBC News. "Blog Death Threats Spark Debate." *BBC News Technology*, March 27, 2007. http://news.bbc.co.uk/2/hi/6499095.stm.

Beebe, Barton. "An Empirical Study of U.S. Copyright Fair Use Opinions, 1978–2005." *University of Pennsylvania Law Review* 158 (2008): 549–624. http://www.bartonbeebe.com/documents/Beebe%20-%20Empirical%20Study%20of%20FU%20Opinions.pdf.

Beggs, John J., Valerie A. Haines, and Jeanne S. Hurlbert. "Urban Contrast: Personal Networks in Nonmetropolitan and Metropolitan Settings." *Rural Sociology* 61 (1996): 306–325. doi:10.1111/j.1549-0831.1996.tb00622.x.

Behm-Morawitz, Elizabeth, and Dana Mastro. "The Effects of the Sexualization of Female Video Game Characters on Gender Stereotyping and Female Self-Concept." *Sex Roles* 61:11–12 (2009): 808–823. doi:10.1007/s11199-009-9683-8.

Belknap, Joanne, Ann T. Chu, and Anne P. DePrince. "The Role of Phones and Computers in Threatening and Abusing Women Victims of Male Intimate Partner Abuse." *Duke Journal of Gender Law & Policy* 19 (2012): 373–406. http://scholarship.law.duke.edu/cgi/viewcontent.cgi?article=1232&context=djglp.

Bender, Geoff. "Resisting Dominance? The Study of a Marginalized Masculinity and Its Construction Within High School Walls." In *Preventing Violence in Schools: A Challenge to American Democracy*, edited by Joan N. Burstyn, Geoff Bender, Ronnie Casella, Howard W. Gordon, Domingo P. Guerra, Kristen V. Luschen, Rebecca Stevens, and Kimberly M. Williams, 61–77. New Jersey: Lawrence Erlbaum, 2001.

Benedict, Helen. *Virgin or Vamp? How the Press Covers Sex Crimes*. New York: Oxford University Press, 1992.

Benet, James. "Conclusion: Will Media Treatment of Women Improve?" In *Hearth and Home: Images of Women in the Mass Media*, edited by Gaye Tuchman, Arlene Kaplan Daniels, and James Benet, 266–272. New York: Oxford University Press, 1978.

Bennett, Susan, Stuart Hart, and Kimberly Ann Svevo-Cianci. "The Need for a General Comment for Article 19 of the UN Convention on the Rights of the Child: Toward Enlightenment and Progress for Child Protection." *Child Abuse & Neglect* 33:11 (2009): 783–790. doi:10.1016/j. chiabu.2009.09.007.

Bennett, W. Lance. "Changing Citizenship in the Digital Age." In *Civic Life Online: Learning How Digital Media Can Engage Youth*, edited by W. Lance Bennett, 1–24. Cambridge, MA: MIT Press, 2008.

———. "The Personalization of Politics: Personal Identity, Social Media, and Changing Patterns of Participation. *ANNALS of the American Academy of Political and Social Science* 644 (2012): 20–39. doi:10.1177/ 0002716212451428.

Berry, John W., Jean S. Phinney, David L. Sam, and Paul Vedder. "Immigrant Youth: Acculturation, Identity and Adaptation." *Applied Psychology: An International Review* 55 (2006): 316–317. doi:10.1111/ j.1464-0597.2006.00256.x.

Berson, Ilene R., and Michael J. Berson. "Challenging Online Behaviours of Youth – Findings From a Comparative Analysis of Young People in the United States and New Zealand." *Social Science Computer Review* 23 (2005): 29–38. doi:10.1177/0894439304271532.

Bharat, Mehra, Cecelia Merkel, and Ann Peterson Bishop. "The Internet for Empowerment of Minority and Marginalized Users." *New Media & Society* 6 (2004): 781–802. doi:10.1177/ 146144804047513.

Binder, Matt. "If you thought these unbelievable reactions to Steubenville would just peter out, I guess you can say you were pretty, pretty wrong." comment on *Tumblr* (March 19, 2013). http://publicshaming. tumblr.com/day/2013/03/19.

Black, Jerome H. "Minority Women in the 35th Parliament: A New Dimension of Social Diversity." *Canadian Parliamentary Review* 20:1 (1997): 17–22. http://www.revparl.ca/20/1/20n1_97e_Black.pdf.

———. "Racial Diversity in the 2011 Federal Election: Visible Minority Candidates and MPs." *Canadian Parliamentary Review* 36:3 (2013): 21–26. http://www.revparl.ca/36/3/36n3e_13_Black.pdf.

Black, Rebecca. "Access and Affiliation: The Literacy and Composition Practices of English Language Learners in an Online Fanfiction Community." *J. Adolescent & Adult Literacy* 49:2 (2005): 118–128. doi:10.1598/JAAL.49.2.4.

———. "Language, Culture and Identity in Online Fanfiction." *E-Learning and Digital Media* 3:2 (2006): 170–184. doi:10.2304/elea.2006.3.2.170.

Blackwell, Bonnie. "How the Jilt Triumphed Over the Slut: The Evolution of an Epithet, 1660–1780." *Women's Writing* 11:2 (2004): 141–161. doi:10.1080/09699080400200225.

Blanchet-Cohen, Natasha, and Christophe Bedeaux. "Towards a Rights-Based Approach to Youth Programs: Duty-Bearers' Perspectives." *Children and Youth Services Review* 38 (2014): 75–81. doi:10.1016/j.childyouth.2014.01.009

Blazak, Randy. "From White Boys to Terrorist Men: Target Recruitment of Nazi Skinheads." *American Behavioral Scientist* 44 (2001): 982–1000. doi:10.1177/00027640121956629.

Bloodshot. "Kindle Worlds." https://kindleworlds.amazon.com/world/Bloodshot?ref_=kww_home_ug_Bloodshot.

Bluett-Boyd, Nicole, Bianca Fileborn, Antonia Quadara, and Sharnee Moore. "The Role of Emerging Communications Technologies in Experiences of Sexual Violence: A New Legal Frontier?" *Australian Institute of Family Studies*, February 2013. http://www.aifs.gov.au/institute/pubs/resreport23/rr23.pdf.

Blum, Lawrence. *I'm Not a Racist But...* Ithaca: Cornell University Press, 2003.

Boldt, Megan. "Osseo High-Schooler Battles Taunts with Tweets." *Pioneer-Press*, September 9, 2012. http://www.twincities.com/education/ci_21656149/osseo-high-schooler-battles-taunts-tweets.

Boler, Megan, Averie MacDonald, Christina Nitsou, and Anne Harris. "Connective Labor and Social Media: Women's Roles in the 'Leaderless' Occupy Movement." *Convergence: The International Journal of Research into New Media Technologies* 20 (2014): 1–23. doi:10.1177/1354856514541353.

Boon, Marcus. *In Praise of Copying.* Camebridge: President and Fellows of Harvard College, 2010.

Bornstein, David. "Fighting Bullying With Babies." *The New York Times*, November 28, 2010. http://opinionator.blogs.nytimes.com/2010/11/08/fighting-bullying-with-babies.

boyd, danah. "Streams of Content, Limited Attention: The Flow of Information through Social Media." *Educause Review* (2010), https://net.educause.edu/ir/library/pdf/ERM1051.pdf.

———. "Why Youth <3 Social Network Sites: The Role of Networked Publics in Teenage Social Life." In *Youth, Identity and Digital Media*, edited by David Buckingham, 119–142. Cambridge: The MIT Press, 2008.

———. *It's Complicated*. New Haven: Yale University Press, 2014.

Brassard, Daniel. "Information Superhighway." http://publications.gc.ca/Collection-R/LoPBdP/BP/bp385-e.htm.

Braidotti, Rosi. *Nomadic Subjects: Embodiment and Sexual Difference in Contemporary Feminist Theory, 2nd Ed.* New York: Columbia University Press, 2011.

British Columbia Civil Liberties Association. "Liberty Awards 2013 Recipients." http://bccla.org/2013-liberty-awards-gala/liberty-awards-gala/2013-awards.

British Columbia, Ministry of Education. "Developing and Reviewing Codes of Conduct: A Companion." http://www.bced.gov.bc.ca/sco/resourcedocs/facilitators_companion.pdf.

———. "Safe, Caring and Orderly Schools: A Guide." http://www.bced.gov.bc.ca/sco/guide/scoguide.pdf.

Brockman, Libby, Dimitri Christakis, and Megan Moreno. "Friending Adolescents on Social Networking Websites: A Feasible Research Tool." *Journal of Interaction Science* 2(1) (2014). doi:10.1186/2194-0827-2-1.

Bronfenbrenner, Urie. *The Ecology of Human Development: Experiments by Nature and Design.* Cambridge, MA: Harvard University Press, 1979.

Bronfenbrenner, Urie, and Ann C. Crouter. "The Evolution of Environmental Models in Developmental Research." In *Handbook of Child Psychology, History, Theory and Methods, 4th Edition*, edited by Paul Henry Mussen and William Kessen, 357–417. New York: Wiley, 1983.

Bronfenbrenner, Urie, and Gary W. Evans. "Developmental Science in the 21st Century: Emerging Questions, Theoretical Models, Research Designs and Empirical Findings." *Social Development* 9:1 (2000): 115–125. doi:10.1111/1467-9507.00114.

Bronfenbrenner, Urie, and Pamela Morris. "The Ecology of Developmental Process." In *Handbook of Child Psychology*, edited by William Damon and Richard M. Lerner, 993–1028. New York: John Wiley & Sons, Inc., 1998.

Brookes, Fiona, and Peter Kelly. "Dolly Girls: Tweenies as Artefacts of Consumption." *Journal of Youth Studies* 12:6 (2009): 599–613. doi:10.1080/13676260902960745.

Brown, Jesse. "Nova Scotia's awful cyber abuse law makes bullies of us all." *Maclean's*, August 8, 2013. http://www.macleans.ca/society/technology/nova-scotias-awful-cyber-abuse-law-makes-bullies-of-us-all.

Brown, Kathryn R. "The Risks of Taking Facebook at Face Value: Why the Psychology of Social Networking Should Influence the Evidentiary Relevance of Facebook Photographs." *Vanderbilt Journal of Entertainment and Technology Law* 14 (2012): 357–393. http://www.jetlaw.org/wp-content/journal-pdfs/Brown2.pdf.

Brown, Mary-Rose. "Edging Towards Diversity: A Statistical Breakdown of Canada's 41st Parliament, with Comparisons to the 40th Parliament." http://www.ppforum.ca/sites/default/files/edging_towards_diversity_final.pdf.

Brown, Rebecca, and Melissa Gregg. "The Pedagogy of Regret: Facebook, Binge Drinking and Young Women." *Continuum* 26:3 (2012): 357–369. doi:0.1080/10304312.2012.665834.

Brunsdon, Charlotte, Julie D'Acci, and Lynn Spigel. "Identity in Feminist Television Criticism." In *Feminist Television Criticism: A Reader*, edited by Charlotte Brunsdon, 309–320. Oxford: Clarendon Press, 2008.

Brunsdon, Charlotte. "The Feminist, the Housewife and the Soap Opera." In *The Feminist, the Housewife, and the Soap Opera*, edited by Charlotte Brunsdon and John Coughie. Oxford: Oxford University Press, 2011. doi:10.1093/acprof:oso/9780198159803.001.0001.

Bryson, Mary. "When Jill Jacks In: Queer Women and the Net." *Feminist Media Studies* 4:3 (2004): 239–254. doi:10.1080/1468077042000309928.

Buckwald, Emile, Pamela R. Fletcher, and Martha Roth. *Transforming a Rape Culture*. Minneapolis: Milkweed Editions, 1993.

Buhrmester, Duane, and Karen Prager. "Patterns and Functions of Self-disclosure During Childhood and Adolescence." In *Disclosure Processes in Children and Adolescents*, edited by Ken Rotenberg, 10–56. New York: Cambridge University Press, 1995.

Burkell, Jacquelyn, Valerie Steeves, and Anca Micheti. "Broken Doors: Strategies for Drafting Privacy Policies Kids Can Understand." http://www.idtrail.org/files/broken_doors_final_report.pdf.

Burkell, Jacquelyn. "The View From Here: User-Centered Perspectives on Social Network Privacy." Paper presented at The Tory Lectures Series, Faculty of Law, University of Ottawa, Ottawa, Ontario, October 24, 2012. http://ir.lib.uwo.ca/cgi/viewcontent.cgi?article=1027&context=fimspub.

Burridge, Joseph. "'I am not Homophobic *But...*': Disclaiming in Discourse Resisting Repeal of Section 28." *Sexualities* 7 (2004): 327–344. doi:10.1177/1363460704044804.

Busse, Kristina. "In Focus: Fandom and Feminism: Gender and the Politics of Fan Production." *Cinema Journal* 48 (2009): 105–106.

Butler, Judith. *Gender Trouble*. New York: Routledge Classics, 2006.

Calhoun Research and Development, C. Lang Consulting, and Irene Savoie. "Girls in Canada 2005." Canadian Women's Foundation. http://www.canadianwomen.org/sites/canadianwomen.org/files/PDF%20-%20Girls%20in%20Canada%20Report%202005.pdf.

Canadian Radio-Television and Telecommunication Commission (CRTC). "CRTC Supports Choice of Internet Services." http://www.crtc.gc.ca/eng/com100/2011/r111115.htm.

——. "Telecom Decision CRTC 2010–255. Bell Aliant Regional Communications, Limited Partnership and Bell Canada – Applications to Introduce Usage-based Billing and Other Changes to Gateway Access Services." http://www.crtc.gc.ca/eng/archive/2010/2010-255.htm#archived.

——. "Telecom Decision CRTC 2011–44. Usage-based Billing for Gateway Access Services and Third-party Internet Access Services." http://www.crtc.gc.ca/eng/archive/2011/2011-44.htm.

——. "Usage-based Billing for Gateway Access Services and Third-party Internet Access Services: 8661-C12-201015975." http://www.crtc.gc.ca/PartVII/eng/2010/8661/c12_201015975.htm.

——. "Availability and Adoption of Digital Technologies." http://www.crtc.gc.ca/eng/publications/reports/policyMonitoring/2013/cmr6.htm.

——. "Here's How to Have Your Say! A Five-Minute Guide to Understanding and Participating in Our Activities." http://www.crtc.gc.ca/eng/info_sht/g10.htm.

Carman, Tara. "Amanda Todd: School Districts Have Limited Reach With Anti-Bullying Tactics." *The Vancouver Sun*, October 16, 2012. http://www.vancouversun.com/news/Amanda+Todd+School+districts+have+limited+reach+with+anti+bullying+tactics/7394300/story.html.

Caron, Caroline. "Getting Girls and Teens into the Vocabularies of Citizenship." *Girlhood Studies* 4 (2011): 13–30. doi:10.3167/ghs.2011.040206.

——. "Sexy Girls as the "Other": The Discursive Processes of Stigmatizing Girls." Paper presented at the Canadian Communication Association Conference, University of British Columbia, Vancouver, British Columbia, June 6, 2008.

CBC News British Columbia. "UBC investigates frosh students' pro-rape chant: Chant condoned non-consensual sex with underage girls." http://www.cbc.ca/news/canada/british-columbia/ubc-investigates-frosh-students-pro-rape-chant-1.1699589.

CBC News Montreal. "Child porn charges laid against 10 Laval teens – police allege boys traded screen grabs of girlfriends' explicit Snapchat photos." http://www.cbc.ca/news/canada/montreal/child-porn-charges-laid-against-10-laval-teens-1.2426599.

CBC News Nova Scotia. "Saint Mary's University frosh chant cheers underage sex: Frosh week leaders, student union executive sent to sensitivity training." http://www.cbc.ca/news/canada/nova-scotia/saint-mary-s-university-frosh-chant-cheers-underage-sex-1.1399616.

CBC News, Science, and Technology. "CRTC's Internet Billing Decision Faces Review." http://www.cbc.ca/news/technology/crtc-s-internet-billing-decision-faces-review-1.1080216.

CCSO Cybercrime Working Group. "Cyberbullying and the Non-consensual Distribution of Intimate Images." http://www.justice.gc.ca/eng/rp-pr/other-autre/cndii-cdncii/pdf/cndii-cdncii-eng.pdf.

CCSO Working Group. "Report to the Federal/Provincial/Territorial Ministers Responsible for Justice and Public Safety: Cyberbullying and the Non-consensual Distribution of Intimate Images." Department of Justice. http://www.justice.gc.ca/eng/rp-pr/other-autre/cndii-cdncii/pdf/cndii-cdncii-eng.pdf.

Centres for Disease Control (CDC). "Sexual Violence: Definitions." http://www.cdc.gov/violenceprevention/sexualviolence/definitions.html.

Chander, Anupam, and Madhavi Sunder. "Everyone's a Superhero: A Cultural Theory of 'Mary Sue' Fan Fiction as Fair Use." *California Law Review* 95 (2007): 597–626. doi:10.2307/20439103.

Chemaly, Soraya. "An Open Letter to Facebook." *The Huffington Post*, May 21, 2013. http://www.huffingtonpost.com/soraya-chemaly/an-open-letter-to-faceboo_1_b_3307394.html.

Chen, Eva. "Neoliberalism and Popular Women's Culture: Rethinking Choice, Freedom and Agency." *European Journal of Cultural Studies* 16 (2013): 440–452. doi:10.1177/1367549413484297.

Chen, Jilin, Werner Geyer, Casey Dugan, Michael Muller, and Ido Guy. "Make New Friends, but Keep the Old: Recommending People on Social Networking Sites." Paper presented at SIGCHI Conference on Human Factors in Computing Systems, Boston, Massachusetts, April 3, 2009.

Cheryl. "May Vogue Visits The Future And The Future Is Missing A Clavicle." *Jezebel*, May 6, 2008. http://jezebel.com/387701/may-vogue-visits-the-future-and-the-future-is-missing-a-clavicle.

Choate, Laura. *Adolescent Girls in Distress: A Guide for Mental Health Treatment and Prevention.* New York: Springer Publishing Company, 2013.

Choma, Becky, Mindi Foster, and Eileen Radford. "Use of Objectification Theory to Examine the Effects of Media Literacy Intervention on Women." *Sex Roles* 56:9–10 (2007): 581–590. doi:10.1007/s11199-007-9200-x.

Christensen, Miyase, and André Jansson. "Complicit Surveillance, Interveillance, and the Question of Cosmopolitanism: Toward a Phenomenological Understanding of Mediatization." *New Media & Society* (2014). doi:10.1177/1461444814528678.

Citron, Danielle Keats. "Law's Expressive Value in Combatting Cyber Gender Harassment." *Michigan Law Review* 108:3 (2009): 373–415. ISSN: 0026-2234.

———. "Misogynistic Cyber Hate Speech." http://digitalcommons.law.umaryland.edu/cgi/viewcontent.cgi?article=2143&context=fac_pubs&sei-redir=1&referer=http%3A%2F%2Fscholar.google.ca%2Fscholar%3Fq%3

DDANIELLE%2BKEATS%2BCITRON%2Bcybermisogyny%26btnG%
3D%26hl%3Den%26as_sdt%3D0%252C5#search=%22DANIELLE%20
KEATS%20CITRON%20cybermisogyny%22.

——. "Revenge Porn Should Be A Crime In U.S." *CNN*, January 16 2014.
http://edition.cnn.com/2013/08/29/opinion/citron-revenge-porn/.

Citron, Danielle Keats, and Mary Anne Franks. "Criminalizing Revenge
Porn." (2014) 49 *Wake Forest L Rev* 345–392, archived at Social Sci-
ences Research Network. http://papers.ssrn.com/sol3/Delivery.cfm/
SSRN_ID2473705_code829721.pdf?abstractid=2368946&mirid=1.

Clark, Levina, and Marika Tiggemann. "Appearance Culture in Nine
to 12 Year Old Girls: Media and Peer Influences on Body Dissatisfaction." *Social Development* 15:4 (2006): 628–643. doi:10.1111/
j.1467-9507.2006.00361.x.

Clavert, Clay. "Sex, Cell Phones, Privacy and the First Amendment: When
Children Become Child Pornographers and the Lolita Effect Under-
mines the Law." *The Catholic University of America CommLaw Conspectus*
18 (2009): 1–65. http://commlaw.cua.edu/res/docs/articles/v18/18-1/
sexting-12-11-09-to-publisher.pdf.

Cohen, Alex. "Countering the Online World of 'Pro-Anorexia." http://www.
npr.org/templates/story/story.php?storyId=101210192.

Cohen, Jeffrey W., and Robert A. Brooks. *Confronting School Bullying: Kids,
Culture, and the Making of a Social Problem.* Boulder, CO: Lynne Rienner
Publishers, 2014.

Cohen, Julie. "Creativity and Culture in Copyright Theory." *U.C. Davis L.
Rev.* 40 (2007): 1151–1205. http://lawreview.law.ucdavis.edu/issues/40/3/
copyright-creativity-catalogs/DavisVol40No3_Cohen.pdf.

Cohen, Richard. "Tyler Clementi and the Questionable Wisdom of Hate
Crime Laws." *The Washington Post*, March 19, 2012. http://www.
washingtonpost.com/blogs/post-partisan/post/tyler-clementi-and-
the-questionable-wisdom-of-hate-crime-laws/2012/03/19/gIQAlpaENS_
blog.html.

Cohen, Nicole S., and Leslie Shade. "Gendering Facebook: Privacy and Commodification." *Feminist Media Studies* 8:2 (2008): 210–214.

Cohn, Tracy J., and Valerie S. Leake. "Distress Among Adolescents Who
Endorse Same-Sex Sexual Attraction: Urban Versus Rural Differences
and the Role of Protective Factors." *Journal of Gay and Lesbian Mental
Health* 16:4 (2012): 291–305. doi:10.1080/19359705.2012.690931.

Colley, Ann, Zazic Todd, Adrian White, and Tamara Turner-Moore.
"Communication Using Camera Phones Among Young Men and
Women: Who Sends What to Whom?" *Sex Roles* 63:5–6 (2010): 348–360.
doi:10.1007/s11199-010-9805-3.

Collier, Anne. "Why Digital Citizenship's a Hot Topic (Globally)." http://
www.netfamilynews.org/why-digital-citizenships-a-hot-topic-globally.

Collins, Jessica L., and Barry Wellman. "Small Town in the Internet Society: Chapleau Is No Longer an Island." *American Behavioral Sciences* 53 (2010): 1344–1366. doi:10.1177/0002764210361689.

Collins, Rebecca L. "Content Analysis of Gender Roles in Media: Where Are We Now and Where Should We Go?" *Sex Roles* 64:3–4 (2011): 290–298. doi:10.1007/s11199-010-9929-5.

Collins, Sue. "Making the most out of 15 Minutes: Reality TV's Dispensable Celebrity." *Television & New Media* 9:2 (2008): 87–110. doi:10.1177/1527476407313814.

Commission Scolaire English-Montreal. "Registration." http://www.emsb.qc.ca/en/services_en/pages/registration_en.asp.

Cook, Bob. "Lesson From Steubenville Trial: How Jock Culture Morphs Into Rape Culture." *Forbes*, March 17, 2013. http://www.forbes.com/sites/bobcook/2013/03/17/lesson-from-steubenville-rape-trial-how-jock-culture-morphs-into-rape-culture.

Cooper, Robyn M., and Warren J. Blumenfeld. "Responses to Cyberbullying: A Descriptive Analysis of the Frequency of and Impact on LGBT and Allied Youth." *Journal of LGBT Youth* 9 (2012): 153–177. doi:10.1080/19361653.2011.649616.

Coppa, Francesca. "A Fannish Taxonomy of Hotness." *Cinema Journal*. 48 (2009): 107–113. http://www.yalelawtech.org/wp-content/uploads/Coppa_In_Focus.48.4.pdf.

———. "An Editing Room of One's Own: Vidding as Women's Work." *Camera Obscura* 26 (2011): 123–130. doi:10.1215/02705346-1301557.

Cover, Rob. "Performing and Undoing Identity Online: Social Networking, Identity Theories and the Incompatibility of Online Profiles and Friendship Regimes." *Convergence: The International Journal of Research into New Media Technologies* 18:2 (2012): 177–193. doi:10.1177/1354856511433684.

Coyne, Sarah, Jennifer Linder, David Nelson, and Douglas Gentile. "'Frenemies, Fraitors and Mean-em-aitors': Priming Effects of Viewing Physical and Relational Aggression in the Media on Women." *Aggressive Behavior* 38:2 (2012): 141–149. doi:10.1002/ab.21410.

Crenshaw, Kimberley. "Mapping the Margins: Intersectionality, Identity Politics, and Violence against Women of Color." *Stanford Law Review* 43:6 (1991): 1241–1299. http://socialdifference.columbia.edu/files/socialdiff/projects/Article__Mapping_the_Margins_by_Kimblere_Crenshaw.pdf.

Culp-Ressler, Tara. "Study Finds that Sexting Doesn't Actually Ruin Young Adults' Lives." *ThinkProgress*, September 10, 2013. http://thinkprogress.org/health/2013/09/10/2599811/study-sexting-college/.

Daniels, Jessie. "Rethinking Cyberfeminism(s): Race, Gender and Embodiment." *Women's Studies Quarterly* 37:1/2 (2009): 101–124. doi:10.1353/wsq.0.0158.

DAWN Canada. "Women with Disabilities and Violence." http://www.dawncanada.net/main/wp-content/uploads/2014/03/English-Violence-January-2014.pdf.

De Goede, Irene H. A., Susan J. T. Branje, Marc J. M. H. Delsing, and Wim H. J. Meeus. "Linkages over time between adolescents' relationships with parents and friends." *Journal of Youth and Adolescence* 38 (2009): 1304–1315. doi:10.1007/s10964-009-9403-2.

Dean, Jodi. *Blog Theory: Feedback and Capture in the Circuits of Drive.* Cambridge: Polity Press, 2010.

———. *Publicity's Secret: How Technoculture Capitalizes on Democracy.* Ithaca, New York: Cornell University Press, 2002.

Den Hertog, Joanna. "Herstory: Johanna Den Hertog – A Founding Member Keynote Speech at Rape Relief 35th Anniversary." http://www.rapereliefshelter.bc.ca/about-us/herstory/herstory.

Denhem, Elizabeth. "Privacy and the World Wide Web: How the OPC Investigation of Facebook Made Worldwide Waves: Remarks at the IAPP KnowledgeNet Session." http://priv.gc.ca/speech/2009/spd_20091007_ed_e.cfm.

Denzin, Norman K., Yvonna S. Lincoln, and Michael D. Giardina. "Disciplining Qualitative Research." *International Journal of Qualitative Studies in Education* 19(6) (2006): 769–782. doi:10.1080/09518390600975990.

Department of Education. "Provincial School Code of Conduct and School Code of Conduct Guidelines." http://www.studentservices.ednet.ca/sites/default/files/provincial_school_code_of%20conduct.pdf.

Derecho, Abigail. "Gender and Fan Culture (Round Eight, Part One): Abigail Derecho and Christian McCrea." http://henryjenkins.org/2007/07/gender_and_fan_culture_round_e.html.

De Ridder, Sander, and Sofie van Bauwel. "Commenting on Pictures: Teens Negotiating Gender and Sexualities on Social Networking Sites." *Sexualities* 16 (2013): 565–586. doi:10.1177/1363460713487369.

Dewey, John. *How We Think.* Boston: D.C. Heath & Company, 1910.

Dhariwal, Amrit, Jennifer Connolly, Marinella Paciello, and Gian Vittorio Caprara. "Adolescent peer relationships and emerging adult romantic styles: A longitudinal study of youth in an Italian community." *Journal of Adolescent Research* 24 (2009): 594–595. doi:10.1177/0743558409341080.

Di Ionno, Mark. "Exclusive Interview with Dharun Ravi: 'I'm Very Sorry about Tyler.'" *The Star-Ledger,* March 22, 2012. http://blog.nj.com/njv_mark_diionno/2012/03/exclusive_interview_dharun_rav.html.

Dickson, Louise. "Vancouver Island 'sexting' case sparks challenge over charging youth with child pornography." *Vancouver Sun,* September 18, 2013. http://www.vancouversun.com/technology/Vancouver+Island+sexting+case+sparks+challenge+over+charging+youth+with+child+pornography/8928731/story.html.

Dillon, Michele, and Sarah Savage. "Values and Religion in Rural America: Attitudes Toward Abortion and Same-Sex Relations." *The Carsey Institute at the Scholars' Repository* 1 (2006): 1–10. http://scholars.unh.edu/cgi/viewcontent.cgi?article=1011&context=carsey.

Dobson, Amy S. "'Individuality is Everything': 'Autonomous' Femininity in MySpace Mottos and Self-Descriptions." *Continuum* 26:3 (2012): 371–383. doi:10.1080/10304312.2012.665835.

———. "Bitches, Bunnies and Bffs (Best Friends Forever): A Feminist Analysis of Young Women's Performance of Contemporary Popular Femininities on MySpace." PhD diss., Monash University, 2010.

———. "Femininities as Commodities: Cam Girl Culture." In *Next Wave Cultures: Feminism, Subcultures, Activism*, edited by Anita Harris, 123–148. New York: Routledge, 2008.

———. "Hetero-Sexy Representation by Young Women on MySpace: The Politics of Performing an 'Objectified' Self." http://www.outskirts.arts.uwa.edu.au.proxy.bib.uottawa.ca/volumes/volume-25/amy-shields-dobson.

———. "Performative Shamelessness on Young Women's' Social Network Sites: Shielding the Self and Resisting Gender Melancholia." Feminism & Psychology 24 (2013): 97–114. doi:0959353513510651.

———. "The Representation of Female Friendships on Young Women's MySpace Profiles: The All-Female World and the Feminine 'Other.'" In *Youth Culture and Net Culture: Online Social Practices*, edited by Elza Dunkels, Gun-Marie Franberg, and Camilla Hallgren, 126–145. Hershey, PA: IGI Global, 2011.

Doyle, Aaron. "Revisiting the Synopticon: Reconsidering Mathiesen's 'the Viewer Society' in the Age of Web 2.0." *Theoretical Criminology* 15 (2011): 283–299. doi:10.1177/1362480610396645.

Draper, Hannah. "Canadian Policy Process Review 1994–201." http://egirlsproject.ca/research/research-memos-backgrounders/2013-policy-discourses-jurisdictions/#CdnFed.

———. "Canadian Policy Process Review 1994–2011." http://egirlsproject.files.wordpress.com/2013/10/canada-federal-policy-review-2012.pdf.

Driscoll, Catherine, and Melissa Gregg, "Convergence Culture and the Legacy of Feminist Cultural Studies," *Cultural Studies* 25 (2011): 566–584. doi:10.1080/09502386.2011.600549.

Duggan, Maeve, and Aaron Smith. "Social Media Update 2013." *Pew Research Centre*, December 20, 2013. http://www.pewinternet.org/files/2013/12/PIP_Social-Networking-2013.pdf.

Duggan, Maeve, and Joanna Brenner. "The demographics of social media users – 2012." *Pew Research Center's Internet & American Life Project*, February 14, 2013. http://www.pewinternet.org/files/old-media/Files/Reports/2013/PIP_SocialMediaUsers.pdf.

Dunning, Jennifer. "Amanda Todd, sextortion and cyberbullying," *CBC News*, November 13, 2013. http://www.cbc.ca/newsblogs/yourcommunity/2013/11/amanda-todd-and-sextortion.html.

Durham, Meenakshi G. "Articulating Adolescent Girls' Resistance to Patriarchal Discourse in Popular Media." *Women's Studies in Communication* 22:2 (1999): 210–229. doi:10.1080/07491409.1999.10162421.

———. "Constructing the "New Ethnicities": Media, Sexuality and Diaspora Identity in the Lives of South Asian Immigrant Girls." *Critical Studies in Media Communication* 21:2 (2004): 140–161. doi:10.1080/073931804100 01688047.

Dwairy, Marwan, and Mustafa Achoui. "Parental Control: A Second Cross-Cultural Research on Parenting and Psychological Adjustment of Children." *Journal of Child and Family Studies* 19 (2010): 16–22. doi:10.1007/s10826-009-9334-2.

Dworkin, Shari, and Kari Lerum. "Bad Girls Rule: An Interdisciplinary Feminist Commentary on the Report of the APA Task Force on the Sexualization of Girls." *Journal of Sex Research* 46:2 (2009): 250–263. doi:10.1080/00224490903079542.

Dyson, Esther. "Reflections On Privacy 2.0." *Scientific American* 299 (2008): 50–55.

Earl, Jennifer, and Katrina Kimport. *Digitally Enabled Social Change: Activism in the Internet Age*. Cambridge, MA: MIT Press, 2011.

Editorial Board. "Fighting Back Against Revenge Porn." *New York Times*, October 12, 2013. http://www.nytimes.com/2013/10/13/opinion/sunday/fighting-back-against-revenge-porn.html.

Editorials. "Cyberbullying Law Sneaks in Measures on Police Snooping." *Toronto Star*, November 24, 2013. http://www.thestar.com/opinion/editorials/2013/11/24/cyberbullying_law_sneaks_in_measures_on_police_snooping_editorial.html.

Edwards, Lynne. "Victims, Villains, and Vixens: Teen Girls and Internet Crime." In *Girl Wide Web: Girls, the Internet, and the Negotiation of Identity*, edited by Sharon Mazzarella, 13–30. New York: Peter Lang, 2005.

Elias, Nelly, and Dafna Lemish. "Spinning the Web of Identity: The Roles of the Internet in the Lives of Immigrant Adolescents." *New Media & Society* 11 (2009): 533–551.

Elm, Malin S. "Exploring and Negotiating Femininity: Young Women's Creation of Style in a Swedish Internet Community." *Young* 17:3 (2009): 241–264. doi:10.1177/110330880901700302.

Englander, Elizabeth K. *Bullying and Cyberbullying: What Every Educator Needs to Know*. Cambridge, Mass.: Harvard Education Press, 2013.

———. "Low Risk Associated With Most Teenage Sexting: A Study of 617 18-Year-Olds." http://webhost.bridgew.edu/marc/SEXTING%20AND%20COERCION%20report.pdf.

Equal Voice. "Women in Federal Politics." http://www.equalvoice.ca/pdf/women_in_federal_politics_fact_sheet_march_2013.pdf.

ERASE Bullying. "Policy to Action." http://www.erasebullying.ca/policy/policy.php.

Evans, Adrienne, Sarah Riley, and Avi Shankar. "Technologies of Sexiness: Theorizing Women's Engagement in the Sexualization of Culture." *Feminism & Psychology* 20:1 (2010): 114–131. doi:10.1177/0959353509351854.

Fanfiction. "Fanfiction – Unleash Your Imagination." https://www.fanfiction.net/tos.

Farley, Julee P., and Jungmeen Kim-Spoon. "The development of adolescent self-regulation: Reviewing the role of parent, peer, friend, and romantic relationships," *Journal of Adolescence*, 37 (2014): 436–37. doi:10.1016/j.adolescence.2014.03.009.

Feinberg, Lisa. "Facebook: Beyond Friends." *Our Schools/Our Selves* 17 (2008) http://www.policyalternatives.ca/sites/default/files/uploads/publications/Our_Schools_Ourselve/9_Feinburg_facebook_beyond_friends.pdf.

Feltrin, Claire. "Girls Online – Canadian Provinces Policy Review." *The eGirls Project*, May 2013. http://egirlsproject.files.wordpress.com/2013/09/canada-provinces-policy-review-2013.pdf.

Fenwick, Helen, and Daniel Fenwick. "The Changing Face of Protection for Individual Privacy Against the Press: Leveson, the Royal Charter and Tort Liability." *International Review of Law, Computers & Technology* 27 (2013): 241–279. doi:10.1080/13600869.2013.797203.

Fernandez, Maria, and Faith Wilding. "Situating Cyberfeminisms." In *Domain Errors! Cyberfeminist Practices*, edited by Maria Fernandez, Faith Wilding, and Michelle Wright, 17–28. New York: Autonomedia, 2002.

Ferráns, Silvia Diazgranados, Robert L. Selman, and Luba Falk Feigenberg. "Rules of the Culture and Personal Needs: Witnesses' Decision-Making Processes to Deal with Situations of Bullying in Middle School." *Harvard Educational Review* 82:4 (2012): 445–470. http://her.hepg.org/content/4u5v1n8q67332v03/fulltext.pdf.

Fighting Internet: YouTube. "Hitler Gets Netflix and Hits the Internet Cap." http://www.youtube.com/watch?v=y-Mg6pq33Zc.

Findlay, Stephanie. "Bullying Victims are Taking Schools to Court." *Maclean's*, September 14, 2011. http://www.macleans.ca/news/canada/taking-schools-to-court/.

Fine, Gary A., and Ralph L. Rosnow. "Gossip, Gossipers, Gossiping." *Personality and Social Psychology Bulletin* 4 (1978): 161–168. doi:10.1177/014616727800400135.

Fine, Sean. "Tory 'Revenge Porn' Bill Touches on Terrorism, Cable Theft." *Globe and Mail*, November 20, 2013. http://www.theglobeandmail.

com/news/politics/tories-wide-ranging-crime-bill-cracks-down-on-distributing-intimate-images/article15533521/.

Fink, Marty, and Quinn Miller. "Trans Media Moments: Tumblr, 2011–2013." *Television & New Media* 15:7 (2013). doi:10.1177/1527476413505002.

Finkelhor, David. "The Internet, Youth Safety and the Problem of 'Juvenoia.'" http://www.unh.edu/ccrc/pdf/Juvenoia%20paper.pdf.

Fischer, Claude S. *To Dwell Among Friends*. The University of Chicago Press: Chicago, 1982.

Flanagan, Mary, and Austin Booth. "Introduction." In *Reload: Rethinking Women + Cyberculture*, edited by Mary Flanagan and Austin Booth, 1–24. Cambridge, MA: MIT Press, 2002.

Ford, Liam. "Prosecutors: 3 teens posted taped sex assaults of girl, 12, on Facebook." *Chicago Tribune*, May 17, 2013. http://www.chicagotribune.com/news/local/breaking/chi-3-teens-posted-taped-sex-assaults-of-girl-12-on-facebook-20130517-story.html.

Foucault, Michel. *Discipline and Punish: The Birth of the Prison*. New York: Vintage Books, 1979.

Fox, Jesse, and Jeremy N. Bailenson. "Virtual Virgins and Vamps: The Effects of Exposure to Female Characters' Sexualized Appearance and Gaze in an Immersive Virtual Environment." *Sex Roles* 61:3–4 (2009): 147–157. doi:10.1007/s11199-009-9599-3.

Frank, Blye W. "Masculinities and Schooling: The Making of Men." In *Systemic Violence: How Schools Hurt Children*, edited by Junita Ross Epp and Ailsa M. Watkinson, 113–129. London: Falmer Press, 1996.

Franks, Mary Ann. "Unwilling Avatars: Idealism and Discrimination in Cyberspace." *Columbia Journal of Gender and Law* 20 (2011): 224–248, archived at Social Science Research Network: http://papers.ssrn.com/sol3/Delivery.cfm/SSRN_ID2164495_code1224353.pdf?abstractid=1374533&mirid=1.

Fulat, Shareefa, and Raza Jaffrey. "Muslim Youth Helpline: A Model of Youth Engagement in Service Delivery." *Youth & Policy* 92 (2006): 151–171. http://www.youthandpolicy.org/wp-content/uploads/2013/07/youthandpolicy92.pdf.

Gajjala, Radhika. "Internet Constructs of Identity and Ignorance: 'Third World' Contexts and Cyberfeminism." *Works and Days* 33/34, 35/36:17&18 (1999–2000): 117–137. http://www.worksanddays.net/1999-2000/08-Gajjala_Gajjala.pdf.

Gannes, Liz. "NTV Predictions: Online Video Stars." *Gigacom*, December 30, 2007. http://gigaom.com/2007/12/30/ntv-predictions-online-video-stars.

Gannon, Maire, and Karen Mihorean. *Criminal Victimization in Canada, 2004*. Ottawa: Canadian Centre for Justice Statistics, 2005.

Gans, Herbert J. *People and Plans: Essays on Urban Problems and Solutions*. Basic Books: New York, 1968.

Gariba, Shaibu Ahmed. *Race, Ethnicity, Immigration and Jobs: Labour Market Access Among Ghanaian and Somali Youth in the Greater Toronto Area.* Unpublished dissertation. Toronto: Ontario Institute for Studies in Education of the University of Toronto, 2009. https://tspace.library. utoronto.ca/bitstream/1807/19037/1/Gariba_Shaibu_A_200911_PhD_ Thesis.pdf.

Garside, Ruth, Richard Ayres, Mike Owen, Virginia A. H. Pearson, and Judith Roizen. "Anonymity and Confidentiality: Rural Teenagers' Concerns When Accessing Sexual Health Services." *The Journal of Family Planning and Reproductive Health Care* 28:1 (2002): 23–26. http:// jfprhc.bmj.com/content/28/1/23.long.

Gay, Lesbian, & Straight Education Network. "Out Online: The Experiences of Lesbian, Gay, Bisexual and Transgender Youth on the Internet." http://glsen.org/press/study-finds-lgbt-youth-face-greater-harassment-online.

Gee, James P. *New Digital Media and Learning as an Emerging Area and "Worked Examples" as One Way Forward.* Cambridge: The MIT Press, 2010.

General Assembly. "United Nations General Assembly, Declaration on the Elimination of Violence Against Women." http://www.un.org/documents/ga/res/48/a48r104.htm.

Gerstenfeld, Phyllis B., Diana R. Grant, and Chau-Pu Chiang. "Hate Online: A Content Analysis Of Extremist Internet Sites." *Analyses of Social Issues and Public Policy* 3 (2003): 29–44. doi:10.1111/ j.1530-2415.2003.00013.x.

Giddens, Anthony. *Modernity and Self-Identity: Self and Society in the Late Modern Age.* Cambridge: Polity Press, 1991.

Gilbert, Christopher J. "Playing with Hitler: *Downfall* and Its Ludic Uptake." *Critical Studies in Media Communication* 30 (2013): 407–424. doi:10. 1080/15295036.2012.755052.

Gilbert, Eric, Karrie Karahalios, and Christian Sandvig. "The Network in the Garden: Designing Social Media for Rural Life." *American Behavioral Scientist* 53 (2010): 1367–1388. doi:10.1177/0002764210361690.

Gilden, Andrew. "Cyberbullying and the Innocence Narrative." *Harvard Civil Rights-Civil Liberties Law Review* 48 (2013): 357–407. http://harvardcrcl. org/wp-content/uploads/2011/09/CRCL_Gilden_print-version.pdf.

Gill, Rosalind. "Empowerment/Sexism: Figuring Female Sexual Agency in Contemporary Advertising." *Feminism & Psychology* 18 (2008): 35–60. doi:10.1177/0959353507084950.

———. *Gender and the Media.* Cambridge: Polity Press, 2007.

Gill, Rosalind, and Christina Scharff. "Introduction." In *New Femininities: Postfeminism, Neoliberalism and Subjectivity*, edited by Rosalind Gill and Christina Scharff, 1–13. Cambridge: Palgrave Macmillan, 2011.

Girls Action Foundation. *Amplify: Designing Spaces and Programs for Girls, A Toolkit.* Montreal: Girl's Action Foundation, 2010.

Goffman, Erving. *The Presentation of Self in Everyday Life.* Peter Smith Publisher: Garden City, 1999.

Gonick, Marnina. "Between 'Girl Power' and 'Reviving Ophelia': Constituting the Neoliberal Girl Subject." *NWSA Journal* 18:2 (2006): 1–23. doi:10.1353/nwsa.2006.0031.

Gonzales, Amy, and Jeffrey T. Hancock. "Mirror, Mirror on my Facebook Wall: Effects of Exposure to Facebook on Self-Esteem." *Cyberpsychology, Behavior and Social Networking* 14 (2011): 79–83. doi:10.1089/cyber.2009.0411.

Goode, Erica. "Victims Push Laws To End Online Revenge Posts." *New York Times,* September 23, 2013. http://www.nytimes.com/2013/09/24/us/victims-push-laws-to-end-online-revenge-posts.html.

Google Support: YouTube. "How Content ID Works." https://support.google.com/youtube/answer/2797370?hl=en.

Gorton, Kristyn, and Joanne Garde-Hansen. "From Old Media Whore to New Media Troll." *Feminist Media Studies* 13:2 (2013): 288–302. doi:10.1080/14680777.2012.678370.

Government of Canada. "Canada – Permanent residents by category, 2009–2013." http://www.cic.gc.ca/english/resources/statistics/facts2013-preliminary/01.asp.

Government of Canada: Industry Canada News Releases. "Minister Clement Updates Canadians on Canada's Digital Economy Strategy." http://www.ic.gc.ca/eic/site/064.nsf/eng/06096.html.

Government of Newfoundland Labrador. "Violence Against Aboriginal Women fact sheet." http://www.gov.nl.ca/vpi/facts/VAW_EN_Fact%20Sheet_Aboriginal_Women.pdf.

Grabe, Shelly, Monique L. Ward, and Janet Shibley Hyde. "The Role of the Media in Body Image Concerns Among Women: A Meta-Analysis of Experimental and Correlational Studies." *Psychological Bulletin* 134:3 (2008): 460–476. 10.1037/0033-2909.134.3.460.

Gray, Kishonna L. "Deviant Bodies, Stigmatized Identities, and Racist Acts: Examining the Experiences of African-American Gamers in Xbox Live." *New Review of Hypermedia and Multimedia* 18 (2012): 261–276. doi:10.1080/13614568.2012.746740.

Greene, Kevin J. "'Copynorms,' Black Cultural Production, and the Debate over African-American Reparations," *Cardozo Arts & Ent. L.J.* 25 (2008): 1179–1227. http://www.cardozoaelj.com/wp-content/uploads/2013/03/Green.pdf.

Grenoble, Ryan. "Amanda Todd: Bullied Canadian Teen Commits Suicide After Prolonged Battle Online and in School." *Huffington Post,*

November 10, 2012. http://www.huffingtonpost.com/2012/10/11/amanda-todd-suicide-bullying_n_1959909.html.

Grillo, Trina, and Stephanie M. Wildman. "Obscuring the Importance of Race: The Implication of Making Comparisons Between Racism and Sexism (Or Other-Isms)." *Duke Law Journal* 1991 (1991): 397–412. http://scholarship.law.duke.edu/cgi/viewcontent.cgi?article=3148&context=dlj.

Grisso, Ashley D., and David Weiss. "What Are Gurls Talking About? Adolescent Girls' Construction of Sexual Identity on Gurl.Com." In *Girl Wide Web: Girls, the Internet and the Negotiation of Identity*, edited by Sharon Mazzarella, 31–49. New York: Peter Lang, 2008.

Grusin, Richard. *Premediation: Affect and Mediality After 9/11*. New York: Palgrave, 2010.

Haggart, Blayne. "Fair Copyright for Canada: Lessons for Online Social Movements from the First Canadian Facebook Uprising." *Canadian Journal of Political Science / Revue canadienne de science politique* 46 (2013): 841–861. doi:10.1017/S0008423913000838.

Haight, Michael, Anabel Quan-Haase, and Bradley A Corbett. "Digital Divide in Canada: The Impact of Demographic Factors on Access to the Internet, Level of Online Activity, and Social Networking Site Usage" *Information, Communication & Society* 17 (2014): 503–519. doi:10.1080/1369118X.2014.891633.

Hall, Stuart, "Introduction: Who Needs Identity?" In *Questions of Cultural Identity*, edited by Stuart Hall and Paul du Gay, 1–17. London: Sage Publication, 1996.

Haste, Polly. "Sex Education and Masculinity: The 'Problem' of Boys." *Gender and Education*, 25 (2013): 515–527, doi:10.1080/09540253.2013.789830.

Haraway, Donna. "A Cyborg Manifesto: Science, Technology, and Socialist-Feminism in the Late Twentieth Century." In *Simians, Cyborgs, and Women*, edited by Donna Haraway, 149–183. New York: Routledge, 1991.

Harmon, Amy. "Star Wars' Fan Films Come Tumbling Back to Earth." *New York Times*, April 28, 2002, B28. http://www.nytimes.com/2002/04/28/movies/film-star-wars-fan-films-come-tumbling-back-to-earth.html.

Harper, Brit, and Marika Tiggemann. "The Effect of Thin Ideal Media Images on Women's Self-Objectification, Mood and Body Image." *Sex Roles* 58:9–10 (2008): 649–657. doi:10.1007/s11199-007-9379-x.

Harris, Anita. "Introduction: Youth Cultures and Feminist Politics." In *Next Wave Cultures: Feminism, Subcultures, Activism*, edited by Anita Harris, 1–13. New York: Routledge, 2008.

———. "Revisiting Bedroom Culture: New Spaces for Young Women's Politics." *Hecate* 27:1 (2001): 128–138. doi:10.1177/1440783311408971.

———. "Young Women, Late Modern Politics, and the Participatory Possibilities of Online Cultures." *Journal of Youth Studies* 11:5 (2008): 481–495. doi:10.1080/13676260802282950.

Hart, Roger, and Michael Schwab. "Children's Rights and the Building of Democracy: A Dialogue on the International Movement for Children's Participation." *Children and the Environment* 24:3 (1997): 177–191. http://www.jstor.org/stable/29767030.

Hart, Roger, Collette Daiute, Semil Iltus, David Kritt, Michaela Rome, and Kim Sabo. "Developmental Theory and Children's Participation in Community Organizations." *Children and the Environment* 24:3 (1997): 33–63. http://www.jstor.org/stable/29767020.

Hartung, Freda-Marie, and Britta Renner. "Social Curiosity and Gossip: Related to but Different Drives of Social Functioning." *PLoS ONE* 8 (2013). doi:10.1371/journal.pone.0069996.

Hartzog, Woodrow, and Frederic Stuzman. "The Case of Online Obscurity." *California Law Review* 101:1 (2013): 1–50. http://www.californialawreview.org/assets/pdfs/101-1/01-HartzogStutzman.pdf.

Harvey, Laura, and Jessica Ringrose. "Sexting, Ratings and (Mis)recognition: Teen Boys' Performing Classed and Racialised Masculinities in Digitally Networked Publics." In *Children, Sexuality and 'Sexualisation'*, edited by Emma Renold, Jessica Ringrose, and Danielle Egan. Forthcoming, 2015.

Hasinoff, Amy. "Sexting as Media Production: Rethinking Social Media and Sexuality." *New Media & Society* 15:4 (2013): 449–465. doi:10.1177/1461444812459171.

Hearn, Alison. "'John, a 20-Year-Old Boston Native with a Great Sense of Humor': On the Spectacularization of the 'self' and the Incorporation of Identity in the Age of Reality Television." In *The Celebrity Culture Reader*, edited by P. David Marshall, 131–147. New York: Routledge, 2006.

Heilman, Elizabeth. "The Struggle for Self: Power and Identity in Adolescent Girls." *Youth & Society* 30:2 (1998): 182–208. doi:10.1177/0044118X98030002003.

Henry, Nicola, and Anastasia Powell. *Preventing Sexual Violence: Interdisciplinary Approaches to Overcoming a Rape Culture*, edited by Nicola Henry and Anastasia Powell. United Kingdom: Palgrave Macmillan, 2014.

Hess, Amanda. "Why Women Aren't Welcome on the Internet." *Pacific Standard*, January 6, 2014. http://www.psmag.com/navigation/health-and-behavior/women-arent-welcome-internet-72170/.

Hewson, Claire. "Qualitative Approaches to Internet-Mediated Research: Opportunities, Issues, Possibilities." In *The Oxford Handbook of Qualitative Research*, edited by Patricia Leavy, 423–454. Oxford: Oxford University Press, 2014.

Hill, Kashmir. "Dharun Ravi Gets Off Easy In Rutgers Spying Case: Month In Jail and $10,000 Fine." *Forbes*, May 21, 2012. http://www.forbes.com/sites/kashmirhill/2012/05/21/dharun-ravi-gets-off-easy-in-clementi-case-month-in-jail-and-10000-fine.

Hirschman, Celeste, Emily A. Impett, Deborah Schooler. "Dis/Embodied Voices: What Late-Adolescent Girls Can Teach US About Objectification and Sexuality." *Sexuality Research & Social Policy* 3:4 (2006): 8–20. http://link.springer.com/article/10.1525%2Fsrsp.2006.3.4.8.

Hobbs, Renee, and Amy Jensen. "The Past, Present and Future of Media Literacy Education." *Journal of Media Literacy Education* 1 (2009): 1–11. http://digitalcommons.uri.edu/cgi/viewcontent.cgi?article=1000&context=jmle.

Hoder, Randye. "For Teenage Girls, Facebook Means Always Being Camera-Ready." *Motherlode: Living in the Family Dynamic*, March 7, 2012. http://parenting.blogs.nytimes.com/2012/03/07/for-teenage-girls-facebook-means-always-being-camera-ready/?_php=true&_type=blogs&_r=0.

Hodge, Jessica P. *Gendered Hate: Exploring Gender in Hate Crime Law*. Boston: Northeastern University Press, 2011.

Hodge, Matthew J. "Comment: the Fourth Amendment and Privacy Issues on the 'New' Internet: Facebook.com and Myspace.com." *Southern Illinois University Law School Journal* 31 (2006): 104–191.

Hodkinson, Paul, and Sian Lincoln. "Online Journals as Virtual Bedrooms?: Young People, Identity and Personal Space." *Young* 16:1 (2008): 27–46. doi:10.1177/110330880701600103.

Hoelzel, Mark. "New Study Shows Instagram And Snapchat Beating Twitter Among Teens And Young Adults." *Business Insider*, March 13, 2014. http://www.businessinsider.com/instagram-and-snapchat-are-more-popular-than-twitter-among-teens-and-young-adults-sai-2014-3.

Holman, Rebecca. "She's a Homewrecker: The Website Where Women Expose 'Infidelity'. The Internet Just Ate Itself." *The Telegraph*, November 15, 2013. http://www.telegraph.co.uk/women/womens-life/10452482/Shes-A-Homewrecker-the-website-where-women-slut-shame-each-others-infidelity.-The-internet-just-ate-itself.html.

Holmes, Su. "When Will I Be Famous? Reappraising the Debate About Fame in Reality TV." In *How Real Is Reality TV?: Essays on Representation and Truth*, edited by David S. Escoffery, 7-25. Jefferson: MacFarland & Company, 2006.

Horek, Tanya. "#AskThicke: 'Blurred Lines,' Rape Culture, and the Feminist Hashtag Takeover." *Feminist Media Studies* 14:6 (2014): 1105–1107. doi:10.1080/14680777.2014.975450.

Houghton Mifflin Harcourt. "A Conversation with Alice Randall." http://www.hmhbooks.com/readers_guides/wind_done_gone/index2.shtml#conversation.

Huberman, Michael, and Matthew B. Miles. "Data Management and Analysis Methods." In *Collecting and Interpreting Qualitative Materials*, edited by Norman K. Denzin and Yvonna S. Lincoln. Thousand Oaks, CA: Sage, 2000.

Huggins, Christopher M., and Jeffrey Debies-Carl. "Tolerance in the City: The Multilevel Effects of Urban Environments on Permissive Attitudes." *Journal of Urban Affairs* (2014): 1–15. doi:10.1111/juaf.12141.

Humbach, John. "'Sexting' and the First Amendment." *Hastings Constitutional Law Quarterly* 37:3 (2010): 433–485. http://www.hastingsconlaw quarterly.org/archives/V37/I3/Humbach.pdf.

Hurd, Heidi M., and Michael S. Moore. "Punishing Hatred and Prejudice." *Stanford Law Review* 56 (2004): 1081–1146. ISSN: 00389765.

Idle No More. "CStreet Campaign." http://www.idlenomore.ca.

Industry Canada. "Shaping Canada's Strategy for the Digital Economy." http://www.ic.gc.ca/eic/site/ich-epi.nsf/eng/02090.html.

Internet World Stats. "Top 50 Countries With the Highest Internet Penetration Rate." http://www.internetworldstats.com/top25.htm.

Jacobs, J. *The Death and Life of Great American Cities*. Random House: New York, 1961.

Jacobson, Erik. "Music Remix in the Classroom." In *DIY Media: Creating, Sharing and Learning with New Technologies*, edited by Colin Lankshear and Michele Knobel, 27–50. New York: Peter Lang Publishing Group, 2010.

Jakle, John A. "America's Small Town/Big City Dialectic." *Journal of Cultural Geography* 18 (1999): 1–27. doi:10.1080/08873639909478302.

James, Carrie, Katie Davis, Andrea Flores, John M. Francis, Lindsay Pettingill, Margaret Rundle, and Howard Gardner. "Young People, Ethics, and the New Digital Media: A Synthesis from the Good Play Project." *GoodWork Project Report Series*, Number 54. Project Zero, Harvard Graduate School of Education: Massachusetts Institute of Technology, 2009.

James, Kandy. "'I just gotta have my own space!': The Bedroom as a Leisure Site for Adolescent Girls." *Journal of Leisure Research* 33:1 (2001): 71–90.

Jenkins, Henry. "Gender and Fan Studies (Round Five, Part Two): Geoffrey Long and Cathering Tosenberger." http://henryjenkins.org/2007/06/gender_and_fan_studies_round_f_1.html.

Jenkins, Henry. *Spreadable Media: Creating Value and Meaning in a Networked Culture*. New York University Press, 2013.

Jenness, Valerie. "The Hate Crime Canon and beyond: A Critical Assessment." *Law and Critique* 12:3 (2001): 279–308. doi:10.1023/A:1013774229732.

Jewkes, Rachel, Purna Sen, and Claudia Garcia-Moreno. "Sexual Violence." In *World Report on Violence and Health*, edited by Etienne G. Krug, Linda

L. Dahlberg, James A. Mercy, Anthony B. Zwi, and Rafael Lozano, 149–181. Geneva: World Health Organization, 2002.

Jiwani, Yasmin. *Violence Prevention and the Girl Child: Final Report*. Ottawa: Status of Women Canada, 1999. http://fredacentre.com/wp-content/uploads/2010/09/Jiwani-et-al-1999-Violence-Prevention-and-the-Girl-Child-.pdf.

Jiwani, Yasmin, Helene Berman, and Catherine Ann Cameron. "Violence Prevention and the Canadian Girl Child." *International Journal of Child, Youth and Family Studies* 1:2 (2010): 134–156. ISSN: 1920–7298.

Johnson, David, and Geraldine Lewis. "Do You Like What You See? Self-Perceptions of Adolescent Bullies." *British Educational Research Journal* 25 (1999): 665–677. doi:10.1080/0141192990250507.

Johnson, Deborah G., and Priscilla M. Regan. *Transparency and Surveillance as Sociotechnical Accountability: A House of Mirrors*. London: Routledge, 2014.

Johnson, Holly, and Myrna Dawson. *Violence Against Women in Canada: Research and Policy Perspectives*. Don Mills, Ontario: Oxford University Press Canada, 2011.

Johnson, Holly. "Preventing Violence Against Women: Progress and Challenges Volume." https://www.ncjrs.gov/App/Publications/abstract.aspx?ID=241584.

Jones, Lisa M., Kimberly J. Mitchell, and Wendy A.Walsh. "Evaluation of Internet Child Safety Materials Used by ICAC Task Forces in School and Community Settings, Final Report." https://www.ncjrs.gov/pdffiles1/nij/grants/242016.pdf.

Juang, Linda P., and Alvin A. Alvarez. "Discrimination and Adjustment Among Chinese American Adolescents: Family Conflict and Family Cohesion as Vulnerability and Protective Factors." *American Journal of Public Health*, 100 (2010): 3–4. doi:10.2105/AJPH.2009.185959.

Kahne, Joseph, Nam-Jin Lee, and Jessica T. Feezell. "The Civic and Political Significance of Online Participatory Cultures among Youth Transitioning to Adulthood." *Journal of Information Technology & Politics* 10 (2013): 1–32. doi:10.1080/19331681.2012.701109.

Kapur, Ratna. "Pink Chaddis and SlutWalk Couture: The Postcolonial Politics of Feminism Lite." *Feminist Legal Studies* 20:1 (2012): 1–20. doi:10.1007/s10691-012-9193-x.

Karaian, Lara. "Lolita Speaks: 'Sexting', Teenage Girls and the Law." *Crime Media Culture* 8:1 (2012): 57–73. doi:10.1177/1741659011429868.

———. "Policing 'Sexting': Responsibilization, Respectability and Sexual Subjectivity in Child Protection/Crime Prevention Responses to Teenagers' Digital Sexual Expression." *Theoretical Criminology* 18:3 (2013): 282–299. doi:10.1177/1362480613504331.

Katyal, Sonia K. "Performance, Property and the Slashing of Gender in Fan Fiction." *Journal of Gender, Social Policy and the Law.* 14:3 (2006): 461–518. http://www.wcl.american.edu/journal/genderlaw/14/katyal3.pdf.

Kearney, Mary C. "Girls' Media Studies 2.0." In *Mediated Girlhoods: New Explorations of Girls' Media Culture,* edited by Mary Celeste Kearney, 1–16. New York: Peter Lang, 2011.

——. "Productive Spaces: Girls' Bedrooms as Sites of Cultural Production." *Journal of Children and Media* 1:2 (2007): 126–141. doi:10.1080/17482790701339126.

Kee, Jac Sm. "Cultivating Violence Through Technology? Exploring the Connections Between Information and Communication Technologies (ICT) and Violence Against Women (VAW)." http://www.genderit.org/sites/default/upload/VAW_ICT_EN.pdf.

Keller, Jessalynn. "Virtual Feminisms: Girls' Blogging Communities, Feminist Activism, and Participatory Politics." *Information, Communication & Society* 15 (2012): 1–19. doi:10.1080/1369118X.2011.642890.

Keller, Jessalynn. "Fiercely Real?: Tyra Banks and the Making of New Media Celebrity." *Feminist Media Studies* 14:1 (2014): 1–18. doi:10.1080/14680777.2012.740490.

Kelly, Dierdre M., Shauna Pomerantz, and Dawn Currie. "No Boundaries? Girls' Interactive, Online Learning About Feminities." *Youth Society* 38:3 (2006): 3–28. doi:10.1177/0044118X05283482.

Kember, Sarah, and Joanna Zylinska. *Life After New Media: Mediation as a Vital Process.* Cambridge: MIT Press, 2012.

Khazan, Olga. "The Evolution of Bitchiness." *The Atlantic,* November 20, 2013. http://www.theatlantic.com/health/archive/2013/11/the-evolution-of-bitchiness/281657.

Kids Help Phone. "About Kids Help Phone." http://org.kidshelpphone.ca/en.

Kift, Sally M., Marilyn A. Campbell, and Desmond A. Butler. "Cyberbullying in Social Networking sites and Blogs: Legal Issues for Young People and Schools." *Journal of Law, Information and Science* 20:2 (2010): 60–97. ISSN: 0729-1485.

Kimber, Stephen. "Why Are We Using Child Pornography Laws to Charge Children?" *Rabble.ca,* January 14, 2014. http://rabble.ca/blogs/bloggers/skimber/2014/01/why-are-we-using-child-pornography-laws-to-charge-children.

Kindle Worlds. "Content Guidelines and Review Process." https://kindle-worlds.amazon.com/faqs?topicId=A2W2IF5J2WZDKT.

Kirshner, Ben. "Youth Activism as a Context for Learning and Development." *American Behavioral Scientist* 51:3 (2007): 367–379. doi:10.1177/0002764207306065.

Klein, Renate. "The Politics of Cyberfeminism: If I'm a Cyborg Rather Than a Goddess Will Patriarchy Go Away?" In *Cyberfeminism: Connectivity,*

Critique, Creativity, edited by Susan Hawthorne and Renate Klein, 186–207. North Melbourne, Australia: Spinifex Press, 1999.

Knobel, Michele, Colin Lankshear, and Matthew Lewis. "AMV Remix: Do-It-Yourself Anime Music Videos." In *DIY Media: Creating, Sharing and Learning with New Technologies*, edited by Colin Lankshear and Michele Knobel, 205–230. New York: Peter Lang Publishing Group, 2010.

Koenigs, Michael, and Ian T. Shearn. "Tyler Clementi Cyberbullying Trial Begins Today." *ABC News*, February 21, 2012. http://abcnews.go.com/US/tyler-clementi-bullying-trial-begins-today/story?id=15752236.

Koskela, Hille. "'Cam Era' – the contemporary urban Panopticon." *Surveillance & Society* 1 (2002): 292–313. ISSN: 1477-7487.

Koskela, Hille. "Webcams, TV Shows and Mobile Phones: Empowering Exhibitionism." *Surveillance and Society* 2:2/3 (2004): 292–313. ISSN: 1477-7487.

Kryk, John. "Target in 2005 McGill Hazing Horror Speaks Out." *The Toronto Sun*, November 9, 2013. http://www.torontosun.com/2013/11/09/target-in-2005-mcgill-hazing-horror-speaks-out.

Kuznekoff, Jeffrey H., and Lindsey M. Rose. "Communication in Multiplayer Gaming: Examining Player Responses to Gender Cues." *New Media & Society* 15:4 (2013): 541–556. doi:10.1177/1461444812458271.

Lalonde, Julie S. "Online Harassment Isn't Melodrama, But Serious Abuse." http://o.canada.com/technology/internet/online-harassment-isnt-melodrama-but-serious-abuse.

Lampe, Cliffe, Nicole Ellison, and Charles Steinfield. "A Face(Book) in the Crowd: Social Searching vs Social Browsing." In *Proceedings of the 2006 20th Anniversary Conference on Computer Supported Cooperative Work*, 167–170. New York: ACM, 2006.

Lange, Patricia G. *Kids on YouTube: Technical Identities and Digital Literacies*. Walnut Creek, CA: Left Coast Press, 2014.

Lansdown, Gerison, Shane Jimerson, and Reza Shahroozi. "Children's Rights and School Psychology: Children's Right to Participation." *Journal of School Psychology* 52:3 (2014): 4–7. doi:10.1016/j.jsp.2013.12.006.

Laskin, Bora. "The Function of the Law." *Atlanta Law Review* 11 (1973): 118–122.

Latour, Bruno. *Reassembling the Social: An Introduction to Actor-Network-Theory*. New York: Oxford University Press, 2005.

Lau, Andree. "Amanda Todd: Bullied Teen Commits Suicide." *The Huffington Post*, October 11, 2012. http://www.huffingtonpost.ca/2012/10/11/amanda-todd-teen-bullying-suicide-youtube_n_1959668.html.

Laursen, Brett, David Wilder, Peter Noack, and Vickie Williams. "Adolescent Perceptions of Reciprocity, Authority and Closeness in Relationships with Mothers, Fathers and Friends." *International Journal of Behavioral Development* 24:4 (2000): 464–471. doi:10.1080/ 016502500750038017.

Lawler, James P., and John C. Molluzzo. "A Study of the Perceptions of Students on Privacy and Security on Social Networking Sites (SNS) on the Internet." *Journal of Information Systems Applied Research*, 26:3 (2011): 36–41.

Leage, Rodda, and Ivana Chalmers. "Degrees of Caution: Arab Girls Unveil on Facebook." In *Girl Wide Web 2.0: Revisiting Girls, the Internet and the Negotiation of Identity*, edited by Sharon Mazzarella, 27–44. New York: Peter Lang, 2010.

Lee, Jo-Anne. "Amanda Todd, more than bullying." *Antidote*, November, 2012. http://www.antidotenetwork.org/2012/11/amanda-todd-more-than-bullying-part-1.

Lee, Timothy B. "Ars Book Review: 'Here Comes Everybody' by Clay Shirky". *Ars Technica*, April 3, 2008. http://arstechnica.com/features/2008/04/book-review-2008-04-1/3/.

Lehdonvarta, Villi. "Virtual Worlds Don't Exist: Questioning the Dichotomous Approach in MMO Studies." *Game Studies* 10:1 (2010). ISSN: 1604-7982.

Lenhart, Amanda, and Mary Madden. *Teens, Privacy & Online Social Networks*. Pew Internet & American Life Project, 2007.

Lenhart, Amanda, Mary Madden, Aaron Smith, Kristen Purcell, Kathryn Zickuhr, and Lee Rainie. *Teens, Kindness and Cruelty on Social Network Sites: How American Teens Navigate the New World of 'Digital Citizenship.'* Washington, DC: Pew Research Center's Internet & American Life Project, 2011.

Lessig, Lawrence. *Code version 2.0.* New York: Basic Books, 2006.

———. *Remix: Making Art and Commerce Thrive in the Hybrid Economy.* New York: Penguin Press, 2008.

Leurs, Koen, and Sandra Ponzanesi. "Gendering the Construction of Instant Messaging." In *Women and Language: Essays on Gendered Communication across Media*, edited by Melissa Ames and Sarah Himsel Burcon, 199–214. Jefferson: McFarland and Company, Inc, 2011.

Levande, Meredith. "Women, Pop Music and Pornography." *Meridians: Feminism, Race, Transnationalism* 8:1 (2007): 293–321. doi:10.1353/mer.2008.0003.

Library of Congress Rulemaking Hearing Section 1202. Testimony of Francesca Coppa 0119.4-0120.4, May 7, 2009. http://www.copyright.gov/1201/hearings/2009/transcripts.

Lincoln, Sian. "Teenage Girls' 'Bedroom Culture': Codes Versus Zones." In *After Subculture: Critical Commentaries in Contemporary Youth Culture*, edited by Andy Bennett and Keith Kahn-Harris, 94–106. Basingstoke: Palgrave, 2004.

Livingstone, Sonia. "Online Risk, Harm and Vulnerability: Reflections on the Evidence Base for Child Internet Safety Policy." *ZER Journal of Communication Studies* 18:35 (2013): 13–28. ISSN: 1137-1102.

——. "Taking Risky Opportunities in Youthful Content Creation: Teenagers' Use of Social Networking Sites for Intimacy, Privacy and Self-Expression." *New Media & Society* 10:3 (2008): 393–411. doi:10.1177/1461444808089415.

Livingstone, Sonia, and Magdalena Bober. *UK Children Go Online: Surveying the Experiences of Young People and their Parents.* London: Economic and Social Research Council, 2004.

Livingstone, Sonia, and Ellen Helsper. "Balancing Opportunities and Risks in Teenagers' Use of the Internet: The Role of Online Skills and Internet Self-Efficacy." *New Media & Society* 12:2 (2010): 309–329. doi:10.1177/1461444809342697.

Livingstone, Sonia, and Leslie Haddon. *EU Kids Online: Final Report.* London: The London School of Economics and Political Science, EU Kids Online, 2009.

Livingstone, Sonia, and Peter Lunt. "Representing citizens and Consumers in Media and Communications Regulation." *Annals of the American Academy of Political and Social Science* 611:1 (2007): 51–65. doi:10.1177/0002716206298710.

Loader, Brian D., Ariadne Vromen, and Michael A. Xenos. "Introduction: The Networked Young Citizen: Social Media, Political Participation and Civic Engagement." *Information, Communication & Society* 17, (2014): 143–150. doi:10.1080/1369118X.2013.871571.

Lopate, Carol. "Daytime Television: You'll Never Want to Leave Home." *Feminist Studies* 3 (1976): 33–51. doi:10.2307/3177728.

Lopez-Guimera, Gemma. "Influence of Mass Media on Body Image and Eating Disordered Attitudes and Behaviors in Females: A Review of Effects and Processes." *Media Psychology* 13:4 (2010): 387–416. doi:10.1080/15213269.2010.525737.

Los, Maria, and Sharon E. Chamard. "'Selling Newspapers or Educating the Public? Sexual Assault and the Media." *Canadian Journal of Criminology* 39 (1997): 293–328. ISSN: 0704-9722.

Lowder, J. Bryan. "Did Dharun Ravi Really Commit a Hate Crime?" *Slate,* March 20, 2012. http://www.slate.com/blogs/xx_factor/2012/03/20/did_dharun_ravi_really_commit_a_hate_crime_.html.

Lumsden, Kalen. "Bullying and Balancing Rights in AB v Bragg Communications." *IP Osgoode,* November 16, 2012. http://www.iposgoode.ca/2012/11/bullying-and-balancing-rights-in-ab-v-bragg-communications.

Macaulay, Maggie. "Is critique of 'rape culture' enough? Waving the feminist arms in the academy." *Rabble,* September 26, 2013. http://

www.rabble.ca/blogs/bloggers/campus-notes/2013/09/critique-rape-culture-enough-waving-feminist-arms-academy.

Macdonald, Myra. *Representing Women: Myths of Femininity in the Popular Media*. London: Edward Arnold, 1995.

Macgregor, Lyn C. *Habits of the Heartland: Small-Town Life in Modern America.* Cornell University Press: Ithaca, 2010.

MacKay, A. Wayne, Lyle Sutherland, and Kimberley D. Pochini. *Teachers and the Law: Diverse Roles and New Challenges, 3rd Edition.* Toronto: EMP, 2013.

MacKay, A. Wayne. "Safe and Inclusive Schooling = Expensive/Quality Education = Priceless/ For Everything Else There are Lawyers." *Education & Law Journal* 18 (2008): 21–55. ISSN: 0838-2875.

———. *MacKay Report on Inclusion, Inclusion: What is Inclusion Anyway?* New Brunswick: MacKay Report, 2007. http://www.law.hku.hk/hrportal/wp-content/uploads/file/InclusionHighRez-WMackay_000.pdf.

MacKinnon, Catherine. "Reflections on Sex Equality Under Law." *Yale Law Journal* 100(5) (1991): 1281–1328. doi:10.2307/796693.

Madden, Mary. "Teen's Haven't Abandoned Facebook — Yet." *Pew Research Internet Project*, August 15, 2013. http://www.pewinternet.org/2013/08/15/teens-havent-abandoned-facebook-yet.

Malecki, Edward J. "Digital Development in Rural Areas: Potentials and Pitfalls." *Journal of Rural Studies* 19 (2003): 201–214. doi:10.1016/S0743-0167(02)00068-2.

Maltby, John, David Giles, Louise Barber, and Lynn McCutcheon. "Intense-Personal Celebrity Worship and Body Image: Evidence of a Link Among Female Adolescents." *British Journal of Health Psychology* 10:1 (2005): 17–32. doi:10.1348/135910704X15257.

Manago, Adriana M., Michael B. Graham, Patricia M. Greenfield, and Goldie Salimkhan. "Self-Presentation and Gender on MySpace." *Journal of Applied Developmental Psychology* 29:6 (2008): 446–458. doi:10.1016/j.appdev.2008.07.001.

Manago, Adriana M., Tamara Taylor, and Patricia M Greenfield. "Me and my 400 Friends: The Anatomy of College Students' Facebook Networks, their Communication Patterns, and Well-Being." *Developmental Psychology* 48 (2012): 369–380. doi:10.1037/a0026338.

Manesse, Laurence. "Autour du concept d'expérience chez Benjamin" *Revue Appareil* (2011): 7–8. http://revues.mshparisnord.org/appareil/pdf/1172.pdf.

Markham, Annette, and Elizabeth Buchanan. *Ethical Decision-making and Internet Research: Recommendations from the AoIR Ethics Working Committee.* http://aoir.org/reports/ethics2.pdf.

Marwick, Alice E., and danah boyd. "I Tweet Honestly, I Tweet Passionately: Twitter Users, Context Collapse, and the Imagined Audience." *New Media & Society* 13 (2010): 1–20. doi:10.1177/1461444810365313.

———. "The Drama! Teen Conflict in Networked Publics." Paper presented at the Oxford Internet Institute, A Decade in Internet Time: Symposium, Oxford, England, September 22, 2011.

———. "'It's Just Drama': Teen Perspectives on Conflict and Aggression in a Networked Era." *Journal of Youth Studies* 17 (2014): 1187–1204. doi:10.1080/13676261.2014.901493.

———. "The Drama! Teen Conflict, Gossip, and Bullying in Networked Publics." Paper presented at A Decade in Internet Time: Symposium on the Dynamics of the Internet and Society, Oxford, England, September 22, 2011.

Marwick, Alice. "Online Identity." In *A Companion to New Media Dynamics*, edited by John Hartley, Jean Burgess, and Axel Bruns, 355–364. Malden: Wiley-Blackwell, 2012.

———. "Public Domain: Surveillance in Everyday Life." *Surveillance & Society* 9 (2012): 378–393. ISSN 1477-7487.

Mason-Bish, Hannah. "Examining the Boundaries of Hate Crime Policy: Considering Age and Gender." *Criminal Justice Policy Review* 24 (2011): 297–316. doi:10.1177/0887403411431495.

Mathen, Carissima. "Crowdsourcing Sexual Objectification." *Laws.* 2014 3:3 (2014): 529–552. doi:10.3390/laws3030529.

Mathiesen, Thomas. "The Viewer Society: Michael Foucault's 'Panoticon' Revisited." *Theoretical Criminology* 1:2 (1997): 215–232. ISSN: 1362–4806.

Mazzarella, Sharon. "Introduction: It's a Girl Wide Web." In *Girl Wide Web: Girls, the Internet and the Negotiation of Identity*, edited by Sharon Mazzarella, 1–12. New York: Peter Lang, 2008.

McAneny, Barbara. "AMA Adopts New Policies at Annual Meeting." http://www.ama-assn.org/ama/pub/news/news/a11-new-policies.page.

McCaskell, Tim. *Race to Equity: Disrupting Educational Inequality.* Toronto: Between the Lines, 2005.

McCaughey, Martha. "Technology is My BFF: What are New Communication Technologies Doing to/for Girls?" *Media Report to Women* 41:1 (2013).

McCormack, Clare, and Nevena Prostran. "Asking for It: A First-Hand Account from Slut-Walk." *International Feminist Journal of Politics* 14 (2012): 410–414. doi:10.1080/14616742.2012.699777.

McCormack, Mark. *The Declining Significance of Homophobia: How Teenage Boys are Redefining Masculinity and Heterosexuality.* Oxford: Oxford University Press, 2012.

McGill, Jena. "What Have You Done for Me Lately? Reflections on Redeeming Privacy for Battered Women." In *Lessons from the Identity Trail: Anonymity, Privacy and Identity in a Networked Society*, edited by Ian

Kerr, Valerie Steeves, and Carol Lucock, 157–172. New York: Cambridge University Press, 2008.

McNamee, Lacy G., Brittany L. Peterson, and Jorge Peña. "A Call to Educate, Participate, Invoke and Indict: Understanding the Communication of Online Hate Groups." *Communication Monographs* 77 (2010): 257–280. doi:10.1080/03637751003758227.

McPhail, Beverly A. "Gender-Bias Hate Crimes: A Review." *Trauma, Violence, & Abuse* 3 (2002): 125–143. doi:10.1177/15248380020032003.

McRobbie, Angela, and Jenny Garber. "Girls and Subcultures." In *Feminism and Youth Culture: From Jackie to Just Seventeen*, edited by Angela McRobbie, 12–25. Boston: Unwin Hyman, 1991.

——. "Girls and Subcultures." In *Resistance Through Rituals: Youth Subcultures in Post-War Britain*, edited by Stuart Hall and Tony Jefferson, 209–222. London: Harper Collins Academic, 1976.

McRobbie, Angela. "Top Girls?: Young Women and the Post-Feminist Sexual Contract." *Cultural Studies* 21 (2007): 718–737. doi:10.1080/09502380701279044.

——. *The Aftermath of Feminism: Gender, Culture and Social Change.* Thousand Oaks, CA: SAGE Publications Inc., 2009.

Meddaugh, Priscilla Marie, and Jack Kay. "Hate Speech or 'Reasonable Racism?' The Other in Stormfront." *Journal of Mass Media Ethics* 24:4 (2009): 251–268. doi:10.1080/08900520903320936.

MediaSmarts. "Digital Literacy Fundamentals." http://mediasmarts.ca/digital-media-literacy-fundamentals/digital-literacy-fundamentals.

——. "Facing Online Hate." http://mediasmarts.ca/facing-online-hate-portal-page.

——. "Gender Messages in Alcohol Advertising." http://mediasmarts.ca/sites/mediasmarts/files/pdfs/lesson-plan/Lesson_Gender_Messages_Alcohol_Advertising.pdf.

——. "Girls and Boys on Television." http://mediasmarts.ca/lessonplan/girls-and-boys-television.

——. "History." http://mediasmarts.ca/about-us/history.

——. "Little Princesses and Fairy Tale Stereotypes." http://mediasmarts.ca/backgrounder/little-princesses-and-fairy-tale-stereotypes.

——. "Media Literacy Fundamentals." http://mediasmarts.ca/digital-media-literacy-fundamentals/media-literacy-fundamentals.

——. "MyWorld: A Digital Literacy Tutorial for Secondary Students." http://mediasmarts.ca/game/myworld-digitial-literacy-tutorial-secondary-students.

——. "Online Marketing to Kids: Protecting Your Privacy – Lesson." http://mediasmarts.ca/lessonplan/online-marketing-kids-protecting-your-privacy-lesson.

———. "Privacy Pirates: An Interactive Unit on Online Privacy (Ages 7–9)." http://mediasmarts.ca/game/privacy-pirates-interactive-unit-online-privacy-ages-7-9.

———. "Resisting Stereotypes and Working for Change." http://mediasmarts.ca/gender-representation/women-and-girls/resisting-stereotypes-and-working-change.

———. "Stay on the Path: Teaching Kids to be Safe and Ethical Online Portal Page." <http://mediasmarts.ca/stay-path-teaching-kids-be-safe-and-ethical-online-portal-page.

———. "Talking to Kids About Body Image." http://mediasmarts.ca/sites/default/files/pdfs/tipsheet/TipSheet_Talking_kids_about_media_body_image.pdf.

———. "Talking to Kids About Gender Stereotypes." http://mediasmarts.ca/sites/default/files/pdfs/tipsheet/TipSheet_Talking_Kids_Gender_Stereotypes.pdf.

———. "The Privacy Dilemma: Lesson Plan for Senior Classrooms." http://mediasmarts.ca/lessonplan/privacy-dilemma-lesson-plan-senior-classrooms.

———. "Think Before You Share." http://mediasmarts.ca/sites/default/files/pdfs/tipsheet/TipSheet_Think_Before_You_Share.pdf.

———. "Young Canadians in a Wired World, Phase I: Parent and Youth Focus Groups." http://mediasmarts.ca/sites/mediasmarts/files/pdfs/publication-report/full/YCWWI-focus-group.pdf.

———. "Young Canadians in a Wired World, Phase II: Focus Groups." http://mediasmarts.ca/sites/mediasmarts/files/pdfs/publication-report/full/YCWWII-focus-groups.pdf.

———. "Young Canadians in a Wired World, Phase III: Talking to Youth and Parents about Life Online Executive Summary." http://mediasmarts.ca/sites/mediasmarts/files/publication-report/summary/ycwwiii-youth-parents-summary.pdf.

Meier, Brian P., Michael D. Robinson, George A. Gaither, and Nikki .J. Heinert. "A Secret Attraction or Defensive Loathing? Homophobia, Defense, and Implicit Cognition." *Journal of Research in Personality* 40 (2006): 377–394. doi:10.1016/j.jrp.2005.01.007.

Meissner, Dirk. "Amanda Todd's legacy: A look at Canada's anti-bullying efforts a year after her death." *CTV News*, October 9, 2013. http://www.ctvnews.ca/canada/amanda-todd-s-legacy-a-look-at-canada-s-anti-bullying-efforts-a-year-after-her-death-1.1490889.

Mendoza, Kelly. "'WATZ UR NAME?' Adolescent Girls, Chat Rooms, and Interpersonal Authenticity." *Media Education Lab Working Paper Series* 403 (2007): 1–27. http://mediaeducationlab.com/sites/mediaeducationlab.com/files/403_WorkingPapers_Mendoza.pdf.

Meyer, Elizabeth J. "Gender, Bullying and Harassment: Strategies to End Sexism and Homophobia in Schools." https://tesl-ej.org/~teslejor/pdf/ej61/r1.pdf.

——. "New Solutions for Bullying and Harassment: A Post-Structural, Feminist Approach." In *School Bullying: New Theories in Context*, edited by Robin May Schott and Dorte Marie Sondergaard, 209–240. Cambridge: Cambridge University Press, 2014.

Micheti, Anca, Jacquelyn Burkell, and Valerie Steeves. "Fixing Broken Doors: Strategies for Drafting Privacy Policies Young People Can Understand." *Bulletin of Science, Technology & Society* 30:2 (2010): 130–143. doi:10.1177/0270467610365355.

Micole. "Women's Art and 'Women's Work.'" *Ambling Along the Aqueduct*, August 29, 2007. http://aqueductpress.blogspot.com/2007/08/womens-art-and-womens-work.html.

Milford, Trevor Scott. "Girls' Online Agency: A Cyberfeminist Exploration." Master's thesis. Ottawa: University of Ottawa, 2013.

——. "Assessing Girls' Online Experience Through a Cyberfeminist Lens: A Review of Relevant Literature." (2012), unpublished. http://egirlsproject.files.wordpress.com/2012/10/milford_critical-lit-review-memo-sep-19-2011.pdf.

Milford, Trevor Scott and Ciara Bracken-Roche. "Social Surveillance: Feminist Implications for Online Privacy, Self-Disclosure and Gendered Agency." *.dpi – Feminist Journal of Art and Digital Culture* 30 (2014). http://dpi.studioxx.org/fr/no/30-cybersurveillance/social-surveillance-feminist-implications-online-privacy-self-disclosure-and. ISSN: 1712-9486.

Milgram, Stanley. "The Experience of Living in Cities." *Science* 167 (1970): 1461–1468. http://www.cl.cam.ac.uk/~dq209/others/experience.pdf.

Miller, Laura. "Middle-Earth According to Mordor." *Salon*, February 15, 2011. http://www.salon.com/2011/02/15/last_ringbearer/#postID=2042021&page=0&comment=1986322.

Miller, Vincent. "New Media, Networking and Phatic Culture." *Convergence: The International Journal of Research Into New Media Technologies* 14:4 (2008): 387–400. doi:10.1177/1354856508094659.

Ministère de l'Immigration, de la Diversité et de l'Inclusion. "L'immigration permanente au Québec selon les catégories d'immigration et quelques composantes 2009–2013." http://www.midi.gouv.qc.ca/publications/fr/recherches-statistiques/Portraits_categories_2009-2013.pdf.

Moffitt, Terrie E., Avshalom Caspi, Michael Rutter, and Phil A. Silva. *Sex Differences in Antisocial Behaviour: Conduct Disorder, Delinquency and Violence in the Dunedin Longitudinal Study.* New York Cambridge University Press, 2001.

Monahan, Torin. "Editorial: Surveillance and Inequality." *Surveillance & Society* 5:3 (2008): 217–226. http://www.surveillance-and-society.org/articles5(3)/editorial.pdf.

Moore, Dawn, and Mariana Valverde. "Maidens at Risk: 'Date Rape Drugs' and the Formation of Hybrid Knowledges." *Economy and Society* 29 (2000): 514–531. doi:10.1080/03085140050174769.

Moore, Oliver. "Woman's Call to End Video Game Misogyny Sparks Vicious Online Attacks." *The Globe and Mail*, July 11, 2012. http://www.theglobeandmail.com/news/world/womans-call-to-end-video-game-misogyny-sparks-vicious-online-attacks/article4405585.

Morrison, Connie. *Who Do They Think They Are? Teenage Girls & Their Avatars in Spaces of Social Online Communication.* Peter Lang Publishing, New York, 2010.

Moulton, Donalee. "Parrying Thrusts of the Cyberbully," *The Lawyers Weekly,* January 13, 2012. http://www.lawyersweekly.ca/index.php?section=article&articleid=1568.

Mulholland, Monique. *Young People and Pornography: Negotiating Pornification.* New York: Palgrave, 2013.

Munt, Sally. *Technospaces: Inside the New Media.* London: Continuum, 2001.

Murnen, Sarah, Linda Smolak, J. Andrew Mills, and Lindsey Good. "Thin, Sexy Women and Strong, Muscular Men: Grade-School Children's Responses to Objectified Images of Women and Men." *Sex Roles* 49:9/10 (2003): 427–437. doi:10.1023/A:1025868320206.

Murphy, Meghan. "The Steubenville rape case: This is masculinity." *Feminist Current,* March 19, 2013. http://feministcurrent.com/7339/the-steubenville-rape-case-this-is-masculinity.

Nadel, Mark S. "How Current Copyright Law Discourages Creative Output: The Overlooked Impact of Marketing." *Berkeley Technology Law Journal* 19:2 (2004): 785–836. http://www.btlj.org/data/articles/19_02_04.pdf.

Nakamura, Lisa. *Digitizing Race: Visual Cultures of the Internet.* Minneapolis: University of Minnesota Press, 2008.

Ndengeyingoma, Assumpta, Francine de Montigny, and Jean-Marie Miron. "Représentations de l'expérience migratoire d'adolescents africains immigrants avec leur famille au Québec." *Revue québécoise de psychologie* 34:2 (2013): 101–123.

——. "Development of personal identity among refugee adolescents: facilitating elements and obstacles." *Journal of Child Health Care* 18:4 (2013): 369–377.doi:1367493513496670.

Netanel, Neil W. "Copyright and a Democratic Civil Society." *Yale Law Journal* 106 (1996): 283–387. doi:10.2307/797212.

Nicol, Julia, and Dominique Valiquet. *Bill C-13: An Act to amend the Criminal Code , the Canada Evidence Act, the Competition Act and the Mutual Legal Assistance in Criminal Matters Act.* Ottawa: Library of Parliament, 2014.

http://www.parl.gc.ca/Content/LOP/LegislativeSummaries/41/2/c13-e. pdf.

Norman, Moss E. "Embodying The Double-Bind Of Masculinity: Young Men And Discourses Of Normalcy, Health, Heterosexuality, And Individualism." *Men and Masculinities* 14 (2011): 430–449. doi:10. 1177/1097184X11409360.

Norsigian, Judy. "Women, Health, and Films." *Women and Health* 1 (1975): 29–30. doi:10.1300/J013v01n01_07.

Nova Scotia Task Force on Bullying and Cyberbullying. *Respectful and Responsible Relationships: There's No App for That: The Report of the Nova Scotia Task Force on Bullying and Cyberbullying.* Dartmouth: Nova Scotia School Boards Association, 2012.

Nurka, Camille. "Public Bodies." *Feminist Media Studies* (2013): 1–15. doi: 10.1080/14680777.2013.771693.

O'Malley, Patrick. "Responsibilization." In *The SAGE Dictionary of Policing*, edited by Alison Wakefield and Jenny Fleming, 277–279. London: SAGE Publications, 2009.

Obar, Jonathan A., and Leslie Regan Shade. "Activating the Fifth Estate: Bill C-30 and the Digitally-Mediated Public Watchdog." In *Strategies for Media Reform: Communication Research in Action*, edited by Des Freedman, Robert W. McChesney, and Jonathan A. Obar. New York: Fordham University Press, forthcoming 2015.

Office of the Privacy Commissioner of Canada. "Backgrounder: Facebook Investigation Follow-up Complete." http://www.priv.gc.ca/media/ nr-c/2010/bg_100922_e.cfm.

Ofsted. "The Safe Use of New Technologies." http://www.ofsted.gov.uk/ sites/default/files/documents/surveys-and-good-practice/t/The% 20safe%20use%20of%20new%20technologies.pdf.

O'Neil, Susan. *Bullying by Tween and Teen Girls: A Literature, Policy and Resource Review.* Prince George: Kookabura Consulting, Ltd, 2008.

Ontario. *Ontario's Sexual Violence Action Plan.* "Changing Attitudes, Changing Lives." March 5, 2011. http://www.women.gov.on.ca/owd/docs/svap.pdf.

Ontario. *The Provincial Code of Conduct*, Policy No 128, 2012, http://www.edu. gov.on.ca/extra/eng/ppm/128.pdf.

OpenMedia. "About us." https://www.openmedia.ca/about-us.

——. "Regulators Pull Back From Usage-based Billing After Half-a-Million Canadians Speak Out." https://openmedia.ca/news/regulators-pull-back-usage-based-billing-after-half-million-canadians-speak-out.

——. "Stop Telecom Price Gouging." https://openmedia.ca/meter.

——: YouTube. "Our Gouge-Based Heritage." February 17. https://www. youtube.com/watch?v=qoZGkqQvAVw.

Oppliger, Patrice A. *Bullies and Mean Girls in Popular Culture.* Jefferson: McFarland & Company, Inc., Publishers, 2013.

Organization for Transformative Works. "What We Believe." http://transformativeworks.org/about/believe.

Ouellette, Laurie, and Julie Wilson. "Women's Work." *Cultural Studies* 25: 4-5 (2011): 548–565. doi:0.1080/09502386.2011.600546.

Paasonen, Susanna. "Surfing the Waves of Feminism." *Universidade de Brasília: Labrys Estudos Feministas* janeiro/julho (2005). http://www.tanianavarroswain.com.br/labrys/labrys7/cyber/susanna.htm.

Paillé, Pascal, and Adalgisa Battistelli. *L'Analyse qualitative en sciences sociales.* Paris : Armand Colin, 2003.

Park, Sung-Yeon, Gi Woong Yun, Jacqueline McSweeney, and Albert Gunther. "Do Third-Person Perceptions of Media Influence Contribute to Pluralistic Ignorance on the Norm of Ideal Female Thinness?" *Sex Roles* 57:7–8 (2007): 569–578. doi:10.1007/s11199-007-9284-3.

Pascoe, C. J. *Dude, You're a Fag: Masculinity and Sexuality in High School.* Berkeley: University of California Press, 2007.

Pascoe, C.J. "Notes on a Sociology of Bullying: Young Men's Homophobia as Gender Socialization." *QED: A Journal of GLBTQ Worldmaking* (2013): 87–104. doi:10.1353/qed.2013.0013.

Patchin, Justin, and Sameer Hinduja. "Bullies Move Beyond the Schoolyard: A Preliminary Look at Cyberbullying." *Youth Violence and Juvenile Justice* 4 (2006): 148–169. doi:10.1177/1541204006286288.

Pepler, Debra J, Dirsten C. Madsen, Christopher D. Webster, and Kathryn S. Levene. *The Development and Treatment of Girlhood Aggression.* London: Lawrence Erlbaum, 2005.

Pepler, Debra, and Penny Milton. "External Review of the Halifax Regional School Board's Support of Rehtaeh Parsons." http://www.ednet.ca/files/reports/External%20Review%20of%20HRSB%20Final.pdf.

Percy-Smith, Barry. "'You Think You Know? ...You have no Idea': Youth Participation in Health Policy Development." *Health Education Research* 22: 6 (2007): 879–894. doi:10.1093/her/cym032.

Percy-Smith, Barry, and Danny Burns. "Exploring the Role of Children and Young People as Agents of Change in Sustainable Community Development." *Local Environment* 18:3 (2013): 323–339. doi:10.1080/13549839.2012.729565.

Petitmengin, Claire. "Describing One's Subjective Experience in the Second Person, an Interview Method for the Science of Consciousness." *Phenomenology and the Cognitive Sciences* 5 (2006): 13–29. doi:10.1007/s11097-006-9022-2.

Petronio, Sandra. *Boundaries of Privacy: Dialectics of Disclosure.* New York: State University of New York Press, 2002.

Phillips, David J. "Ubiquitous Computing, Spatiality, and the Construction of Identity: Directions for Policy Response." In *Lessons From the Identity Trail: Anonymity, Privacy and Identity in a Networked Society,* edited by Ian Kerr, Valerie Steeves, and Carole Lucock, 303–318. New York: Oxford University Press, 2009.

Piran, Niva, Michael P. Levine, and Lori M. Irving. "GO GIRLS! Media Literacy, Activism and Advocacy Project." *Healthy Weight Journal* 14:6 (2000). ISSN: 1075-0169.

Plant, Sadie. "On the Matrix: Cyberfeminism Simulations." In *Cultures of Internet: Virtual Spaces, Real Histories, Living Bodies*, edited by Rob Shields, 170–183. London: Sage, 1996.

Plaxton, Michael. "Canadian Women Deserve More Than A 'Revenge Porn' Law." *Globe and Mail*, November 22, 2013. http://www.theglobeandmail.com/globe-debate/canadian-women-deserve-more-than-a-revenge-porn-law/article15560839.

Poltash, Nicole. "Snapchat and Sexting: A Snapshot of Bearing Your Bare Essentials." *Richmond Journal of Law and Technology* 19:4 (2013): 1–24. http://jolt.richmond.edu/v19i4/article14.pdf.

Poole, Emily. "Hey Girls, Did You Know? Slut-Shaming on the Internet Needs to Stop." *University of San Francisco Law Review* 48:1 (2013): 221–260. http://www.usfca.edu/uploadedFiles/Destinations/School_of_Law/Academics/Co-Curricular_Programs/(7)%20SAN48-1%20Poole.pdf.

Poteat, V. Paul, and Craig D. DiGiovanni. "When Biased Language Use is Associated with Bullying Dominance Behavior: The Moderating Effect of Prejudice." *Journal of Youth and Adolescence* 39:10 (2010): 1123–1133. doi:10.1007/s10964-010-9565-y.

Powell, Anastasia. "Configuring Consent: Emerging Technologies, Unauthorized Sexual Images and Sexual Assault." *Australian & New Zealand Journal of Criminology* 43 (2010): 76–90. doi:10.1375/acri.43.1.76.

———. "Rape culture: why our community attitudes to sexual violence matter." *The Conversation*, September 16, 2014. http://theconversation.com/rape-culture-why-our-community-attitudes-to-sexual-violence-matter-31750.

———. *Sex, Power and Consent: Youth Culture and the Unwritten Rules*. Melbourne: Cambridge University Press, 2010.

Preibusch, Sören, Bettina Hoser, Seda Gürses, and Bettina Berendt. "Ubiquitous Social Networks: Opportunities and Challenges for Privacy-Aware User Modelling." *DIW Berlin: German Institute for Economic Research, Discussion Papers* 698 (2007): 1–23. ISSN: 1433-0210.

Press, Andrea L. "'Feminism? That's So Seventies': Girls and Young Women Discuss Femininity and Feminism in *America's Next Top Model*." In *New Femininities: Postfeminism, Neoliberalism and Subjectivity*, edited by Rosalind Gill and Christina Scharff, 117–133. Basingstoke: Palgrave Macmillan, 2011.

Privacy Commissioner of Canada. *Privacy for Everyone: Report on the Personal Information Protection and Electronic Documents Act.* Ottawa: Office of the Privacy Commissioner of Canada, 2011. https://www.priv.gc.ca/information/ar/201112/2011_pipeda_e.pdf.

Puar, Jasbir K. "The Cost of Getting Better: Suicide, Sensation, Switch-points." *GLQ: A Journal of Lesbian and Gay Studies* 18 (2012): 149–158. doi:10.1215/10642684-1422179.

Pyke, Karen D. "What is Internalized Racial Oppression and Why Don't we Study it? Acknowledging Racism's Hidden Injuries." *Sociological Perspectives* 53:4 (2010): 551–572. doi:10.1525/sop.2010.53.4.551.

Raacke, John, and Jennifer Bonds-Raacke. "MySpace and Facebook: Applying the Uses and Gratifications Theory to Exploring Friend-Networking Sites." *CyberPsychology & Behavior* 11 (2008): 169–172. doi:10.1089/cpb.2007.0056.

Raphael, Chad, Christine Bachen, Kathleen Lynn, Jessica Baldwin-Philippi, and Kristen McKee. "Portrayals of Information and Communication Technology on World Wide Web Sites for Girls." *Journal of Computer-Mediated Communications* 11:3 (2006): 771–801. doi:10.1111/j.1083-6101.2006.00035.x.

Rapoza, Jim. "'Privacy Policy' as Oxymoron: Current United States (US) Law Prevents Real Progress in the On-Line Privacy Push." *eWeek Magazine* June 15 (2009): 21.

Raynes-Goldie, Kate. "Aliases, Creeping and Wall Cleaning: Understanding Privacy in the Age of Facebook." *First Monday* 15:1 (2010). doi:10.5210/fm.v15i1.2775.

Reay, Diane. "Shaun's Story: Troubling Discourses of White Working Class Masculinities." *Gender and Education* 14:3 (2002): 221–234. doi:10.1080/0954025022000010695.

Regan, Priscilla, and Valerie Steeves. "Kids R Us: Online Social Networking and the Potential for Empowerment." *Surveillance & Society* 8:2 (2010): 151–165. ISSN: 1477-7487.

Regenboen, Christina, Daniel A. Schneider, Andreas Finkelmeyer, Nils Kohn, Birgit Derntl, Thilo Kellerman, Raquel E. Gur, Frank Schneider, and Ute Habel. "The Differential Contribution of Facial Expressions, Prosody, and Speech Content to Empathy." *Cognition & Emotion* 26 (2012): 995–1014. doi:10.1080/02699931.2011.631296.

"Rehtaeh Parsons, Canadian girl, dies after suicide attempt: parents allege she was raped by 4 boys." *The Huffington Post*, April 9, 2013. http://www.huffingtonpost.com/2013/04/09/rehtaeh-parsons-girl-dies-suicide-rape-canada_n_3045033.html.

Reich, Stephanie M., and Kaveri Subrahmanyam. "Friending, IMing and Hanging Out Face-to-Face: Overlap in Adolescents' Online and Offline Social Networks." *Developmental Psychology* 48:2 (2012): 361–365. doi:10.1037/a0026980.

Reid-Walsh, Jacqueline, and Claudia Mitchell. "Girls' Web Sites: A Virtual "Room of One's Own" In *All About the Girl: Culture, Power and Identity*, ed. Anita Harris, 173–218. New York: Routledge, 2004.

Reilly, Ian. "'Amusing Ourselves to Death?' Social Media, Political Satire, and the 2011 Election." *Canadian Journal of Communication* 36:3 (2011): 503–512. http://www.cjc-online.ca/index.php/journal/article/viewFile/2508/2259.

Reiter, Michael D., Katherine Richmond, Amber Stirlen, and Natalia Kompel. "Exploration of Intimacy in Intercultural and Intracultural Romantic Relationships in College Students." *College Student Journal* 43 (2009): 1080–1083. ISSN: 0146-3934.

Rentschler, Carrie A. "Rape Culture and the Feminist Politics of Social Media." *Girlhood Studies* 7 (2014): 65–82. doi:10.3167/ghs.2014.070106.

Rest, James R. *Moral Development: Advances in Research and Theory*. New York: Praeger, 1986.

Reynolds, Graham. "Towards a Right to Engage in the Fair Transformative Use of Copyright-Protected Expression." In *From "Radical Extremism" to "Balanced Copyright": Canadian Copyright and the Digital Agenda*, edited by Michael Geist, 395–422. Toronto: Irwin Law, 2010.

Rheingold, Howard. *The Virtual Community: Homesteading on the Electronic Frontier*. Reading: Addison-Wesley Publishing Company, 1993.

Ringrose, Jessica. "A New Universal Mean Girl: Examining the Discursive Construction and Social Regulation of a New Feminine Pathology, Feminism & Psychology 16 (2006): 405–424. doi:10.1177/0959353506068747.

———. "Sluts, Whores, Fat Slags and Playboy Bunnies: Teen Girls' Negotiation of 'Sexy' on Social Networking Sites and at School." In Girls and Education 3–16: Continuing Concerns, New Agendas, edited by Carolyn Jackson, Emma Carrie, and Emma Renold, 170–182. Maidenhead: Open University Press, 2010.

———. Postfeminist Education? Girls and the Sexual Politics of Schooling. New York: Routledge, 2013.

Ringrose, Jessica, and Emma Renold. "Slut-Shaming, Girl Power and 'Sexualisation': Thinking Through the Politics of the International SlutWalks With Teen Girls." *Gender and Education* 24 (2012): 333–343. doi:10.1080/09540253.2011.645023.

———. "Teen Girls, Working-Class Femininity and Resistance: Retheorising Fantasy and Desire in Educational Contexts of Heterosexualised Violence." *International Journal of Inclusive Education* 16 (2012): 461–477. doi:10.1080/13603116.2011.555099.

Ringrose, Jessica, and Katarina Eriksson Barajas. "Gendered Risks and Opportunities? Exploring Teen Girls' Digitized Sexual Identities in

Postfeminist Media Contexts." *International Journal of Media & Cultural Politics* 7:2 (2011): 121–138. doi:10.1386/macp.7.2.121_1.

Ringrose, Jessica, and Laura Harvey. "Boobs, Back-off, Bits and Blows: Mediated Body Parts, Gendered Reward, and Sexual Shame in Teens' Networked Images." *Continuum* (forthcoming, 2014).

Ringrose, Jessica, Laura Harvey, Rosalind Gill, and Sonia Livingstone. "Teen Girls, Sexual Double Standards and 'Sexting': Gendered Value in Digital Image Exchange." *Feminist Theory* 14 (2013): 305–323. doi:10.1177/1464700113499853.

Ringrose, Jessica, Rosalind Gill, Sonia Livingstone, and Laura Harvey. *A Qualitative Study of Children, Young People and 'Sexting': A Report Prepared for the NSPCC.* London: NSPCC, 2012.

Riordan, Ellen. "Commodified Agents and Empowered Girls: Consuming and Producing Feminism." *Journal of Communication Inquiry* 25:3 (2001): 279–297. doi:10.1177/0196859901025003006.

Roberts, Julian V. "Sexual Assaults in Canada: Recent Statistical Trends." *Queen's Law Journal* 21 (1996): 395–421. ISSN: 0316-778X.

Roberts, Steven, and Aziz Douai. "Moral Panics and Cybercrime: How Canadian Media Cover Internet Child Luring." *Journal of Canadian Media Studies* 10:1 (2012): 1–14. http://cjms.fims.uwo.ca/issues/10-01/DouaiRoberts.pdf.

Rogoyski, Robert S., and Kenneth Basin. "The Bloody Case that Started from a Parody: American Intellectual Property and the Pursuit of Democratic Ideals in Modern China." *UCLA Entertainment Law Review* 16 (2009): 237–264. ISSN: 1073-2896

Roher, Eric M. "Dealing with off-school conduct: Cyberbullying, Drug Dealing and other Activities Off School Property." *Education & Law Journal* 21 (2012): 91–110. ISSN: 0838-2875.

Rooney, Ben. "Women And Children First: Technology And Moral Panic." *TechEurope – The Wall Street Journal*, July 11, 2011. http://blogs.wsj.com/tech-europe/2011/07/11/women-and-children-first-technology-and-moral-panic.

Rose, Nikolas. *Governing the Soul: the Shaping of the Private Self.* London: Free Association Books, 1999.

Rowland, Robert C., and Kirsten Theye. "The Symbolic DNA of Terrorism." *Communication Monographs* 75 (2008): 52–85. doi:10.1080/03637750701885423.

Rukszto, Katarzyna. "History as Edutainment: *Heritage Minutes* and the Uses of Educational Television." In *Programming Reality: Perspectives on English Canadian Television*, edited by Zöe Druick and Aspa Kotsopoulos, 171–186. Waterloo: Wilfrid Laurier Press, 2008.

Russo, Julie L. "User-Penetrated Content: Fan Video in the Age of Convergence." *Cinema J.* 48 (2009): 22–43. ISSN: 0009-7101.

Sag, Matthew. "Predicting Fair Use." *Ohio State Law Journal* 73:1 (2012): 47–91. http://moritzlaw.osu.edu/students/groups/oslj/files/2012/05/73.1.Sag_.pdf.

Salter, Michael. "Justice and Revenge in Online Counter-Publics: Emerging Responses to Sexual Violence in the Age of Social Media." *Crime Media Culture* 9 (2013): 1–18. doi:1011771741659013493918.

———. "Responding to Revenge Porn: Gender, Justice and Online Legal Impunity." Paper presented at Whose Justice? Conflicted Approaches to Crime and Conflict, University of Western Sydney, Sydney, September 27, 2013.

Samuelson, Pamela. "Unbundling Fair Uses." *Fordham L. Rev.* 77 (2009): 2537–2621. http://fordhamlawreview.org/assets/pdfs/Vol_77/Samuelson2_Vol_77_Apr.pdf.

Sandoval, Chela. "New Sciences: Cyborg Feminism and the Methodology of the Oppressed," In *Cybersexualities: A Reader on Feminist Theory, Cyborgs and Cyberspace*, edited by Jenny Wolmark, 247–263. Edinburgh: Edinburgh University Press, 1992.

Schmitt, Kelly L., Shoshana Dayanim, and Stacey Matthias. "Personal Homepage Construction as an Expression of Social Development." *Developmental Psychology* 44 (2008): 499–500. doi:10.1037/0012-1649.44.2.496

Schuster, Julia. "Invisible Feminists? Social Media and Young Women's Political Participation." *Political Science* 65:1 (2013): 8–24. doi:10.1177/0032318713486474.

Schwartz, Daniel. "The fine line between 'sexting' and child pornography." *CBC News.* August 13, 2013. http://www.cbc.ca/news/canada/the-fine-line-between-sexting-and-child-pornography-1.1367613.

Scott-Dixon, Krista. "Turbo chicks: Talkin' 'bout My Generation: Third Wave Feminism is Comfortable With Contradiction Because That's the Only Way the World Makes Sense." *Herizons* 16:2 (2002). http://www.herizons.ca/node/146.

Scully1121, "There is Hope for Vidders." *LiveJournal*, November 16, 2011. http://vidding.livejournal.com/275168o.html.

Seabrook, John. "Streaming Dreams: YouTube Turns Pro." *The New Yorker*, January 16, 2012. http://www.newyorker.com/reporting/2012/01/16/120116fa_fact_seabrook?currentPage=all.

Sedgwick, Eve K. "Paranoid Reading and Reparative Reading or You're So Paranoid, You Probably Think This Introduction is About You," In *Novel Gazing: Queer Readings in Fiction*, edited by Eve Kosofsky Sedgwick, 1–37. Durham, NC: Duke University Press, 1997.

———. *Between Men: English Literature and Male Homosocial Desire*. New York: Columbia University Press, 1992.

Seidman, Karen. "Child pornography laws 'too harsh' to deal with minors sexting photos without consent, experts say." *National*

Post, November 16, 2013. http://news.nationalpost.com/2013/11/16/child-pornography-laws-too-harsh-to-deal-with-minors-sexting-photos-without-consent-experts-say.

Senate Standing Committee on Human Rights. *Cyberbullying Hurts: Respect for Rights in the Digital Age*. Ottawa: Parliament of Canada, 2012. http://www.parl.gc.ca/content/SEN/committee/411/ridr/rep/rep09dec12-e.pdf.

Senft, Terri M. *Camgirls: Celebrity and Community in the Age of Social Networks*. New York: Peter Lang, 2008.

Shade, Leslie R. "Internet Social Networking in Young Women's Everyday Lives: Some Insights from Focus Groups." *Our Schools, Our Selves* (2008): 65–73. http://www.policyalternatives.ca/sites/default/files/uploads/publications/Our_Schools_Ourselve/8_Shade_internet_social_networking.pdf.

——. "Towards a Model of Digital Policy Literacy." Paper presented at the iConference, Toronto, Ontario, February 7–10, 2012. http://dl.acm.org/citation.cfm?id=2132176.

Shade, Leslie R., and Tamara Shepherd. "Youth and Mobile Privacy: Applying a Model of Digital Policy Literacy." *First Monday* 18 (2013). doi:10.1080/00220670009598707.

Shapiro, Lila. "Dharun Ravi Appeals Highlight the Continued Hate-Crime Law Debate." *The Huffington Post*, June 13, 2012. http://www.huffingtonpost.com/2012/06/13/dharun-ravi-appeals-hate-crime_n_1594320.html.

Shariff, Shaheen. *Sexting and Cyberbullying; Defining the Line on Digitally Empowered Kids*. New York: Cambridge University Press, in press, forthcoming 2015.

——. *Define the Line: Clarifying Boundaries Between Cyberbullying and Socially Responsible Digital Citizenship*. Montreal: Define the Line, 2014. http://definetheline.ca/dtl/define-the-lines-facebook-report/.

——. *Confronting Cyberbullying: What Schools Need to Know About Misconduct and Legal Consequences*. Cambridge: Cambridge University Press, 2009.

——. *Cyber-Bullying: Issues and Solutions for the School, the Classroom and the Home*. London: Routledge, 2008.

Shariff, Shaheen, and Andrew H. Churchill. *Truths and Myths of Cyber-Bullying: International Perspectives on Stakeholder Responsibility and Children's Safety*. New York: Peter Lang, 2010.

Shariff, Shaheen and Leanne Johnny. "Cyber-Libel and Cyber-Bullying: Can School Protect Student Reputations and Free-Expression in Virtual Environments?" *Education & Law Journal* 16:3 (2007): 307–342.

Shaw, Gillian. "Amanda Todd's mother speaks out about her daughter, bullying." *The Vancouver Sun*, March 13, 2013. http://www.vancouversun.com/news/Amanda+Todd+mother+speaks_about+daughter+bullying+with+video/7384521/story.html.

Shearer, Cindy L., Ann C. Crouter, and Susan McHale. "Parents' Perceptions of Changes in Mother-Child, Father-Child Relationships During Adolescence." *Journal of Adolescent Research* 20:6 (2005): 662–684. doi:10.1177/0743558405275086.

Shepherd, Tamara. "Young Canadians' Apprenticeship Labour in User-Generated Content." *Canadian Journal of Communication* 38:1 (2013): 35–55. http://www.cjc-online.ca/index.php/journal/article/view/2598/2361.

Shepherd, Tamara, Gregory Taylor, and Catherine Middleton. "A Tale of Two Regulators: Telecom Policy Participation in Canada." *Journal of Information Policy* 4 (2014): 1–12. doi:10.5471jip.v1i0.11.

Short, Donn. *Don't Be So Gay! Queers, Bullying, and Making Schools Safe*. Vancouver: UBC Press, 2013.

Sifry, Micah L. "Children's Crusade: A Primer on How Britain's Students Are Organising Using Social Media." *TechPresident*, November 29, 2010. http://techpresident.com/blog-entry/childrens-crusade-primer-how-britains-students-are-organising-using-social-media.

Simmel, Georg. *The Sociology of Georg Simmell*. New York: MacMillan, 1950.

Simmons, Rachel. *Odd Girl Out: The Hidden Culture of Aggression in Girls*. Boston: Houghton Mifflin Harcourt, 2011.

Sinha, Maire. "Measuring Violence Against Women: Statistical Trends." http://www.statcan.gc.ca/pub/85-002-x/2013001/article/11766-eng.pdf.

Skeggs, Beverley, and Helen Wood. *Reacting to Reality Television: Performance, Audience and Value*. London: Routledge, 2013.

Skreggs, Beverley. *Formations of Sex and Gender: Becoming Respectable*. London: SAGE Publications, 1997.

Soep, Elisabeth. *Participatory Politics: Next-Generation Tactics to Remake Public Spheres*. Cambridge, MA: MIT Press, 2014.

Sorkin, Andrew R., and Jeremy W. Peters. "Google to Acquire YouTube for $1.65 Billion." *The New York Times*, October 9, 2006. http://www.nytimes.com/2006/10/09/business/09cnd-deal.html.

Southern Poverty Law Center, "Misogyny: The Sites." *Southern Poverty Law Center Intelligence* 145: Spring (2012). http://www.splcenter.org/get-informed/intelligence-report/browse-all-issues/2012/spring/misogyny-the-sites.

Southey, Tabatha. "Bill C-13 is About a Lot More Than Cyberbullying." *Globe and Mail*, December 6, 2013. http://www.theglobeandmail.com/globe-debate/columnists/maybe-one-day-revenge-porn-will-be-have-no-power/article15804000/.

Stalnaker, Deidre. "On the Cover, In the Mirror." *Research Magazine*, January 21, 2010. http://research.ua.edu/2010/01/on-the-cover-in-the-mirror.

Standing Senate Committee on Human Rights. *Cyberbullying Hurts: Respect for Rights in the Digital Age*. Ottawa: Parliament of Canada, 2012.

Statistics Canada. "General Social Survey: Victimization." Ottawa: Statistics Canada, 2015. http://www23.statcan.gc.ca/imdb/p2SV.pl?Function=getSurvey&SDDS=4504.

———. "Measuring Violence Against Women: Statistical Trends." Ottawa: Statistics Canada, 2013. http://www.statcan.gc.ca/pub/85-002-x/2013001/article/11766-eng.htm.

———. "The General Social Survey: An Overview." Ottawa: Statistics Canada, 2013. http://www.statcan.gc.ca/pub/89f0115x/89f0115x2013001-eng.htm.

———. "Distribution of Population by Size of Population Centre, 2006 and 2011 Censuses." Ottawa: Statistics Canada, 2011. http://www.statcan.gc.ca/pub/92-195-x/2011001/geo/pop/tbl/tbl10-eng.htm.

———. "Population, Urban and Rural, by Province and Territory (Canada)." Ottawa: Statistics Canada, 2011. http://www.statcan.gc.ca/tables-tableaux/sum-som/l01/cst01/demo62a-eng.htm.

———. "Canadian Internet Use Survey, Internet Use at Home, by Internet Activity, Urban or Rural Distribution." Ottawa: Statistics Canada, 2010. http://www5.statcan.gc.ca/cansim/a26?lang=eng&retrLang=eng&id=3580130&pattern=3580130&csid=.

Status of Women Canada. "Cyber and Sexual Violence: Helping Communities Respond." Ottawa: Status of Women Canada, 2013. http://www.swc-cfc.gc.ca/fun-fin/cfp-adp/2013-2/index-eng.html.

———. *Gender-Based Analysis: A Guide for Policy-Making*. Ottawa: Status of Women Canada, 1996.

Stedman, Kyle D. "Remix Literacy and Fan Compositions." *Computers and Composition* 29 (2012): 107–123. doi:10.1016/j.compcom.2012.02.002.

Steeves, Valerie. "Swimming in the Fishbowl: Young People, Identity and Surveillance in Networked Spaces." In *Digitizing Identities*, edited by Irma van der Ploeg and Jason Pridmore. London: Routledge, 2015, in press.

———. *Young Canadians in a Wired World, Phase III: Cyberbullying: Dealing with Online Meanness, Cruelty and Threats*. Ottawa: MediaSmarts, 2014. http://mediasmarts.ca/sites/mediasmarts/files/pdfs/publication-report/full/YCWWIII_Cyberbullying_FullReport.pdf.

———. *Young Canadians in a Wired World, Phase III: Encountering Racist and Sexist Content Online*. Ottawa: MediaSmarts, 2014. http://mediasmarts.ca/sites/mediasmarts/files/publication-report/full/ycwwiii_encountering_racist_sexist_content_online.pdf.

———. *Young Canadians in a Wired World, Phase III: Experts or Amateurs? Gauging Young Canadians' Digital Literacy Skills*. Ottawa: MediaSmarts, 2014. http://mediasmarts.ca/sites/mediasmarts/files/pdfs/publication-report/full/YCWWIII_Experts_or_Amateurs.pdf.

——. *Young Canadians in a Wired World, Phase III: Life Online.* Ottawa: MediaSmarts, 2014. http://mediasmarts.ca/sites/mediasmarts/files/pdfs/ publication-report/full/YCWWIII_Life_Online_FullReport.pdf.

——. *Young Canadians in a Wired World, Phase III: Online Privacy, Online Publicity.* Ottawa: MediaSmarts, 2014. http://mediasmarts.ca/sites/ mediasmarts/files/pdfs/publication-report/full/YCWWIII_Online_ Privacy_Online_Publicity_FullReport.pdf.

——. *Young Canadians in a Wired World, Phase III: Sexuality and Romantic Relationships in the Digital Age.* Ottawa: MediaSmarts, 2014. http:// mediasmarts.ca/sites/mediasmarts/files/pdfs/publication-report/full/ YCWWIII_Sexuality_Romantic_Relationships_Digital_Age_Full Report_0.pdf.

——. "Hide and Seek: Surveillance of Young People on the Internet." In *The Routledge Handbook of Surveillance Studies,* edited by David Lyon, Kevin Haggerty and Kirstie Ball, 352–360. New York: Routledge, 2012.

——. *Young Canadians in a Wired World, Phase III: Talking to Youth and Parents About Life Online.* Ottawa: MediaSmarts, 2012. http://mediasmarts. ca/sites/default/files/pdfs/publication-report/full/YCWWIII-youth-parents.pdf.

——. "The Watched Child: Surveillance in Three Online Playgrounds." In *Rights of the Child: Proceedings of the International Conference, Ottawa 2007,* edited by Tara Collins, Rachel Grondin, Veronica Pinero, Marie Pratte and Marie-Claude Roberge, 119–140. Montreal : Wilson & Lafleur, 2008.

——. "It's Not Child's Play: The Online Invasion of Children's Privacy." *University of Ottawa Law and Technology Journal* 3:1 (2006): 169–188. http://www.uoltj.ca/articles/vol3.1/2006.3.1.uoltj.Steeves.169-188.pdf.

——. *Young Canadians in a Wired World, Phase II: Trends and Recommendations.* Ottawa: Media Awareness Network, 2005. http://mediasmarts.ca/ sites/mediasmarts/files/pdfs/publication-report/full/YCWWII-trends-recomm.pdf.

Steeves, Valerie, and Jane Bailey. "Living in the Mirror: Understanding Young Women's Experiences With Online Social Networking." In *Expanding the Gaze: Gender, Public Space and Surveillance,* edited by Amanda Glasbeek, Rob Haynen and Emily van der Muelen. Toronto: University of Toronto Press, forthcoming 2015.

——. "Will the Real Digital Girl Please Stand Up?" In *New Visualities, New Technologies: The New Ecstasy of Communication,* edited by Hille Koskela and John Macgregor Wise, 179-201. Surrey, U.K.: Ashgate Publishing, 2013.

Steeves, Valerie, Trevor Scott Milford and Ashley Butts. *Summary of Research on Youth Online Privacy.* Ottawa: The Office of the Privacy Commissioner of Canada, 2010. https://www.priv.gc.ca/information/research-recherche/2010/yp_201003_e.pdf.

Steeves, Valerie, and Cheryl Webster. "Closing the Barn Door: The Effect of Parental Supervision on Canadian Children's Online Privacy." *Bulletin of Science, Technology and Society* 28:1 (2008): 4–19. doi:10.1177/0270467607311488.

Steil, Justin Peter, and Ion Bogdan Vasi. "The New Immigration Contestation: Social Movements and Local Immigration Policy Making in the United States, 2000–2011." *American Journal of Sociology* 119 (2014): 1104–1155, archived at Social Science Research Network: http://papers.ssrn.com/sol3/papers.cfm?abstract_id=2433132.

Stein, Nan. "Sexual Harassment in School: The Public Performance of Gendered Violence." *Harvard Law Review* 65 (1995): 163–173.

Stern, Susannah. "Producing Sites, Exploring Identities: Youth Online Authorship." In *Youth, Identity and Digital Media*, edited by David Buckingham, 95–118. Cambridge, MA: The MIT Press, 2008.

Stokes, Carla E. "'Get on My Level': How Black American Adolescent Girls Construct, Identify and Negotiate Sexuality on the Internet." In *Girl Wide Web 2.0: Revisiting Girls, the Internet and the Negotiation of Identity*, edited by Sharon Mazzarella, 45–67. New York: Peter Lang, 2010.

Suarez, Eliana, and Tehany M. Gadalla. "Stop Blaming the Victim: A Meta-Analysis on Rape Myths." *Journal of Interpersonal Violence* 25:11 (2010): 1–26. doi:10.1177/0886260509354503.

Sullivan, Keith. *The Anti-Bullying Handbook*. Ireland: National University of Ireland, 2011.

Swank, Eric, Breanne Fahs, and David M Frost. "Region, Social Identities, and Disclosure Practices as Predictors of Heterosexist Discrimination against Sexual Minorities in the United States." *Sociological Inquiry* 83 (2013): 238–258.

Sundaram, Vanita. *Preventing Youth Violence: Rethinking the Role of Gender and Schools*. London: Palgrave, 2014.

Taefi, Nura. "The Synthesis of Age and Gender: Intersectionality, International Human Rights Law and the Marginalisation of the Girl-Child." *The International Journal of Children's Rights* 17:3 (2009): 345–376. doi:10.1163/157181809X458049.

Take Back the Tech. "Take Back the Tech: About Campaign." https://www.takebackthetech.net/page/about-campaign.

Tang, Kwong-leung. "Rape Law Reform in Canada: The Success and Limits of Legislation." *International Journal of Offender Therapy and Comparative Criminology* 42 (1998): 258–270. doi:10.11771030662 4X9804200307.

Tayor, T.L. *Play Between Worlds: Exploring Online Game Culture*. Cambridge, MA: MIT Press, 2006.

The Associated Press. "'Most Hated Man on the Internet' Charged Over Plot to Post Stolen Nude Photos." *Toronto Star*, January 24, 2014. http://www.

thestar.com/news/world/2014/01/24/most_hated_man_on_the_internet_
charged_over_plot_to_post_stolen_nude_photos.html.

———. "California: Man is Charged in 'Revenge Porn' Case." *New York Times*,
December 10, 2013. http://www.nytimes.com/2013/12/11/us/california-
man-is-charged-in-revenge-porn-case.html?_r=0.

The Belle Jar. "Rape Culture at the University of Ottawa." *The Belle Jar*,
February 28, 2014. http://bellejar.ca/2014/02/28/rape-culture-at-
the-university-of-ottawa.

The Fifth Estate. *The Sextortion of Amanda Todd*, documentary. Toronto: The
Fifth Estate, 2013.

The Ontario Coalition of Rape Crisis Centres. http://www.sexualassault-
support.ca.

Thiel, Shayla Marie. "'IM Me': Identity Construction and Gender Negotiation
in the World of Adolescent Girls and Instant Messaging." In *Girl Wide
Web: Girls, the Internet and the Negotiation of Identity*, edited by Sharon
Mazzarella, 179–201. New York: Peter Lang.

Thiel-Stern, Shayla. "Femininity Out of Control on the Internet: A Critical
Analysis of Media Representations of Gender, Youth, and MySpace.
com in International News Discourses." *Girlhood Studies* 2:1 (2009):
20–39. doi:10.1177/1461444812459171.

Tiggemann, Marika, Amy Slater, and Veronica Smyth. "'Retouch free': The
Effect of Labelling Media Images as not Digitally Altered on Wom-
en's Body Dissatisfaction." *Body Image* 11 (2014): 85–88. doi:10.1016/j.
bodyim.2013.08.005.

Tiggemann, Marika, and Amy Slater. "NetGirls: The Internet, Facebook,
and Body Image Concern in Adolescent Girls." *International Journal of
Eating Disorders* 46:6 (2013): 630–633. doi:10.1002/eat.22141.

Tincknell, Estella. "Scourging the Abject Body: Ten Years Younger and
Fragmented Femininity under Neoliberalism." In *New Femininities:
Postfeminism, Neoliberalism and Subjectivity*, edited by Rosalind Gill
and Christina Scharff, 83–98. Basingstoke: Palgrave Macmillan, 2011.

Tipper, Jennifer. *The Canadian Girl-Child: Determinants of the Health and Well-
being of Girls and Young Women*. Ottawa: Canadian Institute of Child
Health, 1997.

Tokunaga, Robert. "Social Networking Site or Social Surveillance Site?
Understanding the Use of Interpersonal Electronic Surveillance in
Romantic Relationships." *Computers in Human Behavior* 27:2 (2011):
705–713. doi:10.1016/j.chb.2010.08.014.

Tong, Stephanie Tom, Daria Heinemann-LaFace, Jehoon Jeon, Renata
Kolodziej-Smith, and Nathaniel Warshay. "The Use of Pro-Ana Blogs
for Online Social Support." *Eating Disorders: The Journal of Treatment
and Prevention* 21:5 (2013): 408–422. doi:10.1080/10640266.2013.827538.

Toppo, Greg. "Kids Upload and Unload on School Cafeteria Lunches." *USA Today*, December 2, 2013. http://www.usatoday.com/story/news/nation/2013/12/02/school-lunch-photos/3784625.

Toronto Anarchist Bookfair. "Sexual Assault and Consent Policy Statement." *Toronto Anarchist Bookfair* (2014). http://torontoanarchistbookfair.wordpress.com/sexual-assault-and-consent-policy/.

Torrance, Andrew W., and Eric A. von Hippel. "Protecting the Right to Innovate: Our 'Innovation Wetlands.'" MIT Sloan Research Paper no. 5115–13, Oct. 9, 2013, 18, archived at Social Science Research Network: http://ssrn.com/abstract=2339132.

Tosenberger, Catherine. "Potterotics: Harry Potter Fanfiction on the Internet." PhD diss., University of Florida, 2007.

Trottier, Daniel, and David Lyon. "Key features of social media surveillance." *Internet and Surveillance: The Challenges of Web 2.0 and Social Media*, edited by Christian Fuchs, Kees Boersma, Anders Albrechtslund, and Marisol Sandoval, 89–105. Routledge: New York, 2012.

Trottier, Daniel. "Watching Yourself, Watching Others: Popular Representations of Panoptic Surveillance In Reality TV Programs." In *How Real Is Reality TV? Essays on Representation and Truth*, edited by David S. Escoffery, 273–275. Jefferson: MacFarland & Company, 2006.

——. *Identity Problems in the Facebook Era*. London: Routledge, 2012.

——. *Social Media as Surveillance: Rethinking Visibility in a Converging World*. London: Ashgate Pub. Co., 2012.

Tsoulis-Reay, Alexa. "Omg I'm Online…Again! MySpace, MSN and the Everyday Mediation of Girls." *Screen Education* 53 (2009): 48–55. ISSN: 1449-857X.

Tuchman, Gaye. "Introduction: The Symbolic Annihilation of Women by the Mass Media." In *Hearth and Home: Images of Women in the Mass Media*, edited by Gaye Tuchman, Arlene Kaplan Daniels, and James Benet. New York: Oxford University Press, 1978.

Turkle, Sherry. *Life on the Screen: Identity in the Age of the Internet*. New York: Simon and Schuster, 1997.

Turner, Janice. "Dirty Young Men." *The Guardian*, October 22, 2005. http://www.theguardian.com/theguardian/2005/oct/22/weekend7.weekend3.

Tushnet, Rebecca. "Economies of Desire: Fair Use and Marketplace Assumptions." *William & Mary Law Review* 51 (2009): 513–546. http://scholarship.law.georgetown.edu/cgi/viewcontent.cgi?article=1021&context=facpub.

——. "I Put You There: User-Generated Content and Anticircumvention." *Vanderbilt Journal of Entertainment & Technology Law* (2010): 889–946. http://scholarship.law.georgetown.edu/cgi/viewcontent.cgi?article=1421&context=facpub.

——. "User-Generated Discontent: Transformation in Practice." *Columbia Journal of Law & The Arts* 31 (2008): 101–120. http://scholarship.

law.georgetown.edu/cgi/viewcontent.cgi?article=1068&context=fwps
_papers.

Tynes,Brendesha M., Michael T. Giang, and Geneene N. Thompson. "Ethnic Identity, Intergroup Contact, and Outgroup Orientation Among Diverse Groups of Adolescents on the Internet." *CyberPsychology & Behavior* 11 (2008): 459–465. doi:10.1089/cpb.2007.0085.

United Nations Commission on the Status of Women. *Agreed Conclusions on Access and Participation of Women and Girls in Education, Training and Science and Technology, Including for the Promotion of Women's Equal Access to Full Employment and Decent Work.* New York: United Nations Commission on the Status of Women, 2014. http://www.un.org/womenwatch/daw/csw/csw55/agreed_conclusions/AC_CSW55_E.pdf.

———. *Progress in Maintaining a Gender Perspective Into the Development, Implementation and Evaluation of National Policies and Programmes, With a Particular Focus on Challenges and Achievements in the Implementation of the Millennium Development Goals for Women and Girls*, ESC, 58 Sess., Annex, Agenda Item 3(a), E/CN.6/2014/4. New York: United Nations Commission on the Status of Women, 2014.

———. *International Day of the Girl Child*, GA Res. 66/170. UN GAOR 66th Sess., UN Doc A/RES/66/170. New York: United Nations Commission on the Status of Women, 2012.

United Nations Committee on the Rights of the Child, *The Right of the Child to be Heard*, CRC, 55 Sess., General Comment No 12 UN Doc CRC/C/GC/12. New York: United Nations Convention on the Rights of the Child, 2009.

———. *Convention on the Rights of the Child*, GA Res 40/25, UN GAOR, 44th Sess., U.N. Doc A/RES/44/25. New York: United Nations Office of the High Commissioner for Human Rights, 1990. http://www.ohchr.org/en/professionalinterest/pages/crc.aspx.

United Nations Department of Economic and Social Affairs, Population Division. *World Urbanization Prospects, the 2014 Revision.* New York: United Nations Department of Economic and Social Affairs, 2014. http://esa.un.org/unpd/wup/.

United Nations Entity for Gender Equality and the Empowerment of Women. *Platform for Action: The Girl-Child Diagnosis.* Beijing: United Nations Fourth World Conference on Women, 1995. http://www.un.org/womenwatch/daw/beijing/platform/girl.htm#object1.

United Nations Web Services Section, Department of Public Information. *UN's International Day of the Girl Child.* New York: United Nations, 2013. http://www.un.org/en/events/girlchild.

United States Copyright Office. U.S. Copyright Office, *Public Hearings: Exemption to Prohibition on Circumvention of Copyright Protection Systems for Access Control Technologies 0108.20-0111.15.* Washington, D.C.: Library of Congress, 2009. http://www.copyright.gov/1201/hearings/2009/transcripts/1201-5-7-09.txt.

United States Patent and Trademark Office. *Department of Commerce Private Meeting: Copyright Policy, Creativity and Innovation in the Digital Economy.* Washington, D.C.: Library of Congress, 2013. http://www.uspto.gov/ip/global/copyrights/121213-USPTO-Green_Paper_Hearing-Transcript.pdf.

Updegraff, Kimberly A., Melissa Y. Delgado, and Lorey A. Wheeler. "Exploring Mothers' and Fathers' Relationships with Sons Versus Daughters: Links to Adolescent Adjustment in Mexican Immigrant Families." *Sex Roles* 60 (2009): 559–574. doi:10.1007/s11199-008-9527-y.

Urback, Robyn. "Nova Scotia Cyber Law Turns Bullied Into Bullies." *National Post,* December 8, 2013. http://fullcomment.nationalpost.com/2013/08/09/robyn-urback-nova-scotia-cyber-law-turns-bullied-into-bullies/.

Valkenburg, Patti M., Alexander P Schouten, and Jochen Peter. "Adolescents' Identity Experiments on the Internet." *New Media & Society* 7 (2005): 383–402. doi:10.1177/0093650207313164.

Valkenburg, Patti M., and Jochen Peter. "Preadolescents and Adolescents' Online Communication and Their Closeness to Friends." *Developmental Psychology* 43 (2007): 267–277. doi:10.1037/0012-1649.43.2.267.

——. "Social Consequences for the Internet for Adolescents." *Current Directions in Psychological Science* 18 (2009): 1–5. doi:10.1111/j.1467.

Van Der Velden, Maja, and Khaled El Emam. "'Not all my Friends Need to Know': A Qualitative Study of Teenage Patients, Privacy, and Social Media." *Journal of the American Medical Informatics Association* 20 (2013): 16–24. doi:10.1136/amiajnl-2012-000949.

Van Dijck, Jose. *The Culture of Connectivity: A Critical History of Social Media.* New York: Oxford University Press, 2013.

van Doorn, Niels, Liesbet van Zoonen, and Sally Wyatt. "Writing from Experience: Presentations of Gender Identity on Weblogs." *European Journal of Women's Studies* 14:2 (2007): 143–159. doi:10.1177/1350506807075819.

Van Doorn, Niels. "The Ties that Bind: The Networked Performance of Gender, Sexuality and Friendship on MySpace." *New Media and Society* 12 (2010): 583–602. doi:10.1177/1461444809342766.

van Zoonen, Liesbet. "From Identity to Identification: Fixating the Fragmented Self," *Media, Culture & Society* 35:1 (2013): 44–51. doi:10.1177/0163443712464557.

Venton-Rublee, Jordan. "Rehtaeh Parsons' father speaks at McGill." *The McGill Daily,* October 7, 2013. http://www.mcgilldaily.com/2013/10/rehtaeh-parsons-father-speaks-at-mcgill.

Vermersch, Pierre. "Vécus et couches des vécus." *Expliciter* 66 (2006): 32–47, archived at Academia.edu. https://www.academia.edu/7474892/Vécus_et_couches_des_vécus._Questionner_le_déroulement_d'un_entretien_V3_.

Vickery, Jacqueline R. "Blogrings as Virtual Communities for Adolescent Girls." In *Girl Wide Web 2.0: Revisiting Girls, the Internet and the Negotiation of Identity*, edited by Sharon Mazzarella, 183–202. New York: Peter Lang, 2010.

Vroman, Ariadne, and Philippa Collin. "Everyday Youth Participation? Contrasting Views from Australian Policymakers and Young People." *Young: Nordic Journal of Youth Research* 18:1 (2010): 97–112. doi:10.1177/11033088090180010107.

Walby, Sylvia. "Violence and Society: Introduction to an Emerging Field of Sociology." *Current Sociology* 61 (2012): 95–111. doi:10.1177/0011392112456478.

Walker, Jesse. "Remixing Television." *Reason Magazine*, July 2008. http://reason.com/archives/2008/07/18/remixing-television.

Walker, Kyle E. "Immigration, Local Policy, and National Identity in the Suburban United States." *Urban Geography* 35 (2014): 508–529. doi:10.1080/02723638.2014.890423.

Walters, Mark A., and Jessica Tumath. "Gender 'Hostility', Rape, and the Hate Crime Paradigm." *The Modern Law Review* 77 (2014): 563–596. doi:10.1111/1468-2230.12079.

Wang, Hua, and Barry Wellman. "Connectivity in America: Changes in Adult Friendship Network Size from 2002 to 2007." *American Behavioral Scientist* 53 (2010), 1148–1169. doi:10.1177/0002764209356247.

Warburton, Jaime. "Me/Her/Draco Malfoy: Fangirl Communities and Their Fictions." In *Girl Wide Web 2.0: Revisiting Girls, the Internet, and the Negotiation of Identity* edited by Sharon R. Mazzarella, 117–137. New York: Peter Lang Publishing Group, 2010.

Ward, L. Monique, and Corissa Carlson. "Modeling Meanness: Associations Between Reality TV Consumption, Perceived Realism, and Adolescents' Social Aggression." *Media Psychology* 16 (2013): 371–389. doi:10.1080/15213269.2013.832627.

Wasserman, Michelle. "Rape: Breaking the Silence." *The Progressive* 37 (1973): 19–23. ISSN: 0033-0736.

Weekes, Debbie. "'Get Your Freak On': How Black Girls Sexualise Identity." *Sex Education* 2(3) (2002): 251–262. doi:10.1080/1468181022000025802.

Weinstein, Emily C. "The Personal is Political on Social Media: Online Civic Expression Patterns and Pathways Among Civically Engaged Youth." *International Journal of Communication* 8 (2014): 210–233. http://ijoc.org/index.php/ijoc/article/download/2381/1066.

Welles, Caitlin. "Breaking the Silence Surrounding Female Adolescent Sexual Desire." *Women & Therapy* 28:2 (2005): 31–45. doi:10.1300/J015v28n02_03.

Wellman, Barry. "Physical Place and Cyberplace: The Rise of Personalized Networking." *International Journal of Urban and Rural Research* 25 (2001): 227–252. doi:10.1111/14682427.00309.

Welsh-Huggins, Andrew. "Ohio football players guilty in rape of 16-year-old girl, face year-plus in jail." *National Post*, March 17, 2013. http://news.nationalpost.com/2013/03/17/ohio-football-players-guilty-in-rape-of-16-year-old-girl-face-year-plus-in-jail/.

West Coast LEAF. "#CyberMisogyny: Using and strengthening Canadian legal responses to gendered hate and harassment online." http://www.westcoastleaf.org/userfiles/file/Cyber%20Misogyny%20Report.pdf.

White, Katherine J. Curtis, and Avery M. Guest. "Community lost or transformed? Urbanization and social ties." *City & Community* 2 (2003): 239–259. doi:10.1111/1540-6040.00053.

White, Michele. "Too Close to See: Men, Women and Webcams." *New Media & Society* 5:1 (2003): 7–28. doi:10.1177/1461444803005001901.

Wienke, Chris, and Gretchen J Hill. "Place of Residence Matter? Rural–Urban Differences and the Wellbeing of Gay Men and Lesbians." *Journal of Homosexuality* 60 (2013): 1256–1279. doi:10.1080/00918369.2013.806166.

Wilding, Faith. "Notes on the Political Condition of Cyberfeminism." In *First Cyberfeminist International Reader*, edited by Old Boys Network. Berlin: Old Boys Network, 1997. http://www.obn.org/reading_room/writings/html/notes.html.

Wilding, Faith. "Where is the Feminism in Cyberfeminism?" *N. Paradoxa: International Feminist Art Journal* 2 (1998): 6–13. http://www.ktpress.co.uk/pdf/vol2_npara_6_13_Wilding.pdf.

Williams, Mary E. "Horrifying new trend: Posting rapes to Facebook." *Salon*, May 20, 2013. http://www.salon.com/2013/05/20/worst_horrifying_new_trend_posting_rapes_to_facebook.

Willick, Frances, and Sherri Borden Colley. "School administration didn't probe incident." *The Chronicle Herald*, April 9, 2013. http://www.thechronicleherald.ca/metro/1122506-school-administration-didn-t-probe-incident.

Winch, Alison. "The Girlfriend Gaze: Women's Friendship and Intimacy Circles Are Increasingly Taking on the Function of Mutual Self-Policing." *Soundings* 52 (2012): 1–8.

Winch, Alison. *Girlfriends and Postfeminist Sisterhood*. Basingstoke: Palgrave Macmillan, 2013.

Wirth, Louis. "Urbanism as a Way of Life." *American Journal of Sociology* 44 (1938): 1–24. http://www.jstor.org/stable/2768119

Woolley, Emma. "When a Revenge Porn Kingpin is Busted, Does it Matter Why?" *Globe and Mail*, February 11, 2014. http://www.theglobeandmail.com/technology/digital-culture/when-a-revenge-porn-kingpin-is-busted-does-it-matter-why/article16776273.

Xenos, Michael. Ariadne Vromen, and Brian D. Loader. "The Great Equal-
    izer? Patterns of Social Media Use and Youth Political Engagement in
    Three Advanced Democracies." *Information, Communication & Society*
    17 (2014): 151–167. doi:10.1080/1369118X.2013.871318.
Yager, Zali, and Jennifer A. O'Dea. "Prevention Programs for Body Image
    and Eating Disorders on University Campuses: A Review of Large,
    Controlled Interventions." *Health Promotion International* 23:2 (2008):
    173–189. doi:10.1093/heapro/dan004.
Ybarra, Michele, Kimberly Mitchell, Janis Wolak, and David Finkelhor.
    "Examining Characteristics and Associated Distress Related to Inter-
    net Harassment: Findings from the Second Youth Internet Safety
    Survey." *Pediatrics* 118 (2006): 1169–1177. doi:10.1542/peds.2006-0815.
Youn, Seounmi. "Teenagers' Perceptions of Online Privacy and Coping
    Behaviors: A Risk-Benefit Appraisal Approach." *Journal of Broadcasting
    & Electronic Media* 49:1 (2005): 86–110. doi:10.1207/s15506878jobem4901_6.
Zelizer, Viviana A. "The Social Meaning of Money: 'Special Monies'." *The
    American Journal of Sociology* 95 (1994): 342–377. http://cas.umkc.edu/
    econ/economics/faculty/wray/631Wray/Zelizer.pdf
Zerbisias, Antonia. "Internet Trolls an Online Nightmare for Young Women."
    The Toronto Star, January 18, 2013. http://www.thestar.com/news/
    insight/2013/01/18/internet_trolls_an_online_nightmare_for_young_
    women.htm.
Zernike, Kate. "Judge Defends Penalty in Rutgers Spying Case, Saying It
    Fits Crime." *The New York Times*, May 30, 2012. http://www.nytimes.
    com/2012/05/31/nyregion/judge-defends-sentence-imposed-on-dharun-
    ravi.html?pagewanted=all&_r=0.
Zhang, Yin, Leo Shing-Tung Tang, and Louis Leung. "Gratifications,
    Collective Self-Esteem, Online Emotional Openness, and Traitlike
    Communication Apprehension as Predictors of Facebook Uses."
    Cyberpsychology, Behavior and Social Networking 14:12 (2011): 733–739.
    doi:10.1089/cyber.2010.0042.
Zhang, Yuanyuan, Travis L. Dixon, and Kate Conrad. "Female Body Image
    as a Function of Themes in Rap Music Videos: A Content Analysis."
    Sex Roles 62:11–12 (2010): 787–797. doi:10.1007/s11199-009-9656.
Zubriggen, Eileen, Laura Ramsey, and Beth Jaworski. "Self- and Partner-
    Objectification in Romantic Relationships: Associations with Media
    Consumption and Relationship Dissatisfaction." *Sex Roles* 64:7 (2011):
    449–462. doi:10.1007/s11199-011-9933-4.
Zurbriggen, Eileen L., Rebecca L Collins, Sharon Lamb, Tomi-Ann Roberts,
    Deborah L Tolman, L Monique Ward, and Jeanne Blake. "Report of
    the APA Task Force on the Sexualization of Girls." http://www.apa.
    org/pi/women/programs/girls/report-full.pdf.

Zweig, Janine M., Meredith Dank, Pamela Lachman, and Jennifer Yahner. *Technology, Teen Dating Violence and Abuse, and Bullying.* Washington, DC: Urban Institute, 2013.

Cases Cited

A.B. v. Bragg Communications Inc., 2012 SCC 46, https://scc-csc.lexum.com/scc-csc-scc-csc/en/item/10007/index.do, [2012] 2 S.C.R. 567.

Brown v. Board of Education of Topeka, 347 US 483 (1954) at p. 493.

Campbell v. Acuff-Rose Music, Inc., 510 U.S. 569, https://supreme.justia.com/cases/federal/us/510/569/case.html, 579 (1994).

Cariou v. Prince, 714 F.3d 694, at p. 705–708 (2d Cir. 2013).

Marc R. Poirier, "Statement on Predicate Crimes for Bias Intimidation," May 2, 2012, at p. 6, submitted in *State of New Jersey v. Dharun Ravi* (May 3, 2012) Pros. File #10002681 (Superior Court of New Jersey, Middlesex County, Law Division – Criminal Part) Sentencing Memorandum on Behalf of Defendant Dharun Ravi.

Chamberlain v. Surrey School District No 36, 2002 SCC 86, http://www.scc-csc.lexum.com/scc-csc/scc-csc/en/item/2030/index.do, [2002] 4 S.C.R. 710.

In Re C.S., 2012 CP-39-JV-447-2012." In the Court of Common Pleas of Lehigh County, Pennsylvania Juvenile Division, October 19, 2012. http://www.krautharris.com/documents/In-re-CS.pdf.

Ross v. New Brunswick School District No 15, [1996] 1 S.C.R. 825, https://www.canlii.org/en/ca/scc/doc/1996/1996canlii237/1996canlii237.html, [1996] canLII 237 (SCC).

Seltzer v. Green Day, Inc., 725 F.3d 1170 (9th Cir. 2013).

Sony Corp. v. Universal City Studios, 44 U.S. 417, http://www.law.cornell.edu/copyright/cases/464_US_417.htm, at p. 449 (1984).

State of New Jersey v. Dharun Ravi (August 10, 2011) Pros. File #10002681 (Superior Court of New Jersey, Middlesex County, Law Division – Criminal Part) On Motion to Dismiss the Indictment and Compel Discovery, Brief on Behalf of Defendant Dharun Ravi (photocopies obtained from Superior Court of New Jersey, Middlesex County).

State of New Jersey v. Dharun Ravi (August 13, 2011) File #10002681 (Superior Court of New Jersey, Middlesex County, Law Division – Criminal Part) State's Response to Motion to Dismiss the Indictment and Compel State to Produce Discovery, Brief Submitted on Behalf of State of New Jersey (photocopies obtained from Superior Court of New Jersey, Middlesex County).at p. 11.

State v. Hogan (1996) 144 N.J. 216, http://leagle.com/decision/1996360144NJ216_1229.xml/STATE%20v.%20HOGAN, 676 A.2d 533 at 228-29.

Suntrust Bank v. Houghton Mifflin Co., 268 F.3d 1257 (11th Cir. 2001), http://www.yale.edu/lawweb/jbalkin/telecom/suntrustbank%28appeal%29.pdf.

Legislation Cited

Copyrights, 17 U.S.C. § 107, http://www.law.cornell.edu/uscode/text/17/107>.

Copyright Act (R.S.C., 1985, c. C-42), § 29.21, http://laws-lois.justice.gc.ca/eng/acts/c-42/page-19.html#h-27, (Canadian fair dealing law).

Accepting Schools Act, S.O. 2012 c. 5, http://ontla.on.ca/web/bills/bills_detail.do?locale=en&BillID=2549.

An Act Concerning Bias Crimes, N.J.S.A 2C:16-1(a)(1), (2) and (3), ftp://www.njleg.state.nj.us/20002001/AL01/443_.PDF.

Bill C-13, *An Act to amend the Criminal Code, the Canada Evidence Act, the Competition Act and the Mutual Legal Assistance in Criminal Matters Act*, 2nd Sess, 40th Parl, 2013 (first reading 20 November 2013).

Copyright Modernization Act, S.C. 2012, c. 20, http://laws-lois.justice.gc.ca/eng/annualstatutes/2012_20/FullText.html, s. 29.21.

Cyber-safety Act, S.N.S. 2013, c. 2, http://www.nslegislature.ca/legc/bills/61st_5th/3rd_read/b061.htm.

Education Act, R.S.O. 1990, c. E.2, http://www.e-laws.gov.on.ca/html/statutes/English/elaws_statutes_90e02_e_htm.

Education Act, S.N.S. 1995–96, c. 1, http://www.nslegislature.ca/legc/statutes/education.pdf.

Education Amendment Act (Progressive Discipline and School Safety) S.O. 2007 C. 14, http://www.e-laws.gov.on.ca/html/source/statutes/English/2007/elaws_src_s07014_e.htm.

Ministerial Education Act Regulations, N.S. Reg. 80/97, http://www.novascotia.ca/just/regulations/regs/edmin.htm, s. 47.

New Jersey Code of Criminal Justice, NJ Rev Stat § 2C:16-1 (2013).

Promotion of Respectful and Responsible Relationships Act, S.N.S. 2012, c. 14, http://www.nslegislature.ca/legc/PDFs/annual%20statutes/2012%20Spring/c014.pdf.

Protecting Canadians from Online Crime Act, S.C. 2014, c. 31, http://laws-lois.justice.gc.ca/eng/annualstatutes/2014%5F31/.

Provincial Standards for Codes of Conduct Order, Ministerial Order 276/07, (2007), (*School Act*, R.S.B.C. 1996, c. 412 as am.), http://www2.gov.bc.ca/gov/DownloadAsset?assetId=D4DE4CDF12BD4C5AB1D9EA6D3F8CB222.

School Act, R.S.B.C. 1996, c. 412, http://www.bced.gov.bc.ca/legislation/school-law/revisedstatutescontents.pdf.

School Regulation, B.C. Reg. 265/1989, http://www.bced.gov.bc.ca/legislation/schoollaw/d/bcreg_265-89.pdf, at s. 4.

Contributors

Gillian Angrove is currently a law clerk for the Honourable Justice Donald Rennie at the Federal Court of Canada. She has a BA (honours with distinction) from the University of Victoria and a JD from the Schulich School of Law at Dalhousie University. During law school, she served as research assistant to Professor Constance MacIntosh and Professor Wayne MacKay, whom she assisted on a variety of projects involving health law, human rights law, cyberbullying, and sexualized violence on university campuses. Upon graduating, she received the Muriel Duckworth Award based on her consciousness of women's issues and feminism in the legal community.

Jane Bailey is Associate Professor at the University of Ottawa Faculty of Law in the Common Law Section, teaching cyberfeminism, technoprudence, contracts, and civil procedure. She is the co-principal investigator with Dr. Valerie Steeves on the eGirls Project, which has been funded by a three-year Social Sciences and Humanities Research Council Partnership Development Grant and team leader of Working Group 1 on a seven-year Major Collaborative Research Initiatives project entitled Rethinking Processual Law: Towards Cyberjustice. Her current research is focused on online self-exposure by girls and young women (including sexting and cyberbullying), online harassment and hate, privacy and equality concerns arising from surveillance, and access to justice.

Jacquelyn Burkell is Assistant Dean of Research and Associate Professor in the Faculty of Information and Media Studies at the University of Western Ontario. Dr. Burkell's research focuses on the empirical study of the interaction between people and technology, with a particular emphasis on the role of cognition in such interactions. Specific aspects of this research include the impact of presentation on information use and understanding and the social impact of technology. One particular focus of her research is privacy in the online context: she examines how technology influences privacy, and how privacy perceptions and expectations change in the online context. Dr. Burkell is also involved in research on the credibility of online information and information sources, with particular emphasis on the evaluation of the credibility of online news.

Ashley DeMartini is a PhD student in the Department of Integrated Studies in Education at McGill University. Her research interests are vast and include media and technology, critical reflexivity, as well as commemorative practices around histories of mass violence.

Jordan Fairbairn is a PhD candidate in the Department of Sociology and Anthropology at Carleton University in Ottawa, Canada. Her research explores sexual and intimate partner violence, social media, feminist activism, and the relationship between academia and social change.

Laura Harvey is a Lecturer in sociology at the University of Surrey. Her work takes an interdisciplinary approach, drawing on sociology, gender studies, social psychology, and cultural studies. Her interests include sexualities, everyday intimacies and inequalities, research with young people, the mediation of sexual knowledge, feminist methodologies, and discourse analysis.

Sarah Heath is a doctoral student at the Department of Criminology at the University of Ottawa and a research assistant on the eGirls Project. She has an MA in criminology and a Bachelor's of Social Science in criminology and psychology. Sarah has published and presented various works nationally and internationally on punitiveness, court efficiency, crime prevention, privacy legislation, and research methods. She has experience conducting research and evaluation in the federal government and has been involved in research projects associated with various federal and provincial departments.

Matthew Johnson is the Director of Education for MediaSmarts, Canada's centre for digital and media literacy. He is the designer of the comprehensive digital literacy tutorials "Passport to the Internet" (grades 4 to 8) and "MyWorld" (grades 9 to 12). He has contributed blogs and articles to websites and magazines around the world; has been interviewed hundreds of times in print, radio, and television;and has also presented MediaSmarts' materials on topics such as copyright, cyberbullying, body image, and online hate to governments, academic conferences, and organizations around the world, frequently as a keynote speaker. Matthew is an acclaimed writer of science fiction whose collection of short stories, *Irregular Verbs and Other Stories*, was published in June 2014 to considerable acclaim; he also serves on the board of the Science Fiction and Fantasy Writers of America.

Akane Kanai completed her BA/LLB with honours at the University of Melbourne in 2008. She began her professional career as a lawyer, working in the corporate and not-for-profit sectors before returning to study. She completed her MSc in gender, media, and culture at the London School of Economics with distinction and returned to Melbourne to begin her doctoral study at Monash University. Her research concerns new femininities and the circulation of memes in digital culture. Other research interests include issues of race, masculinities, reality television, and celebrity culture.

Trevor Scott Milford is a doctoral candidate in sociology at Carleton University. His research focuses on gendered agency and risk in online social networking, where he adopts a cyberfeminist perspective to investigate girls' lived experiences of online gender harassment. He also examines potential structural factors that can position girls to engage in online conflict, as well as whether Canadian legislation addressing gender and harassment in virtual spaces functions to promote online gender equality. He is thrilled to be working as a research assistant with the eGirls Project and to have been able to travel to Antwerp, Belgium, to present on his master's research, a cyberfeminist analysis of an eGirls focus group transcript. He has recently joined forces with Canada's Competition Bureau to conduct exploratory research and ultimately develop guidelines on youth marketing in digital contexts. In his spare time, he volunteers with the Innocence Project and sits on the Social Science Research Ethics Board at the University of Ottawa.

Assumpta Ndengeyingoma is Professor at the Nursing Department of the Université du Quebec en Outaouais. She is affiliated with several groups and research centres, including le Groupe interdisciplinaire de recherche en sciences de la santé et milieux favorables (le GIRESSS; the interdisciplinary research group in health sciences and healthy communities), le Centre d'étude et de recherche en intervention familiale (le CERIF; the study and research centre in familial intervention), and la Chaire interdisciplinaire de recherche en littératie et inclusion (la CIRLI; interdisciplinary research chair in literacy and inclusion). Her research interests are focused on the wellbeing and health of vulnerable groups (immigrants, teens) and strategies for inclusive education for health.

Priscilla M. Regan is Professor of Government and Politics in the School of Policy, Government, and International Affairs at George Mason University. Prior to joining that faculty in 1989, she was a senior analyst in the Congressional Office of Technology Assessment (1984–1989) and an Assistant Professor of Politics and Government at the University of Puget Sound (1979–1984). Since the mid-1970s, Dr. Regan's primary research interest has been the analysis of the social, policy, and legal implications of organizational use of new information and communications technologies. Dr. Regan has published over thirty articles or book chapters, as well as *Legislating Privacy: Technology, Social Values, and Public Policy* (University of North Carolina Press, 1995), and co-edited *Transparency and Surveillance as Sociotechnical Accountability: A House of Mirrors* (Routledge, 2014). As a recognized researcher in this area, Dr. Regan has testified before Congress and participated in meetings held by the Department of Commerce, Federal Trade Commission, Social Security Administration, and Census Bureau. Dr. Regan received her PhD in government from Cornell University and her BA from Mount Holyoke College.

Jessica Ringrose is Professor of Sociology of Gender and Education, at the Institute of Education, London. She leads MA and PhD courses in the areas of gender, sexuality, social justice, and intersectionality studies in education. Her recent research explores youth sexting, digital feminist activism, and feminism in schools. She was an academic advisor on the UK Home Office's "Sexualisation of Young People Review" (2010) and is a founding member of the UK Government Equalities Office's "Body Confidence Campaign." Her publications include *Rethinking Gendered Regulations and Resistances in Education* (New York Routledge, 2011, edited), *Post-Feminist Education? Girls and the Sexual Politics of Schooling* (New York Routledge, 2012), *Deleuze and Research Methodologies* (Edingburgh University Press, 2013, co-edited with Rebecca Coleman), and *Children, Sexuality and 'Sexualisation'* (London: Palgrave Macmillan, 2015 co-edited with Emma Renold and Danielle Egan).

Betsy Rosenblatt is Assistant Professor of Law and Director of the Center for Intellectual Property Law at Whittier Law School, where she teaches intellectual property law subjects including patent law, trademark law, and video game law. Her scholarship focuses on intellectual property theory, entertainment law, and gender/sexuality law. Her scholarly publications include "Fear and Loathing: Shame, Shaming and Intellectual Property" (*DePaul Law Review*, 2013), "A Theory of IP's Negative Space" (*Columbia Journal of Law & the Arts*, 2011), and "Rethinking the Parameters of Trademark Use in Entertainment" (*Florida Law Review*, 2009). She is chair of the legal committee of the Organization for Transformative Works.

Madelaine Saginur, BSc, BCL, LLB, is the Executive Director of University of Ottawa's Centre for Law, Technology, and Society. She is also a member of Canadian Blood Services' Research Ethics Board. Previously, she practiced intellectual property law, and also worked as a Research Associate at University of Montreal's Centre de recherche en droit public. She has published in the area of bioethics and health law and recently co-edited *Intellectual Property for the 21st Century: Interdisciplinary Approaches* (Toronto: Irwin Law, 2014).

Leslie Regan Shade is Associate Professor at the Faculty of Information at the University of Toronto. Her research focus since the mid-1990s has been on the social and policy aspects of information and communication technologies (ICTs), with particular concerns towards issues of gender, youth, and political economy. Her research promotes the notion of the public interest in ICT policy; her publications, community outreach, and student supervision have as their goal the promotion of a wider popular discourse on information and communication policy issues and media reform in Canada and internationally for a diverse public and policy audience. Dr. Shade has an ongoing commitment to building participatory scholar-activist networks.

Shaheen Shariff is Associate Professor at McGill University's Department of Integrated Studies, Faculty of Education. Her research and teaching interests focus on emerging online issues such as cyberbullying, free expression, privacy, libel, and criminal harassment. Her work is grounded in the study of law as it impacts educational policy, pedagogy, and practice. She currently holds grants from the Social Sciences and Humanities Research Council of Canada to help educators and the legal community better understand youth online, towards the development of informed laws and policies. She is also one of four recipients globally of Facebook's Inaugural Digital Citizenship Grant. Her work has culminated in several books on cyberbullying; a resource website, www.mcgill.ca/definetheline/; and the Queen's Diamond Jubilee Medal.

Andrea Slane, PhD, is an Associate Professor and Director of the Legal Studies Program in the Faculty of Social Sciences and Humanities at the University of Ontario Institute of Technology (UOIT). Prior to joining UOIT in 2009, she was Executive Director of the Centre for Innovation Law and Policy at the University of Toronto, Faculty of Law. She received her JD degree from the University of Toronto with honours in 2003, and was called to Ontario bar in 2004. She holds a PhD in comparative literature from the University of California, San Diego. Her research interests include privacy, information law, internet law, cyberbullying, and online sexual exploitation of children and youth.

Valerie Steeves is Associate Professor in the Department of Criminology at the University of Ottawa in Ottawa, Canada. Her main area of research is human rights and technology issues. Professor Steeves has written and spoken extensively on privacy from a human rights perspective, and is an active participant in the privacy policy-making process in Canada. She is a co-principal investigator with Professor Jane Bailey on the eGirls Project and the lead researcher on the ongoing Young Canadians in a Wired World Project. Both projects examine young people's experiences and perspective of networked media.

Diana Sweet is a PhD student studying political science in the School of Policy, Government, and International Affairs at George Mason University (GMU). Her dissertation examines the role of national cultural institutions as part of a nation's public diplomacy effort. While at GMU she has also published in the field of political communication. She earned an MA from the European University at St. Petersburg and graduated *summa cum laude* from SUNY Albany with a BA in Chinese and Russian studies.

Rebecca Tushnet is Professor at Georgetown Law, where she teaches intellectual property law, advertising law, and First Amendment law. Her scholarly publications include "Worth a Thousand Words: The Images of Copyright Law" (*Harvard Law Review*, 2011), "Gone in 60 Milliseconds: Trademark Law and Cognitive Science" (*Texas Law Review*, 2008), and "Copy This Essay: How Fair Use Doctrine Harms Free Speech and How Copying Serves It" (*Yale Law Journal*, 2004). She is a member of the legal team of the Organization for Transformative Works, a non-profit dedicated to supporting and promoting fanworks, and has advised and represented several fan fiction websites in disputes with copyright and trademark owners.

Index

Law, Technology and Media

Edited by Michael Geist

The *Law, Technology and Media* series explores emerging technology law issues with an emphasis on a Canadian perspective. It is the first University of Ottawa Press series to be fully published under an open access licence.

Previous titles in this collection

Michael Geist (ed.), *The Copyright Pentalogy: How the Supreme Court of Canada Shook the Foundations of Canadian Copyright Law*, 2013.